THE ILLUSION
OF VICTORY

ALSO BY THOMAS FLEMING

Nonfiction

Fiction

THE ILLUSION OF VICTORY

AMERICA IN WORLD WAR I

THOMAS FLEMING

A MEMBER OF THE PERSEUS BOOKS GROUP
NEW YORK

Published by Basic Books
A Member of the Perseus Books Group

Designed by Lisa Kreinbrink
Set in 11-point Bembo by the Perseus Books Group

Library of Congress Cataloging-in-Publication Data

Fleming, Thomas J.
    The illusion of victory : America in World War I / Thomas Fleming.
        p. cm.
Includes bibliographical references and index.
    ISBN 0-465-02467-X (hard)
    1. World War, 1914-1918—United States.   2. United States—
History—1913-1921.   I. Title.

D570.A456   2003
940.3'73—dc21

                                                2003002616

03 04 05 06 / 10 9 8 7 6 5 4 3 2 1

To Eugene D. Fleming,
brother and friend

There is but one response possible for us: Force,
Force to the utmost, Force without stint or limit,
the righteous and triumphant Force which shall
make Right the law of the world.

WOODROW WILSON

We have got all we want in territory, and our claim
to be left unmolested in the enjoyment of our vast
and splendid possessions, mainly acquired by
violence, largely maintained by force, often seems
less reasonable to others than to us.

WINSTON CHURCHILL

If the war didn't happen to kill you, it
was bound to start you thinking.

GEORGE ORWELL

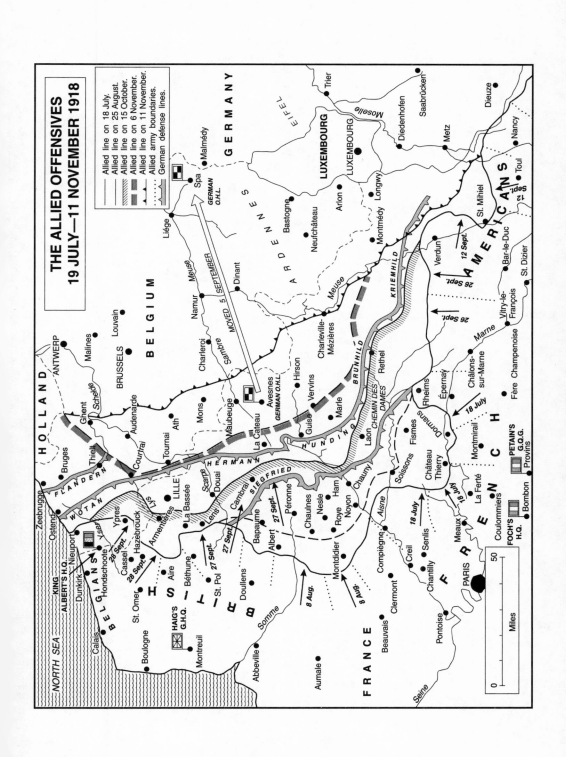

THE ALLIED OFFENSIVES
19 JULY–11 NOVEMBER 1918

Allied line on 18 July.
Allied line on 25 August.
Allied line on 15 October.
Allied line on 6 November.
Allied line on 11 November.
Allied army boundaries.
German defense lines.

NORTH SEA

HOLLAND

GERMANY

LUXEMBOURG

BELGIUM

FRANCE

AMERICANS

FRENCH

BRITISH

BELGIANS

FLANDERN

WOTAN

HERMANN

SIEGFRIED

HUNDING

BRUNHILD

KRIEMHILD

CHEMIN DES DAMES

EIFEL

ARDENNES

Moselle

Meuse

Meuse

Sambre

Scheldt

Lys

Scarpe

Somme

Seine

Marne

Aisne

KING
ALBERT'S H.Q.

HAIG'S G.H.Q.

PETAIN'S G.Q.G.

FOCH'S H.Q.

GERMAN O.H.L.

GERMAN O.H.L.

Zeebrugge
Ostend
Nieuport
Dunkirk
Calais
Boulogne
Bruges
Ghent
Thielt
Courtrai
Ypres
Hazebrouck
Cassel
Hondschoote
St. Omer
Aire
Béthune
St. Pol
Doullens
Montreuil
Abbeville
Aumale
Beauvais
Clermont
Creil
Chantilly
Pontoise
PARIS
Senlis
Compiègne
Montdidier
Albert
Bapaume
Péronne
Chaulnes
Nesle
Roye
Noyon
Ham
Chauny
Soissons
Château Thierry
La Ferté
Meaux
Coulommiers
Montmirail
Bombon
Provins
Épernay
Châlons-sur-Marne
Fère Champenoise
Vitry-le-François
St. Dizier
Bar-le-Duc
Verdun
St. Mihiel
Toul
Nancy
Dieuze
Metz
Saarbrücken
Diedenhofen
Trier
Longwy
Arlon
Montmédy
Neufchâteau
Bastogne
Luxembourg
Spa
Liège
Namur
Dinant
Charleville-Mézières
Rethel
Charleroi
Vervins
Hirson
Guise
Marle
Laon
Fismes
Dormans
Rheims
Avesnes
Maubeuge
La Cateau
Cambrai
Douai
Lens
La Bassée
LILLE
Armentières
Audenarde
Tournai
Ath
Mons
Louvain
Malines
BRUSSELS
ANTWERP

MOVED 5 SEPTEMBER

18 July
18 July
18 July
18 July
8 Aug.
8 Aug.
27 Sept.
27 Sept.
27 Sept.
27 Sept.
28 Sept.
28 Sept.
28 Sept.
12 Sept.
12 Sept.
26 Sept.
26 Sept.
26 Sept.

Miles
0   50

CONTENTS

ACKNOWLEDGMENTS

A great many people have spurred and sustained my lifelong interest in World War I. Not the least is my father, Thomas J. Fleming, Sr., who was a sergeant in the Seventy-Eighth Division and was commissioned in the field when all the officers in his company were killed or wounded. I must also thank the editors of American Heritage, who sent me to Europe in 1968 to write an article on the fiftieth anniversary of the battle of the Argonne. That marked the beginning of my determination to write about the war as a historian. I am equally grateful to the staffs of Yale University's libraries, where I conducted my first in-depth research in 1990, for my novel *Over There*. It was at Yale that I first encountered the women's side of the war.

Since that time, many other people have helped me fill my file drawers. Not least has been my son, Richard Fleming, whose computer expertise and knowledge of Russian and European history have been invaluable. Also in the front rank of my researchers is Steven Bernstein, who helped explore numerous sources in Washington, D.C., and F. Kennon Moody, whose knowledge of the Franklin D. Roosevelt Library at Hyde Park has been a frequent resource. I am in debt to many other libraries and librarians, from the staff of the New York Society Library, who tolerated my endless requests for interlibrary loans, to the staff of the Westbrook Public Library at my Connecticut summer home, who were equally cooperative in this department.

My wife, Alice Fleming, has been a vital supporter throughout the many drafts of the manuscript, as well as a superb in-house editor. I must also add my agent, Ted Chichak, to this list of colleagues. His advice, both from the editorial and business points of view, has been a constant resource. My gratitude also extends to my previous editor at Basic Books, Don Fehr, who encouraged me to tackle this daunting task, and my current editor, Elizabeth Maguire, whose enthusiasm for the project has been an equally sustaining force.

Chapter 1

WAR WEEK

It was time.

At 8:20 P.M. on Monday, April 2, 1917, a grim-faced Woodrow Wilson strode down the main corridor of the White House onto the North Portico. There a black Pierce-Arrow limousine waited in the rain, its motor purring. With the president was his secretary, Joseph Tumulty, his doctor, Admiral Cary T. Grayson, and an army aide, Colonel William J. Harts. The president's second wife, Edith Galt Wilson, his oldest daughter, Margaret, and his closest friend and adviser, diminutive Colonel Edward M. House (his title was an honorary one, bestowed by a Texas governor), had departed in another car at 8:10. Their joint destination was the U.S. Capitol, where Wilson was to give the most important speech of his life.[1]

It had been a long, irritating day of clouds and rain, waiting for the 65th Congress to convene "to receive a communication concerning grave matters of national policy" from the president. Every American who read a newspaper assumed Wilson's communication would contain a request that Congress declare a state of war existed between the United States and Germany. It was a stunning reversal of course for a president who had been reelected five months before on the slogan "He kept us out of war."

Soon after his victory at the polls, Wilson had made an electrifying speech, calling on the warring European powers to let him mediate a "peace without victory." He had been ferociously denounced by former president Theodore Roosevelt and other leading Republicans as something close to a traitor. The warring nations had all rejected Wilson's entreaty, and Germany had added injury to this insult by announcing that on February 1, 1917, it would resume unrestricted submarine warfare in barred zones around the British Isles and the ports of its enemies in the Mediterranean.

Wilson had broken diplomatic relations with Germany, sending its suave ambassador, Count Johann von Bernstorff, back to Berlin on February 3. On March 1, alienation between the two nations had deepened drastically when Wilson authorized the State Department to release a telegram from the German foreign minister, Arthur Zimmermann, to the government of Mexico, proposing an alliance if war should break out between Germany and the United States. The message had been intercepted by British crypt-analysts and discreetly leaked to the American government.

Most diplomats would have dismissed the dispatch as a forgery. But the Germans, imbued with the righteousness of their cause and profoundly disenchanted with the Americans for selling their enemies hundreds of millions of dollars' worth of high explosives and weaponry, admitted every word was true, down to the proposal that a successful war would restore Mexico's "lost territories" of Texas, New Mexico, and Arizona.[2]

Outrage simmered from sea to shining sea. The United States had been on the brink of war with Mexico since Wilson took office, thanks largely to his interference in their ongoing revolution. But Americans regarded the matter as a private quarrel shielded by the Monroe Doctrine.

In mid-March, German submarines sank four American ships in the barred zone, drowning fifteen sailors. A chorus of mostly Republican sena-tors and congressmen called for war. Wilson's cabinet told him they unani-mously favored it. Reflecting this widespread anger, the *New York Tribune*'s April 2 headline virtually shouted: "Congress Ready to Declare State of War Now Exists, Country in a Militant Mood."

On the front page of the same edition, *Tribune* Washington correspon-dent Cass W. Gilbert enlivened his readers with a snide assault that under-scored the paper's long-running disenchantment with Woodrow Wilson. Gilbert bluntly questioned whether the president could inspire the nation to fight a war: "Making war is a great act of the emotions and will. Mr. Wilson is an intellectual. [Can he summon] a great burst of righteous feel-ing [in] the hearts of men?" As for Congress, Gilbert virtually dismissed it as hopeless. "Let Germany do it" (that is, let Germany push the United States into the war) had been Congress's policy for too long. But Berlin's transgressions were quickly forgotten by the fickle American public. Gilbert feared that Wilson, whose "almost physical revulsion" against war had been starkly visible to red-blooded Americans, would do little but present a "legal brief" against Germany.[3]

II

The *Tribune* story was evidence of the Republican Party's hostility toward Wilson—and something deeper: a mixture of bafflement and amazement to find this man president of the United States. In 1910, a mere seven years earlier, Woodrow Wilson had been president of a minor-league New Jersey college called Princeton. He had left that presidency in a cloud of acrimony, having alienated almost everyone on the faculty and the board of trustees.[4]

Former president Grover Cleveland, a member of the board of trustees, had called Wilson a dishonorable man who was careless about facts and had a volatile, vindictive temper. Other Princetonians called Wilson a liar and a demagogue. The one talent Wilson displayed in complicated disputes about a building for the graduate school and reorganizing the college around a "Quad Plan" was a gift for denouncing his opponents as traitors to America's ideals. He accused them of defending privilege against democracy. This got him numerous headlines. Scholars who have investigated the details of these long-forgotten quarrels have dismissed Wilson's charges as sheer fiction.[5]

A man without a future in academe, Wilson accepted the offer of wealthy conservative Democrats to back him for governor of New Jersey. The man behind the offer was an ebullient journalist named George Harvey, editor of *Harper's* magazine, whose contacts included J. P. Morgan, Jr.—like his late father, the undisputed titan of American finance. The conservatives' game plan was to publicize Wilson's gubernatorial performance and use him as a foil to take the Democratic Party away from the Nebraska orator William Jennings Bryan. The so-called Great Commoner had been giving the money men nervous tremors since 1896, when he made the first of his three runs for the presidency on the demagogic cry "You shall not crucify mankind upon a cross of gold!"

Harvey's offer stirred long-suppressed yearnings in Wilson's soul. From his early manhood, he had daydreamed about winning political power. "This is what I was meant for, the rough and tumble of the political arena," he told one of his favorite correspondents. "My instinct all turns that way."

What drove this instinct? Essentially, it was an appetite for fame; deeper in Wilson's psyche was a desire to transcend a frequently critical minister father and his own self-doubts. While courting his first wife, Ellen Axson, the future president confessed "a passion for interpreting great events to the world." He yearned to "inspire a great movement of opinion." Not long after this confession, at the age of thirty-three, he had confided to his diary the outsize hope that his era's political autobiography would be written through his life.[6]

Wilson won the governorship of New Jersey in 1910. During the campaign, he confounded his conservative backers by becoming a fiery progressive. Jettisoned were his publicly stated views that labor unions were bad, that big business monopolies called trusts were legitimate enterprises, and that political bosses were necessary to make parties run smoothly. Wilson's liberal program as governor of New Jersey won him headlines and the Democratic nomination for president in 1912. Ordinarily, this honor would have led straight to the same sort of humiliation William Jennings Bryan had repeatedly suffered at the hands of the well-financed Republican Party. The only Democrat elected president since the Civil War had been Grover Cleveland (1884 and 1892), who talked and acted more like a Republican.

But the United States had been in ferment for the previous decade; progressive ideas about limiting the power of big business and restoring a more equal liberty to American life had been espoused by liberals in both parties. When former president Theodore Roosevelt sought the 1912 Republican nomination as an all-out progressive, the GOP's (Grand Old Party's) conservatives balked and stayed with the current occupant of the White House, William Howard Taft. Roosevelt ran as the candidate of the Progressive Party and split the Republican majority. Woodrow Wilson became president with a mere 42 percent of the vote, leaving the Republicans in a state of shock and disarray from which they had yet to recover.

III

Among the other stories in the *Tribune* and sister newspapers on April 2 were reports on the latest carnage from Europe's battlefronts. As usual, the papers gave readers the impression that the Germans were losing the war. The headline in the *New York Times* read: "Haig Beats Back Foe Three Miles from St. Quentin: British Drive Foe Out of Savy, Three Miles West of the City After Heavy Fighting." Sir Douglas Haig was the commander in chief of the British army in France. Today this dour Scot is high on any list of the worst generals in history. In his 1916 offensive along the Somme

River in northern France, Haig lost 527,000 men to gain a few miles of muddy, shell-pocked earth. The British had declared a victory and promoted Sir Douglas to field marshal.

Americans knew even less about what the Germans were thinking and doing on their side of no-man's-land. More than the traditional fog of war enveloped the battlefields. The murk was compounded by rigid censorship and massive propaganda—and compounded again by a widespread conviction that the untrustworthy Germans were trying to manipulate American public opinion.

Another news story of burgeoning importance was the revolution in Russia. On March 15, 1917, a liberal majority in the Russian parliament had deposed Czar Nicholas Romanoff and announced their intention to create a democratic government. Pro-war newspapers and magazines in the United States had hailed this event as a godsend to the Allied cause. Now the war could be described as a clear-cut contest between despotism and democracy. On April 2 the *Washington Evening Post* carried a vivid story about the president of the Russian-American Chamber of Commerce, who reported the revolution was being acclaimed with wild enthusiasm in Siberia. *The Nation*, one of the leaders of U.S. liberal opinion, excitedly declared: "With a single gesture the Russian people has won its own freedom and lifted a heavy burden from the shoulders of the . . . democratic nations of western Europe."[7]

IV

On April 2, President Wilson, who had been sleeping poorly, was up at dawn to take a last look at his "communication." He had written most of the speech on his portable Hammond typewriter during the morning of March 30 and the afternoon of March 31. He did not finish it until about 10 P.M. on April 1. While working on it, his mood had been vile; he had snapped and snarled at the White House servants, demanding quiet. As usual, the president had delayed writing until the last possible moment; he thought this gave him better command of the intellectual and emotional content of a speech.[8]

There are other versions of how Wilson wrote his speech and what he felt about it. Edith Galt Wilson later told of waking up a night or two before April 2 and finding her husband gone from their bedroom. She searched the darkened White House and finally discovered him on the

South Portico, writing the speech on his portable typewriter by the light of an electric lantern. Edith went to the kitchen, got a glass of milk and a cookie, and left them beside his chair. The story is unlikely, not only because it contradicts the diary of a White House staffer, who recalled the president's bad mood and demands for quiet. The South Portico was not the place a president would be likely to go in the middle of the night, when he had a second-floor office only a few steps from his bedroom. But it reveals Edith's view of herself as Wilson's humble helpmate and silent coadjutor—an image she needed to project in later years because she had been neither silent nor humble in her White House days.[9]

Even more intriguing in some ways—and a far more quoted part of the Wilson legend—is a story that appeared in a biography of Frank I. Cobb, editor in chief of the *New York World*. According to the author of the book, two of Cobb's former colleagues on the *World*, Laurence Stallings and playwright Maxwell Anderson, recalled that Cobb told them he had been summoned to the White House on the night of April 1–2 to discuss Wilson's decision for war. He did not get there until 1 A.M., and they talked into the dawn. Wilson told Cobb he had "considered every loophole" to escape going to war, but each time, Germany deliberately blocked the path of peace with some "new outrage."

Then Wilson began to talk about the impact the war would have on the United States: "He said when a war got going it was just war and there weren't two kinds of it," Cobb said. "It required illiberalism at home to reinforce the men at the front. We couldn't fight Germany and maintain the ideals of government that all thinking men shared. He said we would try but it would be too much for us."

"'Once lead this people into war,' Wilson continued, 'and they'll forget there ever was such a thing as tolerance. To fight you must be ruthless and the spirit of ruthless brutality will enter the very fibre of our national life, infecting Congress, the courts, the policeman on the beat, the man in the street' . . .

"He thought the Constitution would not survive it," Cobb said. "That free speech and the right of assembly would go. He said a nation couldn't put its strength into a war and keep its head level; it had never been done.

"'If there's any alternative, for God's sake let's take it,' he (Wilson) exclaimed. Well I couldn't see any, and I told him so," Cobb concluded.[10]

It is a moving scene. But there are grave reasons for doubting that it happened on the night of April 1–2, or any other night. The White House log contains no record of Cobb's visiting Wilson at 1 A.M. on April 2. A president can sneak people in side doors and avoid the log—but such evasions usually involve secret affairs of state or clandestine national politics.

There are other reasons for doubting Cobb's account. The picture of Wilson summoning Cobb from New York—four hours away by train—for this last-minute plea for advice, when the decision for war had already been made, Congress had been summoned and his speech written, is extremely dubious. Although Cobb was an ardent Wilson man and the president often expressed appreciation for his friendship, he was unlikely to confide such potentially explosive thoughts to him—or any other newspaperman. If Wilson went through such a dark night of the soul, the only believable witness would have been Colonel House.

Loath to lose this heartbreaking image of a tormented chief executive, some Wilson biographers have transferred Cobb's White House visit back two weeks to mid-March, when Wilson made the decision to go to war, after the cabinet meeting in which the vote was unanimous. But the image of Wilson confiding in Cobb, who did visit him at that time, grows equally dubious when we take a closer look at the story's timing—and the two men who supplied the third-hand account.[11]

The story surfaced in 1924, when both Cobb and Wilson were dead. By that time, Laurence Stallings and Maxwell Anderson were both bitterly disillusioned with the U.S. experience in the war and had written a cynical hit play, *What Price Glory,* as testimony. Stallings, who lost a leg in combat, had also published an autobiographical novel, *Plumes,* about a soldier who came back from France "a broken fool," convinced the war had been "a brutal and vicious dance directed by ghastly men."[12]

A far better explanation for the Stallings-Anderson recollection of Cobb's recollection (he left no written account) is the mordant fact that almost everything this pseudo-Wilson predicted would happen to the United States when it went to war against Germany transpired. But the real President Wilson was unlikely to have foreseen these developments, for a very simple reason: He had only the dimmest idea of how the United States would fight the war. At the time he spoke to Cobb, the president—and the vast majority of those who called for war—thought the United States would not have to send a single soldier to France.[13]

The *World* had been fiercely anti-German. Cobb and his colleagues had reason to be grateful to Wilson for several leaks of confidential documents that had put the Germans in the worst possible light—and created sensational news beats for the paper. What better way to win historical forgiveness for the president—and repay a debt—than to remember Wilson foresaw that the war would make a mess of the United States, yet he felt compelled to launch the nation into it? This perspective not only won sympathy, but also gave Wilson high marks for courage and realism—two traits his critics found singularly lacking in his complex character.[14]

Not to be gainsaid as a final ingredient in this blurry picture is the tradition of faking it—fabricating stories that put across a newspaper's point of view. In 1898, Joseph Pulitzer and his fabulous clone, William Randolph Hearst, had collaborated to start the Spanish-American War with this technique, which they had refined but by no means invented. Faking it was widespread in nineteenth-century journalism. After the "splendid little war" with Spain ended, Pulitzer ordered his top editors to gather the staff of the *World* and tell them that henceforth, truthfulness would be the paper's policy. But faking it was by no means extinct in the minds and hearts of numerous reporters and editors.[15]

V

Presidential secretary Tumulty had arrived at the White House before breakfast to dispatch the final copy of the president's speech to the public printer. Later in the morning, in spite of the April showers, the restless Wilson and his wife had played eighteen holes of golf, a game at which he did not excel. It once took him twenty-six strokes to complete a single hole. His wife regularly beat him. He played only because Admiral Grayson had told him it was vital to his precarious health.[16]

Back in the White House, the tense president told Colonel House he was annoyed to discover there was still no word from Congress. What was talking the legislators so long to get organized? He would put off the speech until tomorrow if he could not give it by 3 P.M. He did not want to look as if he were "unduly pressing matters." House, by now a past master of soothing Wilson, persuaded the president that he should give the speech whenever Congress said it was ready to hear him.

After lunch, Wilson read the speech to Colonel House, who told him it was the best thing he had ever written. In his mind (and later in his diary) the colonel smugly took credit for several of the most important ideas.

House asked Wilson if he had shown the manuscript to his cabinet. Wilson shook his head and curtly replied that it would have been "picked to pieces." He had decided to keep it to himself and take all the responsibility. Although House disapproved of Wilson's tendency to ignore and even to humiliate his cabinet, most of whom had been chosen by the shrewd little Texan, he wisely decided to confine this opinion to his diary.[17]

VI

By this time, Colonel House had become more than Wilson's closest friend. He was an alter ego whom the president needed and used constantly. A wealthy progressive Democrat who had helped elect two Texas governors, in 1911 House had chosen Wilson as his vehicle to power politics beyond the Lone Star State. He had won Wilson's friendship with a deft combination of flattery and artful persuasion of key Wilson opponents in the Democratic Party, such as William Jennings Bryan, to back the instant politician from New Jersey.

House was Wilson's political self, his bridge to a world that Wilson was too aloof and often too condescending to tolerate. Wilson's ideal interview with any politician lasted five minutes. House was prepared to spend hours listening, cajoling and listening again. What was House's reward for this often exhausting process? One of the most delicious sensations in the human emotional repertoire, power—plus the almost equally delicious pleasure of recording in his diary his impact on the history of his time.[18]

House's goals were benevolent; he labored to increase the sum of human happiness and reduce the often appalling toll of human misery. But he had little or no faith in the people's capacity to make their way toward these goals on their own initiative. His ideal government was portrayed in a novel he wrote a few years before he met Woodrow Wilson: *Philip Dru, Administrator*. It was the story of a military and political genius who took over a wealthy, disordered, quarrelsome nation and led it into an era of almost superhuman contentment by persuading the people to make him their supreme autocrat.

Few people were aware that this vision was not very different from Woodrow Wilson's view of how things worked best politically. In one of his books, Wilson wrote that the "graver questions" of politics, such as the choice between peace and war, could only be decided by "the selected leaders of public opinion and rulers of state policy." He maintained that in the United States, the leader of public opinion and the most trustworthy architect of state policy was the president. "Congressional government" was a messy, ultimately feckless process, to be avoided at all costs. It was easy to see how in Edward Mandell House's reveries, Woodrow Wilson became Philip Dru.[19]

VII

Most Wilson biographers have been reluctant to look hard at the Philip Dru side of Wilson. Nor have many people bothered to read this rather lugubrious novel. A close examination reveals a surprisingly militaristic side to Dru's approach to political problems. Although the details are submerged in murky generalities, Dru, a graduate of West Point, fights a large-scale civil war with the forces of "privilege" before ushering the United States into an era of domestic peace and harmony.

Wilson's performance as president revealed a similar readiness to resort to military solutions. During his first term, he sent the U.S. Marines into Haiti and the Dominican Republic to support governments that had few backers outside of the business elite and their American friends. Wilson also used the marines to make Nicaragua a virtual protectorate of the United States. The irony of this policy was not lost on Wilson's critics. During his campaign for the presidency in 1912, he had denounced the Republicans for a similar use of force—he called it gunboat diplomacy—to keep order in the Caribbean.

The Dominicans accepted the U.S. military occupation rather passively, but the Haitian invasion turned into a brutal guerrilla war between the marines and the *cacos,* the island's semiprofessional soldiers. The death toll for the *cacos* eventually reached 3,250. One student of these forgotten imbroglios concluded: "In not a few instances, the legacy of American rule was unmitigated hatred of the United States."[20]

Mexico proved even more resistant to Philip Dru–style diplomacy. There a revolution had been sputtering since 1910. More than 75,000 Americans lived and worked in this southern neighbor, running businesses and overseeing the millions of dollars that U.S. banks and corporations had invested in the country. When General Victoriano Huerta overthrew the ineffective reform government of Francisco I. Madero and murdered him, most Americans in Mexico welcomed the soldier as a man who would restore order to the country. Wilson saw the situation differently. Refusing to recognize a "government of butchers," he went to work on undermining the Huerta regime.

The Mexicans resented Wilson's interference in their internal affairs. The president ignored them and announced that he was backing a Huerta rival, Venustiano Carranza, who called himself a Constitutionalist and an heir of Madero. Wilson allowed Carranza to buy arms in the United States, and hinted that he was prepared to help him depose Huerta with several regiments of marines. The president was dismayed to discover that Carranza was no more enthusiastic about U.S. intervention than the Huertistas.

Still determined to settle things his way, Wilson seized on the arrest of a navy paymaster and his whaleboat crew by a Huerta general at Tampico. Although the sailors were released with an immediate apology, Wilson called the incident an insult to the honor of the United States and told General Huerta he would have to salute the American flag with twenty-one guns by way of apology. The Mexican president declined to do any such thing.

While Congress debated whether to give Wilson the authority to intervene in Mexico, Wilson learned that a German ship, the *Ypiranga*, was approaching Vera Cruz with a cargo of weapons for Huerta. To prevent the guns from being unloaded, on April 21, 1914, Wilson ordered the navy to seize the port. The Mexicans resisted, and a day of fighting left 126 Mexicans and 19 Americans dead. Carranza, the man Wilson was backing, denounced the invasion as a gross violation of the rights and dignity of the Mexican people.

Wilson condemned German meddling in Mexico's affairs, unaware that the guns were from the Colt automatic arms factory in Hartford, Connecticut, and had been shipped via Germany to escape the U.S. embargo on arms exports to Huerta. The German government had had nothing to do with the shipment. Meanwhile, anti-American riots erupted in South America.[21]

By this time, the rest of the world had begun to wonder about Wilson's judgment. Such blatant interference in the internal affairs of another country was unusual in modern diplomacy. Although he was shaken by the casualties at Vera Cruz, Wilson remained convinced that it was his duty to back the man who represented the forces of democracy in Mexico. The only trouble was, these "democrats" had a bad habit of murdering priests and nuns and an occasional American.

The U.S. Army and U.S. Navy withdrew from Vera Cruz, leaving behind tons of weapons to arm the Carranzistas, who soon made rapid progress toward Mexico City. General Huerta fled to Spain—but the revolutionaries split into two factions. One was led by the dignified, white-bearded Carranza; the other by his swaggering, rambunctious general, Francisco "Pancho" Villa. Relying on information from the amateur spokesmen whom Wilson persisted in sending into Mexico because he did not trust the U.S. State Department's personnel, the president decided to back Villa—a decision he soon regretted.

Before this messy adventure ended, Wilson was forced to send a 6,675-man Punitive Expedition into Mexico to hunt down Villa, who had begun murdering Americans on both sides of the border. All things considered, Wilson's intervention in Mexico was not a performance worthy of administrator Philip Dru. The real world was considerably more complicated than Colonel House in his fictional daydreams—or Woodrow Wilson in his pursuit of the ideal—imagined.[22]

VIII

In the White House, the day wore on with no word from Congress. The House of Representatives was distracted by a brouhaha within the Republican Party. The Democrats were in the minority. Wilson's whisker-thin reelection in 1916, decided by a mere 4,000 votes in California, had left the people's chamber in nominal Republican control, with the swing vote in the hands of eight independents. The GOP nominated Congressman James R. Mann of Chicago for speaker, over the furious objections of some members of his party, because he supposedly favored the German side in the war. In fact, Mann had gotten in trouble for backing Wilson's call for peace without victory in December 1916. This shift had prompted many newspapers and pro-war Republicans, notably former president Theodore Roosevelt, to denounce him as a tool of the kaiser.

Thanks to the disunited GOP, the gleeful House Democrats reelected their candidate for speaker, Champ Clark of Missouri, who had held the job since 1911. But the Republicans, trying to salvage something from their intraparty contretemps, called for voice votes on the selection of the other officers of the House—a process that took most of the afternoon.[23]

At about half past four, the restless president walked across the street to the ornate State, War and Navy Building and spent some time with Secretary of War Newton Baker. There is a better-than-even chance that they discussed a controversial topic: conscription. Wilson had opposed it publicly in his reelection campaign. Now he was about to endorse it. This reversal seemed to confirm an adage often used by the president's critics: Anyone who followed Wilson down a political path was almost certain to meet him coming in the opposite direction. Theodore Roosevelt maintained that Wilson had taken contradictory stands on almost every political issue under the sun.

Next, Wilson joined Secretary of the Navy Josephus Daniels at a meeting of the navy's general board. The deeply religious Daniels had found the lurch to war a "Gethsemane," but he had reluctantly concurred in Wilson's decision. Cooperation with the British navy was now assumed to be imminent. Rear Admiral William S. Sims had sailed for England on March 31 to work out the details.

The president also paused to discuss with Secretary of State Robert Lansing some minor changes in the proclamation of war that would be issued after his speech. The secretary, who had been urging Wilson to get into the war on England's side for a year, expressed concern for the president's safety on his way to the Capitol. Attorney General Thomas W. Gregory, who happened to be visiting Lansing, earnestly concurred. Wilson dismissed their fears. But the moment the president departed, Lansing called Secretary of War Baker and persuaded him to add a troop of cavalry to Wilson's usual police and Secret Service escort.[24]

Back in the White House, the president learned that the House of Representatives had finally gotten itself organized. Wilson sent word that he would speak at 8:30 P.M. He had dinner with his wife, his daughter, Margaret, and Colonel House in the mansion's private dining room around 6:30. House later recalled that they chatted about "everything excepting the matter at hand." They all knew how important it was to reduce the stress on the edgy president. In 1906, under the comparatively minor strains of the presidency of Princeton, Wilson had suffered a physical collapse that had left him partially blind in one eye. Doctors had diagnosed hypertension and arteriosclerosis and told him he could never work again. Although a six-month vacation in England had restored him, his health remained a source of concern—one of the reasons why his almost constant companion was Admiral Cary Grayson.[25]

IX

Not all Americans agreed with the course the nation was about to take. Throughout the day in Washington, D.C., hundreds of antiwar protesters roamed the streets, carrying placards and handing out pamphlets against plunging the United States into the European cataclysm—this "Great War," which had already killed 5 million men. The newspapers called these protesters pacifists, a pejorative term that made them sound as if they were opposed to all wars and were supinely prepared to let aggressive enemies of their country step all over them. In fact, most of them were opposed to entering this war, for reasons they considered extremely persuasive. They were led by idealistic David Starr Jordan, former president of Stanford University. Less than forty-eight hours earlier, Jordan had been battered and bruised by a mob when he addressed an antiwar meeting in Baltimore. But he accepted command of this last-ditch effort for peace.[26]

Also in the capital were numerous members of Pilgrims for Patriotism, a group organized by the violently pro-war National Security League. Among the league's leaders were Theodore Roosevelt and Alton B. Parker, the Democratic candidate for president in 1904. The members of the league were convinced that the Germans were already enemies of the United States and that anyone who opposed fighting them was a traitor. The Washington police defused a confrontation between the two groups by banning all parades and rallies.

Barred from the White House by a heavy police detail, and repulsed from an attempt to invade the State, War and Navy Building, the antiwar protesters trudged down Pennsylvania Avenue in the rain to the Capitol, where they gathered on the steps. They were led by a young woman carrying a banner that underscored one of the chief reasons that these people objected to Woodrow Wilson's course: "Is This the United States of Great Britain?"[27]

Some protesters ventured into the Senate Office Building, which was patrolled by the Secret Service, the District of Columbia police and even the Post Office Department police, as anxiety mounted over the influx of pro- and antiwar activists. A half dozen proponents of peace from Massachusetts found their way to the offices of their senior senator, Henry Cabot Lodge, who had been urging Americans to get into the war on the English side almost from the day the fighting started. When they insisted on speaking to the white-bearded, sixty-seven-year-old politician, he finally came to the door of his office to hear their dissent from his well-publicized opinions.

The discussion grew heated. Lodge suggested they were degenerates and cowards and started to return to his office. One of the protesters, a husky Princeton student named Alexander Bannwart, shouted, "You're a damned coward."

Lodge wheeled and confronted his accuser. "You're a damned liar," he snarled.

Bannwart threw a roundhouse right at Lodge, who ducked and punched "the German," as he later incorrectly called his attacker, in the face. (Bannwart was an American of Swiss German descent.) Male secretaries from Lodge's office, a passing Western Union messenger, and Capitol police piled on Bannwart and beat him badly. Soon the story swept through the Capitol that Lodge had flattened "the German" with one punch.[28]

At about eight o'clock, the triumphant senator and his fellow solons headed for the House of Representatives to welcome the president. The chamber was rapidly filling with dignitaries. The justices of the Supreme Court, sans robes, sat in places of honor before the rostrum. Off to one side sat the cabinet and the entire diplomatic corps in full gold-laced regalia—the first time they had been welcomed to this sanctum in anyone's memory. In the packed gallery, the wives of the cabinet sat in the front row. They were joined by Edith and Margaret Wilson and Colonel House.

Back at the White House, as the president's limousine rolled through the north gate onto Pennsylvania Avenue, the car was surrounded by a troop of poncho-draped cavalrymen. They cantered beside it, their drawn sabers gleaming in the streetlights. A few hardy souls cheered feebly from the sidewalks. Earlier in the day the streets had been crowded with prospective applauders; most had long since gone home to dinner. Washington bureaucrats, anticipating the president's decision, had decked the city with patriotic bunting, which now drooped soggily in the rain. Up ahead, the Capitol's illuminated dome gleamed in newly installed indirect lights, a gigantic symbol of the republic's power and putative purity.

About a block from the Capitol, other cavalrymen had cordoned off the antiwar protesters. They shouted angry, despairing cries at the presidential limousine. At the east portico of the Capitol, Wilson's cavalry escort halted to permit the president's driver to glide to a stop at the foot of the steps. As Wilson got out of the car, several hundred pro-war demonstrators on the steps shouted cheers of encouragement.[29]

Inside, Speaker of the House Champ Clark, the man Wilson had defeated for the Democratic Party's nomination in 1912, rapped his gavel for order. Two minutes later, the rear doors opened and the vice president of the United States, Thomas R. Marshall of Indiana, entered, followed in a column of twos by the senators, representing the forty-eight states of the Union. Most of the senators were carrying or wore in their breast pockets small American flags. Vice President Marshall looked glum. He was opposed to entering the war. But President Wilson was utterly indifferent to his opinion. Marshall sometimes summed up the insignificance of his office by telling a story: "Once there were two brothers. One of them ran away to sea and the other one became vice president of the United States. Neither was ever heard from again."[30]

The senators were soon in their allotted seats. The speaker banged his gavel once more. Behind him the hands on the big official clock read 8:35. The clerk of the House of Representatives solemnly intoned: "The President of the United States!"[31]

As Wilson came down the aisle, everyone on the floor and in the gallery rose and cheered, shouted, clapped with a wild emotion that made only too clear what they expected him to say—and how they hoped he would say it. Expressionless, Wilson strode to the rostrum, his eyes down, his speech clutched in both hands. He opened it on the lectern and waited for the ovation to subside.

Like many great actors, Wilson often experienced acute nervousness as he approached an audience. But his anxiety vanished when he reached the moment of delivery. Wilson had supreme confidence in himself as a public speaker. He had honed his considerable talents in hundreds of addresses while at Princeton and earlier academic posts. He had won the governorship of New Jersey and the White House with his oratory. He was the first president in 113 years to address joint sessions of Congress. (His predecessors' messages had been read by clerks.) His speeches had already gone far, in the words of an admiring editorial in the *New York Times,* toward "stamping his personality upon his age."[32]

Eventually, there was total silence in the huge chamber. "Gentlemen of the Congress," Wilson began in a voice that one listener found "husky" with emotion. "I have called the Congress into extraordinary session because there are serious, very serious choices of policy to be made, and made immediately, which it was neither right nor constitutionally permissible that I should assume the responsibility of making."

Swiftly he narrated the developments of the last two months, in which the "Imperial German Government" announced its intention to "put aside all restraints of law or of humanity" and use its submarines to sink every vessel that ventured into the barred zone around the British Isles. He briefly recalled that in April 1916, Germany, in response to Wilson's protests, had promised to stop this practice and to order its submarines to give "due warning" to targeted ships to enable the crews to escape. The Germans had also promised to refrain from sinking passenger ships.

The new policy, Wilson somberly declared, had "swept every restriction aside." Once more, ships were going down without the slightest concern for their cargo, their destination or their crews. Even hospital ships and vessels carrying food to "the sorely bereaved and stricken people of Belgium" had been sunk "with the same reckless lack of compassion and principle."

At first, the president said, he was "unable to believe that such things would in fact be done by any government that had hitherto subscribed to the humane practices of civilized nations." But he had been forced to conclude that "German submarine warfare against commerce is a warfare against mankind."

It was also a war against all nations, including the United States. He grieved for the losses of other neutral nations. How each would meet the challenge was up to each country to decide. America's choice would be made with "a moderation of counsel and a temperateness of judgment befitting our character and our motives as a nation."

Solemnly, the president reinforced this point: "We must put excited feeling away." America's motive would not be revenge or a demonstration of its physical might. Instead the United States would fight for "the vindication of the right, of human right, of which we are only a single champion."

For a few months, Wilson said, he had considered arming U.S. merchantmen against the submarines as a way to maintain a precarious neutrality. But the "outlaw" tactics of submarine warfare made this "impracticable."

What choice, then, did the United States have? Wilson's voice darkened, grimness deepened on his somber face. "There is one choice we cannot make, we are incapable of making, we will not choose the path of submission."

As Wilson said these words, Chief Justice of the Supreme Court Andrew White raised his arms in the air, and in the words of a *New York Times* reporter, "brought them together with a heartfelt bang. . . . House, Senate and galleries followed him with a roar like a storm."[33]

It was the response Wilson had been looking for. A new emotion, a mixture of defiance and anger, appeared in his voice. "The wrongs against which we now array ourselves are no common wrongs; they cut to the very roots of human life."

With renewed solemnity, Wilson asked the Congress to declare "the course of the Imperial German Government to be in fact nothing less than war against the people of the United States." It was time to "formally accept the status of belligerent which has thus been thrust upon it; and that it take immediate steps . . . to exert all its power and employ all its resources to bring the government of the German Empire to terms and end the war."

Chief Justice White began cheering in the middle of this declaration of hostilities. By the time Wilson got to the final phrases, White and the entire chamber were on their feet, shouting, applauding. The chief justice's face, reported the *New York Times* reporter, "worked almost convulsively and great tears began to roll down his cheeks."[34]

The president proceeded to describe the program on which the United States would now embark. They would offer "the most liberal financial credits" to the governments now at war with Germany. They would share America's material resources, immediately equip the navy to deal with enemy submarines, and expand the army by at least 500,000 men, "who should, in my opinion, be chosen upon the principle of universal liability to service."

These words were an uplifting way of saying conscription, a draft. Along with this hard choice would be "equitable" taxation to finance the U.S. government's war program and to protect people against the inflation produced by "vast war loans."

More important than these "deeply momentous things" was the necessity to make America's motives clear "to all the world." The goal of the war would be to "vindicate the principles of peace and justice against "selfish and autocratic power." It was "autocratic governments backed by organized force" that made neutrality impossible.

Wilson insisted that he did not blame the German people for this international malaise. "We have no quarrel with the German people. We have no feeling towards them but one of sympathy and friendship. It was not upon their impulse that their government acted in entering this war." The war had been provoked and waged in the interests of "dynasties or of little groups of ambitious men."

In a voice vibrant with emotion, the president launched into a paean to democracy. "Self-governed nations do not fill their neighbor states with spies" or launch "cunningly contrived plans of deception or aggression . . . from generation to generation." Such things can only be done "within the privacy of [royal] courts or behind the carefully guarded confidences of a narrow and privileged class." They were "happily impossible" where public opinion insisted that a government give the people "full information" about the nation's affairs.

At this point Wilson asked the audience if they did not share his enthusiasm for the "wonderful and heartening things that have been happening within the last few weeks in Russia." That nation, he maintained, had always "been democratic at heart." The autocracy that ran the country was an aberration, not even Russian in origin. Now Russia had become a fit partner for a "League of Honor."

Returning to Germany, the president launched a scathing denunciation of the spies and saboteurs that the "Prussian autocracy" had sent to the United States to disturb the peace and disrupt U.S. industries. Even worse was the attempt to "stir up enemies against us at our very doors" by offering Mexico an alliance. This underhanded policy had made it clear that the German government had no "real friendship" for Americans and intended to "act against our peace and security" at its convenience. It was time to "accept the gauge of battle" with this "natural foe to liberty," to fight for "the ultimate peace of the world and for the liberation of its peoples, the German peoples included; for the right of nations, great and small . . . the world must be made safe for democracy."

At first, Senator John Sharp Williams of Mississippi was the only person in the chamber to react to these last words. He began clapping. The harsh sound of his beating hands seemed to take everyone by surprise. A moment later, the entire audience was imitating him.[35]

Wilson reiterated America's disinterested motives. "We have no selfish ends to serve. We desire no conquest, no dominion. . . . We are but one of

the champions of the rights of mankind." He also restated America's lack
of enmity toward the German people. He declared that Americans would
prove this friendship by their actions toward the millions of German-
Americans in their midst. In fact, they would prove their friendship for all
the immigrants and their descendants who were "loyal to the government
and to their neighbors in the hour of test."

Finally, came a soaring peroration:

> It is a fearful thing to lead this great peaceful people into war, into the
> most terrible and disastrous of all wars, civilization itself seeming to be
> in the balance. But the right is more precious than peace, and we shall
> fight for the things we have always carried in our hearts—for democ-
> racy, for the right of those who submit to authority to have a voice in
> their own governments, for the rights and liberties of small nations, for
> a universal dominion of right by such a concert of free peoples as shall
> bring peace and safety to all nations and make the world itself at last
> free. To such a task we can dedicate our lives and our fortunes, every-
> thing that we are and everything that we have, with the pride of those
> who know that America is privileged to spend her blood and her
> might for the principles that gave her birth and happiness and the
> peace which she has treasured. God helping her, she can do no other.[36]

The last line, a paraphrase of Martin Luther's famous defense of his
Protestant faith, guaranteed that this time, there was no need for cheerlead-
ing by Chief Justice White or Senator Williams. Almost every person in the
chamber was standing up, clapping, shouting, waving flags, in some cases
sobbing with the emotion Wilson had ignited. Only a few people noticed
that one man made a point of doing none of these things. A small, sardonic
smile on his wide, creased face, Senator Robert La Follette of Wisconsin,
one of the stellar voices of liberalism in America, folded his arms across his
broad chest and stood there in silent disagreement.[37]

X

Wilson left the House chamber immediately. Only a few people were able
to shake his hand. One was Senator Lodge, who told him that he had "expressed in the loftiest manner the sentiments of the American people."

These were the first kind words Lodge had directed toward Wilson in a long time. The secretary of agriculture, David F. Houston, who had been arguing for war against Germany within Wilson's cabinet as passionately as Lodge had been calling for it publicly, also shook the president's hand and congratulated him. Wilson returned to the White House with Joe Tumulty and Cary Grayson where he found his wife and daughter and Colonel House waiting for him in his study on the second floor.

House told Wilson he had "taken a position as to policies that no other statesman had yet assumed." Perhaps revealing a certain weariness with House's sycophantic style, Wilson disagreed. He said Daniel Webster, Abraham Lincoln and the president's favorite politician, Britain's William Evarts Gladstone, had relied on the same principles. House diplomatically disagreed. "It seemed to me," House told his diary, "he did not have a true conception of the path he was blazing." Was the colonel telling himself he understood the history they were making far better than Philip Dru?[38]

XI

Later, according to Joe Tumulty, he and Wilson adjourned to the Cabinet Room, where the president broke down. "My message today was a message of death for our young men," he said. "How strange it seems to applaud that." The president supposedly launched into a self-pitying monologue, defending his long struggle to keep the United States neutral. He spoke bitterly of how he had been maligned in the newspapers by men such as Theodore Roosevelt and Henry Cabot Lodge. Wilson read Tumulty a letter from a friend who understood what he was trying to do. Finally, Tumulty said, "he wiped away great tears [and] laying his head on the table, sobbed as if he was a child."

Repeated in dozens of history books and Wilson biographies, this touching scene almost certainly never happened. Tumulty wrote it in 1920, when the illusion of victory had been shattered by cruel realities. Like Frank Cobb's imaginary interview, it represents something that Tumulty wished Wilson had said and done. By 1920, Tumulty was one of the few men in U.S. politics who remained loyal to Wilson, in spite of the shameful way the president and his wife had treated him.[39]

Without Tumulty, Woodrow Wilson might never have become president. The shrewd, genial Irish-American from Jersey City had shepherded Wilson through the wilderness of New Jersey machine politics when he ran for governor in 1910. Tumulty had stayed loyal when Wilson did what almost every Irish-American politician in the United States considered unforgivable. He broke his promise that he would not attack James Smith, the powerful Democratic Party boss whom George Harvey had persuaded to offer Wilson the gubernatorial nomination. Instead, to prove his liberal bona fides, Wilson made Smith one of his principal targets. In sticking with Wilson, a man whom fellow Irish-Americans called a liar and an ingrate, Tumulty destroyed his once bright future in the New Jersey Democratic Party.[40]

In Washington, Tumulty had been equally valuable in dealing with Congress and the press during Wilson's first term. He combined abundant charm with shrewd judgment and tact. Nevertheless, after Wilson's reelection in 1916, the president had fired Tumulty. Why? Because Edith Galt Wilson and Colonel House had advised him against having an Irish-Catholic in his White House. Edith considered Tumulty "common." House foolishly joined the First Lady in this effort to dispose of a rival for Wilson's attention, never dreaming that he was next on her hit list.

Tumulty had been the target of attacks by anti-Catholics and politicians jealous of his influence—often one and the same. Too many Irish-Americans assumed he could get them favored treatment on everything from government jobs to freeing Ireland from Britain's grip. In dealing with these problems, Tumulty did nothing to impugn his loyalty or impair his usefulness to the president.

Tumulty wrote Wilson a sad letter, in which he said his dismissal "wounds me more deeply than I can tell you." Although he was "heartsick," he would depart "grateful for having been associated so closely with so great a man." Newspaperman David Lawrence, a former student of Wilson's at Princeton and an admirer of Tumulty, persuaded the president to change his mind. But the old, confident friendship between Tumulty and Wilson was gone beyond recall. The secretary was always aware that Edith Wilson's critical eye was fixed on him—and her opinion often meant more to the president than his advice.[41]

XII

Edith Galt Wilson was by no means the first presidential wife to wield political power behind the scenes. Abigail Adams was known as a "compleat politician," whose counsel her harassed husband, John, frequently sought.

Dolley Madison's political skills were crucial to the survival of James Madison's troubled presidency. Sarah Polk was James Polk's constant confidante and adviser on everything from patronage to fighting the Mexican war.

But these First Ladies had been married to their politician husbands for decades before they reached the White House and had acquired graduate degrees in political sophistication over the years. Edith Galt Wilson's interest in politics was so minimal that she did not even know who was running in the presidential election of 1912, when her future husband won the White House. Even more minimal was her education—only two years of formal schooling. Her adult life had been largely involved with business. Her late husband had owned a jewelry store known as "the Tiffany's of Washington." After his death, she managed the business with the help of a hardworking brother.

Nevertheless, the recently widowed Wilson, in his passionate pursuit of Mrs. Galt, undertook to convert her into a partner in the most confidential aspects of his presidency. He conferred with her about his letters to the German government and his problems with Haiti, Mexico and the Republican opposition. Soon she was telling him, "Much as I love your delicious love-letters . . . I believe I enjoy even more the ones in which you tell me . . . of what you are working on . . . for then I feel I am . . . being taken in to partnership as it were."[42]

After their marriage on December 18, 1915, this partnership became even more explicit. Each morning, Edith joined the president in inspecting "the Drawer," the place in his Oval Office desk where aides placed reports from the State Department or other parts of the government requiring the president's immediate attention. Edith regularly converted into code Wilson's letters to ambassadors or to House when the colonel was conferring with political leaders in London and Paris, and decoded letters from them. She frequently remained in the Oval Office while Wilson dictated answers to urgent letters. When Colonel House returned from Europe, he was amazed when Wilson invited Edith to join them to hear about his supersecret negotiations with the British and French.[43]

This crash course in power politics made Edith Galt Wilson presume a political wisdom she did not possess. The illusion would have a deleterious impact not only on Joe Tumulty and Colonel House, but also on Woodrow Wilson's presidency and the history of the world.

XIII

Elsewhere in the country, the news that the United States had gone to war landed with a dull thud. No one danced or demonstrated in the streets. In New York, newsboys sold extras to the usual crowds in Times Square. But there was no visible response. About a hundred people read the bulletin boards in Herald Square, where the latest news flashes were posted, without the slightest sign of excitement. The contrast between the way the war had begun in Europe, with tens of thousands of Germans, French, and Russians cheering the news, was stark.[44]

There was some mild interest in a *New York Times* story about a hearing before the New York State Senate in Albany to resolve a dispute between Mayor John Purroy Mitchel of New York City and State Senator Robert F. Wagner. The senator had demanded the hearing to clear his name when the mayor accused him of being an agent of the German government. The *Times* reported that the senate gave Wagner a clean bill of patriotic health.

Another story reported that the pro-war president of Columbia University, Nicholas Murray Butler, had expelled one Morris Ryskind of the School of Journalism for writing an article in the college magazine, *The Jester*, calling him a warmonger. Ryskind had also lampooned the pompous president in a poem. The *Times* claimed that the entire university supported the decision to give Ryskind the boot. The opinionated young man went on to Broadway and Hollywood fame as the writer of Marx Brothers comedies and hit plays in collaboration with George S. Kaufman.[45]

Only in the Metropolitan Opera House was there any political drama. That was mostly supplied by the former ambassador to Berlin, James W. Gerard, who was violently anti-German. During intermission, he heard the newsboys shouting on the sidewalk outside. Gerard seized the arm of one of the Metropolitan's directors and urged him to read the news from the stage and have the orchestra play "The Star-Spangled Banner." "No," the director said, "the opera company is neutral."

The enraged former ambassador rushed to his box seat and shouted the news to the startled audience. He urged everyone to cheer President Wilson. Very few of these rich people had voted for the president; the response was halfhearted at first. But patriotism soon inspired a louder hurrah, especially when the orchestra undertook the national anthem.

Satisfied, Gerard sat down to enjoy the rest of the opera. But he and the audience were doomed to disappointment. German-born soprano Margaret Ober, deeply distressed by the news, fainted in the middle of the next act. She had to be carried off the stage, leaving an artistic vacuum through which the other singers floundered to the final curtain.[46]

In Cincinnati, the city's symphony, one of the nation's best, played "The Star-Spangled Banner" in magnificent style when the news arrived. Then the conductor, Ernest Kunwald, turned to his mostly German-American audience with tears streaming down his cheeks and said, "But my heart is on the other side!"[47]

XIV

The next morning, pro-war newspapers and public spokespeople of all stripes made Colonel House's praise of Wilson's "communication" seem tame. Frank Cobb's editorial in the *New York World* declared that the hope of the whole world rested on Wilson's words. The *New York Tribune*, eating Cass Gilbert's sneers, proclaimed: "No praise is too high for Wilson." The *Times* of London, once considered the greatest newspaper on the globe, opined: "We doubt if in all history a great community has ever been summoned to war on grounds so largely ideal."[48]

Private letters loaded with equally extravagant praise poured into the White House and the mailboxes of Wilson's intimates. "The president's address is magnificent," wrote twenty-seven-year old Walter Lippmann, already a star liberal spokesperson on the editorial board of the *New Republic,* in a letter to Colonel House. "It puts the whole thing exactly where it needed to be put and does it with real nobility of feeling."

Other leading liberal intellectuals, such as Columbia University philosopher John Dewey and Oswald Garrison Villard, editor of *The Nation*, were similarly swept away by Wilson's rhetoric. After years of denouncing Theodore Roosevelt, Henry Cabot Lodge, and anyone else who urged the United States to get into the war, these men suddenly saw the president as the leader of a "stupendous revolution" that would change the world.[49]

In Missouri, a thirty-three-year-old farmer named Harry S. Truman was amazed to discover that Wilson's speech had transformed local attitudes toward the war—including his own—from bored indifference to crusading fervor. Although Truman was the chief support of his mother and sister and beyond draft age, he decided to volunteer. "I felt like Galahad after the Grail," he said later—an example of Wilson's ability to tap the latent idealism in the soul of many Americans.[50]

XV

In Washington, D.C., Congress convened at noon on April 3 and spent the first hour noting the avalanche of letters and telegrams its members had received from individuals, mass meetings, impromptu committees of public safety, and state legislatures, most of them endorsing the president's stance. While this chore was filling twenty-four pages of tiny type in the *Congressional Record,* the Senate Foreign Relations Committee was discussing a resolution stating that war had been "thrust upon" the United States by the imperial German government and was now formally declared. The document had been drafted the previous night by the House Foreign Affairs Committee.

The chairman of the Senate committee, William J. Stone of Missouri, startled everyone by casting a negative vote and declining to submit the resolution to the full Senate. At any other time, this defection would have been major news. Stone had played a vital role in winning Wilson the Democratic nomination in 1912 and had worked closely with him in the Senate to pass important domestic reforms. He had wholeheartedly endorsed the president's attempts to mediate the conflict as a neutral.

Wilson's switch to a belligerent posture had dismayed Stone. In February, the senator had issued a statement charging that a "cabal of great newspapers" in the United States was "coercing the government into an attitude of hostility" to Germany. Friends had warned Stone that he was risking political extinction. In deep background, a partner in J. P. Morgan's bank, which had loaned billions to the British, cabled London that he could supply evidence that Stone was "intimate" with the German government.[51]

In place of Stone, Senator Gilbert Hitchcock of Nebraska, once a strenuous opponent of war, undertook the task of presenting the resolution to the Senate. He read the brief document in a matter-of-fact style, obviously assuming that the task was a mere formality. The senator asked his fellow legislators for unanimous consent to consider and approve the resolution. In addition to Wilson's triumphant speech, this sense of foregone conclusion was bolstered by the morning's newspapers, which carried a report of the torpedoing of the armed U.S. merchantman *Aztec*, with the loss of twelve lives. In the press gallery, reporters were poised to scribble news flashes that the United States was practically at war.

A lone voice punctured these assumptions: "I object to the request for unanimous consideration!" Senator La Follette was on his feet, defiance personified. Consternation swept the chamber. Those who understood Senate rules knew this meant that a vote would be postponed for at least a full day. The rule had been created to prevent hasty votes on important topics and to add substance to the claim that the Senate was the world's greatest deliberative body. La Follette asked a startled Vice President Marshall to rule on his request. In a rage, the pro-war senators could do nothing but adjourn. In the cloakroom, they agitatedly conferred, wondering if La Follette would dare to launch a filibuster against the war resolution.[52]

A month before, La Follette's stalling tactics had succeeded when President Wilson had asked Congress for the authority to arm merchant ships as a final attempt to keep the United States out of the war. The Wisconsin liberal and eleven other senators had filibustered until the Sixty-Fourth Congress expired without getting a chance to vote on the proposal. "Fighting Bob" had argued that the proviso would give Wilson the right to declare war—a privilege reserved for Congress—and was a bad idea in the first place. A few guns on a merchant ship were no defense against submarines. The president had denounced the filibusterers as "a little group of willful men" and released the Zimmermann telegram (which he had been sitting on for almost a week) to the press. La Follette and his antiwar colleagues had been roasted in almost every newspaper in the nation. But he stubbornly continued his filibuster, forcing Wilson to arm the merchant ships by executive order.[53]

XVI

While the Senate fumed impotently, other parts of the U.S. government were preparing for war—sort of. At his desk in the State, War and Navy Building, Army Chief of Staff Major General Hugh L. Scott was confronting a threat he considered far more dangerous than the German army: former president Theodore Roosevelt. The large, slow-moving Scott was deaf and frequently fell asleep in his chair; he had a penchant for answering questions using Native American sign language. But Roosevelt had galvanized him into uncharacteristic action.

After maligning Wilson as everything from a coward to a Byzantine lo-gothete for his refusal to go to war, Roosevelt wanted the president to au-thorize him to raise a volunteer division that would sail for Europe immediately to show the flag and hearten the Allies. The idea appalled Scott and all the other aging bureaucrats on the general staff. They vividly recalled TR's performance in the Spanish-American War, in which he not only won fame charging Spanish rifle pits on Kettle and San Juan hills, but also relentlessly criticized the army bureaucracy's appalling lapses in arm-ing, clothing and feeding the soldiers. The general staff had ordered cold-eyed Major Peyton C. March to prepare a paper denouncing the idea of a volunteer division. This document was now in the hands of Secretary of War Baker, making Scott feel that the army was safe from a Roosevelt coup d'état.[54]

Roosevelt was on his way from Florida to make his request for a volun-teer major generalship in person. Further undermining his hopes was a tall, handsome major named Douglas MacArthur, who was serving as Secretary of War Baker's information officer—the army's first venture into public re-lations. MacArthur was ordered to tell reporters that Roosevelt's volun-teerism would mess up the planned draft. The major was already so popular with the fourth estate that a few days later, twenty-nine reporters presented a letter to Baker, praising him as a man who "helped to shape the public mind." All in all, it looked as if the army would win its first battle without shedding a drop of blood.[55]

In the same building, another tall, extremely handsome young man was toiling at his desk in the Navy Department. Assistant Secretary Franklin Roosevelt was possibly the happiest civilian in the government. He had been lobbying overtly and covertly for a declaration of war on Germany for well over a year. He even met clandestinely with his wife's uncle (and his distant cousin), Theodore Roosevelt, Woodrow Wilson's most outspo-ken critic, to discuss how to put pressure on the president.[56]

The younger Roosevelt hoped that hostilities would oust his lethargic boss, Josephus Daniels, and make the thirty-five-year-old New Yorker sec-retary of the navy. Through his worshipful right-hand man, gnomelike Louis Howe (who sometimes signed his letters "Your slave and servant"), Roosevelt had sponsored a series of backstairs attacks on Daniels, calling for his replacement by his "virile-minded, hardfisted civilian assistant," in the words of one complaisant newspaper.[57]

With war virtually declared, Roosevelt began trying to embarrass Daniels almost openly. When a reporter asked him if the fleet had been mobilized yet, the assistant secretary said he did not know, "but you have a right to know. Come along and we'll find out."

He led the reporter into Daniels's office and said, "Here's a newsman. He wants to know, and all the rest of us want to know, whether the fleet has been ordered mobilized."

The portly, mild-mannered Daniels, who maintained an amazing tolerance of Roosevelt's behavior, replied that an announcement would be made in due course.

Out in the corridor, Roosevelt muttered to the reporter, "You see?" With a shrug and a contemptuous look over his shoulder at Daniels's closed door, he added, "It was the best I could do."[58]

Roosevelt's impatience with his slow-moving chief was fueled by the widespread assumption that the major U.S. role in the war would be on the ocean. In the April 4 New York Tribune, Cass W. Gilbert told his readers that the notion of sending a large U.S. army overseas was a "phantasy." There were simply not enough ships to transport men along with the food that England and France needed to feed their civilians and the munitions that would enable their armies to kill more Germans. Underlying this vision of a more or less bloodless war was the assumption that American infantrymen were not needed. It was evident to everyone who read U.S. newspapers that England, France and Russia were winning the war.[59]

Elsewhere in the United States, officials and ordinary citizens braced themselves for a wave of German sabotage. In New York, the police commissioner mobilized no less than 12,000 men equipped with machine guns and rifles to deal with an assault by German army reservists who had supposedly been waiting undercover for hostilities to begin. Armed guards patrolled bridges, railroad yards and other likely targets. The National Guard was already protecting the upstate reservoirs, on the apparent assumption that Berlin was not above ecoterrorism.

More worrisome, according to the New York Tribune, were reports of a German plot to trigger a huge uprising among the South's African Americans, a largely disenfranchised group who might wonder about joining a crusade to make the world safe for democracy. (The Tribune, of course, did not allude to this somewhat glaring fact—or to the way the Southern-born Wilson had permitted his mostly Southern cabinet to extend racial segregation to all parts of the U.S. government.) The shocking goal of the putative plotters was to seize Texas and turn it into a black republic in which "Mexicans and Japanese were to have equal rights with the Negro." In San Francisco, gentlemen in the lounges of the exclusive Bohemian Club were discussing an even scarier possibility: A German-led army invading from Mexico, with cadres of "armed Negroes" in their ranks.[60]

Elsewhere, many people were ignoring Wilson's claim that Americans would prove their friendship with the German people by being nice to the millions of German-Americans in their midst. Men and women with obviously German names were being harassed by superpatriots, investigated for presumed disloyalty and arrested as probable spies and saboteurs. In a Wichita Falls, Texas, exhibition game, Detroit Tigers outfielder Ty Cobb, arguably the greatest baseball player of the day (or any other day), slid into second base with spikes high and badly slashed Charles Lincoln "Buck" Herzog of the New York Giants. Cobb leaped on top of the bleeding Herzog and pounded him with his fists, screaming, "German!"[61]

XVII

On April 4, the Senate reconvened at 10 A.M. in an angry mood. La Follette was the main target of their wrath, which was reflected in numerous newspapers. During the Wisconsin senator's filibuster on the armed-ship bill, *New York World* cartoonist Rollin Kirby had portrayed La Follette at the head of his little column of filibusterers, receiving the Iron Cross. The *New York Times* had assembled thirty-three editorials from around the nation, two-thirds of them denunciations. La Follette had been compared to Benedict Arnold and Judas Iscariot.

Toward the end of the filibuster, Senator Ollie James of Kentucky had rushed at La Follette carrying a gun concealed under his coattails. One of Fighting Bob's allies, Senator Harry Lane of Oregon, spotted the gun and drew a steel file long enough, he later said, to slip under James's left collar bone and "reach his heart with one thrust." Fortunately, several other senators wrestled the berserk Kentuckian back to his seat.[62]

Outrage over the way La Follette had forced the Senate to adjourn without declaring war was even more intense. Students from the Massachusetts Institute of Technology burned him in effigy. At a pro-war lecture by a distinguished sociologist in New York, La Follette's name was greeted with hisses. The Madison, Wisconsin, *Democrat* declared that the senator's home state was "disappointed, chagrinned, indignant," and wondered: "Is La Follette mad?"[63]

Although his Senate supporters had dwindled from eleven to five, La Follette remained undaunted. He had stayed up most of the night working on a speech. Now he waited expectantly while Senator Hitchcock reintroduced the war resolution with the admission that he had "bitterly opposed" the war but had decided that to cast his vote against the resolution would be "doing a vain and foolish thing." The aloof, dandyish Hitchcock was revealing an odd passivity that enabled him to do all sorts of things in the name of party loyalty that contradicted the voice of his conscience. An admirer of Germany, Hitchcock had been severely critical of Woodrow Wilson's supposed neutrality. He and the president had long since arrived at a state of mutual detestation.[64]

Hitchcock was followed by other senators who called for a yes vote, notably Henry Cabot Lodge. His Van Dyke beard giving him a vaguely Mephistophelian air, Lodge reiterated the opinion that had outraged antiwar critics on Monday—the decision was a choice between war and "national degeneracy" and "cowardice." Lodge also predicted the war would heal "the division of our people into race groups, striving to direct the course of the United States in the interest of some other country."[65]

Here Lodge was joining his friend Theodore Roosevelt and Woodrow Wilson in a long-running attack on what the president called hyphenated Americans. The senator was thinking somewhat nervously of the large number of Irish-Americans in Massachusetts who were opposed to becoming England's ally. He went on to echo Wilson's words about a war against barbarism, a war for peace and democracy.

Senator James Vardaman of Mississippi arose to disagree with Lodge and Wilson. A veteran of the Spanish-American War, Vardaman could claim ancestors who had fought in virtually every previous American war. He noted that the president had said on April 2 that if the citizens of the warring countries had been consulted, there would have been no conflict. If the president had consulted the "plain honest people" of America, who would bear the burden of taxation and would fight the battles, the United States would not be trying to declare war on Germany today. Vardaman gravely doubted whether sacrificing millions of American lives and spending billions of dollars made sense to "organize the parliament of man." He did not think the world would accept Wilson's "big ideas" by force of arms and "the methods of the brute." [66]

Senator Stone said that he would not try to answer Henry Cabot Lodge and other pro-war speakers, "although it seems to me [the] answer would be easy." The pro-war advocates claimed to be speaking from facts, he said, but they were using "only part of the facts." Stone was confident that history would eventually tell the whole story. Meanwhile, he would simply say that involving the United States in this war, which Congress clearly intended to do, would be "the greatest national blunder in history."[67]

George Norris, the portly Republican senator from Nebraska, now rose. Like La Follette, he was one of the founders of the progressive movement in America, the political upheaval that had split the Republican Party and had made Woodrow Wilson president. Norris assailed Wilson for not telling the whole truth about why the Germans were attacking U.S. ships in the so-called war zone around the British Isles. The creation of this zone was a response to Great Britain's similar blockade of Germany, by mining the North Sea virtually the day the war started. The Americans had done little or nothing to protest the British blockade. Norris asked why the United States had kept its ships out of the war zone that England had created but refused to recognize the German war zone around the British Isles. Why didn't the United States keep its ships and citizens out of it?

American neutrality, in short, was a sham. Why had the president and so many other people tolerated this situation? Because American bankers and corporations were reaping enormous profits by selling weapons and munitions to the British, the French and the Russians. Now these profiteers wanted to take this covert alliance a step further, into actual war. Norris read a letter written by a member of the New York Stock Exchange to his customers. The Nebraskan had obtained it from another senator, who lacked the courage to read it—and who planned to vote for the war. "The popular view is that stocks would have a quick clear sharp reaction immediately on the outbreak of hostilities," the broker wrote. "They then would enjoy an old fashioned bull market such as followed the outbreak of war with Spain in 1898."

Here, Norris said, was the "coldblooded proposition that war brings prosperity." The senator denounced this "comfortable opinion," which was supported by "a servile press" in league with the pro-war bankers and corporate executives. These profit-hungry Americans, he shouted, had created a war madness that was sweeping the country and Congress into a ruinous conflict: "I would like to say to this war god, You shall not coin into gold the lifeblood of my brethren. We are going into this war on the command of gold. I feel we are putting the dollar sign on the American flag."[68]

Senator Jim Reed of Missouri leaped up to roar, "If that be not giving aid and comfort to the enemy . . . then I do not know what would bring comfort to the heart of a Hapsburg or a Hohenzollern [the ruling families of Austria-Hungary and Germany]!" John Sharp Williams of Mississippi, among the most vociferous of the pro-war majority, shrilled, "If it be not treason, it grazes the edge of treason!" Senator William Squire Kenyon of Iowa rose to issue a cry that would soon become widespread: "It is no time for criticism of the president, of the cabinet, of Congress. . . . It is time for one hundred percent Americanism!"[69]

More pro-war speeches followed. They were challenged by Asle Jorgenson Gronna, a Republican from North Dakota, who said that he had received thousands of letters from his constituents begging him to avoid war. He was going to vote against the resolution. Reminding his fellow senators that they were not the government, he was convinced that if the United States truly wanted to do so, the country could maintain an "honorable peace" with every nation on earth.[70]

XVIII

Shortly before four o'clock came the moment that the other senators and the packed galleries had been awaiting. Robert La Follette took the floor. He opened with a brief, almost curt attack on the idea that every senator should "stand behind the president." What kind of doctrine was that? he asked. What if the president were wrong? That was the crucial question every legislator had to ask. In this case, he knew of no course but "to oppose the demands of the chief executive."

La Follette recalled the filibuster over the armed-ship bill, which had prompted Wilson to call him and his supporters willful men. Yet in his speech on April 2, the president had admitted that the senator and his eleven supporters had been right. Not only was arming merchantmen impractical, it gave the United States none of the rights or the effectiveness of a belligerent. If Wilson was wrong on this issue, might he not also be wrong on this "hotly pressed" decision for war?

The senator said he had received more than 15,000 telegrams and letters, nine out of ten opposing the war. He cited a straw vote in the town of Monroe, Wisconsin, which reported 954 against war, and 95 in favor of it. Introducing a poll conducted by the Emergency Peace Committee in Massachusetts based on 20,000 postal cards, he reported that 66 percent opposed the war and 63 percent opposed conscription. In Minneapolis, a congressman had polled his district and found 8,000 against the war, 800 favoring it. For a half-hour, La Follette put in the record similar communications and asked if these messages did not indicate the American people's deep-seated conviction against entering the war.[71]

Had Germany violated a promise not to resume unrestricted submarine warfare, as Woodrow Wilson had claimed? The answer was no. Germany had agreed to suspend the policy on the assumption that the United States would persuade or force England to modify its illegal blockade, which was threatening the German people with starvation. America's "poor protests" to England had utterly failed to do this. Was it fair to accuse Germany of dishonorable conduct?

Wilson said that Germany's submarine warfare against commerce was "a warfare against mankind . . . a war against all nations." If this were the case, La Follette asked, why was the United States the only nation in the world that objected to it? Norway, Sweden, Spain, the nations of South America—not one had protested Germany's position or felt any compunction to go to war over it. La Follette cited a report in the previous day's newspapers that the Brazilian government was adopting a cold shoulder to Wilson's decision for war.

The senator carried his argument further. Wilson's claim that the U.S. quarrel was with Germany's government, not its people, was absurd. In his next breath, Wilson talked of "practicable cooperation" with England and its allies to prosecute the war. Such cooperation meant joining the British blockade, which was "starving to death the old men, the women and the children, the sick and the maimed of Germany." If the United States cooperated with Great Britain, America would be endorsing London's "shameful methods of warfare," against which it had feebly protested—and been ignored.

The idea of a war to make the world safe for democracy was equally absurd, with England as a U.S. ally. Had the British shown the slightest interest in extending democracy to Ireland, to Egypt's millions, to India's hundreds of millions? Tens of millions of Great Britain's own citizens were denied the right to vote by the oligarchy that ran the country. The other countries in the war, Italy and Japan, were monarchies. Only France and newly baptized Russia were democracies—and La Follette challenged anyone to deny that Wilson would have called for war, whether or not the Russians had tossed out the czar.

The president's denunciations of "Prussian autocracy" made as little sense as the claim that the German people did not support the war. After almost three years of observing Germany's performance as a belligerent, La Follette opined that far more of the German people backed their government than did Americans who supported Wilson's decision for war. Moreover, it ill became crusaders for democracy to tell the German people they could only have peace by giving up their government.

As for Wilson's claim that the war was begun without the consent of the German people—was the U.S. decision for war any different? Could the members of the Senate claim with any certainty that most Americans supported the war? Why didn't the government put things to the ultimate test, and have a referendum? Let the American people vote on it. Instead, the government was already talking about espionage and censorship bills to suppress popular opinion and a draft to force every man to fight, no matter what he thought.

Point by point, La Follette presented a legal brief against Wilson's arguments for war. Often it was a dogged, unemotional argument. He emphasized facts, logic, the principles of international law, as enunciated in the Treaty of London in 1909. This international conclave had codified neutral rights in case of war, specifying which goods were contraband and thus liable to seizure and which were entitled to free passage on the high seas. La Follette cited an admission by Lord Salisbury, one of England's most prominent statesmen, that food for the civilian population was never contraband—a principle that the English were callously ignoring in their blockade of Germany.

As the second hour of La Follette's speech passed, lights were turned on. Many people in the gallery departed, and others took their places. Among the new arrivals were the capital's elite: Wilson's son-in-law, Secretary of the Treasury William Gibbs McAdoo; Secretary of State Robert Lansing; and British ambassador Cecil Spring Rice, whose dislike of Wilson frequently surfaced in his dispatches. In the front row, two of La Follette's oldest friends—journalist Gilson Gardner and reformer Amos Pinchot, pioneer members of the progressive movement—remained for the entire speech. They had not spoken to the senator in five years, because they had backed Theodore Roosevelt for the Progressive Party's nomination in 1912. La Follette had regarded that decision as a betrayal. But they had come to hear him, because they too opposed the war.

La Follette launched a searching appraisal of the origins of the war. Germany was only partly responsible. All the belligerent powers bore some blame. But the overarching cause was England's determination to destroy Germany as a commercial rival. He devoted several minutes to England's unsavory conduct in the 1911 crisis over Morocco. Here, Germany, England and France had signed a treaty permitting individual Germans to do business in the country. But England and France executed a secret treaty, agreeing to drive the Germans out. In return, France abandoned its claims to commercial rights in Egypt. When England backed the expulsion of the Germans, Europe almost went to war. La Follette quoted the English journalist William T. Stead, who called this underhanded diplomacy "an almost incredible crime against treaty faith."[72]

Grimly La Follette reiterated: "It was our absolute right as a neutral to ship food to the people of Germany." It was a right the United States had asserted since its foundation as a nation. "The failure to treat the belligerent nations alike, to reject the illegal war zones of both Germany and Great Britain, is wholly accountable for our present dilemma." Instead of admitting this failure, the country was trying to "inflame the mind of our people into the frenzy of war."[73]

There were only two ways out of this quandary. The first would be for the United States to admit its mistake and enforce its rights against Great Britain as strenuously as it had insisted on its rights against Germany. The other alternative would be to withhold food from both sides.

Without attempting a peroration beyond this stark choice, La Follette stopped speaking at 6:45 P.M. Tears streamed down his cheeks. To Amos Pinchot, he looked like a despairing man who had "failed to keep his child from doing itself irreparable harm." Gilson Gardner turned to Pinchot and said, "That is the greatest speech we will either of us ever hear."[74]

XIX

Senator John Sharp Williams of Mississippi leaped to his feet and began living up to his middle name. Williams had his own agenda. He saw the war as a chance to redeem the secessionist South in the eyes of the ruling North. In his speeches, he often dilated on how Southerners would volunteer en masse and go to war to the strains of "Dixie." This vision added fuel to his ire. La Follette, he sneered, had given a speech "that would have better become Herr Bethmann-Hollweg," a reference to Theobald von Bethmann-Hollweg, the chancellor of Germany. Williams called the speech "pro-German, pretty nearly pro-Goth and pro-Vandal." It was also "anti-American president, anti-American Congress and anti-American people." The Mississippian continued insulting La Follette, violating all the rules of Senate courtesy, for another seven pages of the *Congressional Record*. No senator tried to stop him. Several times, he drew guffaws from the galleries.[75]

Williams's harangue was followed by more oratory, all of it pro-war. Finally, at eleven minutes after eleven, the Senate voted. The crowded gallery listened in absolute silence. Many of the lawmakers' voices quivered with emotion. La Follette's "No" rang out with characteristic firmness. When the clerk announced the final tally, 82 to 6, not a hand clapped, not a voice cheered in the galleries. Somehow, declaring war no longer seemed a cause for celebration. In the corridor, as Senator La Follette walked to his office, a man handed him a rope.[76]

XX

The following day, April 5, was the House of Representatives' turn. The congressmen slogged to their task through a city whipped by a mounting northeast storm. Some of them may have noticed a lamppost on Fourteenth and H Streets decorated with a yellow-striped scarecrow. The thing had two recognizable faces: One was Senator Stone of Missouri; the other, Senator Vardaman of Mississippi.[77]

The *New York Tribune* crowed over the Senate vote and praised John Sharp Williams for his scurrilous denunciation of Senator La Follette. It also warned of a national conspiracy of "pacifists" plotting to disrupt the war effort. The *Los Angeles Times* assured its readers there were no plans to send an American army overseas. All that the Allies needed to win the war was munitions. In New York, a young man who called Americans "a lot of skunks" at an antiwar rally got six months in jail.[78]

The House galleries were only half full when debate began. With the Senate vote, the conclusion probably seemed foregone. But the onlookers saw some fireworks early in the session. Congressman Fred A. Britten, a Republican from Illinois, stirred a furor when he estimated that 75 percent of the representatives secretly opposed the war but were afraid to say so. Dozens of friends had told him they "hate[d] like the devil" to vote for the war resolution, but were going to do it anyway. A startling wave of applause swept the House and the galleries. An emboldened Britten concluded that "something in the air," perhaps the "hand of destiny" or "some superhuman movement," seemed to be forcing them to vote for war when, "deep in our hearts," they were just as opposed to it as their people back home.[79]

Numerous congressmen leaped up to rebut Britten. Some drew applause for flights of patriotic oratory. Others rose to defend him. Chicago Republican William Ernest Mason, who had been a strong proponent of the Spanish-American War, said flatly, "I am against this war because I know the people in my state are not for it." The debate went back and forth while the northeast wind drove sheets of rain against the huge skylight above the speakers' heads.[80]

A pro-war Republican, Clarence B. Miller of Minnesota, enlivened things by reading a supposedly suppressed paragraph in Herr Zimmermann's telegram to Mexico: "Agreeably to the Mexican government, submarine bases will be established in Mexican ports, from which will be supplied arms, ammunition and supplies. All [German] reservists in the United States are ordered into Mexico. Arrange to attack all along the border."

Antiwar congressmen rushed a messenger to the State Department, which denied the existence of any such paragraph. But Miller kept insisting on its authenticity and waved the paper at them to the end of the session.[81]

The next surprise came when Claude Kitchin of North Carolina, the Democratic majority leader, announced that he was voting nay: "After mature thought and fervent prayer for rightful guidance, [I] have marked out clearly the path of my duty, and I have made up my mind to walk it, if I go barefooted or alone." Robert La Follette, who was among the spectators, led a burst of applause.[82]

Implicitly agreeing with La Follette, Kitchin denounced the failure of the United States to protest England's violation of the right to trade with Germany. He described the North Sea as "strewed with hidden mines." Kitchin maintained that this failure to treat the two belligerents alike was a fatal flaw in Wilson's declaration of war.[83]

James Heflin of Alabama told Kitchin that he should have resigned as majority leader before he made such a statement—and then resigned his seat. John Lawson Burnett of Alabama said that Heflin ought to prove his patriotism first by enlisting in the army as a private. A shouting match erupted, adding a touch of low comedy to the scene.[84]

Hour after hour, the speeches, limited to ten minutes by Speaker Clark, marched on, many making the same or similar points. Like La Follette and Norris, the antiwar minority argued that sinking a handful of ships and killing some American sailors did not constitute a cause for war. They pointed out that the Mexicans had killed far more Americans in Villa's raids and skirmishes with the Punitive Expedition. Like Kitchin, they blamed the government and U.S. corporations for sending ships into the war zone declared by Berlin—while tamely submitting to the war zone declared by the English blockade of Germany.

The pro-war speakers answered with outrage over Germany's "barbaric tactics." They descanted on how the British only violated property rights in their blockade, whereas the Germans were committing murder. They extended their oratory to a general denunciation of the way Germany was fighting the war in Europe, "raping" neutral Belgium and despoiling the large chunk of France it occupied. They exalted the purpose of the war, as defined by President Wilson. A war for democracy, for the rights of mankind.

Among the orators who enjoyed the loudest applause was bearded eighty-one-year-old Joseph "Uncle Joe" Cannon of Illinois, for many years the Speaker of the House in its days of Republican majorities. He rose to dilate on the power and resources of the United States, "greater than any other nation on earth." It was time to commit them to the cause of peace. Pounding on his desk, he roared, "I—shall—vote—for—this—resolution."[85]

The antiwar representatives achieved some poignant (and totally forgotten) moments. Most notable was Edward J. King of Illinois. The lawmaker said that a vote for war on the president's arguments, with conscription thrown in, would qualify an American soldier to join the men of other nations in W. K. Enwer's heartbreaking poem "Five Souls":

> *First Soul.*
> *I was a peasant of the Polish plain;*
> *I left my plow because the message ran—*

Russia in danger needed every man
To save her from the Teuton; and was slain
I gave my life for freedom—this I know
For those who bade me fight had told me so.

Second Soul.
I was a Tyrolese, a mountaineer;
I gladly left my mountain home to fight
Against the brutal, treacherous Muscovite;
And died in Poland on a Cossack spear.
I gave my life for freedom—this I know,
For those who bade me fight had told me so.

Third Soul.
I worked in Lyons at my weaver's loom,
When suddenly the Prussian despot hurled
His felon blow at France and at the world;
Then I went forth to Belgium and my doom.
I gave my life for freedom—this I know
For those who bade me fight had told me so.

Fourth Soul.
I owned a vineyard by the wooded Main
Until the fatherland begirt by foes
Lusting her downfall called me and I rose
Swift to the call, and died in fair Lorraine.
I gave my life for freedom, this I know
For those who bade me fight had told me so.

Fifth Soul.
I worked in a great shipyard on the Clyde;
There came a sudden word of wars declared,
Of Belgium peaceful, helpless, unprepared
Asking our aid. I joined the ranks and died.
I gave my life for freedom—this I know
For those who bade me fight had told me so.

King added to this tragic parade a sixth soul from America.

> *Sixth Soul.*
> *I worked upon a farm in Illinois.*
> *The squad appeared; I marched away.*
> *Somewhere in France, amid the trenches gray*
> *I met grim death with many other boys.*
> *I gave my life for freedom—this I know.*
> *For he who bade me fight had told me so.*

America was going to war, King said, driven by "armed plutocracy crying 'Onward Christian Soldiers.'"[86]

At 7 P.M., with no end of speakers in sight, Champ Clark said they would stay in session all night if necessary. At 9 P.M., Clark began to limit the speeches to five minutes. On went the oratory, until at 2:30 A.M. on April 6, the number of speeches had passed one hundred. At 2:45, the legislators at last fell silent and the weary Clark called for a vote.

The voices reciting yes and no echoed dully in the empty galleries and drifted eerily into the darkness around the skylight. The count went swiftly until the clerk of the house reached the name Rankin. There was a strained silence—and the clerk went on to other names. Uncle Joe Cannon hobbled from his seat to where Representative Jeannette Rankin of Montana sat virtually paralyzed. As the first woman elected to Congress, she had received a bouquet of flowers and an ovation when the House convened on April 2. Now, confronting her first vote, she was in torment.

Cannon leaned over her and said, "Little woman, you cannot afford not to vote. You represent the womanhood of the country. I shall not advise you how to vote but you should vote, one way or another, as your conscience dictates."

On the second call, when the clerk reached her name, Rankin was again speechless. Finally, she struggled to her feet and said, "I want to stand by my country, but I cannot vote for war. I vote no."

She sank into her seat and began to sob. The roll call continued until the clerk reached the last name and reported the tally to the speaker. The House of Representatives had voted for war, 373 to 50. Over half the nays were from progressive Republicans in the West, political blood brothers of

Robert La Follette and George Norris. The Northeast produced only one negative vote—Meyer London, the socialist member from New York City. Four of the Democratic no votes came from Mississippi, somewhat dulling the edge of John Sharp Williams's rhetoric. Nine of Wisconsin's eleven representatives supported La Follette.[87]

Speaker Clark signed the war resolution on the spot, but Vice President Marshall, whose signature was also needed as president of the Senate, had long since gone to bed. He signed it the next day, a little after 12 noon. The resolution was immediately rushed to the White House, where the president was having lunch with his wife and his cousin Helen Woodrow Bones. They put down their knives and forks and hurried to the chief usher's desk in the lobby. There, Rudolph Forster, the White House's executive clerk, was waiting for them with the document. Edith Galt Wilson handed the president a gold pen he had given her as a gift, and he signed the document without the slightest fanfare or ceremony.

Forster dashed off to notify reporters. They raced to their telephones. A young naval officer ran out on the sidewalk in front of the White House. Looking like someone fighting off a swarm of insects, he waved his arms to send a semaphore message to an officer in the State, War and Navy Building. Within minutes, wireless operators were flashing the news to navy ships and shore stations around the world. It was 1:18 P.M. on April 6, 1917—which happened to be Good Friday. The United States of America was at war with Germany.[88]

Chapter 2

BIG LIES, GREED, AND OTHER HOARY ANIMALS

Almost a century after that dramatic week in April 1917, can we make sense out of its tangle of pro- and antiwar passion, the rhetoric of violated rights and democratic visions, the opposing denunciations of the war's chief antagonists, Germany and Great Britain? The conduct of other wars and the research of numerous historians have shed some light, particularly on the reason why so many Americans—a majority, if the votes of Congress accurately reflected national sentiment (a still debated question)—favored Great Britain, and its allies, France and Russia.[1]

To understand the aggressive, often angry pro-war sentiment of the apparent American majority, we must go back thirty-two months, almost three years before April 6, 1917, to one of the most important but largely forgotten episodes of World War I. In the misty dawn of August 5, 1914, the 1,013-ton British ship *Telconia*, an aptly named layer of undersea cables, hove to in the North Sea off the German port of Emden. On August 4, after a month of halfhearted attempts to defuse the crisis created by the brutal assassination of Archduke Franz Ferdinand and his wife, Sophie, heirs to the Austro-Hungarian empire's throne, by a Serbian terrorist, the war had begun. An Austrian army assaulted Serbia. Russia, determined to defend its Slav cousins, attacked Germany and Austria from the east. The French, allied with Russia, attacked from the west. The German army marched into Belgium and Luxembourg as part of its plan to outflank French forts and armies along the Franco-German border, capture Paris, and end the war on the Western Front in a month.

That same day, Great Britain had demanded Germany's immediate withdrawal from Belgium, citing a decades-old treaty Europe's major powers had signed guaranteeing that country's neutrality. Only a handful of people knew the real reason for England's intervention. Years earlier, Foreign Secretary Sir Edward Grey had negotiated a secret understanding with the French to join them in resisting a German attack. He had negotiated an equally secret alliance with the Russians. Most of the British cabinet did not know about these agreements, which included extensive consultations between the French and British military staffs. They were also concealed from the British Parliament. While his fellow liberals talked peace and forbearance with Germany, Grey had become a confirmed German hater, who saw Berlin's rising power as a mortal threat to the British empire.

London's ultimatum had expired at midnight on August 4, while the *Telconia* was en route to its rendezvous point off Emden. Fathoms beneath the ship's keel lay a network of five cables that wended south from Germany through the English Channel, one to France, one to Spain, one to North Africa and two to New York City. On board the *Telconia* were huge grappling hooks that enabled the ship to retrieve malfunctioning cables from the sea bottom for repairs. Down slid the grapples into the cold, gray depths, and soon, one by one, the five mud-covered sheaths of copper-covered wires were hauled aboard. Each was hacked apart and dropped back into the sea. Henceforth, Germany could communicate securely with the Western Hemisphere only through a subsidiary cable that ran from Liberia to Brazil, a line that was largely U.S. owned.

Six months later, after some friendly persuasion from London, which undoubtedly included plenty of pounds sterling, this link too was eliminated by one of *Telconia*'s sister ships. That meant Berlin had to depend on Guglielmo Marconi's newly invented and somewhat undependable wireless—and all these messages could be intercepted and deciphered by British cryptanalysts.[2]

The *New York Times* reported the cutting of the main cables on August 6, 1914. The reporter dutifully noted that from now on, "all word of happenings in Germany must pass through hostile countries—Russia on the east, France on the west, and England on the north." (These three allies would soon be known to newspaper readers as the Triple Entente.) The consul general of Germany's chief ally, Austria-Hungary, in one of the greatest understatements of the twentieth century, told the *Times:* "The cutting of that cable may do us great injury. If only one side of the case is given . . . prejudice will be created against us here."[3]

A week after Great Britain entered the war and began frantic efforts to ship an expeditionary force to Belgium, Parliament passed a Defence of the Realm Act, soon to be known as DORA, which gave British censors the power to scrutinize every word that went from England to the United States and elsewhere in the world. American reporters in England and at the battlefronts in France soon learned this meant only stories that favored the Triple Entente would leave the British Isles. Some reporters tried to cover the war from Berlin, but they had to send their stories through the neutral Netherlands to London for cabling to the United States. The British censors also read their copy. On August 2, 1916, a group of American correspondents in Berlin signed a protest complaining that their dispatches were constantly "suppressed, mutilated or delayed" by the London censor. Americans were not getting the "vital half" of the most important events of the war.[4]

II

Within a month of declaring war, the British prime minister, Herbert Asquith, put his friend and member of Parliament, Charles F. G. Masterman, in charge of propaganda. A journalist and author of some note before he turned to politics, Masterman took over several floors in Wellington House, a London office building not far from Buckingham Palace. Masterman warned his staff that they would toil in secret and be thanked or honored by no one for their efforts. He swiftly convened meetings with top British authors, such as H. G. Wells, Rudyard Kipling, Arthur Conan Doyle and John Galsworthy, to enlist them in the large effort he contemplated. They consented without a demur. On September 19, 1914, fifty-three writers subscribed to a statement in the *Times* of London, calling on Englishmen to "defend the rights of small nations" against "the rule of Blood and Iron." Wells, who liked to describe himself as an extreme pacifist, was soon to declare: "I hate Germany, which has thrust this experience upon mankind, as I hate some horrible infectious disease."[5]

Masterman early saw the importance of a separate propaganda department for the United States. Its immense wealth and resources were essential for the survival of His Majesty's empire. For this task, Masterman chose a fellow member of Parliament, Sir Gilbert Parker, a Canadian-born bestselling author of novels about the Canadian Northwest (a region he had never visited). The books featured absurdly unrealistic characters and numerous scenes of blood and gore.

Although Parker's novels were trash and a British newsman described him as "an ass and self-promoter," he was a clever, enormously energetic man. Thanks to his books and frequent visits, he had many friends in the United States. He assembled an excellent staff of assistants, which included historian A. J. Toynbee of Oxford. They combed *Who's Who in America* and other sources to assemble a mailing list of 260,000 influential men and women. Sir Gilbert also arranged for a weekly report from the British embassy in Washington, the *American Press Résumé*, to keep him in close touch with the public mood as it manifested itself in America's 20,000 newspapers. He supplied 360 papers in less populated states with a weekly "newspaper" that purveyed London's line on the war. He arranged for American reporters to interview more than one hundred prominent Englishmen, from the prime minister to the Archbishop of Canterbury. The numerous VIP speakers Parker dispatched to the United States to win hearts and minds also provided him with voluminous reports on what stories and themes worked best. By 1917, Parker had 54 people working for him.

In March 1918, when the Americans were safely in the war, Parker published an article in *Harper's Monthly* in which he bragged about his role in persuading the United States to intervene. He claimed that he always cautioned British speakers to avoid exhorting Americans to join the hostilities. These missionaries had embarked on a task of "extreme difficulty and delicacy," and the results could only be obtained by letting the Americans make up their own minds that "German policy is a betrayal of civilization." The latter remark is a graphic glimpse of Parker's objectivity.[6]

Also very much in the propaganda field were voluntary British organizations, such as the Union of Democratic Control (a revealing juxtaposition of terms) and the Central Committee for National Patriotic Organizations (CNPO). The Central Committee was almost as formidable as Wellington House. Created on November 21, 1914, soon after the British Expeditionary Force had been bloodied in its first encounter with the German army in Belgium, the CNPO had affiliates in all the neutral countries and a separate committee that concentrated on the United States. This group too sent pamphlets, books and speakers to America.[7]

In the former colonies (aka, the United States) voluntary organizations sprang up that also became valuable channels for British propaganda. One of the most important was the Navy League. Its members included dozens of major bankers and corporate executives, from J. P. Morgan, Jr., to Cornelius Vanderbilt. "What a band of patriots," Senator Robert La Follette exclaimed when he saw their membership list. "Owning newspapers, periodicals and magazines and controlling through business relations the editorial good will of many others."

Virtually confirming the senator's comment, in the fall of 1914 one of Morgan's partners remarked: "In America [at present] there are 50,000 people who understand the necessity of the United States entering the war on [England's] side. But there are 100,000,000 Americans who have not even thought of it. Our task is to see that those figures are reversed."[8]

Equally potent was the National Security League, which was created to preach preparedness but soon spent much of its time and energy echoing British propaganda handouts and warning of the danger of German "reservists" operating under cover in the United States. These homegrown Anglophiles were almost all situated in the Northeast, with the heaviest concentration in New York City, whose newspapers dominated editorial opinion in the rest of the country.[9]

Also not to be discounted were the numerous immigrants from the British Isles and Canada, many of them fairly well-to-do, who eagerly volunteered to help the mother country in its hour of peril. Woodrow Wilson's four grandparents and his mother were among these nineteenth-century arrivals. Unlike American immigrants with foreign-sounding names and scant knowledge of English, these British (in Wilson's case, Scottish and Scotch-Irish) newcomers had won ready acceptance in American middle- and upper-class society. They had access to men and women of power and influence.[10]

III

The Wellington House propaganda machine had a ready-made supply of themes on which to elaborate. Since 1896, the Conservative Party, with the avid cooperation of press tycoon Alfred Harmsworth, a low-rent version of Joseph Pulitzer and William Randolph Hearst, had been ranting about Germany's "militarism" and its intention to attack England. The Tories sneered at Germany's boasts about its *Kultur* and the prosperity of its working class, who enjoyed pensions and health care while most of England's workers had neither and lived in some of the worst slums in Europe. The Germans, according to Harmsworth, were thick-necked helots who obeyed the orders of the generals and Prussian aristocrats who ran the country. Harmsworth also portrayed Wilhelm II, Germany's kaiser, as a bully and a menace.

Elevated to the peerage as Lord Northcliffe, Harmsworth owned a megachain of newspapers and magazines, including the venerable *Times* of London, which struggled to retain some vestiges of respectability in his sordid grip. The seat of Northcliffe's power was his flagship, the *Daily Mail*. With a circulation of more than a million, it was a veritable epitome of yellow journalism.[11]

In 1906, Northcliffe sponsored and serialized a novel by William Le Queux, dramatizing a brutal German conquest of Britain with the help of a secret civilian army of reservists disguised as waiters, clerks, hairdressers and bakers. The book, unimaginatively titled *The Invasion of 1910,* sold over a million copies worldwide and was popular in the United States. To advertise the serial, Northcliffe had sandwich men dressed as German soldiers, complete with spiked helmets, parading London's streets.[12]

Wrapping this hate propaganda around the cry of preparedness, Northcliffe almost single-handedly revived the British Conservative Party in the elections of 1912. He was backed by the National Service League, which called for a conscription law, and Britain's Navy League, which constantly warned that Germany's decision to build a big navy meant that it was out to dominate the world. Anglophiles in the United States soon transferred this paranoia to the Western Hemisphere, finding evidence of pan-Germanism in German immigrants to Brazil and other South American countries. In fact, Germany's imperialism was timid and indecisive most of the time. German immigrants in southern Brazil, for instance, pleaded in vain for money from Berlin to build a railroad to connect them to the sea. When Germany sent warships to demand payment from Venezuela for long-overdue debts, it scrupulously asked American permission, lest it violate the Monroe Doctrine. The Germans were fearful of offending major powers, especially England and the United States, and worsening their sense of isolation.[13]

The real reason for Northcliffe's hate campaign was economic, not military. For more than a decade, Germany had been challenging England as a competitor in the world marketplace. British economic power was in decline everywhere. Between January and June 1914, Germany's exports and gross national product had exceeded England's for the first time. Senator La Follette cited this competition as the real reason for the slaughter in Europe. George Bernard Shaw said the same thing in an obstreperous pamphlet that outraged the writers who had obediently parroted Wellington House's line. Ultimately, Woodrow Wilson himself would admit this dolorous truth.[14]

Such realistic details never got into Lord Northcliffe's newspapers, of course. When the war erupted in 1914, the press baron and the conservatives were primed to respond with I-told-you-so vituperation that wilted the liberal politicians in the Asquith government who had repeatedly declared their opposition to a war on the European continent. Even more flummoxed by Foreign Secretary Grey's revelation of his secret "understandings" with France and Russia, they soon joined the cry to defend "poor little Belgium."[15]

IV

To an objective observer, Northcliffe and his allies in Wellington House would seem to have had a problem arousing pity for Belgium. In 1904, Sir Roger Casement, a tall, black-bearded Irishman in the British diplomatic service in the Belgian Congo, and Edmund Morel, a young British shipping agent, had revealed to an appalled world a tale of brutality and rapine unmatched in the annals of imperialism. The Congo's blacks had been routinely starved, beaten and shot for trivial offenses while being forced to labor endless hours as slaves to extract millions of dollars in rubber and ivory for their Belgian masters, chief of whom was King Leopold II. For many years, the royal family literally owned the Congo, making an estimated billion dollars out of its exploitation. Behind a screen of unctuous lies about bringing Christianity to the dark continent, an estimated 10 million natives had died—a holocaust that exceeds anything in previous, or subsequent, recorded history. Whole districts were depopulated. Chopping off a man's or woman's hands was a routine punishment for disobedience. At the time, one British writer said Belgium had become "a stench in the nostrils of the world." But in 1914, Lord Northcliffe's newspapers and Wellington House's propaganda machine raised a howl against the violation of "poor little Belgium's" neutrality that obliterated the crimes of the Congo.[16]

In fact, Belgium was about as neutral as Scotland. The Belgian government had secret understandings with France and England. The Belgian border with Germany bristled with forts. On the French border, there were none. The country's official language was French, although half the population, the Flemings, spoke Walloon and had no great enthusiasm for France or French people. When hostilities began, the Germans had asked Brussels for safe passage for their army and had guaranteed to pay for any damage to property as well as for food or drink obtained en route. Neighboring Luxembourg had accepted these terms without a word of reproach.

Belgium was about as democratic as Germany—it had a parliament elected in a system that gave the wealthy as many as three votes. A similar system prevailed in Prussia, Germany's most powerful province. Like Kaiser Wilhelm, Belgium's king, Albert I, son of the monstrous Leopold II of the Congo barbarism, had not a little legislative power. Nonetheless, by sheer reiteration, Belgium became a keystone of the basic British propaganda line: It was a war to defend small, democratic, neutral countries against autocracy and its supposed by-product, militarism.

These claims were supplemented with quotations from the writings of extremists in Germany, such as the members of the Pan-German League, who talked wildly of world power. Another favorite source of hate quotes was retired General Friedrich von Bernhardi, whose 1911 book, *Germany and the Next War,* had chapter headings such as "The Duty to Make War" and "World Power or Downfall." Many more quotations were obtained from books by German socialists and liberals, attacking "German militarism"—a term these critics of the establishment all but coined. Ignored was France's love of military glory and lust for conquest. In the era of Napoleon, the rest of Europe had labeled militarism the French disease. On the eve of the Great War, with a population far smaller than Germany, France had a bigger army, and most of its politicians were obsessed with erasing the stain of their crushing 1870–1871 defeat by Germany in a war that another French militarist, Napoleon III, had started. To satisfy the national appetite for *la gloire,* Paris had established a colonial empire in Africa and Indochina. The British, possessors of the world's biggest fleet and an immense empire ruled by force, were hardly entitled to prate about militarism. But facts seldom if ever deterred the determined men in Wellington House.[17]

Germany's parliament, the Reichstag, with its turbulent mix of political parties, was denounced as a fake, with no real power to rein in the kaiser. There was some truth to this latter claim, but the kaiser also lacked the power to silence his critics in the Reichstag, to his often vocal distress, because they could refuse to fund the annual budgets he submitted to them. When President Wilson called for peace without victory on January 25, 1917, the Socialist newspaper *Vorwärts* and the liberal *Berliner Tageblatt* effusively praised his speech. Nevertheless, Germany was convicted of the crime of "autocracy." Lost in the blasts of war and bleats about poor little democratic Belgium was the secret diplomacy of Foreign Minister Grey and the fact (pointed out by La Follette) that a hefty proportion of the British lower class did not have a vote when the war began.[18]

In 1912, at King Albert's behest, the Belgian parliament increased the army to 340,000 men, a large force for a country of 7 million. Many of these soldiers were untrained "civic guards," who did not wear uniforms, beyond shoulder ribbons or an insignia pinned to their shirts. When these units joined the uniformed regulars in resisting Germany's invasion with gunfire, they ignited an old grievance in the minds of the advancing Germans. In the Franco-Prussian War of 1870–1871, after the Germans smashed the French army and the government surrendered, there was an attempt to arouse a *levée en masse.* This idea of citizen resistance originated in the wars of the French Revolution, in which the entire population was summoned to resist invaders. Thousands of civilian *franc-tireurs* (French sharpshooters) took up the fight, inflicting many casualties on the Germans.

In Belgium, the Germans decided the civic guards were *franc-tireurs,* symptoms of a *levée en masse.* Compounding the Germans' rage was the threat from the east, where only a few divisions were on the defensive against the oncoming Russian hordes. Time was of the essence, and Belgian resistance was fatally delaying the German goal of a quick victory against the French. Also in this explosive mix was the inexperience of the German army's rank and file. The nation had not fought a war since 1870. Spooked by rumors of *franc-tireurs* everywhere, the Germans frequently opened fire on each other in the darkness, inflicting numerous casualties and deepening their rage against the recalcitrant Belgians and their obviously spurious neutrality. Retaliation was virtually inevitable—and bloody. Civilians were seized and many were executed. Towns and villages, including Louvain's world-famous medieval library, went up in flames. Wellington House soon had a new propaganda theme: atrocities.[19]

A flood of stories portrayed the Germans as monsters capable of appalling sadism. Eyewitnesses described infantrymen spearing Belgian babies on their bayonets as they marched along, singing war songs. Accounts of boys with amputated hands (supposedly to prevent them from using guns) abounded, without even a hint of a blush for the way the Belgians had done the real thing in the Congo. Tales of women with amputated breasts multiplied even faster. At the top of the atrocity hit parade were rape stories. One eyewitness claimed that the Germans dragged twenty young women out of their houses in a captured Belgian town and stretched them on tables in the village square, where each was violated by at least twelve "Huns" while the rest of the division watched and cheered. At British expense, a group of Belgians toured the United States telling these stories. Woodrow Wilson solemnly received them in the White House.[20]

The Germans countered these tales with equally extreme stories of wounded soldiers found with their eyes gouged out and German officers shot dead at the dinner tables of their treacherous Belgian hosts. Berlin permitted eight American news reporters to follow the German army through Belgium. On September 3, 1914, they sent a telegram to the Associated Press: "IN SPIRIT FAIRNESS WE UNITE IN DECLARING GERMAN ATROCITIES GROUNDLESS AS FAR AS WE ARE ABLE TO OBSERVE. AFTER SPENDING TWO WEEKS WITH GERMAN ARMY ACCOMPANYING TROOPS UPWARD HUNDRED MILES WE UNABLE REPORT SINGLE INCIDENT UNPROVOKED REPRISAL. ALSO UNABLE CONFIRM RUMORS MISTREATMENT PRISONERS OR NON-COMBATANTS . . . NUMEROUS INVESTIGATED RUMORS PROVED GROUNDLESS . . . DISCIPLINE GERMAN SOLDIERS EXCELLENT AS OBSERVED. NO DRUNKENNESS. TO TRUTH THESE STATEMENTS WE PLEDGE PROFESSIONAL WORD."[21]

Early in 1915, the British government asked Viscount James Bryce to head a royal commission to investigate the atrocity reports. Bryce was one of the best-known historians of the era; he had written widely praised books on the

U.S. government and on Irish history, sympathetically portraying the Gaels' hard lot under British rule. In 1907, he had collaborated with Roger Casement to expose the horrendous exploitation of indigenous people on the Amazon by a British rubber company. From 1907 to 1913, he had served as British ambassador in Washington, where he became a popular, even beloved, figure. It would have been hard to find a more admired scholar.

Bryce and his six fellow commissioners, an amalgam of distinguished lawyers, historians and jurists, "analyzed" 1,200 depositions of eyewitnesses who claimed to have seen atrocious German behavior. Almost all the testimony came from Belgians who had fled to England as refugees; some were statements from Belgian and British soldiers, collected in France. The commissioners never interrogated any of these eyewitnesses; that task was left to "gentlemen of legal knowledge and experience," namely, lawyers. Since the asserted crimes took place in what continued to be a war zone, there was no on-site investigation of any report. Not a single witness was identified by name; the commissioners said this was justified in the case of Belgians by the fear that there might be German reprisals against family members. British soldier witnesses remained equally anonymous, for no apparent reason. Yet Bryce stated in his introduction: "In dealing with the evidence we have recognized the importance of testing it severely."[22]

The Bryce Report was released on May 13, 1915. Wellington House made sure that it went to virtually every newspaper in the United States. The impact was stupendous, as the headline and subheads in the *New York Times* make clear:

GERMAN ATROCITIES ARE
PROVED, FINDS BRYCE
COMMITTEE
Not Only Individual Crimes, but
Premeditated Slaughter in
Belgium

YOUNG AND OLD MUTILATED
Women Attacked, Children
Brutally Slain, Arson and
Pillage Systematic

COUNTENANCED BY OFFICERS
Wanton Firing on Red Cross and
White Flag: Prisoners and
Wounded Shot

CIVILIANS USED AS SHIELDS[23]

On May 27, 1915, the *American Press Résumé*'s editors gleefully reported to Wellington House: "Even in papers hostile to the Allies, there is not the slightest attempt to impugn the correctness of the facts alleged. Lord Bryce's prestige in America put skepticism out of the question." Charles Masterman told Bryce: "Your report has *swept* America."[24]

Among the few critics of the Bryce Report was Sir Roger Casement. "It is only necessary to turn to James Bryce, the historian, to convict Lord Bryce, the partisan," Casement wrote in a furious essay, "The Far Extended Baleful Power of the Lie." By this time Casement had become an advocate of Irish independence and did not hesitate to compare British crimes in Ireland to Belgium's in the Congo. Few people paid any attention to his dissent, which was dismissed as biased.[25]

Clarence Darrow, the famously iconoclastic American lawyer who specialized in winning acquittals for seemingly guilty clients, was another skeptic. He went to France later in 1915 and searched in vain for a single eyewitness who could confirm even one of the Bryce stories. Increasingly dubious, Darrow announced that he would pay $1,000, a very large sum in 1915—more than $17,000 in twenty-first-century money—to anyone who could produce a Belgian or French boy whose hands had been amputated by a German soldier. There were no takers.[26]

After the war, historians who sought to examine the documentation for Bryce's stories were told that the files had mysteriously disappeared. This blatant evasion has prompted most historians to dismiss 99 percent of Bryce's atrocities as fabrications. One called the report "in itself one of the worst atrocities of the war."[27]

More recent scholarship has scaled down the percentage of the Bryce Report's fabrications; several thousand Belgian civilians, including some women and children, were apparently shot by the *franc-tireur*-enraged Germans in the summer of 1914. Bryce more or less accurately summarized some of the worst excesses, such as the executions in the town of

Dinant. But even these latter-day scholars admit that Bryce's report was seriously "contaminated" by hysteria and war rage.[28]

Correspondence between the members of the Bryce committee survived the destruction of the documents; it revealed severe doubts about the tales of mutilation and rape. One of the committee's secretaries admitted that he been given numerous English addresses of Belgian women supposedly made pregnant by German rapes but could not locate a single case. Even the story of a member of Parliament sheltering two pregnant women turned out to be fraudulent. This dearth of corroboration is hardly surprising. Tales of spearing babies and cutting off the breasts of murdered women were standard hate-this-enemy fables hundreds of years old. So were mass rapes in fields and public squares. Lord Bryce the scholar should have rejected such fabrications out of hand. Instead, he lumped them all into a general condemnation of the German army.[29]

In spite of its patent lies, the Bryce Report was a huge propaganda victory for the British, convincing millions of Americans and other neutrals—the report was translated into twenty-seven languages—that the Germans were beasts in human form.[30]

V

The British piled the Bryce Report on top of another propaganda bonanza handed to them by the Germans—the torpedoing of the passenger liner *Lusitania* off the Irish coast on May 7, 1915. Of the roughly 2,000 passengers on board, 1,198 died, including 291 women and 94 children. American dead numbered 128; among them were Broadway producer Charles Frohman and millionaire sportsman Alfred Gwynne Vanderbilt. Fueled by the British claim that the submarine had fired two torpedoes, causing the ship to sink in less than twenty minutes, American outrage was intense. Theodore Roosevelt called for an immediate declaration of war. The British distributed graphic accounts of the bodies of women and children floating ashore on Irish beaches. An Irish grand jury indicted the kaiser for murder.

No one told the Americans (or the *Lusitania's* passengers) that the liner was carrying 4.2 million rifle cartridges (the equivalent of ten tons of gunpowder) and 1,250 cases of shrapnel shells (supposedly empty) in its hold. Insiders such as Secretary of State Bryan and Dudley Field Malone,

Collector of Customs in New York, suspected these explosives, not a second torpedo, were the source of the blast that sank the ship so swiftly. But the Wilson administration said nothing in public to counteract British claims of a second torpedo.

Shortly before the *Lusitania* sailed, the German government had published a warning in New York newspapers, urging passengers not to travel on the liner. But Woodrow Wilson's administration maintained that American citizens had a right to take belligerents' ships, even when they were sailing into the war zone. The British, determined to prove Britannia still ruled the waves, had scoffed at the danger.[31]

Later in 1915, the Germans gave the British another propaganda victory that in some ways equaled the *Lusitania*. Dame Edith Cavell was a British-born nurse working in a Belgian hospital. The Germans discovered that she had helped more than two hundred Belgian, English and French wounded soldiers escape to their own lines or to the neutral Netherlands. A five-man military court found her guilty, and she was executed at dawn on October 12, 1915. "I realize patriotism is not enough," she told the British clergyman who consoled her on the eve of her death. "I must have no hatred or bitterness for anyone." Wellington House made those words, which it may have fabricated, as famous throughout the United States as Nathan Hale's farewell utterance. A delighted American colleague wrote Sir Gilbert Parker that Cavell "gave us an occasion for another outburst of real sentiment."[32]

The cumulative impact of Cavell's execution, the *Lusitania*'s sinking and the Bryce Report is visible in a *New York Times* editorial on October 23, 1915. The writer admitted that the Germans had a legal right to shoot Cavell and then conflated her death with "countless other acts of like kind, all the fruit of the stern blind devotion to the ruthless ideas of militarism and state power." This was why "the civilized world had turned against Germany . . . and hopes and fervently prays for [her] defeat in arms, lest by triumph her unspeakably horrible ideals should come into dominance and the hands of the clock of civilization be turned back 1000 years."[33]

A separate Wellington House campaign focused a substantial share of this anti-German rage on the kaiser. Wilhelm II was a juicy target, as Lord Northcliffe had demonstrated long before the war began. A grandson of Queen Victoria, Wilhelm had a prickly relationship with his British royal cousins and a tendency to shoot off his mouth about Germany's martial prowess and its right to a "place in the sun." He was also fond of discoursing on the danger of "the yellow peril"—the growing power of Japan—and the superiority of white, northern European Protestants. Prone to nervous breakdowns—he suffered three in the five years preceding the war—he was extravagantly fond of gorgeous military uniforms, perhaps an attempt to achieve masculinity in spite of a withered arm. At his desk, he sat in a saddle because it made him feel like a warrior. His gaunt face, which featured haughtily curled mustaches, made him a hostile cartoonist's dream.[34]

Soon the kaiser, who had little more control over his armies than King George V of England had over the British Expeditionary Force, was being blamed for rapes and murders in Belgium and called a megalomaniac with a hunger to rule the world. From here it was only a short step to calling him "the Mad Dog of Europe" and "the Beast of Berlin." In one book, *The Unspeakable Prussian,* the author argued that "madness has always dogged the steps of the Hohenzollerns." Among his proofs of Wilhelm's insanity was his open dislike of his mother, Victoria, "England's Princess Royal."

A Dutch cartoonist, Louis Raemakers, was employed by Wellington House to portray the kaiser as a cross between a Cro-Magnon primitive and a slavering crocodile. The British hailed Raemakers as a great artist and distributed books of his caricatures in the United States, one of them with an introduction by Prime Minister Asquith. When the artist visited the United States, Woodrow Wilson invited him to the White House.[35]

In the wake of this tidal wave of hate, it was hardly surprising to discover that by March 1917, the Reverend Newell Dwight Hillis, pastor of the Plymouth Congregational Church in Brooklyn, was telling his well-heeled flock that he was prepared to forgive the Germans "just as soon as they are all shot." Then, to fill his cup of happiness to the brim, he wanted to see "the sight of the Kaiser . . . hanging by a rope."[36]

Totally forgotten was the supplement devoted to the kaiser in the *New York Times* on June 8, 1913, on the twenty-fifth anniversary of his coronation. On its front page, along with a handsome portrait of the monarch in a navy uniform, was an effusive salute to him from the paper's editors. The headline read "Kaiser, Twenty-Five Years a Ruler, Hailed as Chief Peacemaker." The accompanying story called Wilhelm "the greatest

factor for peace that our time can show"—and credited him with frequently rescuing Europe from the brink of war. Along with the newspaper's praise came tributes from prominent Americans, including
Theodore Roosevelt; his White House successor, William Howard Taft;
Columbia University president Nicholas Murray Butler; and steel tycoon Andrew Carnegie, whose full-page commentary concluded that all
the citizens of the civilized world were the kaiser's "admiring loving
debtors" for his service to the cause of peace.[37]

What a difference a war makes.

VI

What the British and the Germans really thought about neutral countries
was exemplified by Greece. A democracy with roots in the ancient past, it
was aggressively, even obnoxiously neutral. The Greek king, Constantine,
was of German descent but wanted nothing to do with the war. His rival
for power, Premier Eleutherios Venizelos, had other ideas. He saw that the
Serbians were almost certain to be thrashed by the Austrians and the
Germans, and hoped to replace them as the Balkan ally of the Triple
Entente.

The entente became more than eager to listen to this siren song after
the disastrous failure of the British attempt to land an army at the
Dardanelles and knock Germany's halfhearted ally, Turkey, out of the war.
Still hoping to launch some sort of foray at the southern flank of the
Central Powers, the British soon wangled an invitation from the devious
Venizelos to land an army in Greece. When the first British and French
troops came ashore at Salonika in October 1915, the premier, realizing that
no one, especially the king, bought his diplomacy, protested the violation
of Greece's neutrality—and resigned.

It did not matter what anyone in Greece said or did. The British and the
French were in Salonika to stay. They were soon joined by 150,000 Serbs,
the remnants of the army that had been smashed by a German-led Austrian
offensive, in alliance with Bulgaria. The Serbs, French and British sat in
Salonika for the next three years, doing little but skirmishing with the
Bulgarians and treating the Greeks as second-class citizens in their own
country.[38]

VII

The Germans were unprepared for the British propaganda onslaught of 1914. As a newcomer to international power politics—Germany was barely forty years old in 1914—the country had paid little attention to this time-honored British custom of slandering their enemies. In the sixteenth century, the predecessors of Wellington House had pinned the label "barbarians" on the Irish, thereby putting them outside the usages of international law and the mercies of Christianity. When the British fought the Spanish for imperial hegemony in the New World and in Europe, London's Grub Street flacks created the *Leyendra Negra*, the "Black Legend," which used the Spanish Inquisition to paint a portrait of Spaniards as uniquely cruel, bigoted, fanatical, treacherous and greedy.

When the American revolutionists under George Washington became the foe, no less a literary heavyweight than Samuel Johnson was hired by Parliament to label them "Negro drivers" and a "mongrel" mix of Irish, Scottish, German, Dutch and English, unworthy of being considered true Englishmen. Other scribblers spread the story that George Washington revolted because he had spent all his rich wife's money on gambling and loose women. The Bew Letters, supposedly written by Washington, portrayed him enjoying the sexual favors of his washerwoman and any other female within reach. When the French under Napoleon challenged England's growing world power, hordes of London pamphleteers and journalists pictured their Continental rivals as bloodthirsty madmen with a guillotine in every village square. Napoleon was the subject of caricatures at least as vicious as those visited on the kaiser.[39]

A major flaw in the German character in World War I was a naive righteousness. No one in Berlin gave any thought to creating a Wellington House to respond to the British defamation campaign with similar whoppers about the British Expeditionary Force, Lord Northcliffe, and other ripe targets such as Arthur Balfour, the quintessential aristocrat who headed the Conservative Party before the war and eventually joined the war cabinet. In the early 1900s, Balfour asked a friend, "What exactly *is* a labor union?" Instead, the Germans earnestly tried to refute British and French slanders. They defended shooting Belgian *franc-tireurs* who had fired on their army and the civilians who supported them. When the Cavell execution detonated in their faces, they pointed out that the French had shot two German nurses as spies in 1915. The story did not stir an iota of sympathy in America.

When the kaiser's men captured Brussels, they searched the Belgian Foreign Office files and found ample evidence that Belgium had a virtual alliance with France and England. Again, the refutation of "poor little neutral Belgium" was barely noticed. Berlin tried to answer the uproar over the *Lusitania* by denying that there was a second torpedo and arguing that the ship was a floating explosion waiting to happen, thanks to its cargo. Again, yawns and rampant skepticism. As any student of modern-day spin can tell you, the story that gets there first gets the most attention.[40]

The Austro-Hungarian empire, headquartered in Vienna, with less-than-total power over provinces that included restless Czechs, Hungarians, Poles, Croatians, Bosnians and Serbs as well as Germans, was even less prepared to cope with the publicity war in the United States. Vienna took the better part of six months to send someone to the United States to explain why it was the one party in the whole mess with a legitimate reason for going to war. The Serbian terrorist who shot Archduke Ferdinand and his wife had patent links with government plotters in Belgrade.

Thanks to the astute German ambassador, Count Johann von Bernstorff, the kaiser's men in the United States mounted a propaganda counterattack fairly quickly. Bernstorff persuaded the *New York Times* to give him a full-page interview in their Sunday magazine on August 30, 1914, in which he denounced England for cutting the undersea cables and blamed Russia for starting the war by mobilizing its huge army to defend Serbia. By September 1914, the German Information Service (GIS) was up and running in New York. It had established radio contact with Berlin and other European capitals through the Trans-Ocean News Service, which operated from Sayville, on the south shore of Long Island. But the GIS's numbers never came close to the manpower that Wellington House and the British voluntary organizations, supplemented by Lord Northcliffe's numerous reporters and American Anglophile volunteers, brought to the fray.[41]

VIII

Ambassador Bernstorff's team asked for help from the 8.3 million U.S. citizens who proudly called themselves German-Americans. By far the most affluent immigrant group in the United States, they had enclaves in numerous Midwest cities and towns, and politicians were sensitive to their opinions. In 1908, a survey of how other Americans viewed immigrant groups had ranked the Germans as the most admirable. They were hard-working, law-abiding, patriotic—tens of thousands had fought for the Union in the Civil War.

The German-American response to the war in Europe was staunchly pro-fatherland. In their numerous newspapers, they fulminated against the prejudices of U.S. papers, which quickly became saturated with Wellington House propaganda. Mass meetings in major cities—Chicago, New York, Cincinnati—hailed the "idealism of Germany" and damned the English for cutting the cables and gaining a monopoly on the flow of information about the war. They set up a Literary Defense Center, which sponsored hard-hitting books by American writers, defending Germany and Austria-Hungary with titles such as *Who Is to Blame for the War?*[42]

A star German-American writer soon emerged: George Sylvester Viereck. He had come to the United States as a boy, graduated from New York's City College, and won a reputation as an experimental poet and a progressive political journalist. With backing from the German Information Service, he began editing an English-language weekly, *Fatherland,* which swiftly achieved a circulation of 100,000. But Viereck blundered badly when he defended the sinking of the *Lusitania* as proof that "Germany was not bluffing in this war" and maintained that burning Louvain's famous library taught a valuable lesson to other countries that were thinking of ordering their civilians to participate in the war. Naive Germanic self-righteousness skewed even Viereck's seemingly sophisticated judgment.[43]

Also active was a national group, the German-American Alliance. Until the war began, they had confined themselves to fighting prohibition, the growing political movement to ban alcoholic drinks from the United States. They now organized mass meetings in Washington to demand an embargo on the sale of munitions to England and France. They also indulged in outbursts of authoritarianism when their local numbers gave them power. They called for firing schoolteachers who espoused the Anglo-French cause in their classrooms and the banning of pro-Entente books in public libraries. These activities raised the hackles of the National Security League and other Americans, whom Wellington House had turned into Germanophobes. They began claiming that the alliance was a "vast engine of the German government."[44]

Germany also had some spokesmen in the academic world. Shortly after the war started, the *New York Times* gave Hugo von Munsterberg, professor of history and psychology at Harvard University, a respectful hearing when he blamed Russia for igniting the explosion. Another Harvard professor, Edmund von Mach, launched a weekly column, "The German Viewpoint," for the Boston *Evening Transcript*. After the *Lusitania* went down, the editors decided their readers were no longer interested in the German viewpoint and fired him. Munsterberg was similarly isolated. He stopped coming to Harvard faculty meetings because former friends refused to sit near him.[45]

The Germans tried to counter Belgian atrocity stories with tales of monstrous deeds by Russians on the Eastern Front. Berlin's lack of imagination was almost pathetic. The best they could muster was a familiar recital of women with amputated breasts, impaled children, and virgins ravished by gloating Cossacks. These obvious retreads impressed no one.[46]

The German Information Service sponsored or originated more than 1,500 books, pamphlets and articles. But they seldom disguised the source of this propaganda; with that same naive self-righteousness, they usually did not even try. They never came close to matching the covert way Wellington House distributed British propaganda through American friends and pliable reporters. Nor did the Germans ever find an advocate with Viscount Bryce's instant credibility. The GIS's first spokesman, Bernhard Dernburg, was a clever man and a skillful writer. But he was soon labeled the Kaiser's mouthpiece by the pro-British New York press. When he tried to defend the sinking of the *Lusitania*, the American response was so ferocious, Ambassador von Bernstorff sent him back to Germany.[47]

Ironically, numerous American politicians, including Woodrow Wilson, worked themselves into a state of considerable outrage at the Germans for trying to "tamper" with American public opinion. No one ever said a word against Wellington House, for a very simple reason: Its existence was unknown to all but the top people in the British government.

IX

The Germans had seemingly formidable allies in the second largest ethnic group in America, the Irish-Americans. Four million strong, with powerful political machines that controlled major cities such as Chicago and New York, the Irish had a grievance against Great Britain, which some of them were not shy about expressing: the long history of oppression in their home-land. The famine of 1847, which killed 1.5 million Irish, while the British feasted on beef and barley exported from Ireland, was still a vivid memory. In 1911, the slums of Dublin had a higher death rate than Calcutta.[48]

In the *Gaelic American* and the *Irish World,* the two largest newspapers read by Irish-Americans, Great Britain was abused with a pugnacity and pertinacity that the Bernstorff team must have found heartwarming at first. The papers praised Irish-Americans who stormed movie theaters showing British propaganda films and shut them down. They published in large black type a protest against the U.S. government's pro-British tilt by the United Irish-American Societies, whom they pointedly described as "the largest aggregation of citizens in Greater New York"—a warning to vul-nerable politicians. Not far behind these two papers was the American Truth Society, headed by Jeremiah O'Leary, which tried to expose British lies as fast as Wellington House churned them out. Among O'Leary's favorite quotations was an editorial in the *London Chronicle:* "The debt that England owes the newspaper world of America cannot be overestimated. . . . We have no better Allies in America than the editors of the great papers." O'Leary also began publishing a monthly magazine whose title spoke for itself: *Bull.*[49]

These Irish-Americans pointed out that the British empire controlled some 13 million square miles of the earth's surface, with a subject popu-lation of 444 million. In this vast expanse, the only people with the right to vote were a minority of Britons in their home islands, and in the do-minions of Australia, New Zealand, Canada and South Africa. The Irish occasionally noted that if you threw in the Russian empire, the two gov-ernments controlled half the earth's surface, each a colossus built "on the ruins of small nations." London's claim to be fighting for democracy was a sick joke. The top 2½ percent of Britain's population controlled 98 per-cent of the country's wealth. England, wrote John Devoy, the editor of the *Gaelic American,* was "the incarnation of greed. Her arrogance and in-solence are only equaled by her conscienceless cupidity."[50]

With this viewpoint, it was hardly surprising that Devoy and his fellow supporters of Irish independence rooted for a German victory. They argued that Ireland, Poland, Finland, Egypt and India would become free democra-cies. They scoffed at the atrocity stories flooding New York newspapers, and urged a political union of Irish-Americans and German-Americans that would be "more than a match for the pro–British intriguers who have been using press, pulpit and platform to promote England's interests."[51]

For a while, these inflamed Irish spokespersons were supported by the semiofficial newspapers of the Roman Catholic Church, which was strongly sympathetic to the Catholic rulers of Austria-Hungary, the Hapsburgs. The church was also extremely cool to embattled France, where anticlericalism was part of the political creed of French liberals and had prompted the government to expel numerous religious orders from the country in 1904.[52]

The alliance that the Irish-Americans and the German-Americans tried to concoct to meet the British propaganda onslaught soon revealed serious weaknesses. The circulation of the *Gaelic American,* the *Irish World,* and *Bull* barely exceeded 200,000 a week. The *New York Times* alone reached 300,000 readers each day, and the total circulation of the other New York papers, most of them even more pro-British, came to ten times that figure. Only William Randolph Hearst's chain of newspapers (circulation 4 million) scoffed at British claims and called for genuine neutrality. The old adage, it takes one to know one, seemed to apply here. Hearst readily saw Lord Northcliffe's yellow-journalist hand in Wellington House and ordered his newspapers to resist London's line.

The great mass of Irish-Americans were not passionately concerned with Irish independence—or into hating the British in the violent style of Devoy, O'Leary and company. They were as repelled by the German atrocity stories as most other Americans and were equally dismayed by the sinking of the *Lusitania* and the execution of Edith Cavell. As one woman put it some years later, there was too much "Deutschland go-bragh" in the onslaught of the Irish independence men for most Irish-Americans to swallow.

Confusing matters even further were ferocious assaults on the independence men by fellow Irish-Americans, such as the distinguished lawyer and bibliophile John Quinn. His contacts with British writers had turned him into a critic of his own people. Quinn said he would like to see Paul von Hindenburg (Germany's top general) as governor general of Ireland for six months. Not only would he get rid of the likes of Devoy and O'Leary, but he would "teach the [home] Irish industry, order, efficiency, economy [and] cleanliness." One can almost hear the ghost of that earlier British propagandist, Samuel Johnson, repeating his famous remark: "The Irish are a fair people—they never speak well of one other."[53]

Perhaps most important, the vast majority of the Irish-Americans were Democrats, and in early 1916, Woodrow Wilson made a series of speeches condemning "hyphenates." He accused them of "pouring poison into the veins of our national life." The speeches had a chilling effect on support for Germany among the Irish-Americans who did not regularly read the independence-for-Ireland press. Wilson was reviving memories of their persecution in the previous century by nativist organizations such as the Know-Nothing Party and the American Protestant Association, which questioned their loyalty to the United States. When Devoy and his friends tried to respond to the president by calling an Irish Race Convention in 1916 to create a semblance of Celtic unity, numerous leading Irish-Americans such as Senator James O'Gorman of New York declined to attend.[54]

Then came a dramatic turnaround. On Easter Sunday, 1916, Irish rebels seized key buildings in Dublin and proclaimed a republic. The British quickly crushed the rebellion. With a stupidity that more than matched the German execution of Cavell, the London government sentenced most of the leaders to death—and the Wilson administration, with equally incredible stupidity, made no protest against the barbarity.

The executions caused a huge uproar in the Irish-American community and gave new influence to the independence men. Easter martyrs also solidified the Irish link to Germany, which lost no time issuing a statement that it recognized Ireland's right to independence. "The Irish are with us," gloated the secretary of the German American Alliance."[55]

The independence men's antagonism to Wilson was intensified by the *Gaelic American*'s claim that the U.S. government had betrayed the Easter rebellion after Secret Service agents raided the office of the German consul in New York and discovered correspondence between Devoy and Roger Casement about a shipload of arms and ammunition that Casement had obtained from Germany. The Wilson administration had supposedly turned the letters over to the British, who captured Casement and forced the panicked German captain to scuttle his ship. Casement was executed for his role in the rebellion, and his reputation smeared by the publication of diaries purporting that he was a homosexual. Throughout the rest of 1916, the *Gaelic American* repeatedly accused Wilson of being the evil genius behind this tragedy.

Again revealing the minority status of the independence men, the accusation had little impact on the Irish-American vote for Wilson in the 1916 election. No mean debater, Wilson used the violent hostility of the Devoy-O'Leary circle to bolster his call for ethnic support for his frequent declarations of neutrality. When Jeremiah O'Leary sent Wilson a snide telegram predicting his defeat, the president replied: "I would feel deeply mortified to have you or anybody like you vote for me. Since you have access to many disloyal Americans and I have not, I will ask you to convey this message to them." Joseph Tumulty, Wilson's Irish-American secretary, later claimed this telegram galvanized the president's reelection campaign.[56]

It was, as the saying goes, a famous victory. But the time was not far off when Wilson would pay dearly for alienating these outspoken Irish-Americans.

X

Throughout the argument over submarine warfare, the Germans said they only wanted a fair hearing—something the British made sure they never got. The London government had a very different agenda in mind—one that extended beyond public opinion. From the opening of the war, British newspapers portrayed the submarine as an outlaw weapon, used by the Germans to kill unarmed sailors on merchant ships. Woodrow Wilson and most other Americans accepted this idea. Much of Wilson's dialogue with the German government before the declaration of war was about his insistence that the submarine should act as a surface raider, and give sailors time to abandon ship before their vessel was sunk. The British praised the president for this stance.

In their war at sea, however, the British went to great lengths to make these "cruiser rules" extremely dangerous if not impossible for the U-boats. The admiralty under First Lord Winston Churchill warned ship captains that they would be prosecuted if they tamely surrendered their ships. The admiralty ordered crews to ram or fire on U-boats whenever possible. Churchill also ordered that the survivors of sunken U-boats be treated as felons rather than prisoners of war, meaning they could be shot if this was the "most convenient" way of dealing with them.[57]

British ships were ordered to sail with no names or registry numbers. When they were in the barred zone around the British Isles, they were told to fly a neutral flag, preferably American. On the voyage before it was sunk, the *Lusitania* had used this tactic as it approached the Irish coast. Although the Wilson administration objected to this misuse of Old Glory, the president was ignored as usual and did nothing as usual.[58]

The sinking of the British steamer *Falaba* on March 29, 1915, was a good example of England's deft combination of resistance and propaganda. The story as it was told by Wellington House for the New York newspapers portrayed a ruthless German submarine captain who sank the cargo-passenger liner without warning, killing 110 people, including one American, by triggering a "terrific explosion" in the engine room. After the war, historians found that the U-boat captain had given *Falaba*'s master three warnings to abandon ship, waiting a total of twenty-three minutes while the Englishman made excuses and radioed for assistance. Only when a British warship appeared on the horizon did the Germans unleash a torpedo, which blew up 13 tons of ammunition in the *Falaba*'s hold, accounting for the heavy casualties.[59]

Another British innovation that made it difficult if not impossible for the U-boats to follow cruiser rules was the Q-ship. This disguised merchantman had a well-trained crew and almost as many concealed guns on its decks as a royal navy destroyer. If a submarine surfaced and ordered one of these craft to abandon ship, the U-boat was answered with a hail of shellfire.[60]

In August 1915, the *Baralong,* a Q-ship flying the U.S. flag, destroyed a German submarine that had surfaced to attack another British vessel, the *Nicosian.* Adding outrage to this injury, the *Baralong*'s crew executed the submarine's survivors. The chancellor of Germany went before the Reichstag to denounce this "bestial" high-seas murder. He called the *Baralong* a *franctireur* ship, demonstrating that the Germans still thought their execution of Belgian civilians the previous August was justified.[61]

Winston Churchill's correspondence as first lord of the admiralty offers evidence that getting the United States into the war on Britain's side was a major consideration. He urged the British government to offer the cheapest possible insurance rates to neutral shippers: "It is most important to attract neutral shipping to our shores in the hope especially of embroiling the United States with Germany." The more neutral "traffic," the better, Churchill insisted. "If some of it gets into trouble, better still."[62]

XI

In early October 1914, two months after the war began, Charles Schwab, the president of Bethlehem Steel, was in London, eager to do business with the British government. Bethlehem was one of the world's biggest arms merchants. After picking up orders for millions of artillery shells, Schwab visited First Sea Lord Sir John Fisher, who told him England was desperate to acquire more submarines, fast. This stance differed a good deal from what Fisher's government was saying about the submarine's being an underhanded, weapon, but Schwab was not the sort to let such seeming contradictions bother him. He told Fisher he could build ten 500-ton undersea boats at crash speed. With a handshake, the deal was done.

Back in the United States, U.S. Navy inspectors at Bethlehem were distressed to discover British submarines under contract. They informed Schwab the deal violated a law that was 120 years old. In the 1790s, during the Napoleonic wars, the French government tried to outfit privateers in American ports. Fearing this would embroil the country in a war with England, Congress banned the practice. During the Civil War, the Confederate raider *Alabama,* built in Great Britain, wreaked havoc on Union shipping and brought U.S.-British relations to a low point. Schwab replied that he was not *actually* building the submarines for Great Britain. He was going to ship the parts to Canada, where they would be welded together by another company.

The navy men—and some newspapers—did not agree, and the matter soon attracted President Wilson's attention. He asked Robert Lansing, at that time the State Department's counselor, for a legal opinion. A Watertown, New York, lawyer who had been involved in much international litigation, Lansing was an Anglophile from his cravat to his wingtips. He quickly produced some dense legalese that sanctioned Schwab's maneuver. Wilson wrote back, telling Lansing that he still wanted the submarines stopped. Lansing ignored him, and in June 1915, the ten 500-ton subs sailed from Quebec for the war zone. Neither President Wilson nor the U.S. Department of Justice said a word. In the next year, 1916, Bethlehem Steel earned $61 million, more money than the company's total gross for its previous eight years.[63]

The Bethlehem story is a pithy summary of the evolution of the United States into a branch of the British armament industry during the thirty-two months of its neutrality. Wilson talked—and talked and talked—about neutrality and apparently convinced himself that he was neutral. But the United States he was supposedly running was not neutral, in thought, word or deed, thanks to Wellington House in London—and the international banking firm of J. P. Morgan in New York. The storied founder of the firm had died in 1913; it was now headed by his son, "Jack" Pierpoint Morgan, who spent six months of each year on his English estate and was a totally committed Anglophile. Morgan and his fellow bankers were the key players in the shift from genuine to sham neutrality. The war was barely two days old when the French government, through Morgan's Paris branch, requested a loan of $100 million.[64]

Morgan replied that he feared the U.S. government would object—and he was right. Secretary of State William Jennings Bryan opposed the loan and told President Wilson: "Money is the worst of all contrabrands because it commands everything else." He warned Wilson against letting "powerful financial interests" get involved in the war. They had the ability to influence many other parts of society, especially the press and politicians.[65]

In spite of Bryan's three losing runs for president on the Democratic ticket, he still had a strong following inside the Democratic Party. Wilson had made the Nebraskan secretary of state because Bryan had switched his support to him at a crucial moment in the 1912 nominating convention. Like most Midwesterners, Bryan viewed the Great War as an outbreak of European insanity from which the United States should distance itself. Wilson asked Robert Lansing for his legal opinion of the French request for a loan. The State Department counselor produced a brief, declaring it "compatible with neutrality."[66]

Bryan vociferously disagreed, and Lansing backed down. Wilson supported Bryan, personally composing a statement: "Loans by American bankers to any foreign government which is at war are inconsistent with the true spirit of neutrality." An ecstatic Bryan thought a major threat of war had been eliminated. The Nebraskan soon discovered it was only the first inning of a long ball game. As British and French orders for ammunition and other war matériel filled the books of U.S. companies, the pressure for financial assistance to pay for them grew more and more acute.[67]

Meanwhile, Bryan became distracted by the dispute over submarine warfare, which British propaganda and the Anglophile tilt of Wilson's cabinet skewed in England's favor. Bryan's protests against the British blockade, particularly England's refusal to allow U.S. foodstuffs into Germany, which he found especially reprehensible, were muted by Wilson's ambassador to London, Walter Hines Page, who totally identified with the British cause. A former editor of the *Atlantic Monthly* and a longtime Wilson friend and supporter, Page "thanked heaven he was of [English] race and blood," and regularly presented Bryan's protests to Foreign Secretary Grey with dismissive comments. During one of his presentations, Page said: "I have now read the dispatch but I do not agree with it; let us consider how it should be answered."[68]

As the war continued, Wilson edged Bryan to the diplomatic sidelines. He sent his confidential adviser, Colonel House, to London, Paris and Berlin to explore the possibilities of a mediated peace. House was as pro-British as Page, but concealed it out of his desire to blend with Wilson's seemingly neutral stance. In the State Department, Lansing gradually acquired more influence than Bryan, a political rival Wilson never liked or respected. Soon Lansing convinced Wilson that loans might be a violation of America's neutral stance—but the granting of "credits" to England and France by the House of Morgan and other banks was legally justifiable. Wilson accepted this fine distinction, and by the time the United States declared war, Morgan had loaned the two belligerents $2.1 billion, the equivalent of almost $30 billion in 2002, making a neat profit of $30 million, worth $422 million in 2002 dollars. Twenty years later, when a Senate committee investigated the World War I munitions industry, J. P. Morgan was asked about the difference between loans and credits. His testimony made it clear that practically speaking, there was no difference.[69]

When the *Lusitania* was sunk, William Jennings Bryan was one of the few Americans who resisted the hysteria whipped up by Wellington House and its American mouthpieces. Citing the *Lusitania's* cargo manifest, which listed the ammunition as well as material for uniforms and leather belts in its cargo, he told Woodrow Wilson: "A ship carrying contraband should not rely on passengers to protect her from attack—it would be like putting women and children in front of an army." That was an ironic echo of the Bryce Report, which accused the Germans of doing this in Belgium.[70]

Wilson ignored his secretary of state and filed an angry protest with the German government, in which he baldly stated that American citizens "bound on lawful errands" had the right to travel on ships belonging to "belligerents" and Germany would be held to a "strict accountability" if it violated these rights. He followed this with a second note that virtually required Germany to abandon unrestricted submarine warfare. Rather than sign this second note, Bryan resigned, accurately predicting that Wilson's policy was certain to embroil the United States in war with Germany.[71]

Bryan was succeeded by Robert Lansing. Two weeks after he took over the State Department, he wrote himself a private memorandum, which could have been excerpted from a statement by Wellington House: "I have come to the conclusion that the German Government is utterly hostile to all nations with democratic institutions because those who compose it see in democracy a menace to absolutism and the defeat of the German ambition for world dominance. . . . Germany must not be permitted to win this war or even to break even."[72]

Making Lansing secretary of state was one of Wilson's worst mistakes. The president had little or no respect for the man and seldom concealed it. Colonel House had even less respect. He told Wilson that Lansing's "mentality" did not impress him. But the president, like many other holders of the office, considered himself the master of the nation's foreign policy and regarded the secretary as a mere messenger. In this view, House wholly concurred. He opined that the ideal secretary of state was a person with "not too many ideas of his own." Lansing, by no means a stupid man, resented Wilson's (and House's) scarcely concealed contempt for his opinions. He used the power and influence of his office to undermine Wilson's neutrality.[73]

By 1916, the United States was supplying Great Britain, France and Russia with 40 percent of their war matériel. France and Russia were broke, and London was paying for everything. Of the 5 million pounds England spent on the war each day, 2 million pounds—$70 million a week—were spent in the United States. (This computes to $96,000,000 a week in 2002 dollars.) Three British missions were operating in Washington, D.C. The Ministry of Munitions had a staff of 1,600 and bought weapons and ammunition for both Britain and bankrupt France. Ministry agents were in hundreds of U.S. factories where orders were being filled; agents also rode the freight trains and supervised loading at U.S. docks to prevent sabotage. The Board of Trade and an entity called the Wheat Export Company were also hard at work buying immense amounts of civilian goods, cotton and grains.[74]

Simultaneously, the United States did little while the British navy slowly but steadily extended the meaning of the word *contraband* (of war) until the definition included almost every imaginable article produced by farmers or industrialists. Cotton shipped to Germany had to be unloaded in New York and x-rayed, bale by bale, at the shippers' expense to make sure it did not carry concealed contraband. A few months later, cotton itself became contraband. American exporters and companies that did business with the English were ordered to form trade associations that solemnly promised to sell nothing to Germany or Austria. Finally, in July 1916, the British published a blacklist of 87 American and 350 South American companies that were trading with Berlin and Vienna.

Not a few American businessmen resented this arrogant restraint of trade by a foreign nation. President Wilson exclaimed to an alarmed Colonel House: "I am . . . about at the end of my patience with Great Britain and the Allies." But Secretary of Commerce William Redfield, a passionate Anglophile, warned the president that an embargo on further business with England would be "more injurious" to the United States than to the countries at war. According to Redfield, an embargo would cost America the Triple Entente's good will, which the United States would need badly when the war ended. This reasoning was based on the virtually invulnerable American assumption that an Allied victory was inevitable. Wilson, sharing the assumption, retreated into silence on the blacklist.[75]

XII

Watching this performance, Germans in the United States and in Germany became more and more embittered and skeptical about Wilson's protestations of neutrality. "I do not think the people in America realize how excited the Germans have become on the question of selling munitions of war . . . to the Allies," Ambassador James Gerard reported from Berlin. When Colonel House visited Berlin in 1915 on a supposed peace mission, he told Wilson that everyone he met "immediately corner[ed] me . . . to discuss our shipment of munitions to the Allies."[76]

The Germans became even more exercised when a U.S. machine tool company advertised a new lathe that could produce "poison shells" filled with two acids that would explode and cause death "in terrible agony within four hours." Ambassador Gerard reported that a copy of the advertisement had been laid on the desk of every member of the Reichstag. Gerard, who was about as neutral as Robert Lansing, complained that "a veritable campaign of hate" against the United States was swirling through Germany.[77]

In America, not a few members of the German embassy staff began to view the U.S. armaments industry as a branch of the British war machine.

They decided it was their duty to disrupt this flow of weaponry. Their first large-scale attempt was legal and ingenious. They set up a corporation called the Bridgeport Projectile Company (BPC) and funneled several million dollars into its treasury. BPC ordered huge quantities of hydraulic presses, machine tools and rolling mills, depriving companies that were supplying the British with the tools needed for expansion. The Germans also tried to corner the market in carbolic acid, a vital ingredient in explosives. They hired agent provocateurs to stimulate strikes in ammunition factories where immigrants from Austria-Hungary predominated.

All these activities were organized by Heinrich Albert, a self-effacing commercial attaché in the German embassy. He never dreamed that Secretary of the Treasury William Gibbs McAdoo, with President Wilson's approval, had ordered the U.S. Secret Service to begin shadowing him. (They also began tapping the telephones of the German and Austrian embassies.) One hot day in July, Albert, weary from his labors, dozed off on a New York subway, awoke at his stop and dashed off the train, leaving his briefcase behind. The Secret Service agent tailing him grabbed it—itself a violation of America's neutrality. Soon McAdoo and Wilson were examining the briefcase's contents, which revealed almost all Germany's covert operations, from the munitions diversion to fomenting strikes to financing the newspaper *Fatherland*.

McAdoo admitted that none of these operations were the basis for any "legal action" against Germany. But, he claimed, he saw a chance to "scare the whole swarm of propagandists—British and French as well as German." With President Wilson's approval, he gave the contents of Albert's briefcase to the *New York World*, which plastered it all over the front page, topped by screaming headlines:

HOW GERMANY HAS WORKED IN U.S.
TO SHAPE OPINION, BLOCK THE ALLIES
AND GET MUNITIONS FOR HERSELF.
TOLD IN SECRET AGENT'S LETTERS.[78]

German agents operating under deeper cover planted bombs in U.S. armament factories, on docks where the deadly products were loaded, and in the holds of freighters carrying them to Europe. During the night of July 30, 1916, tons of ammunition on Black Tom Island, off Caven Point in

Jersey City, blew up, breaking tens of thousands of windows in that city and in lower Manhattan, just across the harbor. Six months later, a munitions plant in Kingsland, New Jersey, exploded. These acts of sabotage did little to stem the flow of weaponry and munitions to France and England. In the United States, although connections to the explosions were unproved, the Germans were suspects number one, and pro-British advocates in U.S. newspapers had no trouble convicting them in the court of public opinion.

A key player in this spy-versus-spy game was John Revelstoke Rathom, the editor of the *Providence Journal*. Born in Australia, Rathom had been educated in England and was a Germanophobe of manic proportions. He had close connections with Captain Guy Gaunt of the British navy, the man in charge of British intelligence operations in the United States and a confidant of Colonel House. Gaunt leaked stories, some true, on German undercover operations to Rathom, who soon established himself as the premier authority on the matter. The *New York Times* was so impressed, its editors worked out an agreement whereby they bought exclusive rights to reprint the material under the heading "The *Providence Journal* will say this morning . . . "[79]

It was hardly surprising, in the light of what was transpiring in the United States, that the leaders of Germany looked with growing skepticism on Wilson's claim to be an unbiased peacemaker who could mediate a settlement between the warring nations. The kaiser and his ministers had yielded to the president's demands to moderate their submarines' tactics because they were winning the war in Europe. On the Eastern Front, whole Russian armies had been enveloped and destroyed. In the west, the German army's casualties were much lower than those of the French and British forces, and their army's morale remained high.[80]

But as 1916 lengthened, the British blockade began to inflict menacing damage on the German home front. Food riots broke out in some cities. The lower classes were living close to the malnutrition line. These realities—and a London-Paris rejection of Berlin's call for a peace conference—played a crucial part in Berlin's decision to announce unrestricted submarine warfare, knowing that the decision would probably bring the United States into the war. The Germans were gambling that their submarines could starve the British into submission before American troops could reach Europe in significant numbers. The almost total unpreparedness of the American army lent credence to this strategy.

XIII

On the Allied side, another kind of shortage began to assume nightmarish proportions. By January 1917, not even J. P. Morgan could come up with enough money to keep pace with Great Britain's expenditures in the United States. Morgan informed the British that henceforth, all loans (by this time the parties involved were using the correct term) would have to be on a short-term basis, against collateral. By March, it became apparent that Britain was reeling toward bankruptcy. There were only 114 million pounds of gold left in the Bank of England's vaults to cover further loans. Secretary of State Lansing told Woodrow Wilson of a warning from Ambassador Page that "the collapse of world trade and of the whole of European finance" was imminent. This breakdown would mean the cessation of all war orders in hundreds of U.S. factories—a day of reckoning that would have a catastrophic impact on the American economy.

Around the same time, Colonel House received letters from American embassy staffers in Paris and London, warning him that French morale was in danger of cracking. House immediately told Wilson, "If France should cave in before Germany, it would be a calamity beyond reckoning. . . . If we intend to help defeat Germany . . . it will be necessary for us to begin immediately." It was in the shadow of these looming threats that the president decided the Zimmermann telegram and Germany's submarine "outrages" left him no choice but war.[81]

XIV

Is there an explanation for Woodrow Wilson's "unneutral" neutrality? One answer is the president's Anglophilia. He profoundly admired the English system of government; in fact, he thought it was superior to the American system. His greatest political hero was Prime Minister William Evarts Gladstone, who rhetorically thrashed the conservatives and persuaded England to take a more liberal attitude toward Ireland, among other things. In an unguarded moment, Wilson confessed to a friend that he hoped for an Allied victory in the war but was not permitted by his public neutrality to say so.

It does not take a degree in psychology to see how such a man could be heavily influenced by Wellington House's propaganda. Another large factor

was Wilson's peculiar blind spot about economic realities and their influence on people and affairs. The son of a minister father, he went from college into academic life, after a brief brush with practicing law. He had little
or no chance to understand how businesspeople, journalists and politicians
influenced a society. One of his former students remarked that in his lec-
tures, "Mr. Wilson gave us no glimpse of the economic background of the
English ruling class. . . . It was never hinted in his lecture-room that the
British landed gentry, bankers and businessmen enacted laws to protect
their own class and group."

The socialist leader Norman Thomas, another former student of
Wilson's, put it more succinctly: "If he [Wilson] had ever heard of [the]
dictum that the distribution of power follows the distribution of property,
he never discussed it with us in the classroom."[82]

Not to be underestimated in Wilson's worldview was the influence of
Colonel House. The intensity of their friendship was unique in presidential
annals. Wilson repeatedly expressed amazement about how often they
thought exactly alike. Much of this reaction can be credited to House's astute handling of Wilson, who did not like to be contradicted once he had
formed an opinion. There is also no doubt that a great many of Wilson's
opinions about the war were formed by this small, shrewd Texan. Nor is
there much doubt that most of House's opinions on the war were formed
by his contacts with the top people in the English government, all of
whom wined and dined him at their clubs and baronial homes and flat-
tered him relentlessly into accepting their view of the conflict.

The most striking example of Colonel House's Anglophilia was an
arrangement he worked out with Foreign Secretary Edward Grey. Reading
House's letters to "Dear Sir Edward" (signed "Affectionately yours") makes
it clear that this was not a correspondence between two men representing
independent powers with widely differing opinions on the war. In May
1916, for instance, House anxiously warned Grey of a shift in American
public opinion against England because Germany had suspended unrestricted submarine warfare while London persisted in its blockade. In another letter the following day, he discussed whether the "wearing down
process," as far as Germany was concerned, had gone far enough to make it
"sensible of the power we can wield."

Whereupon House informed the British foreign secretary that the president was ready to commit himself to a plan that Grey had sown in the

colonel's brain nine months earlier. Wilson would approve a secret agreement with the British to commit the United States to war on their side, if Germany refused to respond to the president's call for an immediate peace conference. Moreover, House agreed that Wilson would only speak when the British decided the time was ripe for a peace advantageous to them. Could there be a more complete revelation of which way House–Wilson–Philip Dru was tilting?[83]

The House-Grey memorandum was executed, with only one small reservation by the president. He wrote the word "probably" into the statement that the United States would join the war on the side of the Triple Entente if Germany balked at the British peace offer. After the war, Grey would claim in his memoirs that as far as he was concerned, this single word invalidated the plan. But the minutes of the British cabinet meetings at the time tell a very different story. They show Grey weighing the pros and cons of the proposal, with only one thought in mind: Which alternative was likely to be best for England? He consulted British military authorities to find out if they thought England would be "completely victorious"—in which case it would be "better to ignore" the memorandum. After considerable debate, the cabinet hard-liners such as Arthur Balfour, who thought the proposal was "not worth five minutes thought," convinced the majority that Germany was not sufficiently defeated to obtain the total victory they sought. Months went by with no word from Grey while men died by the tens of thousands on the Western and Eastern Fronts.[84]

Soon after Wilson's reelection in 1916, House and the president decided they could wait no longer. They went all out to pressure Grey with cables, letters, messages through third parties into signaling that the president was ready to breathe life into the House-Grey memorandum. They got nowhere. Grey retreated to saying that as long as Field Marshal Haig and his generals thought there was a chance of Britain's winning the war, he could not agree to Wilson's mediation. Ever the diplomat, Grey finessed House and Wilson out the door by warning them that a unilateral call for peace would be considered pro-German.[85]

A cynical explanation for this performance was Grey's assumption that House and Wilson were on Britain's side no matter what he decided and could be strung along indefinitely with such proposals, which fed what House called the president's desire "to serve humanity in a large way." By and large, Grey was right. As a mediator, Wilson had allowed himself (and

House) to be maneuvered into an impossible situation. The British regarded him with bemused contempt. In private letters, Ambassador Cecil Spring Rice mockingly called Wilson "our Savior." The Germans, thanks to Wilson's refusal to limit U.S. trade in weapons and food with the Allies, considered him pro-British. In the crisis weeks of early 1917, when Wilson called for peace without victory, Berlin told Ambassador von Bernstorff that the president's mediation was "positively not desired."[86]

Simultaneously, Secretary of State Lansing did everything in his power to ruin Wilson's last attempt to play the neutral after his reelection. When Wilson sent a note to both sides, asking them to state their peace terms, Lansing held a press conference in which he denied the president's message was a "peace note" and remarked that the United States was "on the verge of war"—presumably with Germany. The statement caused a sensation in the newspapers and panic on the New York Stock Exchange. Next, he called in the British and French ambassadors and privately told them that the United States was on their side and there was no need to take the note seriously.[87]

In England, meanwhile, an even more astute student of the political-diplomatic game took charge of foreign policy and almost everything else in sight: David Lloyd George. The Welsh Wizard, as he was not very affectionately known to many people, became prime minister of a largely conservative cabinet, frankly committed to fighting the war to the finish. Sir Edward Grey and virtually every other liberal British leader vanished into the shadows. Lloyd George desperately wanted to get Wilson into the war. How to do it, with a man who saw himself as a proponent of a peace without victory and a would-be servant of humanity?

With some help from German Foreign Minister Zimmerman and his telegram, the task proved to be almost absurdly simple. Lloyd George sent a message through Ambassador Page that if Wilson wanted to participate with an equal voice at the peace conference after the Allies won the war, the United States would have to become a belligerent. The prime minister claimed that, like America, Great Britain wanted neither territorial nor any other kind of gains from the war, but the other belligerents would almost certainly insist on a vengeful peace unless Wilson joined the struggle.[88]

It was the perfect political bait. Just how totally Wilson swallowed it was visible in a conversation he had with Jane Addams, a pioneer social worker, and a group of fellow peace activists who visited him in the White House in February 1917. The Germans had just launched unrestricted submarine warfare, and Wilson had severed diplomatic relations with Berlin. Wilson told the activists that "as head of a nation participating in the war, the president of the United States would have a seat at the peace table, but that if he remained the representative of a neutral country, he could at best only 'call through a crack in the door.'"[89]

XV

On a PBS documentary about Woodrow Wilson's life, one historian commentator called his April 2 speech the greatest American state paper since Abraham Lincoln's Gettysburg Address. This comment is typical of the extravagant praise Wilson receives from some historians. Unquestionably, the speech was a rhetorical masterpiece. It was perfectly attuned to stir the emotions of a Congress and a country that had been soaked in British hate propaganda against Germany for the previous thirty-two months. Wilson was a masterful orator; one historian has called him the last of the oratorical statesmen in the tradition of Daniel Webster and Henry Clay.[90]

But from a factual point of view, time has not been kind to many aspects of this speech. The president's claim that German submarine warfare was "a war against all mankind" is not substantiated by America's experience in later wars. The submarine has been accepted as a legitimate naval weapon. There is no moral onus for using it in the only way that gives submariners a decent chance for survival against their surface enemies—torpedoing enemy ships without warning. This surprise-attack approach was the policy adopted by the U.S. Navy during World War II. No one, including America's Japanese or German enemies, called the practice a war against mankind.

Wilson's view of the submarine did not even survive the immediate aftermath of World War I. In 1923, Rear Admiral William Sims, wartime commander of U.S. naval forces in the European Theater, wrote in a magazine article that the "vast majority" of German submarine commanders were "decent seamen" who did not fire on defenseless men in open boats and generally acted humanely toward the survivors of sunken ships. Out of the thousands of sinkings during the war, Sims pointed out, only eighteen U-boat commanders were tried for a total of fifty-seven criminal acts after the war, and some of these were acquitted. A submarine commander who sank a hospital ship and then fired on the lifeboats was tried in Germany after the war and convicted.[91]

Wilson's argument becomes even weaker when we examine the statistics (which also confirm Sims's contention.) A total of 66 Americans died when four U.S. ships were sunk by submarines before war was declared. Another 131 were killed while sailing on British ships that were torpedoed, with the *Lusitania*'s 128 deaths accounting for most of these losses. Another thirteen American ships were sunk with no casualties. Even after war was declared, most of the ships sunk had no casualties. This hardly amounts to barbarism, much less a war against mankind.[92]

Equally invalidated by time and experience is Wilson's insistence that American citizens had a right to travel on British ships in the war zone, ignoring repeated warnings by Germany that this was a very dangerous thing to do. No such right exists or ever has existed in the history of naval warfare. Nor did U.S. merchant ships have an absolute right to sail into the war zone declared by Germany around the British Isles. If maritime access to a war zone were a right on a par with free speech and other clauses in the Bill of Rights, William Jennings Bryan, Robert La Follette and other idealistic antiwar leaders would never have urged the president to abrogate such traffic. President Thomas Jefferson, a fervent proponent of the Bill of Rights, banned such commerce in 1807 to keep the United States out of the world war then raging between France and England. Congress, overhauling the neutrality laws in the mid-1930s, passed by huge majorities laws forbidding both practices—laws that were signed without a word of criticism by Wilson's supposed political heir, Franklin D. Roosevelt.

Wilson not only insisted on the right of Americans to travel on belligerent ships, he did not hesitate to call anyone who challenged him on this assertion a traitor to the country. When a Texas congressman named Jeff McLemore sponsored a resolution forbidding Americans to travel on such ships, Wilson fought the measure as if it had originated with Kaiser Wilhelm. A hefty majority of the Democrats in Congress backed McLemore; Speaker of the House Champ Clark told the president the resolution would pass by 2 to 1. But Wilson, using threats of patronage cutoffs and desperate appeals to party loyalty, managed to defeat the proposal. Later he claimed that those who voted for it had failed the "acid test" of true patriotism.[93]

Even more dubious was Wilson's call for "a war without hate." He had watched the British and French tell thousands of lies to make the German army, the German people, and their leader, Kaiser Wilhelm, more hateful than any other nation in recorded history, give or take a few villains like the Mongols under Ghengis Khan. This tidal wave of hate had washed over Americans for almost three years. Did Wilson think he could make it disappear with a rhetorical flourish? Apparently he did.

A corollary to this sad illusion is Wilson's claim that the United States had no quarrel with the German people, only with their government. As Senator La Follette pointed out at the time, this idea came close to an absurdity. It would return to haunt Wilson in his conduct of the war on the home front and in his attempt to make peace abroad. The idea of distinguishing the people from their government came from Colonel House, who got it from Sir Edward Grey. House wanted Wilson to build a "backfire" against the German government in the minds of its own people. The don't-take-this-personally idea was also supposed to placate the German-Americans—something it signally failed to do.[94]

No one seemed aware—or to care—that many other Wilson phrases, such as a war to make the world safe for democracy, were already clichés in the speeches of British politicians and the propaganda of Wellington House. Wilson and America would eventually pay a price for this second-hand rhetoric and the naive idealism that lay behind it: British and French disdain.

Wilson's long resistance to joining the war that had already consumed so many hundreds of thousands of French and British lives had alienated the leadership of America's putative allies. In 1917 and early 1918, the president had repeatedly declared that he saw no difference between the warring powers from a moral or ethical point of view. The culmination of these statements was his "peace without victory" speech. These assertions infuriated the British and French, whose hate campaigns against Germany were predicated on their claim to moral superiority. Andrew Bonar Law, the leader of Britain's Conservative Party, snarled, "What Mr. Wilson is longing for we are fighting for." In Paris, the novelist Anatole France sneered, "Peace without victory is bread without yeast, jugged hare without wine, brill without capers, mushrooms without garlic . . . in brief, an insipid thing."[95]

In Washington, an exasperated Cecil Spring Rice ranted denunciations of Wilson's peace-without-victory policy at Secretary of State Lansing until the shocked secretary was forced to order the British ambassador to desist. When both sides spurned the president's proposal, Spring Rice told his superiors in London that it now seemed likely that the United States would finally "drift into the war." Not exactly a compliment to the president's decisiveness and leadership.

In the same letter, the British ambassador revealed a significant perception of the American public's state of mind. "All I can record for certain is that the vast majority of the country desire peace and would do a great deal to secure peace." The ambassador blamed this lack of enthusiasm for the war on Wilson's failure to wholeheartedly embrace the Allied cause.[96]

In March 1917, Colonel House and Sir William Wiseman, who was in the process of taking charge of British intelligence in the United States, prepared a memorandum for Prime Minister Lloyd George and his cabinet, aimed at giving them a realistic grasp of the U.S. political situation. Before Wiseman sent the statement to London, House persuaded President Wilson to read it and give it his covert approval. The memorandum amply confirmed Spring Rice's estimate of America's lack of enthusiasm for the war. It admitted that sympathy for the Allied cause was largely confined to what Wiseman and House called "broader-minded" Americans. The "mass of the people" were not ardent backers of the Allies. In fact, a substantial number were hostile to Great Britain because of its blockade of Germany, its blacklisting of U.S. firms, and its censorship of war news. Summing up, the memorandum declared: "The people of the United States wish to be entirely neutral as far as the European war is concerned. The Administration, however, have always understood the cause of the war and have been entirely sympathetic to the Allies."[97]

Did this mean that Wellington House's thirty-two months of hate propaganda had failed? By no means. The "broader-minded" Anglophile Americans were Germanophobes to a man—and woman. They controlled most of the press, the universities, the banks, the corporations and the levers of government. But the Spring Rice letter and the House–Wiseman memorandum confirmed the claims of La Follette and his followers in the Senate and House that many people, especially in the Midwest, had profound doubts about the declaration of war.

Ambivalence and barely concealed hostility abroad as well as substantial lack of enthusiasm at home lay just beneath the surface of America's crusade to make the world safe for democracy—along with a visceral hatred of all things German. An even more visceral hatred of Woodrow Wilson emanated from Theodore Roosevelt, Henry Cabot Lodge and their fellow

Republicans. They were convinced, in Roosevelt's words, that "the contrast between Wilson's conduct down to the declaration of war and his subsequent utterances cannot be overcome." As Lodge put it acidly to Roosevelt, if Wilson's speech declaring war was right, "everything he has done for two and a half years is fundamentally wrong."[98]

For the moment, Wilson's oratorical skills had obscured these harsh realities. But they were still there, not unlike the thousands of British mines in the North Sea blockading Germany that the president had ignored throughout the thirty-two months of America's neutrality. These hazards would soon produce a degree of instability in the ship of state beyond the imagination—or talents—of Philip Dru, administrator.

Chapter 3

ENLISTING VOLUNTEERS AND OTHER UNLIKELY EVENTS

The ink was scarcely dry on the declaration of war when Woodrow Wilson found out how little impression his soaring rhetoric and noble phrases had made on the leaders of the Republican Party. Still seething over the president's hairbreadth victory in November on the slogan "He kept us out of war," the GOP was in no mood to let Wilson use his somersault into the global struggle to increase his power and popularity.

On Monday, April 9, Senator John W. Weeks of Massachusetts rose to urge Congress to create a Joint Committee for the Conduct of the War to make sure that Wilson and his fellow Democrats were up to the job of winning victory. The committee, composed of five Democrats and five Republicans, would have the power to subpoena witnesses, from generals to cabinet secretaries to underlings, and inquire into every aspect of the war, from the battlefields to the boardrooms of the arms companies.

Wilson was horrified. As a historian, he had read about a similar committee that had operated during the Civil War, headed by two Radical Republican enemies of Abraham Lincoln, Senators Benjamin Wade and Zachariah Chandler. They had terrorized Lincoln's administration and tormented the army, often accusing defeated Union generals of being secret Confederate sympathizers and pushing their favorite officers, radical abolitionists like themselves, for promotions. Wilson had no doubt that Weeks planned to select anti-Wilson Democrats such as Nebraska's Senator Gilbert Hitchcock for his committee. They would not be hard to find. The president's abrupt switch from neutrality to war had left many members of his party discomfited, even though most had voted for the war resolution.

Wilson rushed from the White House to the Capitol and personally sought out members of the Senate Rules Committee, who controlled the process of bringing legislation to the floor for a vote. He persuaded the Democratic majority on the committee to bury the Weeks proposal. The agitated president preferred this covert suppression to letting the idea come before the full Senate, which almost certainly would have voted for it.

Only seven days after his oratorical triumph, Wilson was forced to admit he had less than wholehearted support in the national legislature. He also had to worry about the near certainty that Weeks would revive his proposal if the war effort floundered.[1]

II

This minicrisis was only a symptom of Wilson's legislative woes. An even more vivid glimpse of trouble ahead had come three days earlier, on April 6, when a war department aide, Major Palmer S. Pierce, testified before the Senate Finance Committee about the army's request for $3 billion to fight the war. The chairman of the committee, Senator Thomas S. Martin of Virginia, was also the Senate majority leader. Martin scowled at Pierce and asked him to explain how the army was going to spend this stupendous sum, the equivalent of at least $50 billion in 2002 dollars. Pierce began listing how much it cost to build training camps and to buy rifles, artillery, airplanes—then added nervously, "And we may have to have an army in France."

"Good Lord!" Martin said. "You're not going to send soldiers over there, are you?"[2]

Few comments better exemplify the almost incredible naïveté that underlay the U.S. decision to declare war on Germany. Were the Americans going to send an army to France? No one in the War Department seemed to have a clue. Nor did President Wilson, the supposed prophet who purportedly told Cobb of the *World* how much anguish and turmoil the war would cause America. Wilson added to this overall impression by insisting that the United States had not joined the Triple Entente as an ally, but as "an associated power."

On April 6, 1917, the U.S. Army numbered 127,588 men, roughly the same size as the army of Chile. On paper, there were also 80,446 men in the National Guard. When these men were summoned to the Rio Grande in 1916 to protect the border against Mexican guerrillas, appalling numbers of them flunked army physical examinations—and a great many failed to show up. Senator Weeks told Congress on April 23, 1917: "A very considerable percentage—probably as many as one half—had never fired a rifle and nearly as [many] had never had an hour's drill."[3]

As late as February 1917, both Wilson and Secretary of War Newton Baker had issued statements in favor of voluntary enlistment. Wilson had made only a passing reference in his April 2 speech to his switch to conscription. He obviously failed to convince Congress that such a move was wise or necessary. On April 18, the House Military Affairs Committee reported out a bill that repudiated the president's plan. By a 13 to 8 vote, the committee recommended a volunteer system. The bill was supported by Speaker Champ Clark, who delivered a fiery denunciation of a draft: "I protest with all my heart and mind and soul against having the slur of being a conscript placed upon the men of Missouri."[4]

House Majority Leader Claude Kitchin, who had voted against the war resolution, was even more vehemently opposed to a draft. The chairman of the Military Affairs Committee, S. Hubert Dent, Jr., of Alabama had made his opinion clear by refusing to bring the bill to the floor, handing the task to the ranking Republican on the committee. Dent insisted the government should try to raise an army of volunteers before resorting to the draft. Senator Thomas W. Hardwick of Georgia introduced a bill that barred draftees from serving overseas. Throughout the South, the idea of drafting Negroes and putting guns in their hands caused widespread hysteria. One North Carolina congressman told Wilson there was no hope of passing the bill unless a volunteer system was tried first.

In the Senate, Jim Reed of Missouri predicted the streets would "run red with blood" if Congress voted for conscription. Senator Robert La Follette warned that the power, once granted, would be attached to the office of the president, "no matter how ambitious or bloody-minded he may be." The Senate Armed Services Committee voted out their version of a conscription bill 8 to 7, with five of the ten Democrats against it, enabling the Republicans to claim credit for rescuing the measure. An alarmed Joe Tumulty told the president, "There is almost panic in our ranks." He meant the ranks of the Democratic Party.[5]

Adding immensely to the furor was the voice of former president Theodore Roosevelt, who was not in the least discouraged by the U.S. Army's attempt to stifle his plan to raise a volunteer division. On April 10, Roosevelt went to the White House to ask Wilson's approval. The two men, by this time ingrained political enemies, managed a surface cordiality. According to Roosevelt, he told Wilson that he only wanted to make the president's war message "good." It had to be translated into "fact" before it would rank as a great state paper. Roosevelt wanted to persuade the nation "to live up to the speech."[6]

It would be hard to imagine a more disastrous approach to a man who regarded his oratory as the very essence of his presidency. Wilson did not think his speech needed any help from Roosevelt, and he was not about to let the hero of San Juan Hill tell the country and the world that TR had been assigned this task by the man he had called a Byzantine logothete.

Nevertheless, Wilson listened patiently to Roosevelt's plan. The volunteer division would be composed of the cream of American manhood. TR had already persuaded Major General Leonard Wood, former army chief of staff and a leading prewar spokesman for preparedness, to add his professional expertise. There would be a German-American regiment to demonstrate that group's patriotism, and a black regiment, with white officers. Descendants of Civil War and Revolutionary War heroes had already volunteered—a Lee, a Jackson, a Sheridan. French nobility, in memory of the services of the Marquis de Lafayette, would serve on the staff. Dozens of young regular army officers were offering to whip these amateurs into fighting soldiers. They would be ready for the trenches of the Western Front by September 1, 1917.

Afterward, according to Joe Tumulty's memoir, Wilson said that Roosevelt was "a great big boy" and claimed he was charmed by his personality. Tumulty added that the president was inclined to overrule the general staff and let Roosevelt have his division. This comment was another attempt to put in Wilson's mouth emotions and ideas that Tumulty wished Wilson shared. The historical record indicates that Roosevelt's push for his volunteer division played a crucial role in Wilson's decision to back conscription.[7]

This much is certain—there was no hint of reciprocal charm in the way Wilson handled Roosevelt's proposal. He used a technique that the British Foreign Office had perfected on American protests against the blockade of Germany: the silent stall.

Meanwhile, Congress began debating the conscription bill. Roosevelt, getting the message from Wilson's silence, was soon telling reporters that he found "great confusion" in the president's mind. He had been forced to explain in almost embarrassing detail why the division was important and how it would work. The implication was all too clear: Wilson, the logothete, the man of words, could not grasp the thinking of Roosevelt, the man of action.[8]

In Congress, the anti-drafters turned to Roosevelt's volunteer division as a perfect excuse to oppose conscription. "If Roosevelt or any other Pied Piper can whistle 25,000 fanatics after him, for Heaven's sake give him a chance," cried Representative Augustus Peabody Gardner of Massachusetts, Henry Cabot Lodge's son-in-law. The remark again revealed the naive assurance that there was no compelling need to send a large number of American soldiers to fight on the Western Front.[9]

TR's voter appeal was still tremendous. Soon, an alarmed Secretary of War Baker was forced to write to Roosevelt, publicly rejecting his volunteer division and urging him to desist. Congress's refusal to pass the conscription bill was brewing a national crisis. Baker might have added that enlistments, which were by no means barred during this uproar, were negligible—a mere 73,000 men had volunteered for the army out of a potential pool of 10 million. Only the U.S. Navy was getting all the men it wanted. This was further evidence of the widespread assumption that there would be no U.S. Army in Europe and that the navy was the only place where a man was likely to see action.[10]

Roosevelt's response was a ferocious public letter to Baker, denying his plan interfered with the draft, which he favored. He lectured the secretary on the "moral effect" of sending his volunteers to France and sneered at Baker's argument that it would be wiser to train an American army at home, while the Allies did all the fighting with U.S. money and munitions. Roosevelt was intimating that this was more of the gutless cowardice endemic in the White House and the rest of the Wilson administration. In a final blast, the former president denounced the entire Army general staff as a bunch of red-tape-entangled numskulls, who would not recognize a good idea if it ran over them.[11]

Neither Baker nor Wilson could have been consoled by the rain of criticism that descended on them from around the country and abroad. Roosevelt was enormously popular in France and England, thanks to his long-running call for U.S. participation in the war. Numerous prominent figures in both countries bombarded the White House with protesting telegrams. Roosevelt, encouraged by this praise of his brainchild, expanded his proposal from a division to an army corps of 200,000 volunteers. General Wood would be in command, and Teddy would be satisfied to lead a division. Roosevelt's four sons proclaimed their readiness to fight beside their warrior father.[12]

For a while, it looked as if Roosevelt would get his way. On April 28, Republican Senator Warren Harding of Ohio added an amendment to the conscription bill, directing Wilson to let Roosevelt raise 100,000 volunteers. The proposal passed, 56 to 31, with Democrats deserting the president in droves. A delighted Roosevelt sent a telegram to Harding, congratulating him for his "patriotic work." But TR's celebration was premature. In the House of Representatives, many conservative Republicans had never forgiven Roosevelt for bolting the party in 1912 to run for president on the Progressive ticket, handing the election to Wilson. Added to these recalcitrants was the bloc of antiwar representatives around Congressman James R. Mann. This group was disinclined to forgive Roosevelt for calling them traitors when they supported Wilson in his peace-without-victory phase. When the Roosevelt amendment came to a vote, it lost by a decisive 170 to 106.

The congressmen, in one of those about-faces that frequently surprise outsiders, now voted overwhelmingly in favor of the administration's conscription bill, 313 to 109. This inspired the Senate to do a similar 180-degree turn and approve the measure 81 to 8. But when the two houses tried to harmonize the bills in a conference, another huge wrangle erupted over Roosevelt's continued pursuit of his volunteer corps. His persistence won him not a little criticism in the press and a public rebuke by the Army League of the United States, a clone of the pro-war Navy League. Roosevelt blasted the Army League for playing petty politics on Wilson's behalf. Anyone else who said he was interfering with the president's wishes was guilty of "hysteria." In the conference, three Republican senators deserted Teddy, and the Harding amendment was dropped from the bill.

Senator Henry Cabot Lodge, by this time alarmed over growing criticism in the newspapers, urged Roosevelt to give up. The former president grudgingly agreed. Whereupon the House of Representatives, obviously hoping to placate Roosevelt's supporters in the electorate, did another about-face and voted 215 to 178 to give Roosevelt some sort of independent command. This reversal produced another week of wrangling in the conference committee, which finally solved the matter by passing the conscription bill and giving Wilson the authority to commission TR and his volunteers if he so desired—something every man, woman and child over the age of six knew was never going to happen.[13]

It was now May 17, six weeks since Wilson had made his war speech. That afternoon, John M. Parker of Louisiana visited the White House. One of the South's major political figures, he had been nominated as vice president by the Progressive Party in 1916. When Roosevelt decided not to run as a Progressive, Parker had campaigned for Wilson and helped him carry several key states. Parker urged the president to give Roosevelt his division and put General Wood in charge of it: "I beg of you . . . at this crisis not to play politics!" he said.

Wilson kept his temper and replied that it was the Republicans who were playing politics: "I do not propose to have politics in any manner, shape or form influence me in my judgment."[14]

The truth—or lack thereof—in those words was demonstrated within twenty-four hours, when Wilson refused to appoint two men to important posts in the War Department, because they were Republicans. One of them was Henry L. Stimson, President Taft's secretary of war. Stimson would have to wait until another war with Germany to win an appointment from a Democratic president. For the present, he satisfied his martial ardor by joining the fighting army as a colonel in the Seventy-Seventh Division.[15]

The president signed the conscription bill on May 18, and added a public rejection of Roosevelt as a volunteer general. "This is not the time for any action not calculated to contribute to the immediate success of the war," Wilson intoned. "The business now in hand is undramatic, practical, and of scientific definiteness and precision."[16]

This rejection surely has to be one of Wilson's strangest utterances. He made the war sound like something that was going to happen in a laboratory. It was not what those who opposed conscription wanted to hear. They still feared that blood would run in the streets on draft registration day. Wilson was responding to those who had opposed volunteerism, because, in Walter Lippmann's words, to make it work would require a newspaper campaign that "manufactured hatred," in the style of the British press. A prominent Boston banking house had made a similar argument in a circular letter, claiming that volunteers could only be obtained by letting the press stir up "an unjustified sense of crisis," which would be bad for the stock market. Once more, we see these insiders assuming that the war was as good as won by the Allies—and Wilson agreeing with them. All concerned were also covertly admitting that enthusiasm for the war was neither deep nor widespread.[17]

In the evening of May 18, Henry Cabot Lodge and two Republican senatorial colleagues visited Wilson in the White House. The atmosphere was superficially cordial. They talked for almost two hours, discussing how to get food to the Allies as fast as possible without causing shortages in the United States, which had experienced two poor wheat harvests in a row. Another topic was censorship—how to deal with war news, good and bad, and with antiwar opinion. Lodge was in an arrogant mood. He and his colleagues enjoyed telling Wilson "some truths which he ought to have heard from those who surround him. . . . Without the Republicans he could not get his legislation." The wrangle over the conscription bill made that fact very clear.

More important than politics was Lodge's personal reaction to Wilson: "I watched and studied his face tonight as I have often done before—a curious mixture of acuteness, intelligence and extreme underlying timidity—a shifty, furtive sinister expression can always be detected by a good observer."[18]

More than political partisanship separated these two men. Lodge was a strong advocate of U.S. involvement in world affairs. From his election as senator in 1893, his greatest ambition was to become chairman of the Senate Foreign Relations Committee. He saw an active foreign policy as crucial to forming America's national character.

Lodge believed that American idealism could become a more significant force in world affairs than the often "sordid" imperialism of Britain, France and Russia. He was also a strong advocate of some sort of international organization that would keep the peace. In 1915, in a speech to Union College's commencement exercises, he said world peace could only be maintained by "united nations" that were willing to use force when necessary.[19]

For Lodge the worst foreign policy sin was inaction and pale neutrality. During the first 2½ years of World War I, Wilson seemed to embody these vices. Wilson's claim that the United States was "too proud to fight" (in a speech after the *Lusitania* sinking) and his pursuit of peace without victory had struck Lodge as close to blasphemy. The declaration of war had not changed his opinion of the president's character.[20]

III

There was another reason why Wilson did not consider it his job to arouse patriotic enthusiasm for volunteerism—or conscription. He had found the right man for this formidable task, and he was already hard at work. His name was George Creel.

A native of Missouri, the forty-one-year-old Creel often styled himself as "the original Wilson man." He had boomed Wilson to run for president as early as 1905, when he was still presiding over Princeton University. At that time, Creel was a muckraking journalist of some renown and a political dreamer who liked to think big. He was also not given to moderation. A journalist friend said: "To Creel there are only two classes of men. There are skunks and the greatest man who ever lived. The greatest man is plural and includes everyone who is on Creel's side in whatever public issue he happens to be concerned with." In a rare moment of candor, Creel admitted this description was not entirely wrong.

In the 1916 campaign, Creel had written a book, *Wilson and the Issues,* and worked hard for the president's reelection. A few days after war was declared, Wilson summoned Creel to the White House to discuss how to deal with the information side of the conflict. In Britain and France, iron censorship was the rule and the generals and admirals in the State, War and Navy Building were demanding a similar setup in the United States. Creel told Wilson it was not *supp*ression but *ex*pression that the country needed. Public opinion about the war had been "muddled," Creel said, by the thirty-two-month battle between German and Allied propaganda. Creel recommended forming a Committee on Public Information that would handle the war news and inspire Americans to see the struggle as a patriotic crusade.[21]

The idea jibed with an approach to news that Wilson had long favored. In his first term, his attempts to ingratiate himself with the Washington press corps had been an egregious failure. Most reporters, he had concluded, were only interested in "the personal and trivial rather than in principles and politics." He had eventually abandoned press conferences and given Joe Tumulty the job of dealing with newsmen. For a while Wilson toyed with the idea of creating a government publicity bureau that would dispense the "real facts" while the newspapers supposedly continued to distort and trivialize them.[22]

The Committee on Public Information would, Wilson hoped, be the realization of this dubious dream. He made Creel chairman of the enterprise. To bolster his authority, Wilson added three cabinet members to the committee, Secretary of State Lansing, Secretary of War Baker and Secretary of the Navy Daniels. Chairman Creel held one meeting with these gentlemen, listened gravely to their advice, and never conferred with them again. "The Committee on Public Information was George Creel," wrote Mark Sullivan, a fellow newspaperman who knew him well. "It continued to be George Creel after a hundred and fifty thousand people were taking part in its incredibly varied and far flung activities."[23]

Creel's goal was to create the "war will." In a democracy, he believed, this will depended on "the degree to which each one of all the people of that democracy can concentrate and consecrate body and soul and spirit in a supreme effort of spirit and sacrifice." That consecration could only be achieved by creating "a passionate belief in the justice of America's cause that [would] meld the people of the United States into one white hot mass instinct with fraternity, devotion, courage and deathless determination." The feverish prose was typical Creel.[24]

Creel was also not shy about playing politics. When the Vigilantes, a patriotic organization that had been fighting for preparedness, offered Creel the services of some eighty leading writers, the former muckraker replied: "We don't want you. You're all Roosevelt men!" Creel was not planning to share his fiefdom with anyone.[25]

Reports from British agents in the United States to Wellington House made it clear that a patriotic state of mind was virtually nonexistent in the United States two months after Wilson's war message. "There is evidence that in many localities the people have only entered the war with reluctance and with a feeling of inevitability rather than with any enthusiasm," wrote the author of the *American Press Résumé* on May 23, 1917. Joe Tumulty nervously informed Colonel House that "the people's 'righteous wrath' seems not to have been aroused." The widespread lack of enthusiasm observed by British Ambassador Cecil Spring Rice and intelligence chief William Wiseman before Wilson's April 2 speech was obviously not overdrawn. [26]

A few days after Creel began to organize his committee, a young man named Donald Ryerson of Chicago burst into his office and told Creel that he headed a group of volunteer speakers who were making patriotic talks in movie theaters. In ten minutes, Creel escalated the idea to a national effort dubbed Four Minute Men, and put Ryerson in charge of it. From its first days, Creel said with typical hyperbole, the Four Minute Men "had the projectile force of a French .75" (the French army's favorite artillery piece). Soon, tens of thousands of these local orators were at work.

In movie theaters across the nation, a glass slide was thrown on the curtain before or after the main feature.

> FOUR MINUTE MEN
> [Name of speaker]
> Will speak four minutes on a subject
> of national importance.
> He speaks under the authority of
> THE COMMITTEE ON PUBLIC INFORMATION
> GEORGE CREEL, CHAIRMAN
> WASHINGTON, D.C.[27]

The Creel committee sent the Four Minute Men various bulletins about the state of the war effort, including several sample speeches written by top advertising copywriters on the committee's staff. The speakers were warned against stereotyped oratory and urged to transform the material into personal statements whenever possible. They soon expanded their operations from movie theaters to lodge and labor union meetings, church halls, lumber camps, and even Native American reservations. Before the war ended, no less than 75,000 Four Minute Men would be orating on Creel-assigned topics, aimed at creating a white-hot war will.[28]

The first topic, on which the volunteer orators spoke from May 12 to May 21, was "Universal Service by Selective Draft." The goal was to infuse draft registration day, June 5, 1917, with moral uplift. The orators were working in tandem with Secretary Baker, who was striving to make the draft palatable. Long before Congress finally passed the bill, he was printing the 10 million forms on which the draftees would register. He wanted to make registration similar to going to the polls to vote.

Baker also did his utmost to keep the army out of sight. The selection of the registered men would be handled by local citizens, under the direction of state governors. On the day Wilson signed the bill, Baker persuaded him to issue a sonorous proclamation, calling on Americans to make registration a "great day of patriotic devotion and obligation." He hoped his fellow citizens would see to it that "every [eligible] male person" was included on "these lists of honor."

The president was telling Americans to report anyone who tried to dodge the obligation. But this unpleasant directive was largely buried beneath the speeches of the Four Minute Men and the complementary oratory urged by Baker on mayors and chambers of commerce throughout the nation. As often as possible, the word "service" was substituted for the harsher "conscription." It was a word that blended nicely with the ideals of progressive reform that had swept the nation in the decade before the war.[29]

Behind the patriotic rhetoric, a mailed fist was also at work. In Snyder, Texas, seven men were arrested on May 22 and charged with seditious conspiracy for "planning to resist conscription by force." Similar arrests took place in Michigan, Illinois, Washington and other states. A Mexican-American was arrested in Los Angeles. Socialists—antiwar to a man—were jailed in Detroit and Cleveland. When two men tried to get a court order to prevent the governor of Missouri from enforcing registration, they also wound up behind bars. In New York, three men were arrested for passing out antidraft literature. Two of them ended up in the federal penitentiary in Atlanta. On May 25, the *Los Angeles Times* ran a headline: "Death for Treason Awaits Anti-Draft Plotters." A week later, the same paper reported that the nation's ports were under surveillance to make sure no one fled abroad to escape registration.[30]

The result of this mixture of exhortation and intimidation was a success that astonished Baker and Wilson and everyone else. Very little blood ran in the streets. In most towns and cities, almost 10 million men registered without a murmur of protest. Resistance was sporadic and widely scattered.

In Butte, Montana, where there was a large Irish-American enclave, six hundred members of a club named after two Easter Rebellion martyrs marched behind a twelve-foot-long red banner inscribed "Down with War!" The protesters were confronted by local militia with fixed bayonets.

In the ensuing melee, shots were fired and about twenty men were arrested. The city was put under martial law. In two Oklahoma counties, a mix of white tenant farmers, blacks and Native Americans fought a pitched battle with sheriff's deputies before fleeing into the hills.[31]

These dissenters amounted to no more than ripples in the immense stream of 9.5 million unprotesting registrants. Baker and Creel had pulled off a feat of national persuasion that was little less than awesome. One explanation may be the words of a Texas father, who was asked why he was ready to let his son fight in a foreign war: "I'd rather have my son go to heaven in France than to hell in America!" Another explanation may be glimpsed in a comment in the *New York Times*: "The Selective Service Draft gives a long and sorely needed means of disciplining a certain rather insolent foreign element in the nation."[32]

Hyphenates, beware!

IV

In Congress, while the Four Minute Men were preaching acceptance of the draft in the American heartland, another brawl raged over an "omnibus bill" that gave the president wide powers to deal with spies, saboteurs and other forms of subversion; to control exports of materials that might be needed for the war effort; and to bar "treasonous" materials from the mail. The quarrel erupted when senators spotted in the middle of the bureaucratese the president's demand for the power to censor the nation's newspapers. Almost as infuriating was an appropriation of $100 million to fund the Committee on Public Information—with no accounting to Congress on how this large sum would be spent. Republicans—and many newspapers—were already viewing Creel's committee as a Wilson publicity machine.

Woodrow Wilson's low opinion of the press and fears of its supposed distortions had not been assuaged by George Creel's arguments in favor of government expression. The president's demand for censorship powers had Democratic support, but Republican progressives such as Senator Hiram Johnson of California went berserk over this attempt to repeal the First Amendment. Predictably, the *New York Times* and other papers agreed, calling the "spy" bill a tyrannous measure.[33]

Another political disaster began taking shape before the White House staff's appalled eyes. Tumulty and other Wilson advisers begged the president to consult with leading figures in the press to create a censorship board composed of (presumably) patriotic newsmen. Instead, Wilson wrote a letter to the *New York Times*, declaring that press censorship was "absolutely necessary to the public safety." He was backed by Attorney General Thomas W. Gregory, Postmaster General Albert Burleson, and Secretary of State Robert Lansing, who added to the uproar by forbidding State Department employees to speak to reporters under any circumstances. Gregory topped this indiscretion by circulating a memorandum to the Justice Department, warning that many newspapers had been infiltrated by German sympathizers. The outrage of the major papers, most of which had led the cry for war, was spectacular.[34]

After weeks of wrangling, in which the president was repeatedly described as a would-be tyrant by the Republicans, Congress finally voted down the sweeping censorship powers Wilson demanded. But the lawmakers left in the hands of the postmaster general the authority to decide which newspapers were seditious and liable to prosecution. The Committee on Public Information also emerged with its power to control official war news largely intact. Even more worrisome—and largely ignored by the bill's opponents—was a passage stating that anyone who made "false reports or false statements with the intent to interfere with the operation or success of the military or naval forces" or interfered with the recruiting of these forces would be subject to a $10,000 fine and twenty years in jail.

These words would soon inflict misery on thousands of Americans. The sponsors of the bill brushed aside worries about free speech expressed by some members of Congress. They were told that "policies of the government and [the] acts of its officers" would always be open to criticism. Only makers of "willfully false" statements would be prosecuted.[35]

V

On June 15, 1917, Wilson signed the Espionage Bill, as it was now called, in spite of its lack of censorship powers. He and Congress might have continued wrangling over this explosive issue and the powers of Creel's committee for the rest of the summer. But a new sense of urgency was injected into the national mood by the arrival of missions from France and England to discuss their nations' military and financial needs. England's was led by former prime minister Arthur Balfour, now foreign secretary in the war cabinet of Prime Minister David Lloyd George. Smooth-tongued and exuding charm, Balfour made a favorable impression on everybody except the Irish independence men, who hated him for his savage repression when he was chief secretary for Ireland.

France's group was headed by former premier René Viviani, who was known as the William Jennings Bryan of France for his fervid oratory. His behavior did not win friends or influence people. When a manicurist failed to keep a 6 A.M. appointment, Viviani flew into such a rage, people wondered if the alliance were about to collapse. The orator announced he would address the Senate—but only if President Wilson was in the audience. Whereupon he spoke in French. The newspapers and the administration gave up on him and made portly Marshal Joseph "Papa" Joffre the star attraction. This affable soldier had been puffed to mythic proportions for stopping the German drive on Paris in 1914. Since then, Joffre had killed even more men than Field Marshal Haig in futile offenses. In early 1917, Papa had been promoted to field marshal and retired to dining out on his past glory.[36]

An alert observer might have spotted a symptom of trouble in the peculiar way the French and British missions operated. They barely spoke to each other. They preferred to talk separately to the Americans. Eventually, however, both the king's men and the heirs of Napoleon Bonaparte informed the astonished Americans that they were on the brink of collapse. The U-boats were sinking 900,000 tons of shipping a month, threatening England with starvation. The French army was in a funk after another failed offensive in April 1917, under a new commander, General Robert Nivelle, who had the Haig-Joffre genius for mass slaughter. Behind the murk of censorship and Wellington House's miasma of hate and bunk, the Germans were winning the war.

What was the answer? Besides massive infusions of American cash into their depleted exchequers, both the French and the British wanted men—the quicker the better. There was no need to train the raw American youths who would soon peacefully register for selective service. British General G. T. M. "Tommy" Bridges urged U.S. Chief of Staff Scott to send "five hundred thousand untrained men at once to our depots in England to be trained there, and drafted into our armies in France."[37]

An appalled General Tasker H. Bliss, the army's assistant chief of staff, told Secretary of War Baker: "When the war is over it may be a literal fact that the American flag may not have appeared anywhere on the line because our organizations will simply be parts of battalions and regiments of their Entente Allies. . . . I have received the impression from English and French officers that such is their deliberate desire."

When Bliss and Chief of Staff Scott expressed doubts about this approach, the British suggested letting them recruit volunteers in the United States, with the help of their propaganda machine. (By this time, Wellington House had been replaced by a bigger and more aggressive government department devoted to official lies.) Backing up the British negotiators was a cable from Prime Minister David Lloyd George: "It is vital that American troops of all arms be poured into France as soon as possible." The April 2 antiwar protester whose placard read, "Is this the United States of Great Britain?" would seem to have been onto something.[38]

VI

The Allied panic was profoundly embarrassing to President Wilson and his advisers—so embarrassing that it was never revealed to the American people. Aside from casting further doubt on Wilson's prophetic conversation with Frank Cobb of the *New York World*, it forces us to ask what impact this revelation had on Woodrow Wilson. Almost certainly, it inflicted a terrible wound in Wilson's self-image as a president. It also shook his confidence in Colonel House, his supposedly all-knowing, roving diplomatic representative. Wilson struggled to deny this wound, to reassert his confidence in his presidential judgment. But the realization that American soldiers would have to die in possibly huge numbers to gain him a place at the peace table soon flowered in Wilson's subconscious as gnawing guilt.

This guilt was intensified by another revelation that Foreign Minister Arthur Balfour made to the president in the privacy of the White House. He told Wilson about a number of secret treaties that the Allies had signed. Russia had been promised Constantinople, a prize for which it had hungered for centuries. France was to regain its lost province of Alsace-Lorraine and a chunk of Germany's mineral-rich Saar basin. The French would also divide Turkey's Mediterranean empire and Germany's African colonies with England.

Japan was promised Berlin's Far East colonies, including control of China's Shantung peninsula, hitherto a German preserve. The crudest and most blatant payoff went to Italy for deciding to enter the war in 1915. Rome was to get the Austrian South Tyrol and Trieste regions in the north as well as control of the Dalmatian coast on the east side of the Adriatic Sea and some colonies in Africa. For Wilson, it must have been profoundly disturbing to discover behind the facade of his noble war for democracy the hoary tradition of who gets what.[39]

At first, Wilson was inclined to insist on a revocation of these testaments to imperial greed before the Allies got another dollar of U.S. aid or before a single American soldier headed for Europe. But Colonel House, his Anglophilia never more nakedly exposed, persuaded the president that such a blunt approach would disrupt the war effort—and victory had become the only thing that mattered. Wilson reluctantly assented; from a practical point of view, House was right. But the decision added another dimension to the guilt that began to fester in Woodrow Wilson's psyche.[40]

Meanwhile, on the practical side, the frantic demand for American soldiers suggested that Theodore Roosevelt was right. There was an urgent need to get some Yanks into the front lines in France to lift the morale, if not fill the ranks, of the reeling British and French armies. This discomfiting truth was underscored by a telegram from Georges Clemenceau, soon to become premier of France, urging Wilson to reconsider and give Roosevelt his volunteer force. The president and the general staff remained united in their opposition to Teddy. But they realized if some sort of American expeditionary force were to go overseas, they had better find a commander for it, fast.

By far the best-known soldier on the horizon was Major General Leonard Wood. Chief of Staff Hugh Scott admired him so extravagantly that, when war was declared, he offered to resign so Wood could take his job. Wood's chief liability was his tendency to play politics. He had joined Theodore Roosevelt to campaign for preparedness while Wilson had been talking neutrality. In January the president told Baker he had "no confidence in General Wood's discretion or his loyalty to his superiors." George Creel voiced a typically over-the-top opinion: "Wood ought to be shot for treason!"[41]

Down in Texas was another major general, who had led Wilson's Punitive Expedition into Mexico in pursuit of the revolutionary leader Pancho Villa for shooting up a New Mexico border town and murdering many other Americans elsewhere. Ramrod straight at fifty-seven, with a brush mustache and a hawkish countenance, John Pershing had not a few things to recommend him. He had led a company of African-American soldiers up San Juan Hill in 1898 alongside Roosevelt's Rough Riders. In the Philippines, he had pacified the island of Mindinao in a deft campaign against fierce Moro tribesmen with the loss of only a handful of men. In 1905, he had married Helen Frances Warren, daughter of Republican Senator Francis E. Warren of Wyoming, who at that time was chairman of the Senate Military Affairs Committee.

Pershing had some liabilities. He was a friend if not a political ally of Theodore Roosevelt, who had promoted him to brigadier general over 862 senior officers. Some of these infuriated gentlemen had spread a whispering campaign that Pershing had fathered several illegitimate children in the Philippines; the story had gotten into the newspapers and Pershing had been forced to obtain affidavits from loyal friends to support his denials. When he was proposed for superintendent of West Point a few years later, an angry newspaper campaign based on these Philippine accusations had killed the appointment.

Pershing's largest liability, however, was an act of fate. On the night of August 27, 1915, a smoky fire had broken out in his family's quarters in the Presidio, outside San Francisco. He had been in El Paso, Texas, trying to keep the Mexican border quiet. Helen Warren Pershing and her three daughters were asphyxiated. A son, Warren, was rescued by an orderly. A man with such a tragedy in his immediate past might seem a dubious candidate for high command. But Pershing had endured the loss with public stoicism; only a handful of close friends and family knew the depths of his grief.[42]

Pershing had performed well in Mexico, except for a tendency to say unkind things about Wilson's refusal to let him pursue Pancho Villa all the way to Mexico City if necessary. He had ceased these after-dinner diatribes when warned by Hugh Scott. There was no doubt that Pershing wanted the new command. In February, after Wilson had recalled the Punitive Expedition without catching Villa, Pershing summoned to his tent some reporters who had been on the campaign and said: "We have broken diplomatic relations with Germany. That means we will send an expedition abroad. I'd like to command it. Each of you must know some way you can help me. Now tell me how I can help you so you can help me."[43]

In his memoirs, Pershing would later claim: "I had scarcely given a thought to being chosen as commander in chief of our forces abroad." In

1917, he thought of little else. He wrote to Chief of Staff Scott, saying he was eager to go overseas. The day after Wilson's war message, Pershing wrote Secretary of War Baker, fulsomely praising the president's speech and adding that he was "prepared for the duties of this hour." On May 2, 1917, Pershing's pulses must have leaped when he received a telegram from his father-in-law, Senator Warren, asking if he could speak French. Pershing immediately wired that he had spent several months in France in 1908 and had learned to speak the language well. He was sure he could quickly "reacquire [a] satisfactory working knowledge."[44]

The next day, May 3, Pershing got a telegram from Hugh Scott, informing him that the War Department had decided to send four infantry regiments and one artillery regiment to France from Pershing's department. The Wilson administration was still hoping that a token expeditionary force would mollify the French and British and raise their morale. By May 10, Pershing was in Washington to discuss matters with Scott.[45]

The conversation left Pershing dismayed at the army's almost total lack of preparation for a major war. The United States had only 285,000 Springfield rifles, 450 light field guns and 150 heavy guns in its armories. "It had been apparent to everybody for months that we were likely to be forced into the war," Pershing later wrote, "and a state of war had existed for several weeks, yet scarcely a start had made for our participation. . . . The War Department seemed to be suffering from a kind of inertia."

Pershing's chief competitor for his job, General Leonard Wood, emphatically agreed. After a visit the previous week, Wood confided to his diary: "War Dept. Dead Sea lively in comparison. . . . Scott helpless."[46]

Another glimpse of what was wrong with the War Department comes from a recollection of Secretary of War Baker. Arriving at the State, War and Navy Building one morning in April 1917, he learned from a puzzled aide that the basement was filled with typewriters—no less than 12,000 of them. The adjutant general, Brigadier General Henry P. McCain, had proclaimed them his property.

Baker asked General McCain why typewriters were overflowing the basement. Were they going to fight the war with typewriters?

"No, Mr. Secretary," McCain chortled. But the declaration of war had alerted him to the certainty that there would be fierce competition for typewriters in Washington, and he had laid his hands on "every free typewriter in the United States."

Baker had to explain to McCain that in wartime it might be a good idea to share some of his typewriters with the navy, the Quartermaster Department, and maybe even with the army's bête noire, the Marine Corps. McCain went away disgruntled. He was typical of the army's bureau chiefs, who regarded their departments as semi-independent fiefdoms over which the general staff had little authority. To make matters worse, most of these men were pushing seventy, having risen to power in the army's rigid seniority system. In the words of a young captain named George C. Marshall, who would rise to fame in another war with Germany, they had all "ceased mental development years before."[47]

Pershing was more encouraged by his meeting with Secretary of War Baker. His first glimpse did not enthuse the general. Baker looked "diminutive" in a large office chair, sitting with one leg curled up beneath him, the other dangling several inches from the floor. But Pershing soon found himself liking the little man's decisive manner and crisp style. Baker said his reading in the history of the Civil War had convinced him that civilian superiors should give generals the authority to fight the war their way and back them up when they needed political support. Pershing left the meeting feeling he had found an important friend.

Pershing did his best to participate in decisions that would affect his mission. He cast an emphatic vote against the amalgamation of the American army into the French and British armies. Baker was convinced and persuaded an uncertain Wilson to back the general. After some hesitation, Pershing also cast a more covert vote against giving his old friend Theodore Roosevelt any role overseas—something that no doubt pleased Wilson.

By this time, Roosevelt was resigned to his rejection and on May 20 wrote Pershing a warm letter, congratulating him on his appointment to command the expeditionary force. The former president asked Pershing if his two sons, Theodore, Jr., twenty-seven, and Archibald, twenty-three, could serve under the general. They had spent two previous summers training at a preparedness camp set up by Roosevelt and General Wood at Plattsburgh, New York. The president had announced that only regular officers would go with Pershing's division. If this rule remained in force, TR said both young men were prepared to serve in the enlisted ranks.

Roosevelt added a touching postscript, saying that if he were not "old and heavy and stiff," he would volunteer as a sergeant. Pershing replied with a promise that he would send for Ted and Archie as soon as possible.[48]

On May 24, two weeks after Pershing arrived in Washington, Secretary Baker took the general to meet Woodrow Wilson for the first time. Although the president was cordial, his conversation was surprisingly superficial. He did not say a word about what was happening in France, nor did he give even a hint of how he thought Pershing should deal with the panicky Allies and their demand for amalgamation.[49]

Four days later, on an afternoon so rainy and foggy that the Statue of Liberty and the New York skyline were invisible, Pershing and a staff of 191 officers and men sailed for Europe on the SS *Baltic*. Although the departure was supposedly top secret, a battery on Governors Island fired a salute—another example of the U.S. Army's reluctance to admit it was fighting a serious war.[50]

VII

Elsewhere in the United States, the reality of the war was being brought home to people in less heroic ways. At Columbia University in New York, President Nicholas Murray Butler fired two professors, one for working with antiwar groups, the other for petitioning Congress not to send draftees overseas. The *New York Times* praised Butler for "doing his duty" by striking this blow against "disloyalty." Historian Charles A. Beard resigned in protest. Many other colleges soon followed Butler's lead, firing professors who declined to support the war.[51]

This attitude was only a portent of a war within the war, which would soon be waged by Woodrow Wilson's Department of Justice, under the leadership of Attorney General Thomas W. Gregory. Earlier, the liberal Gregory had pushed antitrust prosecutions and persuaded Wilson to appoint fellow liberal Louis Brandeis to the U.S. Supreme Court. Now, like most Americans, including the president, Gregory was convinced that the country swarmed with German secret agents and homegrown admirers of Kaiser Wilhelm. How to track them down was the big problem. The Justice Department had only three hundred men in its Bureau of Investigation (BI). Since the government did not provide these agents with automobiles or expenses for taxis, they had to pursue spies on foot or on streetcars.[52]

The answer to Gregory's predicament emerged in Chicago, where a middle-aged businessman named Alfred M. Briggs offered to recruit twenty or thirty affluent men of his vintage who would hunt spies and other hidden enemies of the war effort gratis. They would even provide their own automobiles. Soon Briggs was in Washington, D.C., conferring with A. Bruce Bielaski, head of the BI. Bielaski had used civilian volunteers in the past in one of the first progressive reform campaigns, against the white slave trade. The BI head listened attentively while Briggs proposed a nationwide organization, the American Protective League (APL), which would operate under cover as "Secret Service Divisions" in cities and towns throughout the United States.[53]

Bielaski swiftly persuaded Attorney General Gregory to approve this bad idea. By June the APL had 250,000 activists in its ranks and was rooting out dissent in six hundred cities and towns. It was ridiculously easy to join. A dollar bought a man membership and entitled him to call himself part of the "Secret Service."

Local APL leaders were usually prominent men in their communities—bankers, lawyers, clergymen. Unfortunately, their presumably good education did not include a course on the Bill of Rights. Their methods frequently involved opening suspects' mail, burglarizing their homes and offices, tapping their telephones and planting listening devices in their parlors and bedrooms. Secretary of the Treasury William Gibbs McAdoo, under whom the nation's professional Secret Service agents served, warned Wilson that these amateurs were getting out of hand. Wilson wrote to Attorney General Gregory, opining that it was dangerous to have such an organization operating in the United States: "I wonder if there is any way in which we could stop it." After the APL turned out in massive force to make sure there were no disruptions on draft registration day, Gregory told the president he thought they were a wonderful group of 100 percent Americans, and Wilson dropped the subject.[54]

The president also had nothing to say about the American Defense Society, which turned from preaching preparedness to hunting for spies, saboteurs and dissidents. Nor did he criticize the state Councils of Defense organized by many governors. Like the APL, the councils operated with scant attention to the Bill of Rights.

The government also played a direct role in suppressing dissent. New York police raided meetings of the Friends of Irish Freedom, where harsh things were being said against conscription and demands for immediate peace brought "prolonged cheers." In Boston, labor union members staged a protest parade down Tremont Street, near the Common. They carried banners such as: "If Is This a Popular War Why Conscription? We Demand Peace!" The paraders were attacked by well-organized squads of soldiers and sailors commanded by uniformed officers. For three hours the military pursued, clubbed, kicked and battered the paraders, often forcing them to kiss the American flag on their knees. Afterward, the police, who watched the fracas in bemusement, arrested five of the marchers on charges of assault and battery. The *Boston Journal* called the riot a disgrace that would "harden the hearts of our already numerous skeptics of our war for democracy." [55]

In West Virginia, the state secretary of the Socialist Party wrote a pamphlet attacking the draft as a foreshadowing of a "militarized America." He got six months in jail. In Philadelphia, another socialist was sentenced to six months in jail for possession of an antiwar pamphlet, *Long Live the Constitution of the United States*. The U.S. Supreme Court eventually upheld the sentence; liberal Justice Oliver Wendell Holmes affirmed the legality of the Espionage Act under the doctrine that in time of war, antigovernment critics can be "a clear and present danger" to victory. [56]

At first, some judges dismissed charges against men and women who distributed literature or spoke out against the draft. Popular among the protesters was the pamphlet *The Price We Pay*, which described the war in France in horrific terms. In Albany, a man named Pierce gave a copy to one John Scully, who was holding forth against the draft in a saloon. Scully was working undercover for the American Protective League, and Pierce was soon in jail. His indictment declared that the statements in the pamphlet, which included a diatribe against fighting for J. P. Morgan, were "wholly false and untrue." Therefore Pierce was obstructing the war effort. When Pierce was convicted, this interpretation of the little-noticed clause in the Espionage Act swiftly became gospel in courts across the country. [57]

The government soon broadened this mandate for total patriotism from printed words to speech. John White, an Ohio farmer, received twenty-one months in the penitentiary for declaring that the murder of women and children by German soldiers was no worse than the crimes that American soldiers committed in the Philippines during the 1900–1902 insurrection there. An elderly South Dakota farmer got five years for urging a young man not to enlist in a war that was "all foolishness." [58]

Also in the mix was some old-fashioned revenge. A prime target was strident Wilson critic Jeremiah O'Leary. His magazine, *Bull*, was suppressed by Postmaster General Burleson, and O'Leary was arrested for obstructing the draft, which he had attacked in numerous speeches. Convinced that he had no hope of getting a fair trial, O'Leary jumped bail and fled to the state of Washington, where he changed his name and became a farmer.[59]

Wilson did not seem interested in or even aware of this ruthless repression of dissent. On July 27, 1917, when Lucius W. Niemann, the editor of the Milwaukee *Journal*, urged him to take a strong stand against draft resisters in Wisconsin, the president told Joe Tumulty that "anybody is entitled to make a campaign against the draft law provided they don't stand in the way of the administration of it by any overt acts or improper influences." But the president showed the other side of his contradictory nature when he told the cabinet that a man who had publicly hoped Secretary of War Baker would become an early casualty should be arrested "and given the 33rd degree and then the story of his comment given to the public so he would be forever damned by the people."[60]

VIII

Another large administration worry was unrest among African-Americans. The newspaper stories of German plots to foster a black revolution in the South that surfaced during the first week of the war were only a symptom of this concern. White fears were not assuaged when the National Association for the Advancement of Colored People (NAACP) held a convention in Washington, D.C., in May 1917. Behind the scenes, W. E. B. Du Bois, the association's brightest intellect, wrote most of the resolutions, which declared: "The real cause of this World War is the despising of the darker races by the dominant groups of men." The convention called for the extension of the principle of the consent of the governed "not only to the smaller nations of Europe but among the natives of Asia and Africa, the Western Indies and the Negroes of the United States." The NAACP insisted that American blacks were loyal to the United States and pledged their support of the war, but "absolute loyalty in arms and civil duties need not for a moment lead us to abate our just complaints and just demands."

In spite of these noble words, most of America's blacks remained skeptical of, if not antagonistic to, Wilson's claim that the United States was fighting to make the world safe for democracy. After the war, an African American writer admitted that many blacks who "whooped it up for Uncle Sam" would not have been terribly upset if the kaiser took charge of

Memphis and other cities in the South. "Any number of intelligent Negroes expressed the opinion under their breath that a good beating would be an excellent thing for the soul of America."

Black idealism did not improve in June 1917, when the Confederate veterans held a reunion in Washington, D.C., and were received with rapturous acclaim by Congress and the president. Francis J. Grimke, the leading black cleric in the capital, wondered how patriotic orators could work themselves into "spasms of indignation" over German atrocities and remain unmoved by "the equally atrocious conduct of southern lynchers."

The Justice Department's Bureau of Investigation began to monitor "Negro activities," beginning a pattern of surveillance that would continue throughout the war. The fear that German agents were recruiting blacks to join a Mexican army persisted. When 150 black men appeared at the railroad station in Memphis to go North in search of jobs in the booming war economy, they were forbidden to leave town until the authorities made sure they were not heading for Mexico. A BI agent reported 700 blacks had recently left for Cincinnati, their railroad tickets paid for, and wondered if disloyal German-Americans in that city had recruited them for some nefarious purpose. In New Orleans the BI interrogated a black man who said he would gladly join the kaiser's army tomorrow and shoot white American soldiers with pleasure.[61]

These simmering tensions exploded in East St. Louis, Illinois, on the state's southwestern border. The city had attracted thousands of Southern blacks to work in its mills and factories. Some had come as strikebreakers, which angered not a few white workers. Labor unions told the mayor they wanted "drastic action" to get rid of recently arrived blacks. Adding tension to the city's already volatile race relations was a rumor that 300,000 Negroes, who mostly voted Republican, had been "colonized" in Illinois, Ohio and Indiana to swing the states into the GOP camp in the 1916 presidential election. When Illinois went Republican in 1916, the Wilson justice department ostentatiously investigated claims that thousands of blacks had registered illegally in the months before Election Day. Black-white clashes in May 1917 forced the governor to send in National Guard troops to keep order in East St. Louis. On July 2, two carloads of white men roared through the city's black neighborhoods, shooting into homes and stores. No was hurt or killed, but blacks reached for their guns. When more cars with whites appeared, the blacks opened fire, killing two detectives. A reporter riding with the victims published a vivid account of the crime, with pictures of the riddled patrol car.

The next day, hundreds of armed white workers invaded black neighborhoods, beating and shooting blacks, including women and children, and setting three hundred of the mostly wooden houses on fire. At least 39 and possibly 110 blacks were killed, and hundreds wounded. Eight whites also died. Smaller riots erupted in New York, Chester, Pennsylvania, and other cities.

The federal investigation in East Saint Louis was superficial and hid behind a suggestion that the upheaval had been triggered by German agents. Investigators did not interview a single black person. The NAACP newspaper, *The Crisis,* embarrassed the Wilson administration by publishing a twenty-page report replete with dozens of eyewitnesses, black and white.[62]

The riot created a crisis among African-Americans. In Chicago, attorney Ferdinand L. Barnett, whose wife, Ida Wells-Barnett, had long led a crusade against lynching in the South, declared that the time had come for blacks to arm themselves. The local BI division superintendent responded by smearing Barnett as "rabidly pro-German." The BI was ordered to find grounds to arrest the lawyer, but it failed to persuade a single black person to testify against him.

Throughout the uproar, Woodrow Wilson said nothing. When prominent African Americans journeyed to Washington to complain in person, he refused to see them. The only major white politician to speak out was Theodore Roosevelt. On July 6, appearing on a program to greet representatives of the new democratic government of Russia, the former president called the riot "an appalling outbreak of savagery" and demanded that Wilson take action. Samuel Gompers, the ardently pro-war head of the American Federation of Labor, was also on the program. When he tried to blame the violence on black strikebreakers, Roosevelt all but dismembered him in public. He asked Gompers how he could try to excuse such "unspeakable brutalities committed upon colored men and women" at a meeting to hail the birth of freedom and justice in Russia.[63]

On July 28, 8,000 black New Yorkers marched down Fifth Avenue to the beat of muffled drums, carrying banners that read, "Mr. President, Why Not Make America Safe for Democracy?" and "Your Hands Are Full of Blood." The police confiscated one banner, a blowup of a newspaper cartoon showing Wilson holding a speech on democracy while a black mother and two children pleaded for help in the ruins of their burned home. Two weeks later, on August 15, Wilson issued a statement deploring black-white violence. Most blacks thought it was much too late and too little in the bargain. It did nothing to counteract the "lukewarm aloofness" with which the president had approached the situation.

Events soon suggested the blacks were right. On August 22, trouble erupted in Houston when white police officers raided a black crap game. The blacks were all members of the Twenty-Fourth Infantry, one of four black regular regiments that had been in the army since the Civil War, serving mostly in the West. The soldiers already resented Houston's segregation and white hostility. When some of the gamblers fled to the home of a nearby black woman, a Houston policeman abused her verbally and perhaps physically. One of the black soldiers got into a fistfight with the cop and was arrested. Later in the day, a military policeman from the regiment was shot at and arrested by the same policeman.

In their camp outside Houston, members of the Twenty-Fourth Regiment's third battalion seized their guns and headed for the city, where they began shooting every white they saw. By the time order was restored by white troops rushed to the scene, fifteen whites and four blacks were dead. Forty-one black regulars were sentenced to long terms in the army prison at Fort Leavenworth, and thirteen were hanged almost as soon as the court martial board handed down the sentences, making an appeal impossible.

Secretary of War Baker informed Wilson that "some feeling was aroused" by the speedy executions. He suggested henceforth that military death sentences ought to be reviewed in Washington. During the Civil War, this policy had been routine. It was hard for most people to believe that Baker and Wilson did not know this.[64]

In a black newspaper in San Antonio, an article praised the executed men for trying "to protect a Negro woman from the insult of a southern brute in the form of a policeman." The editor of the paper was arrested and given two years in Leavenworth under the Espionage Act.[65]

IX

On June 8, General Pershing and his staff arrived in England to be greeted by a few dignitaries and an honor guard of the Royal Welch Fusileers. While his baggage was being unloaded, Pershing was embarrassed into a press conference by waiting reporters. He said he and his men were glad to participate "in this great war for civilization." Ashore, he sent a cable to the War Department, asking for absolute power to censor anything and everything reporters wrote about him. This was ingratitude, at the very least. The journalists had lavished extravagant phrases on the general. Heywood Broun said: "No man ever looked more the ordained leader of fighting men." Floyd Gibbons called him "lean, clean, keen."[66]

The next day, Pershing met King George V at Buckingham Palace. The king, illustrating how much moonshine was floating between the two allies, said he looked forward to seeing some of the 50,000 planes the Americans had produced while waiting to get into the war. Pershing cleared his throat and informed His Majesty that the U.S. Army Air Service had a grand total of fifty-five training planes. He might have added, but probably didn't, that most of them were obsolete.[67]

Pershing also met Admiral William Sims, who informed him that the British were losing the war at sea; 1.5 million tons of ships had gone to Davy Jones's locker in April and May. This news cast grave doubt on the possibility of bringing a large American army to France. Equally worrisome was a meeting with General Sir William "Wully" Robertson, chief of the imperial staff. Robertson was Field Marshal Douglas Haig's boss and the gruff defender of Haig's mass slaughters in Flanders. Robertson immediately urged Pershing to bring his men to the British sector of the Western Front. When Pershing informed Wully that he and his staff had decided to operate in Lorraine, on the right flank of the French army, Robertson became visibly less charming. He curtly informed Pershing that there was no hope of finding enough ships to bring an American army to France. Equally unencouraging was a visit with Prime Minister Lloyd George, who told Pershing the British were going to need every available ship to feed their home front.

Pershing and his chief of staff, Major James Harbord, also visited a British training camp. There they got a quick lesson in trench warfare, with its emphasis on hand grenades and mortars, two weapons that were receiving scant attention in the U.S. Army. Harbord was appalled by the undernourished, uninspired draftees, a glimpse of what the British class system produced in the slums of London and other cities.[68]

After five days in England, the Americans headed for France aboard a channel steamer. At Boulogne they endured a ceremonial reception that took hours. Harbord confided to his diary that even Pershing questioned out of the corner of his mouth how many times the band was going to play the "Star-Spangled Banner" and the "Marseillaise." There were endless speeches in French, which neither Pershing nor 99 percent of his staff understood. But they got the essential message: The French were extremely glad to see them.

One reason for the long ceremony was the French desire to have Pershing reach Paris as people were finishing their day's work. The government wanted the maximum number of *citoyens* to see him. Arriving at the Gare du Nord (the huge, vault-roofed train station) at 5:20 P.M., Pershing and his staff endured another rendition of the two national anthems and joined the top politicians in the French government, plus Marshal Joffre and other generals, in a motorcade to the Hôtel Crillon.[69]

The two-mile journey should have taken fifteen minutes. Instead it consumed an hour of the most frantic emotion that the dazed Americans had ever witnessed. Streets, rooftops, windows, were packed with French men and women who wept Niagaras of tears and screamed, "*Vive l'Amérique!*" and "*Pair-shang!*" until it seemed as if the din would shatter glass and even concrete, not to mention eardrums. Men and women burst through the police lines to kiss the hands and cheeks of officers and enlisted men and shower them with roses.

Major Harbord, riding in the second car, lost sight of Pershing in the car ahead of him as the berserk French engulfed the motorcade. Harbord began to wonder somewhat nervously if people climbing onto his car thought he was Pershing. One enlisted man almost had his arm wrenched off when he tried to shake hands with the swarming welcomers. The motorcars, not built to run in low gear for long periods, began smoking ominously. "Though I live a thousand years," Harbord later wrote, "I shall never forget that crowded hour."

In front of the Crillon, thousands more people were packed shoulder to shoulder in the immense Place de la Concorde, screaming, "*Pair-shang! Pair-shang!*" French officials prevailed on the general to step out on a balcony to acknowledge the frantic cheers and prevent the crowd from storming the building. There were French and American flags at each end of the balcony. A breeze blew the Tricolor toward Pershing. Though he usually froze when confronted by a large crowd, this time his presence of mind did not desert him. He kissed the fluttering folds and the crowd erupted into even wilder frenzy.[70]

Pershing found the demonstration immensely touching—and alarming. These people obviously regarded him as the savior of France. How could he manage that feat with a single division? The general's uneasiness intensified later that night, when U.S. Ambassador William C. Sharp gave a dinner for Pershing and a roster of French and American dignitaries. In a brief speech, the ambassador hailed the soldiers' arrival and closed with an unnerving "I hope you have not come too late."[71]

The Germans made it clear that this was precisely their opinion. "The arrival of the general without an army was turned into a triumphal march," sneered Berlin's press bureau. If the kaiser's men had seen a memorandum inserted into the U.S. Army files on May 28, their sneers would have been even more triumphant—and the French might have greeted Pershing with curses rather than cheers. Acting Chief of Staff Tasker Bliss (Chief of Staff Hugh Scott had been sent to Russia with a U.S. mission) wrote that "General Pershing's expedition is being sent . . . to produce a *moral* effect. . . . Our general staff has made no [other] plans for prompt dispatch . . . of considerable forces to France."[72]

Two days later, Pershing met the writer Dorothy Canfield Fisher, an old friend from the days when he headed the ROTC at the University of Nebraska. Fisher had been living in France for several years. She told him the French were as good as beaten. They had lost 2 million men to wounds and death in the last three years. "There is a limit to what flesh and blood . . . can stand . . . and the French have just about reached that limit," Mrs. Fisher said.

This dose of gloom became acute when Pershing visited General Henri-Philippe Pétain, the acting commander of the French army, at his headquarters outside Paris. Pétain gave him the details of General Nivelle's failed offensive in April. Nivelle had claimed to have a formula for smashing through the German army in forty-eight hours. Instead, the Germans, forewarned of his attack, had inflicted 120,000 casualties on the massed French infantry before they even reached the main defense line. Whereupon the French army not only stopped fighting—it mutinied. One division attempted to march on Paris to overthrow the government. "Down with the war!" they shouted. The rebellion spread swiftly through sixteen army corps until there were only two divisions that showed any readiness to fight.

Pétain had raced up and down the battle line, arresting some of the more outspoken mutineers, placating others by promising better food, more leaves and an absolute end to mass attacks. "We must wait for the Americans," he said. If Wilson had not declared war on April 2, a German victory would have been inevitable. Instead, the mirage of a vast American army on its way enabled Pétain to stabilize the situation—though he admitted to Pershing that many divisions were still mutinous and the whole army could be described as being in a state of "collective indiscipline."[73]

There were signs that defeatism had also penetrated the French government. Pétain urged Pershing to cable Wilson, asking him to say something to the politicians that would "strengthen their resolution." The general was not imagining things. A thirty-five-year-old Socialist named Pierre Laval had recently told the French Chamber of Deputies: "We are not here to lie to ourselves. There is in France a weariness of war and a pressure for peace." The deputies had exploded into prolonged applause.[74]

Pétain relapsed into a morose silence, which continued at a lunch for Pershing and his staff. As the Americans struggled to make small talk with Pétain's staff in spite of the language barrier, the French general burst out, "I hope it is not too late!" By this time, Pershing had no illusions about what he and Woodrow Wilson were confronting on the Western Front: defeat.[75]

Chapter 4

CREELING AND OTHER ACTIVITIES THAT MAKE PHILIP DRU UNHAPPY

Oblivious to the looming disaster in France, George Creel's Committee on Public Information was hard at work creating the war will in America. By July he had assembled a small army of writers, editors, artists, actors and speakers who were churning out patriotic pamphlets, books, films and speeches for the American public. An upper echelon of former muckrakers, all ardent progressives like Creel, were given prominent roles. The CPI's motto was "faith in democracy . . . faith in fact." The Four Minute Men were urged to rely on facts and avoid "hymn[s] of hate."

Ethnic groups were a major target. Creel put an idealistic social worker, Josephine Roche, in charge of a department that began creating "loyalty leagues" in ethnic communities. Within a year, she was working with no less than twenty-nine nationalities. Pamphlets were printed in the various languages, including German, to explain how the United States got into the war. On July 4, 1918, Irish-America's favorite tenor, John McCormack, sang "The Battle Hymn of the Republic" while representatives of these groups stood in reverent silence outside Washington's tomb at Mount

Vernon. This event is a good example of why Creel's penetration of ethnic opinion on the war remained at the skin-deep level.[1]

The mailed fist was by no means eliminated from the government's propaganda policy. A committee of university professors was organized to read ethnic newspapers looking for "material that may fall under the Espionage Act." Although Creel did his utmost to conceal it, the propaganda chief was part of the Wilson censorship apparatus. "In no degree was the agency [the CPI] an agency of censorship, a machinery of concealment or repression," he later declared in his usual take-no-prisoners style. In fact, Creel was a member of the Censorship Board, established by Wilson's executive order on October 12, 1917, as a clearinghouse for censors operating throughout the government. The board had representatives from the Post Office, the War Department, and the War Trade Board, who conferred regularly with Creel.[2]

Another government worry was the labor movement. Already, the flood of war money from Great Britain and France had sent prices into an inflationary spiral. Workers were restless, and the Germans' idea that strikes could be induced by skillful agitators was by no means a fantasy. Creel had an enthusiastic supporter in Samuel Gompers, the short, pugnacious former English cigar maker who headed the American Federation of Labor (AFL). Well before 1917, Gompers had proclaimed his dislike of the radical union, the International Workers of the World (IWW), the Socialists, and others with negative attitudes toward American capitalism. When the war turned them into critics of J. P. Morgan, Charles Schwab and other bankers and industrialists who were making millions out of supplying the Allies, Gompers's attitude became uncompromising detestation. In a shrewd move, Wilson gave the AFL boss a seat on the Advisory Commission of the Council of National Defense. Gompers felt he—and the labor movement—were halfway to nirvana.[3]

A CPI department of industrial relations won Gompers's unqualified endorsement. He warmly approved Creel's policy of filling factories and offices with dramatic posters and slogans aimed at convincing wage earners that they had a stake in the war. Creel spun off a separate organization, the American Alliance for Labor and Democracy, to answer the attacks of the Socialists and the IWW and put Gompers in command of it.

Along with the Four-Minute Men, the centerpiece of Creel's early propaganda effort was the *Official Bulletin,* an eight-page daily newspaper (eventually thirty-two pages) in tabloid format, which went to every paper in the United states, as well as to government agencies, military camps and the nation's 50,000 post offices. Below its title were the words "Published Daily Under Order of the President by the Committee on Public Information, George Creel, Chairman." Individuals could subscribe for five dollars a year, and the circulation climbed rapidly to a peak of 115,031. The paper published nothing but good news about the U.S. war effort. Wilson considered this hybrid creature his invention—which it was in some respects. Creel had initially opposed the idea. The president gleefully told Joe Tumulty that the *Official Bulletin* was an immense success. He added that Creel was astonished by the way it was being lapped up and reprinted by thousands of newspapers.[4]

Score one for Philip Dru.

II

Not all reporters believed the *Official Bulletin* was trustworthy, in spite of its lofty origins. Not a few saw it as a government plot to co-opt their jobs and chafed under the restrictions imposed by the "voluntary" censorship that the newspapers had promised to maintain about war news. On July 4, this skepticism caught Creel in the first of many mistakes. The five regiments Pershing had selected, now called the First Division, arrived in France just in time to celebrate the Fourth of July in Paris. Creel decided the successful voyage merited a similar celebration in the United States. The CPI ground out a story of the soldiers' perilous trip across the Atlantic, during which their escorting warships had fought off repeated attacks by German submarines, and several of the undersea "pirates" had been sunk. It made the July 4 front page of almost every newspaper in the country. Editorial writers burbled about this first proof of America's fighting prowess coming on the nation's birthday.

An Associated Press reporter in England interviewed the officers on the escort ships, who laughed out loud at Creel's version of the voyage. They said there had been no attacks on the convoy and no submarines had been sunk. Secretary of the Navy Josephus Daniels picked up the phone and scorched the ears of Melville Stone, the president of AP, demanding the story's retraction. The thoroughly cowed Stone sent out a "kill" order. But across the nation, the presses were already rolling and thousands of dismayed editors were calling Creel picturesque names, few of them printable.[5]

After more hugger–mugger, a new, mildly exciting version of the story was published on July 7. There were two minor brushes with submarines, both of which lasted only a few minutes. "No Attack in Force" said a subhead in the *New York Times,* although the paper tried hard to get some excitement out of the second encounter, claiming the submarine was "blown up" by a depth charge. In a nearby column, the paper reported that Republican Senator Boise Penrose of Pennsylvania called Creel's overheated version a national disgrace and demanded an investigation of the Committee on Public Information. A *Times* editorial seemed to agree with the senator; it called Creel's appointment a blunder. A few weeks later, the paper wryly referred to the CPI as "the Committee on Public Misinformation." In many papers, a new word, "creeling," became synonymous with government hot air.[6]

III

With progressive reformers heading the army (Secretary of War Newton Baker) and the navy (Secretary Josephus Daniels) and with a late convert to progressivism in the White House, the U.S. government was determined to make sure the vast mobilization of the nation's men had a positive moral outcome—in addition to winning the war. One of the by-products of progressivism was the social purification movement, which inveighed against saloons, brothels and the red–light districts that were tolerated in many cities. Wilson put an energetic thirty-three-year-old reformer, Raymond B. Fosdick, in charge of making the army and navy training camps and their neighborhoods "clean."

The administration inserted a clause in the Selective Service Act that made it a crime to sell or give a drink to a serviceman. Fosdick ruthlessly closed down saloons and brothels in the vicinity of army camps and shipped some 15,000 women convicted of prostitution to detention centers, where most were held until 1920. By the end of 1917, Fosdick was boasting that he had wiped out 110 red-light districts. Much of the policing was done by women volunteers, formed into local Protective Leagues. These volunteers were equally tough on amateurs, arresting any woman who behaved promiscuously with soldiers and subjecting her to a physical examination to see if she had venereal disease.

Along with police work came hours of exhortation to the new soldiers and sailors to resist sexual temptation. Spokesmen for the Committee on

Training Camp Activities (CTCA) orated on the way venereal disease destroyed a soldier's "efficiency." Pamphlets asked: "You wouldn't use another fellow's toothbrush. Why use his whore?" They urged soldiers to stop thinking about sex. "A man who is thinking below the belt is not efficient." The CTCA tried to help this process by running athletic programs and dances in "hostess houses," where the soldiers could meet respectable women.

Supplementing these moral and social appeals were a series of films that drove home the horrors of venereal disease in the era before wonder drugs. Men and women in the late stages of syphilis were shown with sightless eyes and with noses, ears, and other organs rotting off their bodies. In case morality and terror failed, the army also lectured on the use of condoms and the importance of prophylactic treatment after casual sex.

The ultimate goal was the creation of what Secretary of War Baker called "moral and intellectual armor" that would sustain the soldiers when they went overseas and were beyond the U.S. government's "comforting and restraining and helpful hand." The reformers were acutely aware that the French and British governments had a very different approach to the problem of social purity. One of Premier Georges Clemenceau's gestures of solidarity with France's new ally was an offer to set up brothels for the American army, staffed by French prostitutes. When Baker heard about it, he gasped, "For God's sake . . . don't show this to the president or he'll stop the war!"[7]

IV

Over in France, General Pershing was making big decisions and accumulating even bigger worries that went far beyond sexual purity. He had no difficulty persuading General Pétain to assign the American Expeditionary Force (AEF) to training camps in Lorraine, south of Verdun, where they could eventually launch attacks against key German railroads and important coal and iron mines. But Pershing was troubled by the lack of unity between the British and French. Their centuries-old antagonism had not been healed by their wartime alliance.

The French accused the British of fighting mainly to defend the part of France from which Germany could attack England. The British had a bigger army than the French, but they defended only a third of the front.

Fistfights between French and British officers were not uncommon in Paris cafés. One brawl involved eighty men and required several squads of gendarmes before it was halted.

As for the army of "brave little Belgium," the French said it was good at only one thing: issuing communiqués. The British agreed. Even lower was the French and British opinion of the Italians. They could not even beat the Austrians. When the French Chamber of Deputies heard that a British warship had mistaken an Italian submarine for a German U-boat and sunk it, the legislators cheered. At the bottom of these strata of contempt were the Serbs, whose joke of an army had been chased all the way to Salonika by the Austrians and Bulgarians, with some discreet help from the Germans.[8]

From the Eastern Front came even more dismaying reports. In July the revolutionary Russian government had launched a "liberty offensive" against the Germans and Austrians. By the first week in August, the attack had floundered into almost total disaster, with the Russian army virtually ceasing to exist. The specter of a vastly reinforced German army on the Western Front began taking nightmarish shape.

Pershing soon decided he could not rely on the general staff in Washington for anything. It took weeks to get a reply from them. Acting Chief of Staff Tasker Bliss wrote orders with the stub of a pencil and hid urgent telegrams under his blotter while he made up his mind what to do about them. Pershing decided to set up his own general staff in France—a far more efficient one than the fumbling team in Washington.[9]

Alfred Thayer Mahan, the son of West Point's famed military philosopher, Dennis Mahan, was fond of saying that war was business. As commander of the AEF, Pershing proved it. Until he took charge, each army bureau and department had its own supply officer with its own budget. Back in the United States, this compartmentalization caused immense confusion and duplication of effort and expense. Pershing organized the AEF's purchases around a general purchasing board, headed by an old friend and future vice president, Charles G. Dawes. A canny businessman, Dawes had absolute authority to buy anything and everything the AEF needed from the French and British at the best possible price.

The decisions Pershing and Dawes made to prepare their men for battle were awesome. They placed an order for $50 million worth of French airplanes and did not report the purchase until it was too late for Washington to countermand it. "He did it without winking an eye, as easily as though ordering a postage stamp," Pershing's chief of staff, James Harbord, noted in his diary. Pershing and Dawes also bought French 75mm field guns for their artillery; English Enfield rifles, steel helmets, and French light machine guns (Chauchats) for their infantrymen; and, later, French light tanks (Renaults) for an embryo tank corps.[10]

Pershing decided to make an AEF division 28,000 men, twice the size of an Allied or German division. He wanted an organization with the staying power to sustain an attack in spite of heavy casualties. Unfortunately, he did not double the size of the new division's artillery, the first symptom of his inability to appreciate the lethal increase in firepower that had transformed warfare on the Western Front.[11]

Pershing also strove to put his own stamp on the AEF. "The standards for the American Army will be those of West Point," he announced. "The upright bearing, attention to detail, uncomplaining obedience to instruction required of the cadet will be required of every officer and soldier of our armies in France." Every private a Pershing was an impossible dream, but the general never stopped striving for it.

The British and French had trouble distinguishing between American officers and enlisted men. Pershing ordered officers to wear the British Sam Browne belt across their chests and authorized the use of canes. The first item was hated by many officers, and the latter was derided by enlisted men. But Pershing never wavered in his insistence on both.[12]

The AEF commander also played a part in deciding what his troops would be called in the newspapers. British soldiers were "Tommies," short for Tommy Atkins, the typical man in the ranks of Rudyard Kipling's poems. French soldiers were *poilus*—"hairy ones"—because in the trenches they seldom had a chance to shave or get their hair cut. Pershing took an intense dislike to "Sammies," the name the French and British reporters first fastened on the Americans. He ordered the *Stars and Stripes,* the army newspaper, to push for "doughboys." Military etymologists still argue over this term's origin. The most likely explanation traces it back to the Philippines, where infantry would return from long marches on dusty roads in tropic temperatures, caked with thick, white dust resembling dough. Pershing spent many years in the Philippines, another reason why he would have favored the nickname. It would take another six months for "doughboys" to catch on with the press.[13]

Although he could relax with close friends and make dramatic gestures, such as kissing a French flag, for photographers or admiring crowds, the one thing Pershing could not do was inspire soldiers or civilians with a ringing phrase. He was keenly aware of his limitations as a speaker. His staff wrote a speech for him to make at Lafayette's Tomb on July 4, 1917. The closing line hit an oratorical high note: "Lafayette we are here!" Pershing crossed it out and wrote: "Not in character" beside it. He assigned the speech to a staff colonel who spoke good French.

The scene at Lafayette's Tomb was the climax of a parade through Paris by the Sixteenth Infantry, one of the regiments of the First Division that had arrived at Saint-Nazaire on June 28. Pershing had told Marshal Joffre that these first arrivals would be regulars, the best soldiers in the American army. The AEF commander was horrified by what he saw marching past the reviewing stand. Rank after rank was out of step, their uniforms a mess, their rifles held at all sorts of weird angles.

The Sixteenth Infantry were regulars in name only. Most of the veteran noncoms and officers had been kept in the States to train the army's burgeoning horde of conscripts. These marching men were largely volunteers with only a few weeks' training. One American overheard a French soldier say, "And they sent that to help us?" But the Parisians did not care how unmilitary the Americans looked. The march was a replay of Pershing's arrival. A huge crowd screamed and wept. Women kissed the flank marchers and hung wreaths of flowers on their hats and rifles.

At Lafayette's Tomb, Colonel Charles E. Stanton gave a stem-winding speech worthy of William Jennings Bryan. He damned the kaiser and prophesied glorious victory before reaching his famous announcement to Lafayette. The line became inextricably attached to Pershing, no matter how often he denied saying it. On the historic day, he was persuaded to add a few terse remarks, which one American listener praised as "precisely the right thing, in perfect taste."[14]

V

Back in Washington, Woodrow Wilson was putting in place the men who would run the home front. Herbert Hoover was an almost inevitable choice for food administrator. A wealthy former mining engineer, he had made a worldwide reputation as the man who headed an immense effort to feed captive Belgium in spite of the British blockade. General George Goethals,

builder of the Panama Canal, took command of a vast shipbuilding program. A staggering $649 million was committed to producing an American
air fleet, under the guidance of automobile executive Howard E. Coffin and
Major General George O. Squier. Bernard Baruch, who had made millions
on Wall Street speculating in copper and other raw materials, was put in
charge of marshalling these resources for the war effort. Within nine
months, Wilson would make this tall decisive South Carolinian head of the
War Industries Board, in virtual command of the entire economy.

Reports from Europe generated a crisis atmosphere. On June 28,
Ambassador Walter Hines Page warned from London that "financial disaster to
all the European allies is imminent" unless there was another huge infusion of
U.S. cash. From now on, along with sustaining France and Italy, His Majesty's
cabinet hoped Washington would undertake to pay "all purchases made by the
British government in the United States." Otherwise there was going to be "a
general collapse." Early in July, Pershing said it was imperative to have 1 million
trained men in France by May 1918. Around the same time, Admiral Sims
cabled Secretary of the Navy Daniels: "At the present moment we are losing
this war. This is due to the success of the enemy submarine campaign."[15]

VI

Instead of inspiring all concerned to pull together for victory, these seismic
shocks from abroad only made Congress more critical of the administration's lack of preparation to wage war. Unquestionably, they had a point.
Wilson's 1916 preparedness program had been mostly cosmetic, to fend off
Theodore Roosevelt and other Republican advocates of seriously arming
the United States for war. The president had met strong resistance inside
the Democratic Party and accepted a woefully inadequate compromise.

Meanwhile, other players on the national scene revealed that George
Creel had not yet created the war will that inspired universal self-sacrifice.
Farmers, alerted to the serious grain shortage, began hoarding their crops
while the price of wheat and other grains spiraled upward. Others in the
food business consigned huge amounts of eggs, meat and similar perishables
to cold-storage warehouses to make a similar killing. Screams of distress from
angry consumers assailed the White House. The only answer seemed to be
price controls, but Congress refused even to consider them. A Food Control
Bill submitted by the Department of Agriculture went nowhere. Hours were
wasted on oratory about the greatness of the free-enterprise system.

Next, a new fly got into the political ointment: prohibition. The idea that the United States, as a God-fearing, Christian nation, should ban alcoholic beverages had been working its way around Protestant America for years. One of its biggest supporters was William Jennings Bryan. By now the so-called drys had a substantial following in Congress, and they suddenly emerged from cover to attach a ban on beer and wine as a rider to the House of Representatives Food Control Bill.

A huge uproar erupted, much of the cry led by German-American beer drinkers, whose enthusiasm for the war was lukewarm at best. Wilson urged Democratic senators to detach the rider from their version of the bill. For his efforts, he was snidely informed that very few members of his own party felt "well enough disposed" toward him to do the job.

When the president tried to get the public involved by throwing Herbert Hoover into the fray, he discovered that the food administrator was a man without a party. No one even knew whether he was a Democrat or a Republican. This encouraged many senators to make him their favorite political target. Senator James Reed of Missouri, the same gentleman who had predicted blood in the streets on draft registration day, descanted on Hoover's hunger for power. He called him a market manipulator in a class with Jay Gould and other discredited nineteenth-century tycoons.[16]

Senator Gore of Oklahoma, angry at the president because no new army camps had been built in his state, announced his indifference to the Food Control Bill. Senator George E. Chamberlain of Oregon, a Democratic progressive, struggled to keep it alive, while the politicians began horse trading over whose crops and products would be controlled and whose would escape the regulatory net. Eventually, wheat and coal, two fundamentals in every citizen's budget, were regulated but cotton escaped, thanks to the preponderance of Southerners in the Senate's Democratic majority—a compromise that would cause Wilson much future political pain.

As a climax to this legislative auto-da-fé, the Senate Republicans attached yet another rider on their version of the Food Control Bill—again calling for a Committee on the Conduct of the War. Another Democratic senator from disgruntled Oklahoma, Robert I. Owen, sponsored the measure, supposedly to demonstrate his nonpartisan spirit. The president denounced the idea of subjecting him to "daily espionage," but 14 Democrats joined the Republicans in a 53 to 31 vote in favor of creating the watchdog panel.

The maneuver could not have come at a worse time. General Goethals and another member of the Shipping Board, William Denman, had gotten into an argument about whether the United States should build wooden ships or steel ships to meet the challenge of German submarines. A lot depended on the decision. The British were building only 100,000 new tons per month and were losing nine times that amount. General Goethals, who favored steel, did not disagree agreeably. He took the dispute public. Though hopelessly outgunned, Denman volleyed back. The Hearst papers reported that Denman stood to profit from certain connections with California timber interests. The ballooning brawl-cum-scandal forced Wilson to ask both men for their resignations.[17]

Meanwhile, the president was rallying Democratic support in the House of Representatives to eliminate if not kill the Committee on the Conduct of the War. When Republican minority leader James R. Mann put up a fight, Democratic newspapers recalled earlier gibes from Theodore Roosevelt and others about Mann's patriotism and the discomfited Chicagoan abandoned the effort. Mann's capitulation did not stop the Senate from trying to bulldoze the idea through the conference committee that met to harmonize the two versions of the Food Control Bill. But Senator Frances E. Warren of Montana, General Pershing's father-in-law, voted with the Democrats, and once more, to Wilson's vast relief, the Committee on the Conduct on the War was deep-sixed. Warren had made a similar switch to kill Theodore Roosevelt's volunteer division. The choice of Pershing was turning out to be one of Wilson's better political moves, even though the results were largely coincidental. The president's chief motivation had been his detestation of General Leonard Wood.[18]

Undiscouraged, Senator Weeks announced his determination to attach Conduct of the War Committee resolutions to every bill brought to the floor for the rest of the decade, if necessary. The president grimly told his supporters in the House of Representatives that he was depending on them to frustrate this Republican attempt "to get their hand on the steering apparatus of the Government."[19]

VII

The Washington summer weather was more beastly than usual, adding to Wilson's woes in this pre-air-conditioning era. If the critical shouts and murmurs emanating from the Capitol were not enough to drive a president to distraction, another group of critics clustered at the White House gates, day in and day out, wearing skirts. Representatives of the Women's Party, better known as suffragettes, had been picketing the executive mansion since January, demanding the president to back votes for women by a constitutional amendment.

On June 20, when a delegation from the new Russian republic was greeted by the president, the suffragettes saw a unique opportunity. In their rush to liberation from the czar, the Russians had given women the right to vote. As the delegation approached the White House gates, the suffragettes unfurled a big yellow banner, informing the startled Slavs: "America Is Not a Democracy. Twenty Million Women Are Denied the Right to Vote. President Wilson Is the Chief Opponent of Their National Enfranchisement."

Infuriated spectators ripped down the banner. Several days later, the suffragettes blocked traffic and harassed White House visitors, virtually forcing the police to arrest them. "They seem bent on making their cause as obnoxious as possible," Wilson wrote to a family correspondent. His wife, Edith, could barely conceal her detestation of the suffragettes and their goal. She loathed the idea of "masculinized" voting women. But the president portrayed himself as the soul of patience and quickly arranged for the "Suffs" to be released from jail.

Women had already won the vote in nine western states. Their support could spell the difference in a close election. Many suffragettes claimed that women's votes in California had given Wilson a second term. The president had been on all sides of the issue. He had opposed woman suffrage when he was president of Princeton and governor of New Jersey. Throughout his first presidential term, Wilson refused to support it in Congress. But he had persuaded the Democrats to put a lukewarm suffrage plank in the party platform in 1916, suggesting that the issue be solved at the state level. Now he seemed more inclined to accept the inevitable. He urged several House leaders to set up a special committee on woman suffrage.[20]

VIII

In the midst of these political brawls, Wilson struggled to preserve some shreds of private life. He and Edith often took one- or two-day trips on the presidential yacht *Mayflower*, though he usually brought along a briefcase full of paperwork and his private secretary to take dictation. Wilson and his wife continued to play a lot of golf and, at Dr. Grayson's suggestion, took up horseback riding. Grayson also suggested cycling as an alternative exercise. Edith, who had never been on a bicycle in her life, tried to learn inside the White House. The result was considerable danger to the lives and limbs of the mansion's staff, as well as to the wallpaper and works of art with which she collided. She finally gave up the venture as hopeless.

On July 27, the president found time to write a letter to his daughter Jessie, who was spending the summer on Nantucket with her two children. Her husband, Francis B. Sayre, had recently left for Europe to work for the YMCA with American troops.

> *My Precious Daughter,*
>
> *I cannot put into words the thoughts, the loving wistful thoughts, I have had of you and the dear little ones since Frank went away; and they have been with me at all sorts of times, amidst all sorts of business and all sorts of public anxieties. Edith and I are on the* Mayflower *today to get away from the madness (it is scarcely less) of Washington for a day or two, not to stop work (that cannot stop nowadays) for I had to bring Swem [his private secretary] and my papers along, but to escape people and their intolerable excitements and demands. This is, therefore, the first time in weeks that I have had any chance at all to turn to my private thoughts and to the dear little girl whom I so dearly love in Nantucket and try to say some of the things that are in my heart.*
>
> *I know Helen [his cousin, Helen Bones] has written to you and I have tried to keep track of you as best I could; but that is not the real thing,—that does not satisfy my heart. I hope that the visit Margaret [Jessie's older sister] is planning to pay you may come off soon. . . . We try to take things light-heartedly, and with cool minds, but that is not always possible, and I fear I notice little signs of it telling on Edith. As for myself, I am surprisingly well, by all the tests that the doctor can apply, though very tired all the time. I am very thankful. I do not see how any but a well man could safely be trusted to decide anything in the present circumstances. . . .*
>
> *My heart goes out to you, my darling Jessie, with unbounded love and solicitude! Please, when you have time, write how things are going with you, what you hear from Frank, if a real message has had time to get through yet, and all the things, big or little, that you know I want to hear; and I do not know of anything I do not want to know about you in your new home.*

Edith joins me in warmest love to you all and I send you, for myself, all the love that a father's heart can give to a dear daughter whom he admires as much as he loves.[21]

Behind the president's cold, professorial demeanor lived a deeply caring man. This carefully concealed reality added dangerous intensity to the clashing emotions in Woodrow Wilson's wartime soul.

IX

Soon after this letter reached Nantucket, the president was engulfed in another congressional brawl, this time over taxes. Republican and Democratic progressives in both houses had joined Wilson's call for war with great reluctance. They had listened closely to the denunciations of Senators George Norris and Robert La Follette about the millions J. P. Morgan and his friends were making, and the legislators were determined not to let them keep very much of it. Soon a slogan swept the House of Representatives: "the conscription of wealth."

Squadrons of bankers and other business executives descended on Washington to testify before the Senate Finance Committee, all solemnly avowing that high taxes would be bad for the war effort. The senators clucked sympathetically, but in the House, antiwar Majority Leader Claude Kitchin promoted a tax bill that performed major surgery on corporate profits while farmers paid almost nothing.[22]

The administration, scoured of the illusion that the Allies had the war as good as won, did not help matters by sending Secretary of the Treasury McAdoo, to Capitol Hill to ask for another $5 billion as soon as possible. Once more, cries of bad planning and lack of foresight rained on the White House. The business leaders urged Wilson to raise this new mountain of cash through loans. Wilson disagreed, and nothing could budge him on that important point. As much as possible, he wanted to operate on a pay-as-you-go basis. But the progressives in the Senate, no friends of Wilson in the first place, went him and Claude Kitchin one better. They called for a business tax rate of 80 percent. Only such drastic numbers would stop the profiteers from "plundering the public."[23]

Republican newspapers said this was more than conscription of wealth, it was confiscation. The senators were denounced as demagogues. Business spokesmen such as Senator Warren Harding of Ohio portrayed the nation's captains of industry as pathetic victims of proto-revolutionaries. Senator Henry Cabot Lodge conjured the frightening prospect that the war might become "unpopular" with the business community. The senator did not elaborate on what might happen next: Collective indiscipline à la French army? Excessive liquor consumption at the Harvard Club?

Theodore Roosevelt shocked Republicans by yielding once more to the progressive siren song. In a Labor Day speech, he said an 80 percent business tax rate seemed just about right to him. But Roosevelt was a mere onlooker. Secretary of the Treasury McAdoo insisted that a 31 percent bite was adequate, and the 80-percenters were defeated by crushing Senate majorities. Unfortunately, the senators were unable to remove the agrarian bias from the House version of the bill. In the final version, farmers, including those unregulated cotton producers in the South, paid practically nothing. Business leaders saw themselves as victims of Democratic prejudices and damned the president. City factory workers, having heard senators denounce "predatory" Eastern capitalists and accuse the government of favoring the Morgan-led cabal that had supposedly gotten the United States into the war, were even more disillusioned. Chickens were being hatched that would come to roost as vultures, eager to devour Woodrow Wilson's political corpse.[24]

X

While these domestic excitements were swirling through the White House, a daunting new challenge to Wilson's leadership appeared from abroad. Pope Benedict XV called on the warring governments to make a peace of mutual forgiveness and forbearance. As a starting point, the pontiff proposed the restoration of Belgium, disarmament, arbitration machinery to prevent future wars, and freedom of the seas for all nations.

To the Americans, the timing of the Pope's message seemed almost devilishly unpropitious. In Stockholm, international socialists had convened a peace conference to appeal over the heads of the warring rulers to the workers of the world. In Petrograd, the Bolshevik wing of the Russian revolution had already called for peace on the basis of no annexations and self-determination for all peoples and had bullied the so-called Provisional Government of Russia into going along with them.

The Germans and the Austro-Hungarians promptly accepted the Pope's proposal, although Berlin avoided specific commitments. The provisional Russian government also welcomed the papal mediation. The leaders of France and Italy, with largely Catholic, extremely war-weary populations, were transfixed with alarm. Although they wanted a fight to the finish, they hesitated to take issue with the Pope. The English, even more determined to go for what Prime Minister Lloyd George called a knockout blow, decided to let Wilson answer for all of them.

At first the president was inclined to say nothing. He seemed angry at the Pope's intrusion into the war. However, as the impact of the pontiff's appeal grew larger, Wilson decided he had to reply. The Pope was saying many of the same things Wilson had said before he opted for war. Now, as British Ambassador Cecil Spring Rice wryly pointed out, the president was doing "his utmost to kindle a warlike spirit throughout [the] states and to combat pacifists." No wonder the Pope's appeal gave Wilson indigestion.[25]

Colonel House strongly seconded this presidential decision—and warned Wilson not to dismiss the Pope's proposals out of hand in his reply. The new Russian ambassador in Washington had informed House that alarming splits were appearing in the revolutionary government, with the call for immediate peace one of the chief issues. A dismissal could lead to the overthrow of Russia's moderate leader, Alexander Kerensky.

House also revealed that the Pope's proposal had evoked a sympathetic response in him. The colonel wondered if it would be a good thing in the long run if "Germany was beaten to her knees." A German rout might leave a vacuum in central Europe, which the Russians would be eager to fill. Before the declaration of war, Wilson had agreed with this balance-of-power viewpoint. It had been the idea behind his appeal for a peace without victory.[26]

Secretary of State Robert Lansing sent Wilson an acrid memorandum, in which he opined that the Pope was working with the Germans and the Austro-Hungarians to create a push for peace while they were winning the war on land and the submarine campaign "appears successful." His Germanophobia becoming more visible with every line, Lansing argued that the Pope's proposals would depend on "the good faith of the powers" that signed such a peace treaty. But there could not be "two opinions" of the good faith of the German government. "The German rulers cannot be trusted."[27]

The secretary of state reminded Wilson of the invasion of Belgium, the mistreatment of the civilian population, and the way the Germans "broke their word" about submarine warfare. Lansing even saw the Russian call for peace as the product of German intrigue. The Vatican's—and Berlin's—goal, Lansing concluded, was to "break up the alliance and avoid paying the penalty for the evil they have wrought."[28]

Wilson toiled long and hard on his reply, conferring repeatedly with Colonel House, at one point sending him a draft. Issued on August 27, the statement began on an affirmative note: "Every heart that has not been blinded and hardened by this terrible war must be touched by this moving appeal of His Holiness the Pope." But how could any of the pontiff's noble goals be reached by agreement with the present German government? Wilson now condensed Lansing's Germanophobia into one long, raging sentence:

> The object of this war is to deliver the free peoples of the world from the menace of a vast military establishment controlled by an irresponsible government, which, having secretly planned to dominate the world, proceeded to carry the plan out without regard either to the sacred obligation of treaty or the long established practices and long cherished principles of international action and honor, which chose its own time for the war, delivered its blow fiercely and suddenly, stopped at no barrier either of law or mercy, swept a whole continent within the tide of blood, not the blood of soldiers only, but the blood of innocent women and children and also of the helpless poor, and now stands balked but not defeated, the enemy of four fifths of the world.

Wilson next shifted to House's favorite tactic—denying that the German people were responsible for their government. "This power is not the German people. It is the ruthless master of the German people." Then he was back to his new iron-leader mode. "It is no business of ours how that great people came under its control or submitted with temporary zest to the domination of its purpose; but it is our business to see to it that the history of the rest of the world is no longer left to its handling."

In a gesture to the Russians, Wilson argued that if the Allies accepted peace now, there would be a need for a perpetual military alliance to protect Russia from the "manifold subtle interruptions, and the certain counter-revolution which would be attempted by the malign influence to which the German Government has of late accustomed the world."[29]

When it came to demonizing Germany, Wilson the war leader needed no lessons from Wellington House. Ignoring the president's apparent determination not merely to beat Germany to its knees but to knock it flat, Colonel House told Wilson that his artful mixture of hate and idealism was a "charter of democratic liberty." George Foster Peabody, an aide to Secretary of War Baker, said the reply convinced him that God had sent America "the Master Mind of the World in this crisis."[30]

While Wilson was solemnly assuring everyone that he was determined to protect Russian democracy from German autocracy, America's chief ally, Great Britain, was telling the new commander of the Russian army, General Lavr Kornilov, something else. Kornilov despised Alexander Kerensky only slightly less than he detested the Bolshevik leader Vladimir Ilych Lenin. London urged the general to march on Petrograd and restore order at the point of a gun. When Kornilov and his men headed for the Russian capital, the British cabinet hailed his move by declaring the would-be dictator "represented all that was sound and hopeful in Russia."[31]

XI

The confusion swirling through the alliance against Germany disturbed Wilson. He was also troubled by the somewhat glaring fact that he had rejected the Pope's offer without proposing an alternative peace plan. Running the war and coming up with a detailed proposal was beyond his—or anyone else's—capacity. The president asked Colonel House to round up a group of scholars and liberal thinkers such as Walter Lippmann to research a comprehensive settlement that would be just to both the victors and the vanquished.

Financed out of secret White House funds, the group's first name was the War Data Investigation Bureau. But the staff soon changed this mouthful to "the Inquiry." By October, the experts were toiling in the bowels of the New York Public Library on Forty-Second Street. Their leader was Sidney Mezes, president of City College, who happened to be Colonel House's brother-in-law. Also prominent was House's son-in-law, international lawyer Gordon Auchincloss. When it came to staying on top of a political situation, it was hard to match the adroit Texas colonel. Lippmann, also devoted to House, moved to New York to serve as the Inquiry's general secretary.

Although they hoped to operate in secret, the Inquiry's existence soon seeped through the pro-war intelligentsia's grapevine and they were bombarded with letters from historians, political scientists, and assorted thinkers of every imaginable stripe, all eager to serve. Within a year their staff ballooned to 126, proving, if nothing else, they were a genuine government agency, with the hunger for expansion that infests the heart of every bureaucrat.[32]

XII

At a late August cabinet meeting, Josephus Daniels wondered aloud if the war were popular and reported that Senator William Squire Kenyon of Iowa had told him two-thirds of the people in his state did not favor it. Wilson remarked that if the Germans captured New York, most Iowans would applaud. It was ever thus, Wilson said. People in the boondocks resented the opinions of the capital—or in New York's case, the de facto capital—of the country. New York was ardently pro-war. Therefore, Iowa was antiwar.[33]

Worries about the American perception of the war were not so easily dismissed. During the summer and fall of 1917, Wilson tolerated and occasionally encouraged ferocious attacks on dissenters of every stripe, with the brunt of the public's wrath falling on German-Americans. Wilson did not seem to realize that his denunciations of the German government added fuel to these rancorous flames. Senator La Follette had observed that the president's distinction between the Berlin "autocracy" and its people did not make sense. Others, such as the hugely popular evangelist Billy Sunday, were even more blunt: "All this talk about not fighting the German people is a lot of bunk," Billy said.[34]

At times, in his calls for all-out war, the president portrayed every German-American as a potential enemy. In his June 14 Flag Day address, he accused "the military masters of Germany" of sowing "unsuspecting communities with vicious spies and conspirators." Worse, these persons "seek to undermine the Government with false professions of loyalty to its principles."[35]

Coalescing with the hate propaganda spewed by Wellington House and its American collaborators, these sentiments inspired the American Protective League and thousands of other freelance patriots to join in a nationwide attack on German-Americans and the German language and culture. The *Saturday Evening Post*, already one of the nation's biggest magazines, announced that it was time to rid America of "the scum of the melting pot." An article in the *Atlantic Monthly* accused the German language press of mass disloyalty. The *New York Times* agreed that German-language newspapers never stopped trying to surreptitiously support Berlin's cause. A rear admiral suggested taxing them out of business. Cartoons portrayed fat Germans waving an American flag out the window while drinking a stein of beer to "Hoch der Kaiser" (Hail the Kaiser). The Lutheran Church was attacked because its ministers refused to urge the sale of war bonds from the pulpit—a violation, they maintained, of their sacred mission.[36]

Soon, Lutheran schools were described as hotbeds of disloyalty, where the "Star-Spangled Banner" was never played and German heroes such as Bismarck displaced Washington and Lincoln. When a wealthy German-American who had already bought a substantial amount of Liberty Bonds to finance the war declined to buy more and remarked to a pesky seller, "To hell with Liberty Bonds!" he was arrested and fined. Vigilantes set up a machine gun outside the Pabst Theater in Milwaukee to prevent the production of Schiller's *Wilhelm Tell*, a world-famous protest against tyranny.

The German language was banned from school curriculums and German music barred from auditoriums. Famed violinist Fritz Kreisler was denounced by the Daughters of the American Revolution when he tried to take the stage in Pittsburgh. When Baltimore, Washington and Cleveland also canceled performances, Kreisler retired for the duration. Karl Muck, the Swiss-born conductor of the Boston Symphony, was arrested and interned because he declined, on aesthetic grounds, to play the "Star-Spangled Banner" at the opening of each performance. The pro-German director of the Cincinnati Symphony, Ernest Kunwald, suffered a similar fate.[37]

In September, Congress attached a rider to an unrelated bill, giving the government even greater control over the expression of opinion among German-Americans. Wilson signed the bill into law on October 6, 1917. Henceforth, German-language newspapers were required to supply the post office with English translations of "any comments respecting the Government of the United States . . . its policies, international relations [or] the state and conduct of the war." The cost of providing these documents put many marginal newspapers out of business and had a chilling effect on the editorial policies of those that survived.[38]

The Mennonites, a German-American pacifist religious sect, refused virtually to a man to submit to conscription, but said they would be willing to serve in noncombatant roles, as long as they did not have to don uniforms. They had come to the Midwest in the 1870s, after receiving an explicit promise from President Ulysses S. Grant that they would never have to serve in the American army. Mennonite leaders rushed to Washington to ask Secretary of War Baker if he would approve their stance. Baker advised them to tell their young men to submit to conscription, on his promise that their religious beliefs would be respected.

Unfortunately, Baker, a prewar pacifist himself, had succumbed to the war will. He sent a confidential order to the commanders of army camps to make a major effort to persuade conscientious objectors to change their minds. While they were being persuaded, they were to wear uniforms, live in barracks, and undergo military training. Baker theorized that camaraderie with young men their own age, plus pressure from military superiors, would do the trick. On paper, he was proven correct: About two-thirds of the objectors—some 16,000—abandoned their beliefs and became fighting soldiers.

How this change was accomplished is not a pretty story. Harassed camp commanders, already grappling with shortages of everything, had little time to give much thought to the techniques of persuasion. At most camps, the "conchies" were left to the untender mercies of sergeants and lieutenants, who called them yellow-bellies, cowards and pro-Germans. The Mennonites, who resisted all forms of persuasion, had a particularly bad time. At one camp, officers sent a dozen of them into an open field, where they were pursued by men on motorcycles until they collapsed. At another camp, a Mennonite resister was scrubbed with brushes dipped in lye. Sadists in another camp billeted them with men infected with venereal disease. Not too surprisingly, many resisted this brutal treatment and were court-martialed. Some 110 were sentenced to the Fort Leavenworth, Kansas, army prison for terms ranging from ten to thirty years. One martyr to his faith and conscience wrote to his parents from his prison cell: "You cant emagen how it is to be hated. If it wasent fore Christ it would be empossible."[39]

XIII

The Creel-Wilson determination to create a war will meant deep trouble for the radical union, the International Workers of the World. One of the opening volleys was fired by Senator Harry Ashurst of Arizona. On August 17, 1917, he told his fellow solons that IWW stood for "Imperial Wilhelm's

Warriors" and called for the union's extirpation. Ashurst's antipathy was sharpened by the IWW's tendency to cause trouble in Arizona's copper mines, whose owners were among his chief supporters. The same could be said for many other Western governors and members of Congress who regularly denounced the IWW. The union had very few friends in high places.[40]

The Wobblies, as they were called, were the loose cannons of the labor movement. A forerunner of the Committee for Industrial Organization (CIO), the IWW aimed at unionizing the unskilled and uneducated workers, people largely ignored by the craft-oriented AFL. The union had about 60,000 paid-up members in 1917, the twelfth year of its turbulent existence. The union returned with interest the violent hostility of the employers and their friends in the ruling "tendom." Wobbly rhetoric reeked with class warfare and calls for revolution. Their constitution candidly declared that they were out to "abolish the wage system."

Not too surprisingly, the IWW took a dim view of Wilson's war. Its stance was almost perversely designed to please no one. On May 3, 1917, a month after the United States entered the war, the Wobblies' one-eyed president, William D. "Big Bill" Haywood, told a lieutenant, "While being opposed to the Imperial Government of Germany, we are likewise opposed to the Industrial Oligarchy of this country."[41]

While Congress was arguing over the draft law, the Wobbly newspaper, the *Industrial Worker,* published a poem that was not likely to please Woodrow Wilson or anyone else in Washington:

> *I love my flag, I do, I do*
> *Which floats upon the breeze*
> *I also love my arms and legs*
> *And neck and nose and knees.*
> *One little shell might spoil them all*
> *Or give them such a twist*
> *They would be of no use to me*
> *I guess I won't enlist.* [42]

In the spring of 1917, with the defiant sangfroid that had won it the admiration of romantic liberals, the IWW was conducting strikes in the lumber and copper industries, hampering the construction of the long-promised fleet of 50,000 (sometimes reduced to 22,000) American planes, barracks for draftees, and the flow of weaponry to the British and French armies in Europe. It was easy for journalists and politicians to see treason in these work stoppages. Ignored was the June 8, 1917, explosion and fire in the North Butte Mining Company's Speculator Mine, which killed 164 miners and enraged workers throughout the industry. Three days later, 10,000 Butte miners struck to demand recognition of their union and the abolition of the "rustling" card, a certificate issued by a company-dominated union to blacklist Wobblies. The owners announced they would shut down the mines and flood them rather than talk to "anarchistic leaders." Newspapers suggested that German money was behind the strike.

Montana Congresswoman Jeannette Rankin, one of the Wobblies' few friends in Washington, told the government that the miners were hoping for presidential intervention to win them a just settlement. Behind the scenes, Bernard Baruch, in frequent touch with copper tycoon John D. Ryan, blocked Labor Department attempts to mediate the strike and pushed for the preservation of the status quo.

Similar unrest threatened to shut down Arizona's copper mines, which produced 28 percent of the nation's ore. While the government looked the other way, shotgun-toting vigilantes organized by the Citizens Protective League, a clone of the American Protective League, rounded up some 1,200 Wobblies and other dissidents in Bisbee, Arizona, and deported them in railroad cars to the desert town of Hermanus, New Mexico, with dire warnings not to return. For the next four months, the Citizens Protective League ran Bisbee, issuing passports to local residents and deporting anyone who did not meet the league's test of loyalty. The *Los Angeles Times* hailed the operation as "a lesson that the whole of America would do well to copy." Theodore Roosevelt also applauded the direct action of Bisbee's loyal citizens, saying he had no doubt the deportees were "bent on destruction and murder."[43]

The president's secretary, Joe Tumulty, with his roots in Jersey City's working class, was appalled by the deportations and urged the president to issue a condemnation. Wilson chose to wire the governor of Arizona, urging him not to let people take the law in their own hands. He also appointed federal mediators—a move condemned by many antilabor newspapers. One editorialized that it was crazy to "confer with a mad dog." The only sensible thing to do was "shoot the dog."[44]

In Butte, Montana, vigilantes seized the IWW's most dynamic spokesman, Frank Little, who represented the extreme left wing of the union.

After Congress declared war, Little had persisted in calling for strikes, draft resistance and sabotage to undermine the American military effort. The assailants dragged Little through the streets tied to the rear bumper of a car and hanged him from a railroad trestle. The *New York Times* deplored the lynching, but added that IWW agitators like Little were "in effect and perhaps in fact agents of Germany."[45]

Similar warfare was waged on the IWW in towns around the iron mines of Minnesota. In Duluth, men carrying IWW cards were jailed for vagrancy. In Minneapolis, saloons known to be frequented by "sowers of sedition" (frequented by the IWW) were shut down by the police. The Minnesota Public Safety Commission appealed to the federal government to smash the Wobblies. Governors of Western states added their voices to the rising chorus of denunciations in Congress. Dozens of newspapers called for suppression of "the traitorous organization." Not a word was said in the Wobblies' defense by the already co-opted Samuel Gompers and the American Federation of Labor.[46]

Attorney General Thomas Gregory decided to act. With Wilson's approval, he launched an investigation of whether the IWW was being supported by German money. When no evidence surfaced, Gregory ordered a massive assault on IWW offices in no less than thirty-three cities. Homes and apartments of IWW leaders were also raided. Tons of records, including personal diaries and letters, were seized and studied for evidence of violations of the Espionage Act. It was almost ridiculously easy to find in Wobbly rhetoric the quotations needed to "prove" the union members' guilt.

On September 28, 1917, 166 IWW officers were indicted using their own words to prove that they had violated eleven laws and proclamations related to the war, conspired to interfere with employers trying to fulfill vital government contracts, urged fellow Wobblies to refuse to register for conscription, and plotted to create insubordination in the armed forces. There was little doubt what the Wilson administration had in mind. The Philadelphia federal attorney stated it candidly in a letter to the attorney general: "Our purpose . . . as I understand it, [is] to put the I.W.W. out of business."[47]

XIV

Few people in the United States were inclined to criticize this rampaging war will that Creel and Wilson were creating. One of the few was Senator

Robert La Follette. Appalled by what the war was doing to the American spirit, he became more and more convinced that an early peace was imperative. When journalist Lincoln Steffens returned from Russia and told him that the new revolutionary Russian army was faltering because its soldiers had been told the Allies were fighting to fulfill greedy secret treaties of conquest, La Follette became even more disgusted with Woodrow Wilson's war. Next, the German Reichstag adopted a resolution declaring that Germany sought "a peace of mutual agreements and enduring reconciliation of peoples." La Follette decided to introduce a resolution in the Senate, calling for a restatement of U.S. war aims that would be conducive to a negotiated peace.[48]

Numerous senators, notably John Sharp Williams of Mississippi, rose to denounce La Follette as a traitor. The Senate refused to consider the resolution. When the Russian army collapsed and the Germans began advancing rapidly into Russia, newspapers reprinted anonymous articles making the preposterous charge that La Follette was responsible for the mounting disaster. An anxious Lincoln Steffens wrote to his friend, warning about "war rage," which he said was "as dangerous as madness and as unapproachable to reason."[49]

Undaunted as usual, La Follette accepted an invitation to speak to the Nonpartisan League, an organization composed largely of small farmers in the states of the old Northwest. When he arrived in Saint Paul, Minnesota, on September 19, 1917, he found his hosts in a state of high anxiety. The meeting was being harassed by Secret Service men and self-appointed patriots, who warned of major trouble if La Follette criticized the war. This was exactly what the senator had intended to do, with a special focus on the refusal of the rich to pay a decent share of the financial burden.

The sponsors grew even more jittery when they read La Follette's speech. They begged him not to deliver it, and he reluctantly agreed to say only a few extemporaneous words. When La Follette arrived at the auditorium, he found the placed packed with 10,000 people. Another 5,000 jammed the streets outside, agitating to get in. As he walked to the stage, the crowd rose and cheered so fervently, the sponsors changed their minds. Whacking the senator on the back, they shouted, "Go ahead, Bob, make your speech!"

Unfortunately, the senator had left the speech in his hotel room. But he accepted the challenge of speaking without notes, and began by recalling his fight against corporate power in Wisconsin. He was still fighting for the same principles in the Senate of the United States—for fairness and justice for average citizens. The big issue, as he now saw it, was how to pay for this war—which, he added wryly, he had not been in favor of fighting.

The words were greeted with huge cheers. La Follette added: "I don't mean to say we hadn't suffered grievances; we had, at the hands of Germany. Serious grievances. . . . They had interfered with the right of American citizens to travel on the high seas—on ships loaded with munitions for Great Britain."

From somewhere in the audience a voice shouted, "Yellow!" The interruption only spurred the senator to continue down this dangerous path. He still thought "the comparatively small privilege of the right of an American citizen to ride on a munitions-laden ship, flying a foreign flag, is too small to involve this government in the loss of millions . . . of lives."[50]

He compared the victims who died on such vessels to someone who went to France and camped near an arsenal. Getting more and more carried away, La Follette said that America should have considered more carefully what it had at stake when it went to war. He also asserted that the *Lusitania* was carrying munitions and that Secretary of State Bryan had asked Wilson to stop Americans from sailing on it but the president had done nothing.

If the only things at stake in the war were loans made by the House of Morgan to foreign governments, and the profits of munitions makers, such things should be weighed, "not on a hay scale, but on an apothecary's scale." The implication, of course, was obvious: They were too small for a hay scale. The senator cited Daniel Webster, who questioned the Mexican War when it was at "full tilt," asking whether there had been "sufficient grievance" to start such a bloody explosion.[51]

La Follette went on to argue for bigger taxes on the rich, and ended with a swipe at Congress for failing to live up to its constitutional responsibility to oversee the war. In fact, every American had the right "to discuss freely whether this war might be terminated with honor . . . and the awful slaughter discontinued." He was still angry about the Senate's refusal to take up his war aims resolution.

The audience gave the senator an ovation. While La Follette and his wife were on a train back to Washington, an Associated Press reporter filed a story quoting the senator as saying: "We had no grievance against

Germany." It produced huge headlines everywhere. In the *New York Times,* it became "La Follette Defends Lusitania Sinking." Theodore Roosevelt called the senator the worst enemy of democracy alive. The governor of Minnesota announced that La Follette might be arrested under the Espionage Act. Nicholas Murray Butler, Columbia University's president, called for La Follette's expulsion from the Senate. Butler compared allowing La Follette to speak freely to putting poison in the food of men on troopships to France.[52]

The day after the speech, Secretary of State Lansing released to the newspapers the text of an intercepted message that Germany's former ambassador, Count von Bernstorff, had sent to Berlin, asking for $50,000 to influence Congress. The timing of the release was hardly accidental. The newspapers splashed it across their front pages. An Alabama congressman called for an investigation, declaring that he could name thirteen or fourteen members of Congress who had "acted in a suspicious manner." Called before the House Rules Committee and ordered to name names, he mentioned three congressmen and Senator La Follette. Meanwhile, the secretary of state hastily retreated, saying he had no evidence connecting any legislator with German propaganda.

A week later, La Follette gave another speech in Toledo, Ohio. The city was in the grip of manic war rage. "Vigilante groups hounded, horsewhipped and tarred and feathered war-resisters," said one minister, who had been dismissed from his church for his antiwar views. Several hotels refused to rent the senator a room, fearing they might be burned down. Forty policemen guarded the packed hall, and when La Follette appeared at a side door, they urged the senator to cancel his speech. He ignored them and spoke about the imperative need for a statement of America's war aims. He got another ovation, and a local reporter wrote in a puzzled tone that he gave "no special cause for offense."

Back in Washington, La Follette learned that the Minnesota Public Safety Commission had petitioned the U.S. Senate to expel him. Petitions from similar groups, from the National Security League to the Grand Army of the Republic, soon followed. These appeals were referred to the Subcommittee on Privileges and Elections for investigation. On October 3, the Democratic governor of Wisconsin staged a mass meeting in Madison, at which Secretary of the Treasury McAdoo was the featured speaker. Along the secretary's parade route were illuminated signs calling La

Follette a slacker and a copperhead. Another one read, "La Follette misrepresents Wisconsin. GET HIM OUT." In his speech, McAdoo made clear his opinion of dissenters: "America intends these well-meaning people who talk inopportunely of peace . . . shall be silenced." Warming to his theme, he added, "Every pacifist speech in this country made at this inopportune and improper time is in effect traitorous."

That same day, Secretary Lansing informed Senator Frank Kellogg of Minnesota, who had presented the first expulsion petition to the Senate, that there was no record that former Secretary of State Bryan knew ammunition was aboard the *Lusitania*. Lansing had telephoned Bryan, who said he did not find out about the ammunition until three or four days after the sinking. Bryan made a statement to the press corroborating this claim. The administration was now indubitably involved in trying to destroy La Follette.

On October 5, the *New York Times* reported that the Senate's Privileges and Elections Subcommittee was going to study the evidence while Congress was in recess and hold public hearings on the senator's possible expulsion in December. Federal Judge Charles F. Amidon of North Dakota wrote to the senator: "It is a time when all the spirits of evil are turned loose. The Kaisers of high finance . . . see this opportunity to turn war patriotism into an engine of attack. They are using it everywhere." He urged La Follette to somehow keep his spirit "unclouded by hatred."[53]

La Follette needed this advice. On the last day of the Senate's session, he defended himself in a three-hour speech, quoting excerpts from famous statesmen who had spoken out against wars in their time—including Prime Minister David Lloyd George, a fierce critic of the Boer War. Senator Joseph Robinson of Arkansas answered him in a speech that filled five pages of the *Congressional Record*. He came down the aisle and shouted insults in La Follette's face. Robinson told La Follette to apply to the kaiser for a seat in the Reichstag, implied that the senator had taken German propaganda money, and declared there were "only two sides to this conflict—Germanism and Americanism; the Kaiser or the President."[54]

XV

In another part of the war, John J. Pershing was making good on his promise to Theodore Roosevelt to bring his sons to France. No slouch at the political side of his job, when Pershing said farewell to Secretary of War Baker, the general asked how he would react if Pershing cabled a request for the two older boys, Ted and Archie. Baker did the handsome thing and replied that not only did he have no objections, but the two young men should serve as officers. The secretary made Ted a major and Archie a lieutenant.

Pershing passed the word to TR, and the Roosevelts went to work on wangling a berth on a transport. They sailed for France on June 20 aboard a lumbering French ship named, for some unknown reason, *Chicago*. The family came from all directions for a festive farewell party. TR was, of course, the centerpiece. Young Ted's wife, Eleanor, was more than a little upset when the former president announced in his ebullient way that he expected at least one of his sons to be wounded and possibly killed in France.[55]

Escorted by a French destroyer, *Chicago* reached Bordeaux without mishap. The two Roosevelts were besieged by Frenchmen asking how many more Americans would arrive soon. The French were crestfallen when they learned the brothers were "not the vanguard of an enormous army which would follow without interruption," Ted told his father. The scene was repeated when they shared a compartment with a group of French soldiers on the trip to Paris.

Pershing assigned the brothers to the First Division, which was training in Lorraine, and Ted was given command of a battalion in the Twenty-Sixth Infantry. Archie soon managed to get himself seconded to the same battalion. Their father thought this was a very bad idea, but they ignored his advice. They both went to work on turning the ragtag collection of discards and raw volunteers into fighting soldiers.

The second oldest Roosevelt son, Kermit, had only spent a few days at the Plattsburgh training camp, not enough to win a commission in the U.S. Army. He decided to volunteer for the British army. His father asked Ambassador Cecil Spring Rice, a close friend, to arrange for Kermit to enlist in Canada. Soon the young man was en route to England to pick up his commission and report to the general in command of the British army fighting the Turks in Mesopotamia. One suspects that Spring Rice had something to do with this assignment. British army lieutenants on the Western Front tended to have very brief careers.

Kermit was the son to whom Roosevelt was closest—and who worried him most. A heavy drinker, given to bouts of the blackest gloom, he had traveled to Africa with his father to shoot lions and later survived a horrendous

trip with TR down the River of Doubt, a tributary of the Amazon. Kermit
was the only one who could tell his father he had little enthusiasm for the
war. He would much prefer to stay home with his wife and newborn son.
"The only way I would have been really enthusiastic about going would
have been with you," he wrote later.[56]

XVI

Roosevelt's youngest son, twenty-year-old Quentin, was as ebullient as
Kermit was melancholy. Everyone agreed he was the one who most resembled his father. A gifted writer, he had published surprisingly mature poems
and stories in the Groton School magazine. He had the same omnivorous
interest in history, literature, languages and politics. Another gift baffled the
entire family: Quentin seemed to have an uncommon talent for dealing with
machines—to the point of majoring in mechanical engineering at Harvard.

This fondness for technology led him to take a very different path to the
war. He joined the U.S. Army Air Service and began flight training at
Mineola on Long Island not far from Sagamore Hill, the family home in
Oyster Bay. He regularly buzzed the big house to waggle his wings at his
father. Another target was the mansion of Harry Payne and Gertrude
Vanderbilt Whitney in nearby Old Westbury. There lived the love of
Quentin's life, beautiful Flora Payne Whitney, heiress to an immense fortune.

These two privileged young people had slowly, warily, fallen in love over
the previous two years. They were both aware of the social distance
between them. Flora's father and mother regarded Theodore Roosevelt as a
political revolutionary. Quentin's father had an even lower opinion of "the
dull purblind folly of the very rich . . . their greed and arrogance." When
Quentin proposed in the spring of 1917, he added in a note: "I haven't yet
seen my family. I wonder if they'll approve."[57]

He soon discovered their parents were only part of their problems.
Quentin's proposal produced a crisis in Flora's mind and heart. She revealed
for the first time how much Quentin intimidated her with his quotes from
Dostoyevsky, his insider's political observations, his literary gifts. Flora feared
she was "too ordinary" for him. Quentin responded with the timeless philosophy of lovers: "If two people really love each other nothing else matters.
. . . I might be a Mormon and you an Abyssinian polyandrist and everything
would be all right because you can't get beyond love."[58]

By the end of May, Quentin had the answer he was seeking, and it was his turn to be intimidated. "I don't yet see how you can love me," he wrote. "I feel as if it were all a dream from which I shall wake . . . with nothing left to me but the memory of the beauty and the wonder of it all. You see I know how very ordinary I am and how wonderful you are."[59]

Meanwhile Quentin was learning to fly in cumbersome Curtiss Jenny aircraft that could barely make sixty miles per hour. Nevertheless there was a tremendous thrill in conquering the sky. Quentin had had to overcome some rather serious physical disabilities to get into the air. His eyesight was terrible; he had been forced to memorize the eye chart in advance. He had also managed to conceal a bad back, injured in a fall from a horse during an Arizona camping trip the previous summer. Between them, these limitations made him a less than first-class pilot. His landings were clumsy and his takeoffs often hair-raising. But there was no doubt that he would graduate from Mineola's rudimentary training school. The U.S. Army Air Service had a grand total of thirty-five pilots and was inclined to give a commission to anyone who could get a plane off the ground and keep it in the air for a while.[60]

Quentin and Flora mutually dedicated themselves to persuading their families to accept them as a couple. In a matter of weeks, Flora had utterly charmed Theodore Roosevelt and defrosted much of the chill in his far more disapproving wife, Edith. A glimpse of his mother's attitude is visible in a note Quentin wrote to Edith, remarking he was glad she liked Flora, now that she "had got past the fact that she was a Whitney and powdered her nose."[61]

With an absolute minimum of thought, the War Department decided that Quentin and his group of ten barely trained fliers would go to Europe as an advanced guard of what Secretary of War Newton Baker called "an army of the air." For Quentin and Flora, the decision meant the most painful word in love's vocabulary, separation. In mid-July 1917, a week before he sailed, Quentin brought Flora to dinner at Sagamore Hill and confided to his parents that they were engaged. They did not perform a similar ritual in Old Westbury. There the secret remained unspoken, while Flora struggled to find the courage to tell her parents.

On July 23, 1917, Flora joined Edith and TR at the Hudson River pier where Quentin's troopship was docked. When the sailing was delayed, the elder Roosevelts tactfully went home, leaving the lovers alone. They walked up and down for hours, waiting for the cry of All Aboard. Finally, Quentin sent Flora home to her family's mansion at 871 Fifth Avenue. There, she told Quentin, "the accumulated sea of tears" became a great gulf in her throat. Still she did not weep. She had decided it would be unworthy of their love.[62]

In Quentin's pocket when the troopship sailed was a letter from Flora, written on July 19. "All I do from now on will be for you," she wrote. "I will do something—wait and see—so when you do come back I will be more what you want—more of a real person and a better companion and you will care for me as much as I care for you."[63]

Quentin confessed to his parents that he felt down after Flora went home. He tried to cheer up them and himself by confidently predicting he would be "back sometime within a year." To Flora he admitted his hopes were tinged with darkness: "If I am not killed, there will be a time when I shall draw [sail] into New York again, and you will be there on the pier, just as you were when I left, and there will be no parting for us for a long time to come."[64]

XVII

While the Roosevelts headed for the war, their cousin Franklin continued to do his utmost to unseat his boss, Secretary of the Navy Josephus Daniels. The assistant secretary invited the well-known American historical novelist Winston Churchill, an Annapolis graduate, to do a study of the navy's efficiency and morale. The writer found many faults and sent to the president (a personal friend) a confidential report that gave Daniels some hard knocks for "dilatoriness." At one point, Churchill opined that the secretary's slow-motion style threatened to "paralyze the activities of the naval service." But Wilson made no move to reprimand much less fire Daniels, and Franklin glumly concluded in a letter to Eleanor that it would "take lots more of the Churchill type of attack."[65]

Franklin's rumor-mongering assistant, Louis Howe, was still hard at work trying to crank up such an assault in the nation's newspapers and magazines. This campaign came to an abrupt stop when George Creel appeared in Franklin's office and "let [Howe] have it right between the eyes." Creel was an ardent Daniels backer and had helped quash calls to replace him during the 1916 presidential campaign. He had gotten Admiral George Dewey, the hero of Manila Bay, to issue a glowing encomium of the secretary. As head of the CPI, Creel had put tracers on the "old canards" about Daniels's inefficiency and unpopularity that were sprouting in various newspapers. The tracers led straight to Howe, who spluttered that he was actually trying to defend Daniels. Creel replied that if he heard any more of his "phony explanations" he would tell the whole story to President Wilson, "who had a very precise idea of what constituted loyalty."[66]

Franklin may have been able to bear his aborted ambition with equanimity for a very personal, extremely private reason. He was in love. The object of his passionate affection was twenty-six-year-old Lucy Mercer, a willowy, brown-haired descendant of one of the first families of Maryland, whose alcoholic father had dissipated not only himself but also his wife's fortune.

Eleanor hired Lucy as her private secretary in 1914, when she was feeling overwhelmed by raising five children and playing Washington hostess. Her tender heart was undoubtedly touched by Lucy's sad family story and its similarity to her tormented childhood with her own alcoholic father, Elliott Roosevelt. The charming Miss Mercer soon became a member of the family, often invited to fill out dinner parties and join the Roosevelts on Potomac cruises about the Navy yacht *Sylph*. She even impressed Franklin's formidable mother as "sweet and adorable."

When Lucy and Franklin became lovers is uncertain, but there is little doubt that they were deeply involved by the summer of 1917—and Eleanor was uneasily suspecting the worst. She terminated Lucy's employment, but the charming Miss Mercer immediately enlisted in the navy and was—surprise surprise—assigned to duties in the State, War and Navy Building.[67]

When the time came for Eleanor to take the children to their summer home on Campobello Island in the Saint Lawrence River, she resisted and delayed and finally accused Franklin of trying to get rid of her. Franklin called her a "goosey girl" and finally persuaded her and their brood to depart. He was soon writing her soothing letters about how much he missed her and "hated the thought" of their childless Washington house. He casually mentioned in his letters more cruises on the Potomac and other outings that included Lucy and Nigel Law, a young British diplomat who was acting as his complaisant beard. As for coming to Campobello, Franklin suddenly found the press of navy business overwhelming and canceled several departure dates.

Gossip began swirling through Washington while Eleanor's uneasiness mounted. Theodore Roosevelt's daughter Alice, married to Congressman Nicholas Longworth, himself a notorious womanizer, saw Franklin and Lucy tooling along a Maryland lane in an open car and sent him a sly note. Alice promptly invited the couple to a dinner party. "He deserved a good time," Alice reportedly said. "He was married to Eleanor."[68]

When Franklin came down with a sore throat and high fever, Eleanor rushed to Washington to nurse him. Before she left him on August 14, they apparently had a major argument about just when he was coming to Campobello. The next day she wrote with uncharacteristic sternness: "I count on seeing you the 26th [of August]. My threat was no idle one." Had she threatened to discuss her suspicions with his mother, who held the family purse strings? This time Franklin showed up and stayed long enough to restore Eleanor's confidence in his affection.[69]

That fall, after Eleanor and her children had returned to Washington, with no warning Lucy Mercer was discharged from the service "by special order of the Secretary of the Navy." The ostensible reason was the illness and death of her father, but at least one Roosevelt biographer has opined that rumors of her affair with Franklin had reached Josephus Daniels's ears. A deeply religious man, he did not consider adultery a mere peccadillo.

If Daniels or Eleanor thought the assistant secretary would be discouraged by threats or veiled rebukes, they soon discovered how wrong they were. The lovers continued to see each other in the Maryland or Virginia countryside, and wrote passionate letters celebrating their trysts.[70]

XVIII

Other things were on the Roosevelts' minds—and on the minds of many other Americans—in the summer and fall of 1917. "General Wood has been here," Eleanor wrote a friend. "& F. has been fearfully depressed by what he tells. Hopeless incompetence seems to surround us in high places." Leonard Wood was doing his utmost to repay Woodrow Wilson for refusing to appoint him commander of the AEF. He knew that Theodore Roosevelt's cousin would be more than willing to listen to his horror stories about the Wilson war effort.[71]

In May, the War Department abruptly transferred Wood from Governor's Island, where he was in command of the Eastern Department and had access to dozens of reporters as well as Theodore Roosevelt. Sent to Charleston to command the Southeast Department, Wood told a friend: "I . . . shall set the South on fire." He did exactly that. In Charleston, Atlanta and other Southern cities, he was welcomed with parades and speeches. Spotting a small Confederate flag in an old man's hand, Wood said, "That is an honorable flag. Men have died for it." Thereafter he could do no wrong in Dixie.[72]

Wood toured the many new camps in the South and was dismayed by what he found. "Old broken-down colonels" were in command, without a clue about how to train a new generation of officers. "Their lack of energy . . . acts like a brake on all progress." Wood saw the oldsters as another illustration of the War Department's "dead cold hand of inefficiency."

Everywhere, the general made speeches emphasizing "the little done, the undone vast," an all-but-explicit criticism of the Wilson administration. In a July letter to TR, Wood wrote: "They are beginning to ask why isn't something being done. They cannot be much longer fooled by throwing dust in the air and shouting 'Onward Christian Soldiers.'"[73]

Again, with no warning, the War Department transferred Wood to Kansas. This was a blunder. Wilson had said he was keeping Wood home the way the British had retained their biggest hero, Lord Kitchener, in England, to train troops. Southern papers fulminated at the president's hypocrisy and accused him of mixing politics with the battlefield. A friend assured Wood, "You have got the East and South ablaze, and God knows what you will do with the Middle West."[74]

In command of the new Eighty-Ninth Division at Camp Funston in Kansas, Wood told a friend on September 6, 1917, "Our men are coming in and we are without arms, without artillery and pretty much everything we need, including uniforms, and there is not much prospect of them in the near future." He sardonically wondered how a nation "of our numerical and financial strength" could have watched a great war come nearer and nearer and now found itself, five months after war was declared, unable to equip the small number of troops called to the colors so far.

In a letter to Theodore Roosevelt, Wood said the situation in Washington reminded him of a neophyte driver pushing down on the clutch with one foot while the other one is on the accelerator. "The engine is whirling around and a tremendous noise is being made, but there is no application of power."[75]

As summer ebbed and the icy winds of fall swept across the great plains, Wood became more alarmed than sardonic. "A thousand men slept cold last night, with only one blanket to a man," he told his diary. There was also a "great shortage of hats." Next he discovered that the wells on which the camp depended for drinking water were infected with *E. coli* bacteria. When it rained heavily, Camp Funston became a sea of mud, with many buildings entirely surrounded by water. As fog and general dampness seeped from the nearby Kaw River, Wood called the place a "death-trap for pneumonia."[76]

If he had been given "a free hand" in April, Wood told Roosevelt, he could have had 600,000 men in France by the first of December. Now, the situation was "terrible beyond words." He feared that we would "dribble" men into France and let the Germans beat them "in detail."[77]

XIX

In France, things were not going much better in the disorganized American war effort. Almost everything that arrived from the United States for the AEF was defective. One-third of the bullets were duds. Gas masks were little more than sieves. In boxes marked men's underwear, one quartermaster found infants' night shirts. Trucks arrived without motors, wagons without wheels. Even worse was the deluge of totally unusable civilian items. A desperate Pershing cabled: "Recommend no further shipments be made of following articles . . . Book cases, bath tubs . . . chairs except folding chairs, cuspidors, office desks, floor wax, hose except fire hose, step ladders, lawn mowers, refrigerators, safes except iron field safes, settees, sickles, stools, window shades."[78]

Not too surprisingly, Charles Dawes became Pershing's lifeline to hope and sanity. The canny Nebraskan and his agents whizzed around war-battered Europe buying food, lumber, clothing, and firewood, as well as weapons and ammunition. Pershing made his friend a brigadier general so that Dawes could deal as an equal with officers from the Allied armies and tolerated his incredibly unmilitary style with a good humor that amazed the AEF staff. Dawes's collar was perpetually unbuttoned, his uniform a mess; he frequently saluted with a large cigar in his mouth.[79]

There was another bond between Pershing and this dynamic man, who bought 10 million tons of supplies before the war ended. In 1912, Dawes had lost his only son, Rufus, in a swimming accident. One day when he and Pershing were riding through Paris, they experienced a kind of telepathic fusion. Dawes was thinking of "my lost boy." He realized Pershing was thinking of his lost wife and daughters. Tears streamed down both their faces. "Even this war can't keep it out of my mind," Pershing said.[80]

For the first 2½ months after he arrived, Pershing worked in Paris, in a private building on the Rue de Constantine. As many as five staff officers were crammed into one of the small rooms. They and their general worked ten hour days, but, *oo-la-la!* the nights were something else. The Americans swiftly discovered why the cynical French called a staff job in Paris *la guerre de luxe*. The staff was swamped with invitations to dinner parties from the well-to-do members of the American community. At the top of the glamour list was heiress Louise Cromwell Brooks, who had shed a lackluster husband and was enjoying liberation, Parisian style. She saw herself as Pershing's Madame Pompadour and regularly hurled her beautiful body at him.

To Louise's chagrin—and the occasional distress of Pershing's staff—the general chose a woman who was completely outside the circle of glamour and wealth that descended on him. Micheline Resco was a petite, blonde twenty-three-year-old French-Rumanian artist who met Pershing at a reception in the Hôtel Crillon on the day he arrived in Paris. She had boldly announced she wanted to paint his portrait, and he agreed to sit for her.

Micheline spoke almost no English. Pershing's French remained primitive. But love flowered between them before the summer of 1917 faded into a troubled fall. A glimpse of an explanation is her story of the general's struggle to get her to stop calling him "Pair-shang." After innumerable tries, she gave up and called him "General Darling."

In September, Pershing moved his headquarters to Chaumont, a town sixty miles from Paris. But he continued to visit Micheline's apartment on the Rue Descombes at night, riding in front with his chauffeur, the windshield signs with the four stars and the U.S. flag laid flat on the dashboard. There, on her phonograph, they listened to her favorite music: Wagner's *Lohengrin* and the march of the heroes into Valhalla. Ironically, no one in the United States could play such quintessentially German music without fear of being reported to the American Protective League or some other vigilante group.[81]

XX

For many Americans with husbands and sons in the new American army, General Wood's warning about pneumonia soon took on lethal meaning.

One of these was the family of Representative Augustus Peabody Gardner, Henry Cabot Lodge's son-in-law. The senator was very fond of "Gus," as everyone called this ebullient, outspoken man. He had a knack for extracting campaign cash from what he called "the unemployed plutocrats" of the Bay State. Lodge once told a friend that Gardner had "wrung something like ten thousand dollars" from members of the elite Somerset Club, "who never gave a dime to any public object before."[82]

Gardner was not above spoofing the rituals of Congress in letters to his young daughter Constance, whom he called Took. In 1903, he told her how he spent his time: "Old Pip [her name for him] plays squash, and rides with Grandpa and walks with the President [TR] and that is all the fun that old Pip has. The rest of the time he runs errands for his constituents. This is a long word, and it means all the people who tell Pip how much they helped him get elected.

"Pip made a speech today in Congress; but no one listened. After he got through all the people who had been asleep or out of the hall shook hands with Pip and told him how much they enjoyed it."[83]

Gardner had been a captain in the Spanish-American War and had remained in the army reserve. As early as 1914, he led the fight for preparedness in the House of Representatives, earning almost as much enmity from Woodrow Wilson as his father-in-law received for his caustic speeches on the same subject in the Senate. When the war began, the War Department summoned the fifty-two-year-old Gardner to active duty. Senator Lodge considered it an act of "petty spite." But the congressman, who admitted he had been "clamoring" for U.S. participation in the war, could hardly refuse the call if he hoped to stay in politics. He concealed a weak heart by avoiding a physical examination.[84]

By October 1917, Gardner was in Camp Wheeler, Georgia, where he was soon writing letters that resembled Leonard Wood's. His division was supposed to have 26,000 men, but when the War Department started transferring regiments every which way, it dwindled to 9,500. "There has been a great deal of pneumonia in camp and everyone has had a cold. The weather has been very cold and many of the soldiers have insufficient equipment," he told his wife.

He also wrote a confidential letter to Joe Tumulty, Wilson's secretary. Another jovial type, Tumulty liked Gardner in spite of their political differences. He had urged him to write if there were things he wanted to say "out of channels." Gardner told Tumulty 10,000 drafted men had just arrived at Camp Wheeler. An appalling 7,000 lacked overcoats and were wearing cotton outer garments and underclothes. None of them had any experience in sleeping out of doors in tents. Many of them came from farms and had never had measles. This disease ran rampant, making the recruits prime targets for pneumonia. Soon 1,500 men were crammed into a camp hospital designed for five hundred. The handful of nurses was overwhelmed. Mournfully, Gardner added in a postscript: "Anyone who supposes this part of Georgia to be warm is very much mistaken."[85]

Like Theodore Roosevelt's sons, Gus Gardner wanted to see action. He took a demotion from staff colonel to major in an infantry regiment a few weeks before the division was to go overseas. On December 28, 1917, he told his daughter Constance, the "Took" of earlier letters, that he preferred to command men rather than a basketful of papers. He threw in a teasing reference to her new status as a mother. She had just given birth to her second child. "Think of you with a brace of Kids! Why you ridiculous person! You are not old enough to be married, even."[86]

That was the last letter Major Gus Gardner wrote. A few days later, he was in Camp Wheeler's hospital, gasping for breath. On January 14, 1918, he died of pneumonia. His death undoubtedly added another layer to the screen of bitterness and anger through which Henry Cabot Lodge viewed President Woodrow Wilson.

XXI

In October, General Pershing visited the First Division. Strung out across twenty miles of Lorraine, sleeping in barns and attics, while being trained in trench warfare by French veterans, the men were still a very mixed bag of soldiers. After watching them stage a mock attack on a supposed enemy trench, Pershing asked for comments. Neither the commanding general, Major General William J. Siebert, nor his staff officers had anything intelligent to say. Pershing exploded and began excoriating everyone in sight. He was already furious with the division for their terrible performance on July 4 in Paris. They had not done much better in a review he had recently arranged for the pompous President of France, Raymond Poincaré.

Out of the ranks stepped an earnest young regular army captain named George C. Marshall, who was acting as the division's chief of staff. He caught Pershing's arm as he stalked away. "General Pershing," he said. "There's something to be said here and I think I should say it."

The captain proceeded to list the division's myriad problems—everything from missing equipment to newly arrived recruits. Other staff officers averted their eyes, expecting Marshall and his career to be annihilated on the spot. Instead, Pershing listened to him with amazing patience.[87]

Marshall did not change the AEF commander's mind about General Siebert, who was soon replaced by a more aggressive general. Pershing cast equally critical eyes on a dozen other major generals whom the War Department sent to France for a quick tour before they returned home to pick up their divisions. Pershing told Washington he had no use for ten of them. They were "too old" or "very fat and inactive" or even "infirm." But the desk generals in the State, War and Navy Building proceeded to send nine of the ten rejects to France, ignoring his advice.[88]

Ironically, one of the few who escaped Pershing's scalpel was the fattest general in the army, Hunter Liggett. Pershing kept him, because Liggett, former head of the Army War College, had a brain. The wisecracking side of Pershing, which remained hidden most of the time behind the mask of the iron general, also probably liked Liggett's defense of his bulk: There was nothing wrong with fat as long as it was not above the collar.[89]

On October 21, 1917, four battalions, one from each regiment of the First Division, went into the trenches northeast of Nancy under the supervision of a French division. The sector had seen little action since 1914. The weather proved more menacing than the somnolent Germans. Icy rain deluged the men, who were still wearing summer uniforms. A Washington bureaucrat had recently informed Pershing that they were holding woolen clothing in the United States to keep the draftees warm. The fellow apparently thought France was in the tropic zone.[90]

The four battalions survived their ten days in the lines with nothing worse than a plethora of bad colds. They even captured a German—an unarmed mail orderly who wandered the wrong way in the dark. The next four battalions had a very different experience. Within hours of their arrival, German shells descended around a strong point occupied by a platoon of Company F of the Sixteenth Regiment. The bombardment was a "box barrage," designed to cut off an outpost from nearby support—the prelude to a trench raid. The American lieutenant in command wanted to call for a counter barrage, but his supposedly wiser French adviser disagreed—not the last time the French would reveal their condescension toward the "Sammies."

In minutes, 213 well-armed Germans emerged from the smoke and fog to storm the American trench. They had used bangalore torpedoes to blast their way through the barbed wire protecting it. A wild melee erupted, with the Germans wielding blackjacks, entrenching shovels and other horrendous tools developed by trench warfare veterans. In fifteen minutes, the enemy departed with a dozen prisoners. They left behind five American wounded and three dead—one shot, another with his throat cut, the third with his skull crushed. The Americans killed two and wounded seven attackers. The Bavarian lieutenant who led the raiding party reported, "The enemy was very good at hand to hand fighting."[91]

When Pershing heard the news, he wept. Not out of grief for the dead but because this small defeat could not have come at a worse time. It coincided with a deluge of bad news from other battlefronts. On October 23, the insertion of seven German divisions into the hitherto feckless Austrian army had produced a stupendous victory at Caporetto in northern Italy. The Italian army had become a fleeing mob, which a young American ambulance driver named Ernest Hemingway would later describe in scarifying detail in his novel *A Farewell to Arms.* Over 300,000 Italian soldiers surrendered; the Germans captured no less than 3,000 abandoned artillery pieces. The British and French rushed eleven divisions—150,000 men—to Italy to stabilize the situation.

Even worse was the news from northern France. Starting on July 31, Field Marshal Douglas Haig tried to win the war without the Americans. He hurled a half million men at German defenses around the Flanders town of Ypres. For the next three months, ignoring horrendous casualties and rains that turned the battlefield into a sea of mud so deep that wounded men drowned in it, Haig continued his attacks. Not until November 6, when the dead and wounded reached 310,000, did the field marshal desist, having gained only a few meaningless kilometers and a ridge on which sat the ruined village of Passchendaele. British historians named the battle after it, instead of calling the disaster the third battle of Ypres, which reminded them of two previous stalemates in the same blood-soaked place.

The news from Russia provided no relief from this deluge of gloom. The new democracy's army seemed to have literally vanished. According to one story swirling through France, anyone could predict that the Germans would advance fourteen kilometers closer to Moscow and Petrograd each day. Why? "That was as far as a tired German can walk."[92]

Pershing knew the deteriorating military situation would lead to renewed demands to amalgamate the American army into the shaken French and British forces. When the First Division planned a retaliatory trench raid of its own, the desperate AEF commander supervised it personally. Alas, it was a humiliating flop. The infantry and the engineers failed to meet in no-man's-land, and without the engineers' bangalore torpedoes, no one could get through the German barbed wire.[93]

Eventually the First Division pulled off a successful raid, led by Theodore Roosevelt, Jr. But these trivial skirmishes only intensified Allied disillusion with Pershing's nonexistent army. As fall ebbed into winter, a mixed cry, half despair, half anger, began swirling through France: *Where are the Americans?* The new French premier, Georges Clemenceau, locally known as the Tiger, bared his claws and remarked that General Pershing's chief occupation seemed to be having dinner in Paris.[94]

Chapter 5

SEEDS OF
THE APOCALYPSE

While military disasters disturbed General Pershing's sleep, the political news that arrived in the White House from Europe gave Woodrow Wilson nightmares. The British blunder of urging General Lavr Kornilov to march on Petrograd had produced a political swing to the far left in the Russian capital. Kornilov's army had vanished when the revolutionary government's commissar of the northern front ordered his soldiers not to obey the reactionary general. On November 7–8, 1917 (October 26 in the Russian calendar), the most radical party on the left, the Bolsheviks, seized power. In March 1917, when the czar abdicated, they had barely numbered 25,000 supporters in all of Russia. By November they only had 115,000 in their ranks. But they were led by a revolutionary genius named Vladimir Ilych Lenin, who was backed by a man of equal genius, Leon Trotsky—and they had access to large amounts of German money. The Germans had smuggled Lenin into Russia from his exile in Switzerland for the express purpose of overthrowing the czarist government. With Berlin's help, by August 1917 the Bolsheviks were publishing seventeen daily newspapers with a total circulation of 320,000 copies.[1]

American reaction to the Bolshevik takeover was a mixture of bewilderment and concern about Russia's ability to stay in the war. Although Wilson had hailed the March revolution and sent a mission to Russia in the summer of 1917 with a promise of aid, his spokesmen made it clear that if the Russians stopped fighting the Germans, the dollars would instantly cease coming. Wilson had taken an equally hard line against the Socialists' Stockholm Peace Conference, joining the Allies in refusing to issue passports to let homegrown Socialists attend it.

With that strategy for background, it is not hard to see why the first foreign policy statement of Russia's new rulers stunned and dismayed the Americans. Lenin, with the approval of a rump parliament called the Congress of Soviets, broadcast to the world a "Decree of Peace," calling on "all belligerent peoples and their governments" to join in "the immediate opening of negotiations for a just and democratic peace." Lenin said this just peace would be built on three principles: no annexations (of foreign territory), self-determination for all foreign nationalities within current empires, and no indemnities.[2]

Blown to smithereens was Russia's solemn 1914 promise to its Entente partners not to make a separate peace. Worse was the way the Bolshevik decree encouraged people everywhere to take the search for peace into their own hands, if their governments proved recalcitrant. It was also evident that no annexations and self-determination meant the abolition of colonies everywhere—an idea that caused instant outrage in London and Paris. The world was getting its first glimpse of what the Bolsheviks would soon call demonstrative diplomacy—aimed at embarrassing other nations. Lenin and his circle were certain that this gambit would produce either an instantaneous peace or an explosion of revolutionary warfare everywhere. At this point in their journey to absolute power, they were true believers in the puissance of their own rhetoric.[3]

On November 12, 1917, Woodrow Wilson made a speech to the American Federation of Labor convention in Buffalo, New York. When he mentioned the Russian Decree of Peace, he made it clear that he had no intention of sharing the ideological leadership of the war with the Bolsheviks. He called them fatuous dreamers and lumped them with American "pacifists," whom the U.S. government was busily silencing, putting in jail, or both. "What I am opposed to is not the feeling of the pacifists, but their stupidity," he said. "My heart is with them but my mind has a contempt for them." Proof of the Russians' low IQs, Wilson thought, was their readiness to negotiate peace with the present German government. That idea violated the first article of faith in Wilson's latest creed.[4]

Back in the White House, early reports from Russia encouraged the president to think that the leader of the provisional government, Alexander Kerensky, would soon regain power. In a letter to a congressman, Wilson expressed confidence that the Russian Revolution, like the French Revolution of 1789, would have to go through some "deep waters," but he was sure the Russians would reach "firm land" on the other side. The president seemed to have forgotten that by the time the French reached firm land, they had killed huge numbers of people in France and neighboring countries and wound up with a dictator named Napoleon Bonaparte.[5]

Leon Trotsky, now in charge of the Russian Foreign Office, had recently spent ten weeks working as a journalist in New York and considered himself an authority on the United States. In a widely reported speech, he said the Americans had decided to intervene in the war "under the influence . . . of the American stock exchange." He went on to describe how much money the Americans were making from the war and suggested they were primarily interested in seeing the other belligerents weaken each other until there was a "hegemony of American capital." Much of this statement would have won emphatic approval from Senators George Norris and Robert La Follette. We can be certain, however, that it did not enthuse Woodrow Wilson.[6]

A few days later, Trotsky began exhuming from the Russian diplomatic archives copies of the secret treaties the Allies had made to divide up the spoils of victory. All the sordid deals cut by the supposed defenders of small nations and universal democracy were suddenly revealed to shocked Americans. No one was more dismayed than Woodrow Wilson to have this dirty linen exposed and his sacred struggle for the "right" held up to ridicule.[7]

By coincidence, representatives from the Allies, including Wilson's confidential envoy, Colonel House, were meeting in Paris to try to coordinate their disconnected and in some cases sagging war efforts. House decided the only way to retain a patina of idealism for the war was a frontal assault on the secret treaties. He called for their repudiation. The French and the Italians reacted with outrage and huffily insisted a deal was a deal, whether it was secret or public. The British gave the colonel support so tepid it amounted to another repudiation. All the conferees could agree on was a lame statement that each nation would communicate with Petrograd in its own way and express a willingness to "reconsider" their war aims as soon as Russia had a "stable government." That gave the backs of their hands to the Bolsheviks, who obviously did not measure up to the Allied definition of stability.[8]

The Allied disarray gave the Germans a chance to play a trump card. On December 2, 1917, they sent their foreign minister before the Reichstag to orate on the moderation of Germany's war aims and its readiness for a compromise peace. The Allies, exposed by the secret treaties as "demanding victory and nothing but victory," were driven by narrow, greedy motives. The foreign minister added that he was ready to discuss with the Bolsheviks a "reorganization of affairs in the east"—code words for a peace conference. The Russians accepted the offer and delegates began talking at German army headquarters in Brest-Litovsk on the Russian-Polish border.[9]

This démarche left the international ideological stage swept bare of players—except for Woodrow Wilson. Colonel House clearly recognized this and urged his alter ego not to make "any statement concerning foreign affairs until I can see you." The colonel obviously thought Philip Dru needed all the help he could get.[10]

II

In the midst of this diplomatic turmoil, on November 2, 1917, the British cabinet, over the signature of Foreign Secretary Arthur Balfour, issued a statement that looms large in retrospect but seemed a minor matter to most of the world at the time. The Balfour Declaration, embodied in a letter that the foreign secretary wrote to Lord Rothschild, the unofficial leader of the Jewish community in England, said that His Majesty's government "view with favor the establishment in Palestine of a national home for the Jewish people, and will use their best endeavors to facilitate the achievement of this object; it being clearly understood that nothing shall be done which may prejudice civil and religious rights of existing non-Jewish communities in Palestine, or the rights and political status enjoyed by Jews in any other country."[11]

This epochal document was created by a complex interplay between the dynamics of the war and personal diplomacy by Jews who had become converts to Zionism, a vision of a regained Jewish homeland articulated by the late-nineteenth-century poet and playwright Theodore Herzl. In England one of Zionism's leading exponents was the gifted chemist Chaim Weizmann, who had intermittently conferred with Balfour and Lloyd George during the preceding decade. Both these powerful politicians developed an attachment to the idea, thanks to their noncomformist religious past. But few if any statesmen allow religious sentiment to guide their policies. The driving force behind the decision to issue the statement at the close of the disastrous year 1917 was visible in a coded telegram that Balfour sent to Sir William Wiseman, the director of British intelligence in the United States and a confidant of Colonel House.

London, Oct. 6, '17

Following from Falsterbro [Balfour] for Brussa [House]

IN VIEW OF REPORTS THAT GERMAN GOVERNMENT ARE MAKING GREAT EFFORTS TO CAPTURE ZIONIST MOVEMENT, QUESTION OF A MESSAGE OF SYMPATHY WITH MOVEMENT FROM H.M. GOVERNMENT HAS AGAIN BEEN CONSIDERED BY CABINET . . . BEFORE TAKING ANY DECISION CABINET INTEND TO HEAR VIEWS OF SOME OF REPRESENTATIVE ZIONISTS, BUT MEANWHILE THEY WOULD BE GRATEFUL IF YOU FOUND IT POSSIBLE TO ASCERTAIN OPINION OF ADRAMYTI [Wilson] WITH REGARD TO FORMULA.[12]

Wiseman swiftly passed this telegram to House, who soon handed it to Wilson. Seven days later, the colonel got the following note from the president.

My dear House:

I find in my pocket the memorandum you gave me about the Zionist movement. I am afraid I did not say to you that I concurred in the formula suggested from the other side. I do, and would be obliged if you would let them know it.[13]

Clearly, the matter was not a major concern, if the president put the memorandum in his pocket and forgot about it. Palestine and the entire Middle East was British turf, in which Wilson and House had little interest.

What interest they had was overlaid by caution. On October 16, Wiseman cabled London, reporting that "Brussa [House] put formula before Adramyti [Wilson], who approves it, but asks that no mention of his approval shall be made when H.M.G. [His Majesty's Government] makes formula public, as he has arranged that American Jews shall then ask him for his approval which he will give publicly here."[14]

III

Onrushing events left little or no time to devote much thought to the Middle East. The United States never even bothered to declare war on Turkey. The European drama absorbed the attention of U.S. politicians. On the heels of the Bolshevik call for an early peace and the diplomatic contretemps over the secret treaties came a startling appeal for an end to the war from one of England's leading conservatives. The Marquis of Lansdowne, former foreign secretary and viceroy of India, published a letter in the *London Telegraph,* saying the murderous conflict had already lasted too long. The marquis had lost two sons in the struggle. Calmly, magisterially, he repudiated the economic jealousy and newspaper-manufactured hatred of Germany, which he blamed for drawing England into the war. Lansdowne urged a peace that would neither threaten Germany with annihilation nor deny its rightful place as the dominant industrial nation of Europe. He added to these ideas a proposal for an international organization that would preserve such a peace.

The British leader clearly differed with Wilson and with his own government about their refusal to negotiate with the supposedly autocratic German government. He did not belabor the point. But he was obviously calling for a peace without victory. German-hating Ambassador Walter Hines Page reported that Lansdowne was supported only by "pacifists and semi-pacifists and a war-weary minority." But the nobleman's appeal put new pressure on Woodrow Wilson to find an answer to these calls for peace and somehow restore the idealistic glow in which his rhetoric had coated the war on April 2, 1917.[15]

IV

The president was scheduled to go before the second session of the Sixty-Fifth Congress on December 4 to give his state-of-the-union address. He realized that House's advice to remain silent on foreign policy was patently impossible. Wilson had to say something, as he pointed out to his alter ego in a terse cable: "SORRY IMPOSSIBLE TO OMIT FOREIGN AFFAIRS FROM ADDRESS TO CONGRESS. RETICENCE ON MY PART AT THIS JUNCTURE WOULD BE MISUNDERSTOOD AND RESENTED AND DO MUCH HARM."[16]

The *New York Times* reported the president looked fresh and determined, and remarked on his colorful, new tie. He struck his main theme hard and early. "Let there be no misunderstanding. Our present and immediate task is to win the war and nothing shall turn us aside from it until it is accomplished." There could be no negotiations, no compromise with "German autocracy." As for principles and goals, Wilson endorsed the idea of "no annexations, no indemnities." They were good principles, but they had been used "by the masters of German intrigue to lead the Russian people astray." When the war was won, "a right use" will be made of these principles. Peace would be based on "generosity and justice, to the exclusion of all selfish claims to advantage, even on the part of the victors. . . . There must be no covenants of selfishness and compromise."

Wilson was telling the Allies what he thought of the secret treaties: not much. He then embarked on an even more unilateral argument. He wished these principles had been "made plain at the very outset" of the war. If that had been done, "the sympathy and enthusiasm of the Russian people might have been once and for all enlisted on the side of the Allies, suspicion and mistrust swept away, and a real and lasting union of purpose effected." Instead, the Russian people had been "poisoned by the same dark falsehoods that kept the German people in the dark, and the poison has been administered by the very same hands."

With rhetoric that soared above any semblance of psychological realism, Wilson claimed he sympathized with the German people, who had allowed their evil leaders to deceive them into thinking they were fighting for their national existence. He expressed similar sympathy for the people of Austria-Hungary and insisted he had no desire to "impair or rearrange" their empire. But to speed the progress to victory, Wilson asked for a declaration of war against Austria-Hungary because it was "simply a vassal of the German government."[17]

This request for a wider war evoked, according to the *New York Times*, an eruption that combined war rage and hatred of hyphenated Americans. "A cheer that came from a dozen places at once broke the silence that had been intensified by the sense of disappointment over the feeling he had created that the day of reckoning with the Vienna Government and particularly with those Austrian subjects in America who were playing Germany's game of intrigue and incendiarism under the nose of the United States was now at hand." The cheering, punctuated by the *yip-yip-yip* of the rebel yell from Southern senators, lasted so long that the president had to step away from the lectern until it subsided.

Only Senator Robert La Follette remained seated, stubbornly refusing to join the acclamation.[18]

The president closed with a call for "vigorous, rapid, and successful prosecution of the great task of winning the war." The struggle, he insisted, was for America one of "high disinterested purpose." The cause was "just and holy" and the settlement must be of "like motive and quality." He was saying the secret treaties must be abandoned, but for the time being, he left the problem in the realm of the ideal.[19]

The *Times* of London called the speech "illuminating and inspiring." Ambassador Walter Hines Page cabled: "It is regarded as his most important utterance"—an indication of how badly the British needed an answer to the Bolsheviks and Lord Lansdowne. A *New York Times* sampling of editorial opinion around the country declared the president had given a definitive answer to the peace seekers. Lloyd George's knockout blow was still in charge of the war.[20]

Behind the scenes there was a dramatic revelation of Wilson's real feelings about this outcome. Not long after he finished his speech, the president conferred with William C. Bullitt, a young Philadelphia journalist whose astute reporting on European affairs, especially inside Germany, had persuaded Colonel House to make him an assistant secretary of state. Bullitt congratulated Wilson on the state-of-the-union address. The president replied, "Wasn't it horrible? All those congressmen and senators applauding every wretched warlike thing I had to say, ignoring all the things for which I really care. I hate this war! . . . The only thing I care about on earth is the peace I am going to make at the end of it."

Tears ran down Woodrow Wilson's cheeks.[21]

V

While the president was trying to hold the western end of the Allied coalition together with rhetoric that combined war will and idealism, a very different drama was taking place in Paris. The new premier, Georges Clemenceau, was struggling to stamp out a plot to overthrow the government and take France out of the war. The defeatism that General Henri-Philippe Pétain had worried about during his first meeting with General Pershing had fermented into a full-blown conspiracy. At its center was a wealthy, bald-headed, left-of-center politician named Joseph Caillaux.

A former premier (in 1911), Caillaux led the largest party in the French Chamber of Deputies, the Radical Socialists. They were mostly small businessmen and farmers, few either radical or very socialistic. But they had a motto, "No enemies to the left," which often led them to vote with the genuine Socialists, France's second largest party, making them formidable. Caillaux was not popular with French conservatives, who accused him of being a friend of Germany—tantamount to treason, in their view. In fact, the former premier believed that enmity between the two nations made no sense. He thought France's best hope for prosperity lay in an economic alliance with Germany's dynamic economy.

Caillaux had not held office since 1914. That year, conservatives had tried to destroy him by persuading the editor of their flagship paper, *Le Figaro,* to publish allegations about his steamy private life, backed by revealing letters supplied by his bitter first wife. His second wife, Henriette Caillaux, who figured largely in the letters, settled matters by shooting *Le Figaro*'s editor dead in his office. She was acquitted in a sensational trial; the jury accepted her lawyers' very French argument that her passion had been uncontrollable. But Caillaux emerged so violently hated by the right wing that no government could survive with him in office.[22]

That did not mean Caillaux and his point of view disappeared from French politics. The Radical Socialists remained passionately devoted to him. So did a very powerful man in the French government, Louis Malvy, minister of the interior in the various governments that rose and fell in the course of the war. Malvy was in charge of internal security. He had secret agents everywhere—and the power to put almost anyone but a member of the chamber of deputies in jail.

Caillaux played a waiting game. He served for a while as an army paymaster, which enabled him to keep in touch with soldiers from his district. He toured South America on a vague trade mission. In Argentina, with its large German colony, he easily got in touch with Berlin's ambassador. Through intermediaries, he made it clear that he thought the war would end in French defeat. Then would come the time for a sensible man to take command of France with the backing of the French army—and the victorious Germans.[23]

By some accounts, Caillaux threw in a long-range plan for a later war against England, with a Latin League composed of Spain, Italy and France supporting the kaiser's government. At the head of this league would be

Joseph Caillaux, maximum ruler of France. The Germans were predictably delighted.[24]

Back in France, Caillaux's protégé, Interior Minister Malvy, kept him fully informed of the inner politics of successive French cabinets and their uneasy relationship with the army. Caillaux also stayed in contact with left-leaning General Maurice Sarrail, who was commanding French troops in Greece. Caillaux had appointed him to his high rank during his premiership.

Meanwhile, Malvy evolved a strategy that he described as co-opting the left, supposedly to prevent them from disrupting the war effort. He sponsored a radical editor, Miguel Almereyda, and his paper, the *Bonnet Rouge,* on the theory that they would discourage violent resistance to the war, while seeming to criticize it. *Almereyda,* incidentally, was an adopted name, an anagram for *'Y a la merde* ("Everything is shitty")—a neat summation of his philosophy of life.[25]

As futile offensives killed hundreds of thousands of Frenchmen, the army's prestige among the politicians steadily declined. Interior Minister Malvy called for confining the military's secret service operations to the battle zone, leaving him in charge of the Zone of the Interior. By 1916, the army's secret police had been driven out of Paris. But they had acquired a deep suspicion of Malvy and sent agents into the interior of France to detect traitorous conspiracies.[26]

The army's agents found evidence aplenty of Malvy's strange tolerance for leftist enemies of the war. Beside Almereyda and the *Bonnet Rouge,* there was Paul-Marie Bolo, a former hairdresser and failed restaurateur who displayed remarkable skill at marrying wealthy women and dissipating their fortunes. On the brink of bankruptcy when the war broke out, Bolo met Abbas Hilmi, the former khedive of Egypt, in Switzerland. No one hated the British more than this embittered Arab. He decided to put Bolo in charge of his financial affairs in Europe and honored him with the rank of pasha. Bolo soon realized that most of the khedive's finances came from Berlin, but that did not bother him.

Bolo Pasha began cutting a glittering swath through *la guerre de luxe,* buying up influential politicians. One of his most eager clients was Senator Charles Humbert, who headed the Military Committee in the French Senate, and published *Le Journal,* the third largest daily in France, with a circulation of 1.1 million. Secretly, Humbert sold control of the paper to Bolo, who paid with money from the khedive, who got it from Berlin.

Bolo was told to lie low for the time being, while the *Bonnet Rouge* led the way in attacking the war. The paper acquired a gifted editor, Émile-Joseph Duval, who made numerous trips to Switzerland and invariably returned with infusions of cash from mysterious investors. This pump priming, plus a government subsidy from Malvy, enabled Duval to expand and improve the paper. Almereyda remained the front man and contact with Malvy, but he spent most of his time enjoying his pick of Paris's 75,000 prostitutes, his fleet of six limousines and other perquisites of the *guerre de luxe,* including a steady supply of heroin.[27]

In December 1916, Joseph and Henriette Caillaux took a trip to Italy. He told various Italian politicians that the current government, headed by Premier Alexandre Ribot, would soon fall. There would be one more pro-war regime, possibly headed by ultranationalist Georges Clemenceau, who would bet everything on "intensifying the war." This last gasp of the offensive spirit would inevitably fail, and then France would be ready for a Caillaux government. As soon as he became premier, he planned to dissolve Parliament, flood Paris with regiments drawn from his election district, and appoint General Sarrail the army's commander in chief. Then he would await an offer from the Germans, sign a reasonably advantageous peace and immediately begin constructing the Latin League he had outlined in South America. Caillaux urged Italy to join him in this realistic realignment of the great powers, which would enable the true Europeans to triumph over the barbarians of the east (Russia) and the greedy offshore capitalists of the west (England).[28]

Events on the battlefield soon made Caillaux look like a prophet. The failed Nivelle offensive and the French army's mutiny left the Ribot government tottering. Unexpectedly, Georges Clemenceau arose in the Senate to launch a ferocious attack on Louis Malvy and the *Bonnet Rouge.* The French police had recently arrested Émile-Joseph Duval at the Swiss border with a check for 150,837 francs in his wallet. His stammered explanation of the source of the check, which came from one Marx, an ironically named German secret agent, was so weak, the police had confiscated it. At Malvy's insistence, the check was returned to Duval. Clemenceau used this episode and Malvy's numerous other acts of favoritism to the *Bonnet Rouge* and similar leftist organizations to denounce him as a betrayer of France.

The French conservative press erupted, accusing Malvy of everything from pacifism to supplying the Germans with military information. The Ribot government arrested Miguel Almereyda and shut down the *Bonnet Rouge.* Also arrested was Bolo Pasha, who talked freely, hoping to save his neck. The story of how he had bought *Le Journal* with German money was soon splashed across the front pages of other papers.[29]

Three weeks later, Almereyda was found in his cell, strangled to death with his own shoe laces. The government claimed he had committed suicide because he was deprived of his heroin. But many believed he had been murdered because he had too many stories to tell about the conspiracy.

At the end of August 1917, Malvy resigned as interior minister and the Ribot government fell with him. But the conspirators were by no means out of business. With the army still tainted by "indiscipline," another French cabinet under Premier Paul Painlevé staggered from crisis to crisis, battered by critics from the right and left. In the political wings Caillaux waited and watched for his moment. For a while the French hoped the American alliance would rescue them. But when Pershing's army failed to materialize, the Italians collapsed and the Russians exited from the war, the Caillaux option began to look better and better.

Caillaux's moment seemed to arrive on November 13, 1917, when Painlevé received a vote of no confidence in the chamber of deputies. The three previous wartime governments had collapsed more discreetly, concealing disagreements by shuffling premiers and ministers. This time there seemed to be a vacuum—and the president of France had the constitutional responsibility to ask someone to take charge. In the Élysée Palace, archconservative Raymond Poincaré saw that he had only two choices: Joseph Caillaux or Georges Clemenceau.

Caillaux could rule from the left, but the passionately nationalist Poincaré distrusted him—even though the leader of the Radical Socialists had recently been taking pains to deny any intention of making peace with the Germans. On the other hand, Poincaré hated Clemenceau. The Tiger had repeatedly attacked him as *la paperasse,* an indecisive functionary who relied more on red tape than brains to do his job. When Clemenceau was briefly premier in 1906, he had managed to displease everyone. The left had called him a dictator, a cop, and "the emperor of spies." The conservatives dismissed him as a "sinister gaffer."[30]

Nevertheless, Poincaré chose Clemenceau. Cynics predicted he would not last two months. The country was in no mood to be bullied. Caillaux assured his followers that his moment had only been slightly delayed.

On Clemenceau's first day as premier, the chamber of deputies waited expectantly—and perhaps fearfully—for his opening remarks. His scraggly mustache drooping, his white hair uncombed as usual, the stooped old man paced the rostrum and glared at the deputies. In the balcony sat Britain's minister of munitions, Winston Churchill, invited by French friends to watch the show. Churchill never forgot what he saw and heard on that November day. It would be in his mind when he spoke defiant words during an as yet undreamed of crisis in another war.

Clemenceau had to read a statement of policy to obtain a vote of confidence in his government. "We present ourselves before you with the unique thought of a total war," he barked. For all of them, there was only one simple duty: "To remain with the soldier, to live, to suffer to fight with him." Grimly, the old man added he would tolerate "neither treason nor half treason—only war! Nothing but war! . . . For these measures, without turning back, we seek the sanction of your vote!"[31]

The Tiger won approval by a huge majority and took personal command of the French government. His cabinet was a collection of nonentities. He relied on only a handful of men, notably hard-nosed General Jean Mordacq to advise him on military matters and Georges Mandel, who became interior minister without the title. The son of a Jewish tailor, Mandel was a totally ruthless keeper of dossiers on every politician in sight and a master of backstairs intrigue. At Clemenceau's order he began shutting down every antiwar newspaper in France.

Clemenceau knew he had to strike soon and hard at the men who were waiting for him to falter—Louis Malvy and Joseph Caillaux. He let one of the archconservative deputies accuse Malvy of leaking military secrets to the Germans. The Tiger solemnly declared that this serious charge should be weighed by the French Senate, sitting as a high court. Malvy eagerly accepted the challenge, claiming he was sure of vindication, and surrendered to the police.

But Caillaux? He had not held any public post since 1914—and as a member of the chamber of deputies, he was legally immune to arrest and prosecution. Mandel went to work. Secret agents hurried to Florence, where the Italian police opened a Caillaux safe deposit box containing the plans for his pacifist coup d'état and his Latin League. From the Almereyda and Bolo Pasha files came Caillaux letters, praising their efforts for peace.

Clemenceau went before the chamber of deputies and asked them to revoke Caillaux's immunity. A parliamentary committee was appointed to consider the request. If the committee said no, Clemenceau would resign and Caillaux would become premier. General Pershing and his trainees in Lorraine and the British army in northern France might find themselves surrounded by triumphant Germans within a matter of days as the poilus went home. The anxious correspondent of the *Times* of London called the vote "the most important non-military event in France since the beginning of the war."[32]

On December 22, 1917, the committee recommended that Caillaux be stripped of his immunity. Key members had undoubtedly received calls from Mandel, reminding them of what was in their dossiers. Undaunted, Caillaux demanded the right to speak. His oration was a brilliant display of his powers. He warned his fellow deputies that they were risking France's republican future and possibly their heads. He reminded Clemenceau of the time when the Tiger had been accused of treason and Caillaux and the Radical Socialists had defended him.[33]

Unmoved, Clemenceau called for a vote. It was almost unanimous in favor of putting Caillaux on trial. With their leaders in jail, the cowed French leftists remained sullenly silent while Émile-Joseph Duval and other members of the *Bonnet Rouge* staff were tried for treason by a military court and swiftly convicted. Next came Bolo Pasha, who also drew a guilty verdict. Bolo and Duval were shot, the lesser fry sentenced to varying prison terms.

In Cell Seventeen of the Prison de la Santé on the Boulevard Araggo, a by no means undiscouraged Caillaux waited grimly for his day in court. His cell was as comfortable as the rules for political prisoners permitted. He had two mattresses, ample furniture, the books of his choice, and writing materials. Each day, he had a half bottle of the best Bordeaux for lunch and another half for dinner. He conferred regularly with his attorney; his wife and a stream of friends visited him. As long as Caillaux remained unconvicted, France's participation in the war depended on the continuing health of a stooped, irascible seventy-six-year-old man whom almost every politician in the country hated.[34]

VI

Editorial writers and sycophantic ambassadors may have praised Woodrow Wilson's state-of-the-union address, and Congress may have cheered his declaration of war on Austria-Hungary—but it did not change many minds about the president and his faltering war effort. The Shipping Board had spent a half billion dollars and had yet to launch a ship; the aircraft program had spent even more and had yet to put a single plane in the sky. Coal supplies were so short, in many cities local officials were seizing coal trains and distributing their contents to their people, leaving other parts of the country fuelless as wintry winds began to blow. Labor was surly and wheat farmers were screaming about price controls.

Particularly damned was George Creel's Committee on Public Information, for resolutely painting everything in a rosy hue. Early in 1918, Creel compounded the government's woes with another episode of "creeling." The CPI made a triumphant announcement: "The first American built battle planes are today en route to the front in France." Reporters soon discovered there was only one battle plane in existence, and it was not exactly on its way to France. It had made a rather shaky flight from the factory to a nearby airport for radiator tests. Creel was forced to admit the story was "overcolored"—even the pictures turned out to be fake. After the war, he claimed that he had taken the fall for Secretary of War Newton Baker, who gave him the phony information.[35]

Very much on the scene was Theodore Roosevelt, who was continuing to lambaste Wilson in the newspapers and from platforms. At a breakfast meeting in New York, TR, General Leonard Wood and Senator Henry Cabot Lodge even blamed Lord Lansdowne's call for peace on Wilson, because it was issued while Colonel House was in London on one of his mysterious overseas missions. The president's men fought back by calling TR and his backers war naggers. But the overall political and military situation unfortunately made their nagging seem all too pertinent.[36]

"We cannot beat the Kaiser by standing silently by Wilson," Senator Lodge proclaimed. Republican senators began visiting army camps. General Leonard Wood supplied them with devastating figures about shortages and sickness.

On December 11, a hefty majority of the Senate called for a "drastic inquiry" into the administration's performance. A desperate *New York World* snarled in response that someone should investigate Congress for passing such slipshod war legislation. Soon no less than five investigations were under way in the Senate, with Wilson's enemies in the Democratic Party gleefully participating in all of them.

Senator James Reed of Missouri again assailed the Food Administration. He accused Herbert Hoover and his aides of violating the great unwritten law of supply and demand and erupted with rage when witnesses tried to contradict him. Reed grew so angry at Hoover's refusal to admit wrong-doing, he would not even allow the food administrator to put a statement in the record in his own defense.[37]

Hoover ignored these gross canards; he was the acknowledged star of the Wilson administration. Using the slogan "Food will win the war," he had persuaded Americans to eat fish and vegetables instead of meat and bread, enabling him to double U.S. exports of wheat to hungry England and France. "Hooverizing" entered the language as a patriotic exhortation to consume less and bring conservation to the kitchen. Walter Lippmann praised Hoover as a man who "incarnates all that is at once effective and idealistic in the picture of America." Colonel House urged Washington hostesses to do everything in their power to keep the food administrator happy so he would stay in Washington in spite of senators like Jim Reed.[38]

But Hoover's success did little to ameliorate the administration's perform-ance in other areas. The rapidly worsening coal shortage was an even riper target for congressional ire. Many cities had to deploy nightstick-wielding policemen to protect factory coal piles from desperate mobs. As temperatures sank to near zero and a blizzard buried most of the country east of the Mississippi, newspapers reported people freezing to death in prisons, orphan-ages and mental hospitals. The fuel administrator, Harry Garfield, was a for-mer college president and an old Wilson friend. The senators belabored him as a living metaphor of the incompetence of the man in the White House.[39]

The War Department provided additional ammunition for this bash-Wilson campaign. General William Crozier, chief of the ordnance branch, was so lethargic, he made Generals Hugh Scott and Tasker Bliss look alert. Nobody—including General Pershing—had a good word to say for him. Crozier must have given everyone in the White House the bends when he admitted he had done nothing to procure weapons and supplies on a war-fighting scale until June, three months after the president's supposedly electri-fying war message to Congress. The general blamed everyone else—Congress for being slow with appropriations, manufacturers for refusing to expand their plants until they saw the color of the government's money.[40]

Crozier had more trouble explaining why the U.S. Army had almost no machine guns. Ordnance had dithered between two types, the Lewis gun and the Browning. General Wood had favored the Lewis, which was used in the British army. Crozier had backed the Browning, although it was largely untried—and he did not get around to putting it into production for months. The Republicans tried to make him admit he was continuing the White House vendetta against General Wood—leaving American soldiers shorn of the war's most important weapon.[41]

Juiciest of all the investigations was the war camps probe. Here the senators had ammunition from hysterical parents who reported sons freezing in summer uniforms and dying of pneumonia. Newspapers had already investigated a number of camps and reported appalling conditions when winter temperatures froze plumbing and barracks ran out of coal. Commanders of several camps were called to testify and mournfully declared they had sent the War Department repeated warnings about shortages and poor construction—and never received an answer. One general described having several thousand sick men in a hospital built to hold 800. The quartermaster general admitted that red tape had left winter uniforms sitting in warehouses while draftees froze. "GENERALS TELL OF HOW RED TAPE FILLED GRAVES," screamed a typical newspaper headline.[42]

A topper of sorts was provided by a group of congressmen who had just returned from France. They reported similar conditions among Pershing's troops. They too were freezing in summer uniforms, eating abominable food, and without vital weapons. One congressman quoted French and British generals who said the Allies were facing imminent defeat unless the United States could ship them 25,000 artillery pieces. Their testimony belied the picture George Creel's committee was painting of well-equipped Americans ready to take on the German army.[43]

Senator Boise Penrose of Pennsylvania rose to announce the immediate opening of the 1918 campaign for control of Congress. It was vital to put competent men in charge of the nation's destiny. Other Republicans denounced Wilson's policy of appointing Democrats and old friends such as Harry Garfield to the top jobs. They called on the president to create a coalition cabinet with a separate Munitions Department—something the British had done with apparent success.

Throughout this public bludgeoning, Wilson maintained a tense silence. He ignored Joe Tumulty's pleas to do or say something "radical" in response to "the tantrums on the Hill." The president was absorbed in writing another speech—a statement of America's war aims. The growing aggressiveness of Bolshevik propaganda, House's failure to persuade the Allies to repudiate the secret treaties, and the beginning of peace negotiations between the Russians and the Germans were the main reasons for his decision. Another large factor was the return of Colonel House from Europe with a pessimistic report on the situation there on both the military and political fronts.[44]

VII

Wilson ordered House to put the War Data Investigation Bureau (the Inquiry) to work on background material for a speech that would settle everything. The oration was supposed to answer the Bolsheviks, cleave the German people from their devotion to the kaiser, repudiate the secret treaties and fuse the American people—and the rest of the world—into idealistic peace seekers committed to the victory of Wilsonian ideals. Such was this president's faith in the power of words.[45]

Working day and night, the Inquiry began redrawing the map of postwar Europe with the improbable goal of peace and justice for all—minorities, captive peoples and the warring powers. Using charts and piles of statistics, they tried to decide which clauses of the secret treaties made sense and which were motivated by greed. After four weeks of minimal sleep, an exhausted Walter Lippmann presented Colonel House with a much-revised memorandum, "The War Aims and the Peace Terms It Suggests." Wilson transferred much of this document wholesale into his proposed speech. On Saturday morning, January 5, 1918, he summoned House to the executive mansion and put together the final outline of his speech. "Saturday was a remarkable day," the colonel told his diary. "We got down to work at half past ten and finished remaking the map of the world, as we would have it, by half past twelve o'clock."[46]

This boast was alarming evidence that Philip Dru was at work again, solving tangled political dilemmas that had resisted decades of diplomacy with a naive belief in the power of pronouncements from on high. Convinced that Wilson's prestige as a preacher of international ideals was in the ascendancy, House was serenely confident in his alter ego's power to transform the globe.

A rude shock from not-so-merrie England punched a hole in this optimism. In London, Prime Minister Lloyd George made a speech to the British Trades Union Congress. The British leader said many, even most, of the same idealistic things the president was planning to say. British intelligence chief Sir William Wiseman told Colonel House that the speech was written by Lord David Cecil, a leading British liberal. It was the first but by no means the last glimpse of Lloyd George's fondness for working both sides of the political street.[47]

An infuriated Wilson told House there was no longer any point in making his speech. The agitated colonel had to work very hard to persuade Wilson that Lloyd George had "cleared the air"—and that made it "more necessary" for Wilson to speak. A semiapologetic cable from Foreign Secretary Balfour helped House persuade Wilson to go ahead. Balfour claimed that Lloyd George had been forced to appease the trade unions without delay. Surly over the government's boycott of the Stockholm Conference, they were in a state of collective indiscipline that almost matched the mood of the French army.[48]

Wilson remained unmollified for another two days. On January 8, he finally decided to go ahead. Giving Congress only a half hour's notice, the president went before the legislature again to deliver what many consider his most famous speech. In it he proclaimed "Fourteen Points" that were fundamental to America's war aims. He spent the first several minutes expressing sympathy with the Russian attempt to negotiate peace with the Germans. He even went so far as to imply that the Bolsheviks were the authentic voice of the Russian people. In a flight of moving eloquence, he portrayed the Russian masses negotiating with the "grim power" of Germany with "a largeness of view, a generosity of spirit" that was bound to win "the admiration of mankind." He reported that German terms of "conquest and domination" were so greedy, the Russians had broken off the negotiations, refusing to abandon their "humane and honorable" ideals or "desert others that they themselves may be safe."[49]

Unfortunately, this was rhetoric from never-never land, like Wilson's previous pronouncements about the Mexican revolution. The Bolsheviks were not the authentic voice of the Russian people. They were a splinter party, at best. In elections held six weeks earlier, a huge majority of the

Russian people had repudiated them. Contrary to a January 3 *New York Times* headline, Lenin had not broken off negotiations with the Germans. He and Trotsky were doing exactly what Wilson praised them for not doing—deserting the Allies to preserve their grip on power. As for humane and honorable ideals, the Bolsheviks regarded such notions as leftovers from the era of "rotten liberalism."[50]

Next Wilson tried to deal with German peace initiatives. He said no one could tell whether they came from "liberal leaders and parties" or those who "insist upon conquest and subjugation." He wondered if the two sides were not in "hopeless contradiction." On the other hand, there was no "confusion of counsel" among the Allies—"no uncertainty of principle, no vagueness of detail." Only the Germans clung to "secrecy of counsel" and "lack of fearless frankness."

These claims were so far from the truth as we now know it, one can only take it as a measure of Wilson's desperation. The president was finessing British, French and Italian intransigence on the secret treaties and Clemenceau confronting left wing peace proponents with firing squads. The president tried to manage this verbal prestidigitation by proclaiming a new era. "The day of conquest and aggrandizement is gone by, so is also the day of secret covenants entered into in the interest of particular governments." The processes of peace would involve "no secret understandings of any kind."[51]

Wilson now outlined his "program of the world's peace":

1. Open covenants . . . openly arrived at.
2. Absolute freedom of navigation upon the seas.
3. The removal of all economic barriers [tariffs] to trade.
4. Adequate guarantees of a reduction of armaments.
5. A free, open-minded, and absolutely impartial adjustment of all colonial claims, based on the interests and opinions of the people involved.
6. The evacuation of all Russian territory by German armies.

The next seven clauses dealt with rearranging the map of Europe, from restoring Belgian independence and returning Alsace-Lorraine to France to creating an independent Polish state. Several dealt with such particular questions as giving Serbia "free and secure access to the sea"—not exactly an issue that would inspire Americans to fight to the death. In the four-teenth point, Wilson returned to a supremely idealistic goal: "A general association of nations must be formed under specific covenants" to guarantee political independence and territorial integrity "to great and small states alike" around the world.

These were the purposes for which Americans were prepared to do battle against "the Imperialists." Again, one is almost boggled by the way Wilson fastened this term of opprobrium on Germany, while England and France between them had several hundred million people in their colonial grip. Wilson's goal became clearer in his closing words, in which he insisted that "we have no jealousy of German greatness and there is nothing in our program that impairs it." He praised Germany's achievements in science and culture. He only wanted to see it accept a place of "equality" among the peoples of the world—"instead of a place of mastery."

Next came an even more startling statement. "Neither do we presume to suggest to her [Germany] any alteration or modification of her institutions." He only wanted to know whether Germany's spokesmen "speak . . . for the Reichstag majority or for the military party and the men whose creed is imperial domination." Wilson was appealing over the heads of Germany's rulers to this liberal group, whose existence he had hitherto denied.

The president ended in a soaring tribute to the basic tenet of his program: "Justice to all peoples and nationalities, and their right to live on equal terms of liberty and safety with one another, whether they be strong or weak." On this principle, "the culminating and final war for human liberty" would be fought.[52]

The Fourteen Points speech received extravagant praise in the United States. Even Theodore Roosevelt approved of it, at least in public. The *New York Tribune,* long a harsh Wilson critic, called it "one of the great documents of American history" and compared it to the Gettysburg Address. Senator Henry Cabot Lodge grudgingly admitted the speech met with "general approbation," but too much of it was "general bleat about virtue being better than vice."[53]

In Europe praise was lukewarm, at best. The British made it clear that they had no intention of surrendering their best imperial weapon, the blockade, to absolute freedom of the seas. Lord Northcliffe's *Times* muttered that Wilson assumed "the reign of righteousness on earth is already within our reach." The French were even more skeptical. In private, Premier Clemenceau, who already disliked Wilson, remarked that God was satisfied with ten commandments but Wilson wanted fourteen. All concerned were miffed by Wilson's omission of a very important term: reparations.

Neither England nor France nor Italy said an official word about the speech. As far as changing anyone's mind about the secret treaties was concerned, the Fourteen Points were a flop. The speech also accomplished zero minus with the Bolsheviks. Leon Trotsky dismissed it as capitalist hot air and said the Allies, including Wilson, secretly backed the tough German negotiating stance at Brest-Litovsk. The Bolshevik newspaper, *Pravda,* sneered that "the American President Wilson, in the tones of a Quaker preacher, proclaims to the peoples of the world the teaching of highest government morality."[54]

VIII

Buoyed by a deluge of domestic praise, the president turned his attention to the attacks on the administration still erupting on Capitol Hill. He grew visibly irritated when Senator George Chamberlain of Oregon sponsored a bill calling for a secretary of munitions who would take over all the procurement functions of the War and Navy Departments. Chamberlain had been a staunch Wilson supporter since the war began, frequently defending the administration against Republican attacks. The Oregon solon and another Democratic backer of the bill, Senator Gilbert Hitchcock of Nebraska, went to the White House to discuss the defects of the war effort with the president.

After the meeting, Chamberlain felt they had gotten nowhere. The president "seemed impatient with us," he later said. Visible evidence of Wilson's opinion came in the form of a letter, curtly dismissing the idea of a munitions secretary. The letter was simultaneously released to the press. Such public humiliation was not likely to warm Senator Chamberlain's heart.[55]

Next came a shock that threatened to become a political earthquake. With no warning, Fuel Administrator Garfield shut down all the factories in the country east of the Mississippi River for a week. Thereafter, factories not directly related to the war effort were to be limited to a five-day (instead of a six-day) week until March 25. Wild-eyed reporters called presidential secretary Joe Tumulty at midnight on January 17, 1918, to ask for an explanation. The flabbergasted Tumulty could only stammer that it was the first he had heard about it—which meant Woodrow Wilson knew even less. Here was visible evidence that the administration's right hand did not now what its left hand was doing.[56]

Labor unions roared protests over lost wages. Business leaders bombarded Congress and the White House with squawks over diminished profits. A staggering 30,000 plants were closed in New York City alone. Garfield tried to explain that he was trying to funnel enough coal to East Coast ports to supply dozens of ships with fuel to get war matériel to Europe. Even the *New York World* gave up on Wilson's old friend and urged the president to jettison him. The paper called "Garfield's blunder" the first American defeat of the war. The Senate voted 50 to 19 to delay the order, with dozens of Democrats defecting. Wilson stonily defended the order and Garfield. In a letter to Bernard Baruch, he dismissed people who "wince and cry when they are a little bit hurt."[57]

The contretemps inspired Senator Chamberlain to present yet another bill, proposing to take even more power away from the president. This one called for the creation of a War Council of "three distinguished citizens" who would work with the president on the prosecution of the war and largely supersede the existing cabinet. Most newspapers hailed the idea as a stroke of legislative genius. Even the usually pro-Wilson *New York Times* liked it.[58]

On January 19, the same day that his new bill was introduced in the Senate, Chamberlain spoke to a joint meeting of the National Security League and the American Defense Society at New York's Manhattan Club. No fewer than 1,900 of these patriots had gathered to hear him. At the head table were Theodore Roosevelt, who was an old Chamberlain friend, and Elihu Root, former secretary of war under McKinley and Roosevelt and the grand old man of the GOP.

Root set the stage when he introduced Chamberlain. He pointed out that England, France and Italy had been forced to change governments and governmental structures in the course of the war. He hailed Chamberlain as a "wise and patriotic" leader who was trying to persuade the United States to do the same thing. Chamberlain proceeded to fulfill Root's fondest Republican hopes. He painted a portrait of a war effort in near-total disarray: "The military establishment of America has fallen down. . . . It has almost stopped functioning. Why? Because of inefficiency in every bureau and in every department of the Government of the United States."[59]

These words made headlines coast to coast. Woodrow Wilson fired off a furious letter to Chamberlain, demanding an explanation or a retraction. The senator replied that he did not intend his blast as a personal attack. It was the system that was at fault. He was only trying to correct it for the sake of the Democratic Party as well as the country. Wilson responded with a public letter aimed at nothing less than Chamberlain's dismemberment.

The president called the senator's speech "an astonishing and absolutely mystifying distortion of the truth." The charge of inefficiency in every department of the government "show[ed] such an ignorance of the actual conditions as to make it impossible to attach any importance to his statement." Wilson defended Secretary of War Newton Baker on all points, calling him "one of the ablest public officials I have ever known," and dismissed the Senate investigations as a waste of time. Also dismissed with breathtaking contempt were Chamberlain's War Council and Munitions Secretary bills. The president said he could only draw one conclusion: Chamberlain was opposed to "the administration's whole policy"—in a word, he was a traitor the Democratic Party.

The Portland *Oregonian* accused Wilson of trying to politically assassinate the senator "to prevent the overthrow of his entire military administration by Congress." The newspaper may have somewhat exaggerated the president's intention, but its appraisal of what was at stake in this brawl was definitely on target. Theodore Roosevelt made this clear by rushing to Washington to rally Republicans for a final assault that would force Wilson to accept the War Council and Munitions Secretary bills. If he did so, the president would be all but forced to appoint prominent Republicans to some of these jobs. In a moment of overconfidence, Roosevelt told reporters he was "going after the man in the White House."[60]

With Republicans cheering from the sidelines, Chamberlain rose in the Senate to spend three hours defending his proposals and his record as a supporter of the president. Accusing him of being a traitor to the party was "the unkindest cut," the senator cried, rehearsing the number of times he had helped rescue Wilson from legislative defeat. Chamberlain did not quite call Wilson a liar in return but he came close. He said the president was so busy, he did not have time to "ascertain the truth" about the collapsing war effort. The senator read into the record heart-wrenching letters from mothers and fathers whose sons had died in the army's freezing, unsanitary camps, and did his utmost to portray Secretary of War Baker as a national menace. [61]

Baker demanded the right to appear before Chamberlain's Military Affairs Committee to refute the senator's charges. He had already made one appearance, in which he had displayed a flippant, rather dismissive condescension that many people found irritating. This time Baker was more solemn, but no less intransigent. He spent most of his time refuting the more sensational charges against the War Department, insisted most of the others were exaggerated, and blamed some problems on the unexpected freezing temperatures. He demonstrated his skill in political combat by noting that the sites of several army camps with the worst health problems had been chosen by General Leonard Wood.[62]

As for the number of men in France, Baker declared that the numbers were far from the "trickle" Chamberlain and the Republicans claimed. The U.S. had "five times as many" troops overseas as they had originally planned to send by this time. This was equivocation with a capital E—originally Wilson and Baker did not plan to send any men and then had consented to Pershing's token division. Only when military defeat stared them in the face did the numbers suddenly change.[63]

Democratic newspapers, desperate for something good to say about the administration, heaped praise on Baker's performance. Behind the scenes, Wilson readied a counterattack that revealed his taste for political brinkmanship. He sent the Senate a bill that gave him the power to reorganize the entire government; he wanted to be able to create, merge or abolish agencies and bureaus without so much as a by-your-leave from Congress, and generally operate as the autocrat to end all autocrats.

One senator said the bill would make Wilson a king; all he needed to do was claim to rule by divine right and he and the kaiser would be twins. Senator Hitchcock seized on the image and, in a bitter speech, arraigned Wilson for remaining secluded in the White House, surrounded by a band of flatterers and favorites like witless Louis XVI of France.

Although Congress eventually gave the president the power he demanded (which he barely used), the net effect of this barrage of abuse was a distinct slump in Democratic Party morale. Colonel House confided to his diary the fear that both Wilson and Secretary Baker were out of touch with what the country was thinking about the war and the way the United States was fighting it. Philip Dru's creator expressed regret that the president did not consult him on domestic politics. He had consented to the arrangement, because foreign affairs was his bailiwick of choice. But the

Garfield coal order mess had made him decide that it was time to give Wilson a helping domestic hand "whether he asks for it or not."[64]

In an astonishing display of his unofficial power, House summoned Secretary of War Newton Baker to his New York City residence for a long conference on Sunday, January 20, 1918. Baker spent several hours with the colonel, discussing the administration's numerous critics. The meeting did not go well. Baker coolly defended the War Department's performance, leaving House more than a little nonplused.[65]

Probably the most important political result of this contretemps was the emergence of Theodore Roosevelt as the untitled but acknowledged leader of the Republican Party. Before leaving the capital for his home in Oyster Bay, TR gave a speech at the National Press Club that heaped scorn on the "college professor" in the White House. Roosevelt's daughter Alice and congressman husband, Nicholas Longworth of Ohio, gave him a farewell dinner at their Washington home at which the Old Guard mingled with Republican progressives in a not-so-subtle tribute to the party's new unity.[66]

IX

The winter of 1917–1918 was as severe in France as it was in the United States—and it found the four American divisions in Lorraine unprepared for the harsh conditions. Still in summer uniforms, the men shivered in unheated barns and attics of farmhouses as the temperature sank to seven below zero. Some soldiers started calling it their Valley Forge winter. They were baffled—and sometimes angry—by the way their country had seemingly abandoned them. Stirred by a letter from his son Archie reporting that his company had worn out its shoes and had no replacements, the former president shipped the doughboys 200 pairs, paid for out of his own pocket.[67]

One division had only two trucks to distribute supplies in the fifty square miles across which its men were scattered. They tried to buy horses from local farmers; to a man they refused, making the Americans less than enthusiastic about fighting to save them from the kaiser. French disillusion with the war was all too visible. "A strong feeling of 'Oh what's the use?' was spreading . . . throughout France," wrote one perceptive American officer.[68]

Even more troubling was the number of Americans who returned from their training forays to the front convinced that no one was ever going to break through the enemy's fortified trenches. Even General Robert Lee Bullard, the new commander of the First Division, confided to his journal: "We cannot beat Germany. She has beaten Russia . . . she is now beating Italy." On December 13, 1917, Pershing was forced to issue a strenuous letter denouncing the "deep pessimism" pervading his embryo army. Any officer caught saying the war was already lost would be relieved instantly as unfit for command.[69]

By this time Pershing had seen quite a lot of the Western Front. He had also watched Americans training under French instructors. He decided the French (and the British) would never break the prevailing deadlock. Their tactics practically ignored the rifle and bayonet. The grenade and the entrenching tool were the weapons of choice. He was appalled by the way the poilus dug foxholes and trenches, almost by reflex, the moment they stopped advancing. Only the Americans could change the situation by restoring the rifle to preeminence and using the "fire and movement" tactics preached by generations of West Point military thinkers, to create "open warfare."

When Pershing tried to explain these ideas to a group of American reporters, an Associate Press correspondent asked him if he realized it sounded arrogant to announce he had a recipe for victory without having fought a battle. Pershing glared at the man and snapped, "Of course the Western Front can be broken. What are we here for?"

The newsmen took an acute dislike to Pershing, which the general cordially reciprocated. When a brash young United Press correspondent named Westbrook Pegler showed up at the AEF's Chaumont headquarters, he talked his way into Pershing's office and breezily announced, "I'm Pegler of the United Press. Can you give me a statement on the general situation?"

"Pegler," Pershing growled, "get the hell out of my office."[70]

Journalist Heywood Broun, who followed Pershing around France for a while, was bewildered by the general's appetite for details. He climbed into haylofts and discussed onions with cooks to make sure that the men were being billeted in reasonable health and comfort. He also sternly insisted on West Point basics—crisp salutes, shined shoes and fresh uniforms.

Broun mocked Pershing's assumption that he could "read a man's soul through his boots or his buttons." He found a junior officer who thought Pershing's favorite biblical figure was Joshua "because he made the sun and moon stand at attention." Like many people, Broun noted Pershing made little attempt to win his men's affection. "No one will ever call him Papa Pershing," Broun wrote. Pershing's staff was outraged and wordily rebutted this latter charge. They also urged Pershing to kick Broun out of France. Pershing canceled the rebuttal, but Broun was soon on a New York–bound ship.[71]

In a way, Pershing had to believe in his vision of open warfare. Without it he might have lost control of his army. French and British disappointment with America's failure to join the fighting continued to grow. As 1918 began, Pershing's four divisions looked more and more pathetic as a serious army. A disgusted British journalist told an AEF intelligence office, "After eight months . . . you haven't really fired a damned shot!" An exasperated Pershing told his military censor, Major Frederick Palmer, he feared the worst. "Look at what is expected of us and what we have to start with! No army ready and no ships to bring over an army if we had one."[72]

With Russia out of the war and the failure of Field Marshal Douglas Haig's Passchendaele offensive, the desperate British and French decided their only hope of victory was changing Pershing's mind about amalgamating American troops into their armies. In a few months, the Germans would be able to marshal 250 divisions on the Western Front. To meet them, the Allies would be able to muster only 93 French and 54 British divisions, mostly understrength and composed of war-weary soldiers who had lost all confidence in victory.

David Lloyd George, who was totally disgusted with Field Marshal Haig but did not have the nerve to fire him, because he feared a backlash from Lord Northcliffe and his fellow conservatives, began the new amalgamation campaign with an urgent cable to Colonel House in Washington. The prime minister warned that the situation on the Western Front was about to become "exceedingly serious." The British cabinet wanted "an immediate decision" on putting regiments or companies of American troops into British units. Otherwise, England might be on the receiving end of the "knockout blow" the prime minister had repeatedly said he was determined to give Germany.[73]

House, Wilson and Secretary of War Baker wavered toward surrender. They only wondered if the situation was as critical as Lloyd George claimed. Baker cabled Pershing that they would depend on his judgment—though they regarded "loss of identity of our forces" as secondary to meeting the emergency that seemed to be developing. Pershing promptly replied: "Do not think emergency exists that would warrant putting companies or battalions into British or French divisions."[74]

Thus did John J. Pershing of Laclede, Missouri, pit his judgment against the combined opinions of the commanders of the French and British armies, the prime minister of England, the premier of France, and their cabinets. Further complicating his woes was the appointment of Major General Tasker Bliss as the U.S. military adviser to the newly formed Allied Supreme War Council. Although they were ostensibly friends, Pershing's opinion of Bliss was low. He had never seen action. His entire career had been in staff and administrative jobs.

Meanwhile, Pershing found himself confronting the former chief of the British imperial staff, General William "Wully" Robertson. As part of Lloyd George's attempt to get Field Marshal Haig's appetite for slaughter under control, the prime minister had transferred Robertson to the Supreme War Council in Paris. There he approached Pershing with a proposition that might be called "partial amalgamation." Robertson wanted to bring 150 American battalions (150,000 men) to France immediately for insertion into depleted British regiments. They would be taken from divisions that had only begun training in the United States and were not slated to arrive overseas until 1919.

Pershing wavered, though he wondered where and how the British had suddenly found the ships to transport these men. In the previous amalgamation go-round, London said if the Americans insisted on transporting full divisions, they would have to find their own shipping—the British merchant marine could not handle the job. In mid-January 1918, Pershing cabled a cautious approval of Robertson's proposal. But he insisted it should be a "temporary measure" that would not interfere with American plans to ship enough divisions to create an independent army.

Getting tougher by the minute, Pershing demanded that Robertson give him a frank statement of Britain's current military manpower. Pershing had picked up rumors that Lloyd George was holding large numbers of men in England to restrain Field Marshal Haig from another futile offensive.

Robertson blustered and essentially told Pershing nothing. In fact, there were a staggering 1.5 million Tommies in England at this time, either trained or in training. The British also had another 1.2 million men fighting in other theaters to protect their empire.

Meanwhile, the British worked overtime on General Bliss when he arrived in London. Lloyd George orated on the desperate need for these 150,000 men; he was followed by three other prominent British politicians who said the same thing in less dramatic tones. General Robertson chimed in, soldier to soldier. Obviously, the British saw this concession as a very large foot in the door that would enable them to lay their hands on hundreds of thousands more Americans for Haig's mincemeat machine. "They all seem to be badly rattled," Bliss reported to Washington. "They want men and they want them quickly." Actually, it was Bliss who was rattled.[75]

Robertson followed Bliss to Paris to cement the deal. There they found a different Pershing. He had been talking to the French, who had no desire to see the British get away with kidnapping the American army. They pooh-poohed the British claim of imminent outnumbering and said the Germans could not muster 250 divisions on the Western Front. A more probable figure was 190. Nor would the new arrivals be first-class troops. The Germans had been skimming the best soldiers from the Eastern Front for years. The shipping shortage was another British mirage. Thanks to the addition of the American navy, the Allies had enough warships to launch a convoy system, which was sharply curtailing losses to the Uboats.

His jaw set, the AEF commander told Bliss and Robertson he had changed his mind. If the British could transport 150,000 unattached American infantrymen, they could also convey six complete divisions—and that was what Pershing now wanted. While Bliss tut-tutted in Robertson's favor, Pershing said he would let the six divisions train with the British and if an emergency arose on the northern front, Haig could use them. Robertson stamped out in a fury and telegraphed Lloyd George for political reinforcements.

In one of the most momentous confrontations of the war, Pershing and Bliss met without "Wully" to thrash out their differences. If Pershing had lost the argument, the history of the war would have been altered, almost certainly for the worse. Bliss tried the standard gambit of the staff officer—bucking the decision up the line. He said they should cable Secretary of War Baker their differing opinions and let him decide. Pershing went into his commander-in-chief mode. "Bliss, do you know what would happen if we should do that? We would both be relieved from further duty in France and that is exactly what we would deserve."

Bliss capitulated. "I think you are right and I shall back you up in the position you have taken," he said.[76]

Lloyd George, Robertson, Haig and a phalanx of other British generals and politicians tried to change Pershing's mind. For two days they argued, not always in friendly tones. Pershing bluntly asked why they had so many men in Palestine if a real emergency existed on the Western Front. Would it do any good to beat the Turks if the Germans meanwhile occupied London? At one point, he bluntly accused Haig of double-talk, and the field marshal frigidly suggested that he spoke English better than Pershing. The baffled British turned to Bliss and were dismayed to hear him say: "Pershing will speak for us."[77]

Badly outmaneuvered by the general from the show-me state, the British had to settle for transporting the six complete divisions, a large step toward giving Pershing what they did not want him to have—an independent American army. Much later, Pershing's chief of staff, James Harbord, said: "No greater responsibility [was] ever placed on an American commander than that which now rested on Pershing. He risked the chance of being cursed to the latest generation if, through his failure to cooperate, the war were lost."[78]

X

Back in the United States, the stalled war effort, the savage infighting on Capitol Hill and anxiety about Russia's defection stirred new war rage in superpatriots and government officials. President Wilson led the way in his Flag Day speech on June 14, 1917: "Woe to the man or group of men who seeks to stand in our way in this day of high resolution." A few months later, Attorney General Thomas Gregory warned dissenters to expect no mercy "from an outraged people and an avenging government." The *New Republic* printed a letter from a popular writer recommending that anyone who impeded America's efficiency in "this righteous war" should be executed. The *New York Times* declared: "The patience of . . . the country has snapped." [79]

One of the first victims of this deepening rage was movie producer Robert Goldstein, who had worked with D. W. Griffith on the controversial 1915 film *Birth of a Nation*. That movie portrayed black-white violence in the post–Civil War South in pro-Southern terms. President Wilson had screened the film in the White House and praised it, helping to make it a huge success. While the United States drifted toward war, Goldstein produced *The Spirit of '76,* which attempted to apply Griffith's epic treatment and strong opinions to the American Revolution. One of the most vivid scenes dramatized the 1778 Wyoming Valley massacre, in which British troops and Iroquois Indian allies laid waste the fertile settlement along the banks of the Susquehanna River, burning an estimated 1,000 homes and killing women and children as well as American militiamen. British soldiers were portrayed spearing babies on their bayonets, the way German uhlans had supposedly killed Belgian children, according to Wellington House and Lord Bryce.

Goldstein opened *The Spirit of '76* in Chicago in the summer of 1917 and ran afoul of the local police censor. The producer went to court and successfully argued for his right to exhibit the film. But the bad publicity kept moviegoers away, and Goldstein headed for Los Angeles, where he made another try at attracting an audience after getting the approval of local censors by removing several scenes. In the exhibited film, he restored the scenes—and was promptly arrested.

The film was seized and Goldstein was soon in court. The docket read *United States vs the Motion Picture Film The Spirit of '76*. In the prevailing atmosphere of war rage, no one regarded this listing as even slightly ironic. The judge found Goldstein guilty of exhibiting "exaggerated scenes of British cruelty," which might make people "question the good faith of our ally, Great Britain." The court held that the film was likely to sow disloyalty and insubordination in the armed forces and thus violated the Espionage Act. He sentenced the stunned moviemaker to ten years in the federal penitentiary.[80]

In Missouri, local vigilante groups began sending out white and blue and red cards to those suspected of dissent. The white card meant the person was under surveillance. The blue card meant he or she was in danger of arrest. The red card meant the Secret Service would soon be visiting. The State Council of Defense reported that so far, it had not been necessary to send a red card. The white and the blue induced silence. Other state councils issued booklets urging people to report anyone who offered "destructive criticism" of the government. In Hartford, the Connecticut Home Guard invaded a Socialist meeting and demanded a pledge of allegiance to the flag. "This city must be purified," the Home Guard's leader declared. The *New York Tribune* reported on January 22, 1918, that ten-year-olds were being organized in an "Anti-Yellow Dog League" to detect disloyalty among their neighbors.[81]

The Bolshevik seizure of power and the Russians' defection from the war intensified American ire at critics of capitalism. Many Americans, including the editors of the *New York Times,* made little or no distinction between Lenin's far left radicals and American Socialists. "Thanks to Russian Socialism," the *Times* wrote on December 13, 1917, "the Germans now outnumber the French and British on the Western Front."

Part of the reason for the *Times's* near hysteria was the New York mayoral election of 1917, which pitted an openly antiwar Socialist candidate, Morris Hillquit, against the incumbent mayor, John Purroy Mitchel, and the Democratic candidate, John F. Hylan. The *Times* endorsed Mitchel, a progressive reformer who was embarrassed by his Irish roots. To prove his patriotism, Mitchel used smear tactics against Hylan and Hillquit, calling them both pro-German (the way he had earlier smeared State Senator Robert F. Wagner). Hylan won easily, but Hillquit polled 142,178 votes, only a few thousand less than Mitchel's total.[82]

Elsewhere in the country, the campaign against the Socialists was conducted with a ruthlessness that went far beyond editorial condemnations. In South Dakota, when the state chairman of the Socialist Party said he was a conscientious objector, he was sentenced to twenty years in the state penitentiary. In Newport, Kentucky, Herbert S. Bigelow, a prominent Cincinnati minister and progressive reformer, was seized by masked men on his way to address a Socialist antiwar meeting. Driven into the countryside, Bigelow was stripped and lashed with a blacksnake whip. His head was shaved and he was drenched in crude oil. In Milwaukee, former Socialist congressman Victor Berger wrote in his newspaper, the *Milwaukee Leader,* that Congress was simply "a rubber stamp of Woodrow Wilson and the Wall Street clique." Postmaster General Burleson banned the *Leader* from the mails—a tactic that had already silenced many other Socialist journals.[83]

The IWW was now considered synonymous with the hated Bolsheviks. A writer in *Forum* Magazine wrote that they were so closely allied, "if you prick one the other bleeds." On December 26, 1917, the *New York Times* saw a "worldwide anarchist plot" that linked the Bolsheviks and the IWW with revolutionaries around the globe. The idea was not wholly fanciful. In Australia, the IWW had been banned for treason and "wholesale arson."[84]

Early in January 1918, a group of sailors and a few civilians stormed Seattle's Piggott Printing Company, which printed Socialist and IWW publications. They wrecked presses, smashed typefaces, and warned that the next time they visited, "it will mean death." The leader of the raid was acquitted on the grounds of "mental irresponsibility" because the seditious articles printed by Piggott enraged him into taking the law in his own hands.[85]

XI

War rage also complicated Senator La Follette's attempt to defend himself against the campaign to expel him from the Senate. The Wilson administration refused to give him access to files that would prove his claim that the president knew the *Lusitania* carried ammunition in its hold. The senator found an unexpected ally in Dudley Field Malone, a progressive Democrat who had been Collector of the Port of New York when the liner sailed. Malone expressed outrage at the administration for closing its files and said he had notified Secretary of State Bryan of the ammunition. The senator also obtained from a member of the *New York Times* Washington bureau a statement that Bryan had told him he had warned Wilson about the *Lusitania*'s deadly cargo.[86]

Meanwhile, La Follette was under ferocious attack from the Vigilantes, the group of mostly Republican writers and illustrators whose services George Creel had spurned. One of their leading members, Samuel Hopkins Adams, wrote an article in the *New York Tribune*, "Is Wisconsin Against America?" claiming that La Follette had undermined the loyalty of the state. An accompanying cartoon showed the senator jamming a German helmet on the head of a crouching woman, labeled "Wisconsin."[87]

In Washington, Woodrow Wilson issued a statement through Senator Atlee Pomerene of Ohio, claiming he did not want La Follette expelled from the Senate, because it would make him a martyr. Meanwhile, the subcommittee on privileges kept postponing a hearing, partly because Bryan refused to testify under oath, and partly because they wanted to keep the political pot boiling.

The hate campaign against La Follette continued to mount in ferocity. *Life*, in those days a humor magazine, published a "Traitor's Number," featuring La Follette receiving the Iron Cross from the kaiser. Another set of cartoons showed Satan inducting La Follette into the "Traitor's Club," with Judas Iscariot, Benedict Arnold and other members eagerly welcoming him. Early in January, Vice President Marshall announced he had received dozens of letters from the Vigilantes, demanding La Follette's expulsion from the Senate. He was sending them to the senators of the states in which the writers lived.[88]

The *New York Tribune* and the *Washington Post* published excerpts from the letters. Most of these famous writers have been long forgotten. One said La Follette "speaks the language of Berlin." Another called him a "frank seditionist." A third claimed that the senator was the victim of "distorted mental machinery." Perhaps the lowest blow was struck by Irvin S. Cobb, who wrote a story for the *Saturday Evening Post,* portraying a thinly disguised La Follette as an outright traitor.[89]

In his home state, La Follette endured humiliations that wounded him deeply. Various clubs expelled him. The state legislature passed a joint resolution accusing him of sedition. The faculty of the University of Wisconsin voted 421 to 2 to condemn his "unwise and disloyal utterances." A saddened La Follette noted in his diary that "my picture was taken down from where it was hanging in all of the university buildings." His son Phil, a student at the university, had to endure face-to-face insults and sneers.[90]

La Follette was not completely abandoned. In later years, he liked to note that a third of all the letters he received in his nineteen years in the Senate came in 1917, and they ran more than 60 to 1 in his favor. Socialist Party leader Eugene Debs praised "your courage, your manhood and your devotion to the cause of the people in the face of the bitterest and most brutal persecution to which the lawless looters of this nation and their prostitute press ever subjected a faithful public servant."[91]

But the "Get La Follette" campaign continued. The American Defense Society submitted an elaborate brief, drawn by prominent New York lawyers, to the subcommittee on privileges, arguing the legality of La Follette's expulsion. On January 8, 1918, the day the subcommittee was scheduled to finally meet (its original date had been December 3, 1917), the *New York Sun* ran a story on the brief under the headline "New Proof of La Follette's Sedition Filed." That same day, the senator's son, Robert, Jr., collapsed with an acute streptococcus infection and had to be hospitalized. La Follette asked the committee to postpone the hearings, and his day of reckoning—or justification—was delayed, and delayed again, as young Bob hovered between life and death.

Eventually, Bob La Follette began to recover. But the senator used his son's poor health as a way to evade the hearing while war rage convulsed the country. As weeks stretched into months, it became apparent that Wilson had won. Senator Robert La Follette had been reduced to silence.

XII

In the White House, a very different drama was taking place. Woodrow Wilson and Colonel House began to think they might achieve the kind of peace they wanted—the overthrow of the military men around the kaiser and the emergence of a liberal majority in Germany. One reason for this ballooning hope was information the State Department was receiving about the situation on the German home front. The addition of ships from the U.S. Navy enabled the British to create a virtually impenetrable blockade. In the words of one historian, "the goal of preventing the arrival of even a single loaf of bread in Germany was all but achieved."[92]

Germany's civilian economy was rapidly reaching a crisis point. Its foreign trade had fallen from $5.9 trillion in 1913 to $800 million in 1917. Shortages of everything—rubber, tin, copper, clothing, household items, and, above all, food—were endemic and worsened by a poor harvest in 1917. Civilians were living on 1,800 calories a day, little more than half the 3,300 minimum requirement. Fats and meat had all but vanished from the German diet. The death rate was climbing ominously. By the end of 1917, it was 32 percent above the 1913 figure. The tuberculosis rate had doubled.[93]

On August 13, 1917, the U.S. State Department reported: "The death rate among old people [in Germany] is huge, as it is with small children. There is great discontent in the Navy. The food is very bad." An American named Lang, who had recently left Germany, presumably via a neutral country, and returned to the United States, reported that hundreds of people "drop in the streets, faint from hunger." Lang himself had lost fifty-five pounds while living on the standard food ration. Another report said the average weight loss was thirty-five to forty pounds and the mortality among people over forty-five was "immense." In January 1918, labor unions called a general strike, and a million workers walked off the job in a half dozen cities.[94]

Senator La Follette's condemnation of the British blockade as an attack on defenseless women, children and old people would seem to be confirmed by these reports. But in the White House, there was not even a glimmer of guilt about killing innocent civilians. On January 31, Colonel

House gleefully told Wilson: "It looks as if things are beginning to crack. I do not believe Germany can maintain a successful offensive with her people in their present frame of mind." The House-Wilson team all but gloated when the foreign minister of Austria-Hungary and the chancellor of Germany replied to his Fourteen Points address in conciliatory tones, stressing their desire for peace. Both enemy leaders accepted the general points, freedom of the seas, lowered tariffs, a league of nations.

A closer reading of the two replies considerably lowered House-Wilson hopes. The new German chancellor, Georg Hertling, maintained that arrangements between Germany and Russia were a separate matter and was ambiguous about Belgium. Count Ottokar Czernin, the Austro-Hungarian foreign minister, stiffly rebuffed Wilson's interference in the "territorial" problems of his nation. In short, they mostly rejected Wilson's concrete proposals. But the desire for peace seemed genuine, and there were encouraging rumors of sharp differences between Quartermaster General Erich Ludendorff, the German army's field commander, and Count Czernin.

Journalist Carl Ackerman, one of House's many informants, wrote him a long letter from Bern, Switzerland, reporting on labor unrest in Germany and urging a reply to Hertling and Czernin. It might help discredit the "German War Party," which was still determined to fight to the finish. But Ackerman noted an unsettling problem: Too much talk of peace might also inspire the war-weary populations of France, England and Italy to start calling for an immediate armistice.[95]

Meanwhile, the Allied Supreme War Council, obviously nervous about this possibility, met in Paris and, after much behind-the-scenes wrangling, issued its own reply to the peace feelers—a curt rejection that claimed the German negotiators at Brest-Litovsk had revealed new plans for "conquest and spoliation." Wilson was infuriated and fired off a cable to the American representatives at the Supreme War Council, ordering them to make it clear that their presence at the meeting did not mean the United States approved of anything the council said. Wilson was invoking his insistence that the United States was an "associated power," not an ally.[96]

The clash persuaded Wilson and House that the president should make a public reply to Hertling and Czernin to undo the Supreme War Council's gaffe and preserve the momentum (as they imagined it) of a peace agreement with German liberals. William Bullitt had collected a number of recent antiwar statements by German socialists and had sent them to House. The colonel recommended incorporating them in the speech.[97]

The president found it extremely difficult to write this speech. When Wilson read it to House on February 8, 1918, the colonel informed his diary that it was "a remarkable document but [I] knew that much of it would have to be eliminated." Never before, House remarked in a later diary passage, had he found so much in a Wilson speech that needed to be jettisoned. On the day before Wilson spoke, House felt the speech "still lacked something," and he virtually dictated a paragraph picturing the entire world ready for peace—except the German war party. It was another glimpse of a growing divergence between House and Wilson in their thinking about the right route to peace. Wilson was becoming more and more dubious about the idea that the German people could be distinguished from the kaiser and his generals. War rage was beginning to distort his psyche.[98]

On February 11, Wilson went before Congress to give his speech. He remained unenthusiastic about this oratorical effort, and it was soon easy to see why. The first half was a complicated argument with Czernin and Hertling about rearranging the map of Europe. There were arcane references to the Congress of Vienna, an 1815 peace conference that had settled matters after the Napoleonic wars. One doubts many members of Congress had heard of this conclave, and it is a virtual certainty that for 98 percent of the American people, the term meant nothing. In the second half of the speech, Wilson fell back on by now familiar rhetoric. "We are striving for a new international order based upon broad and universal principles of right and justice. . . . Each part of the final settlement must be based on the essential justice of that particular case." Et cetera, et cetera. Not too surprisingly, Congress, completely out of the loop on what the president was trying to do, listened to the speech in baffled silence.[99]

In terms of achieving the goal of this public diplomacy, the speech was an almost total disappointment. A peace feeler from Austria-Hungary surfaced in Spain, but further conversations went nowhere. This bad news was minor compared to what emerged from Russia on March 3, 1918. While Wilson was playing House's public diplomacy game, the Germans and the Bolsheviks had been negotiating a harsh peace at Brest-Litovsk. There, another rhetorician, Leon Trotsky, had learned some hard lessons about the difference between words and deeds.

Trotsky had strutted on stage at Brest-Litovsk hurling denunciations at German imperialism and confidently predicting that the workers would overthrow the kaiser. The Germans ordered their armies to keep advancing. The battered remnants of the Russian army were unable to stop them. In a few weeks, the Bolsheviks were facing the possibility of German troops in Petrograd and Moscow—and they lamely settled for a far worse deal than the Germans had originally offered them. Lenin fired Trotsky as his negotiator and sent a new delegation to sign the Treaty of Brest-Litovsk.[100]

The agreement gave independence to the Ukraine, Poland, Finland, Estonia, Latvia and Lithuania, with the assumption that they would become German client states. Russia lost roughly 30 percent of its population, and the Bolsheviks humbly promised to cease all revolutionary agitation in the surrendered lands. The appalled British called Brest-Litovsk the greatest seizure of territory by conquest since the days of the Roman empire. In Germany, people celebrated. Only a few stubborn Socialists still talked peace. Victory over Russia had added cubits to the stature of hulking Quartermaster General Erich Ludendorff and his titular commander, aging Field Marshal Paul von Hindenburg, the men who had smashed Russia's armies in stupendous battles during the first years of the war. They began using Brest-Litovsk to weld the German army and people into a feverish unity for a final campaign. The prevailing motto was "Three cheers for General Ludendorff! On to the Western Front!" In the State Department, a glum William Bullitt reported: "A scathing indictment of German policy in the East would serve merely to unite [the German] people behind the government. For the present . . . we had better fight and say nothing."[101]

Chapter 6

THE WOMEN
OF NO-MAN'S-LAND

While Pershing's warriors froze and fumed and were dribbled into the trenches by the cautious French for ten-day tryouts, American women became the first to see the real war. They managed it by ignoring a ukase issued by the AEF commander not long after he arrived in France: No American woman related to a soldier would be tolerated in Europe. This proclamation was soon escalated to no women, period, except army nurses and a cadre of female telephone operators. Seldom has a military order been more flouted. The women came anyway, first in a trickle, then in a flood. Before the war ended, no less than 25,000 skirted Yanks from twenty-one to sixty-something had made it over there.[1]

One evening in the summer of 1917, Pershing found himself seated next to Eleanor Roosevelt, wife of Theodore Roosevelt, Jr., at a Paris dinner party given by the Count de Chambrun, a descendant of Lafayette. Mrs. Roosevelt had left her three children with her mother to follow her husband to France, and was working for the YMCA. Pershing was amused to find someone so pretty in the prim and proper YM and remarked she must attract mobs of men to her canteen.

Suddenly, to Mrs. Roosevelt's dismay, the general's face "set like the Day of Judgment" and he growled, "How do you happen to be here anyway? No wives are allowed to come overseas. Where are your children? You ought to be with them. . . . I think you should be sent home."[2]

Mrs. Roosevelt went back to her Paris house and wrote an angry letter to her husband, who had met Pershing many times at his father's home. The next time the general inspected the First Division, Major Roosevelt saluted and said, "My goodness sir, but you're in bad with my wife. What on earth did you do to her at the Chambruns?"

The next time Eleanor Roosevelt met Pershing in Paris, he took both her hands and said, "I know about the work you're doing and it's good. Can we be friends again?"

The general had discovered the best way to deal with the women-in-France issue was a graceful surrender. He was learning firsthand what many historians took much longer to realize: The modern woman strode onto history's stage, not in the Roaring Twenties, but in the Tempestuous Tens. The progressive movement liberated a lot more than wage slaves from the tyranny of big business. As one writer put it, "Sex o'clock in America struck in 1913, about the same time as the repeal of reticence." Articles on birth control, prostitution, divorce and free love filled magazines and newspapers. Women were becoming doctors and lawyers and journalists. Why couldn't they go to France? Theodore Roosevelt was telling every male in America that the war was the "Great Adventure" of their generation. These modern women were determined to share it.[3]

II

About half this skirted Western Front brigade became nurses. The rest did a wide variety of work. Many drove ambulances, others ran canteens financed by the Red Cross and the YMCA. Some, such as a sixteen-woman unit from Smith College, worked with French civilians in devastated areas just behind the front lines, helping them restore shattered towns and villages. A few women were war correspondents. They had a terrible time getting accredited by the male chauvinists in the U.S. Army. One described the military mind "like a steel mask with the key lost." Nevertheless, several got to the front. That was the ambition of almost every woman who came to France, and a remarkable number realized it.[4]

For Marian Baldwin, who arrived in Paris in July 1917 to do canteen work, the excitement started almost immediately. "Last night I witnessed my first air raid," she told an unnamed correspondent. "It was every bit as thrilling as anticipated. I was awakened out of a sound sleep by the most gruesome sirens imaginable." Soon French pursuit planes were in the air, each with a glowing light on its wingtip. They looked like falling stars as they climbed and dove on the German bombers. Next French antiaircraft guns opened up. "I didn't believe there could be anything louder and then suddenly a bomb dropped and the deafening crash completely obliterated for a second all the other sounds," Baldwin wrote.[5]

In the morning, a long list of dead and wounded was in the newspapers. "The war has suddenly become a reality," Baldwin told her correspondent. She went for a walk with a young American friend, Billy Tailer, who was on his way to a French flying school. Impatient for action, Tailer had joined the Lafayette Escadrille, a group of Americans flying for the French army. As yet the American Air Service was as nonexistent in France as Pershing's army. Tailer told her the average life of an aviator at the front was six months. Half jocularly, he said he would arrange with friends to let her know if he "got it."

A few weeks later, Baldwin was telling her pen pal the Paris reaction to the news that gave Woodrow Wilson and John J. Pershing restless nights— the collapse of the Russian army. "Isn't the Russian news fierce? I've never seen anything like the way it has taken the punch out of every one. I was down at the Gare du Nord yesterday doing a little work for the Red Cross, distributing cigarettes etc among the outgoing French soldiers. We couldn't seem to cheer them, and I didn't see any of the usual smiles. The ray of light which the U.S. troops brought when they began coming over has, for the moment, been completely obliterated."[6]

A few months later, Baldwin was in an even more somber mood: "Billy Tailer, the best of friends and the most splendid of men, has been killed while flying over German lines. I always knew in a vague way I would be terribly cut up if anything happened to him but I never knew it would be like this. Somehow I feel ten years older and the war has become a more hideous reality than ever. . . . Every street corner of this city [Paris] reminds me of Bill, and the whole place seems alive with memories of his radiant boyish face."[7]

III

While some American airmen were in combat with the Lafayette Escadrille, Quentin Roosevelt and his vanguard of the American Air

Service were having a miserable time at Issoudon, some 240 miles south of Paris, where they had set up a flying school. Chosen by the French, Issoudon was the worst imaginable site. The clayish soil turned to gumbo when it rained, making it impossible to take off or land. Rain and bone-chilling cold were constants. One night, Quentin awoke to find a thunderstorm sending a small river flowing through his tent. He was soon calling the place "a god-forsaken hole."[8]

Quentin and his friends, who included his Groton and Harvard classmate Hamilton Coolidge, discovered that the Curtiss Jenny, the plane in which they had learned to fly, had almost no resemblance to the planes they would be piloting at Issoudun, French-made Nieuport-28s. The French air service had discarded this second-rate fighter for faster, more maneuverable Spads, and sold the castoffs to the Americans. Among their many defects, Nieuports had a habit of shedding their wing fabric in a dive. The AEF high command had bought them because there was nothing else available. General Halsey Dunwoodie, the man in charge of army procurement, glumly admitted at the end of the war: "We never had a plane that was fit to use."[9]

Back in the United States, Flora Payne Whitney had become a constant visitor at Sagamore Hill. Even there she found pain. Every time she went up the road to the big rambling house, she remembered how happy she had been in the spring when Quentin was training at Mineola. She still hesitated to tell her parents about their engagement. "I never talk about you or mention your name," she wrote. "I . . . will, though."[10]

Flora began to find the separation almost unbearable. "Oh Quentin, sometimes it's all I can do to keep from just giving in and breaking down completely," she wrote in November 1917. "It's so hard and there is so little satisfaction. I want you so desperately. The hollow blank feeling that is a living nightmare almost kills me at times. . . . Why does it all have to be? It isn't possible that it can be for any ultimate good that all the best people in the world have to be killed."

Her parents were not Flora's only problem. She was still very much a member of society. At parties and dinners she met more than a few young men who were eager to woo her. One asked her point blank if she was engaged to Quentin and told her he thought it was "pretty rotten" when she declined to say yes or no. When she told Quentin about this exchange, he because upset. He did not want to think about Flora surrounded by amorous young men.

Flora told Quentin that his father wanted to see them married and would do everything in his power to "fix it" with her parents. Quentin hesitated. He was afraid marriage would be "selfishness on my part and might cause you pain in days to come."[11]

He was telling her how dangerous the air service was.

It was also exhausting. Along with learning to fly the tricky Nieuports, Quentin was the supply officer. This job had him racing all over France for equipment to get the airfield up and running. His back tormented him and he was forced to take to his cot one day a week. He lay there, thinking of Flora, writing her letters.

Theodore Roosevelt and his wife invited Flora to come to Canada with them to hear TR address the Canadian parliament. The invitation carried more than a hint that TR wanted to accustom Flora to becoming a political wife. There were other indications that he had selected Quentin as the son with the ideal combination of talents and personality to succeed him in this demanding career. Quentin's sister Ethel explained the politics behind the trip—Canadians were debating whether to vote for a conscription law similar to America's. TR planned to urge them to vote yes.

Flora told Quentin she had "the most thrilling time" in Canada. She was "open-mouthed" at the enormous crowds, the gigantic receptions TR's presence inspired. But the experience left her feeling inadequate. "Please don't go into politics," she begged Quentin. "My tongue gets paralyzed and my brain gets paresis [meeting so many strangers]. I can only say 'what wonderful air up here.'"

Quentin was nevertheless pleased that Flora had participated in a typical Roosevelt adventure. Incidentally, Canada voted yes for conscription.[12]

In Issoudun, Quentin developed a perpetual cold and cough. By mid-November, he had pneumonia. The camp doctor sent him to Paris for a three-week leave. He stayed with Eleanor Roosevelt, where he soon encountered his brothers Ted and Archie. Ted, an all-too-typical oldest brother, regarded Quentin with disapproval because he had not performed well at the prewar Plattsburgh preparedness training camp. He began calling Quentin a slacker for hiding out at Issoudun while he and Archie and their other brother, Kermit, were on their way to the front.

Quentin was enormously upset. He appealed to his father and wrote a tense, revealing "apologia" to Archie, defending himself and the American Air Service. No American pilots had been sent to the front, because there were no planes for them to fly. Only the two best pilots at Issoudun had been sent to England for advanced training. He was not one of them. "Father's pull" had gotten him into the air service in spite of his bad back and poor eyes, but pull could not make him the best or second best flier in the service.[13]

This brotherly imbroglio filled Quentin with a fierce desire to get to the front. It also paradoxically emboldened him to express his growing desire to have Flora come to Europe and marry him. His father's letters repeatedly encouraged him to ask her. TR felt every young man should have his "white hour" with the woman he loved before he went into combat.[14]

Flora shared Quentin's wish, but found herself enmeshed in family and government complications. Pershing's ukase had become a War Department regulation, barring relatives of soldiers and all Americans under twenty-one from entering the war zone. Flora had a brother in the air service, still training in Texas, and she would not be twenty-one until July 29, 1918. Considering how other women flouted the War Department regulation, there is little doubt that Flora, backed by TR and her wealthy parents, could have managed it. But her parents were still unenthusiastic about the match, and they worried about German submarines and the deteriorating military situation on the Western Front.[15]

Flora still found it very hard to talk to her family about Quentin. "No one quite understands," she told him. Quentin returned to Issoudun and was made a training squadron commander. His health continued to be bad. He had constant colds and a wracking cough. Once, he had a dizzy spell while performing acrobatics and almost crashed. On another flight, the motor of his decrepit Nieuport quit in midair and he landed in some trees, reducing the plane to kindling wood and badly wrenching his wrist. Yet he badgered his commanding officer with demands to be sent to the front. He extracted a promise that he would get the first available opening. His friend Hamilton Coolidge wangled a similar pledge.

Quentin wrote letter after letter to Flora denouncing the climate and the muddled U.S. war effort, which had yet to produce a single fighter plane. He was haunted by a recurring dream.

"I am coming back to the states wounded, one arm in a sling and my left foot gone. I have not been permitted to telephone from Quarantine to let you know I am coming. The steamer docks at Hoboken. I am planted there with my luggage and no way to carry it because of my arm. I am stuck in Hoboken. Freud says all dreams have meaning. I should like to have him translate that for me."

In later versions of the dream, he met a huge military policeman with a red brassard on his arm. The man ordered him onto an outward-bound transport. "Just as I realize . . . with awful despair I shall never come back, I wake up."[16]

In New York, an anxious Flora wrote: "Quentin I am so worried about you. I am sure you are not a bit well and I wish—oh so much—you could get away somewhere . . . in the south of France. . . . I hardly dare say this but . . . I think with your bad back you ought not even to be in aviation. . . . At the bottom of your heart don't you think there is a good deal of sense in that?"[17]

IV

The boom of 6,000 artillery pieces drowned out Flora's loving voice. On March 21, 1918, Quartermaster General Erich Ludendorff launched Germany's massive attempt to win victory on the Western Front. The *Kaiserschlacht* (kaiser battle) began at dawn with a stupendous bombardment on the thirty-four divisions of the British Third and Fifth Armies along a forty-three-mile front south of Arras. The Fifth Army was guarding the "hinge" between the British and French fronts, always an inviting target. An officer called the rain of shells "more like a convulsion of nature than the work of man. The noise was so immense, it was impossible to hear an order beyond a few yards, even when shouted through a megaphone."[18]

Unlike previous bombardments on the Western Front, the German artillery was on target from the first round. Thanks to ingenious artillerymen and painstaking mapmakers, the Germans had figured out how to fire the big guns accurately without the messy business of "registration," which had previously consumed days and eliminated all surprise from French and British attacks. The man in charge of the rain of destruction was Colonel Georg Bruchmuller, whom black humorists on the general staff called *Durchbruchmuller* (Breakthrough Muller). After almost four years of study, he had composed a deadly symphony, called a fire waltz, that combined precise combinations of poison gas and high explosives, carefully orchestrated to wreak specific havoc on different sections of the battlefield.[19]

Mustard-gas shells were aimed at the flanks of the enemy defenses, because mustard dispersed slowly and could hinder attackers as well as

defenders. Odorless phosgene gas was for the forward trenches, the immediate target of the attack. Huge quantities were also fired into the enemy
rear to immobilize their artillery. These shells were mixed with shells containing diphenyl chloramine, which fouled gas masks and forced men to
breathe the deadly phosgene.

Undetected by Allied spies, patrols or aircraft, Ludendorff had managed
to concentrate sixty-seven divisions on the forty-three-mile front, giving
him a 2-to-1 manpower advantage. For a final touch, the German high
command unveiled a new set of tactics. Certain units had been designated
Angriffdivisionen (attack divisions); they had been trained as *Sturmtruppen*
(storm troopers) with a radically different approach to the battlefield.

Instead of trying to seize specific objectives, storm troopers were given
what are now called mission-oriented orders. They were equipped with
light machine guns and mortars and told to break through the weakened
British defenses in squads and companies, leaving to the rest of the army
the job of mopping up holdouts in the forward battle line. Previously,
storm troopers had been elite units, trained to bring off trench raids. The
Germans were betting they could imbue whole divisions with their reckless ardor. Experiments on the Eastern Front had convinced Quartermaster
General Ludendorff this could be done.[20]

At 9:30 A.M., after five hours of merciless pounding by Bruchmuller's
guns, the storm troopers emerged from the ground fog. Their rifles
remained strapped to their backs; their favorite weapon was the hand
grenade. Lieutenant Ernst Junger, who commanded a company, urged his
men forward with wild emotion, convinced they were about to win the
war. "They . . . had gone over the edge of the world into superhuman per-
spectives," he later wrote.[21]

He and other companies rolled up trench after trench of British officers
and men dazed and panicked by the bombardment. Thousands of other
Tommies fled. Others were stunned to discover Germans attacking their
strong points from the rear. "I thought we had stopped them," recalled one
machine gunner, "when I felt a bump in my back." The bump was a
revolver in the hand of a German officer. "Come along, Tommy, you've
done enough," he said.[22]

So swiftly did the storm troopers advance, they were soon in rear areas
where bacon sizzled on the stoves of abandoned mess halls. They paused to

eat, stuffed their haversacks and kept going. By nightfall, they had burst through the center of the Fifth Army into open country.

In 1916, on the Somme, Field Marshal Haig had lost 500,000 men fighting across these same woods and fields, to gain a grand total of 98 square miles in six blood-soaked months. On March 21, 1918, the Germans gained 140 square miles in twenty-four hours, at a cost of 39,329 casualties. While John J. Pershing talked about it, Ludendorff and his fellow generals had invented a type of open warfare that worked.[23]

Bluff Irish-born General Hubert Gough realized his Fifth Army was in imminent danger of a rout. He pleaded for reinforcements, but Field Marshal Haig, jittery about the rest of his battle line, sent him only a single division. (Haig, out of touch as usual, thought the Fifth and Third Armies were holding their own and sent them warm congratulations.) Gough turned to the French, who were supposed to rush men across the hinge if the British got in trouble (and vice versa). The French sent only a handful of riflemen. The day before the attack, the Germans had leaked disinformation that convinced General Pétain that an assault on Rheims was imminent.

On the third day of the battle, the British Third Army also began to crumble. Their commander had crammed most of his men in forward trenches. They put up a strong defense at first, but when the storm troopers finally broke through, there were no reserves to stop them. An appalled Haig realized there was no alternative but to retreat south of the Somme River.[24]

It was a devastating humiliation for the British army. Having paid a half million men to win this part of France, they presumed they would stay. Huge fuel and ammunition dumps had to be destroyed, entire hospitals and airfields evacuated. Soon Gough's fear of a rout became reality. As thousands of beaten Tommies, many of them wounded, trudged south in a disorganized mob without officers, a cry went up: "German cavalry!" In seconds the panicky infantrymen stampeded down the road, flinging wounded men into ditches, throwing away packs, rifles, gas masks.[25]

Ironically, this headlong retreat was probably the best tactic the harried British could have devised. It kept at least part of the disintegrating Fifth Army and the crumbling Third Army out of the grasp of the oncoming Germans. By this time, some 90,000 British soldiers had surrendered and were on their way to prisoner-of-war camps. Ludendorff ordered one of his armies to seize Amiens, a vital rail center. Another army was told to keep smashing its way down the hinge, to separate the French and British. The Germans encountered some French troops, finally sent by the cautious Pétain, but they were too few and too late.

Inexplicably, the German drive began to run out of steam. Lieutenant Rudolf Binding, a division staff officer, saw one reason on March 28. "Today the advance of our infantry suddenly stopped near Albert," he wrote in his diary. "I began to see curious sights . . . men driving cows before them . . . others who carried a hen under one arm and a box of notepaper under the other. Men carrying a bottle of wine under their arm and another one open in their hand . . . Men staggering. Men who could hardly walk."[26]

Binding described the British back areas as "a land flowing with milk and honey." Along with seeking food, not to mention wine, that was better than they saw in their own army's blockade-shriveled rations, the storm troopers also stopped to equip themselves with warm English boots, jackets and raincoats. They fed their half-starved artillery horses on "masses of oats and gorgeous foodcake." An unanticipated problem was getting their artillery across the devastated battlefield to keep up with the advance, which neared 40 miles by the end of March. The sheer distance, and the added burden of the loot the infantrymen were carrying, were the main reasons why, on April 4, the first phase of the Kaiserschlacht came to a halt, with Amiens uncaptured. Still the Germans had acquired another 1,200 square miles of France, inflicted 164,000 casualties on the British and 70,000 on the French—and thrown panic into the ranks of both the French and British armies.[27]

Only two companies of American engineers, who happened to be working temporarily with the Fifth Army, participated in this great battle. They suffered seventy-eight casualties. The rest of the AEF was still earnestly training for open warfare in Lorraine. Their brief tours in quiet sectors of the front lines had no impact whatsoever on the war. The stunning success of the Kaiserschlacht made many people wonder if John J. Pershing's refusal to amalgamate his army with the French and British was a ruinous mistake.[28]

V

One American woman volunteer saw this cataclysm from a uniquely terrible viewpoint. Shirley Millard was a New Yorker whose heart "thumped admiringly to the tune of Over There." Her parents kept telling her she was much too young to go to war, and she did not have an iota of training to drive an ambulance or nurse wounded men. But she had two valuable assets, "a fair knowledge of French and the determination that goes with red hair." When she heard the French were recruiting Americans to serve in their depleted nursing corps, she volunteered. On March 16, 1918, her awed fiancé, about to begin training as a lieutenant at New York's Camp Upton, saw her off with kisses and presents, urging her "not to win the war" before he got there.

Millard enjoyed every minute of her eight-day voyage across the Atlantic, in spite of the ubiquitous submarines. She read a handbook on nursing in secret, still pleased that she had managed (so she thought) to bluff the French recruiters into taking her. She assumed she would be given some sort of training when she arrived in France. She had no idea that France had been chronically short of nurses since the war began. Nursing was not an accepted profession for Frenchwomen. It had been left to nuns—and in France's ongoing war between the secular left and the religious right, many religious nursing orders had been driven out of the country.

On March 24, 1918, Millard and the nine other members of her unit landed in Bordeaux. They were instantly ordered aboard a train to Paris, where they were told they were needed at an emergency hospital near the front. Soon they were in an odoriferous, covered *camion* (truck) that had just carried a load of mules to the front. They shrugged into their uniforms as the camion roared through the night at headlong speed. They told each other how lucky they were to get to the front without boring delays.

As darkness fell, they reached their hospital, a big, rambling old château near Soissons. Around it on the lawns loomed numerous barracks for wounded enlisted men. Wounded officers were treated in the château. In the distance, the newcomers could hear the boom of artillery. Heavy fighting was obviously in progress. On the grounds between the château and the barracks were hundreds of men, who they assumed were sleeping.

A French doctor looked them over and beckoned them to follow him. Often they had to step over the men on the ground as they hurried toward the barracks. Their ears picked up pathetic cries for water, food, a priest. They realized the prone soldiers were all wounded, lying there waiting for treatment. Moments later, an airplane exploded and burned in the black sky above them. By that time, Shirley Millard was at the door of Barracks

Forty-Two. The doctor opened the door only wide enough to shove her inside. She would soon learn that lights drew German bombers.

She found herself in a long, low room, with cots so jammed together it was hard to walk between them. Light came from flickering candles. Nurses, doctors, orderlies rushed up and down the center aisle. Someone shoved a huge hypodermic needle into her hand and told her every man who came in must have a tetanus shot. Then she was to get them ready for the operating table. Millard stared at the hypodermic. She had no idea how to use it. "I'd never even *had* one [an injection]," she thought. "And what did 'get them ready' mean?"

She watched another nurse snap on the glass tube containing the anti-toxin, fill the syringe and give a man his injection. She followed the same procedure, but when she tried to plunge the needle into her man's arm, it bent. A passing orderly told her the man was an Arab, with skin as tough as leather. She found another needle and tried again. It worked! Ditto the second, third and fourth times. "Soon I am going like lightning."

Then she found out what getting them ready meant. She watched a French nurse as she undressed several wounded men, "removing all their clothing, boots leggings, belts, gas-masks." Then she washed their wounds and wrapped them in a clean sheet to prepare them for surgery. Taking a deep breath, Millard went to work. Most of the men were caked with mud from head to foot; they screamed and cursed her as she struggled to undress them without causing more pain.

Beneath one set of blood- and mud-soaked bandages, she found an arm hanging by a tendon. *Roses Are Blooming in Picardy.* The plaintive British war song started wailing in her head as she went on to the next man. She bathed a "great hip cavity" where a leg once was. Next was a man with no eyes. She could see into the back of his head.

She stared at a chest ripped open by a shell as the exposed lungs slowly shuddered to a stop. Next came a burly Breton, who reminded her of the porter in the hotel in Dinard where she had stayed with her parents years before. "I slit him open!" he babbled. "Open I tell you! Goddamn his soul!"

For three sleepless days and nights, Millard lived this nightmare on the edge of the *Kaiserschlacht.* She watched Dr. Le Brun, a brilliant young surgeon from Lyons, who stayed on his feet, gulping black coffee, operating, operating, for the entire seventy-two hours. Toward the end, he hung onto the door of the operating room and muttered, *"La gloire, la gloire! Bah! C'est de la merde!"* (Glory, glory, it's all shit!)

Finally, one of the French nurses led Millard away to a bedroom in the château. She lay there, listening to "Roses Are Blooming in Picardy" wailing in her head and Dr. Le Brun saying, *"La Gloire . . . la gloire . . . "* She thought of her fiancé at Camp Upton. She felt years and years older than him. She had crossed a river of blood since she had seen him. "How would I feel about him when we met again?" she wondered.[29]

VI

The Smith College volunteers also had a terrifying brush with the *Kaiserschlacht.* They were working at Grecourt, a French town in the path of the oncoming Germans, close to the hinge between the two Allied armies. They received all sorts of assistance from both French and British officers who admired their work in eleven surrounding villages.

The Smithies had organized local women into a sewing and knitting industry, replanted fruit trees, set up libraries, and restocked farms with cows, goats and pigs. At first their worst enemy was the cold. A woman correspondent from the *New York Evening Sun* lived with them for a while and reported on the weather, among other things. "After your first day there, you've discarded silk stockings and are wearing one if not two pair of the heaviest made woolens, and you've borrowed every available woolie not in use."[30]

On March 21, the crash of Bruchmuller's guns was soon followed by a British officer who told them to flee. The Germans had broken through and were coming on like a tidal wave. There was no hope of stopping them. Instead, the Smith women decided to stay and help their villagers to escape. They drove down roads jammed with retreating troops and fleeing civilians to take old people to hospitals and railroad stations. They also fed hungry exhausted Tommies. Mile by mile, often with German shells falling close, they retreated with the British to Amiens. There they endured an air raid that had bombs "popping like cannoncrackers" from 8:30 P.M. until 4 A.M.

The next day they decided to find safer quarters and settled in Beauvais, where they did their best to feed refugees and wounded Tommies as they were loaded on hospital trains for evacuation to England. Gradually the Smithies realized there would be no more reconstruction work until the war was over. But they remained determined to stay in France, no matter how many miles the Germans gained. Grimly, they headed back to Paris and began volunteering as ambulance drivers, canteen workers and nurses.[31]

VII

In Paris, the Smith women found a city in a state of near hysteria. To keep the French off balance while the storm troopers demolished the British army, General Ludendorff had moved three gigantic guns into the forest of Crépy-en-Laonnois, near Laon, seventy miles from Paris. Called *Wilhelm Geschütze* in honor of the kaiser, the superguns were manned by German sailors, who nicknamed them "Big Berthas," after a member of the Krupp family. The specially designed 112-foot-long barrels fired a 200-pound shell into the stratosphere, from whence it descended into the middle of Paris.

The first shell landed at 7:26 A.M. on March 23 and was followed by twenty-two others, killing sixteen people and injuring twenty-nine. Three days later, another shell struck the crowded church of Saint-Gervais during services, killing seventy-five worshippers and wounding ninety. The bombardment continued through March 30. By that time, the Parisians had calmed down and decided the Berthas were no worse than the sporadic German air raids. The civilians accepted the inevitable casualties with the same stoicism that the poilus displayed at the front.

Technical problems with the Big Berthas soon limited their rate of fire. One gun exploded, killing or wounding seventeen of its crew. The guns were erratic. On some days, shells missed Paris entirely, exploding in the countryside beyond the city. French long-range guns and planes retaliated with shells and bombs that forced the Germans to move the guns to new positions. The Berthas would fire again in coming weeks, but there was no longer any danger of panic. Subways and buses continued to run, Parisians went about their business, more or less ignoring the rain of random death. But this brutal weapon deepened French hatred of Germany and spelled future trouble for Woodrow Wilson's dreams of world peace.[32]

VIII

For the moment, peace was not on anyone's mind. The success of the storm trooper tactics in the first *Kaiserschlacht* encouraged Quartermaster General Ludendorff and Field Marshal von Hindenburg to attempt one of their wildest dreams—the isolation of the British army in France by cutting its supply lines to the channel ports. The Germans were aware that the French army had lost its enthusiasm for the war. A British defeat would virtually guarantee an early French surrender. So Ludendorff ordered Colonel Bruchmuller to work on another section of the British front.

At 4:15 A.M. on April 9, which happened to be Ludendorff's birthday, Bruchmuller unleashed another rain of steel and gas on a mere eleven miles of a far more crucial British sector—Flanders. Little more than fifteen miles behind the lines lay Hazebrouck, a rail center through which was funneled almost all the supplies for the British Expeditionary Force. Without it, the royal army would become a marooned whale, bereft of food and ammunition.

Four attack divisions of General Ferdinand Quast's Sixth Army converged on a single Portuguese division holding a central piece of this eleven-mile front. The Portuguese were a 20,000-man token force, sent by their government to affirm their centuries-old alliance with England. The men had no enthusiasm for this murderous war, nor did their officers; their commanding general spent most of his time in Paris. Why the British entrusted such a vital part of the line to them can only be explained as further proof of Field Marshal Haig's appalling generalship.

Their uniforms stained yellow with gas, the men from the Iberian Peninsula sprinted for the rear at a pace that made the soldiers of the British Fifth Army look like slowpokes. Not a few of them stole the bicycles of a British cycle battalion that rushed forward to support them and did not stop pedaling until they reached the English Channel at Le Havre. Another 6,000 surrendered on the spot.[33]

Storm troopers poured through the gap and assaulted British divisions on the flanks, producing more panic and a less rapid but no less ominous retreat. The British First Army fell back five miles, while General Sir Herbert Plumer's Second Army was thrown back from Messines Ridge, which the British had captured at horrendous cost in the battle of Passchendaele. Soon Quast's Sixth Army had linked up with General Sixt von Armin's Fourth Army, which had joined the offensive north of Armentières. By April 12, the breach was thirty miles wide and ten miles deep. Hazebrouck was only five miles away.

A desperate Haig issued an order that had the trumpet of doom in it. "There is no other course open to us but to fight it out. Every position must be held to the last man; there must be no retirement. With our backs to the wall, and believing in the justice of our cause, each of must fight on to the end. The safety of our homes and the freedom of mankind alike depend on the conduct of each one of us in this crucial moment."[34]

Haig did more than write apocalyptic orders. He put Plumer, his best general, in charge of the battle, and rushed Australian reinforcements from Amiens. The Aussies had become the storm troopers of the British army. When the going got tough, Haig invariably turned to them. They paid a horrendous price for their devotion to the empire. Their casualties at war's end were a staggering 87 percent of their expeditionary force.

Fighting stubbornly and at times ferociously, the British began making the storm troopers pay for every foot of ground. The French also moved several divisions into Flanders. Although they did not go into action, they threatened the German left flank, forcing Ludendorff to divert troops from the drive on Hazebrouck. Slowly, as the month of April dwindled, the storm troopers ran out of steam again. On April 29, Ludendorff called off the offensive, with Hazebrouck uncaptured. But in a final show of confidence, the German commander ordered an attack on a French division holding Mount Kemmel, one of the key heights in the monotonously flat Flanders plain. The poilus fled in disorder, convincing Ludendorff that a blow at the French lines near Paris would panic them into withdrawing their forces from Flanders. Then he and Colonel Bruchmuller would swing north to throw a final haymaker at the British Expeditionary Force.[35]

IX

These German victories added up to bad news for General John J. Pershing in more ways than one. After the first *Kaiserschlacht* had annihilated the British Fifth Army and mauled the Third Army, the frantic Allies convened a summit conference at Doullens, to which they did not even bother to invite Pershing or any other American. The only general who seemed interested in fighting was short, fiery Ferdinand Foch, until recently in disgrace for squandering his men in slaughterous attacks. The politicians persuaded Haig and Pétain to accept him as a supreme commander to coordinate the collapsing battle line.

Instead of sulking for being ignored, Pershing made his only grand gesture of the war. He drove to Foch's headquarters outside Paris and in reasonably good French declared: "I have come to tell you that the American people would consider it a great honor for our troops to be engaged in the present battle. I ask you for this in their name and my own." Everyone applauded the performance. It made headlines. But Pershing soon learned he had embraced a rattlesnake.[36]

Pershing thought Foch would put the four available American divisions into line as an Army corps. Instead, Foch assigned them to quiet sectors, piecemeal, after the battle for Amiens subsided. Next Foch dispatched a cable behind Pershing's back, telling President Wilson that unless 600,000 infantrymen were shipped to Europe in the next three months, unattached to any divisions for use as replacements in the French and British armies, the war was lost.[37]

Pershing fought the Frenchman with his only weapon—an immense stubbornness and rocklike faith in his vision of an independent American army. Even when Secretary of War Newton Baker was cajoled into backing Foch by the devious Tasker Bliss, who seized the first opportunity to revoke his capitulation to Pershing, the AEF commander clung to his determination.

In May, after the second German offensive, the Allies convened another conference at Abbeville. This time, Pershing was invited; in fact, he was the principal reason for the meeting. Every leading politician and general in France and England was determined to change his mind. Alone, Pershing faced Prime Ministers Lloyd George, Clemenceau and Italy's Vittorio Orlando; plus Foch, Haig and a half dozen other generals and cabinet officers. Bliss, who was also present, did not say a word in Pershing's support. The others raged, screamed, cursed and pleaded—but Pershing refused to let the Americans fight in units smaller than a division—and he insisted even this concession would be temporary, pending the formation of an American army.

"You are willing to risk our being driven back to the Loire?" Foch shouted.

"Gentlemen," Pershing said. "I have thought this program over very deliberately and will not be coerced."[38]

Pershing's gamble was growing more awesome with every passing day. Even his chief of staff, James Harbord, admitted that if he had been British or French, he would have favored amalgamation. Only his old friend and shrewd head of the General Purchasing Board, Brigadier General Charles

Dawes, retained his faith in Pershing's judgment. "John Pershing, like Lincoln, recognized no superior on the face of the earth," Dawes wrote in his diary.[39]

X

A sense of foreboding was settling deep in the spirit of many Americans. Marian Baldwin had joined the YMCA and had been assigned to Aix-Les-Bains, a resort town where the AEF had taken over numerous buildings, including a mammoth gambling casino, for a leave center. On February 27, 1918, Baldwin wrote anxiously to her favorite correspondent: "The papers are certainly discouraging reading now, and the facts that don't get printed make one sick. Great things are brewing up the line and the trainloads of boys that leave here every day to go back, carry the most determined lot you ever saw, although every one knows what his fate may be."[40]

Aix-Les-Bains was Pershing's solution to the social purity problem. He had emphatically endorsed the stateside ideal of a "clean" army, free of venereal disease. One of his early edicts was a regulation making venereal disease a court-martial offense, meaning it would go into a man's permanent record. He also decreed ferocious punishments for any doughboy who molested an unwilling Frenchwoman.

The First Division had barely landed in France when a peasant girl claimed she had been attacked while bringing her cows in from her family's pasture. The soldier claimed she had flirted with him and he had only been trying to kiss her. Within twenty-four hours, the stunned man was court-martialed and sentenced to thirty years in Fort Leavenworth, the army prison.[41]

To keep the AEF out of Paris, with its 75,000 prostitutes, Pershing set up Aix-Les-Bains and similar centers, where sports, concerts, nature walks, movies and a small staff of American women (fifteen at Aix-Les-Bains) strove to offer an alternative to the mademoiselles. The women were an important component of this program. They were there to remind the doughboys of the girls back home, to whom many had pledged their affection.

Not all the doughboys bought the YMCA approach to the problems of life and love in a foreign land. Woodrow Wilson's moralism and Pershing's drive for discipline and military efficiency had formed a somewhat strange alliance to sponsor the YM's role in the war. Wilson wanted the doughboys to remain "clean" so their crusade to make the world safe for democracy would remain unsullied. Pershing wanted the lowest possible venereal disease rate, because an infected man was as useless as a casualty. The British had 23,000 men in the hospital for VD on any given day during the war and the French reported more than a million cases of syphilis and gonorrhea. Pershing flatly stated that "continence" was the ideal he expected from every doughboy. It was an ideal Pershing himself had not practiced; he had contracted gonorrhea twice in his early army days. Throughout the war, he continued to visit Micheline Resco in Paris.

Probably the general regarded the exhortation as standard hot air that no one with any sophistication was expected to practice. Some proof of this presumption was the officers' venereal disease rate—27.7 per thousand, almost thirty times higher than the enlisted men's rate.[42]

More evidence of skepticism is visible in a poem given to Marian Baldwin by a "mischievous doughboy" who took (she said) a "sly crack" at the "doctrines of the Y."

> *I*
> *My parents told me not to smoke—*
>   *I don't.*
> *Nor listen to a naughty joke—*
>   *I don't.*
> *They made it clear I mustn't wink*
> *At pretty girls; or even think*
> *About intoxicating drink—*
>   *I don't.*
>
> *II*
> *To flirt or dance is very wrong—*
>   *I don't.*
> *Wild youths chase women, wine and song*
>   *I don't.*
> *I kiss no girls, not even one,*
> *I do not know how it is done;*
> *You wouldn't think I had much fun—*
>   *I don't.*[43]

Still, Baldwin felt most of the men who came to Aix-Les-Bains were full of gratitude, for the little they were able to do for them here. "Girlie," one said to her, "it will seem just like a dream when we get back there." Baldwin could only hope that "whatever seemed beautiful to them in this short 'dream' will stand by them to make life, and even death, easier 'out there.'"

The day before, Baldwin continued, she had gone down to the station to see one of the troop trains off. She knew practically every man on it. Several of the women stood at the end of the platform and shook hands with each soldier as the train moved past. "They were still hanging out of the windows with hands outstretched, the setting sun shining full on their eager boyish faces, and many of them smiling bravely through a mist of tears," Baldwin wrote. Every person left on the platform, including several army officers, was crying by the time the train vanished around a distant curve.[44]

XI

In her hospital, Shirley Millard was settling into the life of a nurse. "The big [German] drive is over, and the terrific rush has stopped, at least temporarily," she told her diary. "But the hospital is still filled." Most of the men were too badly wounded to be moved. The hospital desperately needed their beds, because they were being swamped by a new horror: influenza.

"I thought influenza was a bad cold, something like the grippe but this is much worse than that," Millard wrote. "These men run a high temperature, so high that we can't believe it's true, and often take it again to be sure. It is accompanied by vomiting and dysentery. When they die, as about half of them do, they turn a ghastly dark gray and are taken out at once and cremated."

The hospital had become better organized. There were special wards for influenza, and others for gangrene cases, major gas burns, meningitis, fractures, and spinal injuries. "I have worked in all of them and cannot make up my mind which is worse," Millard told her diary.[45]

Another worry was the German air force. Planes bombed the hospital almost every night. Often as many as forty aircraft were overhead. Millard's heart went out to the wounded men, "helpless in bed, with arms strapped up or down . . . or legs in casts." They knew the sound of German motors.

"Boche planes have quite a different noise from ours. It is a dismal groan, several tones deeper than the French."

One day at dawn, Millard was on duty when the barracks next to hers took a direct hit. She rushed out to stare at "an unforgettable sight." A tree that spread its bare, wintry branches over the barracks had "blossomed horribly with fragments of human bodies, arms and legs, bits of bedding, furniture, and hospital equipment." It looked, she thought, like a Christmas tree in a nightmare. Heightening the horror was "the blood red sky of sunrise."[46]

XII

Around the same time, the French decided to give the U.S. First Division a chance to do something more than occupy quiet trenches. They selected as a target the village of Cantigny, which sat on a ridge opposite the division's lines, fifty-five miles northwest of Paris. The whole division was not needed to make the attack. Pershing designated the Twenty-Eighth Regiment to do the job, and told the commander, Colonel Hanson E. Ely, "no inch" of any ground gained was to be yielded to the inevitable German counterattacks. On April 30, another German trench raid had mauled a battalion of the Twenty-Sixth Division in the lines south of Verdun, further dimming the AEF's prestige. Lloyd George had snidely commented that this was the sort of thing that would happen again and again if the "amateur" Americans were allowed to form their own army. Pershing made it clear to everyone in the First Division that the AEF's reputation was at stake.[47]

The French, anxious for the Americans to succeed, backed the operation with 386 long-range guns, trench mortars, twelve heavy tanks, flamethrower teams, and air cover. Unintentionally, the Germans also cooperated with the AEF. Quartermaster General Ludendorff was in the midst of planning his left hook at the French army's solar plexus, to persuade them to pull their troops out of Flanders. He withdrew the crack Thirtieth Division from the Cantigny lines and replaced them with the Eighty-Second Reserve Division, which was full of overage veterans, teenage recruits and assorted other flotsam, including former railway guards. AEF intelligence rated the Eighty-Second as "third class."[48]

At 4:45 A.M. on May 28, French and American artillery hurled hundreds of shells into Cantigny, smashing its ruins to total rubble. At 6:45 the doughboys advanced behind a rolling barrage and sheets of machine-gun fire. They found the soldiers of the Eighty-Second Reserve Division dazed and demoralized by the bombardment. The appearance of the clanking French heavy tanks added to their panic. Tanks were a new weapon to these Germans—they had made their first appearance on the battlefield only six months earlier, in the British assault on Cambrai. There, tougher German divisions had quickly learned how to deal with them. Many of the Eighty-Second Reserve Division surrendered; others ran. In a few hours, the Americans had occupied Cantigny with less than a hundred casualties.[49]

The next morning, the French trumpeted this tiny American victory in their newspapers and the headlines echoed around the world. Then, strange things began to happen. The French tanks, airplanes, flamethrowers and artillery vanished. The Germans had launched an offensive forty miles southeast of Cantigny and the French needed every soldier and weapon they could find to stop it. The Americans were left on their own to cope with German counterattacks to regain Cantigny.

Now it was the German artillery that came cascading down on the doughboys, who were dug into open slopes, with Pershing's orders not to yield an inch of ground. German planes strafed them with impunity and gave their artillery information that murderously improved its accuracy. The American cannon, mostly French 75s, did not have the range to reach the German heavy guns.

The Eighty-Second Reserve Division's counterattacks were as mediocre as the rest of its performance. The division never managed to coordinate its attacks with the artillery; the Americans easily beat them off. But the German big guns did not need the infantry to inflict awful damage on the Americans. Within twenty-four hours, a third of the Twenty-Eighth regiment was dead or wounded. On May 29, Ely reported his front line was "pounded to hell and gone." His men had to be relieved in twenty-four hours, or he would "not be responsible" for what happened next.[50]

Ely's words of warning were reinforced by visible evidence of imminent breakdown. One American lieutenant went berserk, leaped out of his shell hole, and began shooting at fellow Americans. Before they could fire back, a German shell shredded him. The Germans were using 210-mm guns, whose eight-inch shells, Captain George Marshall glumly noted, "rip[ped] up the nervous system of everyone within a hundred yards of the explosion." Still, General Robert Lee Bullard, the First Division's commander, was loath to relieve Ely's men. "The whole world is watching the Twenty-

Eighth Infantry," Bullard told the worried colonel. "We must continue to hold Cantigny at all costs." The general did not want to reveal that the American victory was turning into a semidefeat.[51]

On the third day, a staff officer from Bullard's headquarters visited Ely and told him, in the cheerful tones often used by those who are safe from flying bullets and shrapnel, that he was sure the Twenty-Eighth Regiment could hold. In response, Ely roared, "These men have been fighting for three days and three nights. . . . There are three other regiments [in the division] who have had their sleep. . . . It is an injustice not to relieve the[se] men." He added that five of them were not worth what one was worth when they attacked—and caustically suggested the staffer could "put it [all] down in your notebook" and quote him verbatim to General Bullard.

That night, the Eighteenth Regiment relieved Ely's battered men. He described them coming out of the front line "hollow-eyed and with sunken cheeks," so exhausted that they fell asleep if they sat (or fell) down. More than 1,000 of their buddies were killed or wounded, which Ely thought "was a high price to pay for an unknown village of relatively little value." But Cantigny was not about winning the war. It was about proving that Americans could handle combat on the Western Front.[52]

Pershing's friend, Dorothy Canfield Fisher, who had told him that the French were finished, had dinner with the general and his staff not long after Cantigny. She described their almost manic elation at this "success." At the top of their voices they told each other the conduct of Ely's men had been "magnificent." Pershing became so excited, he slammed his fist on the table and shouted, "I am certainly going to jump down the throat of the next person who asks me, 'Will the Americans fight?'"

The AEF commander cited Cantigny in a cable to the War Department, asserting that the battle proved that all further talk about amalgamation should be dismissed out of hand. "It is my firm opinion that our troops are the best in Europe and our staffs the equal of any," the general declared. The Americans should "start organizing our own divisions and higher units" as soon as possible. Pershing's reaction was more a comment on the psychological beating he had taken from the French and British since he came to France than a realistic assessment of the military situation. Forty miles southeast of Cantigny, the German army was close to winning the war.[53]

XIII

Once more concealing his movements with astonishing success, Quartermaster General Ludendorff had moved his attack divisions south and concentrated them around the town of Laon, opposite the French Sixth Army north of Soissons. The front line ran along a commanding ridge, the Chemin des Dames, named for a carriage road hacked out of the limestone escarpment and used for outings by the ladies of France's ancien régime. The French had captured the ridge the previous autumn in a limited offensive, one of two minor pushes General Pétain ordered to camouflage the morale of his mutinous army. A press officer at headquarters had christened the ridge the outer rampart of Paris. It was rugged country, with numerous small deep valleys and steep hills.

On May 27, Ludendorff had forty-one divisions in and around Laon. Facing him were eleven understrength French and British divisions, all decidedly second or third class. The four British divisions had been mauled in the March and April offensives and had been sent to the Chemin des Dames for a rest. There had scarcely been a shot fired in the sector for almost a year. It was known as the sanitarium of the Western Front. Among the French divisions was one that had been especially mutinous in the 1917 upheaval—its men had never forgiven the commander of the Sixth Army, General Denis Duchene, for his ruthless use of firing squads to restore order.

Pétain, still the commander of the French field army, had issued orders for a defense in depth. But Ferdinand Foch, flexing his command muscles as generalissimo in chief of the entire Western Front, had canceled the order and insisted that the front lines be fully manned, to make sure not a millimeter of France's sacred soil was surrendered. The obedient Duchene had packed almost every man in the Sixth Army into a three-mile wedge between the Chemin des Dames and the Aisne River—perfect targets for Colonel Bruchmuller's orchestra of big guns.

When Foch was appointed generalissimo in late March, the *New York Times* had devoted a full page of its Sunday edition to him, calling him "The First Strategist in Europe." He was about to flunk his first test.[54]

Ironically, an American intelligence officer, Captain Samuel T. Hubbard, with nothing better to do—the semitrained AEF divisions had yet to be organized into a serious army—predicted that the next German offensive would hit the Chemin des Dames. The French loftily ignored his warning. General Duchene, known as "the Tiger" to his admirers, spent the night of May 27 in Paris with his mistress.[55]

At 1 A.M. multicolored Very lights soared into the sky, signals for Bruchmuller's gunners. In seconds, the colonel's orchestra was in full crescendo, with 3,719 guns pouring gas and high explosives on the hapless poilus and Tommies trapped by Foch's interference and Duchene's over-confidence. At dawn the storm troopers surged forward, their ranks bolstered by mountain troops to handle the difficult terrain. On the Chemin des Dames, they found little but corpses and dazed survivors eager to surrender. The mutinous French division evaporated, and others swiftly imitated them. Only the British did any serious fighting, and they were soon driven over the Aisne River.

So swift was the German advance, scarcely a bridge over the Aisne was blown. A French army corps thrown in to restore the front found itself outflanked by hundreds of surging storm companies and was itself swiftly routed, causing its commander, General Joseph Degoutte, to burst into tears. In twelve hours, all the objectives designated by Ludendorff as the limits of the offensive had been taken. But the exultant storm troopers kept going. They crossed the swift and narrow Vesle River on May 28 and headed south for the Marne, chewing up division after French division as they debouched onto the battlefield.

A glimpse of the terror and despair created by the German onslaught is visible in the experience of a lance corporal in the Sixteenth Bavarian Reserve Regiment. Known to his comrades as "Adi," Adolf Hitler had been fighting on the Western Front since 1914. As a runner bearing messages between the front lines and headquarters, he had one of the most dangerous assignments in the German army. By this time his officers considered him an outstanding soldier. Their reports frequently mentioned the Austrian-born Hitler's "exceptional courage," his "admirable unpretentiousness," and his "profound love of country."

On the morning of the assault over the Chemin des Dames, Hitler was carrying a message to a battalion that had broken through and vanished on the chaotic battlefield. Spotting a French helmet in a nearby trench, Hitler whipped out his pistol and captured twelve dazed poilus. He marched them back to headquarters and turned them over to his colonel. A few weeks later the courageous corporal received the Iron Cross, First Class.[56]

Soon Fère-en-Tardenois, a key road junction in the center of Champagne, was in German hands. Premier Georges Clemenceau, who had rushed to the front, came very close to being captured; his car fled out the south end of Fère-en-Tardenois as the Germans entered from the north. Then Soissons, a vital rail center, fell. Only around Rheims, where the French had built a network of fortifications, did the poilus hold. By May 30, the storm troopers were on the Marne, having captured more than 60,000 men and eight hundred guns.

Suddenly, Paris, the original goal of the German invasion, was only forty miles away. Postponing his plan for a knockout blow at the British in Flanders, Ludendorff summoned every available soldier from other parts of the front to exploit this colossal breakthrough. But once more, the French and British, by headlong flight, had given themselves time to muster more reserves and throw up a new if shaky defense line. When a German battalion crossed the Marne on May 30, its men found themselves isolated by a rain of French shells that made reinforcement a form of suicide. The storm troopers would have to wait until German artillery came forward to support a renewed offensive.

East of Soissons, the poilus and a British division also successfully resisted a German attempt to link the huge salient created by this third offensive with the bulge carved in the Somme Valley in March. By hanging onto the hinges of the new salient, the French and British narrowed the focus of the German advance. But this modicum of good news did little to minimize the menace of the immense breakthrough, with its forward echelons poised to leap the Marne and devour Paris.

On May 30, General Pershing had supper at Generalissimo Foch's headquarters. "It would be difficult to imagine a more depressed group of officers," the AEF commander later said. "They sat through the meal scarcely speaking a word as they contemplated what was possibly the most serious situation of the war." In Paris, people were fleeing the city by the thousands. The French government was packing records and talking of retreating to the Pyrenees.

After dinner Foch renewed his demand to amalgamate future American arrivals into the British and French armies. Pershing reiterated his opposition, but offered every division he had in France to meet the crisis. Foch accepted his terms, but insisted the Americans would have to fight under the command of French generals. Pershing reluctantly agreed to this arrangement.[57]

Major General Omar Bundy's Second Division went into position west of Château-Thierry while Major General Joseph Dickman's Third Division manned the banks of the Marne east of that strategic river town. The Forty-Second Division, popularly known as the Rainbow Division, because its troops came from all parts of United States, became part of the French Fourth Army, closer to Rheims. As the Americans moved up, thousands of beaten poilus streamed past them, shouting, "*La guerre finie!*"

Except for some lively skirmishing, the Germans did not attack the Americans. Their infantry went over to the defensive while the generals brought up the artillery and tried to decide what to do next. The option of another massive blow at the British army in Flanders was still on the table. But Paris remained a supremely tempting target, just over the horizon.

XIV

In the French capital, Premier Georges Clemenceau went before an almost hysterical chamber of deputies on June 4. Members shouted insults at him and screamed demands that he fire Foch and Pétain and negotiate peace. Even the deputy premier, Frederic Brunet, abandoned Clemenceau and made a menacing speech, asking if those in high positions should not be called to account for a failure to do "their whole duty." Why should the law come down with "crushing force" upon the soldier who fails to do his duty and spare the leader who is responsible for these "irretrievable defeats"?[58]

Clemenceau summoned all the considerable eloquence in his aged frame to answer these challenges. He asked the deputies if they wanted him to abandon men (Foch and Pétain) who "deserved well of their country" and sow doubts in the souls of the poilus at this crucial moment in France's history. He rejected such an alternative as a crime "for which I would never accept responsibility." He told them that only yesterday, the Supreme War Council, meeting in Versailles, had restated their "high confidence" in General Foch.[59]

The deputies called this nonsense. "It was you who made them [the War Council] do it," one man shouted. Clemenceau ignored this accusation and asked them if they wanted to indict a man who was reeling from exhaustion, whose "head droops over maps." Were they going to add to his burden a demand for an explanation of why he did this and did not do that? Wild-eyed deputies responded by swarming onto the rostrum and driving Clemenceau into the hall. The chamber erupted into total anarchy, with Clemenceau backers wrestling and punching his attackers to clear the podium.

Order of sorts restored, Clemenceau emerged once more to speak of "tragic truths" and his responsibility to France. They were not fighting alone, he reminded them. The British and the French may be exhausted, but "the Americans were coming." These words magically transformed the chamber. A cheer exploded against the ceiling. Catching fire, Clemenceau exhorted them to keep faith with "those who have fallen." It was intolerable to surrender now and confess they had died in vain. More cheers were followed by a vote on whether to call Pétain and Foch to explain the oncoming Germans. A fight to the finish, sans explanations, won by 337 to 110.[60]

In his cell at the Prison de la Santé, Joseph Caillaux was no doubt thoroughly aware of the situation and was waiting tensely for Clemenceau's fall. A former premier told Brigadier General James Harbord, newly promoted to command of the two U.S. Marine regiments in the Second Division, that in a secret session of the Chamber of Deputies, many members said that if "Caillaux were made premier and General Serrail given command of Paris," the war would end in three weeks.[61]

On June 5, General Henry Wilson, the British representative on the Supreme War Council, journeyed to London to discuss the evacuation of the British army from France. General Wilson had no confidence in Foch. He was convinced that the generalissimo "could not see beyond his nose," and the entire French army was on the brink of collapse. "It was a very gloomy meeting," the secretary of the war cabinet, Sir Maurice Hankey, noted in his diary.[62]

XV

General Joseph Degoutte, the French commander of the sector east of Château-Thierry, was, like Ferdinand Foch, an apostle of the school of attack that had done little thus far but pile up bodies in front of German machine guns. Finding himself in possession of fresh American troops, Degoutte ordered an assault on Belleau Wood, which stood on commanding ground about a half mile from the American lines. He found a willing collaborator in Colonel Preston Brown, the Second Division's chief of staff, who was burning to demonstrate American fighting prowess. Brown accepted at face value French reports that the Germans held only the northern corner of the wood. In fact, its 1,000-yard width and 3,000-yard length were occupied to the last inch by infantry and machine gunners with interlocking fields of fire.[63]

At 5 P.M. on June 6, without sending out a single patrol to find out more information, Brown and Brigadier General Harbord ordered the two U.S. Marine regiments forward in a frontal assault. In the myths that have accumulated about the battle of Belleau Wood, the marines have been pictured as hard-bitten veterans of numerous battles in Haiti, Santo Domingo and other overseas combat assignments. In fact, 95 percent were new recruits, in the corps less than a year. Their officers were equally unprepared to fight on the Western Front. They led their men forward in massed formations unseen since 1914. Astonished German machine gunners mowed them down in windrows. The slaughter revealed the horrendous limitations of General Pershing's version of open warfare.

Today, it is painful to read the naïveté with which those young marines advanced to their deaths. They seemed amazed to discover that machine guns killed people. One platoon was commanded by an army lieutenant named Coppinger. "Follow me!" he said and led them up a ravine raked by machine guns. At the top of the rise, he looked around and said, "Where the hell is my platoon?" Only six of the fifty-two marines were still on their feet. Even more appalling was the attack of a battalion led by Major Berton Sibley. They advanced in formation, under slow cadence, as if they were on a parade ground. Shells and machine gun bullets tore awful gaps in their ranks. The commander of the regiment, Colonel Albertus Catlin, declared the advance "one of the most beautiful sights I have ever witnessed." Catlin stayed on his feet, admiring this performance, until a machine gun bullet tore through his chest, leaving him paralyzed.[64]

For the next twenty days, the marines, reinforced by the two army regiments in the Second Division and a regiment from the nearby Third Division, struggled to oust the Germans from Belleau Wood. The Germans fed elements of four divisions into the struggle, which began to acquire a "moral" dimension in their eyes. They were determined to prove that the American army was not the equal, much less the superior, of the German army. In the United States, headlines made the battle seem one of the most important of the war. "Our Marines Attack, Gain Mile at Veuilly, Resume Drive at Night, Foe Losing Heavily," reported the *New York Times*. "Marines Win Hot Battle, Sweep Enemy from Heights Near Thierry," shouted the

Chicago Daily Tribune. Not a word about the fields carpeted with the bodies of dead and dying young marines.[65]

The Americans eventually captured the mile-square forest after the French withdrew the marines and treated the German defenders to a fourteen-hour artillery barrage that left only a few dazed survivors to contest the marines' final assault. The marine brigade lost 126 officers and 5,057 men, more than 42 percent of its force. Until the marines attacked the Japanese on Tarawa, it was the bloodiest battle in the history of the corps. The Second Division's two army regiments lost another 3,252 officers and men. Pershing rewarded Harbord by making him commander of the Second Division, replacing the overage Omar Bundy, who had stood around letting Harbord and Preston Brown make their reckless opening attack without saying a word. In his memoirs, Harbord, a thoughtful man, wrote with evident regret of "the insufficient information on which you are sometimes obliged to send men forth to die."[66]

The desperate French trumpeted Belleau Wood as a major victory in their newspapers, and reporters followed suit around the world. Pershing went along with the hyperbole, because he was even more desperate for proof that his men could stand up to the Germans. The battering he had taken from Foch, Haig and others had narrowed his judgment of what constituted a battlefield success. The man who had once been proud of winning battles with a minimum of casualties had become a virtual convert to Field Marshal Haig's HCI (high casualties inevitable) formula for victory.

Some historians of World War I have portrayed Belleau Wood as a turning point that "proved" Americans could outfight the Germans. General Bullard, commander of the First Division, went even further, claiming that Belleau saved the Allies from defeat. But the German army's subsequent battlefield performance against the Americans showed no decline in determination and ferocity. In his memoirs, Major General Joseph Dickman, commander of the Third Division, which had been in line beside the Second Division while Belleau Wood was consummated, deplored the operation as a waste of men and ammunition: "It was magnificent fighting, but it was not modern war."[67]

XVI

Mesmerized by Paris, and convinced that the storm troopers were an invincible weapon, the German high command decided to try to finish the war where they had almost won it in 1914—on the Marne. Quartermaster General Ludendorff was so overconfident, he sacrificed the key element in the storm troopers' earlier successes: surprise. The Allies knew where the blow would fall—the only question was when. It was difficult, if not impossible, to keep a secret shared by hundreds of thousands of men. Trench raids brought in prisoners who revealed that the new offensive was scheduled to begin at ten minutes past midnight on July 15. The Germans were hoping the French would be sleeping off the July 14 celebration of Bastille Day, their national holiday.

Although some French generals still took Foch's advice and jammed their men into forward trenches, others decided Pétain's defense in depth made more sense. They left only suicide squads up front and targeted their artillery on their own front lines. The rest of their men went underground, into sandbagged dugouts. Precisely at 12:10, Colonel Bruchmuller's artillery orchestra went to work, hurling destruction across forty-two miles of front. Four hours later, the storm troopers went forward—to disaster.

French and American artillery poured concentrated fire into their ranks. In the east, around Rheims, by the time the Germans reached the main defense line, their attacks were scattered, uncoordinated. "Their legs are broken," exulted newly promoted Brigadier General Douglas MacArthur of the Rainbow Division, which was scattered across thirteen kilometers of the front, fighting under French commanders. This impromptu amalgamation was a grim commentary on French lack of confidence in the poilus' staying power.[68]

Along the Marne, riflemen and machine gunners of the Third Division took a terrible toll on the attackers as they paddled through fog and gun smoke in rubber boats. On the Third Division's right flank, a half dozen French divisions evaporated, abandoning a battalion of the Twenty-Eighth Division planted in their midst to strengthen them. But the Third Division stood firm, leaving the 20,000 Germans who had gotten across the river exposed to flank attacks and entrapment. By the end of the first day, the Germans knew the offensive had failed. Lieutenant Rudolf Binding wrote in his diary: "I have lived through the most disheartening day of the whole war."[69]

A discouraged Ludendorff tried to tell himself and his staff that the effort was a success. They had pinned down the entire French army and most of the American army. Now was the time to launch the knockout blow at the British in Flanders. On July 16, after calling off further attacks, he and his staff took a train north to plan the assault without delay. They had scarcely arrived when frantic telephone calls informed the quartermaster general of a totally unexpected development.

On the morning of July 18, out of the Forest of the Retz, east of Soissons, had stormed three divisions of the Allied army, two American and one French. They were biting deep into the exposed right flank of the Marne salient, threatening to trap a half million Germans along the river. A dismayed Ludendorff had to abandon his knockout dreams and rush reinforcements south to blunt this threat.[70]

XVII

In this climactic moment of their struggle to make the world safe for democracy, the Americans of the Second Division rode to the battlefield in trucks driven by Vietnamese from the French colony of Indochina. The First Division had already reached the Forest of the Retz after an exhausting three-day march. There the Americans discovered they would be attacking beside the French army's Moroccan Division, which was a mixture of blacks from Senegal, Arabs and others from North Africa, and a regiment composed of the ex-criminals and lost souls who volunteered for the French Foreign Legion. Fortunately, irony was not a mode of American thought among the doughboys in 1918. They still saw the war as a test of their collective manhood. One member of the First Division wrote in his diary: "The troops which have been massed here are the best of the French army. That we are joining them is a sign that we have gained some prestige."[71]

The commander of the attack was General Charles Mangin, known to the poilus as the Butcher. In an army whose generals had already killed a million men in failed attacks, this was an ominous title. Mangin had decided that the only way to achieve surprise was to attack with no artillery preparation. In the frantic haste with which the offensive was organized, there was virtually no intelligence either. General Harbord and his chief of staff, Preston Brown, obtained a hastily dictated memo from a French staff officer, describing the terrain across which their men were to attack. They had to depend on this rudimentary document to write orders for infantry and artillery.

Moving up through the pitch-dark forest in a driving rain, the Americans encountered monumental confusion. Some machine-gun units became separated from their ammunition. Some infantry battalions attacked without a single hand grenade. Most of the Second Division never got anything to eat. But at dawn on July 18, the 67,000-man assault went forward, stunning the Germans with its size and ferocity. The goal was the railroad that ran through Soissons and Fère-en-Tardenois. It was the main source of food and ammunition for the half million Germans in the Marne salient.

The first day was a sensational success, but on the second day, the Germans recovered from their surprise. Machine guns sprouted everywhere, and American casualties soon mounted to catastrophic proportions. Again and again, the doughboys advanced across open ground without concealment or cover, with predictable results. Typical was the experience of Private Carl Brannen of the Fifth Marine Regiment. It was his second day of the battle and the third without any solid food. "The morning of July 19, we formed our lines . . . for a charge across a sugar beet field. . . . In thirty or forty minutes, our regiment had been almost annihilated. The field which had been recently crossed was strewn with dead and dying. Their cries for water and help got weaker as the hot July day wore on."[72]

In three days, the two American divisions lost more than 12,000 men. The Second Division, already bled by Belleau Wood, collapsed and had to be withdrawn after two days. The First Division, equally battered—its Twenty-Sixth Infantry regiment lost 3,000 out of 3,200 men—was withdrawn the following day. This was hardly the staying power Pershing had envisioned for his double-sized divisions. But he ignored the danger signs and told Harbord that even if the two divisions never fired another shot, they had made their commanders "immortal."[73]

Harbord and Brown stood by the roadside near the Second Division's headquarters and watched the survivors march past them, after their withdrawal. They were "only a remnant," Harbord admitted, "but a victorious remnant; no doubt existed in their mind as to their ability to whip the Germans. Their whole independent bearing, their swagger as they strode by, the snatches of conversation we could hear as they passed, proclaimed them a victorious division."[74]

A general who has lost over 15,000 men in a month needed to see these things to keep up his own morale. A more realistic report of the aftermath of Soissons came from Marine Private Brannen: "The surviving Marines who left the battle line were a terrible looking bunch of people. They looked more like animals. They had almost a week's growth of beard and were dirty and ragged. Their eyes were sunk back in their heads. There had been very little sleep or rest for four days and no food. . . . The boys were more despondent than I ever saw them after this last battle and no wonder. I was the only survivor of Overton's platoon of about fifty men. There were eight able to walk away from the front, out of 212 on the company roster."[75]

Yet it was a victory. Although the attackers did not cut the railroad line, they forced the Germans to abandon all thoughts of crossing the Marne to Paris. Instead, General Ludendorff was forced to shorten his lines—a euphemism for the ugly word *retreat*. In his war memoirs, Field Marshal von Hindenburg wrote: "How many hopes, cherished during the last few months had possibly collapsed at one blow! How many calculations had been scattered to the winds."[76]

XVIII

The American infantrymen who fought at Cantigny and Belleau Wood were constantly harassed by German planes. They frequently cursed America's nonexistent air service. Their criticism added intensity to Quentin Roosevelt's desire to reach the front. At first, from Flora's letters, he thought they might be married before he headed for the war zone. For a while her parents seemed amenable to a trip to Paris. Influential friends were enlisted to approach the War Department.

This hope soon faded. Flora was told that the answer from the War Department was no. Flora's pilot brother, Sonny, now scheduled to go overseas, was the ostensible reason. Mournfully, Flora wrote to Quentin: "It looked so cheerful, the prospects of my coming, it is really . . . mean they should be dashed away so suddenly." Quentin's response was a brash cable: "SO SORRY OUR PLANS IMPOSSIBLE . . . LOTS OF TIME YET. MOVING OUT AT LAST WITH HAM. LOVE, ROOSEVELT."[77]

Quentin also cabled the news to his father, who responded, "My joy for you and my pride in you drown my anxiety." He added it was "very hard" that Flora could not go to France. "I can't help feeling a little more resolution on the part of the Whitneys would have done it."[78]

By this time Quentin's older brothers, Ted, Archie and Kermit, had all seen action. In March, Archie had been badly wounded by an exploding shell that smashed his knee and almost severed an arm. At Cantigny, Ted had been gassed and for a while was forced to sleep in a sitting position. In Mesopotamia, Kermit had commanded an armored car in fierce fighting against the Turks and won the British War Cross for gallantry. This news only redoubled Quentin's desire to see action.[79]

On his way to the front, Quentin stopped in Paris and had a reunion with Archie, who was still in the hospital and deeply depressed. He had undergone a series of operations to try to connect the nerves in his shattered arm. Having seen the reality of the Western Front, Archie was convinced that all four Roosevelt brothers were going to die. Quentin scoffed at this possibility, telling Flora casualties in the air service squadrons already in action weren't "terribly big."[80]

Quentin and his friends were still flying second-rate Nieuports. German pilots were flying sleek, maneuverable Fokkers and Albatros DVs—far superior planes. Early American Air Service tactics resembled the naive optimism of the infantry vis-à-vis the machine gun. The Americans sent up three- and four-man patrols, which were constantly outnumbered by the Germans' aggressive *Jagdstaffeln* (hunting flights) tactics. The Jastas, as they were usually called, put as many as twelve planes in the air, trained to fight as a team.

When Quentin arrived at the Ninety-Fifth Aero Squadron, the commanding officer made him a flight commander. Quentin immediately called together the three other pilots in the flight and said, "Any one of you knows more about [this] than I do." As soon as they left the ground, the most experienced pilot would take command.[81]

On June 25, Quentin told Flora about his first patrol, "a sort of private Boche hunting party." They did not see any German planes but "Archies"—German antiaircraft shells—burst near enough "to turn me inside out." On the ground, he found a big shrapnel hole in his wing.[82]

"Things are getting hotter," Quentin told Flora a few days later. On a recent patrol, four planes tangled with six "Boche." The Americans shot one down but lost two pilots. Off duty, Quentin spent most of his time resting his back and working on his Nieuport, which had a cranky motor. He frequently fell behind other members of his flight while on patrol. He found high-altitude patrols exhausting. "Four miles up is mighty high," he said. Oxygen masks were a thing of the future.

Quentin was quartered in a nearby château, which overlooked some woods through which he sometimes wandered. The green shadowy silence made him think "however long the war lasts peace will come again and just you and I [will enjoy] our island. That's what I almost forget over here. War is only an interlude."

In another letter, he was brutally realistic. "If I do get it, Ham is going to take care of my things. I'm leaving a letter for you in my trunk. Of course this all sounds foolish. I love you too much not to come back, my darling."[83]

Then came a letter charged with excitement. "I think I got my first Boche," Quentin wrote on July 11. He had become separated from his flight and found himself alone over the front. In the distance, he saw three planes. Thinking they were friendly (an indication of how bad his eyes were), Quentin followed them over the German lines. Suddenly the leader turned, and Quentin saw the black crosses on his wings. A less daring flier would have headed for home. But Quentin "put my sights on the end man and let go. . . . He never even turned . . . all of a sudden his tail came up and he went down in a *vrille* (spin)." The other two Germans pursued Quentin, but he made it safely back to the American lines.[84]

French observers confirmed the kill, and Quentin stormed into Paris to celebrate with Eleanor and Archie. Quentin's sister Ethel rushed a triumphant note to Flora. "You must be so happy. Those long weary hours at Issoudun are being gloriously repaid." His father told Ethel, "Whatever now befalls Quentin he has had his crowded hour, his day of honor and triumph. . . . How pleased and proud Flora must be."[85]

On July 13, Archie Roosevelt wrote Flora a more realistic letter from his hospital bed: "Quentin blew in yesterday." Although he looked well, "one can't help being worried. He is in an American squadron and like everything else in our army we have had to take castoff machines from the allies so they have added dangers." Flora responded to this barrage of news and comment with a plaintive: "Oh how I wish it was all over!"[86]

On the morning of July 14, Quentin took off with the three other members of his flight. They had orders to shoot down German observation balloons to help conceal the movements of American infantry, who were preparing to block General Ludendorff's final offensive. Seven red-nosed Fokkers came roaring down on them, with the sun and altitude in their favor.

One of Quentin's flightmates described the ensuing melee. "In a few seconds [they] had completely broken up our formation and the fight developed into a general free-for-all. I tried to keep an eye on all our fellows but we were hopelessly separated and outnumbered nearly two to one. About a half mile away I saw one of our planes with three Boche on him and he seemed to be having a pretty hard time with them so I shook the two I was maneuvering with and tried to get over to him but before I could reach them, our machine turned over on its back and plunged down out of control."[87]

It was Quentin. He was slumped over his instruments with two machine-gun bullets in his brain. The Nieuport smashed to earth behind the German lines near the village of Chamery. In his pocket Quentin carried two letters from Flora, which helped the Germans identify the body. The last one, written on June 19, was full of her yearning to be with him in Paris: "If you were wounded I could be with you and be of some comfort," she wrote.[88]

Quentin's squadron listed him as missing. In the United States, those who loved him clung to shreds of hope. Eleanor Roosevelt, Ted's wife, cabled Flora: "EVERY REASON TO BELIEVE REPORT QUENTIN ABSOLUTELY UNTRUE." Quentin's friend Hamilton Coolidge wrote a letter voicing a similar opinion. But the next day, the German Red Cross reported Quentin had been buried where he fell, with full military honors, including a guard of 1,000 men.

"How am I going to break the news to Mrs. Roosevelt?" TR said when a reporter on duty at Sagamore Hill told him Quentin was dead. He went into the house and emerged a few minutes later with a statement. "Quentin's mother and I are very glad that he got to the front and had a chance to render some service and show the stuff there was in him before fate befell him." Then he telephoned Flora.[89]

Four days after Quentin died, the American-led attack at Soissons slammed the German war machine into reverse. Soon Quentin's grave was in Allied territory—and it swiftly became a kind of shrine. Infantrymen hiked miles to see it and decorated it with flowers and mementos. For soldiers fighting to make the world safe for democracy, the death of a president's son was proof that Americans practiced what they preached.[90]

For Theodore Roosevelt, his son's death had a very different meaning. Quentin had died flying a second-rate French plane, because Woodrow Wilson's administration had refused to prepare for war and after war was declared the president's appointees had failed to produce a single aircraft, in spite of spending almost a billion dollars. There was only one way to give Quentin's death meaning. Woodrow Wilson had to die an equivalent political death. His presidency must be—and would be—destroyed.

Chapter 7

POLITICS IS ADJOURNED, HA-HA-HA

Back in the United States, the exploits—but not the appalling casualties—of American soldiers dominated the headlines. Politics won almost as much space on the front page. It was an election year, and both parties were girding their financial and ideological loins for the struggle. At stake was control of Congress. Democratic majorities were narrow in the House and shaky in the Senate.

Democratic hopes for continuing control of the Senate had been worsened by some cruel blows of fate. No less than ten senators had died in the course of the Sixty-Fifth Congress, eight of them Democrats. Three were replaced by Republican appointees, thanks to GOP governors in their home states.[1]

Woodrow Wilson was anxious to keep control of Congress in Democratic hands. He had attempted to wield his presidential influence in two 1917 by-elections: a contest in the Indiana Sixth Congressional District and another House race in New Hampshire. He had declared both elections were a test of public approval of his conduct of the war. In both cases, he had suffered humiliating defeats. Even more egregious was his venture into the murky politics of Massachusetts, where, at Colonel House's urging, he had endorsed the Democratic candidate for governor—in vain.[2]

On February 12, 1918, GOP leaders met in Saint Louis and elected a moderate Indiana national committeeman, Will H. Hays, as the new party chairman. He had been vigorously backed by Theodore Roosevelt. Hays's selection was additional evidence that the Republicans were recovering from their 1912 split between the Progressives and the Old Guard. Senator Boise Penrose of Pennsylvania, a quintessential OG, whose awesome political machine guaranteed him a lifetime job, sounded the theme of the coming months as the meeting broke up. The senator said that Wilson's muddled war effort was destroying the country's morale. If the voters wanted to win the war, they had better give the GOP control of Congress. The Democrats fired back, implying the Republicans were disloyal. Since ordinary citizens were being arrested for saying such things about the president, the average voter must have felt confused.[3]

The dust had barely settled from these partisan blasts when the president and the nation plunged into an election in Wisconsin to replace Paul O. Husting, a Democratic senator who had died in a duck-hunting accident. A Democrat's only chance in this strongly Republican state was a split in the GOP. Husting had won by only 1,000 votes in 1914, thanks to such a breach. After some jockeying, the election emerged as a contest between the Democratic nominee, an original Wilson backer named Joseph E. Davies, who resigned from the Federal Trade Commission to make the race, and Republican Congressman Irvine L. Lenroot. Also in the race and splitting the progressive Republican vote—or so the Democrats hoped— was a Socialist candidate, Victor Berger, under indictment for openly and repeatedly opposing the war.

Lenroot had supported the 1916 McLemore resolution, which had forbidden Americans to travel into the war zone on ships of the belligerents. The pro-Allied press had castigated this idea and so had Wilson, since it undercut one of his main objections to Germany's submarine campaign. Lenroot's candidacy reignited the press's ire—and the president's. The congressman had also voted against several preparedness bills, supported an embargo on arms shipments to all the belligerents and opposed Wilson's armed-ship legislation. It was easy to smear Lenroot as pro-German, and the national newspapers poured scorn on his candidacy. Davies, meanwhile, declared that a vote for him would prove that Wisconsin stood "four square" behind Wilson.

Encouraged by the national press's abuse of Lenroot, Wilson waded into the fray with a resounding endorsement of Davies and a searing condemnation of Lenroot as a man who had failed to pass "the acid test" of "true loyalty and genuine Americanism" for his vote on the McLemore resolution and other measures. This was vicious stuff. The president was impugning Lenroot's patriotism for his opposition to Wilson's policies before the United States entered the war. He was dismissing the congressman's support of the administration's measures since war had been declared.[4]

Lenroot was by no means the only politician who had differed with the president on these prewar issues. Dozens of Democrats had also committed the same putative sins. The tactic united almost the whole Republican Party behind their candidate. Huge ads endorsing Lenroot, signed by thirty-three of the Senate's forty-four Republicans, ran in every newspaper in Wisconsin.[5]

Urged on by Boies Penrose and Theodore Roosevelt, congressional Republicans built a backfire against Davies by attacking Wilson's mismanagement of the war. They chose a juicy target—the aircraft program. Senator Henry Cabot Lodge and others accused the administration of "criminal negligence" for its failure to produce a single plane after spending $840 million. While they orated, the first great German offensive of the spring was tearing the British army apart. GOP speakers portrayed Tommies and doughboys pounded by unchallenged German bombers because of Wilson's incompetence.

Candidate Lenroot soon joined the attack, abandoning any attempt to defend his prewar "acid test" votes. He also pointed out that his Democratic opponent had been hiding in the government bureaucracy while these acidic issues were being debated. Suddenly Davies was on the defensive. The Democrats sought to rescue him by cranking out lies about the combat readiness of American troops in Europe, most of them told by reporters accompanying Secretary of War Newton Baker, who was visiting the American Expeditionary Force.

It remained a close race until Vice President Thomas Marshall came to Wisconsin on Davies's behalf. Marshall had favored a moderate approach to the 1918 campaign; he thought attacks on Republicans should be kept to a minimum and the Democrats should try to win on an appeal to national unity. Wilson had sharply disagreed and ordered Marshall to flay the GOP in his native Indiana—and do likewise in Wisconsin.[6]

In both states, Marshall obeyed orders. An old stump speaker, he knew how to give the opposition hell. In Wisconsin, the vice president went over the top. He accused Lenroot of pandering to "the sewage vote": pro-Germans, traitors and pacifists. Only a vote for Davies could save Wisconsin's national reputation. "Your state is under suspicion," Marshall roared at an immense meeting in Madison.[7]

That did it. The *Milwaukee Sentinel* declared that "the lash of insult to the loyalty of Republicans in Wisconsin" had united the Republican party "to a degree that has not been seen for twenty years." In a record turnout, enraged Wisconsinites elected Lenroot by 15,267 votes. Even more troubling, as far as standing foursquare behind Wilson was concerned, the Socialist antiwar candidate, Victor Berger, won 110,187 votes—four times the number his party usually received. Berger might well have won the election if it were not for an oblique endorsement of Lenroot by Senator Robert La Follette in his magazine, *La Follette's Weekly*, during the primary campaign. It was the only time that the silenced senior senator from Wisconsin participated in the contest.[8]

II

Emboldened by this repudiation of the president's man in Wisconsin, the Republicans and Wilson-hating Democrats pressed their investigation of the failures of the government's aircraft program. A star performer was Leonard Wood, who testified before Senator George Chamberlain's Military Affairs Committee just after the general returned from several weeks in France. Wood ridiculed the claims of George Creel's Committee on Public Information that 22,000 planes would soon be darkening the skies of Europe. There were only 1,000 American pilots in Europe and not a single U.S.-made plane for them to fly, the general said. In early April, Chamberlain's committee issued a report signed by four Democrats and five Republicans, denouncing the administration's awful performance.

The White House fired the two top officials of the aircraft program, Howard E. Coffin and Major General George O. Squier. Coffin was the chief villain. A classic high-pressure automobile salesman, he had toured the country describing how thousands of planes would smash the German army into submission, making it unnecessary for American infantry to charge machine guns.

Senator Chamberlain added to the White House's distress by trotting out another version of a committee on the conduct of the war. Nothing else could rescue the country from Wilson's ineptitude, the senator intoned. He also wanted authority for his Military Affairs Committee and sundry subcommittees to send investigators into any and every war industry in the nation.

Wilson was rescued from serious embarrassment by Colonel House and Joe Tumulty. Not without difficulty, they persuaded him to appoint the 1916 Republican presidential candidate, Charles Evans Hughes, as a special prosecutor to investigate the airplane mess. Wilson, displaying the supersensitivity that complicated his political life, had previously opposed any appointment for Hughes, a former Supreme Court justice and one of the nation's most distinguished lawyers, because he had been "absolutely false" (i.e., he disagreed with Wilson) during the 1916 campaign. But the president was forced to swallow his doubts and offer Hughes the job. Hughes accepted, and the Chamberlain supercommittee demand was derailed.

This rare—even unique—Wilson experiment in bipartisanship had not a little influence on a fateful speech the president made to Congress on May 27. While grappling with the airplane firestorm, he was also trying to persuade Congress to pass another revenue bill, extracting an additional $7 billion from the tax-hating American public. The idea of raising taxes in an election year was still anathema to the legislators, even if the nation was fighting a war. They balked, and balked, and balked again, while inflation kept climbing.

On May 27, Wilson went before Congress and spoke to the politicians—and the public—about the imperative need for new taxes. The address was a superb example of the American presidency's capacity for wartime leadership. Speaking as commander in chief, Wilson told the legislators he regretted asking them to stay in Washington's summer heat to hammer out a tax bill. But there was only one consideration now, and it made congressional comfort and political expediency seem "trivial and negligible." That was "the winning of the war." They were not only in the war, they were at "the very peak and crisis of it." In fact, on that very day, the German army was storming across the Chemin des Dames and heading for Paris.

Wilson added words that would give him grief—and the nation not a little turmoil. "Politics is adjourned. The elections will go to those who think least of it; to those who go to their constituents without explanations or excuses, with a plain record of duty faithfully and disinterestedly performed."[9]

This was strange stuff from the man who had just injected "the acid test" into the political scene in his attempt to elect a Democrat in

Wisconsin. The volte-face illustrated Wilson's amazing (or dismaying) ability to reverse his political field without even a hint of an apology or an explanation. The politicians confronting him in the chamber of the House of Representatives all but snorted aloud their disbelief. The idea that the elections would be won by those who did not bother to give them any thought would have produced mocking guffaws in any less formal setting.

As with other Wilson rhetorical flourishes (including the acid test), newspapers seized on the phrase. Democratic papers used it to belabor Republicans for their supposedly blatant partisanship. Republican papers told their readers the president was little more than a con artist, trying to intimidate them into passivity. The GOP was particularly annoyed because they had been responsible for rescuing many of Wilson's war measures when congressional Democrats deserted him. They would have been even more outraged if they had known that within days of the speech, Wilson spent several hours with Joe Tumulty discussing tactics for the fall campaign. The secretary advised the president to remain silent and let Roosevelt and the other Republicans rant. At the climax of the campaign, Wilson would release a public letter to some prominent Democrat, crushing the enemy with the accusation of disloyalty in wartime. Wilson concurred with this strategy, which Colonel House praised as "in every way admirable."[10]

III

Infuriated by General Leonard Wood's testimony in the airplane uproar, Wilson and Secretary of War Baker allowed personal pique to lure them into a public relations disaster that inflicted immediate damage to the claim that politics was adjourned. General Wood had returned to Kansas to prepare his Eighty-Ninth Division for shipment to Europe. While the 28,000 men were wending their way to New York for embarkation, Wood received a telegram from the War Department, ordering him to surrender command of the division and take up duties in San Francisco, as commander of the Western Department.

Wood headed for Washington, where he demanded interviews with Baker and the president. Republican newspapers such as the *New York Tribune* erupted. So did former presidents Roosevelt and William Howard Taft, both of whom were writing newspaper columns that regularly attacked the administration. *Life* ran a cartoon of the pint-sized Baker handing a towering

Wood an order: "STAY HOME." The *Tribune* ran a cartoon showing Wood and Roosevelt, with Wilson in the background, as they groused, "Well he kept us out of the war." The Portland *Oregonian* ran a big hand, labeled "Politics," shoving Wood off the dock while his division vanished over the Atlantic horizon. Even the usually pro-Wilson *New York World* said Wood's removal would "give every fair minded man a bad taste in the mouth."[11]

Wood had a bristling interview with Baker and a less hostile one with the president. Both blandly denied they had any animus against him and blamed his removal on General Pershing, who had failed to list Wood as an officer he wanted in Europe. They bypassed the well-documented fact that the War Department had thus far ignored Pershing's lists and recommendations and sent the AEF the generals it preferred. An infuriated Wood muttered darkly about the way he had covered up Pershing's sexual peccadilloes in the Philippines. But he could hardly retaliate on that low road without losing all sympathy. Instead, Wood offered to lead an expeditionary force to Italy. Even one division would boost the Italians' crumbling morale. Wilson said he would think about it.

As he left the White House, Wood met Tumulty, who expressed his sympathy and said "the biggest possible mistake" had been made in the way Wood's relief had been handled. He blamed it entirely on Newton Baker, saying Pershing had been "used"—perhaps willingly. In fact, Pershing did not want Wood in Europe because he feared he would immediately start trying to supplant him. He had enough trouble with Lloyd George, Clemenceau, Haig and Foch on that score.

To complete Wood's humiliation, at the last minute the War Department changed its mind and sent him back to Kansas, where he was ordered to train the new Tenth Division. This was a political mistake; the eloquent general did everything in his power during the next few months to persuade Kansas and neighboring states to vote Republican. Looking ahead to 1920, the city of Salina, Kansas, responded by organizing a Wood-for-President club.[12]

IV

In June, Wilson went from clandestine deceit about the adjournment of politics to public hypocrisy—with a touch of the bizarre. Contemplating the situation in Michigan, where a Republican senator was retiring, Wilson decided to draft Henry Ford as his candidate. Secretary of the Navy Josephus Daniels had explored the idea with Ford and found him ambivalent. Daniels brought the automaker to the White House, where the president told him, "You are the only man in Michigan who can be elected and help bring about the peace you desire."[13]

Swept away, Ford announced his candidacy, and let all and sundry know he hoped he could take advantage of Michigan's cross-filing election law, which would permit him to win both the Republican and the Democratic primaries. Wilson's German-hating backers were boggled: In 1915, Ford had organized a peace ship that sailed to Europe and tried to start negotiations between the belligerents—the last thing the proponents of the knockout blow wanted. The hard-line *Milwaukee Journal*, which had spent the previous year and a half denouncing Senator La Follette, called Ford "not our kind of American." The *New York World* deplored the president's choice, declaring that it would sow discord in the Democratic Party.[14]

Wilson's plan to run Ford as a nonpartisan supporter of the administration blew up in his face. In the August primary, Ford was swamped on the Republican line by a well-financed Detroit businessman, Truman H. Newberry. In this much-publicized campaign, the GOP was able to portray Ford—and by implication, Wilson—as a peace-at-any-price man. They also dredged up the numerous outrageous things Ford had said about patriotism, the flag and American history in his loose-lipped career. The automaker's attempt to win on both electoral lines also gave the Republicans an opportunity to blast Wilson with the epithet he was fond of laying on Kaiser Wilhelm—autocrat. Senator Henry Cabot Lodge deplored the idea of a senator whose only platform was a promise to vote "in obedience to the president's directions."[15]

V

While the Ford fiasco gathered momentum in the summer of 1918, Wilson sought to tighten his leadership of the Democratic Party. He intervened by telegram and public letter in the primary elections of congressmen and senators who had opposed him. This was tricky business, especially in the South, where a formidable antiwar movement was gaining momentum among the so-called wool-hat voters in rural districts. With newspaper support, Wilson used the acid-test argument to dispose of two contrary Democratic senators, James Vardaman of Mississippi and Thomas W. Hardwick of Georgia. (Vardaman had opposed the vote for war, Hardwick the draft.) In Tennessee, the president singled out Senator John K. Shields "as one of the men I would dearly love to see left out of the Senate because I don't like his attitude or his principles." But Shields passed the acid test and won easily, his enmity to Wilson reinforced.[16]

Not even the acid-test argument got Wilson very far in trying to purge Congressman George Huddleston of Alabama. He failed the test catastrophically. Wilson added to his woes by denouncing Huddleston as "an opponent of the administration." But the congressman had a trump card: friends in high places. House Majority Leader Claude Kitchin and Speaker of the House Champ Clark praised Huddleston in public letters, implicitly giving the backs of their political hands to the president. Huddleston won going away.[17]

Another election in which Wilson had intense interest was the New Jersey race for a senate seat vacated by the death of a Democrat. Like all presidents, he badly wanted to demonstrate his appeal in his home state. Alas, this hope too crashed in flames. A popular governor, Walter Edge, was running on the Republican line, and both houses of the legislature were in Republican hands. The Democratic Party was controlled by a new leader, Frank Hague, the mayor of Jersey City, who had a low opinion of former governor Wilson for his double cross of the party's regulars in 1910. When several people suggested that Tumulty return to the state and oppose Edge, the president's secretary sadly rejected the idea. Making the race "strongly appealed" to him, he admitted to a friend. But he could not muster "a corporal's guard" in Jersey City. His response was graphic testimony that Tumulty's devotion to Wilson had terminated his promising political career.[18]

Meanwhile, the National Security League leaped into numerous primary elections by expanding the president's acid-test list from three issues to eight, and scrutinizing the "war records" (actually, the prewar records) of every member of Congress. The NSL found only forty-seven men survived this stringent examination, and only three were Democrats. The league put its research in the form of a chart and distributed it to 1,800 newspapers. With Theodore Roosevelt as one of the NSL's guiding spirits, this document was really Republican campaign literature.

Soon more than a few Democrats were wishing Woodrow Wilson would give more thought to his political rhetoric. In Colorado, Ohio and Missouri, veteran Democratic members of Congress went down to primary defeats on this largely spurious argument. In Wisconsin, the expanded acid test sent three progressive Republican followers of La Follette into forced retirement. As so often happens, patriotism went hand in hand with conservatism in this strange manipulation of facts and votes.[19]

VI

The Germans' decision to try for a military victory and their initial successes against the British and French deepened war rage in the United States. The president set the tone in April, when he went to Baltimore to open the Third Liberty Loan drive. Before an audience of 15,000 in the Fifth Regiment Armory, where he had been nominated in 1912, he denounced the "the German program." If it were carried out, he said, "everything that America has lived for and loved and grown great to vindicate and bring to a glorious realization will have fallen in utter ruin." There was only one possible response: "Force, Force to the utmost, Force without stint or limit, the righteous and triumphant Force which shall make Right the law of the world." The crowd went wild. British and French newspapers were equally enthusiastic.[20]

By this time the top leadership of the International Workers of the World was in jail, indicted for no less than one hundred separate crimes. In the summer of 1918, a jury would find them guilty on every count, after deliberating a bare sixty minutes. From his cell, the Wobbly president, Big Bill Haywood, sentenced to twenty years, wrote to a journalist friend: "The big game is over and we never won a hand. The other fellow had the cut, shuffle and deal all the time."[21]

The Socialist Party was next on the government's hit list. Many local leaders were already behind bars or under indictment. The party's candidate for governor in Minnesota got five years in jail for accusing the Morgans and the Carnegies of starting the war. A Minnesota Socialist candidate for the senate got four years for saying the United States was playing patsy for the territorial ambitions of England and France. Another Socialist politician, indicted for opposing the draft, committed suicide by exploding a stick of dynamite in his mouth.[22]

Eugene V. Debs, the sixty-three-year-old founding father of the party, decided it was time to make a gesture of defiance. On June 15, 1918, he journeyed to Canton, Ohio, to address a rally. Before he spoke, he visited three Socialists in a local jail. On the platform, he condemned the patriots who "with magnifying glasses in hand" scan the country for disloyalty and "apply the brand of treason" to anyone who opposed the war. He urged his audience to ignore these threats, to stand up for their Socialist principles. "You cannot do your duty by proxy," he shouted. "You have got to do it yourself and do it squarely."[23]

In the audience was the U.S. attorney for northern Ohio, with stenographers who took down every word Debs said. By June 29, Debs was in jail, charged with ten violations of the Espionage Act and a recently passed supplement, the Sedition Act. He pleaded guilty to all the charges. By mid-September, he was convicted, in spite of his fervent claim that the trial made a mockery of the Constitution. He was, Debs said, "the smallest part of this trial. . . . There is an infinitely greater issue that is being tried . . . here before a court of American citizens." At his sentencing the judge praised his courage but offered no quarter to someone who was trying to "strike the sword from the hand of this nation while she is engaged in defending herself against a foreign and brutal power." A stunned Debs got ten years.[24]

VII

George Creel's Committee on Public Information, which had begun the war proclaiming that it was going to win the struggle with facts, not hate, shifted gears as the first anniversary of Wilson's April 2 speech to Congress approached. The posters for the Third Liberty Loan drive screamed, "Stop the Hun!" and portrayed an American soldier seizing a hulking German as he assaulted a cowering mother and child with his bayoneted rifle.

Hollywood also jumped on the propaganda bandwagon. Having learned from the fate of Robert Goldstein, producer of the unfortunate *Spirit of 1776,* what the government wanted, Tinsel Town responded with slander of all things German. One of the most popular films was *My Four Years in Germany,* based on the book by James W. Gerard, former ambassador to Berlin. In the first reel, a card announced, "Fact Not Fiction." The kaiser was portrayed as a man with the IQ of a paranoid six-year-old. He rode a hobby horse as he made plans to invade Belgium. The German general staff was introduced with a series of superimposed images comparing each man to an animal. The "rape" of Belgium was dramatized in horrific terms while a German official boasted that they had nothing to worry about because "America won't fight." The film leaped forward to doughboys slaughtering Germans in hand-to-hand combat. As one Yank bayoneted a Hun, a grinning American told his buddy, "I promised Dad I'd get six."[25]

The Kaiser: The Beast of Berlin opened on Broadway in the spring of 1918. The content more than justified the title. The man whom the *New York Times* had acclaimed as the Prince of Peace in 1913 was portrayed as gloating over slaughtered Belgian civilians and torpedoed ships. To add to the fun, audiences were told that they could "hiss the Kaiser" every time his mustachioed face appeared on the screen. The *New York Times* called the film "a travesty of war and America's serious purpose in it." But *Moving Picture World* disagreed: "The scenes are said to be historically accurate and picture a strong dramatic series of events in a commendable way."[26]

In the hissing department, an actor soon attracted more vituperation from audiences than the kaiser. Erich von Stroheim, with his shaved head and saber-scarred cheek, became the prototypical monstrous German officer. In *The Unbeliever,* he murdered old people and children for the fun of it and raped any woman who caught his eye. In *Heart of Humanity,* he reached a high (or low) point when his lust led him to an attractive Red Cross nurse. In a cradle nearby was her baby. When the child's wails annoyed him, von Stroheim tossed the infant out the window. In both pictures, he got his comeuppance, of course, shot, in *The Unbeliever,* by his own soldiers, and in *Heart of Humanity,* by the nurse's husband, who happened to be home on leave.[27]

Often, these films aroused audiences to such rage, they burned the kaiser in effigy and trashed the theater. Police frequently had to be summoned to restore order. Woodrow Wilson was troubled by what he heard about *My Four Years in Germany.* When Henry Morgenthau, Sr., who had been ambassador to Turkey, returned to the United States and published a virulently hostile book about the Germans, he sent a copy to Wilson and told him it too might be made into a film. Wilson urged him to drop the idea. He felt that Gerard had whipped up more than enough German hatred.[28]

Hearts of the World, a film D. W. Griffith made for the British and French governments, premiered in Washington, D.C., in the fall of 1918. Mrs.

Wilson was among the VIP audience. No doubt with Wilson's approval, she wrote Griffith a letter, urging him to cut or moderate a scene in which actress Lillian Gish was brutally whipped by a German soldier. These deep background gestures were Wilson's only attempt to halt the tidal wave of film hate.[29]

VIII

Spokesmen of all stripes fanned the flames of war rage with shrill pronouncements. A Detroit minister said any American who claimed to be neutral should be "jailed, interned or labelled." The Reverend Newell Dwight Hillis of Brooklyn's Plymouth Church published a book on German atrocities. The tome ended with an exhortation to tell the kaiser and his general staff: "You shall not skewer babes upon your bayonets . . . you shall not nail young nuns to the doors of the schoolhouses . . . you shall not mutilate the bodies of little girls and noble women."

In Chicago the American Protective League kept what one paper called "a steady stream of handcuffed men" marching to jail, because they had been overheard exulting over the progress of General Ludendorff's offensives. Neither in the Windy City nor anywhere else in the country did the APL's 250,000 "Secret Service" sleuths catch a single German spy. Nor did the real Secret Service or the agents of the Bureau of Investigation. This dearth of German spies did not deter John Revelstoke Rathom of the *Providence Journal* from concocting ever more improbable stories of evil German reservists ferreting out information about the war effort and fomenting strikes among hyphenates.[30]

German-Americans became favorite targets of this mounting war rage. They were beaten up on the streets of Terre Haute, Indiana, and many other cities. Theodore Roosevelt supported a call to ban the German language from the schools. Forcing German-Americans to kiss the flag or face some far more unpleasant punishment became so commonplace, newspapers stopped reporting such episodes. German-Americans who failed to subscribe to Liberty Loan drives often got their houses painted yellow. An Illinois German-American doctor who called Secretary of War Baker a fathead (something General Leonard Wood, Senator Henry Cabot Lodge and Theodore Roosevelt did regularly) was thrown into a canal, forced to kiss the flag and told to leave town if he wanted to stay healthy.[31]

Inevitably, this violent spirit escalated into murder. In Tulsa, Oklahoma, a member of the County Council of Defense gunned down a waiter for making a pro-German remark. The killer was acquitted. So was a policeman in an Oklahoma small town who shot a Bulgarian for saying something "seditious." Bulgaria was allied with Germany in the war in Europe.[32]

In Collinsville, Illinois, not far from Saint Louis, German-born Robert Prager worked in a bakery. He had dutifully registered as an enemy alien and claimed he wanted to become a citizen as soon as possible. He had even tried to enlist, but a childhood injury had left him blind in one eye. Prager bitterly resented being refused membership in a local miners' union because of his alien status and attacked the union leaders in a statement that he posted at various places around town. On April 4, he was seized by a drunken mob, stripped of his clothes and wrapped in an American flag. The police made a halfhearted attempt to protect him by putting him in jail. But they did nothing to stop the mob from dragging Prager out of his cell and into the countryside. There, after letting him write a farewell letter to his parents in Germany, the mob lynched him.[33]

The death of this innocent young man shocked the country. Theodore Roosevelt and Woodrow Wilson both condemned it. The *New York Times* editorialized that "a fouler thing could hardly be done in America." But not everyone felt remorse for Prager. The *Washington Post* coolly commented that it was a sign of a "healthful and wholesome awakening" to the reality of Germany's evil in the nation's heartland, which had for too long lagged behind the public mind of the East.[34]

John Lord O'Brian, one of the more liberal members of Wilson's Justice Department, sent the president a memorandum, urging him to speak out against the spreading violence. Wilson replied that he was "very deeply concerned" about the problem. But he remained silent.

Around this time a woman friend asked the president's advice on how to deal with German sympathizers in a school of which she was a trustee. Wilson said if the offense "was merely one of opinion," Americans should "vindicate our claim that we stand for justice and fairness and highminded generosity" in the treatment of such people. On the other hand, if the person was "dangerous to the Government or to the community in which he lives, that is another matter." Wilson, as infected with the disloyalty mania as the rest of the country, was convinced most dissent was "another matter."[35]

While the president said nothing, members of the mob that hanged Robert Prager went on trial in Illinois—and were all acquitted. The case was discussed in the Reichstag and was widely publicized in German newspapers. This uncomfortable development may have been why on July 26, 1918, Wilson finally issued a statement deploring the "mob spirit which has recently . . . shown its head amongst us." Every lynching was "a blow at the heart of ordered law and humane justice." He found this especially deplorable because "we are at this very moment fighting lawless passion. Germany has outlawed herself among the nations because she has disregarded the sacred obligations of law and has made lynchers of her armies." This remark virtually nullified the overall purpose of the statement, to prevent other German-Americans from being lynched. It is further evidence of how war rage was infecting the mind of the man who had called for a war without hate.[36]

Lynching was to be deplored, but dissenting from the president's war policy was still another matter. In May 1918, at Wilson's request Congress increased the government's power to control opinion with a Sedition Act. By a process of reasoning that can only be explained by war rage, various authoritative figures—senators, governors, cabinet officers—maintained that giving the government more power to suppress and punish dissent would reduce the incidence of lynching.[37]

Compared to what some people wanted, the Sedition Law was relatively mild. It punished dissent with fines and jail time. Aiming at hyphenates, Vice President Marshall said every American "not heartily of the Government" should have his citizenship revoked and his property confiscated. Senator John Sharp Williams of Mississippi called for abolishing political parties and amalgamating all voters into a single "loyalist pro-American party." Others wanted to set up military courts that would not be burdened with legal technicalities and red tape.[38]

The new law was swiftly invoked against those who made negative comments of any sort about the war. In Lansing, Michigan, a man named Powell was irked when he was intimidated into buying a $50 war bond. He sounded off to a relative about his disillusion with the war, opining that German atrocity stories were nonsense and American soldiers were dying so the rich could increase their stock portfolios. The relative reported him to the police. Thinking the whole affair was a joke, Powell did not even hire a lawyer. A jury convicted him, and he was sentenced to twenty years in the penitentiary and fined $10,000. Too late, Powell wrote a frantic letter to the National Civil Liberties Bureau (forerunner of the American Civil Liberties Union) begging for help. He had a wife and five children to support. When the mayor of Lansing tried to intervene, the judge cited him for contempt of court. Powell went to jail.[39]

Even more deplorable in some ways was the fate of three German-Americans in Covington, Kentucky. One of them, a former policeman named C. B. Shoborg, ran a shoemaker's shop. The three, ranging in age from midfifties to midsixties, often met there to discuss politics and other matters. Local patriots hired a detective agency to sneak a listening device into the shop. The snoopers soon heard the three friends call Theodore Roosevelt "a damned agitator" and express pleasure at the German army's successful 1918 offensives. Although the men's attorneys argued the conversations were private and could not have interfered with the war effort, they were all convicted under the Sedition Act. Shoborg was sentenced to ten years in prison. The other two men received slightly shorter sentences, but one, who was wealthy, was fined $40,000.[40]

Saddest of all was the fate of fifty-two-year old Edwin A. Seidewitz, a former mayor of Annapolis, Maryland, and one of Baltimore's leading florists. Until the United States entered the war, he had been one of the most prosperous citizens in Baltimore; he served as president of the Rotary Club and was considered one of the "livest" men in the organization. One night at a hotel bar, shortly after war was declared, the florist met some officers from several German ships that had been trapped in Baltimore's harbor since 1914. They were in a gloomy mood, lamenting their long separation from friends and family and the prospect of internment as enemy aliens until the war ended. Seidewitz bought them beer, and they drank together. Touched by their plight, the florist kissed one of them on the forehead in an attempt to comfort the man. Word soon swept Baltimore that Seidewitz had "kissed a German." His floral business collapsed. He was expelled from the Rotary Club, after the directors refused to let him speak to the members in his own defense. On August 24, 1918, Edwin Seidewitz killed himself with a bullet in the head.[41]

IX

The Sedition Act also added to the already considerable power of Postmaster General Albert Sidney Burleson, described by Colonel House as "the most belligerent member of the Cabinet." Early in the war, Burleson had banned or harassed into silence a number of magazines and newspapers, such as the left-wing *Masses*. Wilson had been bombarded with protests from intellectuals, including his devoted follower Walter Lippmann, and had asked Burleson to be more tolerant. Burleson's reply was a combination threat and challenge. "If you don't want the Espionage Act enforced, I can [only] resign. Congress has passed the law and said I am to enforce it." Wilson capitulated and said with an embarrassed laugh, "Well go ahead and do your duty."[42]

The Post Office's solicitor, William H. Lamar, was even more intransigent than Burleson. He could find disloyalty and prospective treason in almost any publication that caught his suspicious eye. He banned one Irish-American magazine from the mails for printing Thomas Jefferson's opinion that Ireland should be a republic. When the National Civil Liberties Bureau published a pamphlet pointing out a court ruling that had overturned one of Lamar's decisions, the solicitor promptly banned the pamphlet from the mails.[43]

The Sedition Act gave the Burleson-Lamar team expanded powers. Anyone who used "disloyal, scurrilous, profane or abusive language" about the U.S. government, the armed forces, the flag, or the Constitution could be fined $10,000 and sentenced to twenty years in prison. When Lamar banned the liberal magazine *The Nation*, its publisher, Oswald Garrison Villard, rushed to Washington to argue his case. Lamar told him his censorship program had three main targets, "pro-Germanism, pacifism, and high-browism"—a strange agenda for an administration headed by the former president of Princeton University. It was one more illustration of the gap between Woodrow Wilson's rhetoric and reality.[44]

X

In another part of the war, politics was being semi-adjourned in the Navy Department. Secretary of the Navy Josephus Daniels had decided it might be a good idea to get his untrustworthy assistant secretary, Franklin D. Roosevelt, out of Washington for a while. Daniels yielded to Roosevelt's almost desperate importunities to go to Europe. On a personal level—and to some extent a political level—FDR was more and more embarrassed by Theodore Roosevelt's four sons on the firing line while he enjoyed Washington's version of *la guerre de luxe*.[45]

Daniels had grown weary of hearing stories from friends about Roosevelt's continuing attempts to denigrate his performance as head of the Navy Department. He began noting examples in his journal, adding a Latin phrase that implied retaliation: *Carthage delenda est.* After one of these entries, he scribbled: "R[oosevelt] . . . not loyal sh'd not hesitate." The secretary was evidently thinking of demolishing his overambitious assistant. But the kindhearted North Carolinian decided that granting Franklin his European wish—which meant a separation of several weeks—might be a better solution.[46]

Roosevelt was ecstatic. He was enjoying every aspect of being a man of authority in a government at war. Early on, he had confided to a friend, "It would be wonderful to be a war president." The trip to Europe added the dimension he felt he badly needed on his war record. He took along his Harvard roommate and boon companion, Livingston Davis, whom he had hired as his aide. Davis had also acquired a Washington mistress and we know from his diary they enjoyed a torrid farewell. Whether FDR had a similar encounter with Lucy Mercer remains in the realm of speculation—but the probability must be considered strong.

By July 10, Roosevelt was aboard a new destroyer, USS *Dyer,* heading for England. While he was at sea, Quentin Roosevelt's plane plunged to earth. The young flier's tragic death created huge headlines in U.S. newspapers. It would have made the stay-at-home member of the Roosevelt clan look terrible. Luck as well as destiny seemed to be on FDR's side as he approached the war zone.[47]

The assistant secretary's trip across Periscope Pond, as the wartime Atlantic was sometimes called, was uneventful, although FDR's diary noted a few hairy moments. One was a narrow escape from a four-inch shell when a green sailor pulled the lanyard of a gun when it was trained too far forward. Another close call was a half-hour lying off Ponta Delgada in the Azores with the *Dyer's* overheated turbines shut down, converting the ship into a proverbial sitting duck for any alert U-boat captain.[48]

In London, Roosevelt stayed in "a magnificent suite" as a guest of the British admiralty. He and the first lord, Sir Eric Geddes, hit it off beautifully, and Geddes invited Roosevelt to accompany him on an inspection tour of several bases in Ireland and Wales. En route, he persuaded Roosevelt to act as a British surrogate in an ongoing dispute with the Italian navy in the Mediterranean. U-boats were sinking ships at a furious rate in that theater, and the Italians declined to let their ships out of port to do any serious patrolling, much less fighting. FDR leaped at the chance to play diplomat and promised to head for Rome as soon as possible.

On July 30, Roosevelt and two aides were driven to Buckingham Palace, where he spent forty minutes with King George V. FDR liked his nice smile and "quick and cordial" greeting. He was surprised to find His Majesty's way of speaking so "incisive." In fact, when they began talking about German atrocities in Belgium, Roosevelt's "jaw almost snapped." The king said many German deeds were "too horrible" to be included in Lord Bryce's report—a mind-boggling comment considering what was included in this Wellington House propaganda triumph. The king seemed to think Americans did not believe the Bryce Report, because they had not declared war on Germany the day after it was published. Roosevelt diplomatically agreed that there had been "a singular unwillingness" in the United States to accept it.

His Majesty remarked that he had a number of relatives in Germany (including Kaiser Wilhelm), but that he had "never seen a German gentleman." Here, indeed, was awesome evidence of the power of Wellington House—as well as the tiny dimensions of the royal brainpower.[49]

That evening, FDR attended a sumptuous official dinner for the War Cabinet. He met Winston Churchill, who was munitions minister, and had a very unpleasant time. Having been first lord of the admiralty, Churchill was apparently underwhelmed by an assistant secretary and treated Roosevelt and his entourage with scarcely concealed indifference. Twenty years later, when FDR dispatched Joseph Kennedy to London as his ambassador, the president spoke with still vibrating anger about the way Churchill "had acted like a stinker" at this dinner.[50]

In France, Roosevelt toured the British front on his way to Paris and got the distinct impression that the German offensives had shaken the Royal Army "to its roots." Many of the towns the Germans had hoped to seize, such as Amiens and Abbeville, were still under attack from German Gothas, which were dropping bombs that weighed 1,750 pounds. The Royal Army was revising its war plans from top to bottom to cope with future stormtrooper assaults. But the closest Roosevelt came to danger was on the highway, where his French driver insisted on hitting eighty-five kilometers per hour, no matter how often he was told to slow down.

In Paris, the assistant secretary hurried to a reception at the Élysée Palace, home of France's president, Raymond Poincaré, and was somewhat discomfited to discover that the French leader and his wife did not even know who he was. The guest of honor was Herbert Hoover, a hero in France, thanks to his work as head of Belgian Relief before the United States entered the war. Later in the day, Roosevelt and his party had a more satisfactory visit with Georges Clemenceau, who shook hands with Roosevelt "as if he meant it." Sitting him beside his desk, the Tiger began denouncing the atrocities the Germans were committing in their retreat from the Marne salient—"slashing paintings, burning homes."

Clemenceau told the assistant secretary the war was far from over. "Do not think the Germans have stopped fighting or that they are not fighting well." Roosevelt went away convinced the Tiger was "the greatest civilian in France."[51]

The next day, Franklin visited Eleanor Roosevelt for tea and found her husband, Ted, lying on the sofa with a badly wounded leg, suffered in the First Division's attack on Soissons. Also in the tea party was Archie Roosevelt, who looked "horribly badly." Everyone was trying to get poor crippled depressed Archie to go home, but he refused to take the advice. FDR pitched in with a suggestion that a sea voyage would do wonders for him. Archie still said no. "They both have really splendid records," Roosevelt wrote somewhat ruefully.[52]

Neither of his cousins told him what they really thought about the war, after seeing it close up in the trenches. When Ted's leg was operated on, the nurse came out of surgery to report he would soon be as good as new and ready to return to the front. "Gee that's tough," Archie said. Ted's brother-in-law, Dr. Richard Derby, who had participated in the surgery, thought, "Poor Eleanor." A surgeon in the Second Division, Derby had operated nonstop during the struggle for Belleau Wood.[53]

Franklin badly wanted a splendid war record. He went back to the Hôtel Crillon and planned a tour of the battlefront that took him as close as possible to flying shells and bullets. A navy captain from the American mission in France, who had orders to give him a safe VIP tour, tried to object. FDR told him off in grandiloquent tones, declaring he did not want "late rising, easy trips and plenty of bombed houses thirty miles or so behind the front."[54]

Heading toward the trenches in a three-car caravan, Roosevelt's party roared past French troops moving up and some captured Germans plodding in the opposite direction. Franklin was struck by the "awful contrast between the amount of intelligence in their faces compared with the French poilus." In spite of this unfavorable comparison, Roosevelt saw in the faces of the French civilians along the road "just as much quiet determination . . . to see this thing through to victory as there was in the beginning." He was blissfully unaware of the French army's mutiny, Caillaux's conspiracy, the poisonous mix of despair and hatred of *la gloire* that Shirley Millard had seen in her French hospital.[55]

Roosevelt's party soon reached Château-Thierry, where they were cordially greeted by General DeGoutte, the French commander in Champagne. He arranged for them to visit Belleau Wood. Roosevelt was awed by the debris of battle: "rusty bayonets, broken guns, emergency ration tins, hand grenades, discarded overcoats, rain-stained love letters . . . and many little mounds, some wholly unmarked, some with a rifle stuck bayonet down in the earth, some with a helmet, and some, too with a whittled cross with a tag of wood or wrapping paper hung over it and in a pencil scrawl an American name."[56]

Immensely proud of "his" (the navy's) marines, Roosevelt plunged into a petty quarrel that had broken out between the army and the marines about who deserved credit for Belleau Wood. The marines had gotten immense publicity in U.S. newspapers when an army censor permitted them to be identified by name. No other American unit had been granted this privilege, because it was considered information that could help the enemy. When General Degoutte renamed Belleau the *Bois de la Brigade Marine*, someone on Pershing's staff had changed it to the *Bois des Américains*. Roosevelt considered this a "mean piece of hocus pocus" and let everyone know it.[57]

Obviously, the assistant secretary did not have very much on his mind. This grew more apparent as he hustled Livingston Davis and the rest of his entourage toward the front, which was now ten miles east of Belleau Wood. The Germans were retreating slowly through Champagne, exacting a heavy toll on the advancing French and Americans. Roosevelt was more interested in collecting evidence of German brutality. In one house, he noted "a wreck of three chairs, one leg of a table gone, and smashed china on the dresser," all evidence of damage done "deliberately and maliciously by the Huns."[58]

North of Fère-en-Tardenois, the assistant secretary got a touch of the thrills he was seeking in a "small straggling village" named Mareuil-en-Dôle.

Roosevelt and his party got out of their cars and proceeded past numerous dead horses and some dead Germans. The group stopped now and then to study the landscape ahead of them through their field glasses in the hope of seeing some combat. They had been told they were out of range of German artillery, although Ludendorff's divisions had abandoned the town only the night before. Suddenly a tremendous explosion sent everyone's pulses into overdrive. What else could it be but a German shell?

Through the subsiding blast they heard raucous laughter. A well-camouflaged American artillery battery was only a few dozen feet away in a thicket, and its crew had decided to give these battlefield tourists a scare. After a round of handshakes, the gunners let Roosevelt pull the lanyard of a 155 and fire a shell toward the retreating Germans. In years to come he would improve on the story, adding an extra round and an Allied plane that reported one shell had been on target. He supposedly went away wondering "how many, if any, Huns I killed."[59]

Immensely pleased with himself, Roosevelt wrote home that "the members of my staff have begun to realize what campaigning . . . with the assistant secretary means." The heroic leader got his doughty band back to General Degoutte's headquarters by 9 P.M., where, after washing off "layers of dust," they sat down to an "excellent dinner." One wonders what the marines of the Second Division, who had gone without food for four days at Soissons, would have said about this sort of campaigning.[60]

Early in August, Roosevelt headed for Rome, where he plunged into conferences with Italian admirals and politicians, including the white-mustached premier, Vittorio Orlando, about the need for the Italian fleet to do some fighting in the Mediterranean. He got nowhere. When he pointed out that the fleet had not even had target practice for a year, one admiral complacently replied that the Austrian fleet had not had any either. To humor Roosevelt, the Italians agreed to form a unified command with a British admiral in charge.

Within days, the arrangement became a diplomatic tempest—something the Italians had probably foreseen. The French objected, and Secretary of State Lansing was soon sending irritated inquiries to Secretary of the Navy Daniels asking who had authorized Roosevelt to play diplomat. President Wilson, already suspicious that Franklin was too chummy with Theodore Roosevelt, curtly warned Daniels against letting people go to Europe "assuming to speak for the government."[61]

After much sightseeing and diplomatic dining in Rome, the assistant secretary returned to France and embarked on a whirlwind tour of the inactive Belgian front, which included lunch with King Albert. Roosevelt rushed up and down the channel coast, visiting navy air bases, then dashed back to England to inspect the British Grand Fleet and America's European squadron. By the time he boarded the SS *Leviathan* for the trip back to the United States, Franklin was a very tired young man, with an aching head and body. A fever of 102 confirmed the ship doctor's suspicions: He had influenza.

By the time Roosevelt reached New York, he had pneumonia in both lungs and had to be carried off the ship on a stretcher. Four orderlies lugged him from a taxi to his mother's townhouse on East Sixty-Fifth Street. His dutiful wife hurried from Washington to his side. As the sick man tossed and turned, she began unpacking his suitcases. Suddenly she was staring at a bundle of love letters from Lucy Mercer. Much later, Eleanor Roosevelt told a friend this was the moment when "the bottom dropped out of my particular world."[62]

XI

In Champagne, on the road outside her hospital, Shirley Millard saw Americans going into action. "They were all grinning like youngsters on the way to a picnic." One of them shouted at her, "Hey listen, where is all this trouble, anyway?" The phrase stuck in her mind, interfering with her sleep. *They don't know what they are in for, but I do,* she thought almost guiltily.

At the same time she was glad and proud to see the doughboys heading for the front. *How can I be glad?* she asked herself. It was all very puzzling. War turned everything upside down and inside out.

Among the items in upheaval was her own heart. She realized she was slowly falling in love with Dr. Le Brun, the handsome French surgeon who operated for seventy-two hours at a stretch. He began inviting her for walks in the fields and woods around the hospital. Le Brun had a "delightful" sense of humor, which Millard warned herself was a "dangerous thing to find out about someone you already like a lot." The surgeon asked her if she had ever been in love. She replied no. She started wondering how her fiancé, Ted, would react if she changed her mind about their engagement. But everything with Le Brun remained on a "spiritual plane."[63]

That was more than Millard could say about another French doctor, who invited her to Paris for the weekend and followed up the suggestion with a passionate kiss. He added all sorts of pet French names, to which Millard replied, *"Absolument jamais!"* (Absolutely never!) It was not very good French, but she hoped he got the message.[64]

Suddenly, in mid-July, the hospital filled with Americans. They lay outside on the ground, "a sea of stretchers, a human carpet." Millard hated to see them pouring in. But she was overwhelmed by their gallantry and "pluck." They never complained. It was "Thank you for every little thing" or "Help him first, he has waited longer than I have."[65]

"I felt they were mine, every last one of them, and their downright grit makes me want to cry all over them," she told her diary. Her "efficient detachment of mind"—something every good nurse needed—was demolished. She was no longer a compassionate sympathizer. She was an "active combatant." From now on "the guns shook our blood; the shells exploded in our very hearts."

As she unwrapped the bandages around the stomach of a Nebraska boy, he told her he had been hit four days ago. Millard recoiled in horror at what she saw: The huge wound was a seething, writhing mass of maggots. She thought the soldier was doomed. But an orderly matter-of-factly handed her a can of ether and told her to spray the strange little organisms. Maggots were a good sign, the orderly said. They prevented gangrene.

Another soldier from Idaho had been blinded in both eyes and lost both feet to shrapnel. She gave him morphine and tried to stop him as he fumbled under the covers to find out what was wrong with his legs. She held him while he screamed and screamed and screamed in despair. Finally the morphine hit and he was still as death.

When one of the older nurses collapsed, Millard volunteered to work in the surgery with Le Brun. To get the job, she had to memorize the French names for dozens of knives, scissors, saws, pincers and probes, any one of which she had to hand Le Brun the instant he asked for it. Soon she was watching amputations, stomach resections, skull trepanning, probing for bullets and shrapnel—the hundreds of medical emergencies created by lethal metal.

One of Le Brun's more memorable explorations was on an American officer who had been shot in the hip. The bullet had hit a watch, smashing it to pieces and driving the fragments down into the man's thigh as far as his knee. Le Brun spent an hour extracting tiny bits of crystal, wheels, springs. He did not get them all and remarked that as the doughboy grew older, he would be surprised to discover little metal souvenirs of the Western Front sprouting through his flesh.

The coming of the Americans did not mean that the French ceased to suffer. One night, after operating into the dawn, Millard began sterilizing the instruments while Le Brun smoked one more of his innumerable cigarettes. Into the operating room an orderly wheeled one more case. The man's face had been shattered by shrapnel from an exploding shell. The entire lower jaw and tongue were gone.

For a moment Le Brun examined the "hideous wound," Millard wrote in her diary. Then his weary eyes flickered to the man's gleaming black hair, his straight, proud nose. He glanced up at Millard, "his face ghastlier than it had ever been from fatigue." He knew the man—and so did she. This was René, one of the surgeon's closest friends. Millard recalled his last visit to the hospital in the uniform of an Alpine chasseur. Le Brun had introduced him. René seemed the personification of the proud, confident young soldier. He had showed her a picture of his fiancée, who lived in Dijon, and jokingly told Millard she too had freckles. Now there was only "the hideous cavernous wound . . . where the laughing mouth had been."

Le Brun ran his fingers through his sweat-soaked hair and cursed for a full minute. Millard felt for René's pulse. It was still fairly strong. But there were a half dozen blue crosses elsewhere on René's body, where the examining doctor at the entrance to the operating room had found other wounds. One of his legs was "completely crushed."

Millard struggled against a swirling dizziness. Was she about to collapse like many other nurses when fatigue and accumulated horror pushed them over the edge? She controlled her nerves with a violent act of the will and began handing Le Brun instruments. He worked quickly, fiercely, but every few minutes he stopped and stared mournfully into space.

Millard lost track of time. She only remembered Le Brun's calling for more anesthesia when René stirred and groaned. "*Encore,*" the surgeon snarled. His voice was harsh. Abruptly, he stopped asking Millard for instruments. Millard knew what it meant. There was no hope for René.

Le Brun stripped off his gloves and stumbled out of the operating room. At the door, he asked Millard to find the address of René's fiancée and write a letter, telling her they had done everything they could. Millard could only nod numbly, wondering if the dying would ever end.

XII

In the White House, Woodrow Wilson was confronted with war on another front. On July 8, 1918, he wrote to Colonel House: "I have been sweating blood over the question of what is right and feasible to do in Russia. It goes to pieces like quicksilver under my touch." The president was under terrific pressure from the Allies to join them in sending an expeditionary force to the chaotic nation. At first, the French and British thought men with guns could rally anti-German sentiment against the Bolsheviks and keep Russia in the war. Paradoxically, even after the Russians signed the treaty of Brest-Litovsk, the Bolsheviks tried to keep this latter hope alive by offering to ignore the treaty and continue the war if the Allies recognized them as the legitimate government of Russia. At the same time, Lenin made it clear that they did not want an expeditionary force.[66]

From the start of the Bolshevik takeover, motivations had been opaque but not entirely invisible. Most British politicians shared Winston Churchill's desire to exterminate this Marxist incubus from the moment it appeared. Their own rigid class society was too vulnerable to a radical upheaval to tolerate anyone shouting, "Workers of the world, unite!" Secretary of State Lansing was not far from this opinion. He told Assistant Secretary of State Breckinridge Long that the Bolsheviks were more dangerous to the United States than the Germans.[67]

After General Lavr Kornilov's British-backed march on Petrograd collapsed, London's agents focused on General Alexei Kaledin, who seemed to be leading some sort of anti-Bolshevik movement in south Russia. At one point Wilson agreed with a plan to funnel him aid through Rumania. The president also looked with some favor on the idea of the Japanese landing an army in Siberia to prevent the Bolsheviks from seizing the huge amounts of war matériel in and around Vladivostok. For a while this scheme was stalled by frantic messages from British and American representatives in Moscow, who were trying to work out some sort of deal with the Bolsheviks. Every Russian from Murmansk to Sevastopol hated the Japanese and if they became Allied surrogates on Russian soil, all hope of any positive relationship with Lenin's regime—or any other Russian government—would cease.[68]

Meanwhile, Woodrow Wilson had acquired an intense dislike for Lenin; he felt the Bolshevik leader had stolen his ideas for world peace. Wilson wanted to believe that he and Trotsky were German agents. When the president got his hands on some dubious documents purporting to prove his case, he published them under the imprimatur of the U.S. government. By May 30, 1918, Wilson had developed an unmistakably belligerent attitude toward the Bolsheviks: "If . . . we were invited to intervene by any responsible and representative body, we ought to do so." But where did such a body exist?[69]

The president finally acquiesced to a Japanese invasion of Siberia. Calling it a "policing action," he ordered 7,000 American troops to join them. Their arrival on Russian soil was preceded by a solemn statement from Wilson that they had no desire to interfere in the Russian Revolution. He soon discovered he might have to interfere in Japan's plans to seize a large chunk of Siberia. The two armies were supposed to be the same size, but the Japanese claimed the Americans had violated the agreement by sending along 2,000 civilians. Tokyo felt this lapse entitled it to expand its army to a whopping 69,000 men. The British, loath to be shouldered out of a sphere of influence anywhere in the world, dispatched 2,000 men to show the Union Jack and urged the French to follow suit.

On the other side of the globe, the French and English had dispatched a force to Murmansk, supposedly to protect war matériel there. In fact, they went busily to work to set up an anti-Bolshevik government. With even greater reluctance than he displayed in the Siberian venture, Wilson dispatched American troops to join them. Scholars have spent the intervening nine decades arguing about what the president thought he was doing. His ongoing dislike of Lenin might well be the best explanation.[70]

Throughout this torturous political exercise, there is no record of Wilson's expressing the slightest interest in the fate of Czar Nicholas Romanoff and his family. When Nicholas was first overthrown, there was talk of the Romanoffs' receiving asylum in England. But their kinship with the British royal family could not overcome Conservative Party fears that their presence might cause labor union unrest. The Provisional Government of Russia was equally reluctant to let the czar and his family go, fearing they could become the focus of a counterrevolution.

Just before the Bolsheviks seized power in Petrograd, the deposed monarch and his family were moved to the remote Siberian city of Ekaterinburg. On July 16, 1918, the Bolsheviks herded them into the cellar of the mansion in which they were living. The czar, his wife, Alexandra, his son, Alexis, and his three daughters listened in disbelief as a death sentence was read to them by a representative of the Ural Soviet. A moment later, they were shot at point-blank range. Their bodies were burned and the ashes flung into a nearby swamp.

From Murmansk to Vladivostok, similar Bolshevik brutality and equally brutal retaliation from their enemies soon rendered Wilson's carefully wrought cautionary words about American intervention irrelevant. A vast civil war had begun; it would kill more Russians than the Germans and Austrians slaughtered on the Eastern Front.

The Russian enigma exposed the president's greatest weakness as a wartime statesman—his tendency to rely on words rather than acts. He and Colonel House were discovering that Philip Dru–style leadership did not work in a chaotic world. Along with a miscomprehension of the outbreak of political evil in Russia, House/Wilson/Dru seemed unable or unwilling to admit what was now driving the policies of England and France: that supposedly evil word, imperialism. The future grew crowded with gloomy portents as the war to make the world safe for democracy thundered to a climax on the Western Front.[71]

Chapter 8

FIGHTS TO THE FINISH

Having seized the initiative, Generalissimo Ferdinand Foch was determined not to relinquish it. For the last six weeks of the summer of 1918, he ordered attacks all around the Marne salient. In the vanguard were American divisions fighting under French generals. This little-studied Aisne-Marne offensive demonstrated the courage of the American infantrymen—and the limitations of their open-warfare tactics. Before it ended in early September, more than 90,000 Americans were dead or wounded.

The Rainbow Division was one of the hardest-fighting outfits in this campaign. Its best-known soldier was Brigadier General Douglas MacArthur, who won attention in several unconventional ways. MacArthur designed his own distinctive uniform; he removed the metal band from his cap, giving it a casual, sporty look. A turtleneck sweater, highly polished leather puttees and a riding crop added to his debonair, soldier-of-fortune image. Equally unusual was MacArthur's fondness for personal reconnaissances into no-man's-land in the darkness, armed only with his riding crop. He scorned the idea of wearing a helmet or using a gas mask and participated in trench raids, winning the Silver Star and the Distinguished Service Cross. Reporters, some of them his admirers from his days as Secretary of War Newton Baker's spokesman in Washington, called him "the D'Artagnan of the AEF." Privately, however, the war was transforming MacArthur's ideas about military glory. After the brutal fighting that stopped the German attempt to cross the Marne on July 15, he found himself haunted by the "vision of those writhing bodies hanging from the barbed wire" and "the stench of dead flesh."[1]

During the Aisne-Marne campaign, MacArthur continued to embellish his hero image, repeatedly exposing himself to German shells and bullets to inspire his men. At one point, between directing attacks and exploring no-man's-land at night, he went without sleep for ninety-six hours. The fighting was frequently ferocious. The town of Sergy on the Ourcq River, defended by the crack Prussian Guards division, changed hands seven times in a single day.

Relieved after nine horrendous days, the men of the Rainbow stumbled to the rear. Father Francis Duffy, the division's chaplain, described them: "Our decimated battalions . . . marched in weary silence until they came to the slopes around Meurcy Farm. Then from end to end of the line came the sound of dry suppressed sobs. They were marching among the bodies of their unburied dead." MacArthur's brigade lost 2,835 men out of 5,135 in its ranks when the offensive began.[2]

Again and again, the Rainbow and other American divisions found their flanks lethally exposed by the failure of a French division to keep pace with their attack. "For Christ's sake, knock out the machine guns on our right," begged one anguished battalion commander. "Heavy casualties. What troops should be on my right and left and where are they?"

The French repeatedly ordered the Americans to make attacks that were close to suicidal and gave them objectives they could never reach. Major General Robert Lee Bullard, now a corps commander of two American divisions, fretted about the casualties but could do little else. He had to take orders from General Joseph Degoutte, commander of the French Sixth Army.[3]

By August 27, 1918, the Germans had retreated to the northern bank of the Vesle River. A French order sent two understrength companies of the Twenty-Eighth Division (about 200 men) across the river to seize the hamlet of Fismette. An appalled Bullard tried to withdraw them—they were the only troops on that side of the river, surrounded by some 200,000 Germans. General Degoutte, with the same indifference to casualties he had displayed at Belleau Wood, revoked Bullard's order. The Germans attacked in overwhelming force from three sides, using every weapon in their armory, including flamethrowers. They killed or captured all but 39 of the isolated Americans.

Bullard reported the disaster to Pershing, who met him a few days later and asked him why he had not disobeyed General Degoutte's order. "I did not answer. It was not necessary to answer," Bullard wrote in his memoir, implying all too clearly that he considered Pershing the man at fault for the messy Aisne-Marne experience.[4]

While the Americans struggled, on August 8, 1918, the British army made a successful attack on the western flank of the salient the Germans had created with their rout of the Fifth Army in March. Supported by tanks and swarms of planes, the British advanced almost twenty miles and captured thousands of prisoners. Foch, the apostle of the offensive, was suddenly the right general in the right place at the right time. "*Tout le monde a la bataille!*" became his mantra. Everyone fights![5]

By this time, five American divisions—more than 150,000 men—were serving under Field Marshal Douglas Haig. Pershing had permitted these divisions to go directly into British training areas when they arrived in Europe. These semi-surrenders of control were the price Foch and Haig wrung from Pershing, with the help of Ludendorff's storm troopers. But the AEF commander never stopped insisting on an independent army.

On August 10 Pershing opened First Army headquarters, and on August 15 he handed Foch a plan for an attack on the Saint-Mihiel salient, another huge bulge in the French lines, south of Verdun. He extracted three of his five divisions from a choleric Douglas Haig and withdrew his other divisions from French control.

On August 28, as the Americans moved into the lines around Saint-Mihiel, Foch descended on Pershing with one last attempt to steal his army. The generalissimo announced the whole German battlefront was one huge salient and should be attacked from the north, the south and the center. Foch wanted Pershing to more or less abort the Saint-Mihiel operation, limiting it to a few divisions while the rest of the American army was transferred back to French control for attacks in Champagne and the Argonne valley.

A stupendous argument erupted. At one point both men were on their feet screaming curses at each other. "Do you wish to take part in the battle?" Foch shrilled, the ultimate insult one general could throw at another.[6]

"As an American army and in no other way!" Pershing replied.

"I must insist on the arrangement!" Foch shouted.

Pershing stuck out his granite jaw. "Marshal Foch, you may insist all you please but I decline absolutely to agree to your plan. While our army will fight wherever you decide, it will fight only as an independent American Army."[7]

After another week of wrangling, Pershing accepted a dangerous compromise. He would attack the Saint-Mihiel salient on September 12 as planned and then transfer the bulk of his 500,000-man army west of the Meuse River to attack through the Argonne valley on September 26 as part of the overall Allied offensive. It was a staggering assignment for a general who had never commanded more than a single division in action and whose staff had yet to plan a major battle. Only a man with Pershing's self-confidence would have tried it.

On September 5, Pershing, disturbed by AEF casualties in the Aisne-Marne offensive, made a stab at defining open warfare. In a general order, he contrasted it to trench warfare, which he claimed was "marked by uniform formations, the regulation of space and time by higher commands down to the smallest details and little initiative." Open warfare had irregular formations, comparatively little regulation of space and time, and the greatest possible use of the infantry's own fire power to enable it to "get forward . . . [with] brief orders" and "the greatest possible use of individual initiative."

It was much too late for this condensed version of storm-trooper tactics to filter down even to division staffs, much less to the captains and lieutenants leading companies. The instructions also omitted some vital components of the storm-trooper innovations—a reliance not on rifles but on grenades and flank attacks to deal with enemy machine guns, coupled with a precise use of artillery and mortars.[8]

At first, Pershing's luck seemed to hold. The Saint-Mihiel offensive was the walkover of the war. The Germans were withdrawing from the salient when the Americans attacked. Resistance was perfunctory. The bag of prisoners and captured guns was big enough to make headlines, although the take was not nearly as large as originally hoped.

Historically speaking, the most noteworthy side of Saint-Mihiel was the first appearance of Americans in tanks. The machines were all French, built by the Renault Motor Company. The Wilson administration had been as feckless in tank production as in aircraft, with a net output of zero, in spite of the usual tens of millions spent. The commander of one brigade, which totaled 174 tanks, was a former Pershing aide, Colonel George S. Patton, Jr.

The top speed of these lumbering vehicles was four miles per hour. Their mission was to precede the infantry and knock out machine-gun nests. Communications were primitive. The tanks had no radios. Attempts to use signal flags were an instant failure; machine-gun fire shredded them. Lead tanks were equipped with carrier pigeons in a basket, but in the excitement of battle, the baskets—and the birds—were soon squashed. In lieu of any better communications system, the captains in command of the companies walked from tank to tank to deliver firing instructions.

Colonel Patton disobeyed the orders of the titular commander of the tank corps, General Samuel D. Rockenbach, and followed the tanks into action on foot. "I will not sit in a dugout and have my men out in the fighting," he told his wife. At one point, Patton mounted the turret of a tank to encourage the crew to attack a village. When German machine-gun bullets struck the tank, the daring colonel reluctantly took cover in a shell hole. At another point, Patton encountered MacArthur on the chaotic battlefield. A German rolling barrage moved toward them. Both refused to take cover, although Patton wryly told his wife they had trouble keeping track of their conversation as the shells got closer.[9]

On the battlefield Patton's tanks encountered a squadron of the Second U.S. Cavalry Regiment. The horsemen had captured a sizable number of German prisoners and were contemptuous of the sluggish, clanking tanks. By this time, forty of the iron steeds had gotten stuck in the mud. Incensed, Patton ordered a patrol of three tanks to attack the main German defenses, the Michel Line, at the bottom of the salient. The tankers fought a point-blank duel with German artillery and returned with the breech block of a knocked-out 77-millimeter gun. That night, Patton excitedly discussed with his officers the possibility of tanks becoming independent of the infantry and smashing through fortified lines to wreak havoc in the enemy rear. It was the first glimmer of the armor tactics of World War II.[10]

II

Pershing and his staff now tried to imitate the Germans and gain surprise in the Argonne. They left most of their veteran divisions in the Saint-Mihiel lines and shifted largely green units west. No significant bottlenecks developed on the few available roads, thanks to the planning genius of Colonel George C. Marshall, now a key deputy of Brigadier General Hugh Drum, the First Army's chief of staff. Fellow toilers at headquarters nick-named Marshall "the Wizard" for managing the sixty-mile move in wretched, rainy weather. The thirty-seven-year old Virginia Military

Institute graduate had obviously not compromised his career by talking back to Pershing in Lorraine a year ago.[11]

On September 26, after a 4,000-gun artillery barrage, Pershing threw 250,000 men in three corps at an estimated 50,000 German defenders in the twenty-mile-wide Argonne valley. A massive hogback (a ridge with steeply sloping sides) ran down the center of this rugged landscape, forcing the attackers into defiles on both sides. It was, Major General Hunter Liggett said, a natural fortress that made the Virginia Wilderness of the Civil War seem like a park. Yet Pershing's plan called for no less than a ten mile line abreast advance on the first day to crack the Kreimhilde Stellung, the main German defense line.

Five of Pershing's nine divisions had never been in action before. The rush to get an army to France had left tens of thousands of soldiers with little or no training. Even experienced outfits such as the Seventy-Seventh Division, which had been blooded under the French in Champagne, were full of raw replacements. On the day before they attacked, the Seventy-Seventh received 2,100 men who had never fired a rifle.[12]

Everything imaginable proceeded to go wrong with Pershing's army. The Germans fell back to well-prepared defenses, and machine guns began mowing down charging Americans. Massive amounts of enemy artillery on the heights east of the Meuse and along the edge of the Argonne forest, which loomed a thousand feet above the valley floor on the west, exacted an even heavier toll.

Rigid orders, issued by Pershing's staff, held up divisions at crucial moments. The Fourth Division could have captured the key height of Montfaucon on the first day, but it stood still for four hours, waiting for the green Seventy-Ninth Division, which had been assigned the objective, to come abreast of it. By the time Montfaucon fell the following day, the Germans had poured five first-class divisions into the Argonne and the American advance stumbled to a bloody halt.[13]

To the north, where the British and French were attacking, the Germans could give ground for 60–100 miles before yielding anything vital. Only 24 miles from the American jump-off point in the Argonne was the Sedan-Mézières four-track railroad, which supplied almost all the food and ammunition to the kaiser's northern armies. In the Argonne, the Germans were fighting to protect their jugular, and by October 4, they had elements of twenty-three divisions in line and local reserve. Ferocious counterattacks demoralized green American divisions. At one point, the Thirty-Fifth Division, farm boys from Missouri and Kansas, teetered on the brink of rout. They were rescued by direct fire from their artillery, including a battery manned by Captain Harry S. Truman. With casualties of more than 50 percent, the division was withdrawn.[14]

Pershing replaced decimated divisions with the veteran units he had left in Saint-Mihiel and tried to resume the attack. He was on the road constantly, visiting corps and division headquarters, urging generals and colonels to inject their men with more "drive" and "push." But Pershing soon discovered that words could not silence a machine gun. Private First Class James Rose of the First Division later told of advancing across an open field to within fifty yards of the German line. Suddenly the air around the men "became a solid sheet of machine-gun and artillery fire. No words could possibly describe the horror of it. Body stacked upon body in waves and piles.... Our boys never faltered, they came, wave upon wave, climbing over the bodies of their fallen comrades with one obsession in mind, to reach and destroy every machine gun that was mowing down our advance." These brave men were obeying the orders of the division commander, Major General Charles Summerall, who summed up his tactical thinking on how to deal with machine guns in two brutal words: "Charge 'em!"[15]

While the doughboys bled, they also began to starve. Monumental traffic jams developed on the few roads into the Argonne. Food did not get forward; the wounded lay unevacuated. Premier Georges Clemenceau, caught on one clogged road, lost half a day and went back to Paris vowing to get rid of Pershing. Stragglers were another problem. General Hunter Liggett estimated that, at the height of the battle, 100,000 runaways were wandering around the First Army's rear. One division reported an effective front line strength of only 1,600 men. Early in October Pershing authorized officers to shoot any man who ran away—proof of his growing desperation.[16]

Worsening Pershing's woes was a visit from Foch's chief of staff, General Maxime Weygand, while the Americans were withdrawing the wreckage of the divisions that had opened the battle. The Frenchman announced that Generalissimo Foch thought Pershing had too many men in the Argonne and proposed shifting six divisions to nearby French armies. Pershing told him to go to hell, and Foch retaliated with a formal, on-the-record letter ordering the Americans to attack continuously "without any [further] interruptions."

Behind the scenes, Clemenceau wrote a savage letter to Foch, urging him to call for Pershing's replacement. "Our worthy American Allies," he sneered, "who thirst to get into action and who are unanimously acknowledged to be great soldiers, have been marking time since their forward jump on the first day. . . . Nobody can maintain that these fine troops are unusable; they are merely unused." This was too much even for Foch to swallow. He replied with a defense of Pershing's problems.[17]

Killing fire from enemy guns east of the Meuse River stopped the veteran divisions when they attacked without artillery preparation in a vain hope of achieving surprise. German counterattacks drove them back again and again. Only the First Division, under grim-eyed General Summerall, gained some ground, plunging up the left defile for a half dozen miles, at the cost of 9,387 casualties. On October 8, Pershing sent two divisions east of the Meuse to join the French in an attempt to silence the murderous artillery. The attack faltered and collapsed into a pocket on the banks of the river, deluged by gas and shell fire.[18]

III

More embarrassing was the plight of a battalion of the Seventy-Seventh Division, which had been assigned to the Argonne forest. Attempting to correct the rigid line-abreast advance his staff had decreed for the original assault, Pershing ordered all units to keep attacking "without regard to losses and without regard to the exposed conditions of the flanks." Such tactics were worthy of Charles "the Butcher" Mangin; they were another index of Pershing's desperation.

On October 1, the commander of the First Battalion of the Seventy-Seventh Division's 308th Infantry Regiment, Major Charles Whittlesey, warned that further attacks would be disastrous. The French army that was supposed to be protecting the division's left flank, west of the Argonne forest, was nowhere to be seen. The Germans could easily cut them off. The division's commander, following Pershing's orders, told Whittlesey to attack anyway. Within four hours, the entire force of 550 men was surrounded. Christened "the Lost Battalion" by reporters, it more than conformed to the name. The men had almost no food and little ammunition. Attempts to supply them from the air repeatedly failed. The tall, bespectacled Whittlesey, a

Wall Street lawyer in peacetime, with a remarkable resemblance to Woodrow Wilson, stonily refused German demands to surrender.

The Germans attacked with mortars, machine guns, showers of hand grenades, even flamethrowers. The Americans beat them back. The Seventy-Seventh Division artillery tried to help with a barrage. Many of the shells fell on the Americans, killing and wounding 80 men. One shell struck the battalion's sergeant major; only his helmet and pistol survived the explosion. For five nightmarish days, the battalion held out. At the end of the fifth day, a patrol from the Seventy-Seventh Division reached the battalion. The Germans, intimidated by the gains of the First Division east of the forest, had withdrawn. A grim Whittlesey led 194 exhausted survivors to the rear. He barely responded when the division commander told him he had been promoted to lieutenant colonel and was being recommended for the Medal of Honor.[19]

IV

Pershing drove himself as hard as he pushed his men. He stayed up until 3 and 4 A.M. reading reports and pondering maps. Rumors drifted into headquarters that Foch and Clemenceau were urging Wilson to replace him with Tasker Bliss. One day, in a car with his aide, Major James Collins, the exhausted general put his head in his hands and moaned to his dead wife, "Frankie, Frankie, my God sometimes I don't know how I can go on."[20]

No one else saw anything but the iron general, still in charge. "Things are going badly," he told Henry Allen, commander of the Ninetieth Division. "But by God! Allen, I was never so much in earnest in my life and we are going to get through." George C. Marshall considered this Pershing's finest hour.[21]

Others think Pershing's finest hour came a few days later. Reluctantly, ruefully, with that amazing objectivity about himself that was one of his most remarkable traits, Pershing realized he did not have the answer to the Argonne. On October 12, he gave Hunter Liggett command of the First Army and created a Second Army to operate east of the Meuse under Robert Lee Bullard. Pershing became the commander of the army group, a chairman of the board instead of a CEO.

The First Army continued to attack for another seven days, meeting fierce German resistance that inflicted heavy casualties. The Rainbow Division was in the thick of this carnage, and Douglas MacArthur continued to play a hero's role. One of the chief obstacles to the American advance was the heavily fortified hill, the Côte de Chatillon. General Summerall, promoted to corps commander, visited MacArthur's command post on the night of October 13–14. An attack on Chatillon was scheduled for the next morning. "Give me Chatillon or a list of five thousand casualties," Summerall said.

MacArthur, who had been badly gassed the day before—he still stubbornly refused to wear a mask—replied, "If this brigade does not capture Chatillon you can publish a casualty list of the entire brigade with the brigade commander's name at the top." It took the Americans three nightmarish days and the loss of 4,000 men to accomplish—but Chatillon became American territory. In the thick of the flying bullets and shells virtually every moment, MacArthur won a second Distinguished Service Cross.

The capture of Chatillon was considered a breach, if not a breakthrough, of the Kreimhilde Stellung, the main German defense line in the Argonne. It had taken three weeks and 100,000 casualties to achieve what Pershing and his staff had thought they could do in a single day.[22]

At this point, the First Army was, in the opinion of one staff officer, "a disorganized and wrecked army." Liggett promptly went on the defensive. When Pershing persisted in hanging around headquarters, talking about launching another attack, Liggett told him to "go away and forget it." Pershing meekly obeyed.[23]

V

Shirley Millard was still working beside Dr. Le Brun in the French hospital near Soissons. But their relationship had undergone a probably inevitable change. Millard had met her fiancé, Ted, in Paris, on his way to the front and decided she still loved him. The surgeon accepted the news philosophically, and they remained friends and colleagues in the operating room.

But Millard had a new problem. She could not shake the dread that swept over her as American casualties poured into the hospital. On September 15, she went to a funeral for four Americans who had died the previous day: Donnelly, Wendel, Goldfarb and Auerbach. Millard wept so hard that her fellow nurses became alarmed, fearing a breakdown. An inner voice asked, *What's the sense of it? Why did they have to be killed before they had even begun to live?*

For the first time, Millard found wisdom in Pershing's decision to ban relatives and fiancées of soldiers from France. Every wounded man she saw made her imagine Ted with similar wounds. "It required enormous effort to perform tasks that had been easy before," she told her journal.

On September 20 came news that multiplied her dread tenfold: Ted was wounded. Dr. Le Brun gallantly arranged for Millard to make an emergency trip to Paris. In a hospital there, she found Ted with a fractured leg and a wounded left arm suspended in a frame. "Oh darling," she gasped. "Thank God you're not hurt!"

It took some doing to soothe an outraged Ted into accepting her explanation that "hurt" meant a wound to the head, the chest or the stomach. Those were the ones that often proved fatal. A thoughtful nurse drew a screen around Ted's bed, and soon Millard's greeting became something they would joke about for the rest of their lives.

Back in the hospital, Millard found she could concentrate on her work again, with Ted in relative safety. But the anguish of seeing Americans with mortal wounds was still acute. One man, a sergeant in the Second Engineers named Charlie Whiting, came very close to breaking her heart. He had been shot in the spine and was totally paralyzed. "He is so loveable, clean and sweet as spring water," Millard told her journal. "He cannot speak more than one or two words at a time, in a gasping whisper, but he manages to say Thank you and smiles with his eyes whenever anything is done for him."

The doctors put Whiting in the *salle de mort*, the death room. There was no hope. "He cannot move a muscle except his eyes and two fingers of his left hand," Millard wrote in her journal. One day Whiting tried to say something to her. She bent her head close to his lips and heard "My mother . . ." With his two fingers, he managed to direct her to his pocketbook, where she found his mother's name and address.

Millard promised to write to her. Tears filled Whiting's eyes. It was the first time he had cried. Millard realized he was weeping not for himself but for his mother. "I patted his hand and busied myself, fighting back my own tears."[24]

VI

On September 17, 1918, YMCA canteen worker Marian Baldwin confided exciting news to her American correspondent. Her life was about to undergo a dramatic change. She had been invited to join another woman in a permanent connection with the 148th Infantry Regiment of the Thirty-Seventh Division. She and her partner, Alice, were given a camouflaged Ford camion, "chuck full of supplies" and orders for each day with "official looking road maps" to tell them where to go. They also got a one-eyed driver who had grave doubts about women getting mixed up with a war.

Ideally, they were supposed to reach a town ahead of the regiment and set up their canteen, laying out cigarettes, chocolates and writing paper for letters home. At their first stop, a little room at a convent in the town of Moyen, they were swamped when the regiment arrived. "The boys sat all over the floor and on the window sill and we had a very merry time until well after dark, when taps sounded and they all disappeared in the most amazing manner," Baldwin wrote.

A few days later, on another move, they lost the regiment and drove all night down bad roads, with their YMCA driver cursing and "Lizzie," as they called their camion, close to running out of gas. At a crossroads, an officer stopped them. A huge truck convoy was just behind them. Where in the #%&@ did they think they were going? he asked. He was stunned when a woman's voice answered him. Alice used her flashlight to show him their map and he gasped with surprise. "Alice!" he said.

"Jim!" exclaimed Alice. They were old and close friends, thousands of miles from "God's country."

After getting directions, they found themselves in a huge column of trucks heading for the Argonne. Whenever they passed a truck, they waved and the doughboys in it came alive. "Honest-to-God American girls!" they shouted and waved their helmets. In Fains, they caught up to their regiment and set up shop in a French barracks with a dirt floor. It was quickly jammed with their "boys."

Two nights later, the women were part of the final massive movement toward the jump-off point for the Argonne attack. At the town of Revigny, they went to Fifth Corps headquarters to ask where their regiment was camped. The major general in charge took one look at them and wrote on their orders: "These two ladies are to be returned at once to their Y.M.C.A.

On April 2, 1917, Woodrow Wilson asked
Congress to declare war on Imperial
Germany. Five months earlier, he had been
reelected to a second term on the slogan,
"He Kept Us Out of War." Fifty members of
the House of Representatives, including
the Democratic majority leader, voted no.

Colonel Edward Mandell House was Woodrow Wilson's alter ego as well as his confidential advisor on foreign policy. House did not realize he had a secret enemy: Edith Galt Wilson, the president's formidable second wife.
BETTMANN/©CORBIS

Joseph Tumulty helped elect Wilson governor of New Jersey, his first step to the White House. As the president's secretary, the genial Irish-American dealt shrewdly with the press and Congress on the president's behalf.
COURTESY OF FRANKLIN D. ROOSEVELT LIBRARY

William Jennings Bryan was Wilson's first secretary of state. Intensely anti-war, he objected to America's arms trade with England and France. Bryan resigned when Wilson took a belligerent stance toward Germany after the sinking of the British liner, Lusitania.

In Russia, radical Bolsheviks seized power with German backing and negotiated a separate peace. Here, three of their top leaders, Leon Trotsky, Vladimir Ilyich Lenin and Lev Kamenev, confer. Woodrow Wilson called them "fatuous dreamers."

Woman suffrage was one of Wilson's major political headaches during World War I. Suffragettes picketed the White House and were often arrested for acts of civil disobedience. Here they march up Fifth Avenue in New York.

Former president William Howard
Taft's support for a League To Enforce
Peace made him Woodrow Wilson's ally
for a while. But he found grave fault
with Wilson's confrontation with
Congress and became a critic.

Former president Theodore
Roosevelt played a key role in
defeating Woodrow Wilson's plea
to elect a Democratic congress in
1918. TR was virtually guaranteed
the Republican presidential nomination in 1920. But he died in his
sleep in early 1919.

Quentin Roosevelt, Theodore
Roosevelt's youngest son, fell in love
with Flora Payne Whitney, heiress to a
$100,000,000 fortune, while he was at
Harvard. At first, both sets of parents
disapproved of the match.

Quentin Roosevelt poses in his second-rate French-made fighter plane in May 1918. When his two older brothers were wounded in action, he demanded to be sent to the front. On July 14, 1918, he was shot down and killed.

Energetic Secretary of the Treasury William Gibbs McAdoo was Woodrow Wilson's son-in-law. But when McAdoo ran for president in 1920, Wilson refused to endorse him. He wanted the nomination for himself.
COUTESY OF THE LIBRARY OF CONGRESS

General John J. Pershing and two members of his staff are welcomed by French officers at a Paris railroad station. Relations between the allies were far from cordial. The French and British repeatedly called for amalgamation of AEF troops into their armies.
COURTESY OF THE LIBRARY OF CONGRESS

General Henri-Philippe Petain was pessimistic about France's chances of winning the war. When he met Pershing in the summer of 1917, he said: "I hope you are not too late."
PHOTOS OF THE GREAT WAR

Generalissimo Ferdinand Foch became supreme commander of all the allied armies in France in the spring of 1918. An apostle of the attack, he had been sidelined because of the heavy casualties suffered by troops under his command.
PHOTOS OF THE GREAT WAR

British Field Marshal Douglas Haig makes a point with Prime Minister David Lloyd George while France's Marshal Joseph Joffre watches. Lloyd George yearned to fire Haig but his conservative backers in Parliament would not hear of it.
PHOTOS OF THE GREAT WAR

Kaiser Wilhelm II sometimes talked boastfully of German power. But he was unsure of his masculinity, had frequent nervous breakdowns, and hated to make a decision. He let Germany's generals run the war.

Matthias Erzberger was the leader of the Catholic Centre Party in the German Reichstag. An advocate of a negotiated peace in 1917, he signed the Armistice under protest and denounced the Treaty of Versailles. Nevertheless, he became a symbol of defeatism and was assassinated in Berlin by right wing extremists.

Quartermaster General Erich Ludendorff's victories over the Russians elevated him to demi-god status. In 1918, with Russia out of the war, Ludendorff convinced Germany's leaders that total victory was within their grasp.

Slim sallow Austrian born Corporal Adolf
Hitler was a messenger in the Sixteenth
Bavarian Infantry Reserve Regiment.
When he received the Iron Cross for
courage under fire, he wrote to a friend
that it was "the happiest day of my life."
PHOTOS OF THE GREAT WAR

More than 25,000 American women came to
France to participate in the war. Some enter-
tained troops with theatrical performances.
Others drove ambulances or worked for the
YMCA or the Salvation Army, often running
canteens close to the front.
PHOTOS OF THE GREAT WAR

American wounded
emerge from the
front lines in the
Argonne. This fierce
47-day battle cost
the AEF more than
100,000 casualties. At
one point, a desperate
Pershing issued
orders to shoot any
man who ran away.
COURTESY OF FRANKLIN
D. ROOSEVELT LIBRARY

Brigadier General Douglas MacArthur was called the "D'Artagnan of the AEF." He designed his own uniform and refused to wear a helmet or gas mask at the front. He won two Distinguished Service Crosses. PHOTOS OF THE GREAT WAR

Although Wilson declared that America would fight a war without hate, his administration was soon selling war bonds with a naked appeal to dark instincts. Hollywood produced films such as "The Kaiser, The Beast of Berlin." COURTESY OF THE LIBRARY OF CONGRESS

Eugene V. Debs, head of the American Socialist Party, attacked the war in this speech in Ohio. He was arrested and sentenced to ten years in prison under the Espionage Act, which made it a crime to criticize the government.
EUGENE V. DEBS FOUNDATION

Liberal Republican Senator Robert La Follette of Wisconsin made a four hour speech opposing Woodrow Wilson's call for war. He later denounced the Versailles Peace Treaty as "a spoils-grabbing compact of greed and hate."
WISCONSIN HISTORICAL SOCIETY (5455)

Conservative Republican Henry Cabot Lodge of Massachusetts opposed Wilson's version of the League of Nations. Lodge was not an isolationist. He believed America had an important role to play in world affairs.
COURTESY OF THE LIBRARY OF CONGRESS

General Leonard Wood was a former army chief of staff and political ally of Theodore Roosevelt. Wood relentlessly criticized the Wilson administration's conduct of the war. Bettmann/©CORBIS

Eamon de Valera was president of the as yet unrecognized Irish republic. He helped lead Irish-American opposition to the League of Nations when Wilson refused to ask the British government to grant Ireland independence. Courtesy of the Library of Congress

Assistant Secretary of the Navy Franklin D. Roosevelt and his boss, Josephus Daniels, gaze at the White House from a balcony of the State, War and Navy building. Roosevelt repeatedly tried to ruin Daniels' reputation so he could get his job. Courtesy of Franklin D. Roosevelt Library

Secretary of State Robert Lansing under-mined Wilson's efforts to achieve a negoti-ated peace early in 1917. He saw nothing wrong with U.S. arms trade with the Allies. After the war he made little attempt to con-ceal his contempt for the Treaty of Versailles.
PHOTOS OF THE GREAT WAR

Woodrow Wilson accepts the plaudits of the Paris crowd in this carriage ride with French president Raymond Poincaré. The two men soon hated each other. Poincaré attacked Wilson as pro-German. Wilson blamed him for demanding a vengeful peace.
COURTESY OF FRANKLIN D. ROOSEVELT LIBRARY

Woodrow Wilson told King George V of England to stop calling the Americans cousins and advised him that the term "Anglo-Saxons" was also out of date. The King later called him an "entirely cold academical professor — an odious man."
COURTESY OF THE LIBRARY OF CONGRESS

Many thought Wilson blundered in his selection of the American delegation at the Paris Peace Conference. From left to right, they were: Colonel Edward House, Secretary of State Robert Lansing, the president, retired diplomat Henry White and former chief of staff General Tasker Bliss. White was the only Republican. Wilson rejected advice to invite a leading Republican member of the Senate.

To speed up the interminable peace conference, major decisions were reserved for the "Big Four" (left to right): David Lloyd George, prime minister of Great Britain, Vittorio Orlando, premier of Italy, Georges Clemenceau, premier of France, and President Wilson. Orlando went home in a rage when Wilson appealed over his head to the Italian people.

Woodrow Wilson salutes wellwishers from the upper deck of the liner George Washington on his return from Europe. With him is his physician and close friend, Admiral Cary Grayson, guardian of the president's precarious health.
COURTESY OF FRANKLIN D. ROOSEVELT LIBRARY

In the summer of 1919 race riots erupted in Washington D.C., Chicago and other cities. Here a crowd gathers on a Chicago corner. No fewer than 2,600 strikes, involving 4 million workers, also roiled the country. War-driven inflation had sent the cost of living soaring.
CHICAGO HISTORICAL SOCIETY DN-0071297

Many newspapers supported Wilson in the struggle over the peace treaty. Here, New York World cartoonist Rollin Kirby skewers three opponents, Senators Hiram Johnson, Henry Cabot Lodge and William Borah.
COURTESY OF THE LIBRARY OF CONGRESS

In St. Paul, one of the first stops on his 1919 speaking tour, Woodrow Wilson seemed rested and confident. He expected to rally people behind his version of the League of Nations. But attacks by ethnic groups and senatorial critics soon turned the trip into an exhausting nightmare.

Dandyish Gilbert Hitchcock of Nebraska was the leader of the Senate Democrats in the struggle over the Versailles treaty. Afterward he called his vote against the amended treaty, cast on Wilson's orders, the greatest mistake of his life.

Woodrow Wilson and his wife take their first auto ride after the president's cerebral thrombosis. White House Chief Usher Ike Hoover said: "There never was a moment when he was more than a shadow of his former self. He had changed from a giant to a pygmy."

Democratic presidential nominee Governor James Cox of Ohio and his running mate, Franklin D. Roosevelt, campaign at a Toledo parade. Backing Wilson's call for a "great and solemn referendum" on the League of Nations, they were buried by a stupendous Republican landslide.

headquarters at Bar le Duc." The general told them he could not allow them to stay in Revigny. It would soon be under bombardment from German artillery. He had two daughters at home just their ages. "I admire the work you are doing but this is no place for women," he said.

Ignoring the general's orders, they stayed in Revigny and listened to the thunder of American artillery as the Argonne offensive began. A week later, Baldwin, Alice and two other "Y girls" revolted, took their bedding rolls and musette bags and began a search for their regiments. After days of wandering they reached Auzeville, which had been shelled mercilessly by the Germans only the day before. Nearby was the Thirty-Seventh Division's headquarters, where they received a cordial welcome. Told that their regiment was at the front, the women went to work anyway, standing in the cold mud handing out tobacco and chocolates to "hundreds and hundreds of men"—trivial gifts, they knew, but a way of saying America's women were with the doughboys in spirit.

At last, the 148th Regiment came out of the lines. "Their faces were lined and their eyes glazed with the fatigue they had seen," Baldwin wrote. She and Alice rushed to greet them, calling out, "Where's Joe? How's Bill?" Too often the answer was a muttered "Gone west." That night, Baldwin confessed, "Our hearts were pretty heavy as we crept into our blankets."[25]

VII

In the United States, another fight to the finish, almost as savage as the one taking place on the battlefield, was raging in the newspapers and on podiums and platforms across the nation. The Republicans, led by an enraged Theodore Roosevelt, were going for Woodrow Wilson's jugular. Doubling Roosevelt's ardor was a growing sense that he could capture the Republican nomination for president in 1920. Early in August, he had arranged a public reconciliation with former president William Howard Taft. More and more people saw TR as the man who could unite the Old Guard and progressive wings of the GOP in a landslide victory.

Months before his son Quentin died in his decrepit Nieuport, Roosevelt had made a speech to Maine Republicans that set the general tone of the fall campaign. He had circulated a draft to Old Guarders such as Senator Henry Cabot Lodge and Elihu Root and progressives such as Senator Hiram Johnson before he spoke. The address was a savage attack on

Woodrow Wilson's Fourteen Points and his plans for a negotiated peace. Riding the rising crest of anti-German war rage, Roosevelt pledged the Republican Party to "war to the hilt." The only hope of future peace in Europe, he bellowed, was Germany's "unconditional surrender."[26]

If he felt this way in March, it is not hard to imagine Roosevelt's attitude in August and September, with his youngest son dead, his two older sons badly wounded, and the German army in obvious retreat on the Western Front. An indication was his encounter with Eleanor Roosevelt at a family funeral not long before Franklin returned from his tour of the Western Front. TR took his favorite niece aside and told her, again, that time was running out for her husband. Franklin needed to resign from his desk job and risk sudden death with the rest of the real men of his generation. Eleanor barely concealed her anger as she told Uncle Ted her husband had tried to enlist, but the president had ordered him to stay where he was.[27]

Senator Lodge, TR's close friend and ardent supporter, eagerly joined in the attack on Wilson. The death of Lodge's son-in-law, Congressman Augustus Gardner, added an undertone of bitterness to his politics, not unlike TR's grief for Quentin. Late in August, Lodge made a Senate speech in which he insisted, "We ought not to discuss anything with the Germans at present." He decried the idea of leaving Germany "unharmed" while Belgium and France lay ravaged. "No peace that satisfies Germany in any degree can ever satisfy us," he thundered.[28]

Three days later, in a speech to 100,000 cheering Republicans at Springfield, Illinois, Theodore Roosevelt gave Wilson more of this no-compromise medicine. He urged Americans to beware of milksop internationalists in the administration and the White House. They were all too eager to play the game of German autocracy. "Professional internationalism stands toward patriotism exactly as free love stands toward a clean and honorable and duty-performing family life," TR roared. The key idea on which foreign policy should rest was American nationalism, coupled with a strong army and navy. On that basis, the United States could do justice to all nations and make sure they did justice to America.[29]

From Paris, a *New York Times* correspondent reported that American soldiers agreed with the GOP; like most reporters, he was reflecting what he heard from AEF headquarters. The *Times* of London, German-hating Lord Northcliffe's creature, applauded in an editorial entitled "Dictated Peace."

Secretary of State Lansing, the chief Germanophobe in the Wilson administration before the war began, ruefully noted in his diary that the psychological effect of the Allied victories in France had been "peculiar." It only seemed to produce more bitterness toward the German people. In his Washington, D.C., cocoon, Lansing was apparently unaware of the near psychotic war rage gripping the rest of the country.[30]

Most other Democrats were equally baffled by the way success on the Western Front was failing to obliterate the Republicans, who had been ranting for eighteen months about Wilson's inept war effort. The Democrats were caught flatfooted by the Republicans' switch to attacking Wilson's peace policy, which coalesced beautifully (from the GOP's point of view) with their prewar denunciation of Wilson as a secret pacifist and timid soul who did not have the courage to make war. In many minds, this argument was easily converted into suspicion of the president as a peacemaker who would be too soft on the monstrous Germans. With George Creel and his Committee on Public Information inundating the country with German hatred, the Democrats found it hard to escape this political cul-de-sac.

VIII

Other worries also disconcerted the Democrats. Votes for women were coming to a boil, and the party Wilson led was a two-headed creature, unequipped to deal with the issue. Overcoming his wife's prejudices and his own, the president had endorsed woman suffrage in January 1918 and urged the Senate to pass the Nineteenth Amendment, which would then go to the states for ratification.

But the Southern wing of the party, viewing reality through the myopia of segregation, declined to listen. Among the most outspoken was Senator John Sharp Williams of Mississippi, belaborer of Senator Robert La Follette and everyone else opposed to the war. For six months, the Southerners on the Senate Committee for Privileges and Elections refused to permit the suffrage bill to reach the floor for a vote.[31]

The woman suffrage movement was divided into radical and moderate wings. The radical leader, fiery Alice Paul of New Jersey, saw a Southerner in the White House paying lip service but doing nothing else for her cause. She denounced Wilson repeatedly and called on every woman with a vote to cast it against the entire Democratic Party. The moderate leader, Carrie

Chapman Catt, was almost as difficult. She threatened to rally women voters against a number of western Democratic senators, apparently oblivious to their inability to change the minds of their Southern colleagues.[32]

The Senate's Republicans, determined to win the election and eager to placate the progressive wing of their party, which supported the suffrage amendment, saw another large chink in the Democrats' armor. They caucused in late August 1918 and endorsed woman suffrage. The chink rapidly became a wound.

Joe Tumulty was a passionate supporter of woman suffrage. He politicked on the issue day and night, trying to bring it to a floor vote. Letters signed by the president bombarded the Southern naysayers. When conservative Senator Ollie James of Kentucky died, Tumulty went to his funeral and persuaded the state's governor to appoint a liberal who would support the suffrage amendment. Thanks largely to Tumulty's efforts, the measure finally got out of committee and came to a vote in late September.

Tumulty warmly seconded Treasury Secretary McAdoo's plea for a speech by the president to support the suffragists. An uneasy Wilson, still not a passionate advocate, consented and spoke to the Senate on September 30. He went all out, calling the amendment "vital to the winning of the war." The result was a disastrous humiliation. With Southern Democrats voting in a bloc, the amendment lost by two votes. "When the president says we can't lick Ludendorff [and] scare Bulgaria . . . because nigger women in Mississippi can't vote, I decline to agree with him," Senator Williams said.[33]

The next day, newspapers reported another presidential humiliation. The New Jersey State Democratic Convention had rejected a woman suffrage plank in its election platform. The Newark *Evening News,* no friend of Wilson's, chortled: "It will not be overlooked that while the president was pleading at Washington for the adoption of the suffrage amendment, a Democratic convention in his home state declined to include suffrage in its principles." The implication was all too clear: Wilson was politically impotent or a faker—perhaps both.[34]

IX

Also lurking in the political wings was the Eighteenth Amendment, better known as Prohibition. The movement was an offshoot of the abolition crusade that ignited the Civil War. Having left the freed blacks to the tender mercies of the defeated Southerners, the descendants of these reformers selected the saloon as their next target. They began in a nursery of abolitionism, Oberlin, Ohio, and the weapon they forged was the local option law. By 1900, thirty-seven states had these laws, and the machinery of petitions, letters, telegrams parades and mass meetings was worked out.

By 1914, whole states, especially in the South, had banned alcohol. Oklahoma even entered the Union with a dry constitution. Over 20,000 Anti-Saloon League (ASL) speakers were preaching Prohibition in church halls and other public platforms around the country. World War I gave the ASL and its ally, the Woman's Christian Temperance Union, the opportunity to go national. They had already penetrated Congress with a 1913 law that banned the shipment of "intoxicating liquor of any kind" into dry states.

In 1914 and 1916, the national elections created a Congress in which drys outnumbered wets 2 to 1. The ASL shrewdly supported preparedness, claiming that an alcohol-free America would be far better able to defend itself. The same month that Wilson declared war, the Supreme Court upheld the constitutionality of the 1913 law banning shipments of alcohol into dry states. The ASL said this coincidence was a sign from God and used it to turn state after state totally dry. In Oklahoma, Catholic priests were even forbidden to use altar wine to celebrate Mass.[35]

When Wilson declared war, twenty-seven states were bone dry. On May 18, 1917, after Congress forbade the sale of liquor to men in uniform, the drys launched a new slogan, "Shall the many have food or the few drink?" Congress, worried about feeding not only America's 100 million but the half-starved populations of England and France, responded with a ban on the use of grain to make alcohol. A few months later, Wilson issued a proclamation limiting the alcoholic content of beer to 2.75 percent. Two weeks later, on December 22, 1917, Congress passed the Eighteenth Amendment, turning the whole nation dry—if two-thirds of the states ratified it.[36]

The ASL now unleashed its 20,000 orators on the German-American community, with its numerous brewers a special target. The drys repeatedly linked liquor to disloyalty and claimed that beer drinking was a sign of sympathy with the kaiser and his Huns. The ploy did not work nearly as well as the ASL hoped. By the fall of 1918, only fourteen states had ratified the amendment. But the drys in Congress, undeterred, tacked a rider on an agricultural appropriation bill, establishing national Prohibition as of July 1, 1919.

In the White House, Tumulty denounced the move, warning Wilson that if he signed it, he would alienate millions of ethnic Democratic voters in the big cities, the heart of the party's strength outside the South. "So much in a great broad humanitarian way depends upon your winning the next election," the president's secretary said, "that I look with dread . . . upon anything that stands in its way." His anxiety mounting with every word, Tumulty called the dry rider "mob legislation, pure and simple."[37]

In Wilson's first term, Tumulty's political advice would have been enough to win a presidential veto. But their earlier bond of trust had been damaged if not destroyed by Edith Wilson's interference. President Wilson turned elsewhere for further advice. Colonel House conferred with Secretary of the Treasury McAdoo and Attorney General Gregory and reported they—and he—recommended signing the bill. Wilson did so. It would soon become apparent that Philip Dru and his creator had blown a big one.[38]

X

This was not the end of the Democrats' woes. In the West, fermenting as rapidly as hops once did in now bankrupt breweries, was a farmer's revolt over what Republicans called Wilson's pro-Southern favoritism. To combat wartime inflation, Congress had given the president power to control the price of many commodities, including wheat. With worldwide demand pushing prices up, farmers saw a potential bonanza in their 1918 crop.

Western members of Congress rushed to tack amendments on the agriculture bill, raising the price of wheat per bushel to $3.00. Cooler heads, led by Senator Thomas P. Gore of Oklahoma, reduced it to $2.50, a thirty-cent rise over the 1917 price of $2.20. This sounds modest, until one realizes the harvest would total a billion bushels of wheat. The price jump would have added $300 million to the nation's cost of living. To the Westerners' vast dismay, the president decided to hold the price at $2.20, which was still 109 percent above prewar prices.

In Washington, progressive Gifford Pinchot, close friend of Theodore Roosevelt, had established the Federal Board of Farm Organizations, which sounded official. Pinchot and other Republicans assailed Wilson's decision as one more example of Democratic favoritism for the South, where the crop that mattered was cotton.

Unfortunately for the president, they were right. Wilson had never been able to persuade the Southerners to agree to a price ceiling on cotton. By 1918, it was 400 percent above prewar levels, and Southern planters were raising so much of it, the market was staggering toward a glut. But Wilson was seldom inclined to change his mind once he had decided he was in the right. Even after the House of Representatives shaved ten cents off Senator Gore's price of wheat per bushel and the Senate reluctantly yielded, Wilson still vetoed the agriculture bill.

The West exploded with outrage. Progressive Republican icon Senator William Borah of Idaho claimed to be "utterly demoralized." Senator Gore rushed an article into print, entitled "The Wheat Farmer's Dilemma." An Iowa newspaper ranted: "The . . . farmer would be satisfied with the present price of wheat if he did not know that the Georgia cotton farmer is allowed to sell his product on an unregulated market. He thinks there is politics in that situation, and he is right." A Republican state convention in Nebraska condemned the Democratic administration for "its failure to fix a reasonable price for cotton when it fixed the price for wheat."[39]

As if this were not enough trouble in an election year, House Majority Leader Claude Kitchin and Postmaster General Burleson decided to increase the postage on second-class mail. The nation's newspapers, already irritated by competition with George Creel's Committee on Public Information and the informal but tight censorship on war news, reacted with predictable fury.

A dismayed Joe Tumulty asked Secretary of the Treasury McAdoo if the money could be found elsewhere. The answer was yes, but neither McAdoo nor anyone else in Washington could stop the imperious Wilson-hating Kitchin. In desperation, Tumulty turned to the man who had tried to knife him in the back in 1916, Colonel House. The president's secretary wrote an urgently realistic letter, warning that the postal price rise was "very unwise politically." He never got an answer.[40]

XI

Colonel House had other things on his mind, more important than domestic politics. As it became apparent that Germany might collapse sooner than

anyone expected, the colonel started worrying about Woodrow Wilson's
Fourteen Points. On September 3, 1918, he wrote to the president, asking if
it were not time "to commit the Allies to some of the things for which we
are fighting." Both men were all too aware that the Allied response to the
Fourteen Points speech had been tepid to the edge of negative.

House warned that as the Allies' military successes on the Western Front
mounted, Wilson's influence would diminish. With startling candor, the
colonel described the leaders of the Allied governments as "hostile rather
than sympathetic" to Wilson and his goals. When victory came, liberals in
the Allied countries would support the United States, but "they will be in
the minority and their voices will be heard faintly by the great exultant
throng." This was a long way from the joint crusade to make the world safe
for democracy that Wilson and House used as their rationale to get the
United States into the war.[41]

What was the answer? Another speech, declared House, in his Philip
Dru mode. A speech in which the president would restate his ideals and
stress the importance of a league of nations as part of the peace treaty.
Wilson responded by adjourning to his typewriter. On September 24, an
excited House told his diary that he was just back from Washington, where
he had read the president's latest oratorical effort. As usual, House thought
it was marvelous and when he got to New York, he called Frank Cobb of
the *World* to discuss the kind of editorial he should write after the president
spoke at the Metropolitan Opera House on September 27, 1918.

The ostensible purpose of Wilson's appearance was the kickoff of the
Fourth Liberty Loan drive. The scene was splendid. The great opera house
blazed with Beaux Arts gilt and glitter. Much of the wealth and fashion of
the great city were in the audience. The Republican governor of the state,
Charles S. Whitman, presided. The president began by sounding as if he
agreed with his Republican critics. There would be "no bargain or compromise" with the governments of the Central empires. "We cannot come
to terms with them."

At the same time, the Allies had an obligation to achieve a peace that
embodied "impartial justice in every item of the settlement." The weak as
well as the strong would be treated with the same strict standard. The
instrument for achieving this lofty goal was a league of nations. The president introduced a list of "Five Particulars" that the league would enforce.
These included bans on alliances furthering special interests, selfish eco-

nomic combinations, and secret treaties. Wilson ended with an appeal to the Allied leaders to join the United States in an affirmation of these ideals.

In the audience, House grew more and more alarmed at the reaction to the speech. "Most of it seemed somewhat over the[ir] heads," he later told his diary. "The parts which were unimportant [brought] the most vigorous applause."[42]

What got the greatest applause was Wilson's statement that the United States would not negotiate with the Central Powers. The next day, this was the point that most newspapers featured. House was dismayed by the "lack of discrimination" the nation's editors displayed. It was grim evidence that Republican denunciations of a negotiated peace had coalesced with war rage to achieve significant influence in the public mind. Beside this hulking hunger for revenge, Wilson's abstract ideals looked pale and commonplace in a way that evoked the old saw about familiarity breeding contempt.

Even more disturbing, except for a few congratulatory telegrams from individuals, the Allied governments maintained a cold silence. They were unmoved by Wilson's plea that "unity of purpose" was as "imperatively necessary in this war as was unity of command on the battlefield." The failure of this speech was a shock that Wilson never entirely absorbed. He thought it had been a sensational success. Back at the Waldorf-Astoria Hotel, House described him as "flushed with excitement and altogether pleased with the day's effort."[43]

Meanwhile, Theodore Roosevelt was rampaging through the Western states, ostensibly in support of the Fourth Liberty Loan drive. His real purpose was to flagellate Woodrow Wilson. Everywhere, after urging his listeners to buy bonds, TR blasted Wilson as the purveyor of a "quack peace." He followed this with a denunciation of the league of nations idea, which he dismissed as a scrap of paper that would seduce the United States into disbanding its army and weakening its navy.[44]

Into this political cauldron hurtled a message from imperial Germany. The government was asking for an immediate armistice and a negotiated peace on the basis of the Fourteen Points.

XII

Nightmarish things had been happening in the German psyche since the failure of Quartermaster General Ludendorff's final offensive in July. After persuading the kaiser and the rest of the civilian government that victory on the Western Front was within Germany's grasp, Ludendorff suffered a total failure of nerve when the prize eluded him and Allied counterattacks began. The conduct of some units of the German army during the August 8 British offensive had revealed alarming signs that Bolshevik propaganda was infecting many soldiers. Retreating troops had shouted, "Blackleg [strikebreaker], you're prolonging the war!" at divisions that were replacing them in the lines.

Overall, the August 8 battle was far from a knockout blow. German losses were no worse than the British had suffered in Ludendorff's March assault on the Fifth Army. With its usual skill, the German general staff rushed reserves from the north to seal off the breakthrough and knocked out 300 of the 450 British tanks that had led the first day's assault. But Ludendorff called the setback "the black day of the German army," and on August 10, the quartermaster general told a stunned kaiser that Germany's only hope of salvaging anything from the war was an immediate peace.[45]

When Allied attacks temporarily subsided, Ludendorff got a grip on himself. He decided the German army could stand on the defensive in France, using its superior artillery and local counterattacks to wear the Allies down to the point where both sides would agree to a peace of exhaustion. This was a fatal illusion. Thanks to the British blockade, the German home front was very close to collapse. People were eating four ounces of meat a week. Influenza was killing tens of thousands. Cars, locomotives, tractors, stood idle for want of spare parts. There was no soap, no shoes. Child mortality was soaring. In July the government began confiscating table linens from hotels and restaurants and stripping houses of curtains.[46]

Inevitably, the demoralization of the home front infected the army. As the British, French and Americans renewed their attacks, unprecedented numbers of deserters and malingerers fled the front lines. One German historian estimated their number as high as 750,000 and called it "a covert strike." Soon one of Ludendorff's staff officers was telling his diary that the quartermaster general "despairs of fighting but does not have the courage to bring it to an end."

As September drew to a close, a flood of bad news made it impossible for Ludendorff to deceive himself or anyone else. Bulgaria, reeling from a British-French-Serbian offensive surging from Greece, dropped out of the war. Austria-Hungary announced it wanted a separate peace. Turkey, cut off from German ammunition and other war matériel by Bulgaria's collapse, was also about to quit. On September 28, Ludendorff told the kaiser and the rest of the civilian government that only an immediate armistice could save the German army from catastrophe.[47]

For the previous two years, Ludendorff and von Hindenburg had been the real rulers of Germany, with the kaiser's acquiescence. They had chosen and dismissed chancellors and foreign ministers with unchallenged authority. Now this supremacy was shorn by imminent defeat, and Germany's civilian leaders erupted in a furious demand for political reforms that would make the kaiser and the military subordinate to the Reichstag. A liberal, Prince Max of Baden, became chancellor with the backing of the Social Democratic Party, the Progressives, and like-minded groups.[48]

There was a certain amount of calculation in this transformation. The decision to seek peace based on the Fourteen Points required an infusion of democracy into a political structure that tradition had made authoritarian and the war had reinforced to an unparalleled degree. Quartermaster General Ludendorff acquiesced in this metamorphosis, hoping to save as much of the old order as possible. As one historian put it with fine irony, "the father of German democracy was Erich Ludendorff."[49]

On October 1, Ludendorff told the new civilian government, "Today the troops are holding their own; what may happen tomorrow cannot be foreseen . . . the line might be broken at any moment and then our proposal would come at the most unfavorable time. . . . [It] must be forwarded immediately . . . to Washington." Protesting such haste, the new chancellor sent the epochal message via the Swiss government: Germany was ready to negotiate peace on the basis of the Fourteen Points. Reeling Austria-Hungary added a pathetic footnote, saying it would accept the same terms.[50]

XIII

Woodrow Wilson was as stunned as everyone else by this revelation that Germany was virtually defeated. He immediately telephoned New York to ask Colonel House for advice. It was October 6. The congressional elections were churning to a climax. From that point of view, the timing could not have been worse. There were huge questions that needed to be answered. How could the president make sure the Germans did not use an armistice to rebuild their army? Would the French and the British accept the Fourteen Points? Nine months of silence was not a promising augury.[51]

In a telegram, House told Wilson he should make no direct reply to the Germans. Better would be a statement that he would confer at once with the Allies. Meanwhile, House would start packing for a trip to Paris. He was convinced that it would be a possibly fatal mistake to let this opportunity for peace slip past. Hopelessness could stiffen German resistance. If that happened, the people of Great Britain and France might launch a peace movement that would win Germany better terms than the Allies could impose on it now.[52]

Most of the American press, still engulfed by war rage, dismissed the German offer as a maneuver. Absolute surrender, declared the *Baltimore Sun*, was "the sine qua non for peace." Abroad, French and British papers were equally negative. They hoped Wilson would reject the offer with contempt. The reaction in the U.S. Senate was even more hostile. In a two-hour debate on October 8, not a single speaker had a good word to say for Prince Max's proposal. The *New York Tribune* reported that the solons unanimously demanded its "immediate rejection." Only after a "crushing military defeat" should there be any talk of peace. In an exchange that today sounds almost surreal, Senator Henry Cabot Lodge asked, "Don't you think . . . that an armistice now would mean the loss of the war?" Republican Senator Miles Poindexter of Washington replied, "I do not think that is too strong a statement."[53]

By this time, Robert La Follette had returned to the Senate. With his case still pending before the Committee on Privileges, his lawyer had ordered him to make no extemporaneous speeches until it was settled. He was forced to sit in silence while the rest of the Senate called for continued war. "It wasn't very easy to sit it out but I did," he told his family.[54]

A worried Wilson summoned House to Washington for a face-to-face consultation. The president told his alter ego he was determined not to lose this chance for peace no matter what anyone said. Secretary of State Lansing soon arrived, and he and House examined a reply that Wilson had drafted. Both men recoiled from its mild tone and its lack of guarantees against German deception. House was amazed to discover that Wilson was unaware of "the nearly unanimous sentiment in this country against anything but unconditional surrender. He did not seem to realize how war-mad our people had become." It was a sad commentary on the president's Philip Dru–ish isolation in the White House, talking to few people besides his wife, Admiral Grayson, his staff and a handful of visitors. Wilson's reluctance to consult his cabinet contributed to this seclusion. Another factor was his fragile health. Admiral Grayson did his utmost to limit the president's work week.[55]

Toiling into the small hours, Wilson and House finally concocted a noncommittal message for Secretary of State Lansing to send to Berlin. Basically it was a series of questions designed to find out whether Prince Max's government was prepared to prove that it truly wanted peace and represented the German people, rather than the discredited kaiser and his generals. In the tension and turmoil of this history-in-the-making, House's advice to confer with the Allies was discarded. Not a word of Wilson's reply was shown to any British, French or Italian diplomat in Washington, or to their superiors in Europe.

If Wilson was trying to steer around America's frenzy for unconditional surrender, he soon discovered this was a vain hope. Henry Cabot Lodge and a swarm of anti-Wilson Democrats such as Senator James Reed of Missouri excoriated the president for putting victory on the Western Front at risk. On the hustings in the West, Theodore Roosevelt did likewise.[56]

Republican newspapers published virulent editorials denouncing "the abyss of internationalism" into which Wilson was leading the United States. On the sidelines, Joe Tumulty, although he reluctantly approved the first note, repeatedly warned the president that he was playing with political fire of awesome proportions. If the kaiser stayed in power, the president's secretary said, it would "result in the election of a Republican House [of representatives] and the weakening . . . of your influence throughout the world."

In the Senate, as the Germans replied to Wilson's first note with earnest assurances and he answered them with a demand for specific acts, such as the evacuation of the conquered territories, the debate became frenzied. Republican Senator Poindexter called for a legislative ban on peace talks. He even wanted to make it a crime for the president to answer another note from Berlin: "I . . . think he should be impeached," the senator shouted.[57]

Wilson kept negotiating with Prince Max. He told House he was working on the assumption that if Germany was beaten, it would accept any terms. If it was not beaten, he did not want to negotiate. At the same time, the president insisted he did not desire a vengeful peace. He did not want the Allied armies to "ravage" Germany as the kaiser's army had despoiled France and Belgium. He abhorred such a "stain" on America's honor. House admired these sentiments, but wondered if he could make them realities "with people clamoring for the undesirable and impossible."

Wilson's third note, dispatched on October 14, was aimed at settling things one way or another. He rejected a German request for a separate "mixed commission" to discuss how the occupied territories would be evacuated. Those were details the Allied military leaders would decide. No armistice would be signed that did not provide "absolutely satisfactory safeguards and guarantees of the maintenance of the present military supremacy of the armies of the United States and of the Allies in the field." Nor would there be an armistice as long as Germany continued to practice unrestricted submarine warfare. Finally, he wanted to see convincing proof that the German government spoke for the German people.[58]

These tough terms boggled Quartermaster General Ludendorff and Field Marshal von Hindenburg. They were loath to accept "any conditions that would . . . make a resumption of hostilities impossible." Field Marshal von Hindenburg thought the terms could not be worse "even if we should be beaten." Clearly, the two generals still hoped to use the armistice to revive the German army. They had not abandoned all hope of a semblance of victory.

But Prince Max and his government were no longer listening to the generals. There was too much evidence all around them on the home front that Germany was on the brink of a Bolshevik revolution. Members of Ludendorff's staff covertly informed the new civilian leaders that Foch's three-pronged offensive threatened the German army with annihilation. On October 20, Prince Max decided to accept Wilson's conditions. He agreed to send representatives to Paris to discuss the details of the armistice with Allied military leaders, who had been told to make sure the German army would fight no more. Five days later, the kaiser fired General Ludendorff and renounced all executive powers. Henceforth Wilhelm II would be a toothless constitutional monarch like his cousin, George V of Great Britain.[59]

The president felt triumphant. So did Colonel House, who was en route to Europe to certify the Allies' support for the Fourteen Points. Neither could imagine that such a victory would soon contribute to a ruinous defeat.

XIV

The German concessions satisfied few war-maddened Americans. Most still wanted unconditional surrender, dictated in the wreckage of Berlin. On October 21, Denver's *Rocky Mountain News* editorialized that the real menace to lasting peace was the "Bolshevists" in the Democratic Party. It was absolutely vital to elect a Republican Congress to prevent these leftist creatures from framing peace terms. In New Hampshire, Theodore Roosevelt begged voters to choose Republicans to win "not a Democratic but an American peace." Henry Cabot Lodge said: "The thing to do is lick Germany and tell her what arrangements we are going to make."[60]

An infuriated Wilson went to work on his portable typewriter and produced a blistering denunciation of the Republicans' tactics and ideas, including some very uncomplimentary remarks about Senator Lodge. The president saw this statement as his long-planned appeal to American voters at the climax of the congressional election campaign. When he showed it to the leaders of the Democratic National Committee, they were appalled and begged him to tone it down. He spent another day working on a revision, to which they gave their approval. So did a reluctant Tumulty, who had favored a more oblique approach—a letter to a prominent Democrat, which he (the recipient) would release to the papers. On October 25, the statement was issued to the nation's press as Wilson's direct appeal to American voters.

The president began by claiming he had "no thought of suggesting any political party was paramount in matters of patriotism." But the extraordinary times in which they were living made "unified leadership" imperative. He was not asking for his own sake but "for the sake of the Nation itself." He admitted the Republicans had unquestionably been pro-war, "but they have been anti-administration." The GOP wanted "not so much to support the president as to control him." Wilson claimed this was unacceptable in wartime. Now, if ever, the U.S. government had to speak as one voice. He also warned the voters that "the return of a Republican majority to either House of Congress would certainly be interpreted on the other side of the water as a repudiation of my leadership."

Having situated himself on the outermost tip of the worst imaginable political limb, Wilson solemnly concluded: "If you have approved of my leadership and wish me to be your unembarrassed spokesman in affairs at home and abroad, I earnestly beg that you will express yourselves unmistakably to that effect by returning a Democratic majority to both the Senate and the House of Representatives."[61]

Almost every cabinet member who read the appeal in the newspapers on the following day reacted with dismay. Secretary of the Treasury McAdoo was "thoroughly mad" because his advice had not been sought.

Secretary of the Navy Daniels labeled it Wilson's "first great mistake." Food czar Herbert Hoover was shocked. These reactions were mild compared to the Republicans' response.

The GOP erupted in stupendous fury. "He is a partisan leader first and president . . . second," thundered Theodore Roosevelt. "The president has thrown off the mask," shouted Henry Cabot Lodge. "The only test of loyalty is loyalty to one man no matter what he does." In a private letter to his family, silenced Senator La Follette wrote: "Politics is adjourned—like Hell."

Many other GOP stalwarts rushed to remind voters that a Republican victory would remove from power Democrats such as Claude Kitchin, Champ Clark, James Reed and George Chamberlain, all of whom had repeatedly opposed Wilson and, the Republicans claimed, were lukewarm on the war. GOP party chairman Will Hays raised the cry that had worked well in Wisconsin: Wilson had insulted the loyalty of the Republican Party. In the Senate, the rattled Democrats cut off debate for seven consecutive days by adjourning after the opening prayer.[62]

Tumulty issued a counterblast, noting earlier wartime presidents who had made similar appeals in congressional elections. The combative Irish-American urged the president to make another statement, damming the Republicans for trying to equate the Fourteen Points with a soft peace. The president, intimidated by the negative response of his cabinet, declined, but wrote numerous letters endorsing specific congressmen and senators who needed help.

To make the election an even more unmistakable referendum on Wilson's leadership, the Democratic National Committee ran huge adds in newspapers across the nation, condemning Roosevelt's and Lodge's calls for unconditional surrender. These election-eve broadsides warned that a Republican victory would delay Germany's capitulation and cost thousands of American lives. The *New York Times* added to the drama by calling the election "momentous and epochal beyond any fight for the control of Congress . . . since the Civil War."[63]

Would Wilson pull it off? The president was contending not only against astute, well-financed opponents, but also against war rage and the alienation his administration's attack on civil rights had evoked in millions of German-Americans and Irish-Americans. Then there was the Prohibition-by-stealth bill and the fury of the Western farmers about the uncontrolled price of cotton. But the news from the battlefront continued to be sensationally good. The German army continued its retreat. The nation and the world watched and wondered—while American voters went to the polls.

XV

Colonel House arrived in the French capital on October 26, a week before the election. He had a commission as "Special Representative of the United States of America" and a letter from Wilson, stating he was the president's "personal representative." He knew the election was in doubt. He had heard about Wilson's appeal shortly after he arrived in Europe and had reversed his previous opinion of the idea; he now considered it a mistake. That made House feel an extra urgency to get the Allies to agree to negotiate peace on the basis of the Fourteen Points as soon as possible. With help from Walter Lippmann and Frank Cobb of the *New York World*, who happened to be in Paris, the colonel prepared detailed interpretations of each point, which he brought to his meetings with the British, French and Italian leaders.

These enlargements by no means eliminated the Allies' opposition to a Wilsonian peace. Both David Lloyd George and Georges Clemenceau opened the discussion with bristlingly hostile remarks. The British prime minister had stated his own peace terms months earlier and saw no reason why Wilson's should have primacy. Premier Clemenceau growled that he had been in politics for fifty years, Wilson for seven. Who should be getting, and who should be giving, instructions?

It was starkly evident that the Wilson-House decision to negotiate unilaterally with the Germans had been a colossal blunder. The president's solo performance reignited the Europeans' already substantial hostility to Wilson's autocratic style and moral arrogance—not to mention their long-standing anger at his thirty-two months of neutrality. With radio and undersea cable communications at his disposal, it would have been a simple matter to bring the leaders of the three major allies into the negotiations. Wilson's refusal to do so struck all these veteran statesmen as a calculated affront.[64]

Things grew heated. Prime Minister Lloyd George reiterated that he would never endorse absolute freedom of the seas, which would deprive Britain of the weapon that had won the war, the blockade. Clemenceau insisted that the French and Belgians must have billions in reparations to pay for the damage the Germans had wreaked in their four-year occupation. British diplomats arrived from London to report the cabinet wanted the Germans to pay for every ship sunk by the U-boats. The Italians—and the French—scoffed at the idea of a league of nations. In a sweeping dismissal, the Italian foreign minister called for informing Wilson that for the time being, there was no agreement whatsoever on endorsing his Fourteen Points.

If this was the Allied position, House said, that left the Americans only one alternative. They would have to discuss peace with Germany and Austria on their own.

"That would amount to a separate peace," Clemenceau said.

"It might," House said.

"My statement," House later cabled the president, "had a very exciting effect on those present."[65]

Some Wilson biographers have given readers the impression that the Allies' opposition collapsed at this point. This was hardly the case. These politicians were not stupid men. They knew from a practical point of view that House's threat was meaningless. They were well informed on what was being said and done in the congressional election campaign. The AEF was locked in mortal combat with the Germans in the Argonne. An offer of a separate peace would have made the Germans instant victors over the French and British. Given the prevailing war rage, such a move would have triggered a massive explosion of congressional and public fury that might well have led to Wilson's impeachment.

Lloyd George said even if the Americans made a separate peace, England would continue the blockade, which would win the war for the Allies. The French and the Italians made no such heroic noises, but they prepared elaborate memorandums with a host of objections to various points. Still a French satellite, Belgium also chimed in with some complaints. When Clemenceau prepared to read his objections, House indulged in an even more fantastic bit of brinkmanship. He said that if the French premier presented his statement, the president would be forced to lay the matter before Congress, so that they could see "what Italy, France and Great Britain were fighting for." It would then be up to Congress to decide whether to continue the war. Given the things that were being said about Wilson's diplomacy in the Senate, letting Congress into the debate was the last thing on earth the president would ever have done.[66]

Nevertheless, Clemenceau decided not to present his statement. All the Europeans seemed to sense that demanding too much now might, at the very least, trigger a last-ditch psychology in the Germans. Irritating Wilson might be even more dangerous. He was very much an unknown quantity—and enormously popular with the voters of their respective countries.

If the Allies had seen what Wilson was telling House from Washington, D.C., they would have been even more wary. The president was infuriated by the British criticism of the principle of freedom of the seas. At one point he said he had no patience with British navalism, which was just another form of militarism. At another point he said if he were forced to turn to Congress for advice, he was sure it would "have no sympathy or wishes that American life and property shall be sacrificed for British naval control."

House omitted this threat. But he put to good use other things Wilson said in the same cable. The president admitted that freedom of the seas was a question that needed "the most liberal exchange of views" in the peace conference. Wilson insisted he was sympathetic to the "necessities of the British . . . with regard to the sea." House used these words to lure Lloyd George into a more favorable attitude toward the disputed principle. But the prime minister still refused to endorse it without an explicit reservation, clearly stating that the British retained the right of blockade. Wilson's demand for freedom of the seas had been seen by too many English as an attack on the blockade of Germany. The prime minister claimed if he gave the point a blanket endorsement, he would be voted out of office and his successor would soon be in Paris saying the same thing.[67]

House said he was sure Wilson would accept a British affirmation of the freedom of the seas, with the reservation that the issue needed further discussion in the peace conference. Lloyd George and Foreign Secretary Arthur Balfour said this satisfied them. They added that along with insisting on the right to blockade in wartime, they wanted it understood that the current blockade against Germany would remain in force until a peace treaty was signed. House, mesmerized as usual by British savoir faire, agreed.

The British now teamed up with House to persuade the French, the Italians and the Belgians to drop their reservations about other points for the time being, except for an insistence on reparations for German destruction of civilian property. House proclaimed himself satisfied with this qualified affirmation of the Fourteen Points. He made no further attempt to change the generally negative attitude toward Wilson that prevailed in these meetings from start to finish.

On November 5, House cabled Wilson: "I consider that we have won a diplomatic victory. . . . This has been done in the face of a hostile and influential junta in the United States and the thoroughly unsympathetic personnel constituting the Entente governments." Walter Lippmann euphorically wrote House that this was "the climax of a course that has been as wise as it was brilliant. . . . The president and you have more than justified the faith of those who insisted your leadership was a turning point in modern history."[68]

From a distance of almost a hundred years, it is hard to see what House and Lippmann were crowing about. House had avoided a rupture with England, the linchpin of his Anglophiliac diplomacy since 1914, at a terrible price. The ongoing British blockade would become the greatest atrocity of World War I. The colonel seemed to think he could brush aside the profound hostility all the major Allies had demonstrated toward the president with a phrase about "unsympathetic personnel"—ignoring the indubitable fact that these same people would be back to negotiate the peace treaty. Calling the Republican Party a junta was an even more grotesque distortion of political reality.

Both these supposedly brilliant political thinkers also seemed to have forgotten an important point. On the very day of their illusory diplomatic triumph, American voters were going to the polls to decide whether to support or repudiate President Woodrow Wilson.

XVI

Only 50 of the 435 seats in the House of Representatives were genuine contests. The rest were in solidly Democratic regions, such as the South, or mostly Republican, such as the Midwest. Unfortunately for the Democrats, most of the contested seats were in the West, where farmers were still seething about Wilson's favoritism to the cotton growers of the South. With the Democrats clinging to control of the House by only 3 seats, their prospects in the popular chamber were not promising.

The Senate was another matter. There the Democrats went into the election with a 10-seat margin. There were 37 contests before the voters, 5 of them being special elections to replace senators who had succumbed to the scythe of death that had thinned the Democrats' ranks. Still, Wilson's party started with 11 seats guaranteed in the Deep South, a nice edge. Elsewhere, however, an unnerving number of Democratic senators were involved in bruising contests with well-financed opponents, while only a handful of Republicans had reason to worry about their survival.[69]

On November 6, giant headlines shouted the results: The Republicans had swept the West and won 37 of the 50 contested House seats. They would prevail in the lower chamber by a comfortable 237 to 193. The Senate still hung in the balance, with several states counting votes into the dawn to determine who had won. Not until the following day, when results trickled in from Michigan and one or two other states, did the *New York Times* announce that the Republicans had "apparently" carried both houses of Congress. The margin of victory in the Senate was 2 seats.[70]

Since Vice President Marshall gave the Democrats an extra vote in case of a tie, the Senate margin was actually 1 seat. In several states, such as New Hampshire and Delaware, fewer than 1,000 votes separated the Republican winner and the Democratic loser. Henry Ford amazed everyone by coming within 7,000 votes of winning a Senate seat in Michigan. A dismaying number of Democratic voters—21 percent—had stayed home. The drop in the Republicans' turnout was 17 percent, suggesting that Wilson's appeal for a Democratic Congress may have enraged just enough GOP stalwarts to win.

In some states, other issues complicated Wilson's appeal for support. Nebraska postmortems blamed the American Protective League, whose persecution of German-Americans had turned them into an anti-Wilson bloc. In Oregon, the feud between Senator Chamberlain and Wilson caused the Democratic turnout to drop by 42 percent, dooming a Chamberlain supporter who ran against a Republican incumbent. In Indiana, Vice President Marshall, obeying Wilson's orders, made another stump speech at the state Democratic convention, calling Republicans disloyal. Enraged GOP voters wiped out the state's Democratic congressmen en masse.[71]

The Republicans did not allow such minor details to deflate their self-congratulations. Senator Lodge called it "a wonderful election." He attributed the failure of Wilson's appeal to the American people's refusal to elect "a dictatorship or an autocracy." Not even the "vast machinery of the government" in wartime enabled Wilson to win, though the president used it "ruthlessly for the benefit of the Democratic Party." A few weeks later, Lodge told two other correspondents the Republican victory was "a country-wide revolt against dictatorship" and its magnitude was "unbelievable."[72]

Theodore Roosevelt saw the victory as a repudiation of Wilson's Fourteen Points. He declared that the Republicans had "made the fight on the unconditional surrender issue" and the people had voted their uncompromising support. Another former Republican president, William Howard Taft, blamed the defeat on Wilson's "crass egotism." He also thought the president's peace notes to Berlin had "alarmed the people."[73]

By far the best explanation came from the liberals. The *New Republic* and *The Nation* both blamed Wilson for failing to maintain the Progressive-Democratic coalition that had elected him in 1916. He had allowed war rage and the actions of Attorney General Gregory and Postmaster General Burleson to create an atmosphere of repression and fear, which turned tens of thousands of liberals against the administration. Committee of Public Information Director Creel ruefully confirmed this conclusion in a gloomy letter to the president: "All [your] radical or liberal friends . . . were either silenced or intimidated. There was no voice left to argue for your kind of peace."[74]

For Senator La Follette, the results produced a political resurrection. Suddenly all sorts of pro-war Republicans, who might have voted for his expulsion, were rushing over to shake his hand and tell him the election proved it was time "to unite all Republicans." The *New York World,* which had called for La Follette's expulsion, glumly concluded that with "Battle Bob" holding the balance of power in the Senate, the likelihood of further prosecution of the senator was close to zero. This prophecy was soon fulfilled. On November 22, the Privileges and Elections Committee voted to drop its investigation, 9 to 2.[75]

For Wilson the ironies of this election were large and painful. He had gambled his standing as the political leader of his country and lost. With his well-known preference for a parliamentary system of government, someone might have argued the president should resign, as Clemenceau or Lloyd George would have been forced to do, if they had lost a similar election. But the U.S. Constitution guaranteed Woodrow Wilson two more years of presidential power, and he soon made it clear he had no intention of abandoning the helm of the ship of state. To one influenza-stricken

Democratic congressman who sent a sympathetic telegram from his sick bed, the president replied:"You may be sure the stubborn Scotch-Irish in me will be rendered no less stubborn and aggressive by the results."[76]

Unfortunately, this attitude was not a formula for future political success.

XVII

In Europe, the politicians ordered the generals to set conditions that would render the German army incapable of renewing the war if peace negotiations failed. Field Marshal Haig's proposed terms were surprisingly mild. He thought the Germans should be allowed to retreat across the Rhine with the honors of war. His reasons were bluntly practical. The German army was by no means broken. As Lloyd George, speaking for Haig, put it, "Wherever you hit them they hit back hard and inflicted heavy casualties." Haig added that the Germans showed no symptoms of a disorganized army. Their retreat was being conducted "in perfect order and with the greatest skill."[77]

Generalissimo Foch had other ideas. He demanded the surrender of a third of Germany's artillery, 5,000 cannon, and half their machine guns— 30,000—plus 3,000 trench mortars. In addition, he wanted 5,000 locomotives and 150,000 freight and passenger cars. He also insisted on bridgeheads on the east bank of the Rhine and Allied control of Germany west of the Rhine. Premier Clemenceau strongly backed these draconian measures.

On the naval side, Great Britain's admirals were not nearly as moderate as its generals. The sailors demanded the internment of the entire German surface fleet at their Scapa Flow naval base in the Orkney Islands off Scotland. Some 150 submarines were to be towed away to other ports.

When Secretary of War Baker cabled General Pershing asking for his thoughts on armistice terms, the AEF commander replied that he favored unconditional surrender. He thought the Germans needed to be thoroughly beaten and he had the army to do the job. The statement infuriated Wilson and Baker. They suspected it was the opening gun of a Pershing run for the presidency. More likely, it was a combination of the general's objective view of the military situation and his ongoing friendship with Theodore Roosevelt, who had made him a general. Under fierce pressure from Wilson, Pershing accepted the idea of an armistice. But he remained convinced it was a mistake.[78]

The politicians, after days of wrangling, took Foch's advice. They were receiving worrisome reports of Bolshevik agitation in Germany. They decided it was vital to end the war as soon as possible and leave the German army with enough guns to preserve order—but not enough to resume the war. They also approved the terms demanded by the British navy.

The final scenes of the armistice drama took place in the saloon carriage of Marshal Foch's railway train in the forest of Compiègne, west of Paris. The German delegates arrived on the morning of November 7. Foch met them at 9 A.M., accompanied by his chief of staff, General Weygand, and two British naval officers. It was no accident that Americans were not included. The omission was the opening gun in the Allied campaign to dilute and if possible dismiss the Fourteen Points—and the American contribution to victory.

The two delegations sat down at a table, facing each other. Foch turned to his interpreter and said in an icy stage whisper: "Ask these gentlemen what they want."

Matthias Erzberger, the liberal Catholic leader of the German delegation, replied in German that they were here to receive the Allies' proposals for peace.

Foch replied that he had no proposals to make. The generalissimo started to get up from his chair, as if he were going to end the conference then and there. The flustered Germans asked if they could say they were there to hear the conditions of the armistice. Another German said in French, "How would you like us to express ourselves?"

Foch again replied he had no conditions to offer. Totally bewildered, the Germans read aloud Wilson's latest note to their chancellor, saying Foch was authorized to make known the conditions of the armistice.

The generalissimo replied he could only do that if the Germans *asked* for an armistice. Swallowing hard, Erzberger said yes, they were asking for an armistice.

Foch ordered General Weygand to read the "principle paragraphs" of the terms. The devastating clauses made it clear that Germany was defeated and would remain defeated. The rest of the document was presented to the delegates in written form.

The Germans were staggered by the scope of the demands, which exploded once and for all any hope that some sort of face-saving armistice could be brokered. These were terms that spelled DEFEAT in capital letters for their own people and the rest of the world.

A request for an immediate cease-fire was curtly rejected. A protest that they might need machine guns to keep order in Germany was also denied. Foch told them to get the guns from their reserve divisions. The Germans replied that there were no reserve divisions. Every available man was already in the lines. Foch still insisted on 30,000 machine guns.[79]

The Germans were given seventy-two hours to make a decision. A courier with a copy of the terms departed for German army headquarters in Spa, Belgium, where the kaiser and his generals were waiting. In Berlin, Prince Max was getting news from other parts of Germany that added to the mounting atmosphere of collapse. In province after province, workers and soldiers councils were taking over government offices and proclaiming a republic. Munich and Cologne were flying the red flag of Bolshevism. Next came word that all of Bavaria was tottering in the same revolutionary direction. On the evening of November 8, Prince Max phoned the kaiser and told him to abdicate "to save Germany from civil war." The monarch furiously refused to consider the idea.[80]

Wilhelm II was reconciled to the inevitability of an armistice and a loser's peace. But he still dreamed of placing himself at the head of his army and marching on Berlin to restore order. The following day, the kaiser learned that several elite regiments in the capital had joined the revolution. Field Marshal von Hindenburg still supported the idea of a march, but he did not think it would succeed. The man who had replaced Ludendorff as quartermaster general, Wilhelm Groener, told the kaiser the brutal truth: "Sire, you no longer have an army. The army will march home in peace and order under the command of its officers . . . but it no longer stands behind your Majesty."[81]

A few hours later, Prince Max telephoned the kaiser to report the rapid growth of the revolution in Berlin. He reiterated that only Wilhelm's immediate abdication could prevent a civil war. Soon came truly stunning news. Prince Max had announced the kaiser's abdication and followed it with his own departure. He had handed over the post of chancellor to Friedrich Ebert, leader of the Social Democratic Party. One of Ebert's lieutenants, hoping to stem the Bolshevik tide, had announced the formation of a German republic. Wilhelm II's long reign as kaiser was over.

Instead of struggling to retain his power, the kaiser began to fear for his life. The fate of his cousin Czar Nicholas II and the czar's family loomed before his eyes. "I am hated everywhere in the world," he told one of his aides.[82]

XVIII

When the American First Army resumed the offensive in the Argonne on November 1, Pershing urged it forward with ferocious intensity, hoping it could smash the German army before the armistice negotiators agreed on terms. Rested and reorganized, with new tactics to deal with enemy machine guns, the Americans opened the attack with a massive barrage that mixed poison gas and high explosives, as well as a blizzard of bullets from heavy machine guns. By nightfall the divisions in the center had driven a five-mile wedge into the German lines, forcing the enemy to abandon the Argonne in headlong retreat. A triumphant Pershing said: "For the first time, the enemy's lines were completely broken through."[83]

On November 5, Foch made yet another attempt to steal a chunk of Pershing's army. He asked for six divisions for an attack in Lorraine, under the command of Charles "Butcher" Mangin. No doubt recalling the staggering casualties of Soissons, Pershing growled that he could have the divisions, but only if they fought as a separate American army, with no French interference in their operations. Foch demurred and the idea was abandoned.

The proposal reignited Pershing's ire at Foch and his boss, Clemenceau. The AEF commander retaliated with a ploy that seriously endangered the fragile alliance. He decided the Americans would capture Sedan, the city where the French had ingloriously surrendered to Kaiser Wilhelm I's Germans in 1870. Ignoring a boundary drawn by Foch that placed Sedan in the zone of the French Fourth Army, Pershing ordered the First Army to capture the city and deprive the French of the symbolic honor.

The order directed the U.S. Army's First Corps, spearheaded by the Forty-Second Division, to make the main thrust. But the details were so vague that General Summerall, by then commander of the V Corps, was encouraged to march the First Division across the front of the Forty-Second Division to win the prize. In the darkness and confusion, the First Division captured Brigadier General Douglas MacArthur. His unorthodox uniform made the doughboys suspect he was a German spy. It was a miracle the two divisions did not shoot each other to pieces. Meanwhile, the French Fourth Army liberated Sedan, as originally planned.[84]

By this time, everyone knew armistice talks were under way. But Pershing's order to keep attacking was still in force. Generalissimo Foch, it should be added, bolstered Pershing's order with an attack order of his own on November 9. Major General Charles Summerall decided this meant he should attempt to cross the Meuse River to continue the pursuit of the retreating enemy. By this time Summerall not only accepted heavy casualties, he exulted in them.

On the afternoon of November 10, Summerall spoke to field grade officers at the Second Division's headquarters. He told them he wanted a bridgehead on the east bank of the Meuse by morning. "The lateness of the hour demands heroic action," he said. Increasing the pressure was the only way to bring the Germans to terms. "I don't expect to see any of you again," Summerall added. "But that doesn't matter. You [will] have the honor of a definite success. . . . Report to your commands." Eleven years later, an officer would still remember "the cold anger" Summerall's merciless words generated.[85]

A battalion of U.S. Marines from the Second Division and a battalion of doughboys from the Eighty-Ninth Division were ordered to make the crossing. In cold, rainy darkness, the marines tried to get across on a footbridge swept by German machine-gun fire. It was little short of a massacre. Only about a hundred men made it to the other side, where they were pinned down by more machine-gun fire. A second marine battalion tried to cross on another footbridge, which had been holed by artillery. Many were killed and wounded by shell fire before they got to the bridge. A German shell dumped the battalion commander and his staff into the river. But enough marines made it to the east bank to create a bridgehead and send out patrols.[86]

The battalion from the Eighty-Ninth Division arrived at the river almost two hours after the marine assault. Its commander, Major Mark Hanna, bore a famous name. His uncle had been the man who made William McKinley president in 1896. Totally fearless, Hanna led his men across on the footbridge. Twice, while dozens died, he survived sheets of machine-gun fire. The company that led the assault was reduced to 19 privates and 2 noncommissioned officers. On the third attempt, Major Hanna's luck ran out. But about 300 men made it to the other side.

Further down the river, in another battalion of the Eighty-Ninth Division, Sergeant Ralph Forderhase wondered why headquarters "seemed unable to visualize the effectiveness of the German rear guard tactics." An earlier attempt to cross the Meuse by his battalion had been a calamitous failure. The acting battalion commander, Captain Arthur I. Wear, had asked for volunteers to swim the cold, deep river to explore German strength on the opposite bank. Only a handful survived the machine-gun and artillery fire. Few of these brought back information of any value. As Sergeant Forderhase later recalled it, Captain Wear thanked them for their heroism and "walked a short distance into the dark and somber woods and shot himself in the head with his service pistol."[87]

This time Sergeant Forderhase and his battalion crossed the river on rafts, unopposed. In the morning, they moved forward in a dense fog toward the village of Pouilly. Forderhase heard a voice calling his name. It was Captain Wear's replacement, pointing in amazement at two Germans manning a machine gun. The Americans had stumbled on them in the fog, and they had surrendered without firing a shot. The captain wondered why the gunners had not slaughtered them.

Forderhase knew enough German to ask them for an explanation. The Germans told them the war was ending at eleven o'clock and they saw no reason "to sacrifice their lives, or ours, needlessly." The skeptical Americans took them prisoner and continued to advance until they were stopped by sniper fire. They took cover and debated what to do next. Suddenly the snipers stopped shooting. Forderhase looked at his watch. It was eleven o'clock.[88]

Up and down the Western Front, other guns also fell silent. In the stunning stillness, men emerged from their trenches and dugouts, amazed to find themselves alive. In the Thirty-Third Division, two privates, one a German-American who spoke fluent German, crossed no-man's-land and exchanged souvenirs with the enemy. In the sky above the battlefield, Captain Eddie Rickenbacker, America's leading fighter pilot, with twenty-four kills, looked down on the historic scene. The Great War was over.[89]

XIX

The beginning of the end took place in Germany at 5 A.M. on November 10, when the kaiser and his aides headed for Holland in automobiles. His special train traveled in the same direction, empty. They had decided the train was too likely to be stopped by revolution-minded soldiers. At the border, the royal entourage talked their way past army guards and by eight o'clock were conferring with a Dutch diplomat, who had been alerted to the kaiser's arrival.

The former supreme war lord was told that he would have to await the decision of a ministerial council in The Hague to grant his request for asylum. He boarded his imperial train when it arrived from Spa, but was disconcerted to find large numbers of people, many of them Belgian refugees, on the platform making threatening gestures and noises. The police finally cleared the station and stood guard until word arrived from Dutch Queen Wilhelmina that asylum had been granted. The kaiser and his party were ordered to proceed to the town of Maarn, where they would be quartered in nearby Amerongen Castle.

The trip from the border to Maarn was not without its anxieties. Almost every station platform was full of people shaking their fists and shouting insults. At Maarn, Wilhelm was greeted by Count Godard von Aldenburg Bentinck, proprietor of Amerongen Castle. At the castle, the count's daughter greeted him cordially and Wilhelm relaxed, his fear of imminent assassination subsiding.

People were struck by how unaffected, charming and courteous the kaiser became. He had never been comfortable as a supreme war lord. He was happiest when he was entertaining or being entertained in regal fashion—as on his visits to England to see his grandmother, Queen Victoria, and his royal cousins. Groping for a shred of comfort, Wilhelm turned to his host and said, "What I should like, my dear Count, is a cup of tea—good hot English tea."[90]

XX

In her hospital, Shirley Millard felt overwhelmed by a deluge of new wounded. Many were mustard gas cases. "They cannot breathe lying down or sitting up," she wrote. "They just struggle for breath. But nothing can be done. Their lungs are gone. Some with their eyes and faces entirely eaten away by the gas and bodies covered with burns. . . . One boy, today, screaming to die. The entire top layer of his skin burned from his face and body. I gave him an injection of morphine."

On November 10, Charlie Whiting died. Millard held his hand as he stopped breathing and "could not keep back tears." Near the end, he saw her crying and patted her hand with his two living fingers to comfort her. "I cannot describe that boy's sweetness. He took part of my heart with him," Millard wrote in her journal.

Minutes after Whiting died, someone rushed in to shout, "Armistice! The staff cars have just passed by the gate on their way to sign an Armistice!"

The shouter did not realize he was in the *salle de mort*. Millard angrily shushed him. One of the dying men began to sob. She talked soothingly to him. "But what could I say, knowing he would die before night?" The chapel bell began ringing wildly. A nurse burst in to tell Millard they were opening champagne in the dining hall. Millard told her to get out. She sat there, thinking, "My heart is heavy as lead. . . . Can't seem to pull myself together."[91]

XXI

At Compiègne, the German delegation had finally received permission to sign the armistice agreement on the night of November 10, around the time the kaiser began sipping his tea. While hundreds of Americans were dying along the Meuse, the two sides wrangled about minor details. Finally, at 5:10 A.M., the Germans signed the documents. Matthias Erzberger read a statement denouncing the terms, saying they threatened his nation with anarchy and starvation: "A nation of seventy million suffers but does not die."[92]

Generalissimo Foch immediately ordered messages sent to every part of the Western Front, announcing that hostilities would end at 11 A.M. on November 11. At American First and Second Army headquarters, the news had no discernible impact. Pershing's insistence on continued pressure was still in effect. Attacks planned for that morning went ahead as scheduled. One commander, Brigadier General John H. Sherburne of the black Ninety-Second Division, tried to get an assault canceled. His request was curtly denied, and the black men and their white officers went forward behind the usual barrage. German machine guns chattered and high-explosive shells created familiar carnage. "I cannot express the horror we all felt," Sherburne said later.[93]

Pershing still thought the armistice was a mistake. "If they had given us another ten days, we would have rounded up the entire German army, captured it, humiliated it," he later growled. Haig, Foch and Pétain, commanding armies that had used up their last reserves, did not agree. Nor did the politicians, growing more and more nervous about Germany going Bolshevist.

The AEF commander headed for Paris, where he found himself the toast of a delirious city. In the Place de la Concorde, his car was mobbed. Celebrating doughboys rescued him, fending off the ecstatic Parisians, some of whom tried to get into the back seat to kiss the iron general. Later, celebrating in private with some old friends, Pershing inadvertently summed up the doughboys' contribution to the victory: "The men were willing to pay the price."[94]

XXII

What was the price of winning Woodrow Wilson a seat at the peace table? The Americans had been in combat two hundred days—approximately six months. In that time, 50,300 doughboys were killed. Another 198,059 Americans were wounded in action. Another 62,668 died of disease—an appalling 38,815 of these in training camps in the United States. Another 4,503 were killed in accidents. Almost 1,000 committed suicide. Adding in minor causes, the total deaths were 120,139. In 1930, the Veterans Bureau estimated that war-related diseases, wounds and other kinds of trauma inflicted on the Western Front had raised the total cost to 460,000 deaths. Men disabled by gas attacks were particularly prone to die young. More than 41,000 doughboys were shell-shock victims, listed as psychiatrically disabled. Many of these men were hospitalized for the rest of their lives.[95]

In the 47 months of World War II, U.S. Army and Marine casualties totaled 259,376 dead and 768,207 wounded. In Korea, 37 months of combat cost 53,886 deaths and 103,000 wounded. In eleven years of fighting in Vietnam, American losses were 57,000 dead and 154,000 wounded. Obviously, the price that the doughboys paid in little more than six months on the Western Front was, in the words of one historian, "disproportionately large." The main reason was the lethal firepower of the German army and the AEF's primitive tactics, which relied on Belleau Wood–style frontal assaults until the last days of the war.[96]

XXIII

In Paris on November 11, 1918, while General Pershing was being mobbed by delirious French citizens in the Place de la Concorde, Colonel House was cabling Woodrow Wilson: "AUTOCRACY IS DEAD. LONG LIVE

DEMOCRACY AND ITS IMMORTAL LEADER. IN THIS GREAT HOUR MY HEART GOES OUT TO YOU IN PRIDE, ADMIRATION AND LOVE."

As celebrations erupted in cities across the United States, President Wilson gave federal employees the day off and released an announcement to the people of the United States: "The armistice was signed this morning. Everything for which America has fought has been accomplished. It will now be our fortunate duty to assist by example, by sober friendly counsel and by material aid in the establishment of just democracy throughout the world."

The illusion of victory was sweet while it lasted.[97]

Chapter 9

PEACE THAT SURPASSES UNDERSTANDING

For Woodrow Wilson, sour notes began to appear in the peace process soon after people stopped dancing in the streets. The president assumed that the Allied leaders would welcome his announcement that he was coming to Europe for the peace conference. Instead, they advised Colonel House that they would be much happier if he stayed home. Georges Clemenceau, in his blunt way, told House that Wilson's presence "seems to be neither desirable nor possible." The Allied leaders cooked up an argument that was legalistic and ultimately silly. As president of the United States, Wilson was a head of state, on a par with kings and emperors. If one head of state came to the conference, they would also have to invite the kings of England, Italy, Greece, and perhaps Montenegro, as well as President Poincaré of France, whom Clemenceau despised.[1]

Behind this political hot air was a deep suspicion and not a little dislike of Wilson's overbearing political style. To the president's dismay, this negative attitude coalesced with a burgeoning opinion among his liberal American admirers that it would be a mistake for him to mingle in the gritty details of peacemaking. Better for him to stay in Washington, above the battle, and let Colonel House and others do the negotiating.

Even before the armistice, Frank Cobb of the *World* sent a long memorandum to House, elaborating on this argument. Wilson would have only one vote at the peace conference, Cobb warned. His ability to appeal to the conscience of America and the world would be fatally weakened, if not destroyed. It would be far better if Wilson fought on his "home ground," Washington. "Diplomatic Europe is enemy soil to him." Cobb said he had come to Europe assuming that Wilson should attend the peace conference. A sojourn in Paris had changed his mind.

Even more dismaying for Wilson was the discovery that Colonel House shared this opinion. In a cable on November 14, House told the president, "Americans here . . . are practically unanimous in the belief that it would be unwise for you to sit in the Peace Conference." Instead of arguing against this assertion, House reiterated Clemenceau's opposition and added, "The same feeling prevails in England." House would only approve Wilson's coming to Europe to participate in a "preliminary conference," in which the general terms of the peace treaty would be worked out.[2]

Wilson was infuriated. He cabled House that this idea "upsets every plan we [have] made." The "we" was not a reference to House—Wilson was almost certainly referring to Edith Galt Wilson, who not only urged him to go, but had persuaded the president to take her with him. Wilson dismissed the head-of-state argument, calling it "a way of pocketing me." He suspected the British and French leaders wanted to exclude him from the conference "for fear I might . . . lead the weaker nations against them." Growing more exercised with every word, Wilson stormed, "It is universally expected and generally desired here that I should attend the conference."[3]

This was one more example of Wilson's tendency to ignore political realities. He had just gambled his prestige as America's political leader in the congressional elections and had lost. The results were a stunning refutation of his claim that American voters "universally expected and generally desired" him to attend the peace conference. In fact, there were grave reservations among many people about his going to Europe at all.

During World War II, Americans grew used to having their presidents fly around the world to summit conferences. In 1918, however, people looked askance on the president's leaving the country for any reason. William Howard Taft abandoned his habit of vacationing in Canada when he became president. President McKinley had considered a tour of Europe after the Spanish-American War, but dropped the idea. The U.S. Constitution did not (and still does not) provide for any transfer of power to the vice president when the president leaves the country. Many people feared there would be no supreme authority in a national emergency. Lord Bryce, before he became the purveyor of fake atrocities, had concluded from his popular study of the American Constitution that it seemed "impossible for the president to leave the U.S."[4]

The day after the armistice, Secretary of State Lansing urged Wilson not to go. The president dismissed the advice with a look that spoke "volumes," the secretary later glumly noted in his diary. In the White House, Joe Tumulty could muster very little enthusiasm for Wilson's decision, especially when he was told the president was leaving him behind. In 1918, there was no large White House staff to handle the thousand and one details of the executive office. Almost single-handedly, Tumulty would have to worry about the demoralization of a Democratic Party that had just lost control of both houses of Congress, the hostility of the Republican-controlled Congress, Wilson's long-deteriorated relations with the press and the oncoming 1920 elections. The secretary's attitude grew even more negative when he discovered the men Wilson had chosen to take with him in the American delegation.

Tumulty—and many other Wilson men—saw this delegation as crucial to their hopes for an enduring peace. A treaty would have to win the advice and consent of two-thirds of the GOP-controlled Senate. Tumulty urged Wilson to include at least one prominent Republican in the delegation. He proposed Elihu Root. Along with being the grand old man of the GOP, Root had been secretary of war under McKinley and secretary of state under Roosevelt, winner of a Nobel Peace Prize for improving U.S. relations with Latin America and Japan—and a public backer of a league of nations. Wilson dismissed him as too conservative.[5]

Attorney General Gregory, one of the cabinet members most dismayed by Wilson's midterm election appeal to the voters, next told the president there was only one way to repair the political damage inflicted by the November disaster. He had to invite not one but two prominent Republicans to join the peace conference delegation. Gregory gave him the names of two senators, one a former secretary of state, and four other prominent members of the GOP, including Root and former president Taft, who was also a supporter of a league of nations. Wilson rejected them all.[6]

Instead, Wilson chose Colonel House as one of the peace commissioners, a gesture that needlessly elevated his alter ego to official status, ruining the role he played best, backstairs negotiator and adviser. Secretary of State

Lansing was included because the British and French were bringing their foreign secretaries. Since Wilson already disliked him, Lansing was worse than useless from the start. As a third commissioner, the president chose General Tasker Bliss, a faceless nonentity to most Americans. Like House, Bliss was already in Paris and could have served just as well as an unofficial adviser. For a Republican spokesman, Wilson selected Henry White, a genial old man with long diplomatic experience—but who had been retired for ten years and had no political power whatsoever inside the GOP.[7]

White's choice infuriated the Republicans. William Howard Taft said he was "more of an Englishman than an American." White had never played a part in the councils of the GOP. Much of his adult life had been spent abroad. In the Senate, the Republicans expressed outrage and opposition in scathing oratory. There was talk of sending a committee of senators to Paris to report on the peace conference independently.

George Harvey, one of Wilson's earliest backers, was now publishing a weekly devoted almost entirely to criticism of the president. At one point during the war, there was a serious discussion at a Wilson cabinet meeting about suppressing the publication. Harvey contrasted Wilson's delegation to President McKinley's choices for negotiating a peace treaty at the end of the Spanish-American War. He had chosen two prominent Republican senators and the leader of the Democratic minority.

Harvey put Wilson's choices in three columns to underscore their insignificance.

Name	Occupation	Representing
Woodrow Wilson	President	Himself
Robert Lansing	Secretary of State	The Executive
Henry White	None	Nobody
Edward M. House	Scout	The Executive
Tasker H. Bliss	Soldier	The Commander in Chief

In short, Wilson had appointed himself four times.[8]

Henry Cabot Lodge praised Harvey's assault, but urged fellow Republicans not to attack Wilson's decision to go to Europe. He was sure the trip would add to the president's political woes. He also did not object to the choice of Henry White, who was a personal friend. Instead, he persuaded White to meet with him and other GOP senators and made sure the elderly diplomat conferred with Elihu Root and Theodore Roosevelt as well. Lodge gave White a long memorandum on his own peace ideas. He dismissed a league of nations as fuzzy Wilsonian idealism, but favored strong alliances with France and England to prevent another war.[9]

Lodge did his best to add to Wilson's woes by building a political back-fire against him in England. On November 25, the senator wrote a long letter to fellow conservative Arthur Balfour, the British foreign secretary, telling him that "the overwhelming desire of Americans without distinc-tion of party" favored a harsh peace for Germany. Lodge recommended splitting the country into two or three parts and excluding the Germans from the peace conference until the final terms were settled. There should be "no opportunity for anyone to play . . . the mediator," he wrote, an obvious dig at Wilson. "If the . . . Allies stand firm," Lodge insisted, they would win "the general approbation of American public opinion."[10]

II

On December 2, Wilson gave his annual state-of-the-union address to Congress. Seldom did the president reveal how badly he needed Colonel House to discuss and hone a speech before presenting it. The occasion was a great opportunity to win the American people's support—and even Congress's support—for his trip to Europe. But the vital words, the strong emotions, were missing. Most of the speech was a perfunctory report on the satisfactory condition of the American economy and the steps being taken to return to a peacetime mode. At the close, Wilson asked the people to support him on his mission to Europe. But he made no attempt to spell out his goals.

Congress's response was zero. Secretary of the Navy Daniels called it an ice bath. Applause was minimal and confined entirely to Democrats; not a few of them also sat on their hands, a sign that Congress as a whole was affronted by Wilson's failure to select one of them as a peace commissioner. The nation's newspapers criticized the president's failure to communicate. Some complained that he was treating the American people like college freshmen, who were expected to bow low before an all-knowing professor.

Senator Robert La Follette described the speech as "pretty punk—poorly delivered and received." A few days later, he added an insightful comment. The president "had the appearance of being a whipped man."

There are good grounds for suspecting that Wilson, in spite of his bluster about fighting back, felt that way, when he found himself face-to-face with the politicians he had tried to trump with his appeal to the people.[11]

At midnight the following day, Wilson; his wife, Edith; his daughter, Margaret; his physician, Admiral Cary Grayson; and a small White House staff motored to a sleeper car in Washington's Union Station. The next morning, they arrived in Hoboken, where they boarded the *George Washington* for the trip to Europe. The third biggest passenger liner in the world, it had been seized from Germany when war was declared. As the ship headed down New York Harbor toward the open sea, hundreds of vessels sounded their whistles and sirens. Soon, navy planes and a dirigible appeared overhead. A few miles outside the Narrows, in the open sea, ten destroyers swung in line to port and starboard and the battleship *Pennsylvania* steamed just ahead. America's commander in chief was on his way to create a peaceful world.[12]

From a sickbed in New York City's Roosevelt Hospital, where he was being treated for rheumatism and general exhaustion from his efforts in the congressional election campaign, Theodore Roosevelt issued a statement that did nothing to enhance Wilson's prospects in Paris: "Our Allies and our enemies and Mr. Wilson himself should understand that Mr. Wilson has no authority to speak for the American people at this time. His leadership has just been emphatically repudiated by them. The newly elected Congress comes far nearer than Mr. Wilson to have a right to speak the purposes of the American people. Mr. Wilson and his Fourteen Points and his four supplementary points and his five complementary points . . . have ceased to have any shadow of right to be accepted as expressive of the will of the American people."[13]

III

To handle the publicity side of the American mission, Wilson brought along George Creel. The president was still devoted to the mercurial head of the Committee on Public Information, in spite of the trouble his loose tongue and hyperbolic style had stirred during the war. As the president's spokesman, Creel adopted many of his attitudes toward Congress. He talked of Senator Hiram Johnson's "abnormal vanity" and said Senator James Reed deserved "contempt and ridicule" for his character and abilities, which were equally abysmal. He suggested Henry Cabot Lodge's mind was like the soil of New England, "highly cultivated but naturally sterile."

In May 1918, Creel journeyed to New York for a speech at the Church of the Ascension. Not a few members of the audience were hostile to the war. Toward the end of a rather acrimonious discussion, someone asked him what he thought of "the heart of Congress."

The crowd tittered, and Creel, obviously considering the question absurd, replied, "Oh I have not been slumming for years."

The words were on the front page of several newspapers the next morning. Members of Congress who consulted their dictionaries discovered they had been described as being "poor, dirty, degraded and often vicious." Creel's numerous enemies in Congress quickly persuaded their confreres to demand Creel's banishment. "Uncle Joe" Cannon, former speaker of the House, said that the former muckraker "ought to be taken by the nape of the neck and the slack of the pants and thrown into space."[14]

Wilson enjoyed every minute of this contretemps. He telephoned Creel to tell him not to worry about the "antics of Congress." Some historians think Wilson took Creel to Europe to rescue him from his congressional enemies, who would have tried to devour him without the protection of his friend the president. Even before he reached France, Wilson began to realize this generous gesture was a mistake. Creel had been a congenial and sometimes helpful adviser on domestic politics, as well as a dynamic leader of the Committee on Public Information. But his all-or-nothing style was not suited to the world of diplomacy.[15]

IV

Before he sailed, Wilson had seen a report of a speech David Lloyd George had given to a group of liberals in England. The prime minister had declared that "no settlement that contravenes the principles of eternal justice will be a permanent one. . . . We must not allow any spirit of greed, any grasping desire, to override the fundamental principles of righteousness." He also called for a league of nations to preserve the peace. Wilson had cabled his "sincere admiration." The president declared himself delighted to discover "such community of thought and counsel in approaching the high task now awaiting us."[16]

While the *George Washington* and its escorts plowed through the heavy seas of the wintry North Atlantic, Lloyd George was doing much the same thing in England, politically speaking. He had called an election to solidify his grip on the House of Commons. The prime minister had begun his career as a liberal. He had not only opposed the Boer War, but also been a strong proponent of home rule for Ireland. But the war government he headed was mostly composed of conservatives. His repeated rejections of German peace proposals and calls for a knockout blow were Tory policies.

While the prime minister was hurling the noble apostrophes to peace and justice that had thrilled Wilson at some two hundred leading English liberals, elsewhere in London conservative leader Andrew Bonar Law was reading a letter from Lloyd George in which he pledged himself to a Tory program at home and abroad. Not by accident was the prime minister known as "the Welsh Wizard." His political principles were extremely elastic; many said they were nonexistent.[17]

Inevitably, rumors about this attempted double play got into the newspapers, and soon Lloyd George heard from Lord Northcliffe. The press baron had spent the war lashing his newspapers into ever wilder vituperation against "the Hun"—and there was no letup after the armistice was signed. Northcliffe wanted the kaiser and his circle tried as war criminals and Germany billed for every shilling England had spent on the war. "Make Germany Pay!" "Hang the Kaiser!" shrilled his headlines.

Northcliffe had revealed an interest in joining Lloyd George's government but was rebuffed. The prime minister also ignored a suggestion to make him a delegate to the peace conference. But Lloyd George soon discovered he could not ignore the readers of the *Daily Mail* and the *Times*. They assailed him with hundreds of letters, demanding to know what he was going to do about the kaiser and Germany. At public meetings, when the prime minister orated about helping disabled veterans and building public housing, a cry invariably went up: "What about the Hun?" "Are you going to hang old Bloody Bill?"

Soon Lloyd George was giving speeches in which his liberal social program was barely mentioned. Instead he expostulated on the need for reparations from Germany. He pointed out that Berlin had demanded reparations from France after winning the Franco-Prussian War in 1871 and had thereby established "the principle." Now it was Germany's turn. As for the kaiser, was it fair to punish private soldiers for committing criminal acts and let the biggest criminal of them all live in luxury in Holland?

On December 5, while the *George Washington* pitched and rolled on the North Atlantic to the acute inner distress of most passengers (but not the president), Lloyd George called for the kaiser's prosecution because he had started the war and the war was "a crime." The prime minister wanted reparations from Germany and promised to set up a commission to figure out exactly how much the Germans could pay.

This was not good enough for Lord Northcliffe. A telegram demanded that the prime minister set an exact figure. Two days later, in another speech, Lloyd George said Germany could and should pay 24 billion pounds—$120 billion ($1,428 billion in twenty-first-century dollars). He vowed he would make the Huns cough up this incredible sum "to the last penny." If need be, he would "search their pockets" for the final farthing.[18]

With Northcliffe satisfied, Lloyd George now executed the secret bargain he had struck with Bonar Law and the Tories. Bonar Law and company would tolerate no more than 150 liberals in Parliament. To eliminate 260 others, the prime minister announced he would not endorse anyone who had voted against him in a tempest stirred by an army officer's accusation of government misconduct nine months before. The supposed grudge was sheer pretext—the numbers did not even add up. But soon there were 159 liberals, 364 conservatives and 18 independents with "the coupon," as the newspapers called Lloyd George's endorsement. It was one of the dirtiest deals ever seen in English politics, but it worked magically from Lloyd George's point of view. Demonstrating the potency of the German hatred that Northcliffe, Lord Bryce and Wellington House had sown in the souls of British voters, the prime minister's coalition emerged from the election with the largest majority in the history of the House of Commons—525 of 707 seats. The liberals had been reduced to an infinitesimal band of some 30 hapless survivors. If Lloyd George was right, and the war was "a crime," they had been cruelly punished for their share in starting it.[19]

V

For a while, the significance of the British elections was shoved aside by the sheer dimension of the president's welcome in Europe. He and Mrs. Wilson arrived in Brest on Friday, December 13, a date that made the superstitious sailors aboard the *George Washington* wince. But Wilson was exultant. He claimed thirteen was his lucky number. He had thirteen letters in his name. In fact, he had urged the captain to cut the ship's speed so they would arrive on the supposedly unlucky day.

On the president's last night at sea, nine American battleships and twenty destroyers from the European squadron joined Wilson's flotilla. France sent almost as many warships; a veritable armada escorted the president into Brest, where generals and admirals and government officials by the dozen welcomed him. Soon he was aboard a train to Paris, where reporters glimpsed the first indications that Wilson had already achieved semidivine status. In many villages, people knelt beside the track in the dark, their hands clasped in worship, as the train thundered past.[20]

Wilson's reception in the French capital was one of the most spectacular events of the twentieth century. Two million Parisians jammed the streets, screaming, *"Vive Wilson!" "Vive l'Amérique!"* A huge banner saluted *"Wilson le Juste."* Preceded by an honor guard of cavalry, Wilson rode beside President Raymond Poincaré, acknowledging the delirious cheers with sweeping waves of his high silk hat. Henry White, whose memories of such celebrations went back to Napoleon III, said he had never seen anything like it.

The Wilsons and their party took up residence in the palace of Prince Joachim Napoleon Murat, a descendant of Napoleon's sister. The magnificent mansion was the size of the White House, surrounded by ten-foot walls to keep the masses at bay. Beautiful drawing rooms displayed Napoleon's portrait everywhere, an ironic reminder that the Germans were not exactly the inventors of militarism. It was a setting worthy of an emperor. Coupled with his reception by the people of Paris, it is easy to imagine Wilson developing delusions of Philip Druish political grandeur. He was already convinced that he, rather than the politicians of Europe, was in closer touch with the wishes and hopes of their people. Didn't the hysterical adoration of those screaming Parisians prove it?

If the peace conference had begun, Wilson might have made political capital from the aura of that frenzied reception. Instead, the president discovered to his dismay that domestic politics was keeping Lloyd George and Clemenceau busy. He and Edith spent the next few days going from ceremony to ceremony—an honorary degree at the Sorbonne, a reception at the Hôtel de Ville—with no opportunity for him to do more than spout glittering generalities.

During the next week, House arranged for Wilson to meet Clemenceau twice. The first time was mere friendly chitchat, which House found encouraging. The second time, Wilson broached the idea that had become the centerpiece of his peace program, a league of nations. The French premier was polite but extremely skeptical. He doubted whether a league could be formed or whether it would be workable. A meeting with the Italian premier, Vittorio Orlando, proved equally frustrating. He declined to relinquish an iota of the territory Italy had wangled in the secret 1915 Treaty of London, no matter what the Fourteen Points said about self-determination.[21]

The French tried to fill Wilson's days with visits to battlefields. They wanted him to see firsthand the damage the Germans had done to France and Belgium. He resisted the idea, claiming that he did not need to view the havoc to become convinced that the peace treaty should provide "just punishments" for the enemy's depredations. He became more than a little angry when the French declined to be satisfied with these assurances. Paris newspapers began asking why Wilson refused these invitations. The president finally yielded and made a hurried trip to Rheims, where he committed an unforgivable (to the French) faux pas. He remarked that the famous cathedral was not as badly damaged as he had been led to believe.

On Joe Tumulty's advice, the president and his wife saw another side of the war firsthand. They visited French and American hospitals in Paris. Wilson was visibly shaken by some of the wounded men he saw there—many were blinded, more than a few were amputees. He had sent these young men to the Western Front to give him a seat at the peace table. The president absolutely refused to have his picture taken with them. There was a limit to how much political capital his conscience permitted him to make of their fate.

To his mounting frustration, Wilson next learned that the peace conference had been postponed until January 18, 1919. At the Murat Palace, most of his days were devoted to receiving delegations from distant parts of Europe, all seeking his help to win the right of self-determination in the new world order he had promised. Aboard the *George Washington,* Secretary of State Lansing had confided to his diary the growing conviction that this idea was the worst of Wilson's Fourteen Points: "The phrase is simply loaded with dynamite!"

In Paris, the same realization began to dawn on Wilson. The idea had opened a political Pandora's box that would be difficult if not impossible to close. Albanian warlords, tribal chieftains from obscure valleys in the Caucasus and Carpathian mountains, would-be politicians from Armenia, the Ukraine and Bessarabia appeared at the gates of the Murat Palace seeking redress and recognition. Among the more exotic was a delegation from the mountains of northern Austria. They spoke Polish and did not want to be part of the new nation of Czechoslovakia. Would the great "Voodrow Veelson" please solve their problem?[22]

Partly to escape this ordeal, Wilson decided to make ceremonial visits to Great Britain and Italy. He had planned to visit both countries at some point in his European sojourn. Why not now, when a warm reception would, he hoped, enhance his political potency at the peace conference?

Wilson's welcome in London was not as emotional as Paris. But it was hardly tepid. "Two Million Londoners Give Wilson the Reception of His Life," boomed Northcliffe's *Daily Mail*. The president's talks with Lloyd George and other British leaders were not nearly as warm. The fevered enthusiasm of the masses did not change the statesmen's minds about Wilson. Mourning almost a million dead men, the British leaders remembered the president saying he was "too proud to fight" after the sinking of the *Lusitania* and calling for peace without victory—an idea the election results in both England and the United States had just repudiated.

Wilson's remarks in his several speeches reflected this underlying tension. "I have conversed with the soldiers," he said in one speech. "They fought to do away with an older order and to establish a new one." He was neglecting "imperative tasks" at home to lend his support to the creation of this new order, which was the "great, may I not say, final task of humanity."[23]

Wilson was telling the British that American intervention had won the war and he was now in charge of reordering the world. Very few prominent Britons were prepared to swallow this claim without gulping hard. They compared Pershing's floundering in the Argonne to the rapid advances Haig's soldiers had made in the closing weeks of the war. Already taking shape was the fixed opinion that the British, not the Americans, had won the war.

Wilson compounded this alienation by suggesting that his new order might well require considerable changes in the British empire. In a talk with Lloyd George, he emphatically insisted that Germany's colonies should not be handed over to the winners. Instead, they should be placed under the supervision of the League of Nations, as trusteeships or "mandates" destined for eventual independence. He also opposed punitive reparations against Germany, the issue on which Lloyd George had just won a huge election victory. When Lloyd George reported all this to his Tory-packed cabinet, consternation and outrage were the order of the day.

Years later, in his memoirs, David Lloyd George recalled Wilson's appearance at a royal banquet in his honor at Buckingham Palace. The hosts were wearing "resplendent uniforms of every cut and color." It was a holdover from the nineteenth century's love of pageantry. The president walked in, "clad in an ordinary black suit without a medal to adorn his breast." To Lloyd George and others, it was the second coming of Oliver Cromwell.

At the banquet, the king greeted the president with warm words of friendship. Wilson replied, Lloyd George said, "with the perfect enunciation, measured emphasis and cold tones with which I was to become so familiar in the coming months. There was no glow of friendship or of gladness at meeting men who had been partners in a common enterprise and had so marvelously escaped a common danger." In his remarks, Wilson did not say a word about the sacrifices the British had made in the four long, bitter years of the Great War.[24]

In a private talk at Buckingham Palace, Wilson told King George V that Americans were neither cousins nor brothers, and he wished the king would not use these expressions. He also advised His Majesty not to refer to Americans as Anglo-Saxons. The term could "no longer be applied to the people of the United States." Nor was there any special importance to sharing the same language. There were only two things that could "establish and maintain closer relations" between the two countries: "community of ideals and of interests."[25]

Afterward King George told his private secretary, "I could not bear him. An entirely cold academical professor—an odious man."[26]

VI

While Wilson was making political waves in England, heavier weather was brewing in France. Premier Georges Clemenceau decided he needed a vote of confidence from the Chamber of Deputies. Were the Radical Socialists and other followers of Joseph Caillaux still interested in a peace of reconciliation with Germany? Caillaux remained in jail, but in August 1918, when Germany's imminent collapse was far from visible, the French senate had tried his right-hand man, Louis Malvy. Ignoring reams of evidence that Malvy had been collaborating with German agents, the senators let the former interior minister off with a small fine and a sentence of five years' exile in Spain. A band of cheering Radical Socialists had escorted him to the railroad station, where they asked him what he planned to do in Spain. "Wait!" Malvy said.

After calling for a debate on France's posture in the peace conference, Clemenceau did not say a word for five days, while arguments raged around him. He sat at his desk, taking occasional notes, and mostly scowling at the speakers. Finally, after the differences between liberals and conservatives had been thoroughly aired, he rose and gave one of his most ferocious speeches. Calling on the deputies to support the toughest possible terms with Germany, he appealed to their patriotism and hunger for vengeance. He won overwhelming support—almost a 4 to 1 majority.

Especially disturbing was Clemenceau's declaration that France should rely on the old system of a balance of power to keep a revived Germany at bay. Alliances were far more dependable than the *noble candeur* of President Wilson. In French, *candeur* means both "simplicity" and "naïveté."

An agitated Colonel House informed his diary that Clemenceau's victory—and comment—were "about as bad an augury for the success of progressive principles at the Peace Conference as we could have." He gloomily noted that it came "on the heels of the English elections." If the congressional elections in the United States were added to the picture, "the situation strategically could not be worse." House thought Wilson's only hope was to remind the Allies that they had agreed on the Fourteen Points before they signed the armistice. By now House undoubtedly knew that this acceptance had been mere lip service to pry the guns out of the Germans' hands. Clinging to it only underscored his growing anxiety.[27]

VII

On Armistice Day, Wilson had gone before Congress to announce the good news of the war's cessation and the approach of a peace of "disinterested justice." He pointed to the way the victorious governments were displaying their "humane temper" by a unanimous resolution in the Supreme War Council to supply the people of Germany and Austria-Hungary with food and fuel to relieve "the distressing want that is in so many places threatening their very lives."[28]

In the preliminary talks about the Fourteen Points, House had already pushed the importance of feeding a starved German population. But he had been unable to alter the British determination to maintain the blockade. House's solution was an urgent cable to Woodrow Wilson, asking him to send Herbert Hoover, the savior of starving Belgium, to Paris as soon as possible to take charge of the problem.

Few people knew that Hoover had spent as much time arguing with the British as with the Germans about getting food to the Belgians. The "poor little Belgium" of British propaganda meant little to the British admirals and bureaucrats who were sure the Germans would make off with the victuals. First Lord of the Admiralty Winston Churchill, who favored letting the Belgians starve and blaming the Germans, called Hoover "a son of a bitch." Hoover responded by calling the admiralty "the sanctuary of British militarists."[29]

Hoover was proud of his achievement in Belgium and instantly accepted the challenge of feeding the defeated enemy—and the rest of Europe, which was almost as hungry. Before he departed, he arranged for the shipment of 250,000 tons of foodstuffs to various European harbors. On the day he sailed, Hoover issued a statement from shipboard, calling for a relaxation of the "watertight blockade." He warned that otherwise, anarchy would reign and there would be no government to make peace with and no one to pay for the damage done to Belgium and France.[30]

The exhortation and Hoover's unilateral shipment of food had zero impact. When Hoover got to London, one of the top people in the British Food Ministry told him to stop making public statements about the blockade. The British government was opposed to lifting it "until the Germans learn a few things." Not quite able to believe what he had heard, Hoover watched numbly as Lloyd George waged his "make the Hun pay" election campaign. In London's newspapers, stories about German hunger were headed "Feeding the Beast" and "Germany Whines—Limits of Endurance Reached." Worsening matters was a British decision to forbid the German Baltic fishing fleet to catch so much as a herring, depriving the enemy of a source of food they had depended on throughout the war. This extension of the blockade began the day the armistice was signed. Heretofore, the British navy had had no access to the Baltic Sea.[31]

From London, Hoover sent an assistant into Germany to obtain a thorough report of the country's situation. He brought back a study by the German National Health Office, describing a nation on the brink of mass starvation. To verify this portrait, Hoover sent a three-man team of

American experts, who brought back even more dolorous facts. Most Germans were suffering from chronic malnutrition. The grain harvest, normally 30 million tons, had fallen to 16 million because of bad weather and lack of hands to harvest it. In north Germany, eight hundred adults were dying of starvation every day.[32]

Hoover reported the situation to Wilson, still in Washington, and the president ordered House to present a plan to the Allied governments, making Hoover director general of relief with the authority to lift the blockade and get food into Germany without delay. The Allies' reaction was coldly negative. With almost incredible meanness, they accused Hoover of shipping food from the United States because American cold-storage warehouses were overcrowded with a surplus of pork and dairy products. They turned thumbs down on a Wilson proposal to put Germany's merchant marine at Hoover's disposal to ship more food, because the Allies wanted to seize the ships for their merchant fleets. They also balked at the idea that Hoover should run the emergency food program. At a London meeting between Lloyd George, Clemenceau and Orlando, they announced plans to "investigate" how much food Germany needed—and how much reparations it could pay, a chilling linkage. Significantly, Hoover was not invited to the meeting.

Giving up on the British, Hoover moved his operation to Paris in mid-December. By that time, Wilson had received his tumultuous welcome in the City of Light. But Hoover found the atmosphere "miasmic" when it came to getting food into Germany. "The wolf," Hoover cried, "is at the door of the world." Clemenceau's reply was a vicious wisecrack: "There are twenty million Germans too many."[33]

The French, led by their vengeful premier, became even more intransigent than the British. They joined the Belgians in announcing the discovery that Germany had $570 million in gold in its Berlin vaults. When the armistice agreement was renewed on December 13, the gold was the only topic discussed. The commissioners added an amendment prohibiting Germany from disposing of this hard money for food or anything else, to make sure it was available for reparations. As for food, the commissioners simply rubber-stamped Article 26 of the agreement, stating that victuals would be provided "as shall be found necessary" and did nothing.

The day after Wilson reached Paris, House told him of Hoover's problems. The president contacted Lloyd George, Clemenceau and Orlando, and all three immediately agreed to approve Hoover as the director of an Allied food program. When Hoover went to British officials with his new authority, they stonewalled and proposed an inter-Allied committee to run things. Nevertheless, Hoover managed to wangle an agreement to permit food to be shipped to neutral countries around Germany, such as Denmark and the Netherlands, where it could be traded for German commodities.

Next Hoover asked Admiral William Benson, the courtly, white-mustached chief of U.S. naval operations, to persuade the British to lift the Baltic blockade against the German fishing fleet. Benson was the Americans' senior naval adviser at the peace conference. He got nowhere. Surly British Admiral Edward Browning, president of the Allied Naval Armistice Commission, had only one idea in his head: Make the Huns squirm and plead. Then came stunning news from London: Officials of the British, French and Italian governments had revoked permission to ship food to neutral countries. The blockade remained in wartime force.

These same officials canceled orders for 200 million pounds of American bacon, already cured and ready for shipment to England. Also deep-sixed were contracts for 100 million bushels of wheat and hefty orders of beef, pork and dairy products. This was a neat way of saying "Drop dead" to the Americans, who were stuck with the surpluses. It also meant the Allies would be able to claim they had no food to spare for Germany.[34]

Hoover was a Quaker, but he cast aside meekness when he saw people doing unspeakable things. He paid a visit to Admiral Benson and asked him "if the Allies had any right to stop ships flying the American flag and carrying food to people dying of starvation."

"Not as long there is a ship left in our fleet," Benson replied. Like many American navy men, he was thoroughly sick of condescending British admirals and delighted to have an excuse to tell them off.

Benson soon informed Hoover that the British had dropped their objection to shipping food to neutral nations. The director of relief next convened a meeting with diplomats from France and Italy and talked them out of canceling their food contracts. They had done it under British pressure, and their people needed the food. But these victories were all but destroyed by a British-French counterattack. The Allied Blockade Committee forbade any sale of forthcoming American food to Germany from the neutral countries. Hoover stubbornly shipped the food anyway and stored it in Copenhagen and other cities. Soon neutral warehouses were bulging with $550 million worth of fats, wheat, pork and other products—and Hoover began to worry about a financial disaster that would rebound on American farmers.[35]

After more wrangling, Hoover became head of a compromise organization, the Supreme Council of Supply and Relief, with representatives from all the Allied governments. At their first meeting on January 11, 1919, the delegates informed Hoover that not a pat of butter or a peck of wheat would go to Germany until it surrendered its merchant fleet. They claimed this was necessary to alleviate a world shipping shortage, caused by the depredations of the U-boats. In fact, there was no shortage. By this time, shipbuilding efforts by the British and Americans had replaced 90 percent of the tonnage the U-boats had sent to Davy Jones's locker. What the Allies wanted was the German merchant fleet, which had been omitted from the armistice accords.[36]

Two days later, Wilson, Lloyd George, Clemenceau and Orlando took up the problem of getting food to Germany. The French again insisted Germany could not pay for any food from its gold supply, and Belgium backed them up, once more underscoring its Paris satellite status. The desperate Germans were willing to surrender their merchant marine if they could get a guarantee of some food. But the French ban on paying for it in gold made any and all shipments impossible. The Germans could not raise money by selling goods in foreign markets from their factories. The Armistice Commission had banned German exports. For the next two months, this impasse continued, while tens of thousands of men, women and children succumbed to malnutrition and starvation in Germany and Austria.[37]

A member of Hoover's mission sent back the following description of German children in one city: "You think this is a kindergarten for the little ones. No, these are children of seven and eight years. Tiny faces with large dull eyes, overshadowed by huge puffed rickety foreheads, their small arms just skin and bones, and above the crooked legs with their dislocated joints, the swollen stomachs of the hunger edema."[38]

This was a long way from the "humane peace" that Woodrow Wilson had promised Congress he would deliver in his mission to Europe. Wilson—and the rest of the American delegation—were finding out that cheers on the Champs Élysée and in Trafalgar Square did not translate into political power.

VIII

On January 1, in a royal train provided by the Italian government, Wilson and his wife headed for Rome. As the train wound through the snow-covered Alps, the monks of Saint Bernard's Abbey were forced to slaughter six of their famous rescue dogs because they had run out of food. Oblivious to such details, the president reveled in the adoration of the Italian people. His arrival in the Eternal City was a replay of his reception in Paris. Masses of Romans chanted, "Viva Wilson, god of peace." Low-flying planes dropped flowers on his triumphal procession. There were pictures of him in every shop window. The streets were sprinkled with golden sand, a tradition that went back to ancient Rome's days of imperial glory.

Prime Minister Vittorio Orlando and his fellow politicians already viewed Wilson with not a little anxiety. The president still objected to their attempt to claim the Dalmatian coast and other territories promised them in the 1915 Treaty of London. Lately they had been claiming the city of Fiume and portions of the new defunct Turkish empire in the Middle East. One of the most outspoken proponents of this view was an editor named Benito Mussolini, whose Milan newspaper proclaimed on January 1, 1919, that "imperialism is the eternal, the immutable law of life."

The Italian government tried to keep Wilson busy at state dinners and similar ceremonies. No speeches to the people were on his schedule. In the midst of these official rituals, Orlando's government suddenly informed the president that famous visitors to Rome normally made a gift of $10,000 to the poor. An embarrassed Wilson protested that the U.S. Congress had not authorized such an outlay and he personally could not afford it. This bit of theater was patently designed to make the president look bad.

Only after strenuous insistence did Wilson manage to meet the socialist leader Leonida Bissolati. The day before Wilson arrived, Bissolati had resigned to protest the government's greedy determination to seize the territory promised Italy in the Treaty of London. He told the president, "The Italian people are the most Wilsonian in Europe, the most adapted to your ideals." The interview created a sensation. At a reception in the American embassy, a pumped-up Wilson took a jab at Italy's leader. He remarked that New York had become the biggest Italian city in the world, thanks to recent immigration. Was Orlando going to claim that, too?

On January 4, Wilson visited his erstwhile peace-terms adversary, Pope Benedict XV. As if to emphasize his own faith in liberalism, the president preceded his audience with a visit to the monument of the man whose leadership had created the Italian republic, Giuseppi Garibaldi. Thereafter Wilson's route to the Vatican became another triumphal procession. Arriving a half-hour late, the president spent twenty minutes with the pontiff, talking of nothing but the League of Nations. The pope gave the idea his blessing.

Later that day, from his balcony in the Quirinal Palace, Wilson planned to give a speech to the people of Rome, urging them to abandon Orlando's territorial ambitions. To Wilson's dismay, the plaza abutting his residence remained devoid of people. Troops had cordoned it off, leaving Wilson without an audience. The president made some intemperate remarks to the press and left Rome at nine o'clock that evening in an exceedingly foul mood.[39]

In northern Italy, on his way back to Paris, Wilson's popular reception was equally hysterical. He was hailed as "the Savior of Humanity" and "the Moses from Across the Atlantic." In many homes, families lit candles before his picture, an honor hitherto reserved for saints. Before a huge crowd in Milan, he delivered a bluntly radical speech, in which he proclaimed the superiority of the working classes. They were the foundation of all societies, and they were establishing "a world opinion" in favor of a league of nations and the abandonment of the old system of military alliances and imperialistic greed for territory.

This was not a message Premier Vittorio Orlando was inclined to applaud. It did not seem to occur to Wilson or his advisers that making critical speeches to enthusiastic crowds was unlikely to endear him to the politicians whom he would soon meet at the peace conference.

IX

In the United States, after forty-four days of medical treatment, Theodore Roosevelt had left the hospital and was back at his Sagamore Hill mansion, overlooking Oyster Bay. He was still a sick man; bouts of inflammatory rheumatism hampered the use of his left arm. Mysterious fevers, left over from his almost fatal exploration of Paraguay's River of Doubt in 1914, weakened him. Quentin's death still depressed him. But he was by no means ready to abandon politics. As he was leaving the hospital, a worried doctor tried to hold his arm to make sure he did not fall. "Don't do that," TR snapped, brushing the helping hand away. "I am not sick and it will give the wrong impression."[40]

In the hospital, he had written out a progressive platform for a presidential campaign. It would be his last fight, he told his sister Corinne. There was not much doubt in the Republican party that the 1920 nomination was his for the asking. Will Hays, the party chairman, was 100 percent behind his candidacy. A Midwestern Republican leader remarked to a GOP big-city boss that Roosevelt would be nominated by acclamation. "Acclamation, hell," the boss said. "We're going to nominate him by assault!"[41]

TR was still grimly and vociferously opposed to Woodrow Wilson and all his works. In a recent article, he had called the Fourteen Points "fourteen scraps of paper." He told a visiting Henry Cabot Lodge he would like to be left alone in a room with "our great and good president" for about fifteen minutes. Then he would "cheerfully be hung."[42]

On the last day of the old year, the government's citation honoring Quentin's death arrived. That same day, newspapers carried an account by the German flier who had shot him down. Both spread wisps of gloom through Sagamore Hill. For the next few days, Roosevelt spent most of his time upstairs on a sofa, gazing mournfully at wintry Oyster Bay. His wife wrote their son Kermit that he was in constant pain. On January 5, a wan Flora Payne Whitney came for a visit. She had been spending much of her time with the Roosevelts. TR had told her he hoped she would find happiness with "another good and fine man," but she remained devastated by Quentin's death.

The doctors had assured the former president he was going to recover but it would take time. TR promised he would be patient and tried to get some work done. On January 5, he seemed on the way to resuming a normal schedule. He dictated a letter to Kermit and saw several visitors. He read the proofs of a magazine article and worked on an editorial for the *Kansas City Star*, in which he found more fault with Wilson's ideas about a league of nations. TR favored forming a limited league with the victorious Allies. At the peace table, the United States should make sure "real justice is done" by demanding "the sternest reparation" from Germany. Only after this just peace was achieved might it be possible to admit other countries into the league.[43]

Relaxing on a sofa after dinner, TR seemed contented until he suddenly called his wife to his side. He said he had just felt a strange sensation: A great, shadowy hand seemed to be seizing his body, crushing breath out of his lungs. His wife summoned a doctor, who could find nothing wrong. About midnight, TR's former White House valet, James Amos, helped him upstairs to his bedroom and dozed in a corner chair while the sick man went to sleep.

At about 4 A.M., Amos was awakened by a strange rattling noise. It was TR; something was very wrong with his breathing. The valet rushed to awaken Mrs. Roosevelt and TR's nurse. By the time they reached the bedroom, Theodore Roosevelt was dead of a pulmonary embolism at the age of sixty-one.[44]

Woodrow Wilson heard the news in the railroad station of Modena, Italy, on his way back to Paris. Two reporters on the platform watched him as he unfolded the telegram. His first reaction was shock; next came a smile of "transcendent triumph." The Republicans had no one of Roosevelt's stature to oppose the peace treaty that Wilson, having drunk the adulation of Paris, London and Rome, was now sure he could impose on Europe and the United States.[45]

X

While Wilson was feasting on worshipful applause in Italy, Germany was confronting a Bolshevik onslaught. Soldiers and People's Councils had taken over many cities. Berlin remained unconquered, but it was teetering on the brink. Demonstrations, strikes and armed mobs were everywhere. Behind most of the demonstrations was the Spartacus Union, a radical group that found inspiration in the story of the gladiator Spartacus, leader of a revolt against Rome in 73 B.C. The Spartacists were led by Karl Liebknecht, son of a founder of the German Socialist Party, and Rosa Luxemburg, a brilliant Polish activist. Behind them was the Bolshevik leader Vladimir Lenin, who shipped them gold from Russia's treasury and ordered them to turn Germany into a Soviet satellite.

The new German chancellor, Socialist leader Friedrich Ebert, felt more and more helpless. He saw control of the capital and the rest of the country slipping away from him. As his panic mounted, Ebert made a fateful decision. Not long after the armistice, he had received a call from General Wilhelm Groener, the man who had replaced Quartermaster General Ludendorff, asking if he wanted or needed the army's support. Ebert gratefully accepted the offer. Other Socialists angrily criticized his decision. They called for dismantling the army and replacing it with a democratic militia that would elect its own officers.

Ebert dithered and at first agreed to let them try to arm workers. They turned out to be useless soldiers. Public disorder increased exponentially, and an emboldened Karl Liebknecht decided the capital was ready for revolution. (Rosa Luxemburg disagreed.) On the night of January 5–6, 1919, thousands of armed leftists poured down Berlin's broad streets. They swiftly captured major buildings in the center of Berlin and prepared to take over the capital.

By this time the Spartacists had changed their names to the Communist Party, leaving no doubt about their goals. Ebert called on the army for help. Into action went thousands of demobilized veterans, recruited into new units called Free Corps. Their generals told them: "The place of the Imperial Government has been taken by that of Reichschancellor Ebert. . . . [He] needs strength for the struggle on our borders and the struggle within. . . . Plunder and disorder are everywhere. Nowhere can one find respect for law and justice, respect for personal and government property. . . . Therefore, we must intervene!"[46]

On January 10, an all-out battle erupted in the center of Berlin. The army used flamethrowers, machine guns, hand grenades, mortars and artillery to smash the Communists out of major buildings and improvised street forts. An estimated 1,000 bystanders and pedestrians were killed in the ferocious fighting, which left several buildings gutted. Hundreds of Spartacists were executed on the spot, even when they tried to surrender under white flags. Rosa Luxemburg and Karl Liebknecht were hunted down and dragged to a nearby hotel for a brief interrogation, then ordered to the Moabit Prison. En route their heads were smashed by rifle butts. Pistols added a coup de grâce. Luxemburg's body was thrown into a canal, where it rotted until the end of May. The government issued a communiqué, declaring the two revolutionaries had been shot while trying to escape.

The *New York Times* Berlin correspondent all but congratulated the Free Corps for disposing of "fomenters of robbery, murder and anarchy." A member of a special U.S. mission sent to investigate conditions in Germany wrote a more accurate epitaph for the Spartacists. They had attracted recruits because of "the serious food and economic situation, resulting in hunger, disease and unemployment . . . [and] the fact that they are in control of large sums of money principally from Russian sources."[47]

A liberal visitor to Germany, Oswald Garrison Villard, editor of *The Nation*, blamed Woodrow Wilson for Germany's descent into chaos. With a vehemence worthy of his abolitionist grandfather, William Lloyd Garrison, Villard accused the president of trying to keep secret the continuation of the blockade and the deaths of thousands of women, children and old men from starvation and malnutrition. "The godly Presbyterian from the White House . . . could not be induced to make a public stand against this indefensible cruelty to noncombatants; the screw of starvation was kept turned in order to compel the vanquished to sign whatever treaty might be drafted."[48]

A cable Wilson had sent to Washington from Rome would seem to support Villard's wrathful contention. The president asked for an appropriation of $100 million to buy food for the relief of European people "outside of Germany." In a follow-up cable, Wilson declared "food relief is now the key to the whole European situation and to the solution of peace." An appalled Robert La Follette listened as senator after senator rose, "each straining to outdo the others to make sure not a cent should go to feed a German."

"Can these Americans have forgotten Grant at Appomattox, sending rations to feed Robert E. Lee's starving army and letting the soldiers take their horses home to plow their farms?" Senator La Follette wondered. Here were grown men gloating at the prospect of "denying a starving German child something to eat." La Follette began to think that Wilson's peacemaking enterprise was a case of "the blind leading the blind," abroad and at home. The senator made a ferocious attack on Wilson's proposal, but the appropriation passed the Senate with the German exclusion intact, 53 to 18.[49]

XI

On January 18, 1919, in the gilded Salle de la Paix of the French Ministry of Foreign Affairs on the Quai d'Orsay, the Paris Peace Conference finally began. Bearded, pudgy Raymond Poincaré, the president of France, opened the first plenary session with a speech that he read in a monotone, perhaps on the assumption that only a small percentage of the room understood French. Before him, around a horseshoe-shaped table sat representatives from thirty-two Allied and associated states, representing about 75 percent of the world's population. Absent from the table were any representatives from Russia or from Germany and its allies. Russia's Bolshevik rulers had refused to come. The enemy had not been invited.[50]

Poincaré's speech, translated into English by red-bearded Paul Mantoux, had worrisome overtones for true believers in the Fourteen Points. It also revealed why the French had delayed the opening date of the peace conference. "On this day, forty-eight years ago," the French president declared, "the German Empire was proclaimed by an army of invasion in the Château at Versailles. . . . Born in injustice, it has ended in opprobrium. You are assembled to repair the evil it has done and to prevent a recurrence of it. You hold in your hands the future of the world."[51]

Poincaré was describing the event that he had made the centerpiece of his political career, the German victory in the Franco-Prussian War. He had dedicated his life to revenging this calamitous defeat, which had engraved blind hatred of Germany in his soul. He was the architect of the prewar alliances with Russia and England, which had convinced the Germans they were being encircled as a prelude to extermination.

After a moment of embarrassed silence, Woodrow Wilson rose to nominate Premier Georges Clemenceau as chairman of the peace conference. He praised the old man extravagantly. Lloyd George followed in a seconding speech that was equally effusive. With a twinkle in his eye, the prime minister called him "the Grand Young Man of France."

Clemenceau accepted the accolades with little or no emotion. His acceptance speech went to the heart of the peace conference, as he saw it. The participants' task was to decide who was responsible for the war, who should be punished for it and how much Germany should pay for the terrible depredations that had "devastated and ruined one of the richest regions of France." The premier did not so much as mention a league of nations.[52]

This was confrontational diplomacy of the most blatant kind—a veritable declaration of war on the Fourteen Points. Wilson was not entirely surprised. Since January 12, the five so-called Great Powers—England, France, Italy, the United States and Japan—had been meeting in executive sessions to discuss the issues, the structure, and the machinery of the peace conference. The president soon had no illusions about what the other major powers wanted from the conference: loot. For the time being, Wilson discounted this gritty fact. His mind remained focused on winning the conference's backing for a league of nations that would be intertwined with the peace treaty.

In these preliminary sessions and his earlier talks with the Allied leaders, Wilson worked out a rough strategy for winning support for the league. Two members of the British delegation, Lord David Cecil and Jan Christian Smuts, premier of South Africa, favored the idea. Both had even produced drafts of a possible constitution, or "covenant," as Wilson liked to call it, that were fairly close to the president's ideas. "It would be good politics to play the British game more or less in formulating the covenant," the president told Admiral Cary Grayson, who was rapidly replacing Colonel House as a confidant.

Simultaneously the British decided on an overall strategy of cooperating with Wilson as much as possible. A future alliance with the United States stood to benefit Britain far more than clinging to their ties with battered, war-devastated France. If this made Georges Clemenceau unhappy, so be it.[53]

These backstairs strategies did not come close to solving the conference's burgeoning problems. Incredibly, in spite of the swarms of experts and advisers that all the governments had brought with them—the Americans eventually had 1,300 people in Paris, and the British staff occupied five hotels—no one had produced an agenda. Even more worrisome was the growing hostility of the press. More than 500 journalists had swarmed to Paris (150 of them American) buoyed by the first of the Fourteen Points: "Open covenants of peace, openly arrived at."

Both the press and the American people assumed this meant they would have access to all the details of the peace conference. Wasn't this what the Wilson's "New Diplomacy" meant? Instead, they found themselves barred from all sessions of the Council of Ten (the Big Five and their foreign ministers), which seldom issued more than a five-sentence press release to summarize its doings. This code of silence left the reporters reduced to peering through the doors at the relatively rare plenary council sessions, where little was debated and the lesser delegates were simply asked to ratify the decisions of the major powers.

Wilson had seen open covenants as a way to ban secret treaties such as the prewar accords Foreign Secretary Grey had signed with the French and Russians and the mercenary deal the Allies had cut with the Italians in 1915. He never dreamed people would want to know about the give-and-take of negotiations between foreign ministers and leaders. But the reporters were not interested in the president's clarifications. They called the plenary sessions "washouts" and started writing about a gag rule that made a mockery of Wilson's idealistic promises. It was the old-style diplomacy in the dark all over again.

Behind the scenes, Wilson tried to improve the situation. He persuaded the British and French to stop censoring the Atlantic cable traffic. He asked Admiral Grayson to talk to reporters on his behalf. But it was too late. Alarmed cables from Joe Tumulty back in Washington reported a public-relations disaster. The president compounded the problem by refusing to meet regularly with American reporters for give-and-take press conferences. He tried it only twice, insisting in advance that everything he said was off the record. When two reporters quoted him, he was infuriated and never talked to a newsman again. The other Allied leaders met regularly with the press of their individual countries.[54]

Kansas newsman William Allen White, on his way to fame as the voice of Middle America, summed up the situation in mournful terms. "The newspapermen, for the most part eager to support the American position, were not permitted to know even semi-officially what the American position was. It is not surprising under this state of facts they began to lose confidence in American leadership."[55]

Where was George Creel while this public-relations disaster was occurring? He had been shunted to the sidelines by the astute infighting of Secretary of State Lansing and Colonel House. Lansing detested Creel because the CPI had usurped the State Department's powers and privileges in its overseas propaganda campaign. House disliked Creel's brash style and considered him ill suited to deal with European news reporters and politicians. The colonel had wanted Frank Cobb for the job. But Cobb's conviction that Wilson should not come to Europe had disqualified him.[56]

Another influential American with a negative opinion of Creel was Walter Lippmann, who considered the CPI propaganda campaign in Europe "one of the genuine calamities" of the war. "The general tone of it was one of unmitigated brag accompanied by unmitigated gullibility. . . ." It left Europeans with the impression that a "rich bumpkin had come to town with his pockets bulging."[57]

For want of something better to do, Creel volunteered to go to the newly liberated countries of the Austro-Hungarian empire. He would set up propaganda offices there, touting the Fourteen Points and the rest of the Wilsonian world vision, and distributing wireless sets that would enable people to hear CPI broadcasts. Unfortunately, Creel's performance in Prague and points east left much to be desired from a diplomatic point of view. He described himself as Wilson's secretary and made speeches in which he declared, "America is ready to give you everything." In Budapest, he proposed that the liberated nations of Austria-Hungary should form an American-style federal union, with the Hungarian president as its head. At one point, members of Creel's staff participated in a Czech invasion of the duchy of Teschen, on the border of Poland, to seize its valuable coal mines. All in all, it was a performance that convinced Wilson and the other Americans in Paris that Creel should go home as soon as possible.[58]

Meanwhile, Wilson persevered in his single-minded struggle for the League of Nations, which he saw as the eventual answer to almost every problem confronting the conference. On January 25, he went before the second plenary session and proposed the creation of a special commission to hammer out the structure of the league. Two days earlier, he had persuaded Clemenceau and Lloyd George to accept the league as an essential part of the peace treaty. Now he wanted the plenary session to confirm this decision. Wilson swiftly won the approval he sought—and surprised his colleagues on the Council of Ten by nominating himself as chairman of the commission that would draft the covenant.

Simultaneously, in the Council of Ten, the president was fighting a ferocious battle with his putative allies over the disposition of Germany's colonies. It started on January 24, with two declarations. First, the prime ministers of New Zealand and Australia announced that they wanted Samoa, New Guinea and other Pacific islands formerly controlled by Germany. Second, Jan Christian Smuts, the leader of the Union of South Africa, declared his determination to annex German West Africa, a huge colony just north of his country, now known as Zimbabwe. The three men were backed by Lloyd George, although he piously said he agreed with the U.S. president that most liberated territories should be placed under mandates. But the dominions had a right to insist on these "exceptions." The prime minister also made no objection when France announced it wanted two other German colonies in Africa, Togoland and the Cameroons.[59]

Alone, Wilson stood up to the rest of the Council of Ten, vehemently declaring that these blatant annexations showed "a fundamental lack of faith in the League of Nations." This reproach got him nowhere, because almost everyone in the room lacked this fundamental faith. For days the Allies and their advisers debated the question, while Wilson made ominous noises about their roads to peace fatally diverging. Outside the conference room, the French leaked reports of Wilson's "impracticable ideals," and Paris papers opened a ferocious attack on him. The British tried a subtler approach. They argued that the League of Nations already existed and proposed to divide the colonial spoils as mandates under its aegis.

Jan Christian Smuts proposed creating three types of mandates, labeled A, B and C. Because the C mandates were too primitive for self-government, they would be administered as if they were part of the state to which they were assigned. Lloyd George told Wilson that if he refused this compromise, he might break up the peace conference. Also doing not a little bullying was the prime minister of Australia, William "Billy" Hughes, who had taken a violent dislike to Wilson and his ideas and was fond of pointing out that Australia, with barely a tenth of America's population, had suffered more casualties in the war.

Wilson capitulated, agreeing to let a League of Nations commission decide the disposition of the spoils. In the first week of its deliberations, the peace conference thus undermined the principle of no more annexations, as well as the principle of self-determination. No wonder the watching Germans grew cynical. The Berlin newspaper *Vorwärts* remarked on Wilson's impotence: "It appears more and more as if . . . the Western imperialists [intend] to leave to Mr. Wilson the merely musical declamatory roles of the performance and to reserve to themselves the business end of the show."[60]

XII

A byproduct of the British elections was a political revolution in Ireland. Before the war, most Irish voters had backed the moderate leader John Redmond, who called for home rule for Ireland, on the theory that it would lead gradually to independence. This seemed far more reasonable than a military revolt against the immensely more powerful British crown. But the 1916 Easter Rebellion and the British execution of its leaders destroyed that patient mind-set. In the 1918 elections, a new party, Sinn Féin ("Ourselves Alone" in Irish Gaelic) had swept the field, winning 73 of the 105 seats in England's Parliament.

The Sinn Féin candidates boycotted the British Parliament. Instead, they set up the Dáil Éireann (Assembly of Ireland) and on January 21, 1919, issued a declaration of independence that proclaimed themselves representatives of the "ancient Irish people in National Parliament Assembled." Only 27 of the 73 Sinn Féin members of Parliament were present for the ceremony; the rest were already in British jails for various kinds of civil disobedience. The Dáil appointed three delegates to the peace conference to plead Ireland's cause. Two of the three were in jail. The whole performance seemed closer to playacting than political reality.

On the same day that the Dáil declared Ireland independent, masked men murdered two members of the Royal Irish Constabulary in County Tipperary. The British reacted with the same ineptitude that had characterized their relations with Ireland for the past four hundred years. They rushed in troops and set up what amounted to military governments in every Irish city. They forbade anyone to leave home after 7 P.M. without a permit. Mail was censored, and a virtual state of siege became the order of the day—and night. This rumbling Celtic volcano added up to future trouble for Woodrow Wilson.

XIII

Isolated in the Murat Palace with his adoring wife and his worshipful physician, Admiral Cary Grayson, Wilson was able to convince himself all over again that the League of Nations would right his collapse on the mandates and all other wrongs on the horizon of the peace conference. Ignoring the growing doubts of Secretary of State Lansing, who was never a league enthusiast, Wilson flung himself into a day-and-night effort to draft the covenant.

It was an exhausting business. The league commission's nineteen delegates met in Colonel House's suite at the Hôtel Crillon after Wilson's daylong sessions with the Council of Ten, and often worked until after midnight. They were toiling under the double pressure of the desire of the rest of the peace conference to get to the business of the treaty and a deadline Wilson had imposed—a February 14 departure for a visit to the United States to sign essential appropriation bills and address Congress before it adjourned.

The League of Nations Commission met only ten times in fourteen days, working at night, to write a constitution for the world. One historian has compared this limited time and effort with the twelve intense weeks the delegates of 1787 spent creating the Constitution of the United States.[61] However, Wilson and his group had the advantage of previous drafts of the covenant by House, the president and the British. In fact, Wilson had spent a large part of his time since he arrived in Europe thinking and talking about the league.

Thanks to this head start, the president was able to take charge of the meetings and get his way on many things. He discarded the British idea of creating an executive council of the great powers and insisted on adding some smaller nations to this part of the league's structure (although the major powers remained permanent members of the council). He was able to insist on an article guaranteeing the territorial integrity of all the league's members. Next came a severe struggle with the French, who wanted the league to have an international army to enforce its decisions. Wilson called this proposal "international militarism" and instead relied on the league's provisions for arbitration of disputes and the use of sanctions against offending states. Military action by a concert of the member states' armed forces would be considered only as a last resort.

The French finally accepted this decision with repeated grumbles. A Clemenceau attempt to make the preamble of the covenant an indictment of Germany's conduct in the Great War was voted down. The infuriated French were on the brink of walking out on the commission and sabotaging the league. They were intimidated into a last-minute submission by a blunt British threat to side with the United States and leave them "without an ally in the world."[62]

Finally came a proposal by Japan, whose delegation sat mute most of the time, letting the Westerners do the talking. The Japanese spokesman pointed out that there had been much debate about the equality of nations in the league, whether they were large or small. He hoped the league would add an amendment declaring the equality of all the planet's races. Wilson and House, in preliminary discussions, had approved the idea. But here the British abruptly deserted the Anglo-American alliance. They were not about to tell the tens of millions of Indians, Africans, Burmese, Egyptians, Malayans and other nonwhites in their global empire that they were equal to Englishmen. Foreign Secretary Balfour dismissed the proposition as an eighteenth-century idea. Premier Billy Hughes bellowed he would get the first ship back to Australia if this notion passed.

Wilson let them get away with it. When the Japanese delegate tried to bolster Tokyo's argument by pointing to a Wilson article affirming religious equality, the president sat mute while the British said both racial equality and religious equality should be discarded. Rarely did the gulf between the heirs of the revolutionaries of 1776 and the imperialist descendants of George III yawn so starkly. But Wilson, in his eagerness to get the form of the league adopted, allowed the contradiction to go unchallenged.[63]

These compromises were all done in a frantic rush because Wilson was scheduled to depart for the United States the following day. Also, Wilson had grown disenchanted with the Japanese for their behavior in Siberia and their eagerness to snap up parts of China and numerous Pacific islands. Racial prejudice undoubtedly played a role here. The president who had increased segregation in the federal government was quick to find reasons for disliking people of different skin color. Even though the Japanese were only imitating the white imperialists.

Many Wilson biographers and several historians call the next day, February 14, the high point of Wilson's life. He presented the completed covenant to the plenary council of the peace conference and asked the delegates to adopt it as an integral part of the forthcoming treaty. He saw himself leading the entire world to a new spiritual level, a global incarnation of American idealism. But he was a very tired man. His words did not come close to matching his vision, nor did the text of the league, which had not a single soaring phrase to remind listeners of the Declaration of Independence or the Gettysburg Address. It had been written in haste and showed it.

While rain poured from a gray sky, Wilson read the document word for word to the assembled delegates and followed it with a brief speech, in which he called the league "not a straitjacket but a vehicle of life." He praised some of the features he professed to like best, such as the mandate system, ignoring his recent surrender, which would soon strip the idea of moral meaning. After telling the Japanese that their plea for racial equality was unwelcome, Wilson proclaimed the birth of a single human family: "We are all brothers and have a common human purpose." The ambivalence underlying these words may have had something to do with William

Allen White's appraisal of Wilson's performance. The Kansan thought his "spoken words were as grey and drab and soggy as his reading."[64]

XIV

During these last frantic days before he returned to the United States, Wilson played a major role in another attempt to resolve the Russian problem. In late January, the president issued a statement urging the Bolsheviks and their White Russian enemies to confer with representatives of the peace conference about an end to their civil war. As a meeting place, the president proposed the island of Prinkipo in the Sea of Marmara. The offer made front-page headlines in the United States. "Allies Adopt Wilson Plan to Aid Russians; Recognize Revolution," shouted the *Washington Post*. The paper reported that General Pershing was likely to be the American representative at the conference.[65]

As usual, the newspapers got only half the story. The idea originated with Lloyd George, whose conservative parliamentary supporters were having nightmares about the Bolsheviks taking over Russia. Wilson volunteered to issue a statement that would, they hoped, at least halt the civil war and perhaps lay the groundwork for an agreement that would divide Russia into White and Red spheres.

The Russian Revolution stirred strong emotions in Wilson's soul. It reminded him of the dolorous failure of his attempt to control the Mexican Revolution. He took a similar approach in his pronunciamento to the Bolsheviks.

His statement breathed disinterested idealism. It called for a cease-fire, the removal of internal economic barriers, a general election and some "adequate" arrangement for the repayment of Russia's large debts to France and England.

Wilson was ignoring the vicious names the Bolsheviks had called him. He was playing one of his favorite games: defender of the poor against the forces of "privilege." He was hoping the Bolsheviks would join the Americans in this noble crusade and align themselves with him at the peace conference. It was a hope that only proved the president's ignorance of the Bolshevik mind.

Behind Wilson's back, Secretary of State Lansing cabled the State Department that nothing was likely to come of Wilson's invitation. It had been issued only because Allied military intervention in Russia was failing. Also behind Wilson's back, the French encouraged the White Russians, whom they were supporting with guns and money, to spurn the proposal. The Bolsheviks flung some new insults and declined to agree on a truce. It soon became clear that this dove of peace was dead on arrival. No further appeals for peace in Russia were forthcoming from Woodrow Wilson.

At seven o'clock on Wilson's last day in Paris, Winston Churchill, now minister of war in Lloyd George's cabinet, made a dramatic appearance at the Council of Ten. In his most pungent style, Churchill said the Bolsheviks were winning the civil war. He portrayed Lenin and his followers as an enormous menace to the future peace and stability of Europe and the world. Now or never was the time to stamp out this political disease. Churchill called for an Allied army to invade Russia without delay, crush the Bolsheviks and restore Russia to the comity of nations.

Lloyd George was adroitly absent on supposed political business in London. Although he had opposed Churchill's proposal in the British cabinet, in one of his classic flip-flops the prime minister sent him to Paris in the hope that he might galvanize Wilson into some sort of solution to the Russian nightmare. Clemenceau, who had no liberal illusions about the Bolsheviks, wholeheartedly backed Churchill's plea.

Wilson flatly opposed a military solution. He favored the swift withdrawal of the Allied troops from northern Russia and Siberia. He talked about the need for more information, which was, from his point of view, the main purpose of the Prinkipo proposal. Beside him, Secretary of State Lansing seethed over the thought of even talking to the murderers of Czar Nicholas and his family. Churchill bluntly asked if Wilson was at least willing to spend serious money to arm the White Russians. The president halfheartedly said he might go along if the rest of the council voted in favor of the idea. Whereupon he headed for the *George Washington,* leaving Colonel House in charge of further negotiations.

Talks between Colonel House and anti-interventionists in the British delegation soon torpedoed Churchill's call for action, leaving Clemenceau isolated. From midocean, Wilson approved by wire: "It would be fatal to be led further into the present chaos." Without U.S. support, the bankrupt British and French could do little but fritter around the edges of the Russian upheaval.[66]

XV

On February 23, 1919, the *George Washington,* bearing President Wilson and his party, and several thousand returning doughboys, approached the New England coast. It had been a turbulent voyage. Heavy seas had forced the naval escort to abandon the big liner. Now the ship was groping toward Boston in a heavy fog. Wilson was landing in the capital of New England at Joe Tumulty's suggestion. It was a gesture of defiance to Henry Cabot Lodge. Tumulty had been buoyed by the positive editorial reaction to the draft covenant of the League of Nations, which had been published in American newspapers on February 15, the day after Wilson presented it in Paris.[67]

Wilson was not completely convinced that this foray to Boston was a good move. In Paris, he had received some very different advice from Colonel House. His alter ego had persuaded him to send a telegram to the Senate Foreign Relations Committee and the House Foreign Affairs Committee, asking them not to comment on the league until he had a chance to discuss it with them. The president had invited them all to dinner at the White House on February 26. House had convinced Wilson that this intimate conclave was preferable to introducing the covenant in a speech to both houses of Congress. The colonel felt that the legislators had grown weary of Wilson's lecturing them.

In an exchange of cables with Tumulty while Wilson was at sea, the president had wondered if it would be better to land in Boston and go directly to the train station, where he would make only a few friendly remarks. But Tumulty, his Irish up, had plunged ahead and planned a huge reception. He had invited the governors of all the New England states and persuaded the Democratic mayor of Boston to close the schools for the day. Many businesses followed suit with a day off for their employees.

Congress's reaction to the news that Wilson was planning to make a speech in Boston before meeting with them was ferociously negative. Republican Senators Borah of Idaho and Poindexter of Washington and Democrat James Reed of Missouri unleashed devastating attacks on the League of Nations, calling it a capitulation to British imperialism. They claimed the article on territorial integrity guaranteed the current British empire until the end of time. They excoriated the provision that allotted each of Britain's five dominions a vote in the league's assembly, giving

London six votes to Washington's one. Reed's attack brought the Senate and the galleries to their feet in a wild ovation.[68]

In midocean, the president had received a cable informing him that Premier Clemenceau had been shot by a French anarchist, who had resolved to kill any man who was likely to start another war. The grand old man was recovering from a wound that left a bullet near his lung. A few days later, similar violence erupted in Munich. The German Socialist leader Kurt Eisner had been killed instantly by a right-wing assassin. The deed had plunged the city into a wave of counter-assassinations by left-wing zealots.

These graphic warnings of a Europe in turmoil were echoed by news of similar violence in the United States. Labor unions, infuriated by rising prices and heavy layoffs as industry adjusted to a peacetime economy, were in an ugly mood. In Seattle, stronghold of the Industrial Workers of the World, unions called a general strike. Many people thought it was a step toward a Bolshevik takeover of the United States. The mayor of Seattle, Ole Hanson, asked Secretary Baker for federal troops, and within hours, khaki-clad riflemen were pouring into the city. They pointed to handbills that reminded workers "Russia Did It!" to prove the strike was a Bolshevik plot. Mayor Hanson's defiance made him a national hero. Elsewhere, the American Protective League and other vigilante groups that had spent the war years persecuting German-Americans and dissenters began hunting Bolsheviks.[69]

The threat of violence created massive anxiety as Wilson came ashore in Boston. Troops and police lined the streets; riflemen manned the rooftops. The crowd of 200,000 was wildly enthusiastic, screaming like Romans or Parisians as Wilson's procession of automobiles wound through the narrow streets to the Copley Plaza Hotel for lunch. From there he headed for Mechanics Hall, where 8,000 selected Bostonians were waiting to hear him.

Wilson began with some mild remarks about how good it was to be back in the United States—and a semiapology for how long it was taking to write the peace treaty. But he soon segued to a mood of militant defiance. The key to peace was not a division of the spoils but a summons to forge a new world through the League of Nations. That was the unmistakable wish of the world's people—and the people of the United States. The president dared any politician, anywhere, to resist this surging "spirit of the age." America would not disappoint the world by rebuffing this great moral challenge. He invited critics to "test the sentiment of the nation." His "fighting blood" could barely wait to see the outcome of a contest with these "narrow, selfish, provincial" minds. The overwhelmingly Democratic audience roared its approval.[70]

The Associated Press told its millions of readers that Wilson had "thrown down the gauntlet" to his congressional enemies with these angry words. This was not the warm-up Colonel House had in mind for the crucial dinner with the foreign affairs committees in Washington, two days hence. House had urged the president to be as conciliatory as possible in Boston. Henry Cabot Lodge wrote wryly to a friend: "Mr. Wilson has asked me to dinner. [He] also asked me to say nothing. He then goes to my home town and makes a speech—very characteristic." Later he called Wilson's excursion "a piece of small cunning in which [Wilson] is fond of indulging."[71]

XVI

Two nights later, Wilson sat down to dinner with Senator Lodge and thirty-three other members of the foreign relations committees. Two senators, Borah of Idaho and Fall of New Mexico, had declined to come, declaring the meeting a waste of time. Mrs. Wilson, displaying her political limitations, sat next to Senator Lodge and chattered artlessly about the wonderful reception the president had received in Boston. After she withdrew, the senators and congressmen spent three hours with the president, questioning him about the League of Nations. Admiral Cary Grayson, who talked to Wilson shortly afterward, reported the atmosphere was "free and easy." But the good doctor failed to detect the many hostile undertones.

Lodge and Senator Philander Knox of Pennsylvania, the two men with the strongest backgrounds in foreign affairs (Knox had been President Taft's secretary of state), said little. The jittery Wilson found their silence threatening and hostile; he interpreted it as contempt. Senator Frank B. Brandegee of Connecticut, known for his explosive temper, did much of the questioning. His tone was cool and skeptical. No one said anything in defense of the league except the president, who answered questions in a conciliatory tone. He emphasized, however, that he did not see any room or reason for major changes in the covenant. That would make enormous difficulties for him because he would have to renegotiate the altered articles with the Council of Ten and resubmit them to the Plenary Council of the peace conference.

The chief issue discussed was sovereignty. Was the United States surrendering Congress's constitutional right to declare war? Would the league have the right to decide issues such as immigration to the United States? Would the league control the size of America's armed forces? Would it abrogate the Monroe Doctrine? Wilson stressed the need for trust in the good faith of the league's members and admitted that the United States—and the other nations—would all have to surrender some sovereignty in the name of world peace.

The usually pro-Wilson *New York Times* questioned many of the participants after the meeting and concluded that the president had acquitted himself well. The even more supportive *New York World* reported the same conclusion. But the following day, the hard-line Republican *New York Sun* published an interview with Senator Brandegee that conveyed a very different impression. Brandegee said his visit to the White House had made him wonder if he had been "wandering with Alice in Wonderland and had tea with the Mad Hatter." He sneered that the president had, "with the wide open eyes of an ingenue," relied on "glittering generalities" to meet the legal and constitutional questions he and other senators had raised.[72]

That same day, Henry Cabot Lodge rose in the Senate to give a speech that analyzed the articles of the league covenant, particularly Article 10, which guaranteed the territory of every member of the league. The senator called the covenant crude and loosely written. Lodge said he wanted world peace as ardently as the president. But there were vast issues involved—an abandonment of George Washington's warning against entangling alliances, the relationship of the league to the Monroe Doctrine and to the constitutional powers of Congress. Lodge called on the Senate to retain a critical attitude, to move slowly, and with profound caution, before approving Woodrow Wilson's version of the League of Nations.

That night, the president met with members of the Democratic National Committee at the White House. He seemed to think he was speaking off the record, although a government stenographer was on hand taking down every word. Wilson was supposed to be rallying his demoralized troops after their midterm election defeat. That required a discussion of domestic problems, especially the growing wrath of the labor unions and the need for issues on which to run in 1920. Instead, Wilson orated about the importance of the League of Nations and urged the committee members to tell Congress that the covenant had overwhelming support among the American people. He lashed out at Congress for being psychologically divorced from the rest of the country. "Washington is not part of the United States," he said. Turning his wrath on the congressional opponents of the league, Wilson used words like "contemptible," "blind" and "provincial" to describe them. He sneered that it was "not their character so much that I have contempt for, though that contempt is thoroughgoing, but their minds. They do not have even working imitations of minds." Inevitably, some of these intemperate remarks were soon in the newspapers.[73]

Worse was to come. On March 2, combative Senator Brandegee asked Lodge to consider putting the Senate on record as opposed to the League of Nations. The Connecticut solon brandished a letter from a constituent, calling for such a statement. Lodge conferred with Senator Philander Knox, who suggested a devious device, a round-robin. The three senators soon had the names of thirty-seven senators who were prepared to say they would vote against the league.

On March 3, near midnight, with the Sixty-Fifth Congress one day from adjournment, Lodge rose in the Senate and read the resolution, stating it was "the sense of the Senate" that "the league of nations in the form now proposed" should not be accepted by the United States. Instead, further efforts on the part of the United States should be directed "with the utmost expedition" to negotiating peace terms with Germany. A league of nations could then be taken up "for careful consideration."

When a Democratic senator objected to Lodge's call for unanimous consent to the resolution, Lodge promptly yielded. The last thing he wanted was a vote, which would have buried the proposal. Instead, he read the names of the thirty-seven senators and sat down. If as few as thirty-three Senators voted no, the league would fall short of the two-thirds majority the Constitution required for the approval of a treaty. Lodge knew that the next morning, headlines would blossom across the country reporting that Wilson's league looked dead on arrival.[74]

The Republicans also made sure that when the president went to the Capitol the following day to sign the appropriations bills that Congress was supposed to pass—the ostensible reason for his journey from Paris—he would have nothing to sign. The GOP had filibustered the money measures into oblivion. This tactic meant that Wilson would have to summon the new Congress to an emergency session, enabling the GOP majority to take charge of the legislative branch months before the usual date for

Congress to convene—December 1. Wilson responded with a furious denunciation of "a group of men in the Senate" who for partisan reasons chose to risk throwing the country into financial chaos.

The same day, March 4, Wilson headed for New York, where he had scheduled an appearance with William Howard Taft at the Metropolitan Opera House. The former president was head of a bipartisan organization called the League to Enforce Peace, which had been pushing for an international organization since 1915. He had endorsed the league covenant, even though it was very different from the largely judicial body that Taft and his group had envisioned. Here was another chance—it turned out to be the last chance—for Wilson to say something conciliatory to the Senate. Not all the senators who had signed the round-robin were irreconcilable. The rest—a substantial majority—were not opposed to the league, though many were still sulky about the way Wilson had snubbed them in selecting the delegates to the peace conference.

New York's Democrats poured into the streets to give the president a tumultuous reception that more than equaled Boston's fervor. The cheers no doubt reinforced Wilson's conviction that the people were on his side. The program at the Metropolitan Opera House began on a note of promising harmony. Wilson and Taft came onstage arm in arm. Taft spoke first, defending Wilson's league on virtually all points, and holding out an olive branch to the round-robin senators by admitting that Lodge and other critics had made valuable suggestions about revising the covenant.

If Wilson had followed a similar approach, the fight against the league might have ended that night. Instead his speech bristled with apocalyptic denunciation and arrogant defiance. He proclaimed himself on the winning side, because "the great tides of the world" were with him. Those who opposed this mass movement were certain to be overwhelmed. "The heart of the world was awake and the heart of the world must be satisfied!" Wilson went on to declare that his critics suffered from a "comprehensive ignorance" of what was happening all around them. He despised their "doctrine of careful selfishness." Americans had proven in France that they were willing to die for an idea. Publicly disagreeing with Taft, Wilson said he had heard "no constructive suggestion" from Congress.

Finally, the president repudiated the round-robin's call for a peace treaty first and consideration of a league of nations later. He all but flung a challenge in Senator Lodge's face: "When that treaty comes back, gentlemen on this side will find the covenant not only in it, but so many threads of the treaty tied to the covenant, that you cannot dissect the covenant from the treaty without destroying the whole vital structure." Edith Wilson later said she had never seen an audience go so "wild."[75]

The next day, the *Indianapolis Star* had a very different reaction to Wilson's defiance: "It is hard to escape the impression that President Wilson is riding for a fall."[76]

XVII

Amid the cheers at the Metropolitan Opera House, there was a voice that punctured this moment of illusory triumph: "What about Ireland?" someone shouted. The cry may have come—and probably did come—from a group of Irish-Americans who sat onstage during Wilson's speech. Offstage, the president confronted Joe Tumulty with an angry question: "Is Judge Cohalan in the delegation?"

Tumulty admitted that Judge Daniel Cohalan of New York was among the members of the group on the stage. They were all members of the Committee for Irish Independence and were now waiting for their scheduled meeting with the president. Wilson told Tumulty to get rid of Cohalan. If the judge did not vanish instantly, the president would head for Hoboken to board the *George Washington* for his return trip to Europe.

Wilson's hostility to Judge Cohalan went back to 1912, when the jurist had vociferously opposed his nomination at the Democratic National Convention. The president's animus had deepened when Cohalan criticized America's declaration of war against Germany. In September 1917, the State Department had implied that the judge was on the German secret service payroll. None of this publicity had prevented Cohalan from remaining very popular with Irish-Americans.

Tumulty said snubbing Cohalan would make a terrible impression on the committee. "That's just what I want to do, Tumulty," Wilson said. "But I think it will make a good impression on decent people."

The humiliated Tumulty delivered the president's ultimatum. Cohalan withdrew, and in five minutes, Wilson confronted twenty-three grim-faced, resentful Irish-Americans in a private room at the opera house. They were far from nobodies. One of the leaders was Frank P. Walsh, who had served as joint chairman of the War Labor Board. As a member of the executive committee of the League to Enforce Peace, Walsh had recently toured the country with former President Taft, speaking for the league. But the infuriated Wilson only saw a group of contentious "micks," reiterating the impudent question that had been shouted from the audience: "What about Ireland?"

Joe Tumulty had arranged this meeting after hours of intercession with the hostile president. On February 22, 1919, a new organization, the Friends of Irish Freedom, had convened a gigantic "Irish Race Convention" in Philadelphia. With a unanimity unmatched for decades, the organizers had persuaded swarms of professional politicians, thirty bishops, three archbishops and James Cardinal Gibbons of Baltimore, the leader of the American Catholic Church, to join 6,000 delegates who demanded independence for Ireland. On the platform with Gibbons was Norman Thomas, who would soon become a leader of the Socialist Party; a prominent Philadelphia rabbi; and leaders of many other ethnic groups. The delegates had pledged $1 million to a "freedom fund" to finance a huge public-relations campaign.[77]

The distinguished New York judge, John W. Goff, opened the conversation with Wilson by telling him that the Irish Race Convention wanted him to plead Ireland's case for independence before the peace conference. Wilson curtly refused to do any such thing. Frank Walsh urged the president to at least use "his great influence" to win the delegates from the provisional Irish republic a chance to appear before the conference. With unconcealed irritation, Wilson snapped, "You do not expect me to give an answer to this request now?" Walsh said he was merely asking the president to consider it. Wilson ended the discussion on that sour note.

The president did not express a word of sympathy for Ireland's cause. Later he said he had been sorely tempted to tell the Irish-Americans "to go to hell." He obviously did not much care what they thought of him. He had defeated their attempt to block him from joining the war on England's side with his attack on hyphenates, and by accusing them of being pro-German.

The president who bragged about being in touch with the tides of public feeling was making one of his biggest mistakes. Except for Cohalan, the committee was composed of Irish-Americans who had supported Wilson and the war. As a political issue in the United States, imperial Germany was dead. British policy in Ireland had become more and more brutal since 1916, when they had executed the Easter uprising leaders. Hundreds of leaders of the self-proclaimed Irish republic were in jail. London was ruling by raw terror.

The committee reported the president's snub of Judge Cohalan to the newspapers. A huge commotion erupted. To the distress of Irish moderates such as Frank Walsh, Cohalan became an overnight martyr-hero. Numerous letters from prominent Irish-Americans urged Wilson to "make amends" for insulting Cohalan.

Earlier this same day, by a vote of 216 to 45, the House of Representatives had passed a resolution, calling on the Paris peace conference to "consider the claims of Ireland to the right of self determination." Before the end of March, the Democratic Party's Executive Committee had endorsed the Irish Race Convention's resolutions. So had several state legislatures. Five prominent Democratic senators wrote to the president warning him: "The Irish question has become a very serious matter."[78]

Chapter 10

PEACE THAT SURPASSES UNDERSTANDING II

One of the first things Woodrow Wilson said to Colonel House when they met at Brest on March 13, 1919, was a snarled rebuke: "Your dinner [with the foreign relations committees] was a failure as far as getting together was concerned." Unflappable as always, House replied that the meeting still had some merit. It had diminished press criticism of Wilson's neglect of Congress. Wilson grudgingly admitted this might be true.

The colonel refrained from pointing out that Wilson's Boston speech had undermined the spirit of conciliation he had urged on the president. Nor did he rebuke Wilson for his even more intemperate remarks to the Democratic National Committee, the audience at the Metropolitan Opera House, and the committee from the Irish Race Convention. One wonders if the author of *Philip Dru* had begun to feel like Dr. Frankenstein. Had he created a monster that was running amok?

Wilson had put House in charge of the American delegation in his absence, and the colonel had continued to negotiate with French and British leaders. In her memoirs, Edith Wilson created a scene in which Wilson emerged from an extended conversation with House aboard the *George Washington* in Brest harbor looking dazed and horrified. Edith claims to have seized his hand and cried, "What is the matter? What has happened?"

The president supposedly replied, "House has given away everything I had won before we left Paris. He has compromised on every side, and so I have to start all over again and this time it will be harder because he has given the impression my delegates are not in sympathy with me."[1]

Again, we are dealing with something that Wilson almost certainly never said. For one thing, House did not board the *George Washington,* which had anchored out in Brest's harbor. He had come down to Brest on Wilson's special train and waited for him at the dock. But comments from other participants in the peace conference suggest there is a modicum of truth in the First Lady's recollection. Wilson was extremely dissatisfied with the tenor and direction of the negotiations House had conducted while he was gone.

Aboard the train to Paris that night, House was frustrated by the presence of the French ambassador to the United States, Jules Jusserand, who prevented him from having a serious discussion with the president. But the next morning, before they left the train in Paris, the two men had a long talk. House told Wilson that negotiations on German reparations had gotten nowhere. The British and French refused to modify their astronomical demands. The French were also demanding the Saar basin, with its valuable coal mines, as promised in another secret treaty, and the creation of a "Rhenish Republic" in the Rhineland, which they would control. Both the French and the British wanted to separate the League of Nations from the treaty and conclude a peace with Germany as soon as possible.

House had not opposed the French demands; nor had he rejected the separation of the league and the treaty. He had begun to have grave doubts about Wilson's obsession with the league to the detriment of almost everything else. Germany and much of the rest of central Europe were sliding into chaos and revolution. An immediate peace with Berlin seemed imperative. General Tasker Bliss, a fellow member of the peace commission, felt the same way. He had written a memorandum, saying that if an early peace were concluded with Germany, the American people might be willing to tackle other problems, including Soviet Russia.[2]

Wilson's response to these proposals was dismaying, from House's point of view. The president rejected the transfer of the Rhineland and the Saar to France, because it violated the principle of self-determination. He was even more intransigent on separating the league and the treaty. House did not realize how much Wilson had become involved, politically and emotionally, with his critics in the U.S. Senate. The discouraged colonel glumly noted, "The President comes back very militant and determined to put the league into the peace treaty."

House saw this as a tremendous, potentially earthshaking mistake. Perhaps he could not conceal this conviction. Perhaps he did not try very hard. After all, he was not merely Wilson's unofficial mouthpiece now. At the Paris Peace Conference, Edward Mandell House was almost if not quite Woodrow Wilson's equal. As a peace commissioner, he had one of the most important assignments in American diplomatic history. He desperately wanted this conference to succeed, not only for the sake of Wilson's place in history, but for his own. Their disagreement marked the beginning of the end of the colonel's partnership with Woodrow Wilson.[3]

II

In Germany, American troops had moved into the Rhineland as part of an army of occupation. The Americans—and their British counterparts elsewhere in Germany—swiftly realized from the gaunt faces they saw on the street that the Germans were starving to death. The British began bombarding the War Office in London with horror stories. General Sir Herbert Plumer, commander of the British occupation army, said his soldiers could not stand the sight of hordes of skinny and bloated children pawing through the garbage in British camps. Minister of War Winston Churchill issued a statement, based on evidence he had seen from officers sent to Germany by the War Office: There was grave danger of "the entire collapse of the vital structure of German social and national life under the pressure of hunger and malnutrition." One British journalist was particularly appalled by a visit to a maternity ward in a Cologne hospital. He described "rows of babies feverish from want of food, exhausted by privation to the point where their little limbs were like slender wands, their expression hopeless, and their faces full of pain."[4]

Germany was not the only nation without food. The disparate pieces of the Austro-Hungarian empire were also sinking into starvation and chaos. No one had stopped to figure out how to stitch together the economic connections that the armistice had severed. Prague was devoid of meat, rice, coffee and tea. Its factories had no coal. The death rate for children under 14 was 40 percent. In a Czech mining town, 116 out of 165 children born in 1918 had already died. A wave of typhus was sweeping out of Russia into eastern Europe and Germany. Typhus was carried by lice, tiny crawling creatures that thrived on human bodies when there was no soap to wash them. Soap was made from a surplus of fats. When there was no surplus, the people consumed the fats and did without soap—with disastrous consequences.

On a fact-finding mission to Vienna, one of Colonel House's top aides, Colonel Stephen Bonsal, saw with his own eyes the face of anarchy. As he strolled along one of the streets of the Ring, the circular heart of aristocratic Vienna, he was startled by the rattle of sabers and bursts of gunfire. Infantry and cavalry poured out of courtyards and confronted "a disorderly mob of men, women and barefooted children" emerging from the city's working-class neighborhoods, heading toward the parliament buildings. As they drew nearer, Bonsal could see "how miserably clad they were" and he could hear their cries: "We are starving! Give us bread and jackets! We are famished and we freeze!"

Suddenly shots rang out, followed by volleys, and then by a fusillade. Policemen, soldiers and horses went down. Some of the workers ran away, but other "more resolute" groups pushed on. The troops opened fire with every weapon in their possession, and "soon the Ring was cleared of the living," Bonsal wrote. "Here and there lay groups of dead and tangled masses of writhing wounded." Among the dead was the pretty wife of a British engineer who had come to Vienna to help build factories and create jobs for the underclass. She had been caught in the crossfire while out for a stroll.

Next Bonsal saw something that made him realize what starving people will risk for food. Men and women crept from behind nearby buildings and began hacking chunks of meat from the dead horses, even though the troops continued to fire on them. Bonsal could only conclude that Vienna, the once magnificent capital of the Hapsburg empire, was on the brink of chaos.[5]

More and more people began to wonder what the peacemakers in Paris were doing. Almost five months had passed since the armistice. From Rome, Pope Benedict XV pleaded for the end of the blockade and an early peace treaty. Colonel Henry Anderson, the leader of an American civilian-military commission to aid the Balkan states, issued a similar plea. He described children walking the streets of Bucharest, "their limbs black and blue with cold."

"The slogan of Europe ought to be, 'Get back to work,'" Herbert Hoover said. "To a great extent the whole production is stopped. . . . We have got to have peace as soon as possible." Hoover finally got the blockade lifted for Poland, Czechoslovakia, Rumania and Austria, but not for Germany or Hungary. Unfortunately, this concession made little difference in the desperate situation. The Italians, to reinforce their demands for the territory promised them in 1915, were blocking all attempts to ship food and fuel into eastern Europe.[6]

Rome was also hard at work demolishing Woodrow Wilson's image as the savior of the world. Day after day, Gabriele D'Annunzio, Italy's best-known poet, published newspaper articles denouncing the president as the country's chief enemy at the peace conference. "What peace will in the end be imposed on us, poor little ones of Christ?" the poet cried in his usual extravagant style. "A Gallic peace, a British peace, a star-spangled peace?" D'Annunzio had become devoted to the man he saw as the savior of Italy, Benito Mussolini.[7]

III

The 1½ million American soldiers still in Europe were fighting a new enemy: boredom. At first, convinced that the war was not really over, the U.S. high command had insisted on tough training schedules. The result was endless hours of drilling and maneuvers in cold mud and colder rain. In a month or two, it dawned on the men that it was all meaningless. The newspapers made it clear that the German army had been demobilized as fast as it returned home. Raymond B. Fosdick, in charge of training-camp activities, reported with alarm on what he saw: "A battery that has fired 70,000 rounds in the Argonne fight going listlessly through the movements of ramming an empty shell into a gun for hours at a stretch . . . infantry drill in the muddy roads up and down which columns of American soldiers trudge listlessly and without spirit."[8]

The petty discipline of military life, the requirement to salute every passing officer, to maintain spotless, dust-free barracks, was another irritant. Disillusion with the "Great Adventure" began to seep through the ranks. It persisted, even when Pershing, realizing the peace conference was not going to end soon, began an elaborate sports program and made educational opportunities available in army-operated schools as well as in French universities.

Among the American soldiers in the 200,000-man Allied army of occupation, an unexpected development took shape. The doughboys found the Germans far more pleasant to deal with than the French, who had tried to wring additional francs out of every transaction. The French noted this warmth and found it irritating. The irritation soon got into their newspapers, and someone asked Pershing about it. He replied with characteristic bluntness that the Americans found the Germans likable—so what? They treated the Americans decently. "Our men have the sporting instinct. They don't believe in hitting a man when he is down. There are some people who don't seem to know what that sporting instinct means." He meant the French, of course. Pershing had far more grudges against Clemenceau, Foch and company than he had against General Ludendorff.[9]

IV

As March ebbed into April with no sign of the end of the peace conference, Pershing began to ship some of the disgruntled doughboys home. Along with them went most of the women volunteers who had driven ambulances, nursed, and manned YMCA canteens. A surprising number of these volunteers had severe morale problems. Depression coruscated through the ranks. One woman, Margaret Deland, summed up the reason. "Over in America, we thought we knew something about the war . . . but when you get here the difference is [like] studying the laws of electricity and being struck by lightning." Deland said the only way she kept sane was by concentrating on her "immediate little trivial foolish job." If she lifted her eyes to the "black horizon," she was in serious danger of "los[ing] my balance."[10]

When the guns fell silent, the black horizon loomed larger and larger in the souls of many of these women. One wrote an autobiographical novel that ended aboard a homeward-bound ship in a French port. While the volunteers waited to sail, military police in small boats rowed around and around the vessel to prevent suicides.

Demonstrating that this was fiction based on real experience was the fate of a gifted young poet, Gladys Cromwell, and her twin sister. The two women had worked for the Red Cross, which brought them into close contact with the carnage in the front lines. On the ship returning home, they revealed symptoms of deep depression but no one knew what to do about it.

One night, as dinner was being served, the cry of "man overboard" rang through the ship. The engines abruptly ceased, and an agitated doughboy charged into the dining hall to tell what he had seen. The Cromwell twins had been standing at the rail on a deserted lower deck. The soldier had strolled toward them, hoping to start a conversation. One of them stepped back, then raced to the rail and jumped over.

"Don't!" cried the soldier and rushed to save the second woman. Before he could reach her, she too went over the side with an anguished scream. As she drifted away in the freezing water of the January Atlantic, she screamed again—then there was silence.

The woman who told the story, poet and novelist Eunice Tietjens, remarked, "I believe every one of us on that boat might have done the same."[11]

V

In Paris, Woodrow Wilson made a public announcement that the League of Nations covenant would not be detached from the peace treaty, and persuaded a plenary session of the peace conference to ratify the conjunction. This move multiplied his political woes. Almost immediately, the French press opened a virulent assault on him. The French foreign minister, Stephen Pichon, contradicted the president in public, insisting on a separation of the two entities. The president's insistence also split the American delegation into quarreling cliques.

Not a few people, already jealous of House's influence with Wilson, murmured to the president that the colonel's readiness to compromise amounted to disloyalty. Some talebearers fastened on a remark that House's son-in-law and right-hand man, Gordon Auchincloss, supposedly made, revealing his disillusion with Wilson: "Kings and prime ministers and plenipotentiaries come to the Colonel to get the dope and then we have to tell Woody what to say to them." According to Admiral Cary Grayson, one member of the American delegation threatened to punch Auchincloss in the teeth if he heard him speaking "in that disrespectful manner of the President of the United States." Next came an editorial in the *Times* of London, purportedly inspired by Auchincloss, which opined that Colonel House had rescued the conference from failure while the president was in the United States and was now its sole hope of success. Not surprisingly, the coolness between House and Wilson grew more autumnal with every passing day.[12]

Meanwhile, Wilson had decided to respond to urgent messages from William Howard Taft and several friendly senators to make some modifications in the covenant to satisfy conservative critics in the United States. To try to speed things up, the president accepted Colonel House's proposal to abandon the Council of Ten and confine future discussions to the leaders of France, Great Britain, Italy and the United States. Promptly dubbed "the Big Four" by the newspapers, this conclave of supposedly major minds seemed to promise progress on several fronts—except for one drawback.[13]

The Senate's round-robin vote and their demand for reservations had disastrously weakened the president's negotiating position vis-à-vis Lloyd George and Clemenceau. The British and French leaders now had unique leverage over Wilson. Every time he balked on an issue, they would threaten to torpedo the league by opposing the senate reservations—and Wilson had to capitulate.

The British prime minister made the first move on March 25. He suddenly announced that he could not support Wilson's attempt to strengthen the reference to the Monroe Doctrine in the covenant. In fact, he had become convinced that the league should be separated from the treaty. However, he might change his mind if the president agreed to abandon America's current navy shipbuilding program, which would soon make the U.S. fleet the equal of the British fleet.[14]

A stunned Wilson resisted at first. But he found himself on shaky ground. The league (and the Fourteen Points) called for a disarmament program. He could not claim that the United States wanted an equal fleet because it did not trust the British (Wilson's chief reason for building it). Lloyd George wanted to avoid an arms race that would cripple his cash-strapped nation. After two weeks of dickering, Wilson agreed to sign a memorandum that called for a naval conference that would work out the details of a compromise. Lloyd George suddenly found no objections to a strengthening of the Monroe Doctrine in Article 10 of the covenant.[15]

So began the game of breaking Wilson's resistance to the Europeans' version of peace. Clemenceau now took his turn. He attacked a reservation Wilson wanted, permitting any nation to withdraw from the league. That might leave France friendless. Clemenceau began making outrageous demands on Germany—and insisted on maintaining the blockade. The premier combined his assault with the continuing drumfire of criticism in the Paris press about Wilson's supposed unfriendliness to France.

At one point, when the president resisted Clemenceau's demands, the old man called Wilson pro-Boche and walked out in a huff. "How can I talk to a fellow who thinks himself the first man in two thousand years who knows anything about peace on earth?" the Tiger growled.

Eventually, Wilson agreed to French occupation of the Rhineland for fifteen years. As for the Saar basin and its coal mines, the 650,000 people there had been speaking German for 1,000 years. To compensate France for the French coal mines the Germans had destroyed during the war, Wilson agreed to give France ownership of the Saar's mines for fifteen years, while the region was governed by a League of Nations commission that the French would dominate. Then the people would vote on whether they wanted to belong to France or Germany.

Clemenceau's allies in the Paris press were infuriated by this compromise. France's generals were equally discomfited. They had planned to fortify the Saar and make it a key bastion in the next war with Germany. To keep these critics happy, Clemenceau demanded a treaty of alliance between Britain, France and the United States, promising to defend France against a German attack. Wilson argued that this old fashioned diplomacy implied they had no faith in the League of Nations.[16]

Whenever Wilson preached idealism as a policy—Lloyd George called it his "flight[s] beyond the azure main"—Clemenceau would widen his ancient eyes and turn them to the British prime minister as if to say, "Here he is, off again!" At one point, when Wilson invoked the Marquis de Lafayette role in the American Revolution as a symbol of idealism, the French premier bluntly reminded the president that Lafayette could never have achieved his ideals without force. "Force brought the United States into being and [referring to the Civil War] force again prevented it from falling to pieces."

Wilson capitulated on the treaty of alliance. Only then did Clemenceau approve the change in the covenant, permitting a nation to withdraw from the league. He also approved the modification declaring that the league did not override the Monroe Doctrine. Privately, Clemenceau told his colleagues he thought the Monroe Doctrine was as meaningless as the League of Nations but it was a wonderful bargaining tool.[17]

The Italians soon got into the act, now insisting on Fiume as a city they must have, although the acquisition would deprive the new republic of Yugoslavia of its only deepwater port. Remembering the hysterical crowds that had greeted him as a second Moses in Rome and Milan, Wilson decided to appeal over Premier Orlando's head and release a statement to the press, explaining why he rejected Italy's demands.

If historians ever rate acts of presidential political ineptitude, this maneuver would rank near the top of the list. Clemenceau and Lloyd George begged Wilson not to do it, pointing out that it would make it impossible for Orlando to retreat gracefully. Thomas Nelson Page, the American ambassador to Rome, wrote the president on April 17, warning him that the Italian press had made Fiume as important to Italy as Alsace-Lorraine was to France. Wilson ignored them all and asked the Italians to "exhibit to the newly liberated peoples across the Adriatic that noblest quality of greatness . . . the preference for justice over interest."

The British newspapers called it "Wild-West diplomacy." Premier Orlando summoned his special train and returned to Rome, where he put Wilson's challenge before parliament. Who should the Italian people choose, their premier or this Yankee savior? A Vesuvius of vituperation descended on Wilson, from the Alps to Sicily. Even his erstwhile friends, the Social Democrats led by Leonida Bissolati, attacked the president, pointing out that Wilson did not seem to worry about self-determination when the British and the French were asking for territory.

In the United States, Italian-language newspapers took up the cry "Down with Wilson!" The legislatures of Massachusetts, New York and Illinois passed resolutions backing Orlando. The president only grew more stubborn. "They will never get Fiume while I have anything to do with it," he told his Paris press secretary, Ray Stannard Baker.[18]

Next, in one of the meetings of the league commission, where the revisions in the articles were debated, the Japanese again tried to obtain a statement on racial equality. This time they presented it as "an endorsement of the principal of the equality of nations and the just treatment of their nationals." The Japanese spokesman argued this statement would be valuable in administering mandates and would add weight to the league's commitment to the reform of labor conditions around the world. Wilson favored the proposal, but once more, the British objected on behalf of their polyglot empire, where 98 percent of the people were treated unequally.

Fearful that Lloyd George might make another move to scuttle the league, the president let the prime minister get away with it.[19]

The Japanese now decided to abandon all pretense to idealism, as everyone else was doing. They demanded the Big Four's approval of their takeover of China's Shantung Province and its port of Tsingtao. Here was imperialism at its most naked. Neither China, the nation that possessed the territory, nor the 20 million Chinese who lived there were to be seriously consulted, although the Japanese claimed that the pathetically weak Chinese government had given its approval. To back themselves up, the Japanese flourished the secret treaty they had signed with the British and French in 1917, promising them the peninsula and all the Pacific islands owned by Germany, north of the equator.[20]

Here was another mockery of open covenants openly arrived at. The British insisted their treaty with Japan could not be abrogated. The Japanese threatened to join the Italians in a departure from the peace conference if they did not get their way. Wilson argued in vain with the British. Clemenceau offered no help whatsoever. Finally, the president capitulated, fearful that a Japanese withdrawal on top of the Italian walkout would wreck the conference. Secretary of State Lansing, not consulted as usual, called the deal an "iniquitous agreement." The United States had abandoned China and surrendered its prestige in the Far East for "a mess of pottage—and a mess it is."[21]

At one point in these negotiations, Wilson, almost talking to himself, said, "I am obliged to remain faithful to my Fourteen Points, but without inflexibility." The words convey an image of a man desperately refusing to face the truth about what he was doing—what his precious covenant, for which he had permitted hundreds of thousands of German civilians to starve, was becoming. Behind his back, Clemenceau laughed at the president. "I never saw a man talk more like Jesus Christ and act more like Lloyd George," the French premier remarked. Lloyd George also expressed bemused bafflement. "He believed in mankind but distrusted all men," the Welsh Wizard remarked.[22]

Even more humiliating—and ultimately embarrassing—was the peace conference's disposition of the mandates. Before the diplomats finished divvying up their 1,132,000 square miles (about a third the size of the continental United States), some 17 million people had been handed over to the victorious Allies.

The most flagrant decision in this imperialist landgrab was giving the 3.5 million people of Ruanda-Urundi to Belgium, whose record in the Congo should have disqualified it from running a colony until the end of time. On the A mandate list, the British acquired Palestine and Iraq, and the French got Syria and Lebanon—exactly the way they had divided up the remains of the Turkish empire in a secret agreement signed in 1916. Largely ignored were British promises of independence made to lure the Arabs into the war on the Allied side—and the indubitable fact that all four Middle East countries had manifested strong desires for freedom. An American investigative team Wilson sent to the Middle East found Muslim animosity toward the French particularly strong. These investigators also reported that "anti-Zionist feeling in Palestine and Syria is intense and not lightly to be flouted."[23]

Overall, thanks to Wilson's collapse and the reduction of the mandates to the status of hypocritical fiction, the British empire acquired an additional 8,156,475 people and 862,549 square miles. The French empire gained 5,568,191 people and 238,168 square miles. Neither in the Middle East nor in Africa was there the slightest attempt to apply the principle of self-determination.[24]

Perhaps the best example of the total cynicism that pervaded the Europeans on the mandates was a scene recorded by Harold Nicholson, one of Britain's key players. Lloyd George and his foreign secretary, Arthur Balfour, were arguing with the Italians about what mandates they might get from the breakup of the Turkish empire. In the course of the discussion, they consulted the covenant to make sure they were following the correct procedures. One of them read aloud the lines that an "A" mandate required "the consent and wishes of the people concerned." Nicholson was struck by how heartily everyone laughed. Premier Orlando's eyes filled "with tears of mirth."[25]

Worst of all was Wilson's capitulation on Germany's reparations. For a while, he thought he had Lloyd George on his side in calling for a reasonable figure, based mostly on an estimate of the damage done to property in Belgium and France. But this hope evaporated when Andrew Bonar Law, the conservative leader, arrived from London in a Royal Air Force plane. Bonar Law informed the prime minister that numerous people in England, from Lord Northcliffe to the vast majority of the Tory backbenchers in Parliament, were growing unhappy with the liberal noises Lloyd George was making about Germany. Had the prime minister forgotten he had been elected on a platform of making the Huns pay?

Bonar Law, who had lost two sons in the war, was telling Lloyd George who was really running things. The prime minister got the message. He rushed back to London and made one of his patented somersaults. In ringing terms, he told Parliament by God he would make the Germans pay not only for every ship their submarines had sunk and the damage inflicted by their dirigibles and Gotha bombers, he would insist on their paying for the *pensions* of every British war widow and every crippled soldier for the next six decades.

In France, Clemenceau applauded and immediately added pensions to his already astronomical reparations figures. Wilson could only watch numbly, while his promise to make a peace without punitive damages was blown to shreds by this explosion of the hatred generated by four years of unrelenting anti-German propaganda and the slaughter on the Western Front.

The president was shaken to the core of his being by these defeats. More and more, it became apparent that House and other advisers were right. Woodrow Wilson never should have come to Europe and exposed himself and America's prestige to this political auto-da-fé. At the very least, he should have taken House's advice and separated the league from the treaty when he returned from the United States.

"The league has become a veritable millstone around our necks," Secretary of State Lansing remarked in a letter. Peace Commissioner Henry White, a veteran diplomat, drew the same conclusion: "The League of Nations . . . has been played to the limit by France and Japan in extracting concessions from him [Wilson]; to a certain extent by the British too."[26]

Inevitably, these machinations took a physical as well as a mental toll on this fragile man. For three weeks after Wilson's return from the United States, he spent all day in arguments with Clemenceau, Orlando and Lloyd George and much of the night debating the changes he wanted in the covenant. The closest he came to fresh air and exercise was an occasional session with Admiral Grayson before an open window, during which the physician would work the president's arms back and forth and up and down in a bad imitation of gymnastics. Then the next meeting would begin. Aides began to notice how tired Wilson looked. One noticed a twitch in his cheek below his left eye.

On April 3, in the midst of arguing about the large chunk of Yugoslavia's Adriatic coast that Italy was trying to purloin, Wilson became violently ill.

He took to his bed, complaining of acute pain all over his body. During the night, he was racked by fits of coughing that seemed to threaten him with strangulation. Next came rampant diarrhea and a fever of 103. For a while Grayson wondered if the president had been poisoned. For three days Wilson was a very sick man.[27]

Rumors about the president's health swirled through Paris. Herbert Hoover, who only saw Wilson sporadically in his futile attempts to get food into Germany, suspected he had suffered a stroke—a diagnosis now supported by several neurologists who have studied Wilson's medical history. Grayson thought the illness was a severe case of influenza. Cynics said it was a "diplomatic" indisposition, designed to break off negotiations and resume them from a new angle.[28]

Certainly, the first move the president made from his sickbed was a shocker. He asked Admiral Grayson to find out how soon the *George Washington* could come to Brest to take him home. He also told Grayson to leak this inquiry to Richard Oulahan of the *New York Times,* with tacit permission to cable it to his newspaper. The leak suggests there may have been some basis for the cynics' belief that Wilson was seeking more leverage in the Big Four. But the impulse to flee also revealed how profoundly the mounting political disaster in Paris was affecting Wilson. He was yielding to the inner disgust and revulsion that tormented him as his illusions of power and glory disintegrated before his eyes.[29]

The president soon discovered he was no longer master of his fate. The leak caused a sensation in Europe and the United States. From Washington, D.C., came a panicky cable from Joe Tumulty, reporting that American reaction to the move was alarmingly negative. The press was calling a presidential withdrawal at this time a "desertion."[30]

House meanwhile was negotiating about German reparations in Wilson's place. The colonel capitulated to British and French insistence on adding pensions to the multi-billion-dollar indemnity. On Wilson's first day out of bed, financial experts on the staff of the American delegation begged him to veto this deal. One said it simply was not logical within any possible reading of the Fourteen Points. "Logic? Logic?" Wilson snarled. "I don't give a damn about logic"—and gave the pensions his approval, thereby doubling the reparations package.[31]

These were the words of a man sliding into something very close to despair. Lloyd George, studying the president around this time, said, "A disillusioned prophet is an abject spectacle." Like his fellow cynic Clemenceau, the prime minister seemed to enjoy the sport of puncturing Wilson's idealistic dreams.[32]

By this time, the press was in the game as well. One Associated Press reporter, Charles Thompson, kept a day-by-day record of the peace conference. Much of it concerned Wilson's abandonment of the Fourteen Points. In mid-April, Thompson began to add things up: "The decline and fall of the Fourteen Points, one by one, has been noted from time to time. But it is possible to sum up now what has happened to all or most of them. . . . Of the six points involving general principles, four have disappeared entirely and the two others have dropped into a state of limbo. . . . Other general principles, not in the points . . . have suffered the same vicissitudes. The most notable is the principle of self-determination, with which the name of the president has been conspicuously linked. This principle too has gone the way of the Fourteen Points into . . . oblivion."[33]

VI

While the statesmen wrangled, events in distant India cast a lurid light on Wilson's pretensions to making the world safe for democracy with the British as his chief ally. There, a gaunt Hindu agitator named Mohandas Gandhi was creating major disturbances with his nonviolent protest movement, *Satyagraha* ("fidelity to truth"). One of the flash points was Amritsar, the sacred city of the Sikhs, in the Punjab region of the vast subcontinent. Fifty-five-year-old Brigadier Reginald E. "Rex" Dyer, the army commander of the region, became alarmed when he learned that rampaging mobs had sacked the national bank and murdered the English manager. Another bank and its manager suffered a similar fate, and an Englishwoman riding past on a bicycle was beaten senseless. The telegraph office was smashed and burned, cutting the city off from the rest of the world. Brigadier Dyer decided to take personal charge of the situation.

India had many grievances against its conquerors. Chief among them was the British insistence that they, and not the debaters in the National Congress of India, knew what was best for the country. Also high on the list was the way the government had lured 1.3 million Indians into the British army and into labor battalions to help fight the Great War. The outbreak of Bolshevism in Russia added the danger of a mass uprising.

An English magistrate, Sir Sidney Rowlatt, had conducted an investigation and concluded that drastic measures were in order. He called for legislation to give the central government the power to arrest conspirators at will, try them in secret without lawyers or juries, and sentence them to death without appeal. The so-called Rowlatt Laws, passed in March 1919, had inspired Gandhi to call for nationwide peaceful protests. Unfortunately, Gandhi had only tenuous control over the protesters, who were ready and even eager to go beyond *Satyagraha*.

When Brigadier Dyer arrived in Amritsar, he issued a proclamation banning public assemblies. His timing could not have been worse. Thousands of pilgrims were pouring into the city to celebrate Baisakha, a major Sikh holy day. The next day, April 13, Dyer learned that people were meeting in a field, Jallianwalla Bagh, about the size of London's Trafalgar Square, on the outskirts of the city. In a great rage, the brigadier marched 90 men escorted by two armored cars to the place and found about 6,000 men, women and children listening to an orator. Most of them were country folk who knew nothing about the proclamation against public gatherings.

Without giving the crowd the slightest warning, Dyer ordered his men to open fire at point-blank range and to keep firing until he gave the order to stop. As he saw it, the "wogs" had disobeyed his proclamation and deserved no mercy. The unarmed Indians tried to flee, but there was only one narrow exit and Dyer's riflemen blocked it. When the subalterns reported they were getting low on ammunition, Dyer ordered a cease-fire and marched his men back to town, leaving behind him almost 400 dead and 1,500 wounded. The brigadier did not make the slightest attempt to help the wounded; nor did any other British official in Amritsar. Back in the city, Dyer summoned the leading citizens and told them that any Indians who used the street where the Englishwoman bicyclist had been attacked would have to crawl on their bellies. Agitators against the Rowlatt Laws were flogged in public by British soldiers. In one case, to increase the humiliation, local prostitutes were summoned to witness the punishment.[34]

VII

In the same month of April 1919, the Irish-Americans returned to torment Wilson. On April 11, three members of the committee that Wilson had met in New York arrived in Paris and soon called on Colonel House. They wanted the American delegation to persuade the British to permit Eamon de Valera, the president of the as yet unrecognized Irish republic, and two other spokesmen to ask the peace conference to support their declaration of independence. House arranged for the committee's leader, Frank Walsh, to meet Wilson, who greeted him cordially and said he believed the request "should be granted."

The president told House to ask Lloyd George to meet with the Irish-Americans. The prime minister reacted like a man being asked to make close contact with carriers of the bubonic plague. His already shaky hold on his mostly Tory followers would vanish like so much smoke if they thought he was dallying with Irish independence. Headlines in North-cliffe's papers and speeches in the House of Commons put him on notice. For two weeks the Welsh Wizard stalled. Finally, House persuaded him to let the three Irish-Americans at least go to Ireland to meet with the independence men. An exasperated Lloyd George told General Sir Henry Wilson, his military adviser, that the colonel had wheedled him into letting "the accursed brutes" visit their mother country. Sir Henry was a fierce foe of Irish independence.[35]

In Ireland, the Irish-Americans were hailed as heroes and saviors. They met with President Eamon de Valera and were soon telling large crowds that millions of Irish-Americans backed Ireland's demand for self-determination. It did not take Lloyd George long to start complaining to House about their "scandalous speeches." Lord Northcliffe turned his smear machine loose on the envoys, accusing them of fomenting another Easter Rebellion. In Parliament, Bonar Law claimed that Lloyd George had been double-crossed. Now that he knew the truth about these incendiaries, he would never meet with them. Not only were the Irish-Americans taking part in Irish politics, they were encouraging "a rebellious movement." It was as bad as 1776!

On May 9, as the Irish-Americans arrived to address a crowd in front of Mansion House, where the Dáil Éireann met, British troops seized the building and opened fire from the windows and roof. The shots were aimed over the heads of the crowd, which fled, leaving the American visitors trembling with horror and outrage. They were soon telling everyone that the British ruled Ireland by brute force.[36]

Back in Paris, the Irish-Americans learned there was not a chance of the British permitting De Valera and other delegates to come to Paris.

Undeterred, they demanded the right to go before the peace conference to speak on Ireland's behalf. They also sought a revision of Article 10 of the covenant, specifying that territorial guarantees did not apply to people who had been refused a chance to exercise their right of self-determination.

Walsh and his friends also spread all over Paris their "Report on Conditions in Ireland, with a Demand for Investigation by the Peace Conference," which amplified their assertion about British military rule. They claimed that political prisoners were being held in abominable conditions. They added a list of atrocities, which the British of course denied.

The *New Statesman,* one of England's most respected liberal journals, admitted the report proved "Ireland was being governed by bayonet and machine gun." Oswald Garrison Villard, a close friend of Frank Walsh, made sure the report got space aplenty in *The Nation.* Other American magazines and newspapers gave it major attention as well.[37]

Next came stunning news from the United States. By a vote of 60 to 1, the Senate had passed a resolution calling on Wilson to get a hearing for De Valera and his delegation before the peace conference. An appalled Tumulty cabled Admiral Grayson, with a message for Wilson: "YOU CANNOT OVERESTIMATE REAL INTENSITY OF FEELING BEHIND THE IRISH QUESTION HERE." By this time, Wilson was so enraged with the Irish-Americans, he told his press officer, Ray Stannard Baker, "I don't know how long I shall be able to resist telling them what I think of their miserable mischief making."[38]

Wilson now adopted the British attitude toward Walsh and his committee. He blamed them for the failure to win permission for De Valera and his colleagues to come to Paris. The president claimed that "by our unofficial activity we had practically cleared the way" for the Irish delegation to come before the peace conference. But the Irish-Americans' behavior in Ireland "so inflamed British opinion" that the situation "got quite of hand." There is no evidence of any such pro-Irish "unofficial activity" in the record. The story is one more piece of evidence of how totally Wilson had become Lloyd George's captive.[39]

A frantic Tumulty begged Wilson not to let the "indiscretions" of the Irish-Americans stop him from doing something on Ireland's behalf. It was not the fate of Ireland, but the political survival of Wilson and the peace treaty that worried the embattled secretary back in the White House. He warned that the Irish-Americans' propaganda was deluging "every large city and town." With great reluctance, the president agreed to meet with the committee privately.

The meeting did not go well. Wilson told the Irish-Americans that the Big Four had agreed any one of them had the right to block a small nation that wanted to appear before them. The British were certain to exercise this veto on Ireland. Frank Walsh, his liberal ardor for Woodrow Wilson long since evaporated, bluntly asked the president why he did not go to Ireland and see for himself what was happening there. Wilson angrily reiterated his dubious contention that he had De Valera on his way to Paris when Walsh and his friends "kicked over the apple cart" with their speeches in Ireland. Walsh shot back that they were only trying to help a small nation realize one of Wilson's ideals, self-determination. Had Wilson forgotten that article of the Fourteen Points?

Wilson was staggered. From the lips of this angry Irish-American, a former follower, he heard the ruin and mockery of the illusions he had brought to Paris. "You have touched on the great metaphysical tragedy of today," the president said. "My words have raised hopes in the hearts of millions of people." Wilson admitted he was suffering "great anxieties" because he was unable to fulfill these hopes. Almost pitifully, he admitted he had come to Paris expecting to see his principles triumph. Now he had to admit, "There were a lot of things I hoped for but did not get."[40]

Although Walsh may have been personally moved by this confession, the Irish in America showed Wilson no mercy. Judge Daniel Cohalan and his allies said the president's refusal to act proved he did not give a damn about Ireland. Others scoffed at the president's claim that he needed the unanimous consent of the Big Four, unable to believe how completely Lloyd George had Wilson at his mercy. One Irish-American talked wrathfully of making Wilson himself "the great metaphysical tragedy of the age." This wisecrack would soon become fulfilled prophecy.[41]

VIII

On the other side of the world, another American ally, Japan, found itself confronted by a challenge to its regional imperialism. Since 1910, the Japanese had ruled Korea as a captive province. They had deposed the Korean emperor and installed a governor general with autocratic powers that made the kaiser look like a shrinking violet. They banned the Korean language and ordered schools, newspapers and book publishers to use Japanese. The 20 million Koreans were not happy about this destruction of their ancient country and culture, and many defiant souls fled abroad to seek help. One man, Syngman Rhee, headed for the United States.

There he listened to Woodrow Wilson enunciate his Fourteen Points and various supplementary principles. The one that hit Rhee the hardest was, not surprisingly, the right of self-determination. He and others soon got the news back to Korea, where massive street demonstrations erupted. Hundreds of thousands of Koreans chanted, "Long live Korean independence."

The Japanese responded with six infantry battalions and 13,000 special policemen. They beat, shot, stabbed, hacked, tortured and occasionally burned alive these protesters with exemplary imperial zeal. The final toll, according to Tokyo, was 7,509 killed, 15,951 injured and 46,948 arrested. Koreans claimed the figures should be multiplied by three and possibly five. With effrontery that more than matched the British in India, the Japanese announced that the Koreans seemed to have confused self-determination with independence. They were not the same. Poor Japan was merely trying to keep order in Asia. It was like a clean, hardworking householder "disturbed by family brawls and incompetent sanitation of disorderly neighbors."

There is no record of Woodrow Wilson's saying a word on behalf of the massacred Koreans. The U.S. State Department said that their fate was, like the troubles in Ireland, an internal matter. The State Department incidentally had yet to comment on Amritsar, because the British had managed to make that human rights disaster an official secret.[42]

IX

By this time the peace conference was lurching toward its finale. Clemenceau, Lloyd George and Wilson said they did not care whether the Italians returned or stayed home. The treaty had to be finished without further delay, or galloping Bolshevism would swallow Germany. The swarms of experts were told to finalize everything, and a message was sent to the Germans, telling them to send representatives to Versailles on April 25 "for the purpose of receiving the text of the preliminaries of the treaty, as drawn up by the Allies and Associated Powers."[43]

The Big Four turned their attention to a treaty with Austria-Hungary, a job that could best be compared to putting together pieces of a dropped puzzle. Here Wilson confronted another dismaying problem. The French, still obsessed by their fear of Germany, were unilaterally turning the states born of the breakup of the Austro-Hungarian and Russian empires into military satellites on Germany's borders. French officers and weaponry poured into Poland, Czechoslovakia and Rumania. Poland had raised an army of 600,000, and the Czechs 250,000; the Rumanians were industriously imitating them. All these armies soon began shooting at each other over disputed slices of territory. Ray Stannard Baker, Wilson's press secretary, glumly informed the president that there were no less than fourteen small wars in progress in supposedly pacified Europe.

"Yes," Wilson said wearily. "They all prefer to fight."

Around the same time, Baker overheard Lloyd George denouncing Europe's small states as troublemakers and expensive in the bargain. The prime minister assailed the "monstrous demands of Czechoslovakia" as typical of the "miserable ambitions of the small states."

So much for the war to end all wars on behalf of small countries such as poor little Belgium.[44]

X

Meanwhile, the draft of the final peace treaty was in frantic progress. Staffers toiled on technicalities and wording. Other bureaucrats scurried around Paris to find out what had been decided about Poland's claims to Upper Silesia and similar matters. When it came to the section on reparations, they discovered that no one, including Woodrow Wilson, had paid serious attention to a decision to preface it with a statement asserting that Germany was responsible for starting the war. To the British and the French, this was an article of faith, of course. Their propaganda had reiterated it almost every day for four years. But Wilson was on record as saying no one—or everyone—was responsible.

On the face of it, the accusation was bizarre. No one claimed that the Germans had shot Archduke Franz Ferdinand and his wife in Sarajevo in 1914, nor that this murder of the crown prince of Germany's chief ally did not have a great deal to do with precipitating the conflict. The war guilt clause pretended this central event never happened. Instead, the document curtly demanded that Germany acknowledge its responsibility "for causing all the loss and damage to which the Allied and Associated governments have been subjected as a consequence of the war imposed on them by the aggression of Germany and its allies." Compounding the irony, this statement was written by a former Wilson pupil at Princeton (and future secretary of state), John Foster Dulles.[45]

The source of the assertion was a memoir by Henry Morgenthau, Sr., Wilson's ambassador to Turkey from 1913 to 1916. *Ambassador Morgenthau's Story* told of a secret meeting of the kaiser with Germany's top generals, admirals, industrialists and bankers plus numerous prominent members of the diplomatic corps on July 5, 1914, seven days after the Sarajevo assassinations. "Are you ready for war?" the kaiser had purportedly asked. Everyone except the bankers supposedly said yes. The bankers wanted time to unload securities they held on Wall Street and other financial markets. The kaiser gave the money men two weeks to take care of these matters.

Morgenthau cited the "astonishing slump in prices" on Wall Street from July 5 to July 22 by way of proof that the Germans dumped their stocks. But the pièce de résistance in the evidence department was the ambassador's revelation that he had been told the entire story of the Potsdam conclave by Baron Hans Von Wagenheim, Germany's ambassador to Turkey, who had supposedly attended the meeting. One can easily see why a harried young staffer such as John Foster Dulles might buy this story. In a report filed on March 29, 1919, it had been cited as perhaps the primary piece of evidence by the Commission on the Responsibility for the Authors of the War and on Enforcement of Penalties.

Historians examining the evidence in the next decade concluded that Morgenthau was lying. In the early months of the war, Germany was trying to convince the United States that hostilities had been forced on it. Wagenheim would never have boasted to an American official that the precise opposite was the truth. Nor was there an "astonishing slump" in stocks in July 1914. State Department files show no report from Morgenthau of his conversation with Wagenheim, who had conveniently died in 1915. If such an exchange had taken place, Morgenthau should have (and would have) instantly informed his government.[46]

XI

The Germans, in the midst of fighting Bolsheviks and imminent starvation, had managed to stay in close touch with the peace process in Paris. They had even set up a Bureau for Peace Negotiations, soon shortened by slangy Berliners to *Paxkonferenz*. The bureau's existence testified to the widespread German conviction that Germany had signed a contract with Woodrow Wilson to negotiate peace on the basis of the Fourteen Points. The country put forty bureaucrats to work on Wilson's various statements on peace, backed up by more than one hundred experts on agriculture, industry, education and almost every other conceivable topic that might come up when negotiations with the Allies began.

When the Allied note asking Berlin to send representatives to hear the preliminary terms arrived in Berlin, the German foreign minister, Count Ulrich von Brockdorff-Rantzau, assumed that the document could be picked up by a messenger. He would dispatch an ambassador, an aide and four clerks to do the job. Back came a stiff reply from the Allies. They wanted a delegation of "plenipotentiaries" ready to discuss all aspects of the proposed peace. The count, a veteran diplomat, was not in the least non-plussed. He quickly assembled politicians, soldiers and top-level bureaucrats, and soon, 180 Germans were on their way to Versailles.

When they arrived on April 29, 1919, the French escorted them to the Hôtel des Réservoirs, one of the better hostelries in Versailles. The French dumped their bags in the courtyard and announced there were no porters willing to carry a German suitcase upstairs. Around the hotel was a barbed-wire fence, patrolled by French sentries. For the next week, the Germans waited—and waited—and waited. In Paris the drafting committee was still writing the treaty. Meanwhile, groups of French patriots showed up at the hotel's barbed-wire fence to scream insults at the Germans.

In Paris, the completed treaty, 440 articles in 75,000 words, went to the printer on May 5. It ran to more than 200 printed pages. Before dawn on May 7, messengers rushed copies to Allied delegations and collaborating officials such as Herbert Hoover, who had finally managed to get some food into Germany, though not nearly enough. Hoover received his copy at 4 A.M. Recently the food administrator had written a letter to Wilson, advising him that if they could not get a peace treaty on the basis of the Fourteen Points, "we should retire from Europe, lock stock and barrel."

Hoover finished reading the treaty as dawn brightened the Paris sky. He could not believe his own disappointment. The thing was an abomination, a parody of the Fourteen Points. The economic clauses, aimed at crippling Germany, would "pull down the whole continent." Unquestionably, the terms "contained the seeds of another war." Dressing, the Iowan wandered disconsolately into the streets, where he met the British economist John Maynard Keynes and the South African leader Jan Christian Smuts, both of whom had obviously just finished reading their copies. They stared at each other, disillusion and dismay on their faces.[47]

No one, including Wilson, Lloyd George, Clemenceau or Orlando (who returned from his sulky retreat to Rome on May 5), had read the entire treaty from beginning to end until the day it was presented to the Germans. The cumulative effect of its cynical deals and cruel demands struck almost every American at the conference with the impact of a high-explosive shell, annihilating whatever illusions the participant may have still nourished about their mission in Paris.

Secretary of State Lansing made one of the more powerful statements in a memorandum he put in his files. He called the terms "immeasurably harsh and humiliating." He dismissed Wilson's ploy of putting the league into the treaty, because the treaty made a mockery of the league. The secretary deplored the way the document delivered "peoples . . . against their will into the hands of those they hate." Lansing called the league "an instrument of the mighty to check the normal growth of national power and national aspirations" among the defeated. Instead of a Triple Alliance, he believed the world now had a Quintuple Alliance, "which is to rule the world." The members could surround this alliance with a halo and call it the League of Nations, but it was still an alliance of "the five great military powers." What did it all add up to? "Disappointment, regret, depression."[48]

If this was the treaty's impact on the Americans, not much imagination is needed to picture the German reaction. At 3 P.M. on May 7, Count Brockdorff-Rantzau and five fellow delegates were ushered into one of the most spectacular rooms in the Trianon Château, across the Park of Versailles from the immense royal palace of the French kings. Large windows filled two walls. Outside one window was a flowering cherry tree. A third wall was covered with mirrors, filling the room with reflected light.[49]

The German delegates sat down at a table, which French newspapers had labeled *le banc des accusés*. The table of the accused. Opposite them sat Clemenceau, flanked by Lloyd George and Wilson. Clemenceau rose and spat out a venomous speech. He said it was "neither the time nor place for superfluous words . . . the hour has struck for the weighty settlement of your account." In this "Second Peace of Versailles," the victors were "unanimously resolved" to obtain "all the legitimate satisfactions which are our due."

The reference to the second peace of Versailles made it clear that the French appetite for revenge was still in charge. In 1871, the victorious Germans had forced the French to sign a humiliating peace treaty in the city where France's kings had once dominated Europe. The premier informed the Germans that they would have fifteen days to send "written observations" about the treaty to the Allies—along with a date on which they would sign it.

The Germans registered shock and disbelief. Clemenceau was telling them there would be no face-to-face negotiations. The premier asked if any of the Germans wished to speak. Brockdorff-Rantzau raised his hand, and picked up a speech he and his associates had stayed up most of the night writing. Exhausted and extremely nervous, the foreign minister read his remarks seated, which many people considered a sign of disrespect. (In fact, he was so nervous, he was unable to stand.) The forty-nine-year-old count had been one of the few members of the foreign service who had defied Generals Ludendorff and von Hindenburg and called for an early compromise peace. But he happened to be the kaiser's first cousin and looked like a classic German aristocrat, complete with a monocle and a precise mustache. He began by saying, "We know the intensity of the hatred which meets us" and went on to discuss the clause, already broadcast through newspaper leaks, that fastened guilt for the war on Germany. The count said he would never admit such a thing. "Such a confession in my mouth would be a lie." He told his audience that the continuing British blockade had killed hundreds of thousands of German noncombatants. He reminded them that they had offered peace on the basis of the Fourteen Points.

One British delegate dismissed these words as "the most tactless speech" he had ever heard. Clemenceau's face turned magenta as he listened. Lloyd George's grew so angry, he snapped an ivory letter opener in half. Woodrow Wilson turned to the prime minister while the count was speaking and whispered, "Isn't it just like them?" Earlier in the day, after Wilson had read the full treaty, he had confessed to Ray Stannard Baker, "If I were a German, I think I should never sign it." These were the words of a man who had abandoned interest in fighting for his Fourteen Points.

Back at the Hôtel des Réservoirs, the Germans spent the night translating the treaty. By dawn, they saw what confronted them. Along with the confession of guilt for the war were reparations that would be de-cided later—which meant Germany's economy would be at the mercy of the victors for as long as they pleased. Added to this were the loss of crucial coalfields to the Poles and French; the separation of the Rhine-land, the Saar, and Upper Silesia from the Reich; the loss of the port city of Danzig (given to the Poles); the all-but-total destruction of their army and navy—and a demand that the kaiser and an unspecified num-ber of other leaders be surrendered for trial as war criminals. The terms drove one member of the delegation, a socialist who had risen from the working class to become postmaster general, to drink. In an alcoholic rage, he smashed glasses and shouted, "I believed in Woodrow Wilson until today. I believed him an honest man and now that scoundrel sends us such a treaty!"[50]

XII

The Germans rushed a copy of the translated treaty to Berlin. Overnight, Woodrow Wilson went from the most admired to the most hated man in Germany. In their rage and despair, the Germans printed several thousand copies of the treaty and distributed them all over Berlin. President of the republic Friedrich Ebert called it a "monstrous document." General Ludendorff roared that it was time to tell America to go to hell. Chancellor Philipp Scheidemann called Wilson a hypocrite and said the treaty was "the vilest crime in history." A crowd gathered outside the American military mission to chant, "Where are our Fourteen Points? Where is Wilson's peace?" Chancellor Scheidemann ordered the dele-gates in Versailles to inform the Allies that the treaty was "unbearable and unfulfillable."[51]

Alert American reporters obtained copies of the treaty in Berlin and cabled them to the United States. The document was soon being discussed in American newspapers and magazines. Many liberals, already distressed by Article 10 of the League of Nations, with its implicit support of the British empire in perpetuity, were appalled when they saw the league linked to the punitive treaty. They lost all confidence in Wilson.

Oswald Garrison Villard led the attack in *The Nation*. The league's tilt toward the conservative side of things was bad enough, he said. But now it was tied to a peace of "intrigue, selfish aggression and naked imperialism."

Villard grew more merciless with each succeeding issue. *The Nation* described the peace conference as "the madness at Versailles" and dismissed Wilson as "discredited."

On May 24, 1919, Villard published "Out of His Own Mouth," a collection of quotes from Wilson's speeches, in which the president opposed the venal things that had been done with his apparent approval in fashioning the treaty. Getting to the heart of the matter, Villard asked how anyone with liberal sympathies could expect "the managers of this bastard League of Nations to right the wrongs the treaty contains?"[52]

For the *New Republic*, which had supported Wilson's decision to go to war and had accumulated a heavy burden of doubt as the editors watched him throw Socialists and other dissenters in jail, destroy the International Workers of the World, and muzzle magazines and newspapers, the treaty was the proverbial last straw. On May 24, they published a special issue, "This Is Not Peace." It was, editor Herbert Croly told Justice Louis Brandeis, a confession that the magazine had made a terrible mistake, backing Wilson and his war. Sparing no one, the magazine called the treaty an "inhuman monster" and announced that, thanks to Wilson, liberalism had "committed suicide." Americans would be "fools" to approve a peace that "cannot last." The article saw only one solution—an American withdrawal from the whole sordid business.[53]

Walter Lippmann, after devoting much of the previous two years to Wilson's war, called the League of Nations "fundamentally diseased" and began denouncing it everywhere. When a group of Boston Unitarians invited him to speak on behalf of the treaty, he nonplused them by calling it an unmitigated disaster. In a long letter to Secretary of War Newton Baker, Lippmann did not try to conceal his anger and heartbreak. He went over the treaty, article by article, pointing out the gross violations of the Fourteen Points.

Grimly, Lippmann laid the responsibility for the mess at Wilson's door. He declined to excuse him because he had a "difficult task in Paris." Numerous people had warned the president about the problems he would face—and had urged him not to go. Lippmann blamed part of the disaster on Wilson's inability to delegate responsibility—and tolerate strong men in his entourage. Another reason was the president's "curious irresponsibility in the use of language which leads him to make promises without any clear idea of how they are to be fulfilled."[54]

In the mainstream press, a very different reaction to the treaty prevailed. The *New York Times* editorialized: "It is a terrible punishment the German people and their mad rulers have brought upon themselves. . . . Can Germany live under these conditions? All the world can see that they are terribly severe. But the world knows, too, that they are just." The *Times* demonstrated that German hatred did not make for accurate readings of the future: "The punishment Germany must endure for centuries will be one of the greatest deterrents to the war spirit."

The *New York Tribune*, Germanophobe since 1914, wrote: "The wild beast that sprang at the throat of civilization has been muzzled." The *Chicago Daily News* took a more mocking tone: "What did Germania think—that the Allied nations were going to make her Queen of the May?" The *Cleveland Press* taunted: "It's a hard bed, Heinie, but who made it?" War rage was still alive and well in most of America.

In London, the Tory *Daily Telegraph* still breathed the hatred and envy of Germany that had brought England into the war. In prose that could have been written by Wellington House, the editors gloated that the treaty would leave Germany "an unrecognizable ghost of the empire of five years ago, bloated as it was with criminal annexations, arrogant with wealth, and crazed with the consciousness of unparalleled military power."[55]

XIII

At Versailles, the Germans toiled on a response to the treaty. Count Brockdorff-Rantzau refused to obey his government's order to abandon the argument and retreat to Berlin. He remained convinced that the Germans had signed a contract in the armistice agreement for a peace based on the Fourteen Points. He and his staff sent a stream of objections to Clemenceau, who shared them with Wilson and Lloyd George, and ordered staffers to prepare rebuttals.

The rattled German delegation did not improve its case by objecting to everything, from the reparations to minutiae such as the refusal to permit German missionaries to operate in the surrendered colonies. But most of the delegates' wrath focused on the war guilt clause. They linked this objection to the open-ended reparations article, sensing that if they could eliminate the guilt clause, bargaining on reparations would be tilted in their favor.

The Allies were startled by the intensity of the Germans' resistance to the war guilt charge. But they had no inclination to yield the point, especially after the Germans published the treaty. Once the guilt charge became public knowledge in England and France and United States, hatred of "the Hun" became part of the political atmosphere in which the politicians were operating. Woodrow Wilson felt no compunction about backing it unreservedly, even though it violated his previous statements about the origin of war.

Not a single objection was made in the U.S. Congress or the British Parliament about the treaty's harshness. Instead of backing down, the Allies raised the denunciatory ante by telling the Germans that "the war was the greatest crime against humanity and the freedom of peoples that any nation calling itself civilized has ever consciously committed."[56]

Herbert Hoover was appalled to discover that if Germany refused to sign, the Allies were ready to reimpose the blockade. Clemenceau and Lloyd George had overruled Wilson's objection to this decision. Hoover announced if this atrocity was repeated, he would resign instantly. He and his staff were in "a daily race" against the spread of Bolshevism. The food supplies they were importing barely fed Germany's "pitifully undernourished" children, which left their elders still on the brink of starvation.[57]

While the Allies rebutted the Germans' objections, behind the scenes, Hoover and his relief staff worked to persuade Wilson and other members of the American delegation to make major changes in the treaty. A similar effort began among the British delegation, led by Jan Christian Smuts and John Maynard Keynes. The latter two dissenters made astonishing progress. As Lloyd George absorbed the implications of the whole treaty, his long-dormant liberal conscience began tormenting him. Not a little of these pricks were coming from genuine liberals in England, who were denouncing the treaty as ferociously as their American counterparts. Before long the prime minister was wondering aloud if major changes were needed.

Lloyd George was especially shaken by a letter from Brockdorff-Rantzau on the economic consequences of the treaty, which the liberal *Manchester Guardian* published on May 15. The foreign minister noted that since Germany had become an industrial nation with a population of 67 million, it had been importing 12 million tons of food a year. This food was paid for by exports—about 15 million Germans made their living in foreign trade before the war. Now, stripped of its merchant fleet and its

colonies, which supplied raw materials as well as foodstuffs, this already
dire need for imported food was being compounded by the treaty, which
deprived Germany of 21 percent of its homegrown corn and potato crops.
Simultaneously, a third of its coal was being given to France and Poland,
crippling its industrial capacity. All this added up to the deaths of many
millions of people in Germany in the next few years. The nation's health
was already "broken" by the blockade. The treaty was nothing less than a
mass "death sentence," Brockdorff-Rantzau wrote. Lloyd George was so
disturbed, he summoned the entire British cabinet to Paris for a weekend-
long debate on whether the treaty should be revised.[58]

The American dissenters made no such progress with Woodrow Wilson.
He seemed unbothered when Joseph V. Fuller, one of the best minds on the
delegation staff, resigned with a scorching letter that declared the treaty
"bartered away our principles in a series of compromises with interests of
imperialism and revenge." General Tasker Bliss said he could not sign a
statement that he "heartily and unreservedly" approved the treaty. In a letter to his wife, Bliss summed up his discouragement: "What a wretched
mess it all is." Henry White was similarly despondent: "We had such high
hopes of this adventure; we believed God called us and now we are doing
hell's dirtiest work."

As the German responses to the treaty grew into a 20,000-word document, Jan Christian Smuts wrote to the president, saying he totally agreed
with Berlin's argument that it had signed a contract to make peace on
the basis of the Fourteen Points and the treaty did not come close to
doing this. Press Secretary Stannard Baker told the president the treaty
was "unworkable." Hoover recruited Norman H. Davis of the State
Department to come with him to ask Wilson to revise the treaty. They
pointed to the way Lloyd George was changing his mind and argued that
Wilson could now outvote Clemenceau. Davis urged the president to set
the reparations at a specific amount. Otherwise the German economy
would remain paralyzed. Hoover descanted on the threat of starvation
and Bolshevism.

Wilson was unmoved. He told Ray Stannard Baker that Lloyd George
was just "in a funk." The prime minister was objecting to all sorts of things
he had approved over Wilson's objections. Besides, the British chameleon
would never stand up to Clemenceau face-to-face. To calm the agitation in
the American delegation, Wilson agreed to meet with thirty-nine of them.

Face-to-face with their boss, only Hoover, Davis and Bliss spoke out strongly against the treaty. Wilson listened more or less patiently and then dismissed all the objections by claiming that he had not succumbed to "expediency"; the issue was whether he—and they—were "satisfied in their consciences" that they had done "the just thing." The president insisted the Americans had done exactly that. The treaty was "a hard one," but "a hard one was needed." Why this was so he did not say. Whereupon he ducked into his refuge—the League of Nations. Everything would be solved to everyone's satisfaction when Germany was admitted to the league.[59]

XIV

When Lloyd George learned that Wilson would not consider any changes in the treaty, the prime minister did another political back flip and loaned his private secretary, Philip Kerr, to the Council of Four to draft a general reply to the German demands. Kerr not only rejected every German argument, but interlarded the 30,000-word document with billingsgate straight from Lord Northcliffe's *Daily Mail*. He told the Germans they were responsible not only for starting the war but also for the "barbarous methods" and "criminal character" of the way they fought it. As for complaints that millions of Germans were being handed over to Poland, Czechoslovakia, Italy and France—Berlin had done the same thing to other nationalities at Brest-Litovsk. The treaty sought justice for the dead, wounded, orphaned and bereaved who had fought to free Europe from "Prussian despotism." In a final insult to the liberals and socialists now in charge of Germany, Kerr sneered that there was "no guarantee" that the current government "represents a permanent change" from Kaiserism. Clemenceau, the revenge seeker personified, could not have written a more offensive response. Added to it was an ultimatum: Germany must sign within seven days, or the war would be renewed.[60]

Foreign Minister Count Brockdorff-Rantzau realized he now had only one option—departure. Leaving a token committee behind, he and most of his delegation left for Germany to let the government decide whether to sign the treaty or defy the Allies. On the train, the count and his staff prepared a memorandum, advising a rejection. They called the war guilt clause "hateful and dishonorable" and condemned many other terms as "unbearable and impossible of fulfillment."

The government of the new German republic operated in Weimar, a city 150 miles southwest of Berlin. Famed as the eighteenth-century home of Goethe, Schiller and other poets, Weimar was a symbol of liberalism. There Brockdorff-Rantzau found a cabinet deeply divided between irreconcilables and pragmatists. The latter were led by Matthias Erzberger, the stumpy forty-four-year-old head of the Catholic Center Party, which held ninety seats in the new National Assembly. Erzberger, who had signed the armistice, favored accepting the treaty, even though he called it a "demoniacal piece of work." A refusal to sign would mean a renewal of the blockade and an invasion of Germany. The nation would collapse into chaotic fragments. Sign, Erzberger argued, and let the Allies find out that Germany would not—because it could not—fulfill most of the terms.

A crucial player in this life-and-death game was the German army. The officer corps was incensed by the treaty's reduction of the army to 100,000 men, without tanks, aircraft or heavy artillery. Minor Balkan nations had more men under arms. The operational details of the force were written into the peace treaty. Each soldier would serve twelve years, officers for twenty-five years. They could not serve in a reserve after their tour of duty. The number of field guns, howitzers, machine guns and trench mortars for each division was specified. The general staff was to be dissolved. Overseeing all these details was to be an "Allied Commission of Control."[61]

The government summoned the current quartermaster general, Wilhelm Groener, to Weimar to ask him a crucial question. If they refused to sign the treaty, would the army be able to defend Germany against an invasion? Groener had anticipated the question. He had sent officers into all parts of Germany to find out how much popular support they had for a fight to the finish. The answer that came back was unequivocal: none. Groener told the civilians the army, now barely 350,000 men, could not hope to defend the nation against the Allies, who had 200,000 troops already across the Rhine in bridgeheads established by the terms of the armistice.

Nevertheless, the German cabinet deadlocked. Half favored Erzberger's arguments in favor of signing; half rejected them. The irreconcilables were especially tormented by the guilt clause and the articles that required the surrender of the kaiser for trial as a war criminal, along with an as yet unnamed list of generals and admirals. They called these *Schmachparagraphen*—shame paragraphs. Chancellor Philipp Scheidemann resigned, and his government collapsed.

With two days left in the Allied ultimatum, the president of the republic, Friedrich Ebert, cobbled together another government, led by Socialist Gustav Bauer, who had been minister of labor in the previous cabinet. Taking his cue from Erzberger, Bauer introduced in the National Assembly a resolution to sign the treaty, with the understanding that the new government would try to get the *Schmachparagraphen* eliminated. Through a representative whom Brockdorff-Rantzau had left in Versailles, the Germans said they would sign the treaty with the understanding that they did not accept guilt for the war or an obligation to deliver anyone for trial.

On the same day, June 22, news reached Paris of an event that dashed any hope that the Allies would accept a deletion of the shame paragraphs. The German fleet, interned at Scapa Flow since the armistice, had been scuttled on orders from its commanding admiral. The Bauer government had nothing to do with the move. The admiral decided the navy's honor required him to send the five battle cruisers, nine battleships, seven cruisers and fifty destroyers to the bottom of the sea to prevent them from being used to bombard German ports in the new war that seemed likely to erupt at any moment over the *Schmachparagraphen*.

Lloyd George and the rest of the British delegation were enraged—and not a little mortified by the way the Germans got away with this double cross under the noses of their Grand Fleet. The French wondered aloud if the British let it happen to make sure they remained the world's dominant sea power. Clemenceau had expected to get a hefty percentage of the German ships.

Woodrow Wilson took charge of the situation. He told the Germans that "the time for discussion is past." They had less than twenty-four hours to sign—or be invaded by thirty divisions backed by aircraft—and a renewed blockade that would cut off every scrap of food from the outside world. Herbert Hoover must have winced when the president used the blockade as the ultimate weapon.[62]

It was decision time. President Ebert made one last call to Quartermaster General Groener. He told the general most of the cabinet were ready to fight if they could get the slightest assurance that the army had a chance to win the struggle. Groener asked for two hours to discuss the situation one more time with Field Marshal von Hindenburg. Long before the 120 minutes passed, the two soldiers had decided resistance was hopeless and ultimately suicidal. Along with the invasion from the west,

Germany would have to face a Polish army from the east and a Czech army, commanded by French officers, from the south.

People were marching through Berlin carrying signs: "Peace for God's Sake" and "We Want Bread Not Bullets." Groener told Ebert the despicable treaty had to be signed. The Bauer government informed the National Assembly, but the politicians could not bring themselves to take a final vote. They said their vote on the previous day was sufficient authority, even though the *Schmachparagraphen* remained in the treaty.[63]

The Bauer cabinet sent a note to Paris that made no attempt to conceal its defiance and disgust. "Yielding to overwhelming force . . . the government of the German Republic declares that it is ready to accept and sign the conditions of peace imposed by the Allied and Associated Powers."[64]

XV

Once more the French displayed their appetite for revenge. The signing took place in the Great Hall of Mirrors of the Palace of Versailles, where the Germans had declared Wilhelm I, the current kaiser's father, emperor of Germany in 1871 after signing their victor's peace in the Franco-Prussian war. The Allies' eagerness to finish the business led them to ignore another historical fact, which cast a shadow of illegitimacy over the ceremony. It was five years to the day since the Serbian terrorist Gavrilo Princip had assassinated Archduke Franz Ferdinand and his wife, Sophie, in Sarajevo.

More than 1,000 people jammed into the 240-foot-long room, with its wall of seventeen huge mirrors and its allegorical paintings on the gilded ceiling. On other walls hung immense portraits of Louis XIV, the Sun King, who built the gigantic palace as a symbol of France's power in the seventeenth century, when America was a scattering of settlements on the Atlantic seaboard. Before the mirrors was a long horseshoe table at which the Allied delegates sat. All except the Chinese took their seats. The men from Peking were boycotting the ceremony to protest the Allied surrender of Shantung Province to Japan. In front of the horseshoe table was a small table for the German delegates.

Presently, at Clemenceau's command, two German officials, the secretary for foreign affairs and the colonial secretary, walked to the small table. No one rose in recognition—a petty revenge for Foreign Minister Brockdorff-Rantzau's failure to stand when he spoke at the Trianon on the

day the draft treaty was handed to Germany. Wordlessly, after a brief statement by Clemenceau, the Germans signed. The Americans were next. The
president signed "Woodrow," but had great difficulty completing "Wilson."
Some historians consider this proof of arterial brain damage from the
stroke he may have suffered in April. A psychologist might theorize that he
had to struggle to sign a document that was a parody of his principles.

As the rest of the delegates signed, a battery of guns began firing at the
Saint-Cyr Military Academy. The audience watched with very little sense
of awe or solemnity. The room buzzed with idle chatter. To Lloyd George's
consternation, some spectators asked the German signers for their auto-
graphs. After Jan Christian Smuts signed, he announced he did so under
protest because the treaty was not going to achieve "real peace." In Berlin,
newspapers reported the ceremony with black borders on their front
pages. *Vorwärts*, the more or less official government paper, declared: "We
must never forget it is only a scrap of paper. Treaties based on violence can
keep their validity only so long as force exists. Do not lose hope. The resurrection day comes."[65]

XVI

Woodrow Wilson cabled a message to Joseph Tumulty announcing the
treaty had been signed. He called it "a severe treaty in the duties and penalties it imposes upon Germany, but it is severe only because great wrongs
done by Germany are to be righted and repaired." However, it was "much
more than a peace treaty with Germany." It liberated many other "great
peoples" and ended "an old and intolerable order" that enabled small
groups of selfish men to rule others in the name of autocratic empires.
Most important, it organized the free governments of the world in a permanent league to maintain "peace and right and justice." It was "a great
charter for a new order of things" and ground for "deep satisfaction, universal reassurance and confident hope."[66]

Tumulty rushed this defense of the treaty to Senator Gilbert Hitchcock,
the Democratic minority leader of the Senate. It arrived while the Senate
was debating an appropriations bill. Hitchcock interrupted the debate and
read the text aloud. No one said a word. A copy of the treaty had already
been published in the *Chicago Daily Tribune*. Senator Borah had already read
it into the *Congressional Record*—and had denounced it. In private letters,

Senator La Follette was calling it "a spoils grabbing compact of greed and hate." The senators went back to debating money matters.[67]

In the streets of Washington, D.C., and other cities, there were no celebrations. A reporter for the English *Manchester Guardian* decided the total absence of elation in the United States was explained by "everything that has occurred since the Armistice." The net impact had been a confirmation of "the deep habit of distrusting the European way. Men may differ as to whether France should have the Saar or Britain the bulk of the African colonies, but they agree vaguely that it is not a very inspiring business, one way or another."

In Boston, Eamon de Valera, the provisional president of the yet unborn Irish republic, called the peace treaty a mockery. It would create "twenty new wars in place of the one nominally ended." The League of Nations, he sneered, was simply a new "Holy Alliance." With Great Britain in the driver's seat, it could not "save democracy."[68]

XVII

What did Woodrow Wilson really think of the treaty? At a press conference before he headed home, when Lincoln Steffens asked him if it was a good peace, the president said, "I think that we have made a better peace than I should have expected when I came here to Paris." This reply comes under the category of "What else do you expect a president to say about an enterprise on which he had just spent seven months of his life?" In a private letter written around the same time, Wilson described the results as "much better than at one time I feared." This is a more accurate description of his emotional ups and downs in Paris, but still rather far from the truth.

A more revealing glimpse of Wilson's true feelings was a behind-the-scenes contretemps that erupted when he and Mrs. Wilson were invited to a farewell banquet by President Raymond Poincaré of France. Wilson flatly refused to go. In colorful (for him) language, he expressed his intense dislike for the pompous president, who had been the hardest of the French hard-liners in the demand for a punitive peace. Wilson told Colonel House he would "choke" if he sat at the table with Poincaré.[69]

Only frantic efforts on the part of Colonel House, Henry White and Jules Jusserand, France's ambassador to the United States, changed Wilson's mind. The episode suggests that beneath Wilson's attempts to tell himself and others that the peace treaty was a job well done lay an awareness that it was the betrayal, even the mockery, of the Fourteen Points that the liberals of England and America—and the Germans—said it was.

On June 28, before the president left for Brest, where the *George Washington* was waiting, Wilson had a final conversation with Colonel House. In the last two months of the peace conference, Wilson had shunted House to the periphery of the diplomatic struggle, seldom taking his advice and often not even informing him of what had been decided. The colonel, in a forlorn attempt to regain their old intimacy, again urged him to be conciliatory with the Senate. Wilson's eyes flashed fire. "House," he said, "I have found one can never get anything in this life that is worthwhile without fighting for it."

The colonel murmured that he thought they both understood that "Anglo-Saxon civilization was built up on compromise."

Wilson turned away in silent disagreement.

The exchange was both a commentary on Wilson's ordeal of failure in Paris and an omen of future anguish in the United States. It was also the last conversation Woodrow Wilson had with Edward Mandell House. They never saw each other again.[70]

Philip Dru was on his own.

Chapter 11

CHILLING THE
HEART OF THE WORLD

With battleships and destroyers steaming to port and starboard, the *George Washington* reached New York Harbor on July 8, 1919. The seas had been calm, the voyage refreshing. Woodrow Wilson seemed in fighting trim as he debarked to the cheers of thousands of schoolchildren in Hoboken. Whisked across the river to Manhattan, he enjoyed more acclamation from his fellow Democrats as he rode in an open car to Carnegie Hall, where newly elected Democratic Governor Alfred E. Smith hailed him as the savior of Europe. Wilson responded with a brief speech in which he said he was so glad to be home, even Hoboken had looked beautiful. He paid tribute to the sacrifices of "that army of clean men," the AEF, who were "devoted to the highest interests of humanity." Like them, the peacemakers in Paris had tried to "lift [their eyes] to a distant horizon." But here at home, some people had failed to understand this worldwide vision. They had kept their eyes "too much on the ground." The great task now was to preserve the peace that had been won in Europe.[1]

Anyone who knew anything about the brutalities of Belleau Wood and the Argonne must have concluded from Wilson's description of the AEF that he never had an honest conversation with a doughboy while he was in France. His description of the peacemakers in Paris was even more misleading. Wilson headed for Washington, D.C., where a boisterous crowd cheered him at Union Station. Among them was Alice Roosevelt Long-worth, who gloated that most of the greeters seemed to be run-of-the-mill president gawkers. Proving that she had inherited her father's penchant for over-the-top politics, Alice crossed her fingers and put an Irish curse on Wilson: "A murrain on him," she muttered, with her fingers crossed. "A murrain on him."[2]

In the White House, Alice's curse soon seemed to be working. Wilson toiled over the speech he planned to make when he presented the treaty to the Senate. He could not get it right. Almost certainly, the missing ingredi-ent was Colonel House. If he had brought House home with him, they would have blocked out the speech aboard the *George Washington* and Wilson would have completed it in a few hours as the deadline ap-proached. Wilson blamed his trouble on having "so very little respect" for the audience he was going to address.

On July 10, Wilson went to the Senate with the treaty under his arm. The reception was inauspicious. The minority Democrats gave him a standing ovation; most of the Republicans did not make a sound. Several did not even stand. The president began by calling the treaty "nothing less than a world settlement." But he was strangely uninformative about how the settlement was reached. He claimed there was no need to tell the sena-tors "what was attempted and done at Paris." Instead he chose a "less ambi-tious" course. It was odd to hear a man regarded as one of the best orators in American history apologizing in advance for his speech.

Wilson proceeded to recap why the United States had entered the war and the crucial element the AEF had played in changing the course of the struggle on the Western Front. He called the doughboys "the visible embodiment of America." They had made the nation "a living reality" not only in France but among tens of millions of other people whose freedom was in danger.

The president talked about how the Americans at the peace conference had tried to make the nation's ideals the basis for a lasting peace. He dis-cussed the new countries they had created from the Austro-Hungarian empire, the need to protect racial and religious minorities. Ultimately, he claimed, it had become apparent to everyone that the League of Nations was vital to the treaty, if any kind of lasting peace was to be achieved.

Not a word about the strenuous efforts of the British and the French to jettison the league until the treaty was completed—or the way Wilson had repeatedly sacrificed the Fourteen Points to keep the league linked to the treaty. It is unreasonable, of course, to expect a president to tell the whole truth about what we now call a summit conference. But Wilson's departures from reality struck an especially discordant note in the wake of his earlier condemnations of secret diplomacy. They also ignored the way the treaty had already been denounced by liberals and even by some members of the American peace delegation.

The league was also needed, the president continued, to make sure "the monster that had resorted to arms" would remain "in chains that could not be broken." The League of Nations was the only way to stop future aggression by Germany and other nations. It was the hope of the world. The statesmen of Europe had realized they did not dare disappoint this hope. "Dare we reject it and break the heart of the world?" the president asked.

This was the only memorable line of his speech. But not a single newspaper picked it up and converted it into a slogan, as they had with "the war to end wars" or "making the world safe for democracy." Equally ignored was a statement of religious faith that was clearly very meaningful to the president. The war, American's intervention, and now the peace, Wilson said, "[have] come about by no plan of our conceiving but by the hand of God who led us into this way." Unfortunately, that moving line was followed by rhetoric that was more than a little hackneyed: "We can only go forward with lifted eyes and freshened spirit to follow the vision. . . . America shall in truth show the way. The light streams upon the path ahead, and nowhere else."[3]

The speech was a flop. One Democrat, borrowing a phrase from Lincoln, muttered that it did not "scour." Senator Brandegee of Connecticut dismissed it as "soap bubbles of oratory." More to the point was the comment of Senator Medill McCormick of Illinois, whose family owned the *Chicago Daily Tribune*: "soothing, mellifluous and uninformative." The president had not mentioned a host of topics the senators wanted and needed to understand: why he had given Shantung's 20 million Chinese to Japan; why he had refused to say a word on behalf of Ireland; why he supported Article 10, which many denounced as an obligation to defend the British empire, from Dublin to Singapore to Hong Kong. Senator Harry Ashurst of New Mexico said Wilson reminded him of the president of a troubled company who, instead of giving facts and figures to his board of directors, read them Longfellow's "Psalm of Life."[4]

Is there an explanation for this stunning failure, beyond the absence of Colonel House? Some historians have attributed it—and Wilson's woes in Paris—to his exhaustion, which worsened his chronic hypertension and triggered small strokes that left him mentally incapacitated. But there are other equally cogent explanations: notably, Wilson's awareness of the peace treaty's barbarity, and his all-too-realistic fear that this would poison people's opinion of the League of Nations. On top of this realization was the knowledge that he had blundered by going to Paris in the first place and blundered again by returning in February to subject himself to endless humiliation and scarifying compromises at the hands of Lloyd George and Clemenceau. Wilson's confidence in himself as well as in Colonel House had been grievously damaged by these experiences.

In the speech, the man who wanted to bring peace to the world referred to Germany, where hundreds of thousands of people were still living on the edge of starvation, as a monster that must be kept in chains. He did not say a word about British brutality in Ireland. He talked of Europe's statesmen as converts to the League of Nations, denying Clemenceau's derision, Lloyd George's indifference. This was a man with too many compromises on his conscience, too much anger and anxiety in the depths of his soul. Try as he might to lie to himself and others about it, Wilson knew he had produced a treaty that, in words Senator Robert La Follette had written weeks before the president's invocation of a global longing for peace, "chill[ed] the heart of the world."[5]

II

Another reason for the speech's failure goes beyond Wilson to the country that the United States had become by mid-1919. It was not the nation that had responded to Wilson's soaring call to make the world safe for democracy and the lofty idealism of the Fourteen Points. Wilson's decision to go to Paris had been a mistake that did far more than involve the presidency in the disillusioning game of who gets what. He had also abandoned his leadership of the nation—and the Democratic Party. For seven months, the United States had been adrift, deserted by this stranger president who spent his time taking bows before cheering Europeans while the mediocrities in his cabinet tried to cope with the massive readjustments of the shift from a wartime to a peacetime economy and other upheavals that cried out for creative leadership.

The mounting desperation of the man Wilson had left behind in the White House, Joe Tumulty, personified this leadership vacuum. Tumulty's cables to Wilson in Paris were a litany of woes. "YOU CANNOT UNDERSTAND HOW ACUTE SITUATION IS BROUGHT ABOUT BY RISING PRICES OF EVERY NECESSITY OF LIFE," Tumulty warned on May 12, 1919. But Wilson did nothing to slow the purchases of the wartime Wheat Administration, which kept the price of this crucial staple artificially high. Twenty-six Democrats in the Massachusetts State Legislature cabled Wilson, urging him to come home and do something about the cost of living, "which we consider far more important than the League of Nations."[6]

Eight months after the armistice, the government still controlled the nation's railroads and telephone and telegraph lines, because the United States was, technically, still at war until the peace treaty was ratified. The Republicans in Congress skillfully used this situation to identify the Democrats with socialism, which Americans now considered a first cousin to Bolshevism. "YOU CAN HAVE NO IDEA OF THE INTENSITY OF FEELING OF THE PEOPLE IN THESE MATTERS," Tumulty cabled. "FRANKLY THE PEOPLE ARE SICK OF ALL KINDS OF CONTROL AND WAR RESTRICTION."[7]

The telephone and telegraph companies were run by Postmaster General Alfred Burleson, a walking, talking political disaster. He was hated by management for his provincial Texas hostility to big business and detested by the workers because he discriminated against unions. He gave the back of his hand to telephone workers when they protested their low wages. Burleson topped this performance by raising rates in May, outraging both consumers and workers. Tumulty implored the president to send a message to Congress urging them to return the telephone and telegraph companies to private ownership. Wilson did nothing.[8]

The aging Socialist Eugene Debs was growing sick and depressed in the Atlanta federal prison. He became a cause célèbre among liberals, who bombarded the White House with pleas for a pardon. Tumulty forwarded the requests to Paris, urging Wilson to do the generous thing. Again, the president did nothing.

When Burleson refused to bargain with telephone operators in New England after he raised rates in May, some 8,000 women walked off the job in Massachusetts. Burleson attributed the strike to "radicals" and tried to break it by importing students from Massachusetts Institute of Technology and Harvard to keep the system going. Socialites from Newport were also encouraged to volunteer and bring their maids. The unautomated system depended on trained human beings willing to work ten-hour days, and these unlikely scabs soon vanished. The strike grew until it included 20,000 operators in all five New England states, silencing 610,000 telephones. Businesses floundered and profits plunged. When the public learned that starting operators earned only ten dollars a week, sympathy swung to their side.

Through Tumulty's intervention, the strike was settled after six days by a modest pay raise. But a telephoneless week—and the image of the Democratic Party picking on underpaid women—left voters in an ugly mood. A prominent Massachusetts Democrat told Tumulty that Burleson was "wrecking the party." The postmaster general was symptomatic of the whole Wilson administration. It badly needed an infusion of younger people with new ideas to handle an America transformed by the war. A disconsolate Tumulty told Wilson, "The president ought to get on the job . . . with both feet." But Wilson's feet—and head—remained in Paris.[9]

Before the year 1919 ended, 2,600 labor disputes would roil the country, and more than 4 million workers—one out of every five wage earners— went on strike. Most of these strikes were won by management. The war had been tremendously profitable for big business. DuPont's assets had quadrupled. Bethlehem Shipbuilding's profits had octupled. U.S. Steel, a corporate bellwether, was equally flush. Its chairman, Elbert Gary, arrogantly refused to bargain with the company's 250,000 workers. Wilson sent Bernard Baruch to plead with him. The former War Industries czar got nowhere.[10]

The situation cried out for the propaganda magic of George Creel. Why was the Committee on Public Information not churning out features and articles for newspapers and magazines to create a "peace will" to replace the war will that had carried America to victory? Alas, by the time the president returned to the United States, Creel was like a disembodied phantom, wandering forlornly around Washington, looking for a place to store the CPI's files. With a brutality born of long simmering enmity, the Republican-controlled Congress cut off Creel's funding on June 30, 1919, leaving him without enough money to pay rent on his offices.

In his final report on the committee's work, Creel proved that he learned nothing from the experience: "Congress is the one place in the United States where the mouth is above the law; the heavens may fall . . .

but the right of a Congressman to lie and defame remains inviolate." When it came to nursing (and worsening) grudges, George Creel and Woodrow Wilson were blood brothers.[11]

III

Among America's most unnerving 1919 transformations was Prohibition, which became the law of the land on July 1, 1919, thanks to the rider the drys in Congress had attached to the appropriation bill in 1918—the move Joe Tumulty had denounced as "mob legislation." Working-class Americans were outraged. A consortium of New York City unions threatened a "no beer no work" strike. At its annual convention, the American Federation of Labor voted all but unanimously against the legislation.

Wilson did nothing to block the law, in spite of a spate of cables from Tumulty, urging him at least to permit the sale of beer and wine. The president yielded to the legalistic argument that the law prevented him from acting, because the army had not yet "demobilized"—a term open to wide interpretation. Almost 3 million men had been discharged. About 1 million were still in uniform.

An on-the-job president could have issued a presidential order or a proposal to Congress that would have thrown the drys on the defensive and won him millions of working-class votes. Instead, from the *George Washington* on his voyage home, Wilson rejected a last-gasp appeal from the despairing Tumulty. The new attorney general, A. Mitchell Palmer, worsened the administration's performance by issuing a public statement declaring that violators of the ban would be prosecuted.[12]

Another explosive issue that cried out for presidential leadership was race relations. The war had been a great leap forward for black Americans, economically and psychologically. Tens of thousands had moved north to work in the booming factories. They were determined to enjoy the civil rights that had been denied them in the segregated South. Black spokesman W. E. B. DuBois had summed up their attitude: "We return *from fighting. We return fighting.* Make way for Democracy. We saved it in France and by Jehovah, we will save it in the United States of America." In city after city, tensions between the races mounted.

The South did not help matters by lynching at least ten discharged black servicemen because they persisted in wearing their uniforms after they returned home. Dozens of other black veterans were badly beaten for this supposed offense. A disgusted black paper in Baltimore published a poem, mocking Wilson's League of Nations:

> *How can a nation dare dictate to men*
> *Of foreign climes what their conduct should be*
> *In dealing with their weaker subjects, when*
> *Their own are lynched with all impunity*
> *Restricted and deprived of every right*
> *Because they were born black instead of white?*[13]

In the North, layoffs in no longer busy factories left thousands of blacks, including many veterans, jobless. In Chicago, the Department of Labor reported 99 percent of discharged black servicemen were unemployed. The army noted thousands of black soldiers had announced their intention to settle in the North, rather than return to the Jim Crow South. Black radicals encouraged this attitude. One black Chicago magazine declared: "Any Negro [veteran] who boards a train for Dixie should be derailed into the Mississippi River."[14]

Washington, D.C., still a Southern city, but with a growing Northern consciousness, was a potential volcano of racial unrest when Wilson returned from Europe. In mid-July, a white woman, the wife of a soldier, claimed she was roughed up by two black teenagers. Whites were already complaining about a black crime wave. The next day, about four hundred soldiers, sailors and marines armed with revolvers and clubs headed for the black section of the city. They were joined by some three hundred civilians, who began beating up blacks on the streets. Police broke up the riot, but an incredibly stupid department spokesman blamed the trouble on black veterans who had become intimate with white women in France.

The next night, mobs of whites roamed Pennsylvania Avenue and other main thoroughfares in the District of Columbia, beating any black person they found. Blacks were dragged from streetcars in front of the White House and clubbed bloody. The following day blacks retaliated. Armed with revolvers, they clashed with more than 1,000 equally well-armed whites. A black man emptied his gun at a streetcar full of whites. Blacks in cars roared into posh northwest Washington shooting at any white person they saw. A black on a motorcycle shot a marine in front of the White House.

The next day a distraught President Wilson called Secretary of War Newton Baker and ordered him to summon the U.S. Army. Soon 3,000 rifle-toting infantrymen were patrolling the capital's streets. A heavy rainstorm, breaking the heat wave, also helped calm the seething city. The death toll was at least fifteen, with additional hundreds injured and thousands terrorized.

This Washington upheaval started a chain reaction of race riots that erupted in twenty-five U.S. cities in the summer of 1919. Late in July, a huge riot exploded in Chicago when whites stoned a black teenager who accidentally drifted across a marker segregating a Lake Michigan beach. A rock struck the boy in the head, and he drowned. The resulting riot engulfed Chicago's business district, killing 38 people and seriously injuring 500. More than 1,000 people were left homeless when arson was added to the rioters' weaponry.[15]

Would a Southern-born president do anything about this sputtering time bomb? Apparently not. Especially when all he wanted to talk about was the League of Nations.

IV

Underlying the unrest and disillusion was a growing fear that Bolshevism might invade the United States and cause the sort of upheaval that was desolating Russia. Wilson had withdrawn the two American expeditionary forces from Siberia and Murmansk, but White and Red armies remained locked in a death grapple throughout the huge country, and American newspapers were full of stories about Bolshevik uprisings in Germany, Hungary, and other nations.

Anxiety reached the flash point on June 2, 1919, while Woodrow Wilson was still in Paris insisting in the Council of Four that no changes should be made to the peace treaty with Germany. At 11:15 P.M. that night, Attorney General A. Mitchell Palmer was reading in the front room of his brick house on R Street in northwest Washington. A progressive Pennsylvania Democrat and practicing Quaker who had backed Wilson since 1912, Palmer had been Tumulty's choice to succeed the war-weary Thomas Gregory. With a yawn, Palmer tossed his book aside and strolled toward the bedroom in the back of the house, where his wife was already asleep.

At about the same time, Assistant Secretary of the Navy Franklin D. Roosevelt and his unhappy wife, Eleanor, were parking their car in a nearby garage, on their way home from a dinner party. They planned to walk the few short blocks to their house, across the street from Palmer's. A tremendous blast split the silent spring night. Roosevelt jokingly wondered if an artillery shell he had brought home from France had exploded. His good humor vanished when the wail of police sirens, the clang of ambulances, and hysterical screams of neighbors drifted toward them. Roosevelt broke into a run, leaving Eleanor stumbling behind him in her long skirt. Their eleven-year-old son James was in their house, with their cook.

At the scene, Roosevelt gaped at Palmer's house. The front was smashed into a sagging, windowless ruin. The door dangled from a lone hinge. The dazed attorney general stood amid the rubble on the lawn, his arm around his terrified wife. The front of Roosevelt's house was also windowless—as were those of almost all the other houses within several hundred yards.

In the street was a human leg. Part of another leg was on a neighbor's lawn. Bits of blood and flesh were splattered on the steps of Roosevelt's house. Inside he could hear his cook screaming hysterically. He flung open the door and raced upstairs to James's bedroom. Although the floor was littered with shards of glass, the boy did not have as much as a scratch. He was enjoying the uproar outside. "Father . . . grabbed me in an embrace that almost cracked my ribs," James later recalled.[16]

Back in the street, Roosevelt helped the police gather sheets of anarchist literature that had been scattered everywhere. The police theorized the lone victim of the blast, the bomber himself, had miscalculated how fast he had to run after he lit the fuse of his nitroglycerin bomb. His most salient message was in a pamphlet entitled *Plain Words,* written by someone who signed himself "The Anarchist Fighters."

The writer expressed his rage at the Americans for trying to stop the worldwide spread of revolution. The "working multitude" was going to regain the "stolen millions" the ruling class had made in the Great War. "You jailed us, you deported us, you murdered us whenever you could," the anarchist ranted. But the capitalists could not stop them from "dreaming of freedom" and "aspir[ing] to a better world."[17]

That same night, similar terrorist bombs exploded in front of the private homes of a New York judge, the mayor of Cleveland, two local politicians in Massachusetts, an industrialist in Paterson, New Jersey (the scene of a famous 1913 IWW strike), an immigration official in Pittsburgh, and, for some baffling reason, a Catholic Church in Philadelphia. An elderly woman caretaker in the judge's house was killed. Otherwise, injuries were minor. But the threat of a wave of anarchist terror jangled the nerves of congressmen and senators and the American public.

No one was more exercised than Attorney General Palmer. He saw "the blaze of Revolution sweeping over every American institution of law and order . . . licking the altars of churches . . . crawling into the sacred corners of American homes." Palmer swiftly reorganized the Justice Department's Bureau of Investigation to stamp out this peril. Among the new leaders was a twenty-five-year-old former librarian named John Edgar Hoover, who became head of the General Intelligence Division. Hoover began compiling cross-indexed files on every radical organization in the United States. Franklin Roosevelt, quick to embrace a trend, was soon addressing women's luncheons, telling them that membership in the League of Nations was the best defense against the awful Bolshevik doctrine of free love.[18]

V

This unstable, uncertain, disillusioned America was the setting for Woodrow Wilson's attempt to rescue his League of Nations from rejection by the Senate. After his disastrous speech to Congress on July 10, the president waited a week for a reaction. What he saw in the Senate was not encouraging. On July 15, George Norris of Nebraska rose to deliver a three-day tirade against the league and the treaty. Like Oswald Garrison Villard, Norris's liberal credentials were impeccable. He had long supported disarmament and some sort of international organization to prevent war. He was willing to diminish U.S. sovereignty and even abandon the Monroe Doctrine to achieve these goals. But he could not support a league that was wedded to the peace treaty. He cited Japan's seizure of Shantung as the worst of many immoralities and barbarities in the treaty. The blatant "greed and avarice" of the nations that were going to control the league made it absurd to ask the Senate to permit the United States to lend it America's good name.[19]

Wilson may have been able to disregard a similar conclusion in *The Nation's* articles, which were published while he was in Europe. But he could not ignore this rebuke from one of the Senate's leading liberals. The words must have cut deep. Here, again, was a cruel reminder of his primary mistake, going to Europe to negotiate the treaty, and his repeated failures to defend the Fourteen Points face-to-face with Clemenceau and Lloyd George.

The day before Norris spoke, Wilson had begun to meet with individual senators, who had said they would be satisfied with very modest changes in the covenant. He gave these so-called mild reservationists about fifteen minutes each and encouraged the impression that their modifications would be acceptable to him. But there were not enough of these moderates to make a difference in winning a two-thirds majority. What Wilson needed was someone who could negotiate with those who had strong objections to the treaty and the league. The decision to cut himself off from Colonel House grew more damaging with every passing day.

On July 18, the day after Senator Norris ended his tirade against the treaty, Woodrow Wilson took to his bed, suffering from acute diarrhea and an agonizing headache. Admiral Cary Grayson hustled him aboard the presidential yacht, *Mayflower,* and kept him there for the weekend, in spite of violently stormy weather. After first saying Wilson had a cold, Grayson changed his diagnosis to a dysentery attack. Some historians and doctors who have studied Wilson's medical history think the illness was a stroke. Others see it as a psychosomatic reaction to Norris's ferocious assault. Wilson's digestive system had frequently reacted negatively to stress.

Wilson made a quick recovery from his indisposition, although the political situation did not improve. In the hearing room of the Senate Foreign Relations Committee, Henry Cabot Lodge had begun by reading the treaty aloud, word for word, a task that took two weeks. Next, Lodge announced, would come hearings at which the committee would question those who participated in the peace conference and listen to those who wanted to comment on the results of Wilson's seven months in Paris.

On the surface, there seemed to be strong sentiment among American newspapers and voters in favor of the league. A *Literary Digest* poll of 1,377 daily newspapers found that a majority (718 to 659) favored quick ratification. The League to Enforce Peace claimed that a survey of newspaper editorials showed supporters of the league outnumbering opponents by 5 to 1. GOP foreign policy guru Elihu Root admitted that a majority of the voters, impatient with the endless peace process, wanted ratification "at once."

Some people have accused Lodge of trying to talk the treaty and the league to death. In fact, the senator had a well-thought-out, conservative philosophy, rooted in the Constitution. He was determined not to allow Wilson to stampede the country into a hasty approval of the treaty. Lodge acknowledged to several correspondents that if a vote were taken immediately, the treaty and the league would probably win. Only the small liberal minority disapproved the harsh treatment of Germany. The league at first glance seemed a noble idea, part of the idealism that Wilson had invoked to lead the United States into the war.

But Lodge did not think the Senate should vote on something so important based on a hasty first glance. He believed "the most momentous decision that this country has ever been called upon to make" should be based not on "the passions of the moment" but on the "calm second thought" of the American people. That was one among several reasons why the Constitution gave the Senate the right and obligation to advise and consent on any treaty a president made. Elihu Root echoed this view when he said the Senate should not succumb to "ignorant popular sentiment."[20]

VI

Senator Lodge and Senator Philander Knox now made major speeches, attacking the treaty and the league. Lodge, as majority leader of the Senate and chairman of the Foreign Relations Committee, was restrained. The Republican senators were divided into four groups: irreconcilables such as Norris and Borah; mild reservationists such as the men Wilson was wooing; strong reservationists, who wanted major amendments to the covenant; and a handful who sided with William Howard Taft and his League to Enforce Peace, who favored ratification of Wilson's version of the covenant. Lodge was trying to hold his party together, and his speech tried to offend none of these people. Essentially he argued that the covenant was too open-ended. It was committing the American people to international obligations—in particular to fighting wars—they might on second thought not want to fulfill.

Lodge took a firm stand against this vague internationalism. "I can never be anything but an American," he said. "I must think of the United States first in an arrangement like this." But he did not mean America should withdraw into isolationism. Far from it. He was "thinking of what is best for the world, for if the United States fails the best hopes of mankind fail with it."[21]

Philander Knox was far more scathing. The former secretary of state more than matched Norris in his contempt for the treaty. Knox was the first senator to criticize the vengeful treatment of Germany from the conservative side. He called it "not the treaty but the truce of Versailles." The senator did not think the treaty was tough enough. The terms goaded Germany to evade them and begin planning for another war but did little to prevent it from getting away with a resurrection. For this Knox blamed Wilson and his Fourteen Points. The senator dismissed the League of Nations as simply an alliance of the victors, which would soon fall apart. He ended by calling for outright rejection of this "hard and cruel peace." With those words, Knox joined the irreconcilables—not good news for Wilson. The senator's standing as a foreign policy spokesman equaled and may even have exceeded Henry Cabot Lodge's status in this wordy arena.[22]

For those outside the rather exclusive foreign policy club, the debate began to acquire a strange unreality. The covenant of the league and the treaty were published as a 268-page book. But that was hardly the same thing as educating public opinion on the subject. The document was written in legalistic, diplomacy-speak prose that was virtually impenetrable, as the *Peoria (Illinois) Transcript* remarked: "Nobody is competent to discuss the Treaty of Versailles until he has read it and nobody who would take the time to read it would be competent to discuss it." Presumably because the reader's brain would be dead.[23]

Lack of comprehension did not prevent the public passions aroused by the war and the bungled peace conference from flaring violently. The Irish led the way with a ferocious attack on Wilson and the treaty. The Celtic-dominated Massachusetts legislature passed a resolution condemning "the so called Covenant of the League of Nations claim to commit this republic to recognize . . . the title of England to own and rule Ireland." The Friends of Irish Freedom established an Irish National Bureau in Washington, D.C., which lobbied senators and issued a stream of denunciations of the treaty. Senator Thomas Walsh of Montana went to the White House and implored Wilson to make a statement, declaring that the first order of American business in the League of Nations would be a motion on behalf of Ireland's freedom. Former president of Harvard, Charles Eliot, offered similar advice. Wilson, by this time a confirmed Irish-hater, did nothing.[24]

In New York, Wilson's old enemy, Jeremiah O'Leary, was one of the leading antitreaty voices. O'Leary had been seized in his West Coast hideaway and dragged back to New York for trial in October 1918. He contracted influenza, and the government was forced to postpone his trial until January 1919, when Wilson's coldness toward Irish independence had largely dissipated Gotham's enthusiasm for the war. Conducting his own defense, O'Leary portrayed himself as a martyr to Wilsonian vengeance and the pro-British New York press. He even subpoenaed Adolph S. Ochs, publisher of the *New York Times*, and subjected him to a ferocious grilling about his supposed British sympathies. Acquitted of all charges, O'Leary went to work organizing an Irish-American speaker's bureau to assail Wilson and the treaty.[25]

Italian-Americans, still angry over Fiume, were also making themselves heard. Their newspapers printed a statement Wilson had made in 1902, when he was a conservative Democrat, deploring the immigration "of men of the lowest class from the south of Italy." The countries of southern Europe, he said, were "disburdening themselves of the more hapless elements of their population." The Chinese, Wilson had added, "were more to be desired as workmen if not as citizens." In New York, a young maverick Republican, Fiorello LaGuardia, who had won some modest fame as a pilot in France, switched from supporting the league to damning it in every speech. Soon he was calling for the election of Republican candidates everywhere to show the world that the president was "discredited at home."[26]

The rest of the Republican Party was quick to take advantage of this mass disaffection. Senator Lodge issued a statement to his Italian constituents in Massachusetts, comparing their desire for Fiume to the value the Americans had placed on the port of New Orleans in the early 1800s. State legislators with large Italian constituencies passed resolutions calling on Wilson to do or say something to soothe these outraged hyphenates. Senator Lawrence Y. Sherman of Illinois made Italy's grievance a personal crusade, orating endlessly on Fiume.[27]

The German-Americans also entered the fray. For the first half of 1919, they had maintained a wary silence. The number of German-language newspapers had dropped from 537 to 278, and their leaders were afraid of triggering a new outburst of hostility from the 100 percent Americans of the National Security League and other patriotic watchdogs. When the peace conference began, their newspapers called on German-Americans to "stand by the president" in his struggle to win a peace based on the Fourteen Points. They slowly grew disillusioned when Wilson did nothing to lift the food blockade. When they saw the results of Wilson's personal diplomacy in the final treaty, the German-Americans were stunned and outraged. Although they did not hold mass meetings to condemn it, they united, as one historian wrote, "in sullen opposition" to Wilson's handiwork.[28]

VII

The alienation of the three largest ethnic blocs in the country encouraged Senator Lodge and his Republican confreres. They allowed the Irish, the Italians, and other hyphenates to air grievances against the treaty before the Senate Foreign Relations Committee and gloated over the headlines these witnesses created. Indians and Egyptians also sent spokesmen who condemned English imperialism. A committee of American blacks called for a statement of worldwide racial equality, hoping it might eventually apply to the United States.

The committee also asked members of the American delegation to testify. The first and most damaging witness was Secretary of State Lansing. His problem was how to say something positive about the treaty without revealing how much he detested it. After his first day of laconic testimony, in which he sometimes merely answered yes or no to questions, this troubled man informed his diary that he could have avoided criticism by "a statement of the facts"—but that would have "opened the floodgates of invective against the president." By facts, Lansing probably meant how little he or any other member of the delegation except Colonel House had been consulted by Wilson.[29]

Senator Lodge and his allies nonetheless got the drift of Lansing's evasions. Lodge concluded that the secretary of state knew virtually nothing about how the treaty had been negotiated, which led the senator to conclude that Wilson was "one of the most sinister figures that ever crossed the history of a great country." There was obviously no moderation in Lodge's detestation of the president.[30]

No one knew that Lansing had returned to the United States determined to resign because of the way Wilson had treated him in Paris. But a strange tortured "loyalty," not to Wilson but to the Democratic Party, kept him on the job. The secretary knew his resignation would reveal the breach between him and Wilson at the worst possible time. Lansing was also well aware that if the treaty failed to win ratification, the Democrats' chances of winning the White House in 1920 would sink to nonexistent.

When asked if he thought the Shantung settlement violated the Fourteen Points, Lansing had said yes. This led Lodge to demand from Wilson all the correspondence within the American delegation about this controversial deal. The president dragged his political feet while he and Tumulty decided what not to send. Perhaps the most damaging thing that stayed in the file was a letter from General Bliss, in which he had scathingly denounced the transaction and Japan's growing desire to dominate Asia.

Finally came a climax of sorts—Wilson agreed to meet in the White House with the Foreign Relations Committee. The three-hour and twenty-five-minute session, which the *New York Times* called "epoch making," was occasionally brusque to the point of overt hostility, but Wilson kept his temper and answered tough questions with little or no hesitation. He betrayed his inner anxiety only once, when he was asked when he had first learned about the secret treaties that had so complicated the situation in Paris. Wilson replied that he and Secretary of State Lansing had not known about them until they arrived in Europe to begin the peace conference.

Wilson defenders claim this stonewalling is proof of his cumulative brain damage. But his evasiveness is virtually a replica of a big lie Wilson had told ten years earlier in a dispute with Princeton's trustees before he became a politician. At that time, he claimed never to have seen or read a document which he had signed and approved—and which undermined his claim that his opponents had failed to consult him on a crucial aspect of their quarrel. The brain-damage theorists constantly downplay Wilson's almost obsessive need to win a public controversy.

Admitting that he had known about the secret treaties long before he went to Paris would have raised questions about Wilson's statesmanship—particularly his unilateral dismissal of these agreements in the Fourteen Points. If he had known about them, he should have negotiated with the Allies before he issued the Fourteen Points. But Wilson had yielded to his image of himself as a mystic world savior and decided negotiation was unnecessary. He had foolishly assumed Lloyd George and Clemenceau would humbly beg his pardon and jettison the treaties.

The exact opposite had happened, of course. The lie in the session with the senators is another indication of the destructive inner war raging in

Wilson's mind and body over the intimations of political disaster gathering around him. He got no help from insiders such as the now totally disillusioned Walter Lippmann. In the *New Republic*, Lippmann castigated the president as a liar: "Only a dunce could have been ignorant of the secret treaties." This was not mere rhetorical exaggeration. The treaties had been published in the newspapers when the Bolsheviks revealed them in November 1917 and had been distributed by the antiwar *New York Evening Post* in pamphlet form.[31]

Wilson's external war with the Senate Foreign Relations Committee soon focused on Article 10 of the covenant, to which Senator Lodge and his allies objected because it seemingly obliged the United States to fight foreign wars at the behest of the League of Nations. Wilson tried to finesse the argument by claiming it was a moral, not a legal, obligation, but he complicated the matter by loftily insisting that a moral obligation was more binding than a legal one. Thoughtful men such as Elihu Root were unimpressed. In a letter to Lodge, Root called Wilson's distinction "curious and childlike casuistry." He also said it was "demoralizing and dishonest."[32]

Wilson took an intransigent stand on the question of attaching any serious reservations to the treaty. He claimed this would require renegotiation with the Allies and might endanger the peace. Virtually no one agreed with him on this contention. Democratic as well as Republican senators declared that a majority of their ranks wanted reservations. Wilson remained immovable.

One reason for his obstinacy, now visible to historians, lay behind the scenes throughout this long hot summer. Even before he returned home, Wilson and Tumulty had begun planning a speaking tour that would throw his enemies on the defensive. Colonel House, the alter ego of negotiated compromise, was no longer in the equation. Tumulty, the pugnacious Irish-American who had masterminded Wilson's first political triumph in New Jersey, was now in charge. He was by no means alone in urging such a tour. Secretary of the Treasury McAdoo liked the idea, as did Assistant Secretary of State Frank Polk and J. P. Morgan banker Thomas Lamont, Wilson's chief economic adviser in Paris. Wilson's conversations with individual senators and the Foreign Relations Committee had convinced him that his enemies "wanted not only to defeat the league but to discredit and overthrow" him. He would answer them with his favorite weapon: oratory. He would humble these arrogant Republicans by arousing the American people to join him in a magnificent crusade that would crown his presidency.[33]

VIII

By the end of August, Tumulty had the trip worked out to the last detail. It would cover 10,000 miles and include some thirty speeches. In memoirs written years later, both Mrs. Wilson and Admiral Cary Grayson claim that they tried to talk Wilson out of going. Grayson has a grimly determined Wilson telling him, "You must remember that I, as commander in chief, was responsible for sending those soldiers to Europe. In that crucial test in the trenches, they did not turn back—and I cannot turn back now. I cannot put my personal safety, my health in the balance against my duty."[34]

Wilson may have said something like this. There is no question that he was troubled by guilt for plunging the nation into a war with the naive assumption that there was little likelihood of American soldiers' dying in France. But there are grounds for doubting that his determination to make the speaking tour was framed in such apocalyptic terms. Another contemporary witness, Secretary of the Navy Daniels, reported a very different reaction when he worried aloud that the trip might strain Wilson's health. "You are much mistaken," the president replied. "It will be no strain on me—on the contrary, it will be a relief to meet the people. . . . I am saturated with the subject and am spoiling to tell the people all about the treaty. I will enjoy it." Wilson was basing this optimism on his reaction to previous speaking tours, in particular the highly successful swing through the Midwest he took in 1916 to persuade the Democrats in Congress to vote for a preparedness program—and incidentally demolish the "hyphenates" who opposed it. Daniels added his own observation: "The thought of the trip exhilarated him."[35]

On the evening of September 2, Wilson, his wife, Admiral Grayson and Tumulty boarded his private blue railroad car, the "Mayflower," which had a double bed and a sitting room to give the president a semblance of privacy. Although the crowd was sparse at his first stop, Columbus, Ohio, the numbers built rapidly as the seven-car train rolled into other Midwestern cities. The president's speeches made headlines. The twenty-one reporters on the train agreed with the *New York Times* man's observation that Wilson seemed to be "refreshed as he [went] along."

But the trip soon became a very different experience from previous tours. The opposition to Wilson's appeals for the League of Nations was vocal and well financed. Leading the assault were the Friends of Irish Freedom, which took out two days' worth of full-page ads in the newspapers of every city Wilson visited, denouncing him as a fraud and a hypocrite and an enemy of Ireland. In many cities, the group organized mass meetings to refute his speeches.

At least as potent was a Republican senatorial "truth squad" led by liberal Republican Senators Borah and Johnson and conservative Senator Medill McCormick, who held their own rallies. At these gatherings, some of them markedly larger than the president's, they denounced the League of Nations and the peace treaty with savage sarcasm. Johnson's favorite theme was the clause in the covenant that gave the British six votes in the league's assembly to America's one. In Chicago, where the three senators spoke on the same platform, a huge crowd of mostly German-Americans and Irish-Americans hissed at the mention of Wilson's name and shouted, "Impeach him! Impeach him!"

Anti-Wilson Democratic Senator James Reed of Missouri spoke to another big crowd in Saint Louis with the Catholic archbishop on the platform beside him. Reed lambasted the league as a British plot to rule the world and keep Ireland enslaved forever.

These brutal assaults took a mounting toll on the president's nerves. His speeches, most of which were based on notes, rather than the usual carefully wrought texts, contained unexpected gaffes. At one point he described himself as descended from "old Revolutionary stock." The opposition reminded Wilson that his four grandparents had been born in the British Isles and his mother was born in England. By no stretch could he claim kinship with the Revolutionary generation. The Irish-Americans had a field day with the president's attempt to disguise his British roots.

In Saint Louis came an even more baffling remark. Wilson said the real cause of the war was the rivalry between Germany and England: "This was, in its inception, a commercial and industrial war. It was not a political war." Wilson said this while trying to persuade his audience that U.S. involvement in the league would eliminate such murderous rivalries. He seemed oblivious to the way the admission virtually repudiated his 1917 rhetoric about a war between autocracy and democracy. The words reveal a defensive psychology at work in Wilson's mind. Seven months in Paris left little room for doubt about British economic fear and loathing of Germany.[36]

After the first week of the tour, the exhilaration of the early speeches began to fade. The sheer physical effort of the trip, with its repetitive parades and dinners and speeches to large crowds without benefit of amplifiers, undoubtedly played a part in Wilson's mounting fatigue. The news from Washington played an equally deleterious role. On September 10, the Foreign Relations Committee sent the peace treaty to the full Senate, proposing ratification with forty-five amendments and four reservations—a direct affront to Wilson. Five amendments obliterated the Shantung settlement—hitting Wilson where he was most vulnerable.

Another blow fell on September 12, when newspapers carried blazing headlines about William Bullitt's testimony before the Foreign Relations Committee. The young diplomat who had fed Wilson-House hopes of overturning the German government with words was no longer loyal to the administration. Bullitt told how he had resigned in disgust from the American staff in Paris when he read the treaty, along with several other young associates. Senator Lodge asked Bullitt if any members of the American delegation had expressed their opinion of the treaty to him.

"It is no secret that Mr. Lansing, General Bliss and Mr. White objected very strongly to . . . numerous provisions," Bullitt said.

Lodge said it was "public knowledge" that they objected to the Shantung settlement. Was there anything else they disliked?

Bullitt said he had made a "note" of a conversation with Secretary Lansing. He proceeded to read it. Lansing thought "many parts" of the treaty were "thoroughly bad," especially those dealing with Shantung and the League of Nations. The secretary's opinion of the league could not have been more negative. "I consider that the League of Nations is at present entirely useless. The great powers have simply gone ahead and arranged the world to suit themselves," the secretary said (according to Bullitt). Worse was another supposed remark: "The League of Nations can do nothing to alter any of the unjust clauses of the treaty."

Bullitt had asked Lansing what he thought of the treaty's chances for ratification. Lansing had supposedly replied, "If the Senate could understand what this treaty means, and if the American people could really understand, it would be unquestionably defeated."

Wilson was aboard his train in California when he read the newspaper accounts of this staggering repudiation of the league and treaty by his own secretary of state. "I did not think it was possible for Lansing to act this way," Wilson said. It was a sad commentary on his frequent inability to grasp what was happening in personal relationships. The president had treated Lansing with contempt; he had spoken of him with contempt. Yet he was amazed when he discovered the secretary detested him and most of his works.[37]

These devastating attacks on the treaty added immensely to the strain of Wilson's tour. In California, he was again thrown on the defensive by a warning letter from the state's Irish-American senator, James D. Phelan: "The Irish are in a fair way to leave the Democratic Party." The San Francisco Labor Council followed with a distinctly hostile query about why the president had ignored Ireland at the peace conference. When Wilson tried to speak at a rally that night, Irish demonstrators howled him down for several minutes. Wilson tried to explain how the league would help, not injure, Ireland's fight for independence. In New York, Ireland's president, Eamon de Valera, on a speaking tour of his own, said he was completely dissatisfied with the president's explanation.[38]

Under these attacks, Wilson's temper soured and his speeches acquired an ugly cast. In Saint Paul, he denounced the use of "Irish-American" or "German-American" before a man's name. "It ought not to be there." In Omaha, he warned against a revival of "pro-Germanism"—a low blow that infuriated German-Americans in the audience, who said they had just as much right to criticize the treaty as anyone else. The pro-treaty *New York Times* encouraged this tack by saying the president was outmaneuvering his ethnic critics and the country would soon "turn in resentment" on any immigrant group that tried to block America's participation in the league. The *Times* was remembering Wilson's 1916 triumph over the hyphenates. But 1919 was an entirely new game on a vastly altered playing field.

In Salt Lake City, Wilson said opponents of the treaty came from "exactly the same sources as the pro-German propaganda" of the prewar years. In Cheyenne, he declared the only opposition to the treaty outside the Senate was "the forces of hyphenated Americans." In Denver, he compared ethnic Americans to knives being stuck into the treaty. In the final speech of the tour, at Pueblo, Colorado, the president descended to the most sunken stretch of the low road: "Any man who carries a hyphen about him carries a dagger which he is ready to plunge into the vitals of the Republic."[39]

This was appalling stuff from a president for whom ethnic Americans had responded in overwhelming numbers to fight and die in France. (One in five draftees was foreign born.) The president's obsession with the League of Nations had turned him into a parody of the idealist who had led the United States into World War I. By this time he was a battered man, a punch-drunk political fighter who had taken too many blows to the head and body.[40]

IX

Wilson combined these descents to the low road with repeated affronts to the senators who wanted reservations. He said their opposition was rooted in "downright ignorance" or some malicious "private purpose." The ignorant seemed to have a problem understanding English. As for the malicious, they would be "gibbeted" by historians. At times he spoke as if he had never heard the word "reservations" and ordered his opponents to "put up or shut up"—sign the treaty he had negotiated, or face the wrath of the American people, who were unanimously behind him in this fight for world peace.[41]

How Wilson could say this while the senators who opposed the treaty were addressing huge rallies is a textbook example of a man driven by a compulsion to humiliate his political enemies. A dismayed William Howard Taft, still a supporter of the league, wrote to a friend: "Wilson is playing into their hands [his Senate opponents] by his speeches in the West. It is impossible for him, schoolmaster that he is, to . . . explain the league without framing contemptuous phrases to characterize his opponents. . . . The president's attitude in not consenting to any reservations at all is an impossible one."[42]

Wilson's all-or-nothing approach to politics was so utterly foreign to the American system, even his opponents could not believe their ears at first. The Senate's predictable reaction was outrage. One of the mild reservationists, Senator William Squire Kenyon of Iowa, said: "The Senate is not going to be bulldozed. It has its duty to do, and it will do it."

The more the president talked, the more he convinced a majority of the senators that the treaty needed these reservations to protect the country against a League of Nations run by a leader like Woodrow Wilson—a wild-eyed idealist who would embroil the country in bizarre attempts to perfect the world, without the consent of Congress or the American people.

Wilson was probably correct in his claim that a majority of the people supported the League of Nations. But in his convulsive hatred of Henry Cabot Lodge, and his arrogant condescension toward the "bungalow minds" of the U.S. Senate, he failed to see that this support was encumbered by serious doubts. By this time, it was a treaty with Lodge's reservations that had the support of the vast majority.[43]

X

While Wilson orated on the League of Nations, Congress passed a law that inflicted a serious wound on the American spirit. Called the Volstead Act after the Minnesota congressman who wrote it, the law created a restrictive, totally nonalcoholic regimen that forbade every American from exercising a fundamental freedom. Volstead's goal was to codify and spell out the implications of the Eighteenth Amendment, which had been ratified by forty-six states in January 1919—well beyond the constitutional two-thirds needed to make it the law of the land.

The amendment had banned the "manufacture, sale or transportation of intoxicating beverages." Most people thought these words meant the abolition of the saloon and assumed the word "intoxicating" meant hard liquor. But Volstead and his dry allies in Congress defined "intoxicating" as any beverage that contained more than 0.5 percent alcohol. This decree eliminated all beers and wines. The country was already dry as of July 1, 1919, thanks to the rider Congress had attached to an earlier appropriations bill. But this was a wartime measure that could and probably would have been repealed by the next Congress, especially if the president had urged it.

The Volstead Act transformed Prohibition from a reform to an oppressive restriction. It empowered the federal government to enforce the restrictions with nightsticks, guns and jail terms. Soon millions of Americans would begin breaking this new law, creating an underlying contempt for the government that spread like a virus into other areas of American life. A group of gangsters, known as the Mafia, which had been close to extinction thanks to the heroic efforts of Italian-American detectives, revived and became a seemingly irreversible cancer in American politics and business.

If Wilson had been on the job as president instead of playing world savior, he might have fought the passage of this bad legislation and immediately started rallying enough congressional votes to sustain a veto. He did neither. It was one more piece of evidence that the president had lost sight of his responsibility as leader of the American people.[44]

XI

Woodrow Wilson had barely launched his rhetorical offensive to save his version of the League of Nations when the worst strike of the year reminded people that their elected leader was not minding the nation's store. With war-spurred inflation at 102 percent and other unions getting raises, the nation's policemen began to wonder if they too deserved a piece of the action. Police unions took shape in Washington, D.C., New York and Boston and began talking to the American Federation of Labor. A great many people grew alarmed. The police commissioner of Washington warned that anyone who joined a union was out of a job. The AFL asked for Wilson's intercession. He responded with a telegram urging everyone to stay calm until he returned from his tour.

In Boston, where a Republican mayor and police commissioner held sway, calm did not prevail. Although Commissioner Edwin Upton Curtis, a crusty WASP and former mayor, issued a stern warning, the mostly Irish-American policemen accepted an AFL charter and elected union officials to negotiate with the city. Besides abysmal pay, they had grievances aplenty. The day shift worked seventy-three hours, and the night shift eighty-three hours, per week. The station houses were filthy, cockroach-infested wrecks.

Commissioner Curtis suspended the 19 union leaders on September 8. The next afternoon, 1,117 of Boston's 1,544 cops walked off the job. Curtis had confidently assured the mayor and the governor that he was "ready for anything." Either he thought only a handful of police would walk, or he expected the good citizens of Boston to behave so decorously, it would prove all over again that Beantown was indeed the "city on a hill" that his Puritan forebears had envisioned.

Curtis was wrong on both counts. When the lower orders realized that there was scarcely a cop on duty, they began looting every store in sight. People were held up in broad daylight and stripped of their valuables. Things only got worse as darkness fell. By the following morning, the thugs were more organized. They began carting away stolen goods in trucks. Professional criminals arrived by the trainload from New York and other cities to get a share of the swag.

Curtis tried Postmaster General Burleson's ploy and asked Harvard students to become volunteer policemen. The mobs beat them silly. Boston's frantic mayor called out a regiment of the state guard, and Governor Calvin Coolidge sent another regiment. The 6,700 soldiers, many of them veterans of the Western Front, meant business. They used machine-gun and rifle fire to disperse the looters. Seven people died, but by the following afternoon, order was restored to Boston.

The leader of the police union offered to send his men back to work if the governor and/or mayor agreed to negotiate their grievances. Samuel Gompers of the AFL, no longer a warm admirer of Woodrow Wilson, backed the union men. Governor Coolidge, a man of a few words, said there was nothing to negotiate. Not one of the strikers would ever work as a policeman for Boston again. Even if Curtis's peremptory style had triggered the strike, as Gompers argued, that did not justify "the wrong of leaving the city unguarded. There is no right to strike against the public safety by anybody, anywhere, anytime."

That last sentence shot through the forty-eight states like a lightning bolt. The laconic Coolidge instantly became the kind of hero America wanted in 1919. In the distant west, Woodrow Wilson's comment on the strike came in a pale second. He called it "a crime against civilization." For the thousands of Boston Irish-Americans whose fathers, sons, and brothers had lost their jobs, the president's words only added wormwood to the gall they were drinking. They heard Wilson's sneering attacks on hyphenates behind the word "civilization." They remembered the vicious things the "icicles of Yankeeland" had said about the famine-starved, demoralized Irish when they cascaded into Boston in the middle of the previous century. They were animals, barbarians; they would never become Americans. Their descendants were not inclined to endure similar insults from a president who had refused to lift a hand to help Ireland win its freedom.[45]

XII

On September 23, another dose of bad news reached the Wilson cavalcade, this time from Washington, D.C. The Republican mild reservationist senators whom the president had tried to woo in the White House had negotiated a deal with Senator Lodge. Thanks to Wilson's insults, the Republicans now had the votes to bar ratification of the treaty without reservations.

Numerous Democrats who also favored mild reservations seemed on the brink of joining them.

The news drove Wilson to a near frenzy. At a brief stop in Ogden, Utah, he lashed out at "pro-Germans" and claimed everyone opposed to the treaty was "in cahoots" with Germany. His next major speech, in Salt Lake City, was a rambling, incoherent mess. At one point, he read the Lodge reservation to Article 10, and many people clapped and cheered. The president excoriated the confused applauders, accusing them of wanting to "cut out the heart of the covenant."[46]

At Pueblo, Colorado, after denouncing hyphenates, Wilson sought refuge in idealistic rhetoric. He called the doughboys crusaders. He said their sacrifices had made "all the world believe in America as it believes in no other nation organized in the modern world." He invoked not only the "serried ranks in khaki" who had come home but "the dear ghosts that still deploy upon the fields of France." In their name he called upon the American people to "extend their hand" to the "truth of justice and of liberty and of peace" in the covenant of the League of Nations. Many in the audience were moved to tears by this vision.[47]

But idealism could not silence the ugly passions, the antagonisms, and the hatred that the war had aroused in America. They were loose in Woodrow Wilson's body and mind as well as in the souls of the people. Terrible headaches began to torment the president day and night. As the train climbed to the high altitudes of Denver and Pueblo, he had difficulty breathing. Fits of choking assailed him—grim evidence of arteriosclerosis and congestive heart failure—as well as fateful signs of a faltering crusade.

As the train rolled toward the next speaking date in Wichita, Kansas, Wilson told his wife he felt horribly ill. After sitting with him for a few hours, Edith Wilson summoned Admiral Grayson to the compartment at 2 A.M. Waves of nausea were engulfing the president. He struggled for breath, his face twitched convulsively. The ache in his head had become intolerable.

Grayson awoke Joe Tumulty and told him the rest of the trip would have to be canceled. The president was suffering from nervous exhaustion. "I don't seem to realize it, but I have gone to pieces," a weeping Wilson told the dismayed Tumulty. Outside Wichita, the president's secretary summoned the reporters to tell them Wilson was suffering from a "nervous reaction in his digestive system" and the train was heading back to Washington.

Woodrow Wilson's appeal to the people was over. Not a few of his enemies sneered that he was faking an illness because the trip had been a failure. The president was not the only one who resorted to the low road.[48]

XIII

Back in the White House on September 28, Admiral Grayson ordered complete isolation and total rest for his patient. For a few days, the president seemed to be recovering. His appetite returned. He went for several rides in one of the White House Pierce Arrows. He played pool. He slept fairly well. But he could not escape the political brawl that continued to agitate the nation and the Senate. There, party lines were hardening. The Democrats were declaring themselves committed to a treaty with no reservations. The Republicans were insisting on reservations or no treaty. A stalemate loomed. Only presidential intervention could resolve it.

Another kind of intervention resolved Wilson's dilemma. About 9 A.M. on October 2, White House Chief Usher Irwin "Ike" Hoover received an anguished call from Edith Galt Wilson. "Please get Dr. Grayson. The president is very sick," she whispered over a private wire from the second floor.

Hoover telephoned Grayson and ordered a car to bring him to the White House. Hurrying upstairs to see if the First Lady needed help, Hoover found the door to the president's bedroom shut. When Grayson arrived, he tried the door and found it was locked. Already, Edith Wilson had decided only a select few would find out what was wrong with her husband.

A knock gained Grayson access to the room. Ten minutes later, the admiral emerged to stare at Hoover with an unnerving mixture of horror and dismay. Throwing up his arms, Grayson gasped, "My God! The president is paralyzed!"[49]

In his memoir, Hoover noted that this was the first and last time he heard the word "paralyzed." Grayson swiftly summoned four other doctors, one a well-known Philadelphia neurologist, and a nurse who had cared for Ellen Wilson, the president's first wife, when she died of Bright's disease in 1914. In the late afternoon, Hoover was asked to come into the bedroom to rearrange some of the furniture. He was the only member of the White House staff whose discretion Edith Wilson trusted.

"The president lay stretched out on the large Lincoln bed," Hoover wrote in his memoir. "He looked as if he were dead. There was not a sign of life. His face had a long cut about the temple from which the signs of blood were still evident. His nose also bore a long cut lengthwise. This too looked red and raw."

In her memoir, Edith Wilson would deny these vivid details. But they have the ring of truth. Hoover had nothing to gain from telling what he saw. Edith Wilson had an urgent need to conceal or revise almost every-thing she said and did from October 2, 1919, until she left the White House eighteen months later.[50]

Edith had found her husband on the floor of his bathroom with those ugly cuts on his forehead and nose. Wilson had suffered a stroke and struck his head on the bathtub fixtures as he fell. By the end of the day, "an air of secrecy had come over things," Ike Hoover recalled. This was not an acci-dental development. The doctors conferred, but no one on the White House staff, including Hoover, was told anything. Edith Wilson was deter-mined to keep her husband's collapse a secret.

White House servants knew enough—and whispered enough—to arouse the curiosity of reporters in the press room. The newsmen asked Grayson what was wrong with Woodrow Wilson. For a reply they got a bulletin: "The President had a fairly good night but he is not at all good this morning." Toward the end of the day Grayson amended this vague message: "The President is a very sick man. His condition is less favorable today and he has remained in bed throughout the day."[51]

So began the greatest deception in the history of American politics. Strong-willed Edith Wilson bullied Cary Grayson and Joe Tumulty into joining her in a conspiracy to conceal how sick the president was. Woodrow Wilson had suffered a cerebral thrombosis, which collapsed the lower left side of his face and paralyzed the left side of his body. For a month he hovered between life and death, totally incapable of exercising the powers and responsibilities of his office.

Cabinet members sought information from Tumulty or Grayson. To those they trusted, such as Josephus Daniels, they told the truth. The presi-dent's appointees reacted with bewilderment and horror. Vice President Marshall came to the White House to inquire about Wilson's condition and was told nothing. Only Secretary of State Lansing seems to have real-ized drastic action was required. The Constitution stated that if the presi-dent was incapacitated, the vice president should immediately succeed him. Lansing went to the White House and asked Tumulty for the truth.

Without using the explosive word "paralyzed," Tumulty conveyed Wilson's condition.

The secretary read Tumulty the relevant clause from the Constitution, making it clear he thought it applied to Wilson. Emotion took charge of Tumulty's usually strong intellect. Lansing was already regarded as a traitor, thanks to William Bullitt's testimony before Congress. Tumulty curtly informed the secretary that "the Constitution was not a dead letter in the White House." It was a curious thing to say—because Tumulty, Mrs. Wilson and Admiral Grayson were already in the business of making the national charter exactly that.

Grayson now joined the discussion. In some ways he was more partisan than Tumulty. He had introduced Edith Galt to the president; she had not a little to do with persuading Wilson to promote him over a hundred or so senior officers to the rank of rear admiral. Like Edith (and Wilson), the doctor was a Virginian. Tumulty asked Lansing who would certify that the president was disabled. Lansing said either Tumulty or Grayson could do it. According to his memoir, Tumulty exploded and roared, "While Woodrow Wilson is lying in the White House on the broad of his back I will not be a party to ousting him. He has been too kind, too loyal, too wonderful to me to receive such treatment at my hands." The secretary added that he was sure that Grayson would join him in resisting any attempt to bring an outside authority into the White House to pass such a judgment on the president. Grayson emphatically backed Tumulty's defiance.[52]

Lansing would later deny Tumulty's version of their conversation ever took place. There are grounds for believing the secretary of state. Wilson had been neither kind nor wonderful to Tumulty for a long time. But there is no doubt that Admiral Grayson willingly joined the conspiracy. When Lansing convened a cabinet meeting on October 6 to discuss the situation and summoned Grayson, the doctor blatantly lied about the president's condition. He said Wilson was suffering from a nervous breakdown, indigestion and physical exhaustion. Not a word was said about paralysis or a stroke.

Next came sheer invention: Grayson said the president wanted to know why they were holding a cabinet meeting without his authority. The cabinet members, including Lansing, were intimidated. They claimed they had only gathered to get some information. When Newton Baker asked Grayson to tell the president how concerned they all were, the cabinet instantly became a sympathetic chorus and all talk of incapacity vanished. Almost certainly, Wilson was too sick to be told they were meeting. It contradicted other things Grayson said to the cabinet—that the president had to remain unbothered, because the slightest excitement might kill him.[53]

Tumulty's and Lansing's lies were standard cover-up tales. Compared to the fantasy that Edith Wilson constructed to defend her conduct, her two co-conspirators were mere amateurs in the prevarication game. According to Edith, Dr. Francis Dercum, the neurologist who had rushed from Philadelphia to head the diagnostic team, told her that the president would recover from his stroke, but only if he were isolated from all forms of excitement and responsibility for several months.

Edith, in her version, sweetly asked the physician how this would be possible. Dercum supposedly advised her to "have everything come to you." Edith would "weigh the importance of each matter" and consult with individual cabinet members to see if the problem could be solved without bothering the president. "But always keep in mind that every time you take him a new anxiety or problem to excite him, you are turning a knife in an open wound," the doctor supposedly said. "His nerves are crying out for rest, and any excitement is torture to him."

Sensing how close to absurdity she was treading in this fictionalized version, Edith claimed she asked the doctor, Would the sensible thing be for the president to resign and "let Mr. Marshall succeed to the Presidency?"

"No," Dercum purportedly said, suddenly thrusting himself into the political arena. "For Mr. Wilson to resign would have a bad effect on the country and a serious effect on our patient. He has staked his life and made his promise to the world to do all in his power to get the Treaty ratified and make the League of Nations complete. If he resigns, the greatest incentive to recovery is gone; and as his mind is clear as crystal he can still do more with a maimed body than anyone else. He has the utmost confidence in you. Dr. Grayson tells me he has always discussed public affairs with you, so you will not come to them uninformed."[54]

Of the many quotations in this book that were almost certainly never said, this one ranks at the top. When Edith Wilson published *My Memoir* in 1938, Dercum was as safely dead as Henry Morgenthau's German ambassador. But history has a way of catching up with public liars. In 1991, Cary Grayson's family found in his private files Dercum's report on Woodrow Wilson's "devastating trauma," which Dercum had made to the admiral on

October 20, 1919. This was a follow-up of what the neurologist had obviously told Grayson verbally. The report made it clear that Wilson would never achieve more than a "minimal state of recovery." Dercum also clearly stated that he had told this bad news to Mrs. Wilson and her stepdaughter, Margaret Wilson, early in October 1919.[55]

The Dercum report confirmed what Ike Hoover wrote in his memoir about the aftermath of Wilson's stroke. "It was perhaps three weeks or more before any change came over things. I had been in and out of the room many times during this period and I saw very little progress in the president's condition. He just lay helpless."

Hoover admitted that after three weeks there was some improvement. "He lived on; but oh, what a wreck of his former self! . . . I was with him at some time every day. . . . There never was a moment when he was more than a shadow of his former self. He had changed from a giant to a pygmy in every wise. He was physically almost incapacitated; he could articulate but indistinctly and think but feebly."[56]

From the evasions and vagaries Grayson told the cabinet, the president's physician soon progressed to public lies. On October 9, when Wilson, according to Hoover, was still in a virtual blob state, Grayson told a reporter the president's mind was "as good as it ever was." He said nothing about a prostate condition that had shut down Wilson's kidneys and brought him close to death for several days. At the end of the month, Grayson issued another statement denying that Wilson had the slightest mental impairment, based on the "normal" status of his blood pressure and heartbeat. The doctor's diary and memorandums in his papers make it clear that Edith Wilson had ordered him to avoid specifics and reiterate Wilson's supposedly unimpaired mind.

Is there an explanation for this behavior, beyond the obvious evidence that two men—Tumulty and Grayson—had succumbed to the dictates of a strong-willed woman? From almost a century's distance, the Wilson White House in October 1919 fits the general portrait of a nation—and a world—destabilized by years of hate propaganda and the catastrophic grief the war inflicted on millions of people. In this atmosphere, people were prey to delusions and denial, two psychological mechanisms that lead to bizarre behavior. Edith Wilson was able to convince herself that it was her patriotic duty as well as her loving responsibility to keep Woodrow Wilson in the White House until he recovered his strength and rescued his beloved League of Nations from the hateful Republicans, the enraged Irish-Americans, the evil German-Americans and the hysterical Italian-Americans. To some extent, Cary Grayson and Joe Tumulty shared this illusion of eventual victory.

What none of these deluded conspirators seems to have realized was the potential power of the truth. If they had announced that Woodrow Wilson had sacrificed his health and strength in pursuit of his unreserved commitment to the League of Nations, and handed over the presidency to Vice President Marshall, Senator Henry Cabot Lodge's carefully constructed plan to either defeat the treaty or make it a "Republicanized" document with his reservations would have been swept away in a burst of national sympathy for the fallen president. When Wilson collapsed aboard his train after the Pueblo speech, the *New York Times* had hailed him as a sacrificial hero: "The figure that will stand out in the memory of the Western people is that of a man burning with a restrained passion for a great purpose, for the accomplishment of which he would gladly lay down his life." It is not hard to imagine how powerfully an honest statement about the president's cerebral thrombosis would have affected the Senate—and the American people.[57]

Instead, Edith Wilson's illusion of eventual victory created a web of lies and political ineptitude that inflicted mortal wounds on the Treaty of Versailles, the League of Nations, and America's entire experience in World War I.

XIV

With nothing to go on but Grayson's vagaries, rumors swirled through Washington. Some people said Wilson was insane and pointed to bars on certain White House windows. The bars had been put there during Theodore Roosevelt's tenure to protect the glass from footballs and baseballs flung by the younger members of TR's tribe. Others pointed to the gushes of sympathy in the *New York Times* and other pro-Wilson papers and persisted in seeing his illness as a sham, a last desperate gasp of his losing campaign for the treaty. Total cynics said Wilson was suffering from syphilis, acquired in the bordellos of Paris.[58]

Around the fallen president, Americans grappled with problems that cried out for leadership. Inflation continued to soar and more strikes roiled the economy, as labor leaders were virtually ordered by their rank and file to get more money from corporations. First came a steel walkout that erupted into violence in several cities. At the end of October, the United Mine Workers walked off the job, threatening to bring the country to a dead stop. Coal was the vital fuel on which ships, trains and factories depended—not to mention the millions who used it to heat their homes.

The headless administration floundered. Tumulty took charge of a rump committee composed of the secretary of labor and the head of the nationalized railroads. They drafted an official appeal against the strike, issued over Wilson's name. They called the walkout unjustifiable and unlawful. While the public watched with mounting anxiety, Federal Fuel Administrator Harry Garfield drew up a plan for rationing coal and Tumulty persuaded Attorney General Palmer to agree that a wartime act forbidding strikes in vital industries was still in force.

When the union walked out anyway, federal troops were ordered into the coal towns. Tumulty drew up a statement for the president, calling for a federal injunction. The new president of the United Mine Workers, John L. Lewis, staged the first of his many public tantrums. He was joined by AFL head Samuel Gompers, the administration's wartime ally against the hated Germans. When the court ruled for the government, Lewis called off the strike—but very few miners went back to work. In the coal towns, friction between the troops and strikers grew ominous.

Meanwhile, Harry Garfield had gone to Mrs. Wilson and persuaded her to get a ruling from the president that would limit a wage increase to 14 percent. The union wanted 31 percent. Mrs. Wilson—and the president, if he was compos mentis at this point—had only the dimmest idea of what was going on. The secretary of labor, who thought the miners deserved considerably more than 14 percent, threatened to resign. The entire cabinet voted in a body to support him and implored Wilson to change his mind. After an initial refusal, word finally descended from the second floor that the president agreed. Whereupon Fuel Administrator Garfield quit in disgust and embarrassment, feeling betrayed by his friend the president.

The miners eventually went back to work in late December, with a 14 percent increase and a promise of another increase in the near future, to be decided by a three-man committee representing labor, management and the government. The imbroglio left the public with the image of an administration with so many cooks, it was frequently unable to find the broth. The president's invisibility added to the sense of unnerving confusion.[59]

XV

On the floor of Congress, Representative James Byrnes of South Carolina made an incendiary speech, accusing the Bolsheviks of influencing black Americans to turn against their country. He blamed the reds for the recent riots in Washington, D.C., and Chicago. A Department of Justice investigation of the role of radicals in racial unrest confirmed this accusation. An incident in Texas suggested the problem was much more complex.

John R. Shillady, the white secretary of the National Association for the Advancement of Colored People, journeyed to Austin to improve the relationship between whites and the local NAACP chapter. Shillady patiently explained to the state attorney general that the NAACP had no program for "immediate" racial equality. The association only wanted to ameliorate racial hatred and was opposed to all forms of violence. Not long after, Shillady was badly beaten by a white mob in daylight on an Austin main street.

On November 7, 1919, Attorney General A. Mitchell Palmer ordered federal agents to raid organizations suspected of Bolshevik ties in eleven cities. Hundreds were arrested and held without bail on charges of conspiring to overthrow the government. Many were aliens, and Palmer declared they should be deported as soon as possible. He estimated that there were 60,000 Bolshevik plotters loose in the United States. Virtually confirming this estimate for the jittery public, in Centralia, Washington, a gunfight broke out when the newly founded American Legion, marching in its first Armistice Day parade, detoured to clean out an IWW union hall with baseball bats and pistols. Wesley Everett, the local Wobbly secretary (ironically an AEF veteran) and several others responded with gunfire, killing two legionnaires. Everett was castrated and lynched by a vengeful mob a few hours later. A half dozen Wobblies, selected almost at random, were convicted of murder by a reluctant jury, virtually at the order of the presiding judge. They were sentenced to long prison terms.[60]

A dismayed Walter Lippmann complained that the ship of state was adrift, wallowing haplessly into "severe internal conflict." No one was exercising the slightest leadership to get America back "to some kind of peace footing." Lippmann condemned the tendency to blame the problem on Bolsheviks, blacks and radicals. The administration's leaders had "refused to look ahead, refused to think, refused to plan." The supposed Bolshevik attack on the government was a minor worry compared to "the paralysis of the government."[61]

From the White House came only silence.

XVI

In Ireland, while Wilson had been stumping the American West, a full-scale rebellion took shape. Policemen and soldiers were shot and their guns seized. The British poured in troops until their numbers topped 200,000. But the Irish rebels, buoyed by the support of their American cousins, remained unintimidated. Their growing boldness reached a climax when they opened fire on sixteen soldiers of the Shropshire Light Infantry on their way to church in the town of Fermoy. They killed one man and wounded a half dozen others, seized their rifles and sped away in waiting cars.

The local coroner's jury sympathized with the dead soldier's family, but declined to bring a charge of murder. They claimed the attackers only intended to seize rifles to defend their country and had not intended to kill anyone. The British garrison in Fermoy went wild. Charging down the main street, they smashed more than fifty shop windows and allowed a mob that followed in their wake to loot to their heart's content. The jewelry shop owned by the foreman of the coroner's jury was stripped of every ring, watch and bracelet on the premises.

In Dublin, the Lord Lieutenant of Ireland, Viscount General John French, denounced the Dáil Éireann, Ireland's parliament, as a "dangerous association" and disbanded it. Swarms of soldiers in helmets, rifles at the ready, stormed Sinn Féin headquarters and swept up supposedly incriminating documents. They arrested two Sinn Féin members of the British Parliament who were still boycotting that no-longer-respected body. In retaliation, Irish Republican Army gunmen killed a detective that night not far from a Dublin police station.

This mounting violence made headlines in the United States, where President Eamon de Valera's speaking tour was winning him audiences frequently larger than the president's. Calling Lloyd George's Irish policy "the very bankruptcy of statesmanship," the *Times* of London glumly added that the government's tactics seemed designed to play into the hands of the "anti-British element" in America. That was an understatement. The Friends of Irish Freedom used Ireland's struggle to raise vast sums to fund their ongoing fight to destroy Wilson and the League of Nations.[62]

XVII

In Italy, as Wilson orated his way across the United States, another brand of violence erupted, thanks to the Treaty of Versailles. The poet Gabriele D'Annunzio had been among the leading denouncers of Woodrow Wilson when the president appealed to the Italian people to give up Fiume and the Dalmatian coast in the name of justice and truth. By September 1919, Fiume was occupied by French and Italian troops who were on the brink of open warfare. When an Allied commission blamed the Italians and ordered them out of the city, the fifty-five-year-old D'Annunzio leaped on a motorbike, raced to the scene and persuaded the ousted Italians to join him in a military takeover.

Accumulating supporters along the way, including not a few followers of Benito Mussolini, the poet soon had an army of 4,000 men. He faced down the Italian general guarding the border and marched into Fiume, where he was greeted as a hero by the Italian residents, while thousands of Yugoslavs fled. In a hysterical speech, D'Annunzio proclaimed Fiume part of Italy and called on "Victor Hugo's France, Milton's England and Lincoln's America" to approve his conquest.

In Rome, Premier Francesco Nitti, Vittorio Orlando's successor, denounced the poet and his soldiers as "lunatics and traitors." He was ignored by virtually every Italian in the country. Sailors jumped ship to join the army of Fiume. Hundreds of soldiers deserted their regiments to do likewise. D'Annunzio grandly demanded Nitti's resignation, saying he was "tired of dealing with the dog." The government was paralyzed. When Nitti sought backing from the Chamber of Deputies, a brawl soon had socialists and nationalists kicking and gouging each other on the parliamentary floor. The distraught premier dissolved the government and called new elections.

In Milan, Benito Mussolini took notes on how quickly a few thousand armed and determined men, backed by poetic eloquence, could terminate that stupid idea called democracy.[63]

XVIII

In Germany, a sullen hatred of the Treaty of Versailles pervaded the nation. Politics oscillated violently between socialism and reaction. Judges, many of them holdovers from the old regime, expressed kaiser-like opinions from the bench whenever they could intrude them into a decision. One of the few Socialist judges remarked that there was "a state of war between the people and the judiciary." Meanwhile, the Majority Socialist Party was self-destructing. A plan to socialize all of Germany's factories by continuing wartime controls collapsed in August 1919, when the middle-class parties in the Reichstag united to reject it.[64]

One liberal analyst of the situation, Count Henry Kessler, concluded that "the revolution is provisionally over. Counter-revolution is on the march." When reaction triumphed, Kessler predicted, "that will be Germany's real defeat." The former leaders of the Free Corps, having crushed worker revolts in various parts of Germany, were forming a group called the National Union, which aimed at a military takeover.

In Munich, where martial law reigned and machine guns and barbed wire guarded the entrances of government buildings and hotels, former corporal Adolf Hitler was working as a political officer for the Second Infantry Regiment of the Reichswehr, the new Germany army. In the closing weeks of the war, he had been gassed and shipped to a hospital, where for a while he lay blind. As his sight slowly returned, he had learned of the kaiser's abdication. Overwhelmed with grief, Hitler had listened to the pastor of the hospital tell him and the other patients to accept the armistice "with confidence in the magnanimity of our former enemies." How hollow those words must have seemed now, face-to-face with the Treaty of Versailles.[65]

Hitler was under orders to detect symptoms of communism and socialism in the ranks of the Second Infantry Regiment and to talk the enlisted men out of these disloyal doctrines. For someone with minimal education, and that mostly as an artist, Hitler was a surprisingly effective speaker. Throughout the war, he had spent his spare time reading books. "Even at his battle station," recalled a comrade in his wartime regiment, "he sat in a corner, ammunition bag around his middle, rifle in his arms, and read." His favorite book was Arthur Schopenhauer's *The World as Will and Idea*, which convinced him that the human will could triumph over any adversity.[66]

The officers of the Second Infantry Regiment also employed Hitler as a spy. On September 12, 1919, while Woodrow Wilson was orating his way across the Midwest, Hitler dropped in on a meeting of the minuscule German Workers Party in the back room of a Munich beer hall. About twenty-five forlorn Socialists listened to a professor lecture them on how to create a worker's paradise. Hitler was about to leave when someone suggested Bavaria should secede from Germany and join Austria. The Austrian-born Hitler fiercely denounced the idea. He declared a "greater Germany" was the nation's only hope.

The secretary of the Workers Party congratulated Hitler on his impromptu speech and gave him a forty-page book he had written: *My Political Awakening: From the Diary of a German Socialist Worker.* Back in his room, Hitler threw the book aside and wrote a report dismissing the German Workers Party as a trivial splinter group that would soon crumble. Later in the night, insomnia prompted him to take a look at the book. He was entranced to discover the gist of an idea that had also been taking shape in his own mind—a socialism that was devoted to the German nation, rather than to the mythic international brotherhood of the working class, an idea the war had rendered ridiculous. Also in the tract was another idea that already obsessed Hitler: the Jew as an alien menace to Germany's redemption.[67]

XIX

In Washington, D.C., the fight over the treaty was moving toward a climax. In mid-November, Wilson had recovered sufficiently from his stroke to be able to see a few visitors. By far the most crucial was Senator Gilbert Hitchcock, the acting minority leader of the Senate. Not a Wilson enthusiast—he had opposed the president many times on legislative matters during the war—Hitchcock was trapped between his personal desire to ratify the treaty with reservations and Wilson's intransigence. Most of the time, the Nebraskan performed his role as the Democratic Party's spokesman with a minimum of enthusiasm.

William Gibbs McAdoo urged Wilson to compromise with Henry Cabot Lodge. So did Herbert Hoover, in a three-page telegram. Many other prominent men, including numerous Democrats, offered the same advice, but Mrs. Wilson chose not to trouble the president with such disturbing mail. The solicitor of the State Department issued a formal opinion that Lodge's reservations would not require a renegotiation of the treaty with America's allies. Prime Minister Jan Christian Smuts of South Africa urged ratification. Rejection would "blast the hopes of the world."[68]

Colonel House, back in the United States, sent an emissary to Lodge to explore the possibility of a compromise. The senator jotted some notes on a copy of the covenant, indicating certain changes that would be acceptable to him and—he hoped—to Wilson. An excited House rushed the document to the White House, urging the president to give it serious consideration. Mrs. Wilson, by now the colonel's archenemy, filed it in the wastebasket.[69]

On November 17, Gilbert Hitchcock conferred for a second time with Wilson. Propped up in bed, the president mixed defiance with megalomania. He wanted the votes for and against the treaty "recorded" because when the naysayers came up for reelection he would "get their political scalps." He said the Lodge reservations represented a "nullification" of the treaty. If the Senate approved it with the reservations, he would refuse to sign it.

The discouraged Hitchcock urged compromise. The Democrats simply did not have the votes to ratify the treaty without reservations. Wilson spurned the idea. Rather than bear the odium of rejection alone, Hitchcock drafted a letter for the president's signature. He also needed it to keep wavering Democrats in line. Edith made some minor alterations and stamped the president's signature on it. (His actual signature would have been an instant giveaway of his condition.) She then released it to the press.

Meanwhile, the reasonable and the unreasonable on both sides were in strenuous battle. The League to Enforce Peace issued a statement urging compromise and ratification. The Friends of Irish Freedom dispatched no less than a million telegrams from their members, urging defeat. They had been working closely with the irreconcilables, in particular Senator Borah.

On November 19, 1919, when the Senate convened, Wilson's letter was in the headlines. Lodge read the text to the Senate, adding that he did not think it needed any commentary. All hope of a compromise vanished. After more hours of oratory, the senators voted for the treaty with the Lodge reservations. It lost 55 to 39, 7 votes short of the needed two-thirds. All but 4 Democrats followed Wilson's orders. They were joined by the 13 mostly Republican irreconcilables who were opposed to the treaty in any form. A Democratic senator called for a vote on the treaty without reservations. It lost 53 to 38, most of the irreconcilables voting with the Republicans this time.

Belying their desperation, the Democratic National Committee issued a bulletin, accusing Senator La Follette of being the evil genius behind this second defeat, because he called for a vote, rather than referring the treaty to a committee on conciliation. In a heavy-handed attempt to revive the disloyalty smears that had silenced the Wisconsin senator, the press release sneered: "A few months ago, hardly a senator, Republican or Democrat, would speak to La Follette." Now, the Democrats claimed, he was the "general" of the "Battalion of Death" that had doomed the treaty.[70]

The only scrap of truth in this diatribe was La Follette's opposition to the treaty, which he had denounced in several searing speeches during October and November. During one speech, the senator hung huge maps on the walls of the Senate chamber and used them to illustrate the way the treaty enlarged the British empire. He argued that the League of Nations would also obligate the United States to police the petty states created by the breakup of Austria-Hungary and guarantee unjust territorial rearrangements elsewhere in the world that benefited France, Italy and Japan. It amounted to a promise of American troops to help the Allies "stand guard over the swag."[71]

Two weeks after the Senate rejection, a discouraged Lodge, who had hoped against hope that the treaty would win with the reservations, wrote to Elihu Root, who had clung to the same hope:

> If Wilson had not written his letter to the Democratic caucus . . . the treaty would have been ratified. There would have been enough Democrats voting with us to have done it. It was killed by Wilson. He has been the marplot from the beginning. . . . He can have the treaty ratified at any moment if he will accept the reservations and if he declines to do so we are not in the least afraid to meet him at the polls [in 1920] on that issue.[72]

Those last words were a forecast of Woodrow Wilson's final illusion—and its ultimate defeat.

Chapter 12

ILLUSIONS END

Was the treaty dead? Not in the opinion of the *Washington Post* and many other newspapers.

The *Post* said the president had waged a "gallant fight," but had been beaten "openly and fairly." Reminding Wilson that the American people and Congress had accepted his reelection by only a few thousand votes in 1916, the editors urged the president to "accept the reservations made by the majority" and sign the treaty when it was resubmitted to the Senate. Numerous other papers, including the staunchly pro-Wilson *Baltimore American* and the *New York Times*, said the same or similar things.[1]

None of this well-intentioned advice had the slightest impact on the sick man on the second floor of the White House. Neither did letters from Gilbert Hitchcock and other leading Democratic senators, from General Bliss, from the new ambassador to England, John W. Davis—even William Jennings Bryan got into the act—all urging the president to compromise. Wilson probably never saw these pleas. Edith Galt Wilson remained the guardian of her husband's sickroom, determined to keep disturbing messages to a minimum. Eventually, Joe Tumulty overcame his compulsive loyalty to his chieftain and joined the ranks of the pleaders for compromise—to no avail. He too was denied access to the sickroom and had to couch his messages in evasive terms that did not offend Mrs. Wilson.[2]

In New York, Colonel House watched with mounting dismay as the situation deteriorated. His old friend, Sir Edward Grey, the former British foreign secretary, now Viscount Grey of Falladon, had assured House that

Great Britain and France would accept the treaty with Lodge's reservations. House wrote the president two long letters, urging on him a policy that would rescue the treaty and the league but would enable Wilson to escape most of the humiliation of a defeat.

House suggested the president return the treaty to Congress after it reconvened on December 1, with a message to Hitchcock, giving him permission to negotiate a compromise with Lodge that would win a two-thirds majority. Wilson would then forward the treaty to the Allies with a statement that he had "done his duty" and tried to win ratification of the document they had approved in Paris. If they agreed to accept the Senate's changes, he would do the same thing. "Your conscience will be clear," House wrote. With desperate, almost forlorn flattery, the colonel added that Wilson's willingness to accept reservations rather than have the treaty killed "will be regarded as the act of a great man."[3]

Woodrow Wilson saw neither of House's sensible letters. Mrs. Wilson deemed both unworthy of the president's attention. She ignored an accompanying note, in which the colonel warned Edith that her husband's place in history "hung in the balance." From Edith's point of view, House was as persona non grata as Senator Lodge. When former attorney general Thomas Gregory handed her one of the letters, she made it clear that it was thoroughly unwelcome.[4]

Meanwhile, the *New York Times* and other papers grew uneasy when they learned Wilson had refused to see Senator Hitchcock, the key to any possible movement toward a compromise. To quiet rumors that the president was non compos mentis, Edith Wilson and Admiral Grayson arranged a visit by Hitchcock and Republican Senator Albert Fall of New Mexico on December 5, 1919. With the sick room's lighting reduced to one feeble lamp beside the bed, Wilson was propped up on pillows, concealing his inability to sit up. The covers were drawn to his chin to hide his useless left arm.

In his memoir, Chief Usher Ike Hoover, who was present, called this stage setting "the Great Camouflage." The two senators talked to the president for three-quarters of an hour. As they left the White House, Hitchcock told reporters Wilson was mentally alert and Fall admitted that for a man who had been in bed for ten weeks, the president seemed to be "in fighting trim." The *New York Times* hailed these remarks as "silencing for good the many wild and often unfriendly rumors of Presidential disability."

The senators discussed problems with Mexico, and at the end of the meeting, Hitchcock asked Wilson what he planned to do about the treaty. Wilson replied that it was up to the Senate to figure out what to do. Several days later, when Hitchcock saw Wilson again, the president was even more defiant. When Hitchcock suggested the Democrats might hold out an olive branch, Wilson snarled, "Let Lodge hold out the olive branch!"

On December 14, Wilson went public with his intransigence, releasing a megalomania-tinged statement "from the highest authority in the executive branch" that declared the president had "no compromise or concession of any kind in mind." Philip Dru's ultimate repudiation of House's philosophy of intelligent compromise left the colonel flabbergasted. At the end of a three-hour conference in his New York residence, House asked Thomas Gregory if he was doing the right thing, remaining "quiescent." Gregory told him he did not see how he could do anything else.

Secretary of State Lansing also journeyed to New York to pour out his woes to the colonel. Lansing told House that Wilson was much sicker than Admiral Grayson purported him to be. All Lansing's queries about State Department matters were answered by Mrs. Wilson. When Lansing wrote a Thanksgiving Proclamation for the president, it was returned with Wilson's signature at the top, instead of at the bottom—and it was virtually illegible.

A British diplomat en route home from Washington told House that Vice President Thomas Marshall was growing more and more exasperated by his inability to see the president. He quoted Marshall as saying people "who should be in jail" were seeing Wilson every day. Marshall was supposedly ready to do something drastic, if the treaty was not ratified within thirty days.[5]

A few weeks later, Wilson demonstrated how irrational he had become behind his facade of mental alertness. The president ordered Tumulty to draft a public challenge to the fifty-five senators who opposed the treaty. Let all of them resign and run for immediate reelection to see if the people supported their stand. If a majority of them won in this "great and solemn referendum," Wilson would resign and so would Vice President Marshall. Before this extra-constitutional madness took place, Wilson would name a prominent Republican as secretary of state, making him next in line for the presidency. The Republicans could then do what they pleased with the treaty.

Wilson even conferred with Attorney General Palmer about how the senatorial seats could be legally vacated, before his White House keepers talked him out of this bizarre fantasy. The president's draft of the proposal included dark accusations that the Germans were the secret force behind the failure to ratify the treaty.[6]

II

In Europe, all the major powers had ratified the Treaty of Versailles and were waiting for the Americans. Paralysis was creeping through the initiatives and ideas launched by the peace conference. Nowhere was this more visible than in the thirty-five "commissions of control" set up by the conference to supervise such delicate situations as France's temporary government of the Saar basin, the creation of the free port of Danzig and the corridor connecting it to Poland, as well as plebiscites in Silesia and other disputed territories. Most vital was the reparations commission, whose final judgment hung like a sword of Damocles over the German republic. American participation—even American leadership—had been assumed on these international bodies. Instead, there was only a pathetic remnant of the American delegation still in Paris, without orders or directions from the president or the State Department.

The man most deeply perturbed by the growing vacuum was Georges Clemenceau. His enemies in the Chamber of Deputies were making capital out of Wilson's failed promises. Totally preoccupied by the brawl over the League of Nations, the president had never said a word in support of the treaty he had agreed to sign with France to guarantee the country against a German attack. The treaty was gathering dust in the files of the Committee on Foreign Relations. The Tiger sent a frantic dispatch to Ambassador Jusserand in Washington, begging him to persuade Wilson to allow some American delegates and staffers to remain in Paris to participate in the commissions of control. A withdrawal now would jeopardize "the fruits of victory."

Withdrawal was what the semifunctioning president ordered. Clemenceau rushed to the Hôtel Crillon to ask Assistant Secretary of State Frank Polk if any Americans would remain. Polk grimly replied, "No one." The Tiger was devastated. He knew, among other things, that his political career was over. His enemies, led by Raymond Poincaré, would now crucify him for being too soft on Germany, an irony almost beyond belief. Never an admirer of Wilson, the old man exclaimed to the British ambassador, "What on earth is the Lord Almighty doing that he does not take [Wilson] to his bosom?"[7]

III

In England, the Amritsar massacre was stirring some of the least lovely emotions in the British psyche. A report on the ugly event had reached England in June 1919, but the story did not appear in a British newspaper until December. The British secretary of state for India, Lord Edwin Montagu, professed shock and claimed to have heard about it only when he picked up the newspaper. This was, of course, a blatant lie, which was almost instantly exposed. General Dyer's commander in the Punjab, General Michael O'Dwyer, announced to all and sundry that he had made a full report to Montagu in June.

O'Dwyer and his supporters swiftly mounted a savage attack on the staggered Montagu, claiming that the foreign office and its civil servants were responsible for the unrest in India because they tied the army's hands. Dyer, who had been relieved and placed on "unemployment pay," swiftly joined this assault, claiming that he had made the only possible decision to quell a riot-in-the-making against his outnumbered soldiers.

The British Army Council confirmed the wisdom of Dyer's removal and informed him that there was no longer a job for him in the Indian army. This was the lightest possible punishment. There was no mention of stripping the murderous brigadier of his star or bringing criminal charges against him. The conservative *Morning Post* maintained that even this slap on the wrist was outrageous. It accused the government of sacrificing Dyer to "the susceptibilities of native agitators." The paper announced a fund to ease General Dyer's retirement and swiftly raised 26,000 pounds; among the contributors was Rudyard Kipling.

In Parliament, Edward Carson, the Unionist leader of Ulster, made a motion to reduce Montagu's salary by one hundred pounds to express the House of Commons' disapproval of his treatment of Dyer. An ugly subtext in the affair was Montagu's Jewish blood. Adolf Hitler was not the only person who noted the number of Jews in the Bolshevik revolution. When Montagu argued in the House debate that only a liberal approach could keep India in the empire, one member bellowed, "Bolshevism!" Carson roared that Montagu was blind to the fact that liberalism and Bolshevism had "the same object—to destroy our sea power and drive us out of Asia."

Underscoring the growing ugliness, the *Morning Post* reprinted the scurrilous slander against the Jews, *The Protocols of the Elders of Zion,* which described a global revolution triggered by the overthrow of the British empire by Jewish conspirators. The document had been concocted by Russian anti-Semites in the 1890s. In an editorial, the *Morning Post* wondered about the wisdom of letting a Jew [Montagu] rule India. "The course of events" all looked tinged with "Bolshevik purpose," in their not-so-humble opinion. In a classically British understatement, one liberal member told the *Times* the debate in Parliament was "not free" from ethnic prejudice.

Carson's motion to dock Montagu's salary was defeated. But a few weeks later, the House of Lords voted 129 to 86 to approve a motion deploring the treatment of General Dyer as "unjust to that officer and as establishing a dangerous precedent to the preservation of order in [the] face of rebellion."[8]

IV

In the United States, paranoia about Soviet Russia had similarly replaced paranoia about Germany. The Bolsheviks were blamed for terrorist bombs and the ongoing epidemic of strikes. The U.S. Army patrolled the streets of IWW strongholds, such as Bisbee, Arizona, and Butte, Montana. When workers went on strike in the steel mills of Gary, Indiana; Pittsburgh, Pennsylvania; and other cities, army military intelligence agents worked closely with local police to arrest hundreds of suspected Bolsheviks. On October 16, 1919, the *Pittsburgh Post* wrote that the intelligence men were hunting seven hundred local suspects, and "every third man on the streets . . . seems to be a Government official."[9]

During the fall of 1919, Bureau of Investigation agents under the direction of J. Edgar Hoover arrested hundreds of members of the Union of Russian Workers. In late December, 249 aliens seized in this and similar roundups were marched onto the aging troopship *Buford* and deported to Russia. Newspapers dubbed the ship "the Soviet ark" and gave the story reams of publicity. As the ship got under way, one of the most outspoken radicals, Emma Goldman, shouted, "This is the beginning of the end of the United States!" Hoover, backed by 250 armed soldiers, personally supervised the departure. The State Department said the deportees were "obnoxious" and a "menace to law and order" as well as to "decency and justice." They were therefore being "sent whence they came."[10]

On January 2, 1920, Attorney General Palmer, now certain that he personified the popular will, sent swarms of federal agents into thirty-three U.S. cities in a campaign to break the back of the supposed Bolshevik conspiracy. The BI agents, again led by young J. Edgar Hoover, arrested more than 4,000 people on charges of plotting to overthrow the government. Cooperating with the dragnet were thousands of volunteers from the American Protective League and the other organizations that had kept tabs on German-Americans and dissenters during the war.[11]

Jails overflowed, and their kitchens soon ran out of food. Many of the prisoners went hungry and slept in crowded cells and hallways, with minimum sanitation. Those who were citizens were turned over to state courts to be prosecuted for violating various laws banning "syndicalist" labor organizations (i.e., those that seek the control of factories by workers). Aliens were held for deportation hearings. Palmer had decided deportation was the only legal solution available to the Justice Department, because the wartime sedition laws passed by Congress were no longer relevant.

Liberals were aghast that their former hero, Woodrow Wilson, apparently countenanced Palmer, J. Edgar Hoover and the operations of the military intelligence agents. An agitated Walter Lippmann told Newton Baker, who was rapidly becoming his political therapist, that "the events of the last few months are too disturbing and the behavior of the administration too revolutionary not to put a severe strain upon men's patience." Lippmann accused Wilson's appointees of doing more to endanger fundamental American liberties than any group of men in a hundred years. The Democrats were operating a "reign of terror in which honest thought is impossible," Lippmann wailed.[12]

Not everyone in Wilson's administration admired Palmer's tactics. Secretary of Labor William B. Wilson ordered the department's immigration office to demand strong evidence before approving a deportation order. Soon military intelligence field officers were complaining to Congress that they had to "get a man with a lighted bomb in his hand" before they could deport him. Eventually, Newton Baker reigned in the army's intelligence branch, with an order to stop investigating civilians.[13]

President Wilson was a bystander in this drama.

Meanwhile, Eugene Debs remained in jail, along with hundreds of others imprisoned during the days of war rage. Edith Wilson and her fellow instant expert in national politics and international diplomacy, Admiral

Cary Grayson, decided such minor problems were not worthy of the president's limited attention span.

V

In the White House, Wilson refused to abandon his hunger for a direct appeal to the voters that would crush Senator Lodge and the Republicans. On January 8, 1920, the Democrats convened in Washington, D.C., for their annual Jackson Day dinner, a tribal ritual in which they invoked the populist memory of their founder, Andrew Jackson. Behind the scenes, Tumulty and Hitchcock feverishly concocted a plan for a compromise on the treaty. Hitchcock reported progress in covert negotiations with Lodge. He sent Mrs. Wilson a note warning her that public opinion was virtually demanding some kind of compromise. Tumulty said the same thing in more evasive but equally desperate phrasing.[14]

Instead, Edith, speaking for her husband, ordered Tumulty to draft a letter to be read at the Jackson Day dinner, reiterating the president's absolute opposition to any changes in the treaty or the League of Nations. "We cannot rewrite this treaty. We must take it without changes that alter its meaning, or leave it," Wilson aka Tumulty wrote. Then came truly fateful words: "If there is any doubt as to what the people of the country think on this vital matter, the clear and single way out is to . . . give the next election the form of a great and solemn referendum as to the part the United States is to play in completing the settlements of the war."[15]

When National Democratic Chairman Homer Cummings read these words at the Jackson Day dinner, the party's stalwarts received them, according to one newspaper, with "wild enthusiasm." But a stentorian voice was heard in the tumult, objecting strenuously to the president's proposal. The stunned stalwarts turned to confront William Jennings Bryan, three times their candidate for the White House. The Great Commoner said the idea of a national referendum on a foreign policy dispute was idiocy. American elections were never referenda on any single issue. Besides, there was nothing much wrong with Senator Lodge's reservations. The important thing was to get the treaty signed and the League of Nations working. Even if the Democrats won control of the Senate, waiting for a referendum would put everything off for fourteen months—while Europe and the rest of the world reeled into chaos.

It was one of the wisest statements William Jennings Bryan ever made. But it did not go down well with the Democratic Party's leaders, who saw him as a three-time loser, still jealous of Wilson. "Stand by the President," someone shouted. The cry was taken up from all sides of the room. Bryan sat down, more than a little angry. Within a few days, the *Chicago Daily News* ran a cartoon of Wilson and Bryan driving a wagon carrying the treaty, pulled by a Democratic donkey. Wilson was shouting, "Back up!" Bryan was yelling, "Giddap!"

Bryan still had millions of loyal followers. His opposition increased the likelihood of an electoral disaster in November 1920. The *New York Times,* the *New York World,* the *Dallas News* and a host of other Democratic papers said Bryan was right. Wilson's "great and solemn referendum" looked more wrongheaded than ever.[16]

VI

In the same month of January, two cabinet members, Secretary of the Treasury William Gibbs McAdoo and Secretary of the Interior Franklin K. Lane, weary of working for an invisible president, resigned. Over tea in the White House, Edith Wilson undertook negotiations with their possible replacements. If she was not running the government, the First Lady was giving a good imitation of it. Gossip swirled through Washington in which she loomed larger and larger as the "acting president."

One of the tales that added considerably to Edith's power-god status concerned a contretemps that inflicted yet another wound on the already bleeding Treaty of Versailles. Former British foreign secretary Viscount Grey of Falladon, had come to America as a special ambassador to see if he could help win ratification. He had arrived in Washington the very day that Wilson had collapsed on his speaking tour. Almost blind, Grey wore blue spectacles and could not travel alone. As equerry, he brought with him Major Charles Crauford-Stuart, who had been caught telling a naughty story about Mrs. Wilson in a previous tour at the British embassy.

"What did Mrs. Galt do when the president proposed to her?"

"She fell out of bed!"

Although Crauford-Stuart denied all, the president had demanded his return to London. Now he was back in the role of attendant to the almost blind special ambassador. Edith Wilson sent word that Grey would never enter the White House as long as Crauford-Stuart was in the British embassy. Grey, satisfied that the major was innocent, declined to oblige her. Complicating matters, Crauford-Stuart was engaged to an American woman and strenuously resisted departure. So the viscount waited for an invitation that never came.

Edith Wilson had informants eager to tell her the doings of supposed enemies. When she heard that Assistant Secretary of the Navy Franklin D. Roosevelt and his wife had entertained Viscount Grey for dinner, Edith told the president, who became even more infuriated at the special ambassador for what he considered backstairs intrigue.

In mid-January, Viscount Grey gave up and allowed Crauford-Stuart to lead him back to London. There, no longer conciliatory, Grey published a letter in the *Times* that stirred large political waves in. With the implicit approval of his government (though he claimed to be speaking as a private citizen), Grey said that Great Britain and France had no objections to Lodge's reservations, except for one minor point that could easily be resolved. In an instant, Wilson's main argument, that the reservations would require a renegotiation of the treaty, became null and void.

Did it change what was left of Wilson's mind? Alas, no. Instead, he prepared a statement denouncing Grey, in which he declared that if the viscount had written his dastardly letter in Washington, he would have been kicked out of the country. The White House inner circle managed to suppress this wild-eyed response. But a few days later, the president revealed to the entire world just how shattered his faculties were.

Perhaps because Secretary of State Lansing had tried to arrange a White House meeting with Viscount Grey, or because the president was still brooding over William Bullitt's testimony before the Foreign Relations Committee, or because he had heard that Lansing praised Grey's *Times* letter, Wilson suddenly wrote to the secretary, asking him: "Is it true, as I have been told, that during my illness you frequently called the heads of the executive departments of the government into conference?"

The president was admitting that for four months, while Admiral Grayson was issuing soothing syrup about his steady recovery and his unimpaired intellect, Wilson did not know what was happening in the executive wing of the White House, where his cabinet had met upwards of twenty-five times. Lansing considered the letter an unmistakable request to resign and promptly did so. In a bristling letter, he cited the president's history of ignoring his advice and treating him with disrespect and said he departed "with profound relief."[17]

When Lansing released both letters to the press, Democrats, Republicans—everyone who could read a newspaper—were boggled by their implications. Other cabinet members defended Lansing. Even the *New York World,* for whom Wilson could usually do no wrong, was unable to swallow this performance. The *Saint Louis Post-Dispatch* ran a cartoon of Lansing being tossed off the stern of the ship of state, entitled "Dropping the First Mate."

The *Los Angeles Times* called Lansing's dismissal "Wilson's Last Mad Act." Perhaps impelled to tell the truth by the uproar, one of Wilson's doctors revealed to a reporter that the president had suffered a cerebral thrombosis. This too made headlines, which underscored the breadth and depth of the lies Admiral Grayson had told at Edith Galt Wilson's orders.

The Lansing affair triggered new speculation about the condition of Wilson's brain. Arthur Dean Bevan, former president of the American Medical Association, told a *Philadelphia Press* reporter that Wilson had no hope of a genuine recovery. His brain would always be damaged. Bevan flatly declared that Wilson was "not competent to act as the nation's chief executive." The report sparked a flurry of debate in Congress about the possibility of a joint committee pronouncing Wilson unfit. But it came to nothing. The Republican majority, scenting victory in November, preferred the status quo.[18]

VII

Meanwhile, everyone was reading a book written by John Maynard Keynes, the young British economist who had gone home in disgust when he got a look at the Treaty of Versailles. *The Economic Consequences of the Peace* was a devastating attack on the perpetrators of the Paris Peace Conference, with special venom directed at Woodrow Wilson for saying one thing and doing another from the moment he arrived in Europe.

"The President," Keynes wrote, "was not a hero or a prophet; he was not even a philosopher; but a generously intentioned man" lacking the "intellectual equipment" he needed to deal with David Lloyd George and Georges Clemenceau. The French premier embodied "that culture of the world" that enabled him to outflank Wilson in every argument. Up against Lloyd

George, who had "six or seven senses not available to ordinary men," the president was "a blind and deaf Don Quixote entering a cavern where the swift and glittering blade was in the hands of the adversary." Summing up, Keynes said "there can seldom have been a statesman of the first rank more incompetent than the President in the council chamber." Wilson was also a hypocrite, with "all the intellectual apparatus of self deception." The *New Republic* ran excerpts of *Economic Consequences* and praised it extensively.[19]

With lethally bad timing, Wilson virtually confirmed Keynes's portrait by suddenly intervening in a European problem that he had bungled while he was in Paris. The French and the British had finally worked out a settlement with Italy on the disposition of embattled Fiume. Wilson fired off a note condemning the new arrangement and threatening to withdraw the United States from the league and the peace treaty. One London newspaper said Wilson sounded like "a European monarch of the eighteenth century." The French press said "Czar" was the best one-word description. The Italians had trouble finding enough negative adjectives to describe the man they had once cheered in Rome. Italian-Americans were equally frenzied in their denunciations. The uproar helped convince millions of Americans that the treaty needed reservations to enable the United States to deal independently with the double-talking Europeans.[20]

VIII

Wilson's conduct demoralized the Senate's Democrats. More and more of them wondered if they should continue to take orders from a man who was mentally incompetent. Since a majority of them wanted to vote for the treaty with reservations, Henry Cabot Lodge began to savor the prospects of victory on his terms. Tumulty and Senator Hitchcock warned Wilson that their prospects looked grimmer with each passing day. They hoped the news might persuade the president to seize the initiative and propose some kind of face-saving compromise.

By now it was clear that a vast majority of the American people wanted to join the League of Nations—but only with the safeguards that Henry Cabot Lodge was proposing. The senator had succeeded in persuading not only the Senate but the American electorate to take the sober second look at the treaty that he insisted was at the heart of his opposition.

Beginning in January, dozens of spokespersons for major organizations, ranging from the American Federation of Labor and the National Council of Churches to the American Federation of Women's Clubs, came to Washington and called upon the senators, urging consent with some kind of reservations. The League to Enforce Peace, still doggedly in the struggle, was another strong voice with the same message. An estimated 50 million people were involved in this massive campaign to force a compromise. They were joined by a galaxy of famous names, from J. P. Morgan, Jr. to William Howard Taft to James Cardinal Gibbons.[21]

In the Senate, Lodge shrewdly moved with this popular sentiment. He softened the language of his reservations, dropping, for instance, his original insistence that the Allies would have to cast an affirmative vote for each one. Now he would be satisfied with the tacit acceptance Viscount Grey's letter virtually guaranteed. Democrats as well as Republicans made speeches and advanced proposals, all drenched in this spirit of compromise.

But Woodrow Wilson was already wedded to his strategy of a great and solemn referendum. Rather than surrender (as he saw it) to the hated Senator Lodge, he was prepared to sabotage any compromise and let the American people decide who was right and who was wrong. This determination became brutally clear on March 8, 1920, when he released a letter to Gilbert Hitchcock, commenting on the Senate's recent revisions of Lodge's resolutions.

The long letter was nothing less than a campaign speech. The president focused on Article 10, the heart of the covenant, which committed the United States to defend the territorial integrity of the league's member states. Wilson declared once more that Lodge's reservation amounted to nullification of the whole document. The president said he would never be able to look an American soldier in the face if it were approved. It would destroy America's chance to win a "moral victory" over Germany. In his eagerness to blacken Lodge, Wilson drew on the propaganda rhetoric of the war. He said Lodge's attempt to nullify Article 10 reminded him of the "militaristic party" he had fought in Paris because they endorsed "the ideals of imperialism." He cited the dispute with Italy to prove that these sinister forces were still at work. Finally, Wilson said he saw no difference between a nullifier and a mild nullifier. The president called on all Democrats to resist compromising on a single word.[22]

The almost universal reaction to this letter was disgust and outrage. The *Washington Post* called Wilson "an affirmative irreconcilable." The *New York Tribune* condemned Wilson's "unreasonable acerbity." The *New York Times* threw up its editorial hands and abandoned all hope of ratification. Abroad, the French and British were dismayed to find themselves smeared in this domestic dispute. The French ambassador lodged a protest with the State Department, plaintively asking why Wilson did not communicate such sentiments to him, rather than publish them for the whole world to see. One Paris newspaper opined: "The American nation is directed by an idiot." The president was turning into a one-man international wrecking crew.[23]

The Irish-Americans also remained in the wrecking game. On March 17, 1920 (Saint Patrick's Day), Democratic Senator Peter Gerry of Rhode Island proposed a reservation recommending "self-government" for Ireland and its immediate admittance to the League of Nations. Lodge, who still thought he had a chance of detaching enough Democrats from Wilson to win ratification, resisted vehemently, viewing it as a crude device to split the Republicans. But fear of the Irish-American vote induced senators of both parties to ignore him. The proposal won, 38 to 36, with Senator Gilbert Hitchcock, a professed friend of compromise, voting for it. The desperate Democrats were ready to try anything to shift the blame for rejecting the treaty onto the Republicans.[24]

March 19 was judgment day. By this time, Hitchcock later admitted, 23 Democratic senators had decided to vote with Lodge. If the minority leader could not hold the rest of his party in line, the treaty would win a two-thirds majority. Throughout the long day, Hitchcock worked on wavering senators. On the floor, several Democrats who had decided to disobey the president urged their confreres to follow their example. The most moving speech came from Senator Thomas Walsh of Montana, who had supported Wilson on virtually every issue since 1912. Walsh said he would cast his vote to ratify not because he approved of Lodge's reservations but because a majority of his fellow senators did, and he accepted their judgment. But the overriding issue was the importance of the United States joining the League of Nations, where it would play a vital role in preserving the peace of the world.[25]

The first three Democratic senators to answer the roll call voted yea. Excitement mounted in the packed galleries. Was there going to be a mass defection of the Democrats? The fourth Democrat to respond, gray-haired

Senator Charles Culberson of Texas, hesitated for a long moment, his face revealing not a little uncertainty. Then he voted nay. It was the signal the southern Democrats needed. They began adding nays in obedience to their fellow Southerner in the White House.

Another tense moment came when Gilbert Hitchcock voted. A yea from him—which was what he wanted to say—would have been an even stronger signal to waverers. But Hitchcock remained the sort of politician who can sometimes be the noblest of men, and at other times the saddest, a loyal follower. He voted nay with the president. Years later he would confide to a friend that it was the greatest mistake of his life.[26]

In the end, 49 senators voted yea, and 35 voted nay. That was 7 votes short of a two-thirds majority. Among the Democrats, 21 had voted their consciences and defied the president. But 23 Democrats had remained obedient to Wilson's orders and they were joined by 12 irreconcilables, who would have voted nay no matter what Wilson or Lodge said or did not say. There is little doubt that without Wilson's savage letter of March 8, the treaty and the covenant would have been ratified. But that legislative victory would not have made the treaty a living thing. The deluded man in the White House would have almost certainly have refused to sign it—and still demanded his great and solemn referendum.[27]

IX

About 16,000 men remained on duty in the American sector of the Rhine bridgehead—a mere ghost of the once stupendous AEF. The Americans continued to get on well with the Germans in their sector. The same could not be said of relations in the British and French sectors. In the British sector, German civilians were required to remove their hats when they met a British officer on the street. The Germans soon stopped wearing hats, no matter how low the temperature dropped. The British also imposed draconian controls on local newspapers and regularly opened personal mail. A curfew required all Germans to be in their homes by 7 P.M. every night. All clocks were set for Greenwich Mean Time—as if the British sector were part of the United Kingdom.

The French were even more unpleasant. They published a list of 180 books that were banned and regularly suspended newspapers for comments regarded as hostile to the occupation or the Treaty of Versailles. French officers frequently lashed Germans in the face with their riding crops when they failed to get off the sidewalks quickly enough to permit them to stride past. Even more infuriating from the German point of view was the composition of the French occupation force. Some 25,000 were colonial troops from Senegal and French Morocco. These black and brown-skinned soldiers were selected, the Germans maintained, to humiliate them and violate their women. In no time, newspapers in the rest of Germany whipped up a frenzy about mass rapes of German women that more than matched Wellington House's stories about 1914 Belgium.

On February 1920, while the Americans argued over the treaty and the league, the Allies added to the Germans' rage by abruptly demanding the surrender of the kaiser, his three sons and some eight hundred German generals, admirals and government officials for trial on unspecified charges of war crimes. Articles 227–230 of the treaty entitled them to make this demand. Massive demonstrations swept all parts of Germany. The Netherlands declared it would not surrender the kaiser and his family to anyone. The German army let it be known that it was prepared to fight to the last man to resist this ultimate *Schmachparagraph*. They also hinted strongly that they would seek an alliance with the Russian Red Army to resist an attempt to seize these men by force.

The German government, realizing it would be out of business in twenty-four hours if it surrendered anyone, stalled. Weeks went by without a sign of British or French mobilization. Realizing the Allies had no stomach for an invasion of Germany to enforce their demand, the Weimar government offered to try certain officers on the list in German courts. The Allies lamely accepted this compromise. Sixteen men were eventually tried; six were convicted. They received trivial sentences.

In the midst of this uproar, Adolf Hitler and his supporters reorganized their political movement and gave it a new name, the German National Socialist Workers Party (in German, *Nationalsozialistische Deutsche Arbeitpartei*). Focusing their wrath on the Treaty of Versailles and the men who signed it, the party's slogans became "Down with the November Criminals!" and "Down with the Marxist-Jewish Betrayers of the Fatherland!" The street-corner pronunciation of the first word in the new name soon had everyone calling these angry power seekers the Nazi Party.[28]

X

In the United States, public enthusiasm for the treaty and the league sank rapidly after the second failure to ratify. Popular frustration bred an equally negative attitude toward the entire war. The ongoing chaos in Europe did little to alter this the-hell-with-it mood. The *Los Angeles Times* editors summed up the prevailing atmosphere: "It is quite impossible to tell what the war made the world safe for."[29]

American companies were clamoring for some sort of closure, so they could begin doing business with Germany, once one of America's most important trading partners. The Republican leadership decided the best answer was a resolution declaring the war was over. The United States had entered the war by a majority vote in Congress. Why not end it the same way? If Wilson vetoed it, he would further antagonize the already alienated voters.

The election of 1920 was already on everyone's mind. When the peace resolution was introduced in the House on March 19, 1920, the Democrats reacted with raging speeches that denounced the idea as an underhanded attempt to embarrass the president—which was about 50 percent of the truth. One of the war's chief foes, Congressman Claude Kitchin of North Carolina, went into a denunciatory spasm and suffered a cerebral thrombosis that left him almost as paralyzed as Woodrow Wilson. But the resolution cleared the House by almost 100 votes.

In the Senate, Henry Cabot Lodge and Philander Knox added a very senatorial second thought. They resolved that the war was over, but that the United States retained all the advantages accruing to it under the Treaty of Versailles. This triggered a spate of Democratic speeches castigating this idea as dishonorable and cowardly. The antis tried to portray the move as the equivalent of a separate peace that left the Allies in a lurch. In the light of Wilson's attacks on the French and British as militarists and imperialists, the argument fell flat. The Republicans replied that the only war still in progress was the one Woodrow Wilson was waging "against American citizens and American industry."[30]

Wilson vetoed the joint resolution, calling it "an ineffaceable stain upon the gallantry and honor of the United States." The Republicans failed to muster a two-thirds majority to override it; the desperate Democrats voted as a bloc in both houses. Without an issue besides the treaty, the Democrats clung to Wilson, even though many feared he was trying to walk on water wearing the political equivalent of concrete shoes. The Republicans ended the day all smiles. They sensed the mounting disillusion of the American people with Woodrow Wilson's rhetoric. The next scene in the drama of the great and solemn referendum now shifted from Congress to the national conventions.

XI

One man who watched this uproar with more than passing interest was newly promoted general of the armies John J. Pershing. The title was largely honorific, but it had a very satisfying ring to it. Soon after the armistice, various VIPs nominated the AEF's commander for president. When Pershing admitted he was a Republican, the vice president of the National Republican League thought he was a cinch to repeat General Ulysses S. Grant's performance in 1868. One former senator and old friend urged both political parties to nominate Pershing on a national reconciliation ticket in 1920.

Pershing's father-in-law, Senator Francis Warren, advised him to deny any ambition to be president. That was the best way to stir a groundswell. Besides, there was another general running hard for the White House: Leonard Wood. He was portraying himself as Theodore Roosevelt's heir, the man whose bold embrace of preparedness had helped win the war. By this time, Pershing detested Wood as a loudmouth and grandstander and studiously avoided imitating him.[31]

Pershing's former aide, George Patton, now a tanker with almost no tanks (the army had dissolved the Tank Corps, in effect telling the tankers to rejoin the infantry or the cavalry) worried about Wood's candidacy. If he won, Pershing "would command the island of Guam." Pershing told him not to worry—a Wood victory would produce his instant resignation from the army.

Pershing went to some lengths to deny he was a candidate. He told one lady friend that he would be a "damned fool" to run for president. But Pershing was human. He thought he had won the war and could not resist comparing himself to other generals who had reached the White House. Besides Grant, there was Zachary Taylor, thanks to the Mexican War, and

Andrew Jackson, thanks to the War of 1812. Not to mention George Washington, whose victory in the War for Independence made him the inevitable first president.[32]

Pershing did not object when old friends from Nebraska, which he considered his home state, formed a Pershing for President Club and began touting him as the state's favorite son. For the first few months of 1920, Pershing acted like a candidate, though he never said a word about running. Secretary of War Baker, anxious to avoid a clash between Pershing and the incumbent chief of staff, acerbic Peyton March, sent the general of the armies on a nationwide inspection tour.

Pershing brought along many of his AEF favorites, and the trip took on the character of a royal progress. In thirty-two states, local VIPs held receptions and banquets to welcome the conquering heroes. Pershing turned on the charm, wowing women as usual, kissing children and greeting AEF veterans with hearty handshakes. In speeches, he hailed American patriotism and urged voters to support universal military training so America would never again be caught unprepared to fight a war.[33]

Unfortunately, the general had liabilities that Woodrow Wilson's performance in the White House slowly turned into impediments. Pershing was Wilson's appointee, and the voters' disenchantment with Wilson soon extended to his war. Much if not most of this disenchantment emanated from Republicans. A Pershing nomination could be viewed as an oblique endorsement of Wilson's war. By 1920, this was something most Republicans were unwilling to do. Nor was the push for universal military training the best political move in the prevailing atmosphere of disillusion with the war.

On April 20, Nebraska held a Republican presidential primary. Pershing's friends launched a vigorous campaign, replete with mailings, admiring articles by selected reporters and heavy newspaper advertising. The other candidates were Senator Hiram Johnson of California, one of the liberal irreconcilables, and General Leonard Wood. Pershing finished third. In Michigan, in a field of five candidates, he finished a dismal fifth.[34]

Undaunted, his friends persuaded the general to make a statement at a Washington, D.C., reception in his honor. Pershing said he was not seeking the nation's highest office, but would not "decline to serve" if the people summoned him. The *Washington Post* made it a page-one headline. A few days later, the *Literary Digest* reported a nationwide poll on eight possible

Republican nominees. Pershing ranked eighth. A magazine commissioned a writer to find out why this was happening. He reported a widespread conviction among politicians who had spent some time in France that most of the 2 million doughboys in the AEF would vote no on the proposal to put Pershing in the White House.[35]

Still, the general refused to abandon his by now almost clandestine candidacy. As the Republican convention loomed, he wrote his old friend Charles Dawes, urging him to make sure someone would be on hand to push his name to the front if the delegates deadlocked. It was a hope almost as forlorn as Woodrow Wilson's great and solemn referendum.[36]

XII

The Republicans convened first, on June 8, in Chicago. They were confident but by no means complacent, because they confronted another potentially disastrous split in their ranks. Most of the League of Nations irreconcilables in the Senate were Republicans, and they were led by two hotheads, Hiram Johnson and William Borah. They had already served notice that they might bolt if the idea of ratifying the treaty with the Lodge reservations appeared in the party's platform. The mere suggestion of a replay of the 1912 election gave everyone nervous tremors. Johnson had run for vice president with Theodore Roosevelt on the Progressive Party ticket in that ruinous year.

Senator Henry Cabot Lodge was chosen temporary chairman, a tribute to the parliamentary skills he had displayed in the Senate, holding the fractious GOP majority together. Lodge was determined to repeat the performance in Chicago. This meant a platform that did not upset the irreconcilables, but still paid some sort of lip service to the idea of a league of nations—if not to Wilson's version. After several tries, Lodge and Elihu Root, once more demonstrating his lawyerly brilliance, came up with a plank aimed at being all things to all men—and women, who were voting for the first time. In 1919, the Republican-led Congress had passed the Nineteenth Amendment, giving women the vote, and the necessary number of states had swiftly ratified it.

The plank praised the idea of some sort of international association "to preserve the peace of the world." This association should be based on "international justice" and should "provide methods" that would promote an "instant and general international conference" when war threatened the world. Former Secretary of State Robert Lansing called it "about as near a void as science permits." Nevertheless, given the situation inside the Republican Party, it was a political masterpiece.[37]

Lodge's keynote address more than made up for the lack of specifics in the Republican platform. It was a relentless attack on Woodrow Wilson, the peace treaty and his version of the League of Nations. There were artful taunts, such as noting that after keeping America out of war when America wanted to fight, Wilson had now "kept us out of peace." He praised the Republican senators who had defended America's sovereignty from Wilson's utopian internationalism. At the same time, Lodge insisted that the United States had a role to play in the world, and would play it responsibly, as it did in 1917, when the Republican Party heartily affirmed the decision to throw "our great weight into the wavering scale."[38]

Lodge's speech was considered a huge success. He had proved himself adept at both managing his party and catching the national mood of disillusion with Wilson. His estimate of that mood also led him to collaborate in choosing a candidate that could be artfully guided, if not controlled, in a campaign that caught the same mood. Theodore Roosevelt's death had left a void in the Republicans' leadership. Lodge and Root were too old to seek the presidency. None of the leading candidates, Senator Hiram Johnson, Governor Leonard Wood or Illinois Governor Frank Lowden, commanded a majority of the party. After ten deadlocked ballots, George Harvey, still at his favorite sport of president-making in spite of his disappointment with Woodrow Wilson, called bosses and congressional leaders to his hotel suite. Together they decided that Senator Warren Harding of Ohio was the perfect compromise. He had nothing negative on his record, because he had no record worth mentioning. He had no enemies, because he had no strong opinions on the issues.

In 1920, most people saw Harding as another William McKinley, a kindly, earnest spokesman from the American heartland. The chief motivation for choosing him was a reaction against Wilson's presidential style. Lodge and other leading Republicans thought the American people were tired of being lectured, exhorted and summoned to save the world. "Harding will not try to be an autocrat but will do his best to carry on the government in the old and accepted Constitutional ways," Lodge told Owen Wister, the novelist and close friend of the late Theodore Roosevelt.

By "the old and accepted ways," Lodge meant a president who was inclined to listen to the accumulated wisdom of Congress.[39]

For vice president, the Republicans chose Governor Calvin Coolidge of Massachusetts, the man who broke the Boston police walkout with his blunt denunciation of striking against the public safety. He too represented a reaction against the turmoil the war had created in the United States—in his case against the backwash of the Bolshevik revolution and its rhetoric about power to the people. The Democrats, traditional friends of the working class, could only wince at the way labor issues had become a weapon in the GOP's hands.

XIII

In the White House, the president had made a modest recovery from the most crippling aspects of his cerebral thrombosis. With the help of a physical therapist, he had made some progress in walking, although he required a cane and still dragged his crippled left leg. In April, Wilson attended his first cabinet meeting. His trio of White House helpers brought him to the cabinet room first and seated him at the table before the department heads arrived. He made some feeble jokes and for a few minutes seemed to be able to do some business. But it soon became apparent that he could not follow a train of thought for more than sixty seconds—and when he did follow one, he had nothing to say. After an hour, Edith Wilson and Admiral Grayson, hovering outside the door, abruptly appeared to announce the meeting was over. "This is an experiment, you know," Edith said.[40]

Wilson's White House regimen remained on an invalid's plane. Each morning, he limped to his wheelchair and was taken to the South Portico or out on a part of the grounds where trees and shrubbery shielded him from passersby on the street. Returning to the White House about noon, he invariably watched a movie for an hour before lunch. Since he had difficulty reading books, these films became his favorite recreation. Ike Hoover scoured Washington, D.C., and eventually the entire country to find new releases for the president.[41]

Hoover was not always successful in locating films of decent quality. To his great joy, the head usher discovered five newsreels that Wilson had no objections to seeing more than once. They were footage put together by the U.S. Army Signal Corps showing the president's triumphant receptions in Paris, London, Rome and Milan.

Wilson was so fond of watching these past glories, he frequently invited guests for lunch and asked if they would like to see the film first. It gave the president a legitimate excuse to watch it again. The scene makes one wince with retrospective pain. It also reveals, again, the roots of Wilson's political psychology—the overweening pride in his oratorical ability, which convinced him he did not have to compromise with his opponents, because he could rely on "the people" to support him. In the depths of his tortured soul, the president had the instincts of the demagogue.[42]

Oblivious to the detestation that a majority of Americans now felt for him, Wilson pursued his great and solemn referendum. As the Democratic convention approached, this strategy acquired a new dimension: Woodrow Wilson as the Democratic nominee. A staggered Joe Tumulty begged the president to announce he would not seek a third term. Some Republicans were accusing him of using the fight over the treaty as an excuse to demand another four years in the White House. Wilson refused to issue anything even faintly resembling a disclaimer.

Secretary of the Treasury William Gibbs McAdoo had resigned and announced he was a candidate for the Democratic nomination. Five times in the month of May, McAdoo tried to see his father-in-law and got nowhere. Attorney General A. Mitchell Palmer, also in the running, was similarly spurned. (At the Jackson Day dinner, the Democrats had resoundingly endorsed Palmer's Red hunting.) Feeding the president's fantasy was a *Literary Digest* poll, which showed Wilson running second to McAdoo and well ahead of other announced candidates for the nomination. It represented a triumph of the Edith Wilson–Cary Grayson policy of assiduous lying and a sad commentary on the gullibility of the American press.[43]

In desperation—Tumulty's prevailing state of mind—the president's secretary cooked up a scheme with Louis Seibold, a veteran reporter from the *New York World,* who was anxious to be the first newsman to interview Wilson since his collapse. The week after the Republican Convention, when denunciations of Wilson and the league were fresh in the public's mind, seemed the right moment. Tumulty drew up a set of loaded questions and answers in advance, designed to show that Wilson was very much in touch with things. The league, the treaty, relations with Mexico, the

Volstead Act, taxes, labor, were among the topics covered, with solid answers constructed from Tumulty's energetic research. At the close was a final question about Wilson's desire for a third term—and a carefully phrased statement of renunciation.

Tumulty took this prepackaged interview to Wilson so he would be ready to play his part in the performance. To the secretary's dismay, Wilson dismissed most of the topics. Next came a memo from Edith Wilson, informing Tumulty that Seibold was expected to portray Wilson as ready, willing and able to seek a third term. For once, Tumulty allowed his Irish temper to flare. As he filed the memo, he scribbled on it a fervent hope that Edith Wilson would burn in hell.[44]

Seibold's eagerness to get the interview easily persuaded him to go along with the Wilsons' scam. The reporter told how delighted he was to find the president almost his old self. He joshed with him about running a footrace in a month or two; he would give the president a modest handicap because of his "slight limp." Seibold noted that General Wood, who had almost won the Republican nomination in Chicago, also dragged his left leg, the result of an old injury. As for the treaty and the league, Seibold reported that Wilson demanded a Democratic Party platform that called for ratification without changing a comma. The president was supremely confident that American voters would show their scorn for the "ambiguity and evasion" that the "Prussian-like" Republicans had displayed in the Senate with their reservations.

In obedience to Edith Wilson's orders, Seibold lied shamelessly about the president. "I saw him transact the most important functions of his office with his old time decisiveness, method and keenness of intellectual appraisement," the reporter declared. Seibold claimed to have watched Wilson sign a document "with the same copper plate signature." He even maintained Wilson was functioning better as president than before his "illness" because now he had more time to deliberate on matters.

Admiral Grayson chimed in with a plethora of new lies about Wilson's amazing recovery. The hoary tradition of faking it was still alive and well in Louis Seibold's corner of the *New York World*'s newsroom. For a final irony, the interview won Seibold the Pulitzer Prize.[45]

The next day, a photographer assigned by the *World* came to the White House and took a carefully staged picture of Wilson signing a document, with Edith standing beside him. Seibold also returned for a brief follow-up interview. The picture was taken from the right side, showing the uncollapsed side of Wilson's face and avoiding his useless left hand and arm. The photographer said: "The pictures [he took several shots] speak for themselves." So they did—proving that the camera could lie as convincingly as a reporter—or a president's wife and doctor.

Everyone saw the *World* stories and photographs as a Wilson declaration of readiness to run for a third term. Seeming to confirm this new ambition was a statement from William Gibbs McAdoo, withdrawing from the race for the Democratic nomination. On Wall Street, brokers reported Wilson had become the odds-on favorite among the remaining candidates. Evidence that four more years in the White House were precisely what Wilson had in mind is a document in his papers entitled "Third Inaugural." Random notes thanked the American people for the "overwhelming honor" they had conferred on him and outlined the principles that would govern his new term. The illusion of regained power continued to mesmerize the president.[46]

XIV

The opening scene of the Democratic Convention, which met in San Francisco on June 28, 1920, suggested that Wilson might realize the first step in his third-term fantasy. Moments after the chairman gaveled the conclave to order, a searchlight illuminated a huge portrait of Wilson, draped with American flags. A gigantic demonstration erupted with thousands of delegates prancing in the aisles, waving their state standards. Only the members of the New York delegation remained in their seats, morosely silent. The hardheaded men of Tammany, Irish-Americans almost to a man, wanted no more to do with Woodrow Wilson.

Two members of the delegation thought differently: Mayor George Lunn of Schenectady and Assistant Secretary of the Navy Franklin D. Roosevelt. They asked the state chairman if they could join the celebration. With his permission, they headed for the aisle—until Roosevelt decided to take the New York state standard with him. Judge Jeremiah T. Mahoney, who held it, resisted, and several of his friends rushed to assist him. Mahoney turned for advice to the boss of the party, Charles Murphy, who nodded his approval to let Roosevelt have his way. The assistant secretary joined the tumult in the aisles, waving the prize in triumph.

Roosevelt's private publicity machine swiftly converted the small clash into an epic encounter, in which FDR flattened two Tammany stalwarts with rights, lefts and uppercuts. The man who was there, Judge Mahoney, said the whole thing lasted "about four seconds." Roosevelt contributed to the myth, telling one reporter it had been "a bully fight."

Roosevelt had come to the convention thirsting for political advancement. He entertained the New York delegates aboard one of the battleships of the Pacific fleet. He agreed to make a seconding speech on behalf of New York's favorite son, Governor Alfred E. Smith, whom Murphy planned to nominate for president, although he knew he did not have a chance at this convention. With Wilson an albatross around their necks, Murphy considered the Democrats' cause hopeless and was thinking ahead to 1924.[47]

Convention chairman Homer Cummings followed the demonstration with a keynote speech that made a point of proclaiming the president had approved the address in advance. In a play for a sympathy vote, Cummings blamed Wilson's collapse on Republican harassment. Lodge and his friends had "physically wounded" the president, putting Wilson in the company of such presidential martyrs as Lincoln, Garfield and McKinley. Cummings taunted the Republicans for their evasive platform, calling their Chicago conclave "not a convention but an auction." He deplored the nation's failure to join the League of Nations and uphold Wilson's promise to make the world safe for democracy. The speech was clearly tailored to the president's plan for a great and solemn referendum.[48]

Since Wilson continued to say nothing explicit about being a candidate, William Gibbs McAdoo reentered the race at the behest of his friends. Unfortunately for poor "Mac," he became the lightning rod on which anti-Wilson Democrats vented their disillusion with the party's putative leader. A. Mitchell Palmer soon dropped out of the running. He had looked silly when he predicted a massive wave of terror bombings on May 1, the great Communist-Socialist feast day, and not even a firecracker exploded. Against McAdoo the anti-Wilson men pushed Governor James A. Cox of Ohio, who called for repeal of the Eighteenth Amendment as proof of his bold statesmanship.

Postmaster General Burleson, who had been Wilson's chief lieutenant on party politics, called the White House, pleading for a McAdoo endorsement. Wilson became so enraged, he seemed in danger of another cerebral thrombosis. He ordered Chairman Cummings to bar Burleson from the leadership of the convention and vowed to fire him the moment he returned from San Francisco.[49]

Wilson's game plan gambled on a deadlock. His man in San Francisco was his new secretary of state, Bainbridge Colby, a virtual cipher in foreign policy but a gifted writer and speaker. Dazzled by his ascent to power, Colby had become a Wilson worshipper. He saw nothing seriously wrong with the mentally and physically crippled man who presided at cabinet meetings. Wilson had given him a secret code to communicate directly with the White House. On July 2, Colby sent a wire that Tumulty, unacquainted with the code, passed on to the president. "THE OUTSTANDING CHARACTERISTIC OF THE CONVENTION IS UNANIMITY AND FERVOR OF FEELING FOR YOU. . . . I PROPOSE UNLESS OTHERWISE DEFINITELY INSTRUCTED TO MOVE SUSPENSION OF RULES AND PLACE YOUR NAME IN NOMINATION."[50]

Edith Wilson did not know that her co-conspirator, Admiral Cary Grayson, had defected from this ultimate delusion of glory. His medical training finally in charge of his conscience, Grayson had urged Senator Carter Glass of Virginia to save Wilson from "the juggling of false friends." The admiral must have known when he said this that the foremost false friend was Edith Wilson. Tumulty, who was with Grayson when he spoke to Glass, added his own fervent agreement. Another account has Grayson bringing the same message to Robert Woolley, a Democratic publicist, who told him not to worry about it. Wilson did not have a chance of being nominated.[51]

In San Francisco, Glass spread the word to Homer Cummings, Burleson, Josephus Daniels and other insiders that Grayson had finally told the truth: Wilson could not survive a campaign, much less four more years in the White House. With the convention on its twelfth ballot and no clear-cut leader emerging, Ray T. Baker, a California Democrat, telephoned Tumulty, revealing Bainbridge Colby's plan. A frantic Tumulty begged Edith Wilson to stop the secretary of state. She coldly ignored his note. A second plea also went unanswered.

But Grayson's message had taken on a life of its own in San Francisco. On July 4, when the insiders learned Colby's intentions, they summoned him to a hotel room and all but dismembered him with raging denunciations of his idiocy. The mortified Wilson-worshipper later said they made him feel "like a criminal." He dolefully informed Wilson that the insiders had vetoed his plan because they did not think the president would get enough votes to win the nomination.[52]

For another three days, McAdoo and Cox struggled to win a two-thirds majority. Finally Cox pulled ahead and on the forty-fourth ballot won the nomination. While this struggle absorbed everyone's attention, the cadre of friends and allies Franklin Roosevelt brought with him had been working the hotel rooms and state caucuses, urging FDR as the perfect choice for vice president, no matter who won. He had made a good impression on everyone in his seconding speech for Al Smith. He was from the crucial state of New York, projected youth, was a Wilson man—and the name Roosevelt was a proven vote getter. The day after Cox became the standard bearer, the brash thirty-eight-year-old assistant secretary of the navy was chosen by acclamation as his running mate.

In the White House, the news of the Cox-Roosevelt ticket produced a string of curses from the president that left his valet in a state of shock. Never before had he heard Wilson say anything more violent than an occasional damn or hell. Cox, a total neophyte in foreign policy, had been the president's least favored candidate. Wilson had told Josephus Daniels that Cox's nomination would be a joke. As for Roosevelt, Wilson considered him disloyal for his political flirtations with his cousin Theodore and his dinner with Viscount Grey. The president sent Cox a perfunctory telegram offering "hearty congratulations and cordial best wishes." For FDR, he downgraded the congratulations to "warm" and the wishes to "good."[53]

On Sunday, July 18, 1920, candidates Cox and Roosevelt paid an obligatory visit to the White House. Many of Cox's inner circle had advised against it. They saw their only chance of victory in a campaign that somehow distanced Cox from Wilson. But Cox felt this was impossible, and scheduled the visit. By this time, the euphoric flurry that had produced Wilson's illusory hopes for the Democratic nomination had collapsed into the deep depression that was the president's prevailing mood. The two nominees waited for about fifteen minutes while Wilson was rolled out onto the South Portico. The president's mouth drooped, his long jaw sagged almost to his chest, his staring eyes were fixed on the ground. A shawl covered his useless left arm and paralyzed side.

The two candidates were stunned by his appearance. "He's a very sick man," Cox whispered to Roosevelt as they approached him. Cox's eyes grew moist. Mrs. Wilson later recalled the shock and sympathy on Roosevelt's face.

"Thank you for coming," Wilson said in a weak, strained voice. "I'm very glad you came."

During the brawl over the league, Cox had tried to stay aloof from the struggle. As governor of Ohio, he had no direct stake in it. Now, the sight of Wilson swept aside all equivocations. "Mr. President," he said. "We are going to be a million percent with you and your administration—and that means the League of Nations."

"I am very grateful," Wilson said in the same sad, wavering voice. "I am very grateful."

Back in the West Wing, Governor Cox sat down at Tumulty's desk and drafted a statement affirming that the League of Nations was the primary issue of the campaign and he was in favor of its ratification on Woodrow Wilson's terms.[54]

The great and solemn referendum was on its way.

XV

The Democratic candidates had little choice, when it came to issues. The Eighteenth Amendment was a tar baby that already threatened them with ruin. Although the party platform finessed the issue by trying to ignore it, everyone knew that Cox and Roosevelt were both wets. Their stand put William Jennings Bryan and his followers, all drys to the last man and woman, in a funk. Bryan left San Francisco declaring, "My heart is in the grave." He retired into silence and declined to say a word for the ticket.[55]

The disappointed man in the White House did not do much more for the Cox-Roosevelt team. A few days after the candidates' visit, Wilson unleashed a ferocious diatribe against Roosevelt to Josephus Daniels, who had his own reasons for disliking his assistant secretary. Everyone but Wilson—with the possible exception of Cox and Roosevelt—seemed to know the Democrats did not have a chance. When the secretary of the navy tried to tell Wilson the truth, the president cried, "Daniels, you haven't enough faith in the people!"[56]

Also in the running as the candidate of the Socialist Party was Convict Number 9653 in the Atlanta Federal Penitentiary. Better known as Eugene V. Debs, the man Wilson stubbornly called a traitor to his country, ran on a very simple platform. Wilson was "pro-British and a tool of Wall Street,"

and so was his League of Nations. For added appeal, Debs called for immediate recognition of Irish independence, something neither of the major
parties had been willing to do.[57]

In August, a national German-American Conference met in Chicago.
They disliked the platforms of both major parties and regretted the lack of
a "fearless and patriotic" candidate such as Robert La Follette. But they
still recommended voting for Harding out of fear that a switch to a third
party might permit Cox to win and put "another proxy of Great Britain"
in the White House. Such a calamity would put the seal of "popular
approval" on Wilson's administration, which they characterized as "the
most un-American in the making of our country." George Sylvester
Viereck, who wrote the conference's resolutions, assured Frank Walsh, still
crusading against Wilson for the Irish-Americans, that 5 to 6 million
German-Americans were certain to vote for Harding. "We have decided
there must not be another Democratic president for a generation,"
Viereck told Walsh.[58]

Italian-Americans were equally hostile to Cox and Roosevelt. Their
newspapers called Wilson an enemy of Italy. In New York, 20,000 Italian-
Americans, led by Fiorello LaGuardia, denounced the "Wilsonian peace."
The Federation of Italian Societies in America urged its members to "forget this year any political affiliation and vote for Harding."[59]

The Irish-Americans hated Wilson with an even more vindictive passion, but they had very little enthusiasm for Harding. The Republican candidate had declined to vote for various Senate resolutions calling for
Ireland's independence. If Cox had somehow distanced himself from
Wilson, he might have retained their traditionally Democratic loyalty. But
the candidate's embrace of Wilson sealed his fate with most Irish-American
leaders. "Cox wears Wilson's collar on the League of Nations," John Devoy
wrote in the *Gaelic American*.[60]

From Ireland came news that all but finished Cox with Irish-American
voters. Terence MacSwiney, the lord mayor of Cork, began a hunger strike
when he was arrested by the British for backing the embattled Irish republic. As MacSwiney neared death, prominent Catholic churchmen and Irish-
American leaders bombarded Wilson and the State Department with pleas
for intervention. They only succeeded in arousing the president's antipathy
to hyphenated Americans. Wilson called their appeals "grossly impertinent"
and "a piece of confounded impudence."[61]

In the fall of 1920, Irish-American politicians virtually abandoned the Democratic Party in a body. Few were willing to say a word for Governor Cox out of fear that they would be wiped out on a local level by their enraged followers. When Cox came to Worcester, Massachusetts, the local leaders begged the candidate to make his visit no more than a whistle stop. A long speech about the League of Nations would turn Worcester totally Republican. An amused Henry Cabot Lodge remarked, "The Democratic leadership is motionless in Massachusetts."[62]

Cox tried to deal with these massive defections on the ethnic side by attacking Harding and his Republican Old Guard backers, hoping to retain some of the middle-class progressives who had supported Wilson in 1912 and 1916. A sturdy, even dynamic man, full of energy, Cox traveled 22,000 miles and spoke to more than 2 million people. The Ohio governor denounced the $30 million that the GOP was supposedly raising to guarantee the election, calling it a slush fund and labeling the Republicans' two chief fund-raisers "the Gold Dust Twins." He assailed Harding's "wobbles" on the League of Nations and blasted the Senate "oligarchy." In *Collier's* Magazine, veteran journalist Mark Sullivan wrote that the candidate was so vehement, he made many voters think of him as a frontier "bad man" shooting up the meeting.[63]

Franklin Roosevelt also essayed an over-the-top style. Trying to defend Wilson's decision to give the British six votes in the League of Nations, Roosevelt told an audience in Butte, Montana, that the United States controlled twelve votes in the league. He proceeded to list Cuba, Haiti, Santo Domingo, Panama and other Central American countries that would not dare to vote against the wishes of their big brother, the United States.

This casual endorsement of American imperialism was bad enough. Roosevelt compounded it by claiming that he had run a couple of these "little republics." In fact, he had written Haiti's constitution. "And if I do say so, it's a pretty good constitution."

The assistant secretary of the navy had not written a line of Haiti's constitution—nor did he ever "run" its government. He had done no more than supervise from Washington, D.C., the U.S. Marines' bloody pacification of Haiti in 1915 at Woodrow Wilson's order. To compound his woes, Roosevelt was unaware that *The Nation* was running a series of articles exposing the dark side of Wilson-style imperialism in Haiti and Santo Domingo.

Republicans pounced on the candidate's gaffe. Warren Harding professed to be horrified to learn that "thousands of native Haitians have been killed by American Marines . . . to secure a vote in the League." He called Roosevelt's braggadocio "the most shocking assertion that ever emanated from a responsible member of the government of the United States."[64]

With his usual effrontery, FDR denied saying anything about Haiti, and tried to blame a local Associated Press stringer for misquoting him. The stringer persuaded thirty-one citizens of Butte to swear that Roosevelt was telling a lie almost as big as his claim that he wrote Haiti's constitution. That was the last time Roosevelt mentioned Haiti in the campaign.

In Centralia, Washington, FDR gave a speech that would have brought tears of joy to Attorney General A. Mitchell Palmer's eyes. Roosevelt saluted the members of the American Legion who had been gunned down in the 1919 Armistice Day assault on the IWW union hall, calling them martyrs "to the sacred cause of Americanism." He said not a word about the castration and lynching of Wesley Everett, the IWW local's secretary, by a frenzied mob. Instead Roosevelt orated on the way the legionnaires' deaths had aroused the nation "to the great task of ridding this land of the alien anarchist, the criminal syndicalist, and all similar anti-Americans." He was, of course, only echoing the civil rights policy of the Wilson administration.[65]

XVI

With the electoral tide running strongly in their favor, the Republicans did their utmost to straddle every issue and look confident of victory. In one of his first public statements, Harding summed up the underlying philosophy of his campaign: "America's present need is not heroics but healing; not nostrums but normalcy . . . not surgery but serenity." Most of the time, Harding took a leaf from William McKinley's book and stayed on his front porch in Marion, Ohio, greeting delegations who pledged their fervent support and listening cheerfully to choral groups who warbled

> *We'll throw out Woodrow and his crew*
> *They really don't know what to do.*

At one point, Harding intimated strongly that he had little use for the League of Nations and would reject it. This pleased irreconcilables like

Senators Johnson and Borah. But the Lodge-Root wing of the party protested that a league with reservations was what the people wanted. Consequently, in a succeeding speech, Harding wobbled back to saying that when he became president, he would convene a meeting of the nation's best minds to study the league and see if it were worthy of ratification. In another speech, he said the United States might propose some other form of international association. But there was one point on which Harding never wobbled: Wilson's League. The Republican candidate called it all sorts of nasty names, from monster to fraud.[66]

Even more effective were thousands of other Republican orators who made Wilson the centerpiece of their negative campaign. To remind Irish-, Italian-, and German-American voters how Wilson had treated their homelands, speakers pictured Wilson playing a losing poker game with Lloyd George. "I'll bet you Fiume," says Lloyd George. "I'll raise you Alsace!" says Wilson. The president was portrayed as a stubborn, vain, gullible fool who was taken to the cleaners by the shrewd Europeans. He was described as pounding the table and yelling, "You can never have Fiume!" The orator would add: "Nobody knew where Fiume was, whether one of the Sandwich Islands or a fixed star." In the American heartland, the speech won howls of laughter and applause.[67]

In the closing weeks of the campaign, both Cox and Roosevelt, sensing imminent defeat, heaped abuse on ethnic Americans. Here, ironically, the big influence was Tumulty, who was playing the game that had worked for Wilson in 1916. The candidates began suggesting that German-Americans and Italian-Americans were disloyal and their support tainted Harding's candidacy. Tumulty was delighted and so was Wilson, who hoped Cox would send George Sylvester Viereck an insulting telegram like the one the president had sent Jeremiah O'Leary in 1916.[68]

By October 14, Cox was pointing to "the motley array of questionable groups" backing Harding. Along with the "pro-German party," there were the Italians, the Greeks and the Bulgarians, all putting "nationalistic ambition" above "the welfare of the world" by opposing the League of Nations. In subsequent speeches, Cox began talking about "the enemies of America during the war," attempting to evoke the war rage that had run wild in 1918. In his final speech, Cox reached a predictable low point with the shout "Every traitor in America will vote tomorrow for Warren G. Harding!"[69]

When it came to the low road, Cox's vice presidential candidate was no improvement. Roosevelt regularly castigated the Republicans for soliciting votes from the country's "dangerous element," who had been disloyal during the war. The Democrats scorned such tactics, Roosevelt declared. They wanted "all-American votes only." An Italian-American newspaper sneered that Roosevelt was "a rah-rah boy whose sole asset in politics is his name." Upping the ante, Roosevelt said that Italian-Americans had only "half-consciences" and were "fifty-fifty citizens."[70]

In this Tumulty-inspired game plan, the Irish-Americans were exempted from such attacks. The president's secretary was hoping to appeal to their patriotism and their jealousy of the other ethnics. But the fates foredoomed this shaky strategy, which probably had little impact on the enraged Irish rank and file in the first place. On October 25, hunger-striking Lord Mayor Terence MacSwiney of Cork died, defiant to his last anguished breath. Irish-American leaders promptly proclaimed the Sunday before the election MacSwiney Observance Day. In New York's Polo Grounds, 50,000 Celts heard Wilson and the League of Nations denounced once more as mortal enemies of Ireland's right to self-determination. Similarly huge meetings took place in Chicago and other cities, at which orators told the Irish it was their solemn duty to vote against the Democratic ticket.[71]

Cox and Roosevelt struggled to combine their descents to the low road with repeated apostrophes to the League of Nations. When the league, already operating in Geneva, settled a dispute between Poland and Lithuania, Tumulty urged Cox to point it out to the American people. Roosevelt, in a fog illusionary optimism, replied, "Things are going vastly better. The President's judgment that the League would be the only true issue is wholly borne out."[72]

But Cox soon revealed his desperation when he began saying that he would accept a league with reservations. His would-be vice president began saying the same thing and added a pie-in-the-sky statement that convinced not a few people he had charm but little else to recommend him. Roosevelt declared if Cox were elected, the treaty would be ratified within sixty days. Neither man could see what was obvious to many other people: By this time the main issue was not the league but Wilsonism.[73]

Steve Early, a former Associated Press reporter who served as Roosevelt's advance man aboard his campaign train, was impressed by the young candidate's performance, in spite of his gaffes and a preference for speaking off the top of his head rather than from a prepared text. But Early was depressed by the public's reaction. The Democrats' problem was "the bitterness toward Wilson everywhere. He hasn't a friend." In a halfhearted way, people still wanted to join a league of nations, but not "Mr. Wilson's League." Senator Lodge's call for second thoughts on the league had been an overwhelming success.[74]

No one summed up the Democrats' dilemma better than Franklin K. Lane, Wilson's former secretary of the interior: "Oh, if he [Wilson] had been frank as to his illness, the people would have forgotten everything, his going to Paris, his refusal to deal with the mild reservationists—everything would have been swept away in a great wave of sympathy. But he could not be frank, he who talked so high of faith in the people distrusted them, and they will not be mastered by mystery. So he is so much less than a hero that he bears down his party to defeat."[75]

Tumulty struggled in vain to persuade Wilson to join the campaign. The secretary proposed releasing a weekly address to the American people. Wilson spurned the idea, fearing it would get him into a debate with Harding, whom he had grown to loathe. Not until October 27, with the election only a week away, did the president decide to make a statement. He chose the oddest imaginable audience—a forlorn little band of Republican supporters of the League to Enforce Peace, who clung to accepting the covenant without reservations. They had came to the White House to pledge their allegiance to him.

The LEP remnant listened as the president read his semi-speech from his wheelchair. It was clearly intended not for them but for the nation. "My fellow countrymen," Wilson began. "It is feared the supreme issue presented for your consideration in this campaign is growing more obscure rather than clearer." As he went on, his voice dwindled to a near whisper. But the words were strong and emphatic. He was telling the voters that the election was a national referendum on the league and the treaty. "The nation was never called upon to make a more solemn determination than it must now make." Wilson urged the voters to measure every candidate—those running for the Senate and the House as well as for president and vice president—by the same strict standard: "Shall we or shall we not redeem the great moral obligations of the United States?"[76]

Not once in this final burst of Wilsonian idealism did the president mention the names of Cox or Roosevelt. Was he suggesting that in his

embittered soul he did not think they were worthy of carrying the standard he had lifted before the nation? Perhaps. In the final analysis,
Woodrow Wilson found it hard to share the stage with anyone.

From this summons to the high road, the Democratic campaign lurched
to the lowest imaginable low road a few days later. Hundreds of thousands
of copies of a pamphlet circulated throughout the country, informing voters that Warren G. Harding had "Negro blood," and his election would
result in "international shame and domestic ruin." The author was a race-
baiting history professor named W. E. Chancellor. Rumors about Harding's
ancestry had swirled through Ohio for years. The Republicans had a denial
ready for instant release and threw in a denunciation of "conscienceless
Democratic partisans."[77]

Although by this time the betting odds on a Harding victory had
reached 10 to 1—the highest in anyone's memory—the Republicans
decided a little revenge was in order. They connived with the editor of the
Providence Journal, the Australian-born John Revelstoke Rathom, who had
made a career out of publicizing mostly imaginary German spies during
the war, to unleash a suitably underhanded attack on Franklin Roosevelt.

Rathom's paper had covered some messy problems at Portsmouth Naval
Prison, involving sailors convicted of sodomy. Secretary of the Navy
Daniels had advocated a policy of forgiveness and rehabilitation for these
men, and his assistant secretary had carried it out, ordering them returned
to active duty after relatively brief incarceration. The upper ranks of the
navy had violently opposed this lenient policy and were not averse to leaking their opinions to the press. Rathom used these facts to condemn
Roosevelt for lacking "the qualities of frankness and manliness." Clearly
implying FDR was gay, Rathom sneered that his conduct had earned him
"the detestation and contempt" of every officer in the U.S. Navy.[78]

A flabbergasted Roosevelt summoned newsman Arthur Krock to Hyde
Park to help him draft a reply and filed a $500,000 libel suit against
Rathom. A few weeks earlier, the Democratic candidate had bragged to
friends that his performance on the hustings in the West meant "from now
the vice presidency is going to be a highly respected and live wire office."
Suddenly he was face-to-face with political catastrophe.

Fellow Democrats in the U.S. Department of Justice helped him counterattack in the press. They released documents of a prosecution the government had brought against Rathom in 1918 for claiming he had personally

captured numerous German agents. The government found Rathom had lied about almost every item in his highly colored autobiography. To escape indictment, the editor had made a humiliating confession.[79]

The intrusion of lowlifes such as Chancellor and Rathom into Woodrow Wilson's great and solemn referendum on the League of Nations was the final irony of the 1920 presidential campaign. In the closing days, the Democratic candidates exchanged frantic wires, predicting victory. "WE ARE HAVING THE MOST REMARKABLE MEETINGS I HAVE EVER SEEN," Cox wired Roosevelt. "THE FIGHT IS WON." Roosevelt was so sure they were going to win, he told one of his aides he was looking forward to seeing him at the inauguration on March 4, 1921. The aide, a dour Irish-American named Lynch, brutally punctured this balloon of hope: "Listen, Frank, you're not going to Washington."[80]

In the White House, Woodrow Wilson clung to the same illusion of victory. At a cabinet meeting on election day, several men warned the president that defeat was a strong probability. Wilson replied: "The American people will not turn Cox down and elect Harding. A great moral issue is involved."[81]

On November 2, 1920, the Republican ticket steamrollered through all parts of the nation, crushing Democratic candidates everywhere but in the Solid South. Even there, hitherto Democratic Tennessee and Texas succumbed to the GOP. Harding and Coolidge garnered a staggering 61 percent of the vote—16,141,536 to Cox-Roosevelt's 9,128,488. The Republicans carried 37 states and won 404 of 531 electoral votes. Another 919,799 voters cast their ballots for Convict Number 9653, Eugene V. Debs. In the House of Representatives, the Republican majority swelled to 300 to 135. In the Senate, their edge became 59 to 37. Popular Democrats such as Governor Al Smith of New York and Champ Clark of Missouri were buried in the wreckage. The Cox-Roosevelt ticket lost New York City by 440,000 votes, a hitherto unthinkable beating for a Democratic candidate. Franklin Roosevelt's value on the ticket turned out to be zero-minus. The Democrats did not carry a single county in New York State.[82]

In New Jersey, Boss Frank Hague, seeing every Democratic candidate in sight crumbling before his eyes, went all out to rescue the sheriff's office in his Hudson County home base. The sheriff controlled the selection of the grand jury, a crucial factor if the victorious Republicans sought criminal indictments. The candidate, Thomas "Skidder" Mulligan, was running in spite of a disability that most politicians would have considered daunting: He could not read or write. His campaign slogan was even more unusual: "He was good to his mother." Abandoning all other candidates, the Democratic organization elected Skidder with a majority that was 100 percent stolen. It was a mordant commentary on the durability of Woodrow Wilson's reform of New Jersey's politics.[83]

"We have torn up Wilsonism by the roots," declared Senator Henry Cabot Lodge. The German, Italian and Irish press voiced similar sentiments. The *Irish World* gloated: "The chief fugleman for the conspiracy to make the Republic stand sponsor for the preservation of the British Empire received his answer on the second day of November." George Sylvester Viereck chortled: "T. Woodrow Wilson is the most humiliated president in the history of the United States." A stunned Joe Tumulty said it was not a landslide, it was "an earthquake."[84]

Woodrow Wilson's great and solemn referendum on the League of Nations—and America's participation in World War I—was over. His last illusion of victory had become the debris of humiliating defeat. The president remained impervious to his central role in perpetrating the disaster. Self-righteous to the last, Wilson now blamed the American voters. "They have disgraced us in the eyes of the world," he told the stricken, ever-faithful Tumulty.[85]

Chapter 13

A COVENANT WITH POWER

Historians and biographers sympathetic to Woodrow Wilson have expended an ocean of ink trying to explain away the catastrophic election of 1920. Agreeing with William Jennings Bryan, they have argued that a genuine referendum on the League of Nations or any other issue was impossible because of the local complexities of American politics. The contention undoubtedly has some merit. But Wilson and the Democratic candidates made 1920 as close to a referendum as a presidential election can become. The League of Nations and the Treaty of Versailles were unquestionably the foremost issues. Wilson's enemies undoubtedly misrepresented them in their often furious diatribes against him and his uncompromising ways. It was an imperfect referendum—but it *was* a referendum.

Franklin D. Roosevelt at first blamed the defeat on the ethnic Americans. He ruefully told Josephus Daniels of a postelection conversation with his German-born gardener, Sebastian Baumann. Roosevelt asked him how he had voted. "For Harding," Baumann replied.

Roosevelt asked why. Baumann had worked at Hyde Park for twenty years. He was an American citizen. Baumann said he had received letters from Germany, telling him of mass starvation and terrible shortages of warm clothing. Wilson had joined with England and France to destroy Germany. That made Baumann remember he was a German—and vote Republican. It was a mournful echo of the war's worst atrocity, the British blockade. But Roosevelt, already a ferocious German-hater, did not see it that way. He wanted an explanation of why his performance on the campaign trail had not translated into votes.

Later, with his remarkable ability to revise or avoid the truth—a talent by no means unique to him—Roosevelt blamed the defeat on the pamphlet accusing Harding of having Negro blood. He told one of his 1940 presidential aides that the story had been concocted by Harry Daugherty, Harding's campaign manager, who then cleverly blamed the Democrats, causing a backlash that cost them the election. Aside from giving us a glimpse of Roosevelt's low opinion of the intelligence of the average voter, both these comments make it clear that he declined to see the 1920 election as a referendum, much less a great and solemn one.[1]

The Republicans had no doubt about the election's being both a great and a solemn referendum. In fact, their 7-million-vote margin of victory gradually expanded the referendum's greatness and solemnity. In Warren Harding's inaugural address, the new president said that the United States was ready to confer with "nations great and small" to promote disarmament and any other program that would "lessen the probability of war." But he said nothing about the League of Nations. Some pro-league newspapers wondered if he were repudiating the league. No significant protest came from the public or from members of Harding's cabinet, such as Secretary of Commerce Herbert Hoover, who had strongly backed joining the league with Lodge's reservations.

Five weeks after the inauguration, when Harding addressed Congress for the first time, he said joining the League of Nations would be a "betrayal" of the "deliberate expression of the American people in the recent election." The statement was made with the advice and consent of Henry Cabot Lodge. In a letter written a week after the election, the senator had told the new president that it would be better "to make a fresh start" rather than try to "make over the League" with reservations. The important thing was to sign a swift, early peace with Germany. This formality was soon made fact by a joint resolution of Congress on July 2, 1921, and a separate peace was ratified by both countries in August.

Harding had needed no urging to junk "Wilson's league." He had merely moved cautiously, taking the public pulse before announcing the decision. Lodge claimed to have changed his mind about the league in the course of the 1920 campaign. After orating to thousands of people and talking to hundreds, Lodge became convinced that "the people at large were much more decided about not having anything to do with the League of Nations than the men in public life." Once more, an almost total lack of public outcry seemed to confirm the senator's words.[2]

II

This abandonment of the league did not mean that the United States retreated into total isolation. The world situation, especially the continuing chaos in Europe, made such a posture impossible. Under the auspices of Secretary of State Charles Evans Hughes, a disarmament conference convened in Washington in 1921 and negotiated significant reductions in the world's warships. The French blocked any discussion of land disarmament. But the United States persuaded Japan to sign an agreement returning Shantung Province to Chinese control.

A major share of America's international activity concerned the ongoing question of German reparations and the repayment of Allied war debts. Within a few months of the signing of the Treaty of Versailles, Americans began questioning the wisdom of demanding a huge sum from Germany. Norman H. Davis, one of Wilson's top economic advisers during the Paris negotiations, put it wryly: "Some of the delegates wanted to destroy Germany, some wanted to collect reparations, others wanted to do both." Bernard Baruch warned the American government to reject the British and French policy of forcing Germany to pay "a certain indemnity and yet making it impossible for her to pay."[3]

In 1921, the reparations commission appointed by the peace conference announced that Germany had to pay 132 billion gold marks. In prewar values, when the mark traded at 4.1 to a dollar, this would have been $43 billion, no small sum. (In twenty-first-century money, this is equivalent to $434 billion.) But wartime inflation had decimated the mark, making the real sum close to 750 billion marks—$7.5 trillion in today's dollars. To show they meant business, the commission demanded 1 billion marks within twenty-five days.

The Germans made the first payment, but the succeeding installments were another story. Their bitterness and rage over the Treaty of Versailles impelled them to allow inflation to run wild, hoping to pay off the reparations in depreciated marks. The device escalated out of control, until in November 1923, it took 4.2 trillion marks to equal a single dollar. This hyperinflation meant economic agony to millions of Germans on fixed incomes—and inflicted a fatal wound on their confidence in the government of the German republic.[4]

By this time, that ultimate German-hater, Raymond Poincaré, was premier of France. He sent French troops into the Ruhr valley, Germany's industrial heartland, to make sure future reparations payments had real value. Meanwhile, Britain was demanding that France, Italy and Belgium repay the huge sums loaned them—and the United States was reminding everyone that it expected all its former allies, including Britain, to repay the dollars Uncle Sam had shipped to them. When smaller countries such as Greece and Cuba were included in the astronomical addition, the total owed to the United States came close to $10.5 billion (more than $106 billion in twenty-first-century dollars).

The British tried to persuade the United States to cancel their $4 billion debt, if London canceled the $10 billion supposedly owed it by France, Greece and other allied countries. France too pleaded for debt cancellation. The United States stonily insisted on payment, and Congress created the World War Foreign Debt Commission, which set up a schedule of payments that was going to last sixty-two years, at an interest rate of 2.1 percent.

The United States next played a major role in reorganizing Germany's finances under a commission headed by General Pershing's purchasing wizard, Charles Dawes. The Americans insisted on French withdrawal from the Ruhr and set up a schedule of reparations payments based on a realistic assessment of Germany's ability to pay. The achievement won Dawes the Nobel Peace Prize and prompted Calvin Coolidge to make him his vice president in his successful run for the White House in 1924.

Thereafter, Germany became America's favorite trading partner. American banks and corporations poured millions into its struggling economy, and in 1929, another commission renegotiated the Dawes Plan, again reducing the Germans' reparation debt. All these difficult international labors came to naught as the nations of Europe, saddled with huge internal war debts, sank into recession in the late 1920s. The United States canceled most of the money Italy had borrowed and 60 percent of France's obligations, but these gestures did little to prevent Europe's downward slide into depression.

In 1931, as the American economy too succumbed to the worldwide economic paralysis, President Herbert Hoover, the man who had left Paris deeply disappointed with Woodrow Wilson, decreed a moratorium on all debt payments, including Germany's. America's "special relationship" with Germany continued until Adolf Hitler became the nation's chancellor two years later. By that time, the worldwide economic crisis ended all hope of receiving further payments from any of the debtor countries and also spelled kaput to German reparations. The net effect among average Americans was an even deeper disillusion with World War I.[5]

III

We have torn Wilsonism up by the roots. Did Lodge's triumphant cry reflect a victory over an ideology or a man? What was Wilsonism, anyway? Some Wilson biographers argue that it was a set of principles that guided the president throughout his political career. This argument leads to his portrayal as a prophet without honor in his own country, a tragic figure who refused to compromise his lofty moral standards. In this drama, Republicans such as Henry Cabot Lodge are the villains, saddled with the opprobrious term "isolationists." Ultimately, as Wilson's comment to Tumulty indicated, the true villains become the American people, who were too easily diverted by other issues and/or too selfish to confront the sacrifices necessary to maintain the peace of the world.

These conclusions are debatable, to say the least. The brief against the American people is the easiest to dismiss. What electorate would not have become disillusioned with a president like Wilson? From the time he asked Congress to declare war under the illusion that he would not have to send more than a token force to France to his mishandling of the peace treaty, his conduct of public affairs was deeply flawed. Capping this performance were the seventeen months of lies his wife and doctor perpetrated with his eventual collusion, after his cerebral thrombosis. The verdict the American people rendered in the great and solemn referendum was richly deserved by this president and the Democratic Party that gave him its support.

IV

An examination of Wilson's career forces one to ask, What were his principles? Aboard ship on the way to the Paris Peace Conference, he told his aides and fellow passengers that peace would have to be made "on the highest principles of justice." Otherwise he would "run away and hide." He saw himself as the Solomonic judge who would arbitrate the selfish goals of the Allies. The results of the peace conference revealed how little weight he gave these words.

In his speech calling for a declaration of war, Wilson had said that the German people were not the enemy; the crime of the war lay with their leaders. At the peace conference, he approved Article 231, the infamous war guilt clause. How to explain this total reversal of so-called principle—from lofty forgiveness to low revenge?

The president said he was for absolute freedom of the seas. He nevertheless permitted the British to strangle American commerce with Europe in the name of their infamous blockade and abandoned freedom of the seas along with the rest of the Fourteen Points at the peace conference.

Wilson proclaimed self-determination as a great principle—and then gave away chunks of German-speaking Europe to Czechoslovakia, Poland, Italy and France, sowing the seeds of the next war. Knowing that Austria favored a union with Germany after Vienna lost its empire, Wilson wrote into the Treaty of Versailles an article barring the union, no matter how the Austrians voted.

Wilson himself admitted the irrelevance—even the foolishness—of this so-called principle of self-determination in his talk with the advocates of Irish independence in Paris. He realized too late that it was an irresistible temptation for petty demagogues everywhere. It remains so to this day.

The more one examines the historical record, the clearer it becomes that Wilson regularly applied his rhetoric of principles after the fact or in blithe indifference to the facts. It was an oratorical device, not a well-thought-out philosophy. He took political positions and then cooked up principles to justify them. One might almost call it a bad habit, which caused him immense trouble all his life. When he could not get his way at Princeton, his opponents became advocates of special privilege and enemies of democracy. Until Pancho Villa started murdering Americans in cold blood, the Mexican rebel was the embodiment of Mexico's revolution against privilege in the name of democracy.

No one summed up this side of Wilson better than the man he tried to silence, Senator Robert La Follette. Commenting on Wilson's claim that the peace treaty fulfilled his Fourteen Points, La Follette wrote: "I some-times think the man has no sense of things that penetrate below the sur-face. With him the rhetoric of a thing is the thing itself. He is either wanting in understanding or convictions or both. Words—phrases, felicity of expression and a blind egotism have been his stock in trade."[6]

When Germany's resumption of unrestricted submarine warfare and the effrontery of Foreign Minister Zimmermann's telegram created a crisis, Wilson again invoked principles: Submarine warfare was a war against mankind; Americans had a right to travel on belligerent ships in the war zone and a right to trade with England while making no attempt to invoke a similar right to trade with Germany.

Wilson's tendency to put every dispute and every decision on the high plane of principle has made one historian imagine his reaction when a guest at his Thanksgiving Day table took the last of the white meat for himself. Wilson would never admit he was angry at this act of discourtesy. No, his wrath was because the man called into question "the very notion of an orderly society [and] . . . the social contract." Therefore the greedy fel-low must become a perpetual enemy "because there can be no compro-mise with the forces of anarchy and nihilism."[7]

Wilson had a few fixed ideas, which he had acquired in his academic years. Perhaps the most important was a belief in party government. He refused to bring any Republicans into his war administration, ignoring the example of England and France, both of which created mixed cabinets to sustain national unity. The war within the war that raged between Wilson and Congress had not a little to do with this attitude. He repeated this per-formance by refusing to invite any important Republican to Paris as an American delegate.

Wilson was not a very profound thinker or a good historian. Unlike Theodore Roosevelt's books on the War of 1812 and the history of the western movement, Wilson's biography of Washington and his other books on American history are virtually unreadable today. Only his didactic tract, *Congressional Government*, remains interesting.

Wilsonism would seem to be not a body of ideas or principles but a way of conducting politics—not a very good way. It led inevitably to the voter alienation and outrage that repudiated Wilson more decisively than any president in American history. The public Wilson was not a likable much less a lovable man. When Theodore Roosevelt died, Joe Tumulty, still gripped by the illusion of Wilson's greatness, wrote that it was time to launch a campaign to make Wilson as beloved by the people as TR was. The president, Tumulty noted, was respected, not loved. Within a year, respect for Wilson had evaporated, thanks to his postwar blunders.[8]

If these flaws are so apparent now, why was Wilson at first seemingly successful as a war leader? Because he was a superb orator, who appealed strongly to one side of the deepest dichotomy in American life, the clash between idealism and realism. This conflict threads like a bright, sometimes blood-soaked ribbon through American history, with idealists getting much the greater share of the praise in the history books. Wilson's idealism is why he remained revered in some circles, even in the 1920s and 1930s, when no Republican and few Democrats, including Franklin D. Roosevelt, had a good word to say for him.

But idealism is not synonymous with sainthood or virtue. It only sounds that way. The most dangerous aspect of American idealism is its tendency to become utopian, to propose as ideals a foreign policy or political reforms or a world order that ignores the realities of the way men and women—and nations—live and prosper. Not by accident did the great English statesman Sir Thomas More, the inventor of the idea of utopia, take the term from the Greek word meaning "nowhere."

Wilsonian idealism manifested its utopian derangements again and again. Its most egregious example was Wilson's refusal to entertain any reservations to Article 10 of the league covenant, which committed the United States to sending soldiers to wars around the world on the vote of the League of Nations. The subsequent history of U.S. involvement with world affairs demonstrates rather decisively that succeeding generations have backed Henry Cabot Lodge, not Woodrow Wilson, in affirming an international commitment but retaining control of America's sovereignty.

An ironic footnote to this conclusion was supplied by Henry Cabot Lodge, Jr., the senator's grandson. Writing to one of the senator's biographers, the younger Lodge pointed out that "the United Nations of today falls squarely within the limits of that [Lodge] proposition. The representatives of nations at the United Nations are ambassadors, and for the very reason that the sovereignty of their country is not compromised." Lodge added that the decision of the American people in 1920 "in the light of human experience of the last 30 years, seems remarkably far-sighted."⁹

V

Woodrow Wilson's war shared Wilson's harsh fate. Few people tried to glorify it. Starting with John Dos Passos's *Three Soldiers*, novelist after novelist vented his spleen on its idealistic pretensions. Revisionist historians such as Harry Elmer Barnes attacked Wilson's reasons for intervention and demonstrated the absurdity of the war guilt clause in the Versailles treaty. Politicians who had opposed the war, such as Robert La Follette, became postwar heroes, especially among liberals. In 1924, La Follette ran for president on the Progressive ticket and received 4,822,856 votes—17 percent of the total.

Another source of postwar disillusionment was the memoirs of British and French generals and statesmen, most of whom went out of their way to explain that the Americans had not won the war. They argued that the raw American army could never have succeeded against the German army the European Allies fought from 1914 to 1917. British and French troops had weakened the kaiser's mighty host and thinned its ranks to the point where it was easy for the Americans to deliver a knockout blow. This argument grew so unpleasant, Major General Robert Lee Bullard wrote a book that he sarcastically titled *American Soldiers Also Fought*. In his usual blunt style, Bullard said the former Allies' "patronizing disparagement" had been spread across the United States and "allowed to stand in the public mind virtually unchallenged." He might have added that this sad fact was a tribute to Woodrow Wilson's mishandling of the Treaty of Versailles and the consequent American disillusion with the war.¹⁰

Almost nine decades later, with the fog of propaganda swept away, it is hard to believe that anyone could advance such arguments. German losses on the Western Front were consistently much lower than the combined British and French losses. By the time the Americans arrived in 1918, the British and French armies were essentially beaten men. Nothing else explains the mass surrenders during the German offensives of 1918. Only the Americans faced the Germans with undaunted confidence. There were no British troops and only a single regiment of native-born French soldiers on the opening days of the battle of Soissons, the turning point in the war. As General Bullard put it, "After the long continued lack of success of our Allies, . . . [the] turning of the tide and the decisive results" of mid-1918 could only be attributed to the Americans.[11]

VI

If the United States had refused to intervene in 1917, would a German victory in 1918 have been a better historical alternative? The answer is debatable. By 1918, the Germans, exasperated by the Allied refusal to settle for anything less than a knockout blow, were contemplating peace terms as harsh and vindictive as those the French and British imposed, with Wilson's weary consent, in the Treaty of Versailles.[12]

There is another possibility in this newly popular game of what-if. What would have happened if Wilson had taken William Jennings Bryan's advice and practiced real rather than sham neutrality? Without the backing of American weaponry, munitions, and loans, the Allies would have been forced to abandon their goal of the knockout blow. The war might have ended in 1916 with a negotiated peace based on the mutual admission that the conflict had become a stalemate. As a genuine neutral, Wilson might even have persuaded both sides to let him be a mediator. Lloyd George's argument—that unless the United States intervened, Wilson would have no place at the peace table—was specious at best. Both sides would have needed America's wealth and industrial resources to rebuild their shattered economies.

Germany's aims before the war began were relatively modest. Basically, Berlin sought an acknowledgment that it was Europe's dominant power. It wanted an independent Poland and nationhood for the Baltic states, to keep Russia a safe distance from its eastern border. Also on the wish list was a free trade zone in which German goods could circulate without crippling tariffs in France, Italy, Scandinavia and Austria-Hungary. It is not terribly different from the role Germany plays today in the European Economic Union. But the British Tories could not tolerate such a commercial rival in 1914 and chose war.[13]

Some people whose minds still vibrate to the historic echoes of Wellington House's propaganda argue that by defeating Germany in 1918, the United States saved itself from imminent conquest by the Hun. The idea grows more fatuous with every passing decade. A nation that had suffered more than 5 million casualties, including almost 2 million dead, was not likely to attack the strongest nation on the globe without pausing for perhaps a half century to rethink its policies. One can just as easily argue that the awful cost of the war would have enabled Germany's liberals to seize control of the country from the conservatives and force the kaiser to become a constitutional monarch like his English cousin.

A victorious Germany would have had no need of political adventurers such as Adolf Hitler. Nor would this counterfactual Germany have inserted the Bolsheviks into Russia and supported them with secret-service money. Lenin and Trotsky might have agitated in a political vacuum in Switzerland unto a crabbed old age. Or ventured a revolution in their homeland that would have come to a swift and violent end. On the eve of the war, Russia had the fastest-growing economy in Europe. The country was being transformed by the dynamics of capitalism into a free society. The war created the collapse that gave Bolshevism its seventy-year reign of blood and terror.

VII

Gazing at history's alternatives is a stimulating and even an enlightening pastime. But ultimately it cannot tell us much about how to deal with the history that actually happened in the shrouded, mostly forgotten past.

Best to face the whole truth about World War I. It happened. The United States intervened for reasons that seemed persuasive to Woodrow Wilson and a majority of Congress, however much these justifications seem like half-truths and even untruths almost a hundred years later. Can we describe this intervention in terms that are useful to us today? Or should the war simply be written off as a gigantic blunder?

To write it off would be unwise. There are too many continuities between the Great War and the second, greater war spawned by the peacemakers at Versailles—continuities that remain a basic part of America's world posture today. Perhaps the best way to look at Woodrow Wilson's tragically flawed intervention in World War I is, in the words of the historian Lloyd C. Gardner, as a covenant with power. Painfully, with mistakes aplenty, the United States recognized that power is at the heart of history.

Because it was the strongest, most prosperous nation on the globe, how it used its power was bound to have a large impact on the rest of the world.[14]

At the Paris Peace Conference, Wilson discovered limitations to America's power. He discovered other limitations in the hearts and minds of the American people and the politicians who represented them, when he returned to the United States. Additional limitations resided in the hearts and minds of other peoples, perhaps even in the overused idea of human nature itself, with its tendency to egoism and self interest. Still more limitations lay in the prime illusion of idealism — the expectation that noble words can easily be translated into meaningful realities.

Woodrow Wilson struggled to deal with his inadvertent covenant with power. Like Lincoln, who suspended habeas corpus and jailed hundreds of dissenters during the Civil War, Wilson tolerated a brutally realistic government of the home front. But Wilson corrupted the peace process by proclaiming principles that he failed to support, and by his lack of candor, which culminated in his blatant lie to the Senate Foreign Relations Committee about the secret treaties. Worst of all was his tendency to utopianism — the truly fatal flaw in his dream of flexing America's idealized muscles in the name of peace.

The next man to lead the United States into a great war had even less candor in his political makeup. Wilson evaded the gritty truths about a covenant with power. Franklin D. Roosevelt at first tried to avoid the whole idea. In the mid-1930s FDR did little or nothing to prevent liberals led by progressive Republican Senator Gerald Nye from holding a series of hearings that convinced millions of Americans that the Great War had been fought to enrich J. P. Morgan, Jr., the DuPonts and other tycoons. In discussing the subject with Senator Nye in 1935, Roosevelt remarked that he now thought William Jennings Bryan was right—Wilson's intervention in 1917 was a mistake. He said the same thing in a letter to Josephus Daniels around this same time.[15]

In August 1936, Roosevelt said if another war broke out in Europe, it would be difficult to resist American business leaders who wanted to sell arms to the belligerents. But if the United States had to choose between profits and peace, "the Nation will answer—must answer—we choose peace." This was very close to a total repudiation of Wilson's war by the man who had served in his administration and had been an ardent interventionist.[16]

Not long after World War II began in 1939, Roosevelt became a carefully concealed interventionist. When he campaigned for a third term in 1940, he told the American people he would never send their boys to foreign wars—while ordering his generals and admirals to prepare a war plan that called for an invasion of Europe by 5 million men in 1943. As FDR saw it, American disillusion with Woodrow Wilson's war was still too widespread and too intense for him to tell the truth to the American people.

What had happened? Woodrow Wilson's covenant with power remained a reality, twenty years after he had bungled its presentation to the American people. By breaking his promise to Germany to make peace on the basis of the Fourteen Points, Wilson had also betrayed the liberals who created the Weimar republic at his invitation. In 1941, the republic was dead and Germany was ruled by a man who personified the accumulated rage at that betrayal: Adolf Hitler.

By the time FDR took the oath of office for a third term in 1941, this malevolent dictator had achieved power beyond the kaiser's wildest dreams. He had destroyed the French army and driven the British army back to England, a shattered remnant. On the other side of the world, he had allied Germany with a Japan that sought to dominate Asia. Still Roosevelt feared that a call for intervention would have been defeated in Congress. Instead, he adopted a strategy of provoking Germany and Japan into attacking the United States. He finally succeeded with Japan, though he never imagined that it had the daring or skill to devastate the American fleet at Pearl Harbor.[17]

VIII

During World War II, Woodrow Wilson enjoyed a renaissance of sorts. Numerous writers told Americans that there would have been no Hitler, no Mussolini and no Stalin if Americans had taken Wilson's advice and joined the League of Nations. The Democratic Party campaigned on this proposition in the Congressional elections of 1942—and suffered a ruinous defeat that left Roosevelt on the political defensive for the rest of the war. It would have been more accurate to argue that a genuine peace of reconciliation on the basis of the Fourteen Points might have created a liberal Germany that would have forsworn war and transformed Europe.

The climax of this spate of Wilsonian adulation was the 1944 Darryl Zanuck film *Wilson*, which cost more than *Gone with the Wind* to produce. Portraying Wilson as a prophet tormented by evil isolationists, the movie's climax was the president's final speech at Pueblo, Colorado, in which the movie Wilson predicts a second world war. When the U.S. Senate approved the Charter of the United Nations in 1945, President Harry S. Truman declared that Woodrow Wilson was vindicated.[18]

These belated compliments were another Wilsonian illusion. A close look at Franklin D. Roosevelt's conduct of World War II reveals a man who spent a good deal of time and effort avoiding Wilson's blunders. In 1940, before he ran for a third term, FDR invited two leading Republicans, Henry L. Stimson and Frank Knox, to join his cabinet as secretaries of war and the navy. When the utopian idealism of vice president Henry Wallace, who called for a "New Deal for the World," disturbed voters, FDR jettisoned him and accepted realistic Harry S. Truman as his vice presidential candidate in 1944.

When Roosevelt sought a name for the new international organization he envisioned at the end of World War II, he chose United Nations, the term Henry Cabot Lodge had used in 1915, when he had been a bold proponent of international cooperation. Roosevelt was almost certainly unaware of its origin. But the unintentional conjunction proved to be prophetic. As Henry Cabot Lodge, Jr., noted, the new organization was modeled on Lodge's philosophy, not Wilson's. FDR made this even clearer when he spoke of the postwar world being patrolled by the "Four Policemen," England, the United States, Soviet Russia and China—the concert of great powers that Wilson abhorred. There was very little idealism in this global vision.

Soviet Russia, the problem Wilson had failed to solve, soon disrupted Roosevelt's precarious peace. Within two years of FDR's death, President Harry Truman's joint chiefs of staff and his secretary of state, General George C. Marshall, were telling him that "the ability of the United Nations . . . to protect, now, or hereafter, the security of the United States" was virtually nil. George C. Kennan, the deepest foreign policy thinker of the era, suggested that "the whole idea of world peace has been a premature, unworkable, grandiose form of daydreaming." In short, the realist side of the great American dichotomy had reasserted itself, as the UN's weaknesses turned into virtual paralysis throughout the long decades of the Cold War.[19]

IX

On July 15, 1959, the one hundredth anniversary of the kaiser's birth, the British Broadcasting Company (BBC) produced a film about Wilhelm II. Five days before it was broadcast, its producer, Christopher Sykes, published an article about it in *Radio Times*. He admitted that in his boyhood, even the mention of the kaiser sent "tremors of appalled horror through my nerves." This was not unusual for any Briton who grew up during the era of World War I. The myth of the wicked kaiser had been propagated so relentlessly by British newspapers, even otherwise intelligent political leaders reacted with revulsion when they heard Wilhelm's name.

The film was remarkable as much for what it did not say as for what it said. There was no attempt to explain how the myth of the wicked kaiser came into being. Wellington House got a free pass as usual. The myth was merely stated as a fact that endured for at least ten years after World War I. Meanwhile, a parade of distinguished Britons such as Sir Harold Nicholson exonerated the kaiser from the charge of starting the war. The German ruler's responsibility was described as small compared to leaders in Russia and Austria-Hungary.

The VIPs described meetings with the kaiser before the war and in his postwar years of exile in Holland. Everyone burbled about his amiability and sincerity. There was much talk about his love of England and his devotion to his grandmother, Queen Victoria. The film closed with discussions of Wilhelm's old age and death in 1941, with flattering comments on the way he displayed no bitterness toward those who had slandered him so viciously.

Some pundits speculated that the explanation for the film was the Cold War. Some of the British press were still Germanophobic heirs of Lord Northcliffe. They continued to slander the Germans at every opportunity. Not a few Germans suspected these attacks reflected British government policy. The BBC film may have been sponsored by London to strengthen the British-American alliance with Germany against Soviet Communism. Whatever the motive, the film achieved at least an approximation of the historical truth. One commentator said it also demonstrated what little reliance can be placed on contemporary opinion.[20]

X

In 1962, Arthur Schlesinger, Sr., circulated a poll among historians, asking them to rate the presidents in categories from greatness to failure. One of the recipients was John F. Kennedy, partly because he was a published historian and partly because Schlesinger's son, Arthur, Jr., was working in the administration.

Kennedy wrote the senior Schlesinger that a year ago he would have responded with confidence to the poll. But after twelve months in the White House, he was not so sure. To make a judgment on all but the obvious big names, he would have to subject them to "a long scrutiny after I left this office." Later, talking to the younger Schlesinger, Kennedy added, "How the hell can you tell? Only the President himself can know what his real pressures and his real alternatives are."

Nevertheless, Kennedy was intensely interested in the results of the poll. He was delighted that Harry Truman made the "near great" class and wryly amused that Dwight Eisenhower, whose administration he had fiercely criticized in the 1960 campaign, was near the bottom of the "average" list. But he was shocked that the poll gave such a high rating to Woodrow Wilson—fourth in the list of greats, ahead of Andrew Jackson. Kennedy strenuously pointed out that Wilson had made a botch of his Mexican intervention in 1914, edged the United States into World War I for "narrow legalistic reasons" and catastrophically messed up the fight for the Treaty of Versailles and the League of Nations. This was not the record of a great president.[21]

XI

The broken man who left the White House in 1921 spent the next three years in a comfortable brick and limestone house on tree-lined suburban-like S Street in Washington, D.C., brooding over his defeat. Wilson never admitted making any mistakes in Paris or anywhere else. His mood oscillated between self-pity and consuming bitterness, mixed with occasional delusions of power.

"What else could I have done?" he cried, defending his conduct in Paris during an interview with historian William E. Dodd. "I had to negotiate with my back to the wall. Men thought I had all the power. Would to God I had had such power." Worst of all, he added, was the way the "great people at home" criticized him.[22]

Around the same time, a devoted admirer, Edward Bok, the influential editor of the *Ladies Home Journal,* called on the Wilsons. Bok began a sympathetic discussion of the defeat of the treaty and the league. Wilson erupted in a near frenzy, damning Lloyd George and Senator Henry Cabot Lodge in sulfurous language that shocked the highly proper Bok. In the midst of the tirade, the former president slumped in his wheelchair in the throes of a cerebral spasm. For fifty minutes there was serious concern that he might die.[23]

Wilson clung fiercely to shreds of his presidential power, insisting that he was still the leader of the Democratic Party. When old Senate enemies such as James Reed of Missouri ran for reelection, Wilson called them vicious names and recommended their defeat. He tried to exercise a veto power over the Democratic nominee for president in 1924, publicly rebuking Tumulty for implying he supported James A. Cox.[24]

In 1921 the former president persuaded no less a ghost writer than Supreme Court Justice Louis Brandeis to help him draw up "The Document," a statement of principles for the Democratic Party, binding it inextricably to the League of Nations. It gradually became apparent that Wilson planned to use the statement to launch himself as the candidate for the nomination in 1924. He still believed triumph and ultimate vindication were within his grasp.

When Wilson's associates from the Paris Peace Conference visited the United States, they included a stop at S Street in their itineraries. Lloyd George, dismissed as prime minister by the ruling conservatives, called in 1923 and told the press, with his usual indifference to the truth, that he was amazed by Wilson's alert mind and intense interest in European affairs. In private, the former prime minister deplored Wilson's vituperative comments on the French and the Italians. Wilson had called French president Raymond Poincaré "a cheat and a liar," repeating the phrase "with fierce emphasis." For good measure, Wilson had thrown in a denunciation of Calvin Coolidge, who had just become president after Warren Harding's sudden death, calling him a nobody. Lloyd George concluded that illness had not changed Wilson much. "Here was the old Wilson with his personal hatreds unquenched right to the end of his journey."[25]

Nor did Edith Galt Wilson's animosities subside. When her husband died on February 3, 1924, Senator Henry Cabot Lodge was chosen by the Senate to head a delegation to the funeral. Edith wrote the senator a letter, telling him not to come because his presence would be "embarrassing to you and unwelcome to me." Also barred by Edith's order was the man who had done so much to create Woodrow Wilson the world-reforming politician, Colonel Edward Mandell House. Another victim of her pettiness, the ever-faithful Tumulty, was admitted only at the insistence of William Gibbs McAdoo, via a last-minute telephone call.

XII

Beyond and beneath weighty questions of foreign policy and Woodrow Wilson's hard fate lie the battles the men and women of 1917–1918 fought in France. Whether one considers the war foolish or wise, they dignified it, even sanctified it, with their courage. As a historian I felt obligated to visit the places where so many died—Cantigny, Soissons, Belleau Wood, Saint-Mihiel—and, above all, the Argonne. I spent five days traversing the great valley, imagining it with German shells raining down from three sides.

I labored to the summit of Montfaucon, where a statue of a woman symbolizing liberty stands on a lofty pillar, surveying the rugged rolling terrain, dotted with woods and slashed by ravines, over which the Germans and the Americans fought for seven savage weeks. On another day, I prowled the shallow still-visible trenches in the dim heart of the Argonne forest, where Charles Whittlesey and his Lost Battalion fought so stubbornly. On yet another day, I stood on a road with the forest looming in the distance and pondered a metal pylon engraved with hundreds of names of the First Division's dead. More than once I remembered Shirley Millard's description of the cocky doughboys in their tilted helmets going to their first battle calling, *Hey, listen, where is all this trouble anyway?*

I also visited cemeteries in the Argonne and Champagne, where mute rows of white Carrara marble crosses testify to a soldier's ideals, courage and brotherhood. Each cross was a wound torn in the lives of wives, sons, daughters, fathers, mothers, sisters or brothers. Did these grieving survivors think it was worth the sacrifice of these beloved dead to procure Woodrow

Wilson a seat at the Paris peace table? Somehow, I doubted it. On the contrary, it would not be surprising if many of them thought it was only right that the president too was called upon to pay a heavy price.

General John J. Pershing's last public statement in France was on Memorial Day, 1919, at the Argonne Cemetery, where 14,200 Americans still lie. It was the best speech this laconic soldier ever gave. The closing words evoked echoes of another orator on a battlefield in Pennsylvania, trying to make sense out of an earlier war. But this was a soldier's view of a citizen's responsibilities.

> It is not for us to proclaim what they did, their silence speaks more eloquently than words, but it is for us to uphold the conception of duty, honor and country for which they fought and for which they died. It is for the living to carry forward their purpose and make fruitful their sacrifice.
>
> And now, Dear Comrades, Farewell. Here, under the clear skies, on the green hillsides and amid the flowering fields of France, in the quiet hush of peace, we leave you forever in God's keeping.[26]

XIII

Sobering and saddening as the cemeteries were, the most heartbreaking moment of my historical journey to France was my visit to Chamery, the little village in Champagne where Quentin Roosevelt spun into the earth with German bullets in his brain. Arriving on a gray January day, I spent almost an hour searching for the winding road, barely wide enough for a single car, that led to the cluster of stone houses. Around the village spread rolling farm country, almost as treeless and desolate as Kansas in winter.

Quentin no longer lies in the solitary grave outside the village, although the site is marked by a stone. After World War II, his family moved his body to the Normandy Cemetery to lie beside his brother Ted, who died shortly after he led a brigade of the Fourth Division ashore on D Day in 1944. There is a memorial fountain to Quentin in the center of Chamery. Above the spout, which is a bronze head of a lion, is an inscription in French stating Quentin's age and the date he was shot down. Beneath the lion's head is a line from an article Theodore Roosevelt wrote after Quentin's death: "Only those are fit to live who are not afraid to die."

It was bitterly cold on the day of my visit. The village was deserted. The only sound was the water gushing from the lion's mouth into the fountain's trough. Nearby were bales of hay and a tractor and part of a plow. Across the road a big black dog sat on a barrel, studying the American intruder. It was all very ordinary—until Flora Payne Whitney whispered, *Oh Quentin, why does it all have to be? It isn't possible that it can be for any ultimate good that all the best people in the world have to be killed.*

I could only shake my head and hope the men and women who guide America's covenant with power in the world of the twenty-first century have the courage and the wisdom to manage our country's often perplexing blend of idealism and realism. God helping us, we now can do no other.

NOTES

Chapter 1: War Week

1. Arthur S. Link, *Woodrow Wilson: Campaigns for Progressivism and Peace* (Princeton, 1965), 423.

2. Barbara W. Tuchman, *The Zimmermann Telegram* (New York, 1966), 6–7, 183.

3. Cass W. Gilbert, *New York Tribune,* April 2, 1917.

4. James Kerney, *The Political Education of Woodrow Wilson* (New York, 1926), 12. Kerney was editor of the *Trenton Evening Times.*

5. Henry Wilkinson Bragdon, *Woodrow Wilson: The Academic Years* (Cambridge, Mass., 1967), 328–329. James Kerney said Grover Cleveland predicted Wilson would go far in politics, but when he had finished, there would be very little left of the Democratic Party.

6. Alexander L. George and Juliette L. George, *Woodrow Wilson and Colonel House: A Personality Study* (New York, 1964), 51; and Robert Alex Bober, *Young Woodrow Wilson and the Search for Immortality,* Ph.D. dissertation (Case Western Reserve University, 1980), iv, 202.

7. Link, *Campaigns for Progressivism and Peace,* 394; and *Washington Evening Post,* April 2, 1917.

8. Link, *Campaigns for Progressivism and Peace,* 420–421.

9. Phyllis Lee Levin, *Edith and Woodrow: The Wilson White House* (New York, 2001), 177.

10. John S. Heaton, *Cobb of the World* (New York, 1924), 268–270.

11. Arthur S. Link, "That Cobb Interview," *Journal of American History* 72 (June 1985): 7–17.

12. Jerold S. Auerbach, "Woodrow Wilson's 'Prediction' to Frank Cobb: Words Historians Should Doubt Ever Got Spoken," *Journal of American History* 54 (December 1967): 608–617.

13. See Chapter 3, pp. 86–89, 98–100.

14. Ray Stannard Baker, *Woodrow Wilson: Life and Letters,* vol. 6, *Facing War, 1915–1917* (New York, 1937), 505–507. Arthur S. Link was the first to note Cobb's absence from the White House logs on April 1. But he assigned the interview to mid-March, and subsequent biographers have followed him. Baker cited two other Wilson associates who recollected similar prophecies by the president. These recollections were also long after the fact and suspect for some of the reasons outlined in the text. In his history of the decision for war, Patrick Devlin, *Too Proud to Fight: Woodrow Wilson's Neutrality* (New York, 1975), 681, was inclined to think Wilson expressed sentiments of regret but conceded that Cobb's version of the interview was almost certainly "touched up."

15. W. A. Swanberg, *Pulitzer* (New York, 1967), 254–255.

16. Walter Millis, *Road to War: America 1914–1917* (New York, 1935), 432–433; and *New York Times,* March 22, 1917.

17. Charles Seymour, ed., *Intimate Papers of Colonel House* (New York, 1926), 2:467–468; and Link, *Campaigns for Progressivism and Peace,* 422.

18. Ronald Steel, *Walter Lippmann and the American Century* (New York, 1980), 108, quotes Lippmann's assessment of the House-Wilson relationship: "He was able to serve Wilson because he was in almost every respect the complement of Wilson." Lippmann saw House constantly in 1916–1917 and met and corresponded with Wilson.

19. Bragdon, *Woodrow Wilson: The Academic Years*, 263. Also see George and George, *Woodrow Wilson and Colonel House*, which explores the House-Wilson relationship in depth.

20. Lester D. Langley, *The United States and the Caribbean in the Twentieth Century* (Athens, Ga., 1982), 76–77, 80–83, 85–88, 92.

21. Arthur S. Link, *Woodrow Wilson and the Progressive Era* (New York, 1954), 122–124; and Nancy Mitchell, *The Danger of Dreams: Weltpolitik Versus Protective Imperialism,* Ph.D. dissertation (Johns Hopkins University, 1993), 295.

22. John S. D. Eisenhower, *Intervention! The United States and the Mexican Revolution, 1913–17* (New York, 1993), 165–241.

23. Seward W. Livermore, *Politics Is Adjourned: Woodrow Wilson and the War Congress, 1916–18* (Middletown, Conn., 1966), 10, 14.

24. Baker, *Woodrow Wilson*, vol. 6, *Facing War*, 508.

25. Seymour, *Intimate Papers of Colonel House,* 2:468–470; and Edwin A. Weinstein, *Woodrow Wilson: A Medical and Psychological Biography* (Princeton, 1981), 164–167. Wilson suffered less serious episodes in 1896 and 1904, which temporarily deprived him of the use of his right hand (Weinstein, *Medical and Psychological Biography,* 141–142, 158). Weinstein and others called these traumas strokes. But other physicians, mostly notably Michael F. Marmor, an ophthalmologist at the Stanford University Medical School, have disagreed (Robert H. Ferrell, *Woodrow Wilson and World War I* [New York, 1985], 273–274).

26. Ernest R. Dupuy, *Five Days to War: April 2–6, 1917* (Harrisburg, Pa., 1967), 57–58.

27. Millis, *Road to War*, 433.

28. Ibid., 434.

29. Dupuy, *Five Days to War*, 67.

30. William A. DeGregorio, *The Complete Book of U.S. Presidents* (New York, 1989), 419.

31. Dupuy, *Five Days to War*, 67–68.

32. John Tebbel and Sarah Miles Watts, *The Press and the Presidency* (New York, 1985), 379.

33. *New York Times,* April 3, 1917.

34. Ibid.; and Millis, *The Road to War*, 438.

35. Millis, *The Road to War,* 439–440.

36. Arthur S. Link et al., eds., *The Papers of Woodrow Wilson,* 69 vols. (Princeton, 1966–1994), 41:519–527 (hereafter cited as PWW).

37. Dupuy, *Five Days to War*, 71–72.

38. Edward Mandell House Diary, April 2, 1917, Edward M. House Papers, Yale University Library.

39. Joseph P. Tumulty, *Woodrow Wilson As I Know Him* (Garden City, N.Y., 1921), 256, 259. Link, *Campaigns for Progessivism and Peace*, 427, called the scene preposterous.

40. Eleanor Wilson McAdoo, in collaboration with Margaret Gaffey, *The Woodrow Wilsons* (New York, 1937), 139.

41. John Morton Blum, *Joe Tumulty and the Wilson Era* (Boston, 1951), 120–122.

42. Levin, *Edith and Woodrow*, 75.

43. Ibid., 156.

44. Arthur Marwick, *The Deluge: British Society and the First World War* (New York, 1970), 31.

45. Scott Meredith, *George S. Kaufman and His Friends* (New York, 1974), 402.

46. Millis, *Road to War*, 442; and Dupuy, *Five Days to War*, 75–77.

47. Richard O'Connor, *The German-Americans* (New York, 1986), 406.

48. Link, *Campaigns for Progressivism and Peace*, 428.

49. Steel, *Walter Lippmann*, 112–113.

50. David McCullough, *Truman* (New York, 1992), 104.

51. Link, *Campaigns for Progressivism and Peace*, 362; *Congressional Record,* 65th Congr., 1st sess., Senate, April 13, 1917, 55, pt. 1, 342; and H. C. Peterson, *Propaganda for War* (Port Washington, N.Y., 1939), 22.

52. Dupuy, *Five Days to War*, 85–89.

53. Nancy C. Unger, *Fighting Bob La Follette, the Righteous Reformer* (Chapel Hill, N.C., 2000), 243–244.

54. Dupuy, *Five Days to War*, 100.

55. D. Clayton James, *The Years of MacArthur*, vol. 1, *1880–1941* (New York, 1970), 132.

56. Kenneth S. Davis, *FDR: The Beckoning of Destiny, 1882–1928* (New York, 1971), 446.

57. Geoffrey C. Ward, *A First-Class Temperament: The Emergence of Franklin Roosevelt* (New York, 1989), 339.

58. Ibid., 347.

59. *New York Tribune*, April 4, 1917.

60. Millis, *Road to War*, 445–446; and *San Francisco Chronicle*, April 15, 1917.

61. Dupuy, *Five Days to War*, 111.

62. Belle Case and Fola La Follette, *Robert M. La Follette*, 2 vols. (New York, 1953), 620.

63. Ibid., 650.

64. Millis, *Road to War*, 447.

65. Ibid., 448.

66. *Congressional Record*, 65th Congr., 1st sess., Senate, April 4, 1917, 55, pt. 1, 208–209.

67. Ibid., 210.

68. Ibid., 213–214.

69. Case and La Follette, *Robert M. La Follette*, 655.

70. *Congressional Record*, 65th Congr., 1st sess., Senate, April 4, 1917, 55, pt. 1, 220.

71. Ibid., 225–226; and Case and La Follette, *Robert M. La Follette*, 658–659.

72. *Congressional Record*, 65th Congr., 1st sess., Senate, April 4, 1917, 55, pt. 1, 229.

73. Ibid., 234.

74. Unger, *Fighting Bob La Follette*, 249.

75. Millis, *Road to War*, 452; Unger, *Fighting Bob La Follette*, 249; and Dupuy, *Five Days to War*, 125.

76. Case and La Follette, *Robert M. La Follette*, 666.

77. Dupuy, *Five Days to War*, 132.

78. Ibid., 129, 131.

79. Millis, *Road to War*, 453–454.

80. *Congressional Record*, 65th Congr., 1st sess., House, April 5, 1917, 55, pt. 1, 327.

81. Dupuy, *Five Days to War*, 137.

82. *Congressional Record*, 65th Congr., 1st sess., House, April 5, 1917, 55, pt. 1, 332.

83. Ibid.

84. Dupuy, *Five Days to War*, 137.

85. Ibid., 138.

86. *Congressional Record*, 65th Congr., 1st sess., House, April 5, 1917, 55, pt. 1, 341–343.

87. Millis, *Road to War*, 454–456.

88. Ibid., 458–459.

Chapter 2: Big Lies, Greed and Other Hoary Animals

1. Link, *Campaigns for Progressivism and Peace*, 429n, cites hundreds of letters in the Claude Kitchin Papers at the University of North Carolina revealing an "overwhelming sentiment" against the war. Along with the thousands of letters La Follette and other senators and members of Congress received, these letters constitute evidence that opposition to the war was still "very wide and deep" after Wilson's speech. For more recent scholarship on this relatively uninvestigated subject, see Jeannette Keith, "The Politics of Southern Draft Resistance, 1917–18: Class,

Race and Conscription in the Rural South," *Journal of American History* 87, no. 4 (March 2001): 1335–1361. Keith concludes: "The concept of overwhelming public support for the war becomes less and less tenable."

2. Tuchman, *The Zimmermann Telegram*, 10–11.

3. Stewart Halsey Ross, *Propaganda for War: How the United States Was Conditioned to Fight the Great War of 1914–1918* (Jefferson, N.C., 1996), 27–28.

4. *Congressional Record,* 65th Congr., 1st sess., House, April 5, 1917, 55, pt. 1, 342.

5. Ross, *Propaganda for War*, 30, 38; Cate Haste, *Keep the Home Fires Burning: Propaganda in the Great War* (London, 1977), 25; and Peter T. Scott, "The Secrets of Wellington House: British Covert Propaganda, 1914–18," *Antiquarian Book Monthly,* August-September 1996, 12–15, and October–September 1996, 14–19.

6. Gilbert Parker, "The United States and the War," *Harper's Monthly,* March 1918, 521–531; and H. C. Peterson, *Propaganda for War: The Campaign Against American Neutrality* (Port Washington, N.Y., 1968), 16.

7. Peterson, *Propaganda for War*, 19.

8. Ibid., 21, 31.

9. Ross, *Propaganda for War*, 82, 181–184.

10. Typical of these Anglo immigrants was Toronto-born George H. Doran, whose publishing house issued a stream of books attacking Germany. His memoir, *Chronicles of Barabbas* (New York, 1935), candidly recounts his pro-British activities.

11. Ross, *Propaganda for War,* 78–79; and Robert Rhodes James, *The British Revolution, 1880–1939* (New York, 1977), 365. Northcliffe controlled half the daily newspapers sold in London.

12. James, *The British Revolution,* 285.

13. Nancy Mitchell, *The Danger of Dreams: Weltpolitik versus Protective Imperialism*, Ph.D. dissertation (Johns Hopkins University, 1993), 315–318.

14. Michael Balfour, *The Kaiser and His Times* (New York, 1964), 441–446, offers a wealth of statistics demonstrating that Germany had passed England in virtually every imaginable economic indicator.

15. James, *The British Revolution,* 290–292. As late as July 28, ten of the twenty members of Asquith's cabinet were threatening to resign if England declared war.

16. Adam Hochschild, *King Leopold's Ghost: A Story of Greed, Terror and Heroism in Colonial Africa* (New York, 1998), 200–208, 225–234.

17. Niall Ferguson, *The Pity of War* (New York, 1998), 1–30. No one has done a better job of exploding these half-truths than Ferguson in his opening chapter, "The Myths of Militarism." See also Stuart D. Brandes, *Warhogs: A History of War Profits in America* (Lexington, Ky., 1997), 122–123. Brandes notes the popularity of *Militarism,* a book by Karl Liebknecht, the leader of the radical wing of the Socialist Party in the German Reichstag. It was published in the United States in 1917 and widely reviewed and discussed.

18. Link, *Campaigns for Progressivism and Peace*, 276. In 1910, only 28 percent of British adults could vote. Pressure from the Labor Party forced the upper classes to give significant ground during the war. By 1918, 78 percent could vote. It would take another ten years to achieve universal suffrage (James, *The British Revolution*, 396).

19. John Horne and Alan Kramer, *German Atrocities, 1914: A History of Denial* (New Haven, Conn., 2000), 11–86.

20. Peterson, *Propaganda for War*, 55.

21. Ibid., 69.

22. Viscount Bryce, "Report of the Committee on Alleged German Outrages" (hereafter cited as Bryce Report), World War I Document Archive, available at http://www.ku.edu/~hisite/bryce_report/bryce_r.html.

23. *New York Times,* May 13, 1915.

24. Trevor Wilson, "Lord Bryce's Investigation into Alleged German Atrocities in Belgium, 1914–15," *Journal of Contemporary History* 14 (1979): 370.

25. Angus Mitchell, "James Bryce, Roger Casement and the Amazon," paper delivered to the Oriel College History Foundation, 1997, 10.

26. Gary Mead, *The Doughboys: America and the First World War* (New York, 2000), 39.

27. Peterson, *Propaganda for War*, 58.

28. Horne and Kramer, *German Atrocities*, 235–236, 255. Horne and Kramer, historians at Trinity College in Dublin, estimate 6,500 civilians, mostly men, were killed by the Germans. An American historian, Larry Zuckerman, at work on a similar book about German behavior in Belgium, has a slightly lower figure, 5,521.

29. Bryce Report, 31; and Wilson, "Lord Bryce's Investigation," 374–375. Bryce's report included numerous diaries taken from dead or captured Germans. They recounted shooting supposed *franc-tireurs,* but there was no evidence of mutilation or rape. Trevor Wilson speculates that Bryce left the lurid material in the report because it was what the public wanted to read. More to the point, basing the report only on shooting *franc-tireurs* would have gotten the British into a difficult argument with the Germans, given the abundance of civic guards in the Belgian army.

30. Ross, *Propaganda for War*, 56.

31. Harvey A. Deweerd, *President Wilson Fights His War: World War I and American Intervention* (New York, 1968), 15–16. Diana Preston, *"Lusitania": An Epic Tragedy* (New York, 2002), 389–391, 401–403, explores the numerous investigations of the sinking and concludes there was no second torpedo. But there is little evidence that the second explosion was caused by the ammunition aboard the ship. The cartridges and shells were stowed toward the stern, and the torpedo struck near the bow. The second explosion was probably caused by a ruptured boiler. David Ramsay, *"Lusitania": Saga and Myth* (New York, 2001), 205–217, strongly endorses this conclusion. He also maintains the liner's watertight construction was inadequate and the vessel would have sunk almost as swiftly without the second explosion.

32. Peterson, *Propaganda for War,* 62–63.

33. Ross, *Propaganda for War*, 70–71.

34. William Jannen, Jr., *The Lions of July: Prelude to War, 1914* (Novato, Calif., 1996), 27–28.

35. Haste, *Keep the Home Fires Burning,* 114–115; Ross, *Propaganda for War*, 43–44; and Horne and Kramer, *German Atrocities,* 297–301.

36. David M. Kennedy, *Over Here: The First World War and American Society* (New York, 1980), 74.

37. *New York Times,* June 8, 1913.

38. Dennis E. Showalter, "Salonika," *Quarterly Journal of Military History* 10, no. 2 (winter 1990): 44–55.

39. Nicholas P. Canny, "The Ideology of English Colonization: From Ireland to America," *William and Mary Quarterly,* 3rd series, 30 (October 1973): 575–598, demonstrates how the same manipulation of ideas enabled the English to slaughter the Irish in the sixteenth century and the American Indians in the seventeenth century without a qualm of conscience. For an excellent historical analysis of the Black Legend, see Philip Wayne Powell, *Tree of Hate* (Vallecito, Calif., 1985).

40. Peterson, *Propaganda for War,* 123; and Ross, *Propaganda for War,* 110.

41. Ross, *Propaganda for War*, 115–116.

42. John Bernard Duff, *The Politics of Revenge: The Ethnic Opposition to the Peace Policies of Woodrow Wilson,* Ph.D. dissertation (Columbia University, 1964), 24.

43. Ibid., 27.

44. Ibid., 24–25.

45. Ross, *Propaganda for War*, 103.

46. Ibid., 112–113.

47. Ibid., 124–127.

48. James, *The British Revolution*, 260. The Dublin death rate was 27.6 per 1,000, the highest of any capital in Europe.

49. John Patrick Buckley, *The New York Irish: Their View of American Foreign Policy, 1914–21* (New York, 1976), 10–11; and Jeremiah O'Leary, *The Conquest of the United States: A Book of Facts* (New York, 1915), 28.

50. Buckley, *The New York Irish,* 29.

51. *Gaelic American,* February 3, 1917; and Buckley, *The New York Irish,* 37.

52. Buckley, *The New York Irish,* 23, 37.

53. Ibid., 52.

54. Ibid., 53, 91.

55. Duff, *The Politics of Revenge*, 34.

56. Buckley, *The New York Irish*, 96; and Nancy Gentile Ford, *Americans All: Foreign Born Soldiers in World War I* (College Station, Tex., 2001), 21–22. O'Leary responded with a twenty-three-page public letter to Wilson, in which he angrily denied the slur of disloyalty. He had served in New York's "Fighting 69th" regiment during the Civil War.

57. Haste, *Keep the Home Fires Burning,* 99.

58. Ibid., 100.

59. Ross, *Propaganda for War*, 64.

60. Haste, *Keep the Home Fires Burning*, 99.

61. Horne and Kramer, *German Atrocities,* 259–260; and Ross, *Propaganda for War*, 113.

62. Haste, *Keep the Home Fires Burning,* 100.

63. Ross, *Propaganda for War*, 158–160.

64. Petersen, *Propaganda for War*, 84.

65. Ibid., 86.

66. Louis W. Koenig, *Bryan: A Political Biography of William Jennings Bryan* (New York, 1971), 535.

67. Ibid., 536.

68. Ibid., 538.

69. Matthew Ware Coulter, *The Senate Munitions Inquiry of the 1930s: Beyond the Merchants of Death* (Westport, Conn., 1997), 109–111. See also John E. Wiltz, *In Search of Peace: The Senate Munitions Inquiry, 1934–36* (Baton Rouge, La., 1963), 197.

70. Ross, *Propaganda for War*, 156; and Preston, *"Lusitania,"* 389–390.

71. Ibid., 156–157.

72. Ibid., 155.

73. Devlin, *Too Proud to Fight*, 303–304.

74. Mead, *The Doughboys*, 5–6.

75. Millis, *Road to War*, 114; and Coulter, *Senate Munitions Inquiry,* 115.

76. Ross, *Propaganda for War*, 146.

77. Ibid., 146–147.

78. Mark Sullivan, *Our Times: The United States, 1900–1925,* vol. 5, *Over Here* (New York, 1923), 184–196.

79. Ross, *Propaganda for War*, 206–207.

80. Ferguson, *The Pity of War*, 294–303, demonstrates that throughout the war, Allied casualties exceeded German losses by as much as 35 percent.

81. Link, *Campaigns for Progressivism and Peace*, 381; Baker, *Woodrow Wilson,* vol. 6, *Facing War,* 496; and Devlin, *Too Proud to Fight*, 661. On February 22, 1917, economist John Maynard Keynes told the British government that bankruptcy would occur "four weeks from today."

82. Arthur S. Link, *Wilson: The Road to the White House* (Princeton, 1947), 24.

83. Seymour, *Intimate Papers of Colonel House*, 2:278–280.

84. John Milton Cooper, Jr., "The British Response to the House-Grey Memorandum: New Evidence and New Questions," *Journal of American History* 14, no. 4 (March 1973): 961–965.

85. Link, *Campaigns for Progressivism and Peace*, 28–38.

86. Seymour, *Intimate Papers of Colonel House,* 2:278; and Devlin, *Too Proud to Fight,* 613. As early as June 1916, the German foreign minister wrote to Ambassador Bernstorff: "We entertain but little hope for the result of the exercise of good offices by one whose instincts are all favorable to the English point of view" (Link, *Campaigns for Progressivism and Peace*, 30–31).

87. Devlin, *Too Proud to Fight*, 381–382. When Wilson bluntly asked Lansing if he agreed with his policies, the secretary lied and said he was "unswervedly in support" of the president.

88. Ibid., 646–647. The idea was not original with Lloyd George. Ross, *Propaganda for War,* 37, notes H. G. Wells floated it in his 1914 book, *The War That Will End War.* A few weeks after Lloyd George's message arrived, Secretary of State Lansing wrote the president a memo, saying almost exactly the same thing. Only by going to war would Wilson be able to guarantee a defeated Germany "a merciful and unselfish foe"(Devlin, *Too Proud to Fight,* 665).

89. Link, *Campaigns for Progressivism and Peace*, 414.

90. Robert A. Kraig, *Woodrow Wilson and the Lost World of the Oratorical Statesman*, Ph.D. dissertation (University of Wisconsin–Madison, 1999), vi–vii.

91. Ross, *Propaganda for War*, 261.

92. "U.S. Merchant Ships, Sailing Vessels and Fishing Craft Lost from All Causes during World War I," available at American Merchant Marine at War Web site [http/www/usmm.org]; and U.S. Navy, Historical Section, *American Ship Casualties of the World War, including Naval Vessels, Merchant Ships, Sailing Vessels and Fishing Craft* (Washington, D.C., 1923).

93. John Morton Blum, *Joe Tumulty and the Wilson Era* (Boston, 1951), 99; and Sullivan, *Our Times,* vol. 5, *Over Here,* 143–144.

94. Lloyd C. Gardner, *Safe for Democracy: The Anglo-American Response to Revolution* (New York, 1984), 108.

95. Devlin, *Too Proud to Fight*, 595–607.

96. Sir Cecil Spring Rice, *The Letters and Friendships of Sir Cecil Spring Rice: A Record* (New York, 1929), 387.

97. W. B. Fowler, *British-American Relations 1917–1918: The Role of Sir William Wiseman* (Princeton, 1969), 22–23.

98. William C. Widenor, *Henry Cabot Lodge and the Search for an American Foreign Policy* (Los Angeles, 1980), 264–265. Soon after the declaration of war, Lodge mused in his diary: "I wonder if the future historian will find him [Wilson] out?"

Chapter 3: Enlisting Volunteers and Other Unlikely Events

1. Ray Stannard Baker, *Woodrow Wilson: Life and Letters,* vol. 7, *War Leader* (New York, 1939), 24.

2. Kennedy, *Over Here*, 144.

3. Donald Smythe, *Pershing: General of the Armies* (Bloomington, Ind., 1986), 8–9.

4. John Whiteclay Chambers II, *To Raise an Army: The Draft Comes to Modern America* (New York, 1987), 165.

5. Blum, *Joe Tumulty and the Wilson Era,* 139; Livermore, *Politics Is Adjourned,* 17–18; and Chambers, *To Raise an Army,* 161–162, 327 (note 31).

6. John Milton Cooper, Jr., *The Warrior and the Priest: Woodrow Wilson and Theodore Roosevelt* (Cambridge, Mass., 1983), 324.

7. Tumulty, *Woodrow Wilson As I Know Him,* 288. Chambers, *To Raise An Army*, 135–138, notes that Wilson had repeatedly rejected Army Chief of Staff Scott's call for conscription. But late in March, when Roosevelt announced his plan for a volunteer division, Wilson switched to the draft.

8. Tumulty, *Woodrow Wilson As I Know Him*, 288.

9. Kennedy, *Over Here*, 149.

10. Peterson, *Propaganda for War*, 324. The author's father-in-law, Albert Mulcahey, confirmed this assumption in a personal interview before his death. A football star in his native Yonkers, he was eager to see action and joined the navy in 1917. To his dismay, he never had a shot fired at him.

11. Livermore, *Politics Is Adjourned*, 24.

12. Ibid., 25–28.

13. Ibid., 28–30.

14. Baker, *Woodrow Wilson*, vol. 7, *War Leader*, 71–72; Herman Hagedorn, *Leonard Wood* (New York, 1931), 219–222.

15. Geoffrey Hodgson, *The Colonel: The Life and Wars of Henry Stimson, 1867–1950* (New York, 1990), 83–84.

16. PWW, 42:324–325. Wilson also claimed that regular army officers who would serve with the volunteers were needed to train the draftees and insisted he was acting "under expert and professional advice from both sides of the water."

17. Kennedy, *Over Here*, 151.

18. Baker, *Wilson*, vol. 7, *War Leader*, 73.

19. Widenor, *Henry Cabot Lodge*, 228.

20. Ibid., 83–85, 212–214.

21. Stephen Vaughn, *Holding Fast the Inner Lines: Democracy, Nationalism and the Committee on Public Information* (Chapel Hill, N.C., 1980), 14–19.

22. Tebbel and Watts, *The Press and the Presidency*, 375.

23. Sullivan, *Our Times*, vol. 5, *Over Here*, 427.

24. George Creel, *How We Advertised America* (New York, 1920), 5.

25. Hagedorn, *Leonard Wood*, 217.

26. Peterson, *Propaganda for War*, 323–324.

27. James R. Mock and Cedric Larson, *Words That Won the War: The Story of the Committee on Public Information* (Princeton, 1939), 114–115.

28. Ibid., 118.

29. Kennedy, *Over Here*, 152–153.

30. H. C. Peterson and Gilbert C. Fite, *Opponents of War, 1917–1918* (Seattle, 1968), 25–26. See also Chambers, *To Raise an Army*, 205ff.

31. Peterson and Fite, *Opponents of War*, 28; Sullivan, *Our Times*, vol. 5, *Over Here*, 309; *Washington Star*, June 5, 1917.

32. Sullivan, *Our Times*, vol. 5, *Over Here*, 309; and Peterson and Fite, *Opponents of War*, 24.

33. *New York Times*, April 15, 1917; and *Washington Post*, May 3 and 6, 1917.

34. Livermore, *Politics Is Adjourned*, 33–34.

35. Peterson and Fite, *Opponents of War*, 17.

36. Robert H. Ferrell, *Woodrow Wilson and World War I, 1917–1921* (New York, 1995), 120.

37. Smythe, *Pershing: General of the Armies*, 8.

38. Ibid.; and Kennedy, *Over Here*, 170.

39. Weinstein, *Woodrow Wilson: A Medical and Psychological Biography*, 316.

40. Ibid., 317.

41. Hagedorn, *Leonard Wood*, 217; and Smythe, *Pershing: General of the Armies*, 3.

42. Frank E. Vandiver, *Black Jack: The Life and Times of John J. Pershing* (College Station, Tex., 1977), 595–598.

43. Smythe, *Pershing: General of the Armies*, 4.

44. John J. Pershing, *My Experiences in the World War* (New York, 1931), 1; and Vandiver, *Black Jack*, 675–676.

45. Pershing, *My Experiences*, 2.

46. Hagedorn, *Leonard Wood*, 213; and Pershing, *My Experiences*, 16, 26.

47. Smythe, *Pershing: General of the Armies*, 9–10.

48. Pershing, *My Experiences*, 23; and Smythe, *Pershing: General of the Armies*, 11.

49. Edward M. Coffman, *The War to End Wars: The American Military Experience in World War I* (Madison, Wis., 1966), 48–49.

50. Pershing, *My Experiences*, 42.

51. Kennedy, *Over Here*, 74.

52. Joan M. Jensen, *The Price of Vigilance* (New York, 1968), 15–16.

53. Ibid., 24–25.

54. Ibid., 43–45.

55. Peterson and Fite, *Opponents of War*, 45–46, 74.

56. Ibid., 30–33.

57. Ibid., 34–35.

58. Paul L. Murphy, *World War I and the Origin of Civil Liberties in the United States* (New York, 1979), 130–132.

59. Buckley, *The New York Irish*, 181–182.

60. Baker, *Woodrow Wilson*, vol. 7, *War Leader*, 197; Kennedy, *Over Here*, 88.

61. Mark Ellis, *Race, War and Surveillance: African Americans and the United States Government During World War I* (Bloomington, Ind., 2001), 15–17, 26.

62. Ibid., 31ff; and Peterson and Fite, *Opponents of War*, 87–88.

63. Ellis, *Race War and Surveillance*, 42.

64. Ibid., 46; and Peterson and Fite, *Opponents of War*, 89–90.

65. Peterson and Fite, *Opponents of War*, 90.

66. Smythe, *Pershing: General of the Armies*, 15.

67. Ibid., 16.

68. Ibid., 17.

69. James G. Harbord, *The American Army in France, 1917–19* (Boston, 1936), 79.

70. Smythe, *Pershing: General of the Armies*, 30; Harbord, *The American Army in France*, 79–80; and Pershing, *My Experiences*, 59–60.

71. Vandiver, *Black Jack*, 718–719.

72. Pershing, *My Experiences*, 78.

73. Smythe, *Pershing: General of the Armies*, 21–22.

74. Richard M. Watt, *Dare Call It Treason* (New York, 1963), 251–252.

75. Pershing, *My Experiences*, 75; Coffman, *The War to End All Wars*, 124.

Chapter 4: Creeling and Other Activities That Make Philip Dru Unhappy

1. Kennedy, *Over Here*, 65; and Mock and Larson, *Words That Won the War*, 73, 228.

2. George Creel, *Rebel at Large* (New York, 1947), 161; and Vaughn, *Holding Fast the Inner Lines*, 221–222.

3. Kennedy, *Over Here*, 71.

4. Vaughn, *Holding Fast the Inner Lines*, 197–198.

5. Tebbel and Watts, *The Press and the Presidency*, 383.

6. *New York Times*, July 7 and August 12, 1917; and Baker, *Woodrow Wilson*, vol. 7, *War Leader*, 143. In a postwar defense of the CPI, Creel printed the U.S. Navy's official report of the voyage, which mentioned several attacks and evidence (debris, oil) of one submarine destroyed by a depth charge. He also reprinted newspaper stories quoting enlisted men who claimed six submarines had been sunk. Captain George C. Marshall, who was aboard one of the ships, makes no mention

of a sustained submarine assault in his memoir of his World War I days. One is forced to wonder if the navy's report was "improved" (George Creel, *How We Advertised America* [New York, 1920], 28–41).

7. Ronald Schaffer, *America in the Great War* (New York, 1991), 98–104; Coffman, *The War to End All Wars,* 80–81, 132–133; and Christopher Capozzola, "The Only Badge Needed Is Your Patriotic Fervor: Vigilance, Coercion and the Law in World War I America," *Journal of American History* 88, no. 4 (March 2002): 1370–1373. Capozzola tells of one woman who was given an indefinite term in the Sherburne Reformatory for Women in Massachusetts when the Protective Bureau found her living with a soldier.

8. Smythe, *Pershing: General of the Armies,* 31–32. One cynical Frenchman reportedly declared, "We will fight until not a single Belgian remains on French soil."

9. Richard O'Connor, *Black Jack Pershing: A Candid Biography of America's First Six Star General Since George Washington* (New York, 1961), 171.

10. Richard Goldhurst, *Pipe Clay and Drill: John J. Pershing, the Classic American Soldier* (New York, 1977), 279–280.

11. Ibid., 281.

12. O'Connor, *Black Jack Pershing,* 185.

13. Mead, *The Doughboys,* 67–68.

14. Smythe, *Pershing: General of the Armies,* 33–34.

15. Baker, *Woodrow Wilson,* vol. 7, *War Leader,* 133–134, 149, 151. Margaret L. Coit, *Mr. Baruch* (New York, 1957), 165–174.

16. *Washington Post,* July 17, 1917.

17. Livermore, *Politics Is Adjourned,* 53–54; and Baker, *Woodrow Wilson,* vol. 7, *War Leader,* 187–189.

18. Livermore, *Politics Is Adjourned,* 55–56.

19. Ibid., 57.

20. Baker, *Woodrow Wilson,* vol. 7, *War Leader,* 109–110.

21. Ibid., 181–183.

22. Livermore, *Politics Is Adjourned,* 58.

23. Ibid., 59–60.

24. Ibid., 60–61.

25. Gardner, *Safe for Democracy,* 143.

26. Ibid., 144.

27. PWW, 44:20; and Gardner, *Safe for Democracy,* 143–144.

28. PWW, 44:21–22.

29. PWW, 44:57–58.

30. PWW, 44:83.

31. Gardner, *Safe for Democracy,* 146.

32. Steel, *Walter Lippmann and the American Century,* 127–129.

33. PWW, 44:49.

34. Frederick C. Luebke, *Bonds of Loyalty: German Americans and World War I* (DeKalb, Ill., 1974), 244.

35. Ibid., 234–235.

36. Ibid., 234–240.

37. Ibid., 248–249.

38. Ibid., 241–242.

39. Ibid., 258–259; and Chambers, *To Raise an Army,* 216.

40. Melvin Dubofsky, *We Shall Be All: A History of the IWW, the Industrial Workers of the World* (Chicago, 1969), 368–376.

41. Ibid., 355; and Peterson and Fite, *Opponents of War,* 49.

42. Dubofsky, *We Shall Be All*, 355.

43. Capozzola, "The Only Badge Needed," 1366–1367.

44. Dubofsky, *We Shall Be All*, 384–387; and Peterson and Fite, *Opponents of War*, 55.

45. Peterson and Fite, *Opponents of War*, 60; and Patrick Renshaw, *The Wobblies: The Story of Syndicalism in the United States* (New York, 1967), 205.

46. Dubofsky, *We Shall Be All*, 393–395; and Peterson and Fite, *Opponents of War*, 57–59.

47. Dubofsky, *We Shall Be All*, 406–407.

48. Case and La Follette, *Robert M. La Follette*, 755–757.

49. Ibid., 760.

50. Ibid., 766–767.

51. Ibid., 767–768.

52. Ibid., 770.

53. *New York Times*, October 5, 1917; and Case and La Follette, *Robert M. La Follette*, 780–784.

54. Case and La Follette, *Robert M. La Follette*, 789.

55. Edward J. Renehan, Jr., *The Lion's Pride: Theodore Roosevelt and His Family in Peace and War* (New York, 1998), 132–134.

56. Ibid., 134–135.

57. Morton Keller, ed., *Theodore Roosevelt: A Profile* (New York, 1967), 140; and Flora Miller Biddle Collection of letters between Quentin and Flora (hereafter cited as FMB).

58. FMB, May 12, 1917.

59. FMB, May 28, 1917.

60. Renehan, *The Lion's Pride*, 139.

61. Sylvia Jukes Morris, *Edith Kermit Roosevelt: Portrait of a First Lady* (New York, 1980), 354.

62. Derby Papers, Houghton Library, Harvard University, July 24, 1917 (hereafter cited as Derby Papers).

63. Derby Papers, July 19, 1917.

64. Renehan, *The Lion's Pride*, 144.

65. Ted Morgan, *FDR: A Biography* (New York, 1985), 192.

66. Ward, *A First-Class Temperament*, 339.

67. Ibid., 160–162.

68. Morgan, *FDR*, 203–206; and Ward, *A First-Class Temperament*, 364–366.

69. Morgan, *FDR*, 205.

70. Ward, *A First-Class Temperament*, 373–374.

71. Ibid., 372.

72. Hagedorn, *Leonard Wood*, 214.

73. Ibid., 215, 224.

74. Ibid., 230.

75. Ibid., 235–236.

76. Ibid., 242–243.

77. Ibid., 243–244.

78. Smythe, *Pershing: General of the Armies*, 51.

79. Ibid., 43.

80. Gene Smith, *Until the Last Trumpet Sounds: The Life of General of the Armies John J. Pershing* (New York, 1998), 173.

81. Smythe, *Pershing: General of the Armies*, 296–297.

82. John A. Garraty, *Henry Cabot Lodge: A Biography* (New York, 1953), 176.

83. Constance Gardner, ed., *Some Letters of Augustus Peabody Gardner* (Boston, 1920), 41.

84. Garraty, *Henry Cabot Lodge*, 339; and Gardner, *Some Letters*, 110.

85. Gardner, *Some Letters*, 122–124.

86. Ibid., 126.

87. Smythe, *Pershing: General of the Armies*, 55.

88. Ibid., 54–55.

89. Coffman, *The War to End All Wars*, 250.

90. Smythe, *Pershing: General of the Armies*, 56.

91. Coffman, *The War to End All Wars*, 139–40; and Smythe, *Pershing: General of the Armies,* 59.

92. Smythe, *Pershing: General of the Armies,* 57–58.

93. Frank E. Vandiver, *Black Jack: The Life and Times of John J. Pershing* (College Station, Tex., 1977), 862.

94. Smythe, *Pershing: General of the Armies,* 69.

Chapter 5: Seeds of the Apocalypse

1. Mikhail Heller and Aleksandr M. Nekrich, *Utopia in Power: The History of the Soviet Union from 1917 to the Present,* translated from the Russian by Phyllis B. Carlos (New York, 1986), 34–36; and Peter Kenz, *The Birth of the Propaganda State: Soviet Methods of Mass Mobilization, 1917–1929* (Cambridge, Mass., 1985), 29–32.

2. George F. Kennan, *Russia Leaves the War* (Princeton, 1956), 31, 75–76. The decree was personally drafted by Lenin and did not even mention the United States, calling England, France and Germany "the three mightiest states taking part in the present war."

3. Ibid., 75–76.

4. Ibid., 78–79; and Gardner, *Safe for Democracy*, 149–150.

5. PWW, 45:39.

6. Kennan, *Russia Leaves the War*, 88–89.

7. Ibid., 92–93. Steel, *Walter Lippmann,* 132, calls the revelation "a calamity for Wilson."

8. Ibid., 136–137.

9. Ibid., 144.

10. Seymour, *Intimate Papers of Colonel House,* 3:286.

11. Kenneth Young, *Arthur James Balfour* (London, 1963), 478.

12. PWW, 44:324.

13. Ibid., 44:371.

14. Ibid., 44:391.

15. Seymour, *Intimate Papers of Colonel House,* 3:279; and Baker, *Woodrow Wilson,* vol. 7, *War Leader,* 379.

16. Baker, *Woodrow Wilson,* vol. 7, *War Leader,* 389.

17. PWW, 45:194–199; and Steel, *Walter Lippmann,* 132.

18. Baker, *Woodrow Wilson,* vol. 7, *War Leader,* 390–391.

19. PWW, 45:202.

20. Baker, *Woodrow Wilson,* vol. 7, *War Leader,* 391 n.

21. Sigmund Freud and William C. Bullitt, *Thomas Woodrow Wilson: A Psychological Study* (Boston, 1967), 200–201.

22. Edward Berenson, *The Trial of Madame Caillaux* (Los Angeles, 1992), 71–87, 214–247.

23. Watt, *Dare Call It Treason,* 140–141.

24. Severance Johnson, *The Enemy Within* (New York, 1919), 56–58; and Watt, *Dare Call It Treason,* 141.

25. Johnson, *The Enemy Within,* 62ff; and Watt, *Dare Call It Treason,* 135–137.

26. Watt, *Dare Call It Treason,* 142–143.

27. Ibid., 137–138, 263–264.

28. Ibid., 143–145.

29. Gregor Dallas, *At the Heart of a Tiger: Clemenceau and His World, 1831–1929* (New York, 1993), 486–491; see also 504–505 for timing of arrests.

30. Ibid., 407, 494.

31. Ibid., 501–502. See also the account in Johnson, *The Enemy Within*, 201. He stresses the French Socialist reaction to the Bolshevik takeover in Russia, which heightened the tension in Paris.

32. Watt, *Dare Call It Treason*, 289.

33. Dallas, *Heart of a Tiger*, 506.

34. Johnson, *The Enemy Within*, 218–220.

35. Creel, *How We Advertised America*, 45–46.

36. Livermore, *Politics Is Adjourned*, 64–65.

37. Ibid., 68.

38. Richard Norton Smith, *An Uncommon Man: The Triumph of Herbert Hoover* (New York, 1984), 87–89.

39. Livermore, *Politics Is Adjourned*, 68–69.

40. Ibid., 70.

41. Ibid., 71; and Coffman, *The War to End All Wars*, 38–40.

42. Livermore, *Politics Is Adjourned*, 75–76.

43. Ibid., 72.

44. Seymour, *Intimate Papers of Colonel House*, 3:316–318; and Kennan, *Russia Leaves the War*, 254. The Bolsheviks had warned the Allied governments that if they did not join in an immediate peace conference, the working classes "will be faced with the iron necessity of wresting power" from them.

45. Seymour, *Intimate Papers of Colonel House*, 3:322.

46. Ibid., 3:324–325.

47. House Diary, January 19, 1918.

48. Seymour, *Intimate Papers of Colonel House*, 3:341.

49. Case and La Follette, *Robert M. La Follette*, 838; and PWW, 45:534–535.

50. Kennan, *Russia Leaves the War*, 254–256.

51. PWW, 45:534–539.

52. Ibid.

53. Garraty, *Henry Cabot Lodge*, 340; and Seymour, *Intimate Papers of Colonel House*, 3:344–345.

54. Seymour, *Intimate Papers of Colonel House*, 3:345–346; and Kennan, *Russia Leaves the War*, 261–262.

55. Livermore, *Politics Is Adjourned*, 82–83.

56. Kennedy, *Over Here*, 124–125.

57. Baker, *Woodrow Wilson*, vol. 7, *War Leader*, 480–481.

58. Livermore, *Politics Is Adjourned*, 89.

59. Sheldon Bernard Avery, *A Private Civil War: The Controversy Between George E. Chamberlain and Woodrow Wilson*, M.A. thesis (University of Oregon, 1967), 3.

60. Ibid., 73–74.

61. Ibid., 79.

62. Livermore, *Politics Is Adjourned*, 96.

63. Avery, *A Private Civil War*, 80–81.

64. Diary of Colonel House, January 17, 1918.

65. Ibid., January 20, 1918.

66. Livermore, *Politics Is Adjourned*, 96.

67. Nathan Miller, *Theodore Roosevelt: A Life* (New York, 1992), 558.

68. George C. Marshall, *Memoirs of My Services in the World War 1917–18* (Boston, 1976), 18; Mead, *The Doughboys*, 153; and Smythe, *Pershing: General of the Armies*, 66.

69. Smythe, *Pershing: General of the Armies*, 66–68.

70. O'Connor, *Black Jack Pershing*, 204.

71. Heywood Broun, *The A.E.F. with General Pershing and His Forces* (New York, 1918), 92–93.

72. O'Connor, *Black Jack Pershing*, 167; and Smythe, *Pershing: General of the Armies*, 69.

73. Seymour, *Intimate Papers of Colonel House*, 3:310.

74. Smythe, *Pershing: General of the Armies*, 71–72.

75. Ibid., 74–77.

76. Harbord, *The American Army in France*, 193.

77. Smythe, *Pershing: General of the Armies*, 79.

78. Harbord, *American Army in France*, 190.

79. PWW 42:504; *New York Times,* November 21 and 22, 1917; and *New Republic,* December 22, 1917, 214.

80. Larry Wayne Ward, *The Motion Picture Goes to War: The U.S. Government Film Effort During World War I* (Ann Arbor, Mich., 1985), 118–119. Goldstein's sentence was commuted in 1920. He went back to Europe and made a number of movies in Germany. He was last heard from desperately trying to escape Hitler's Third Reich in the mid-1930s.

81. Peterson and Fite, *Opponents of War*, 151–152; and Capozzola, "The Only Badge Needed Is Your Patriotic Fervor," 1363.

82. Kenneth S. Chern, "The Politics of Patriotism: War, Ethnicity and the New York Mayoral Campaign, 1917," *New York Historical Society Quarterly* 62 (1979): 291–313.

83. Peterson and Fite, *Opponents of War*, 163–164; Murphy, *World War I and the Origins of Civil Liberties*, 164.

84. Paul F. Brissendon, *The IWW: A Study in American Syndicalism* (New York, 1919), 343–346.

85. Peterson and Fite, *Opponents of War*, 168–169.

86. Case and La Follette, *Robert M. La Follette,* 895–896.

87. Ibid., 809.

88. Ibid., 822, 832.

89. Ibid., 833–835. After the war, Cobb wrote a "belated word of contrition" to the La Follettes, saying he had written the story under "the spell of that madness—which we mistook for patriotism."

90. Unger, *Fighting Bob La Follette*, 257–258.

91. Ibid., 257.

92. Charles F. Vincent, *The Post–World War I Blockade of Germany: An Aspect in the Tragedy of a Nation,* Ph.D. dissertation (University of Colorado, 1980), 89.

93. Ibid., 89–90.

94. Seymour, *Intimate Papers of Colonel House*, 3:352; and Ronald Chickering, *Imperial Germany and the Great War, 1914–1918* (Cambridge, 1998), 143–144, 160. Vincent, *Post–World War I Blockade of Germany*, cites reports of people in 1917–1918 standing in line for hours in the bitter cold, to obtain a single egg.

95. Seymour, *Intimate Papers of Colonel House,* 3:354–355.

96. Ibid., 360–363.

97. Ibid., 365.

98. Ibid., 369.

99. Ibid., 369–370.

100. John W. Wheeler-Bennett, *Brest-Litovsk: The Forgotten Peace* (New York, 1971), 246ff.

101. Seymour, *Intimate Papers of Colonel House,* 3:381–382.

Chapter 6: The Women of No Man's Land

1. Dorothy and Carl J. Schneider, *Into the Breach: American Women Overseas in World War I* (New York, 1991), 1–3.

2. Eleanor Roosevelt, *Day Before Yesterday: The Reminiscences of Mrs. Theodore Roosevelt, Jr.* (New York, 1959), 84.

3. James R. McGovern, "The American Woman's Pre–World War I Freedom in Manners and Morals," *Journal of American History,* 55, no. 2 (September 1968): 315–316.

4. Schneider, *Into the Breach,* 196ff.

5. Marian Baldwin, *Canteening Overseas, 1917–1918 (New York,* 1920), 13–14.

6. Ibid., 31.

7. Ibid., 64.

8. Kermit Roosevelt, ed., *Quentin Roosevelt: A Sketch with Letters* (New York, 1921), 44.

9. Hiram Bingham, *An Explorer in the Air Service* (New Haven, Conn., 1921), 126ff; and Stephen Longstreet, *The Canvas Falcons* (New York, 1970), 239–245. The Spad was also very dangerous to fly. One American pilot said it had "the gliding angle of a brick."

10. Derby Papers, FPW to QR, July 31, 1917.

11. Derby Papers, QR to FPW, August 14, 1917; and FMB, QR to FPW, September 9, 1917.

12. Derby Papers, QR to FPW, November 27, 1917; and Chambers, *To Raise an Army,* 328.

13. Theodore Roosevelt Collection, Houghton Library, QR to AR, December 28, 1917 (hereafter cited as TR Collection). The incident is discussed in several other letters in FMB.

14. Elting E. Morrison, ed., *Letters of Theodore Roosevelt,* vol. 8, *The Days of Armageddon* (Cambridge, Mass., 1954), 1347.

15. Derby Papers, FPW to QR, June 17, 1918.

16. FMB, QR to FPW, January 27, 1918.

17. FMB, typewritten letter, no date.

18. John Toland, *No Man's Land, 1918: The Last Year of the Great War* (New York, 1980), 18.

19. Hubert C. Johnson, *Breakthrough!* (Novato, Calif., 1994), 218–219; and B. H. Liddell-Hart, *The Real War, 1914–1918* (Boston, 1930), 390–391.

20. Bruce I. Gudmundsson, *Stormtrooper Tactics: Innovation in the German Army, 1914–18 (New York,* 1989), 151–152.

21. Toland, *No Man's Land,* 21.

22. John Keegan, *The First World War* (New York, 1998), 399.

23. Rod Paschall, *The Defeat of Imperial Germany, 1917–1918* (Chapel Hill, N.C., 1989), 140.

24. S. L. A. Marshall, *The American Heritage History of World War I* (New York, 1964), 268.

25. Toland, *No Man's Land,* 53–54.

26. Rudolf Binding, *A Fatalist at War,* translated from German by Ian F. D. Morrow (New York, 1929), 209–210.

27. John Mosier, *The Myth of the Great War: A New Military History of World War I* (New York, 2001), 317.

28. Vandiver, *Black Jack,* 888 and Smythe, *Pershing, General of the Armies,* 102.

29. Shirley Millard, *I Saw Them Die: Diary and Recollections,* edited by Adele Commandini (New York, 1936), 3–18.

30. Schneider, *Into the Breach,* 75.

31. Ibid., 77–78.

32. Henry W. Miller, *The Paris Gun* (New York, 1930), 1–27, 122ff.

33. Marshall, *World War I,* 272–273.

34. Barrie Pitt, *1918: The Last Act* (New York, 1962), 125.

35. Ibid., 128–129.

36. Vandiver, *Black Jack,* 876.

37. Smythe, *Pershing: General of the Armies,* 103.

38. Pershing, *My Experiences,* 2:28–29; and Smythe, *Pershing: General of the Armies,* 115.

39. O'Connor, *Black Jack Pershing,* 236.

40. Baldwin, *Canteening Overseas,* 74.

41. Marshall, *Memoirs of My Services*, 13–14.

42. Coffman, *The War to End All Wars*, 80–81; and Schaffer, *America in the Great War*, 104–105.

43. Baldwin, *Canteening Overseas*, 170.

44. Ibid., 74-75.

45. Millard, *I Saw Them Die*, 18–19.

46. Ibid., 20–21.

47. Smythe, *Pershing: General of the Armies*, 125, 107–108.

48. Coffman, *The War to End All Wars*, 156–158.

49. Allan Reed Millett, *The General: Robert L. Bullard and Officership in the U.S. Army, 1881–1925* (Westport, Conn., 1975), 363–364.

50. Smythe, *Pershing: General of the Armies*, 129; and Millett, *The General*, 365–366.

51. Marshall, *Memoirs of My Services*, 96; Smythe, *Pershing: General of the Armies,* 127–128; and Millett, *The General*, 366.

52. Smythe, *Pershing: General of the Armies*, 128.

53. Ibid., 128–129; and Millett, *The General*, 367–368.

54. *New York Times,* March 31, 1918.

55. Liddell-Hart, *The Real War*, 412.

56. Charles B. Flood, *Hitler: The Path to Power* (Boston, 1989), 24–25.

57. Pershing, *My Experiences in the World War*, 2:65.

58. Dallas, *At the Heart of a Tiger*, 534.

59. Toland, *No Man's Land*, 375.

60. Ibid., 275–276; and Dallas, *Heart of a Tiger,* 535–538.

61. O'Connor, *Black Jack Pershing*, 263–264.

62. Toland, *No Man's Land*, 277.

63. Robert B. Asprey, *At Belleau Wood* (Denton, Tex., 1996), 141–144. See also Vandiver, *Black Jack,* 896–897.

64. Asprey, *At Belleau Wood*, 178. Laurence Stallings lost his leg to machine-gun bullets in this attack and acquired the disillusion that pervaded his novel *Plumes* and the play *What Price Glory*. He was a marine lieutenant.

65. Toland, *No Man's Land*, 287.

66. Harbord, *The American Army in France*, 296.

67. Joseph Dickman, *The Great Crusade: A Narrative of the World War* (New York, 1927), 267–272.

68. Douglas MacArthur, *Reminiscences* (New York, 1964), 58; and Henry J. Reilly, *The Rainbow at War* (Columbus, Ohio, 1936), 246–247.

69. Binding, *A Fatalist at War*, 254.

70. Robert B. Asprey, *The German High Command at War: Hindenburg and Ludendorff Conduct World War I* (New York, 1991), 437. Asprey sees this attempt to revive the offensive in the north as a forlorn, desperate gesture by Ludendorff, who sensed the failure to break through on the Marne meant the war was lost.

71. Mead, *The Doughboys,* 253; and Douglas V. Johnson II and Rolfe L. Hillman, Jr., *Soissons 1918* (College Station, Tex., 1999), 53. Some 150,000 Vietnamese served in the French army as labor troops. Another 500,000 troops—many of them draftees—came from French colonies in Africa (J. M. Winter, *The Experience of World War I* [New York, 1989], 216–217).

72. Carl Andrew Brannen, *Over There: A Marine in the Great War* (College Station, Tex., 1996), 31–32.

73. *Proceedings* (of the U.S. Naval Institute), November 1987, 60; *Military Affairs,* October 1987, 178; and Pershing, *My Experiences,* 2:167.

74. Harbord, *The American Army in France*, 336–337.

75. Brannen, *Over There,* 35–36.

76. Johnson and Hillman, *Soissons 1918,* 144.

77. FMB, letter undated, cable June 16, 1918. "Ham" is Quentin's Harvard classmate, Hamilton Coolidge.

78. TR Collection, June 18, 1918.

79. Renehan, *The Lion's Pride*, 175–178.

80. Ibid., 193.

81. Edward V. Rickenbacker, *Fighting the Flying Circus* (New York, 1919), 56.

82. FMB, QR to FPW, June 25, 1918.

83. FMB, letters of July 3, 6.

84. Roosevelt, *Quentin Roosevelt,* 163–164.

85. Ethel, FMB collection; and Roosevelt to Whitney, Elting P. Morrison, ed., *Letters of Theodore Roosevelt* (Cambridge, Mass., 1954), 1351.

86. FMB, AR to FPW, July 13, 1918; and Renehan, *The Lion's Pride,* 191.

87. Roosevelt, *Quentin Roosevelt,* 170.

88. Derby Papers, FPW to QR, June 19, 1918.

89. Joseph Gardner, *Departing Glory: Theodore Roosevelt As Ex-President* (New York, 1973), 390.

90. Roosevelt, *Quentin Roosevelt,* 179–181.

Chapter 7: Politics Is Adjourned, Ha-Ha-Ha

1. Livermore, *Politics Is Adjourned,* 115.

2. Ibid., 105–106.

3. Ibid., 106–110.

4. Kennedy, *Over Here,* 237–238.

5. Case and La Follette, *Robert M. La Follette,* 872.

6. Charles M. Thomas, *Thomas Riley Marshall: Hoosier Statesman* (Oxford, Ohio, 1939), 180–183.

7. Ibid., 181. See also Case and La Follette, *Robert M. La Follette,* 870–871.

8. Case and La Follette, *Robert M. La Follette,* 869, 873. Joseph Davies remained a prominent Democrat, serving as ambassador to Moscow in the late 1930s.

9. PWW, 48:162–166.

10. Livermore, *Politics Is Adjourned,* 135; and Blum, *Joe Tumulty and the Wilson Era,* 160–161.

11. Hagedorn, *Leonard Wood,* 283–284, 297.

12. Ibid., 294, 303.

13. Ray Stannard Baker, *Woodrow Wilson: Life and Letters,* vol. 8, *Armistice* (New York, 1939), 209.

14. Livermore, *Politics Is Adjourned,* 159–160.

15. Kennedy, *Over Here,* 238–239.

16. Livermore, *Politics Is Adjourned,* 139–140; 160–162.

17. Ibid., 163–164.

18. Blum, *Joe Tumulty and the Wilson Era,* 155–156.

19. Livermore, *Politics Is Adjourned,* 166–167.

20. Baker, *Woodrow Wilson,* vol. 8, *Armistice,* 75–76. The speech also reflected Wilson's reaction to the Treaty of Brest-Litovsk, which convinced him there was no hope of a negotiated peace with the German government (Wheeler-Bennett, *Brest-Litovsk: The Forgotten Peace,* 364–366).

21. Melvyn Dubofsky, *"Big Bill" Haywood* (New York, 1987), 121. After the war, Haywood was freed on bail while his sentence was appealed. When the higher courts upheld it, he fled to Moscow, where he died in 1928.

22. Peterson and Fite, *Opponents of War,* 184.

23. Nick Salvatore, *Eugene V. Debs: Citizen and Socialist* (Chicago, 1982), 288–289, 292–293.

24. Ibid., 295–296.

25. Ward, *The Motion Picture Goes to War,* 55–56.

26. Ross, *Propaganda for War,* 262–263.

27. Ward, *Motion Picture Goes to War,* 56–57. *Heart of Humanity* also featured a scene in which German soldiers dumped milk donated by the American Red Cross while starving Belgians watched.

28. Baker, *Woodrow Wilson,* vol. 8, *Armistice,* 213.

29. Ward, *Motion Picture Goes to War,* 57.

30. Newell Dwight Hillis, *German Atrocities: Their Nature and Philosophy* (New York, 1918), 139–140; and Peterson and Fite, *Opponents of War,* 183.

31. Peterson and Fite, *Opponents of War,* 195–197.

32. Ibid., 200.

33. Luebke, *Bonds of Loyalty,* 3–10.

34. Peterson and Fite, *Opponents of War,* 203–204.

35. Baker, *Woodrow Wilson,* vol. 8, *Armistice,* 102–103.

36. PWW, 49:98.

37. Peterson and Fite, *Opponents of War,* 210–212.

38. Ibid., 209.

39. Ibid., 224.

40. Ibid., 225.

41. *Washington Evening Post,* August 25, 1918.

42. Baker, *Woodrow Wilson,* vol. 7, *War Leader,* 165 n.

43. Ellis, *Race, War and Surveillance,* 102–103.

44. Ibid., 103–104.

45. Frank Freidel, *Franklin D. Roosevelt: The Apprenticeship* (Boston, 1952), 337–338.

46. Ward, *A First-Class Temperament,* 383.

47. Ibid., 385; and Morgan, *FDR,* 194.

48. FDR Diary, 1918, Franklin D. Roosevelt Presidential Library, Assistant Secretary of the Navy Papers 1913–1920 (hereafter cited as ASN Papers) Box 33, 5.

49. Ibid., 7–8.

50. Ward, *A First-Class Temperament,* 392–399.

51. FDR Diary, ASN Papers, 37.

52. Ibid., 38.

53. Renehan, *The Lion's Pride,* 205–206.

54. Ward, *A First-Class Temperament,* 399; and Morgan, *FDR,* 197.

55. FDR Diary, ASN Papers, 40–41.

56. Ibid., 44.

57. Ibid., 42.

58. Ibid., 46.

59. Ibid., 47; and Ward, *A First-Class Temperament,* 400–401 n.

60. FDR Diary, ASN Papers, 48.

61. Morgan, *FDR,* 199.

62. Ward, *A First-Class Temperament,* 411–412; and Morgan, *FDR,* 200–201.

63. Millard, *I Saw Them Die,* 42–44.

64. Ibid., 37.

65. Ibid., 78.

66. Baker, *Woodrow Wilson,* vol. 8, *Armistice,* 266.

67. Gardner, *Safe for Democracy,* 170.

68. Ibid., 172.

69. Ibid., 177.

70. Ferrell, *Woodrow Wilson and World War I,* 270 n.

71. George F. Kennan, *The Decision to Intervene* (Princeton, 1958), 421.

Chapter 8: Fights to the Finish

1. James, *Years of MacArthur,* vol. 1, *1880–1941,* 156–157, 181.

2. Ibid., 191.

3. Millett, *The General,* 386–387; and Coffman, *The War to End All Wars,* 253.

4. Robert Lee Bullard, *Personalities and Reminiscences of the War* (Garden City, N.Y., 1925), 236–237; and Millett, *The General,* 387–388. By way of compensation, Bullard wryly noted, the French issued a communiqué saying the Americans had stopped a German counteroffensive. Hervey Allen, *Toward the Flame* (New York, 1926), 236ff, describes the Fismette massacre in horrendous detail.

5. Toland, *No Man's Land,* 414.

6. Smythe, *Pershing: General of the Armies,* 176.

7. Pershing, *My Experiences,* 2:247–248.

8. Ibid., 358.

9. Dale E. Wilson, *Treat 'Em Rough: The Birth of American Armor, 1917–20* (Novato, Calif., 1990), 112, 114.

10. Harry S. Semmes, *Portrait of Patton* (New York, 1964), 54–55.

11. Smythe, *Pershing: General of the Armies,* 193.

12. Timothy K. Nenninger, "Tactical Dysfunction in the AEF," *Military History,* October 1987, 180.

13. Paul Braim, *The Test of Battle* (New Haven, 1988), 104–105.

14. Ibid., 115.

15. Toland, *No Man's Land,* 466–467. Summerall blamed the inadequate amount of artillery allocated to each division for the American inability to deal with enemy machine guns. But he was also an early convert to the British doctrine of HCI: high casualties inevitable. Hillman, *Soissons, 1918,* 41, notes Summerall once said: "Sir, when the 1st Division has only two men left, they will be echeloned in depth and attacking toward Berlin!" Hillman adds: "He would have been a wonderful 'talking head' on CNN."

16. Nenninger, "Tactical Dysfunction in the AEF," 180; and Bullard, *Personalities and Reminiscences of the War,* 249ff. General Bullard opined that if the war had continued for another year, the Americans would have had to shoot as many stragglers as the British did annually to keep divisions in the front lines.

17. Coffman, *The War to End All Wars,* 340.

18. Shipley Thomas, *History of the AEF* (New York, 1920), 298–300; and Braim, *Test of Battle,* 126.

19. Toland, *No Man's Land,* 468–473.

20. Smythe, *Pershing: General of the Armies,* 208.

21. Ibid., 209; and Marshall, *Memoir of My Services in the World War,* 176.

22. James, *Years of MacArthur,* vol. 1, *1880–1941,* 217–220; and Smythe, *Pershing: General of the Armies,* 214.

23. Ibid., 217–218.

24. Millard, *I Saw Them Die,* 92–107.

25. Baldwin, *Canteening Overseas,* 125–145.

26. Renehan, *The Lion's Pride,* 178–179.

27. Ward, *A First-Class Temperament,* 409.

28. Garraty, *Henry Cabot Lodge,* 341.

29. Livermore, *Politics Is Adjourned,* 212.

30. Garraty, *Henry Cabot Lodge,* 341.

31. Case and La Follette, *Robert M. La Follette,* 892.

32. Livermore, *Politics Is Adjourned,* 182–183.

33. Blum, *Joe Tumulty and the Wilson Era,* 148; and Case and La Follette, *Robert M. La Follette,* 892.

34. Livermore, *Politics Is Adjourned,* 183–184.

35. Norman H. Clark, *Deliver Us from Evil: An Interpretation of American Prohibition* (New York, 1967), 94ff, 125–126.

36. Ibid., 128–129.

37. Ibid., 129; and Blum, *Joe Tumulty and the Wilson Era*, 149.

38. Blum, *Joe Tumulty and the Wilson Era*, 149.

39. Livermore, *Politics Is Adjourned*, 172, 176.

40. Blum, *Joe Tumulty and the Wilson Era*, 158–159.

41. Seymour, *Intimate Papers of Colonel House*, 4:64–65.

42. Ibid., 71–72.

43. Ibid., 71.

44. Ibid.; and Livermore, *Politics Is Adjourned*, 214.

45. Asprey, *German High Command at War*, 447–450.

46. Ibid., 462. See also Ferrell, *Woodrow Wilson and World War I*, 130.

47. Asprey, *German High Command at War*, 466–467; and Roger Chickering, *Imperial Germany and the Great War, 1914–1918* (Cambridge, 1998), 187.

48. Richard M. Watt, *The Kings Depart: The Tragedy of Germany, Versailles and the German Revolution* (New York, 1968), 136–147.

49. Chickering, *Imperial Germany and the Great War*, 188.

50. Seymour, *Intimate Papers of Colonel House,* 4:73–74; and Chickering, *Imperial Germany and the Great War*, 168.

51. Seymour, *Intimate Papers of Colonel House*, 4:74–75.

52. Ibid., 75.

53. Ibid., 76.

54. Case and La Follette, *Robert M. La Follette*, 896.

55. Seymour, *Intimate Papers of Colonel House,* 4:78–79; and Robert H. Ferrell, *Ill-Advised: Presidential Health and Public Trust* (Columbia, Mo., 1992), 14. Grayson limited Wilson's workday to four hours whenever possible.

56. Seymour, *Intimate Papers of Colonel House,* 4:78–79; and Livermore, *Politics Is Adjourned*, 214–215.

57. Blum, *Joe Tumulty and the Wilson Era,* 163; Livermore, *Politics Is Adjourned*, 216; Baker, *Woodrow Wilson,* vol. 8, *Armistice*, 495.

58. Seymour, *Intimate Papers of Colonel House*, 4:84.

59. Ibid., 75–79; Ferrell, *Woodrow Wilson and World War I,* 130–131; and Asprey, *German High Command at War*, 481.

60. Livermore, *Politics Is Adjourned*, 216; and Garraty, *Henry Cabot Lodge,* 342.

61. PWW, 51:381–382.

62. Baker, *Woodrow Wilson,* vol. 8, *Armistice,* 513–514 n; Blum, *Joe Tumulty and the Wilson Era,* 165; Garraty, *Henry Cabot Lodge,* 342; and Case and La Follette, *Robert M. La Follette*, 899–900.

63. Blum, *Joe Tumulty and the Wilson Era,* 165–166; and Selig Adler, "The Congressional Election of 1918," *South Atlantic Quarterly,* October 1937, 459.

64. Davis, *FDR: The Beckoning of Destiny*, 541. In this first volume of his landmark biography of Franklin Roosevelt (unfortunately unfinished), this remarkably forthright historian saw with an unrelenting eye Wilson's tragic mistakes.

65. Seymour, *Intimate Papers of Colonel House,* 4:160–165.

66. Ibid., 165–169.

67. Ibid., 183–184.

68. Ibid., 188–189.

69. Livermore, *Politics Is Adjourned,* 224–225.

70. Baker, *Woodrow Wilson,* vol. 8, *Armistice,* 558; and Livermore, *Politics Is Adjourned*, 226–227.

71. Livermore, *Politics Is Adjourned,* 230–236; and Thomas, *Thomas Riley Marshall,* 182.

72. Livermore, *Politics Is Adjourned,* 226; and Kennedy, *Over Here*, 244.

73. Kennedy, *Over Here,* 244; and Thomas J. Knock, *To End All Wars: Woodrow Wilson and the Quest for a New World Order* (New York, 1992), 184.

74. Knock, *To End All Wars,* 185–186.

75. Case and La Follette, *Robert M. La Follette,* 902, 910–911.

76. Baker, *Woodrow Wilson,* vol. 8, *Armistice,* 563.

77. Seymour, *Intimate Papers of Colonel House,* 4:121.

78. Harry R. Rudin, *Armistice 1918* (New Haven, 1944), 186.

79. Toland, *No Man's Land,* 551–552; Smythe, *Pershing: General of the Armies,* 231; and Baker, *Woodrow Wilson,* vol. 8, *Armistice,* 570–571.

80. Baker, *Woodrow Wilson,* vol. 8, *Armistice,* 572.

81. Walter Henry Nelson, *The Soldier Kings: The House of Hohenzollern* (New York, 1970), 434.

82. Ibid., 436–437.

83. Pershing, *My Experiences,* 2:375. The author's father, Thomas J. Fleming, was a sergeant in the 312th Regiment of the 78th Division during the Argonne struggle. Commissioned in the field when all the officers in his company were killed or wounded, he went to officers' training school in France after the war. His papers reveal the new tactics Hunter Liggett and his staff devised to deal with machine guns. Charging guns was specifically repudiated. "The platoon that advances all at once plays into the enemy's hands. Even though the position be taken, the enemy is well satisfied with the losses he has been able to inflict." Instead attacks were carried out by twelve-man "platoon gangs" led by corporals. Each gang consisted of three automatic riflemen, two grenade riflemen, three "bombers" (grenade throwers) and three ordinary riflemen. The gangs maneuvered on the battlefield using the firepower of the automatic rifles and rifle grenades to keep the enemy machine guns and supporting infantry busy while the rest of the gang—and nearby gangs—attacked from the flanks (Papers of Lieutenant Thomas J. Fleming, World War I Survey, U.S. Army Military History Institute, Carlisle, Pa.).

84. Smythe, *Pershing: General of the Armies,* 228–229; and O'Connor, *Black Jack Pershing,* 329–330.

85. Rolfe L. Hillman, "Crossing the Meuse," *Relevance (Journal of the Great War Society)* 2, nos. 2–4 (1993): 2.

86. Ibid., 17–18.

87. Mead, *The Doughboys,* 338.

88. Ibid., 338–339.

89. Coffman, *The War to End All Wars,* 356.

90. Nelson, *The Soldier Kings,* 439–440.

91. Millard, *I Saw Them Die,* 108–110.

92. Smythe, *Pershing: General of the Armies,* 232; and Toland, *No Man's Land,* 573–574.

93. Smythe, *Pershing: General of the Armies,* 231.

94. Ibid., 233; and Pershing, *My Experiences,* 2:395.

95. DeWeerd, *President Wilson Fights His War,* 392. Mead, *The Doughboys,* 353; and Schaffer, *America in the Great War,* 202. Some historians have reduced the AEF's days in action to the large-scale combat that began at Cantigny on May 28, 1918, and escalated when the Germans reached the Marne two days later (Arthur Wilson Page, *Our 110 Days of Fighting* [New York, 1920]).

96. Ferguson, *The Pity of War,* 312; Thomas Parrish, ed., *The Simon and Schuster Encyclopedia of World War II* (New York, 1978), 645–649; and Allen Millett and Peter Maslowski, *For the Common Defense: A Military History of the United States of America* (New York, 1984), 504, 542.

97. Seymour, *Intimate Papers of Colonel House,* 4:143; and Baker, *Woodrow Wilson,* vol. 8, *Armistice,* 580.

Chapter 9: Peace That Surpasses Understanding

1. Seymour, *Intimate Papers of Colonel House,* 4:210–211.

2. Ibid., 212.

3. Ibid., 213.

4. Garraty, *Henry Cabot Lodge*, 347.

5. Blum, *Joe Tumulty and the Wilson Era*, 170.

6. Seymour, *Intimate Papers of Colonel House*, 4:223–225.

7. Ibid., 235.

8. Thomas A. Bailey, *Woodrow Wilson and the Lost Peace* (Chicago, 1963), 92; and Willis Fletcher Johnson, *George Harvey: A Passionate Patriot* (Boston, 1929), 263. Humorist Will Rogers, a Democrat, chortled that Wilson had told the Republicans, "We will split 50–50. I will go and you fellows can stay."

9. Garraty, *Henry Cabot Lodge*, 347–348.

10. Ibid., 343.

11. August Heckscher, *Woodrow Wilson: A Biography* (New York, 1991), 496; Bailey, *Woodrow Wilson and the Lost Peace*, 105; and Case and La Follette, *Robert La Follette*, 914–915.

12. Heckscher, *Woodrow Wilson*, 497–498.

13. Seymour, *Intimate Papers of Colonel House*, 4:151; and William E. Leuchtenberg, *The Perils of Prosperity, 1914–32* (Chicago, 1958), 52.

14. Sullivan, *Our Times*, vol. 5, *Over Here*, 436–438.

15. Ira Gregg Wolper, *The Origins of Public Diplomacy: Woodrow Wilson, George Creel and the Committee on Public Information*, Ph.D. dissertation (University of Chicago, 1991), 305–309.

16. Baker, *Woodrow Wilson*, vol. 8, *Armistice*, 592–593.

17. Peter Rowland, *David Lloyd George: A Biography* (New York, 1975), 463.

18. Ibid., 469–470.

19. Ibid., 470–475.

20. Bailey, *Woodrow Wilson and the Lost Peace*, 111.

21. Seymour, *Intimate Papers of Colonel House*, 4:253–254.

22. Sullivan, *Our Times*, vol. 5, *Over Here*, 537–538.

23. Gardner, *Safe for Democracy*, 2.

24. Ibid. At a stag dinner given him by Lloyd George, Wilson spoke warmly of the "bond of deathless friendship" the war had created between the United States and Great Britain. But these off-the-record remarks were never published (Heckscher, *Woodrow Wilson*, 507–509).

25. Gardner, *Safe for Democracy*, 2–3.

26. Levin, *Edith and Woodrow*, 240.

27. Seymour, *Intimate Papers of Colonel House*, 4:255.

28. Baker, *Woodrow Wilson*, vol. 8, *Armistice*, 582.

29. George H. Nash, *The Life of Herbert Hoover, the Humanitarian, 1914–17* (New York, 1988), 65ff; and Smith, *Triumph of Herbert Hoover*, 86.

30. Vincent, *Post–World War I Blockade of Germany*, 134.

31. Ibid., 136.

32. Ibid., 139.

33. Bailey, *Woodrow Wilson and the Lost Peace*, 119; and Vincent, *Post–World War I Blockade of Germany*, 146.

34. Vincent, *Post–World War I Blockade of Germany*, 126, 152–153.

35. Ibid., 154–155.

36. Ibid., 158–159.

37. Ibid., 163–164.

38. Ibid., 173.

39. William Klingaman, *1919: The Year Our World Began* (New York, 1987), 10.

40. Renehan, *The Lion's Pride*, 249.

41. Sylvia Jukes Morris, *Edith Kermit Roosevelt*, 424.

42. Renehan, *The Lion's Pride*, 248.

43. Ward, *A First-Class Temperament*, 421–422.

44. Renehan, *The Lion's Pride,* 221; and Ward, *A First-Class Temperament,* 422.

45. Ward, *A First-Class Temperament,* 422. Arthur Krock, *Memoirs: Sixty Years on the Firing Line* (New York, 1968), 109, presented another version of Wilson's reaction to TR's death. Krock, then a reporter for the *Louisville Courier-Journal*, was on the train platform when Wilson received the telegram. He described Wilson's reaction to the "news that his most powerful adversary had left the lists" as "a kind of spontaneous relaxation." It was followed by a "distinctly sad" expression. Is "spontaneous relaxation" the same as "a smile of transcendent triumph"? Krock was very fond of Wilson. Lloyd George saw Wilson shortly after he returned to Paris and expressed his condolences to the president on Roosevelt's death. "I was aghast at the outburst of acrid detestation which flowed from Wilson's lips," Lloyd George wrote (David Lloyd George, *Memoirs of the Peace Conference* [New Haven, 1939], 1:147).

46. Gordon A. Craig, *Germany, 1866–1945* (New York, 1978), 407–408.

47. Klingaman, *1919,* 35–37; and Craig, *Germany,* 409.

48. Oswald Garrison Villard, *Fighting Years: An Autobiography* (New York, 1939), 397–398.

49. Case and La Follette, *Robert M. La Follette*, 942–943.

50. Charles L. Mee, Jr., *The End of Order: Versailles 1919* (New York, 1980), 45–46; Herbert Hoover, *The Ordeal of Woodrow Wilson* (New York, 1958), 70–71; and Ray Stannard Baker, *Woodrow Wilson and the World Settlement* (New York, 1923), 1:174.

51. Mee, *The End of Order*, 48.

52. Ibid., 49.

53. Knock, *To End All Wars*, 204.

54. Blum, *Joe Tumulty and the Wilson Era*, 172–174.

55. Tebbel and Watts, *The Press and the Presidency,* 387.

56. Inga Floto, *Colonel House in Paris: A Study of American Policy at the Paris Peace Conference, 1919* (Copenhagen, 1973), 69–70. Cobb's close relationship with House in Paris collapsed when the newsman discovered the extent of House's power. He was shocked to find out that "in each U.S. embassy there was one member who was in direct contact with Colonel House and sent him a daily personal report which did not go to the United States." Cobb went back to the United States a confused and troubled man. Wilson was, of course, aware of this arrangement. The episode makes even more unlikely the story of Wilson's unburdening his heart to Cobb on the eve of declaring war. Cobb was clearly not in the presidential loop.

57. Steel, *Walter Lippmann*, 147. It should be pointed out that Lippmann thought he should have gotten Creel's job.

58. Wolper, *Origins of Public Diplomacy*, 320–337.

59. Baker, *Woodrow Wilson and the World Settlement,* 1:256–259.

60. Knock, *To End All Wars*, 212–213; Hoover, *Ordeal of Woodrow Wilson*, 227–228; and Baker, *Woodrow Wilson and the World Settlement,* 1:250–275. Baker devotes an entire chapter to this stormy debate on the German colonies. As he notes glumly at the close, "it was only the first battle of a long and deadly war."

61. Bailey, *Woodrow Wilson and the Lost Peace*, 187.

62. Knock, *To End All Wars*, 222–224.

63. Ibid., 224.

64. John Milton Cooper, Jr., *Breaking the Heart of the World: Woodrow Wilson and the Fight for the League of Nations* (New York, 2001), 52; and Knock, *To End All Wars*, 225–226.

65. *Washington Post,* January 18, 1919.

66. Gardner, *Safe for Democracy*, 239–240; and Floto, *Colonel House in Paris,* 109–112

67. Garraty, *Henry Cabot Lodge*, 350.

68. Bailey, *Woodrow Wilson and the Lost Peace,* 197; and Cooper, *Breaking the Heart of the World,* 60–61.

69. Klingaman, *1919,* 97, 122.

70. PWW, 55:238–245.

71. Garraty, *Henry Cabot Lodge*, 350–351; and Levin, *Edith and Woodrow*, 255, 258.

72. Levin, *Edith and Woodrow*, 257.

73. PWW, 55:309–323.

74. Garraty, *Henry Cabot Lodge*, 353–354.

75. Klingaman, *1919*, 169–170; Levin, *Edith and Woodrow*, 266–267; and Cooper, *Breaking the Heart of the World*, 70.

76. Bailey, *Woodrow Wilson and the Lost Peace*, 208.

77. Alan J. Ward, *Ireland and Anglo-American Relations, 1988–1921* (Toronto, 1969), 172–176.

78. Duff, *The Politics of Revenge*, 84–86.

Chapter 10: Peace That Surpasses Understanding II

1. Edith Bolling Wilson, *My Memoir* (New York, 1939), 245–246.

2. Floto, *Colonel House in Paris*, 111.

3. Ibid., 168; and Levin, *Edith and Woodrow*, 283.

4. Klingaman, *1919*, 141–142.

5. Stephen Bonsal, *Unfinished Business* (New York, 1944), 117–118.

6. Klingaman, *1919*, 159, 207; and Hoover, *The Ordeal of Woodrow Wilson*, 174.

7. Klingaman, *1919*, 69.

8. Coffman, *The War to End All Wars*, 358.

9. Charles T. Thompson, *The Peace Conference Day by Day* (New York, 1920), 184–185.

10. Schneider, *Into the Breach*, 276.

11. Ibid., 280.

12. Floto, *Colonel House in Paris*, 178; and Levin, *Edith and Woodrow*, 293. Grayson became House's secret enemy, filling his diary with condemnations of his supposedly disloyal behavior (PWW, 64:497–498).

13. Seymour, *Intimate Papers of Colonel House*, 4:386.

14. Knock, *To End All Wars*, 248.

15. Ibid.

16. Lloyd George, *Memoirs of the Peace Conference*, 1:141–142.

17. Bailey, *Woodrow Wilson and the Lost Peace*, 216–217; and Knock, *To End All Wars*, 248–249.

18. Knock, *To End All Wars*, 249; and Duff, *Politics of Revenge*, 120–125.

19. Knock, *To End All Wars*, 249.

20. Erik Goldstein, *Winning the Peace: British Diplomatic Strategy, Peace Planning and the Paris Peace Conference, 1916–1920* (New York, 1991), 181–183.

21. Knock, *To End All Wars*, 250; and Robert Lansing, *The Peace Negotiations: A Personal Narrative* (New York, 1921), 256. Wilson managed to procure a verbal promise from the Japanese to restore Shantung to China at some future date. With pressure from the United States, they honored this promise in 1922. He also attempted to protect Chinese interests in other ways, but the Chinese delegation, infuriated by his initial surrender and having no faith in the Japanese promise, refused to accept the compromise (Bruce Elleman, *Wilson and China: A Revised History of the Shandong Question* [Armonk, N.Y., 2002]).

22. Knock, *To End All Wars*, 249; and Lloyd George, *Peace Conference*, 1:149.

23. Baker, *Woodrow Wilson and the World Settlement*, 2:210–215; and Hoover, *The Ordeal of Woodrow Wilson*, 227.

24. Hoover, *The Ordeal of Woodrow Wilson*, 228.

25. Mee, *The End of Order*, 230.

26. Floto, *Colonel House in Paris*, 84, 215.

27. Gene Smith, *When the Cheering Stopped: The Last Years of Woodrow Wilson* (New York, 1964), 48–49.

28. "Wilson's Neurological Illness at Paris," PWW, vol. 58, appendix, 608–640. See also Weinstein, *Woodrow Wilson: A Medical and Psychological Biography,* 336–340. Weinstein diagnosed a combination of influenza and brain damage resulting from either the influenza virus or the associated virus of encephalitis lethargica, which can cause personality changes.

29. Tebbel and Watts, *The Press and the Presidency*, 388.

30. Levin, *Edith and Woodrow*, 292.

31. Knock, *To End All Wars*, 250. Bailey, *Woodrow Wilson and the Lost Peace*, 239–240, 242, points out that at this point, Wilson was not entirely aware of how large the reparations would be. But the president's interest in economics was minimal—a shame, because half the treaty was concerned with economic issues.

32. Levin, *Edith and Woodrow*, 299 (citing Lloyd George's Memoirs). Perhaps the most insightful comment on Wilson's reaction to these defeats is George Kennan's: "His spirit had . . . been broken in the battle over the Versailles treaty" (George F . Kennan, *Russia and the West Under Lenin and Stalin* [Boston, 1960], 143). Weinstein calls Wilson's sudden change in attitude toward the terms of peace a product of his supposed brain damage, which created a false "euphoria." A more down-to-earth way of describing this emotion might be a what-the-hell attitude. Psychological explanations are equally convincing for Wilson's surrenders after the illness. Politically, he was a trapped man (Weinstein, *Woodrow Wilson,* 339–345).

33. Thompson, *Peace Conference Day by Day*, 305–306.

34. Lawrence James, *Raj: The Making and Unmaking of British India* (New York, 1997), 471–473; and J. M. Winter, *The Experience of World War I* (New York, 1989), 217.

35. Duff, *The Politics of Revenge*, 88 n.

36. Ibid., 89.

37. Ward, *Ireland and Anglo-American Relations*, 181.

38. Duff, *The Politics of Revenge,* 97–98.

39. Ward, *Ireland and Anglo-American Relations,* 182–183.

40. Duff, *The Politics of Revenge*, 98–99.

41. Ibid., 100.

42. Klingaman, *1919*, 292–294.

43. Watt, *The Kings Depart*, 398–399.

44. Baker, *Woodrow Wilson and the World Settlement*, 1:394–399.

45. Bailey, *Woodrow Wilson and the Lost Peace,* 249.

46. Ross, *Propaganda for War*, 256–258; and Francis Nielson, *The Tragedy of Europe: A Diary of the Second World War* (Appleton, Wis., 1940), introduction, 8–9, 13.

47. Smith, *Triumph of Herbert Hoover,* 91; and Hoover, *The Ordeal of Woodrow Wilson,* 234–235.

48. Lansing, *The Peace Negotiations*, 272–273.

49. Watt, *The Kings Depart*, 408; and Bailey, *Woodrow Wilson and the Lost Peace*, 288–289.

50. Watt, *The Kings Depart*, 412–413. The actual motive for delaying the reparations figure was a glimmer of realism on the part of the British and French. Lloyd George and Clemenceau, aware that a realistic figure would severely disappoint the voters, put it off to give them time to prepare their constituents for a reduced figure (Craig, *Germany*, 436–437).

51. Ibid., 417.

52. Knock, *To End All Wars*, 254–255.

53. Steel, *Walter Lippmann*, 158–159.

54. Ibid., 159–160; and Knock, *To End All Wars,* 257.

55. Klingaman, *1919,* 309–311; and Bailey, *Woodrow Wilson and the Lost Peace*, 305.

56. Watt, *The Kings Depart*, 443–444.

57. Hoover, *The Ordeal of Woodrow Wilson*, 235.

58. Klingaman, *1919*, 322.

59. Hoover, *The Ordeal of Woodrow Wilson*, 244–245; and Klingaman, *1919*, 310 (White quote).

60. Watt, *The Kings Depart*, 451–452.

61. Ibid., 471–472.

62. Ibid., 486–489, 492.

63. Ibid., 496; and Bailey, *Woodrow Wilson and the Lost Peace*, 301.

64. Watt, *The Kings Depart*, 496–497.

65. Bailey, *Woodrow Wilson and the Lost Peace,* 303.

66. PWW, 61:292–293.

67. Case and La Follette, *Robert M. La Follette,* 969.

68. Klingaman, *1919*, 415–416.

69. Heckscher, *Woodrow Wilson*, 578.

70. Bailey, *Woodrow Wilson and the Lost Peace*, 307–308.

Chapter 11: Chilling the Heart of the World

1. PWW, 61:401–404.

2. Levin, *Edith and Woodrow,* 305.

3. Ibid., 426–436.

4. Thomas Bailey, *Woodrow Wilson and the Great Betrayal* (New York, 1945), 5–6; and Cooper, *Breaking the Heart of the World*, 120.

5. Case and La Follette, *Robert M. La Follette*, 955.

6. Bailey, *The Great Betrayal*, 17; and Blum, *Joe Tumulty and the Wilson Era*, 193–195.

7. Blum, *Joe Tumulty and the Wilson Era*, 193.

8. Ibid., 192.

9. Ibid., 194; and Klingaman, *1919*, 251–252.

10. Klingaman, *1919*, 441; and Kennedy, *Over Here*, 139, 273–279.

11. Sullivan, *Our Times,* vol. 5, *Over Here*, 438; Mock and Larson, *Words That Won the War,* 331.

12. Klingaman, *1919*, 423–424; and *New York Times,* July 1, 1919. One of Congress's leading drys, Republican Congressman Andrew Volstead of Minnesota, argued that demobilization would only become a legal reality when the army's strength was reduced to 175,000.

13. Ellis, *Race, War and Surveillance*, 222–223.

14. Ibid., 225.

15. Ward, *A First-Class Temperament*, 459; and Klingaman, *1919*, 451–453.

16. Nathan Miller, *F.D.R.: An Intimate History* (New York, 1983), 161–162.

17. Robert K. Murray, *Red Scare: A Study in National Hysteria, 1919–20* (New York, 1964), 78–79; Klingaman, *1919,* 352–353; and Ward, *A First-Class Temperament*, 456–457.

18. Ibid., 457–458; and Klingaman, *1919*, 353, 597.

19. Cooper, *Breaking the Heart of the World*, 125.

20. Widenor, *Henry Cabot Lodge*, 313–314; and Duff, *Politics of Revenge*, 148–150.

21. Widenor, *Henry Cabot Lodge,* 317.

22. Cooper, *Breaking the Heart of the World*, 137–138.

23. Bailey, *The Great Betrayal*, 16.

24. Duff, *Politics of Revenge*, 156, 165.

25. Buckley, *The New York Irish*, 248–251; and Ronald H. Bayor and Timothy J. Meagher, eds., *The New York Irish* (Baltimore, 1996), 360–361. O'Leary helped organize the Women Pickets for the Enforcement of America's War Aims, a hugely effective group that gave speeches throughout New York, demonstrated at the British embassy in Washington, and persuaded longshoremen to refuse to load British ships.

26. Duff, *Politics of Revenge*, 123–127.

27. Ibid., 124.

28. Ibid., 128–147.

29. Garraty, *Henry Cabot Lodge*, 367.

30. Levin, *Edith and Woodrow*, 311.

31. Steel, *Walter Lippmann,* 163.

32. Arthur Walworth, *Wilson and His Peacemakers: American Diplomacy at the Paris Peace Conference, 1919* (New York, 1986), 529.

33. Cooper, *Breaking the Heart of the World*, 156.

34. Cary T. Grayson, *Woodrow Wilson: An Intimate Memoir* (New York 1960), 95.

35. Kraig, *Woodrow Wilson and the Lost World of the Oratorical Statesman*, 493.

36. PWW, 63:45–46. The full statement reads as follows: "The real reason that the war we have just finished took place was that Germany was afraid her commercial rivals were going to get the better of her, and the reason why some nations went into the war against Germany was that they thought that Germany would get the commercial advantage of them. . . . This was, in its inception, a commercial and industrial war. It was not a political war."

37. Will Brownell and Richard Billings, *So Close to Greatness: A Biography of William C. Bullitt* (New York, 1987), 97–98.

38. Duff, *Politics of Revenge*, 172–174.

39. Ibid., 180–181.

40. Ford, *Americans All*, 138.

41. George, *Woodrow Wilson and Colonel House*, 294–295.

42. Pringle, *William Howard Taft*, 948.

43. James Dill Startt, *American Editorial Opinion of Woodrow Wilson and the Main Problems of Peacemaking in 1919*, Ph.D. dissertation (University of Maryland, 1965), 273, exhaustively analyzes the newspaper and magazine support for Wilson to bolster this conclusion.

44. Clark, *Deliver Us from Evil*, 130–132. After Wilson was incapacitated by a cerebral thrombosis, Tumulty sent a veto of the Volstead Act to Capitol Hill, pretending it came from the president. With no further spoken or written word from Wilson to back it up, the veto was quickly overridden.

45. Thomas H. O'Connor, *The Boston Irish* (Boston, 1995), 192–193; and Klingaman, *1919*, 498–501.

46. Cooper, *Breaking the Heart of the World*, 183–184.

47. PWW, 63:500–513.

48. Cooper, *Breaking the Heart of the World*, 187–189; and Bailey, *The Great Betrayal*, 131.

49. Irwin Hoover, *My Forty-Two Years in the White House* (New York, 1934), 100–101.

50. Ibid., 102.

51. Smith, *When the Cheering Stopped*, 96.

52. Levin, *Edith and Woodrow*, 339–340; and Ferrell, *Ill-Advised*, 13–14. Grayson's medical credentials were not impressive. He had graduated from the College of William and Mary and obtained an M.D. from the University of the South in a one-year course.

53. Smith, *When the Cheering Stopped*, 99–100.

54. Wilson, *My Memoir*, 288–289.

55. Levin, *Edith and Woodrow,* 344–347.

56. Hoover, *My Forty-Two Years in the White House*, 103.

57. Levin, *Edith and Woodrow*, 333. See also Bailey, *Woodrow Wilson and the Great Betrayal*, 137.

58. Blum, *Joe Tumulty and the Wilson Era*, 215; and Klingaman, *1919*, 577.

59. Blum, *Joe Tumulty and the Wilson Era,* 221–223.

60. Renshaw, *The Wobblies*, 209–212; and Dubofsky, *We Shall Be All*, 455.

61. Walter Lippmann, "Unrest," *New Republic,* November 12, 1919, 1–2. The disillusioned journalist identified the source of this failure: "The government of the United States resides in the mind of Woodrow Wilson. There are no other centers of decision. Whatever thinking is

done, he does. If he is away, the thinking apparatus is away." He went on to castigate Wilson for neglecting to govern because the treaty of peace had not been ratified. Lippmann called this "a fantastic excuse."

62. Klingaman, *1919,* 496–498.

63. Ibid., 520–522; and Dennis Mack Smith, *Mussolini* (New York, 1982), 37.

64. Craig, *Germany,* 430; and Klingaman, *1919,* 474.

65. Flood, *Hitler: The Path to Power,* 34–35.

66. Ibid., 20.

67. Ibid., 67–69.

68. Levin, *Edith and Woodrow,* 380.

69. Cooper, *Breaking the Heart of the World,* 252–257, theorizes that House never sent this document to the White House, but offers no reason for this rather unlikely decision. Walworth, *Wilson and His Peacemakers,* 542, prefers the wastebasket explanation.

70. Case and La Follette, *Robert M. La Follette,* 983.

71. Ibid., 979–981.

72. Garraty, *Henry Cabot Lodge,* 379.

Chapter 12: Illusions End

1. Startt, *American Editorial Opinion,* 254, 257.

2. Blum, *Joe Tumulty and the Wilson Era,* 231–232.

3. Seymour, *Intimate Papers of Colonel House,* 4:509–511. See also Walworth, *Wilson and His Peacemakers,* 545.

4. Walworth, *Wilson and His Peacemakers,* 545.

5. House Diary, December 22 and 27, 1919.

6. Cooper, *Breaking the Heart of the World,* 289–290; and Bailey, *Woodrow Wilson and the Great Betrayal,* 214–215.

7. Walworth, *Wilson and His Peacemakers,* 555–556. Clemenceau ran for president of France in 1921 and was soundly defeated.

8. Helen Fein, *Imperial Crime and Punishment: The Massacre at Jallianwala Bagh* (Honolulu, 1977), 129–144; and James, *Raj,* 478–480.

9. Roy Talbert, Jr., *Negative Intelligence: The Army and the American Left, 1917–1941* (Jackson, Miss., 1991), 191–193.

10. Klingaman, *1919,* 598.

11. Talbert, *Negative Intelligence,* 194–196.

12. Steel, *Walter Lippmann,* 167.

13. Talbert, *Negative Intelligence,* 196–199.

14. Blum, *Joe Tumulty and the Wilson Era,* 233–234.

15. PWW, 64:252–254.

16. Bailey, *Woodrow Wilson and the Great Betrayal,* 218–219.

17. Ibid., 245–246; and Cooper, *Breaking the Heart of the World,* 324–325.

18. Levin, *Edith and Woodrow,* 425.

19. John Maynard Keynes, *The Economic Consequences of the Peace* (New York, 1920), 39ff.

20. Bailey, *Woodrow Wilson and the Great Betrayal,* 252–253. A year later, in the Treaty of Rapallo, Italy and Yugoslavia agreed to make Fiume an independent free state. In 1924, Benito Mussolini, the new fascist dictator of Italy, annexed it.

21. Ibid., 225–226.

22. PWW, 65:8–13.

23. Levin, *Edith and Woodrow,* 435–436; and Bailey, *Woodrow Wilson and the Great Betrayal,* 262.

24. Duff, *The Politics of Revenge*, 221.

25. J. Leonard Bates, *Senator Thomas J. Walsh of Montana* (Urbana, Ill., 1999), 183–184.

26. Bailey, *Woodrow Wilson and the Great Betrayal*, 267.

27. Ibid., 280. Refusing to sign a bill, called a pocket veto, is the president's final resort against legislation he disapproves. He uses it when he knows or fears a veto would be overridden.

28. Flood, *Hitler: The Path to Power*, 91–98.

29. Bailey, *Woodrow Wilson and the Great Betrayal*, 288.

30. Ibid., 291–292.

31. Smythe, *Pershing: General of the Armies,* 270.

32. Ibid., 271.

33. Vandiver, *Black Jack*, 1047–1051.

34. Smythe, *Pershing: General of the Armies,* 272.

35. O'Connor, *Black Jack Pershing*, 348–349.

36. Smythe, *Pershing: General of the Armies,* 272.

37. Cooper, *Breaking the Heart of the World*, 382–383.

38. Ibid., 383–384.

39. Garraty, *Henry Cabot Lodge*, 394.

40. Levin, *Edith and Woodrow*, 441.

41. Hoover, *My Forty-Two Years in the White House,* 107–108.

42. Heckscher, *Woodrow Wilson*, 628.

43. Bailey, *Woodrow Wilson and the Great Betrayal*, 309.

44. Blum, *Joe Tumulty and the Wilson Era*, 243–244.

45. Bailey, *Woodrow Wilson and the Great Betrayal*, 310; Cooper, *Breaking the Heart of the World,* 386; and Blum, *Joe Tumulty and the Wilson Era*, 243–244.

46. Heckscher, *Woodrow Wilson*, 633. A third term was not an entirely new idea, the product of the president's damaged mind. On April 18, 1918, Colonel House asked Admiral Grayson if Wilson could stand another four years in the White House. Grayson said he might last another ten years if nothing "untoward" happened. On August 16, House "sounded him [Wilson] out on another term." House said his "long experience" had enabled him to see evidence of a candidate deciding to run when he was "no more than half aware of it." The colonel was apparently trying to make Wilson aware of this ultimate ambition. House Diary, April 18 and August 16, 1918.

47. Ward, *A First-Class Temperament*, 496–498.

48. Francis L. Paxon, *American Democracy and the World War*, vol. 3, *Postwar Years, Normalcy, 1918–23* (New York, 1966), 157–159.

49. Blum, *Joe Tumulty and the Wilson Era,* 245–247.

50. Smith, *When the Cheering Stopped,* 163.

51. Heckscher, *Woodrow Wilson*, 635; and Smith, *When the Cheering Stopped,* 161–162.

52. Levin, *Edith and Woodrow,* 452.

53. Ward, *A First-Class Temperament*, 514.

54. Ibid., 514–515; and Smith, *When the Cheering Stopped*, 165.

55. Bailey, *Woodrow Wilson and the Great Betrayal*, 318–319.

56. Smith, *When the Cheering Stopped*, 167.

57. Duff, *The Politics of Revenge*, 258.

58. Ibid., 260–261.

59. Ibid., 262–264.

60. Ibid., 264.

61. Ibid., 265–266.

62. Ibid., 267.

63. Mark Sullivan, *Our Times, The United States, 1900–1925,* vol. 6, *The Twenties* (New York: 1923), 130; and Bailey, *Woodrow Wilson and the Great Betrayal*, 322.

64. Davis, *FDR: The Beckoning of Destiny*, 621; and Ward, *A First-Class Temperament*, 535.

65. Ibid., 620; and Frank Freidel, *Franklin D. Roosevelt: The Ordeal* (New York, 1954), 84.

66. Bailey, *Woodrow Wilson and the Great Betrayal*, 326–329; and Sullivan, *Our Times*, vol. 6, *The Twenties*, 121–122.

67. Sullivan, *Our Times*, vol. 6, *The Twenties*, 124–25.

68. Duff, *Politics of Revenge*, 278–279; and Blum, *Joe Tumulty and the Wilson Era*, 252.

69. Duff, *The Politics of Revenge*, 280.

70. Ward, *A First-Class Temperament*, 544; and Duff, *The Politics of Revenge*, 280.

71. Duff, *The Politics of Revenge*, 282.

72. Freidel, *Franklin D. Roosevelt: The Ordeal*, 89; and Blum, *Joe Tumulty and the Wilson Era*, 252.

73. Ibid., 89 n; and Bailey, *Woodrow Wilson and the Great Betrayal*, 323.

74. Ward, *A First-Class Temperament*, 534–535.

75. Ferrell, *Woodrow Wilson and World War I*, 228.

76. PWW, 66:277–280.

77. Ward, *A First-Class Temperament*, 547–548.

78. Ibid., 549–550, 554; and Duff, *Politics of Revenge*, 285.

79. Freidel, *Franklin D. Roosevelt: The Ordeal*, 71 n; and Ward, *A First-Class Temperament*, 553–554.

80. Morgan, *FDR: A Biography*, 231.

81. Bailey, *Woodrow Wilson and the Great Betrayal*, 344.

82. Duff, *The Politics of Revenge*, 286–287; Ward, *A First-Class Temperament*, 556; and Bailey, *Woodrow Wilson and the Great Betrayal*, 342. Later landslides, for Lyndon Johnson in 1964 and Richard Nixon in 1972, equaled Harding's 61 percent, but their opponents received more than Cox's pathetic 35 percent. Debs got 3 percent.

83. Thomas J. Fleming, "'I Am the Law,' a Case History of a Political Machine," *American Heritage* 20, no. 4 (June 1969): 56–57.

84. Duff, *The Politics of Revenge*, 287, 301; and Ward, *A First-Class Temperament*, 556.

85. Bailey, *Woodrow Wilson and the Great Betrayal*, 344.

Chapter 13: A Covenant with Power

1. Ward, *A First-Class Temperament*, 557–558.

2. Garraty, *Henry Cabot Lodge*, 399–400; and Cooper, *Breaking the Heart of the World*, 395.

3. Craig, *Germany*, 436–437.

4. Ibid., 440–450.

5. Frank Trommler and Joseph McVeigh, eds., *America and the Germans*, vol. 2, *The Relationship in the Twentieth Century* (Philadelphia, 1989), 18–29. Financial data from Richard B. Morris, ed., *Encyclopedia of American History* (New York, 1953), 319–323.

6. Case and La Follette, *Robert M. La Follette*, 967.

7. David Fromkin, "What Is Wilsonianism?" *World Policy Journal*, spring 1994, 106.

8. Blum, *Joe Tumulty and the Wilson Era*, 171.

9. Garraty, *Henry Cabot Lodge*, 401.

10. Robert Lee Bullard, *American Soldiers Also Fought* (New York, 1936), vi.

11. Ibid., v–vi.

12. Craig, *Germany*, 282–283. The most complete statement of these late war aims is in Fritz Fischer, *Germany's Aims in the First World War* (New York, 1967).

13. Ferguson, *The Pity of War*, 170–171.

14. Lloyd C. Gardner, *A Covenant With Power: America and World Order from Wilson to Reagan* (New York, 1984), 3–28.

15. Warren I. Cohen, *The American Revisionists: The Lessons of Intervention in World War I* (Chicago, 1967), 161.

16. Ibid., 174.

17. Thomas Fleming, *The New Dealers' War: FDR and the War Within World War II* (New York, 2001). The opening chapters of this book describe Roosevelt's dilemma and his solution in considerable detail.

18. Knock, *To End All Wars*, 272.

19. Ibid., 273–274.

20. F. J. P. Veale, "The Wicked Kaiser Myth," *Social Justice Review,* April 1950.

21. Arthur Schlesinger, Jr., *A Thousand Days* (Boston, 1965), 674–676.

22. Knock, *To End All Wars*, 269–270.

23. House Diary, April 3, 1921.

24. Smith, *When the Cheering Stopped,* 196; and Blum, *Joe Tumulty and the Wilson Era*, 263–264.

25. Lloyd George, *Memoirs of the Peace Conference*, 1:154–155.

26. Smythe, *Pershing: General of the Armies*, 259.

INDEX

11/29.